Choices in Relationships

Choices in Relationships

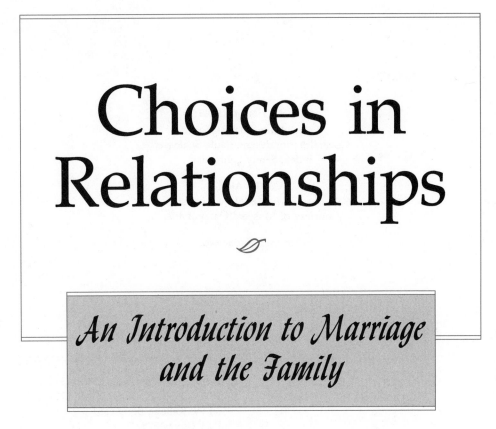

An Introduction to Marriage and the Family

Second Edition

DAVID KNOX
EAST CAROLINA UNIVERSITY

WEST PUBLISHING COMPANY
ST. PAUL NEW YORK LOS ANGELES SAN FRANCISCO

PRODUCTION CREDITS
Copyediting: Mary George
Cover/Interior design: Paula Schlosser
Index: Sandy Schroeder

COVER ART
Le Moulin de la Galette (1876) by Auguste Renoir.
Courtesy of Musée d'Orsay, Paris.

Photo credits follow index.

---

50 W. Kellogg Boulevard
P.O. Box 64526
St. Paul, MN 55164–1003

Printed in the United States of America

95 94 93 92 91 90 89 8 7 6 5 4 3

Library of Congress Cataloging-in-Publication Data
Knox. David, 1943–
Choices in relationships.
Bibliography: p.
Includes index.
1. Family life education. I. Title.
HQ10.K57 1988 306.8 87–22998
ISBN 0–314–61439–7

Contents

IN BRIEF

Contents

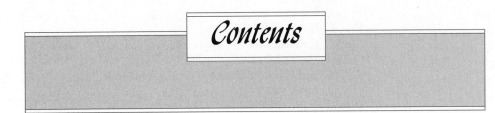

Preface

THE SECOND EDITION of *Choices in Relationships: An Introduction to Marriage and the Family* continues the theme of the first—encouraging you to take charge of your life by making deliberate choices in your personal relationships, especially marriage and the family. Rather than passively reacting to events in your life so that choices are made for you, the text encourages you to actively make choices and select courses of action for your life. By doing so, you increase the control over your happiness and the happiness of those you care about.

The text begins with a new chapter—an overview of some of the more important choices that people make in relation to marriage and the family and a review of the basic facts about choices. Subsequent chapters follow a developmental framework, examining relationships from first meeting through marriage, having and rearing a family, divorce, and remarriage. Along the way, we look at singlehood, gender roles, love, sexuality, communication, violence, dual-income marriages, and stepfamilies.

Each page of the second edition has been reviewed, revised and updated. Examples of new information in this edition include: the best time to marry, romantic scripts, commuter marriages, marriage encounter weekends, marriage across time, one-child families, single-parent families, the feminization of poverty, the biological clock and beginning a family, elderly marriages, responding to teenage drug abuse, Alzheimer's spouses, new laws and the family, and chlamydia—*the* most prevalent sexually transmitted disease in America and the world today.

The following unique features of the text have been developed with one goal in mind: to provide you with a basis for making the best possible interpersonal choices.

CHOICES

At the conclusion of each chapter, a special section emphasizes the choices that are relevant to the content of that chapter. Examples of the issues discussed include: "Is Marriage for You?," "Should You Live with Your Partner?," "Should You Call Off the Wedding?," "How Long Should You Live with Your Parents?," and "Is a Dual Career Marriage for You?". Over 50 choices are examined in 19 chapters.

IMPACT OF SOCIAL INFLUENCES ON CHOICES

A new feature of this edition is an emphasis on how social influences have an impact on the choices you make in your interpersonal relationships. Just as the decision to eat at a particular restaurant is influenced by the person you will eat with, choices such as who and when to marry are also influenced by others. How decisions are influenced by others (social context) and the larger social forces of our society are emphasized.

AGE, RACIAL, AND ETHNIC BALANCE

Another new feature of the second edition is a greater emphasis on choices in relationships made by individuals representing a variety of ages and racial and ethnic backgrounds. Although white students from 18 to 22 years of age comprise the largest percentage of those enrolled in college, increasing percentages of college students are in their mid-twenties or are 35 or older. Enrollments of individuals from different racial groups are also increasing. Black, Hispanic, Asian, American Indian, and foreign students represent about 20 percent of all students in U.S. colleges and universities today. Although many marriage and family choices are similar regardless of racial background, some unique differences will be examined.

Since blacks (27 million or 13 percent of the U.S. population) comprise the largest minority group, their concerns will be emphasized. Some whites may ask, "What difference does the black family make?" Professor Dennis Williams (1986) of Cornell University suggests an answer:

> It is truly amazing that this country can be so blind as to ignore the obvious: blacks are not all that different from everybody else; we are simply ahead of our time. If our kids fall victim to drugs and have babies too young, so will white children. If black men, as some claim, are becoming economically obsolete, is anyone foolish enough to believe that they will be the last to go? If those first affected by domestic trauma were given even the credence of lab mice, we might find answers to save all our families a whole lot of grief. As long as the public sees the plight of our families as a black plague, it will be difficult to develop a vaccine to save everyone else . . ..
>
> Suddenly, and very publicly, black people are reaffirming the obligations of parenthood and sexual responsibility; they are preaching commitment in male–female relationships. On a more symbolic level, it may not be a coincidence that America's favorite family is the steadfastly "normal" television clan of Bill Cosby, who presents a compelling image of fatherhood to a nation that thought we didn't have fathers. These are telling signs: from the wilderness of our despair, black folks just may lead the way to salvation for the American family. You might want to pay attention this time. (p. 7)

Individuals of Spanish origin (15 million or 6 percent of the U.S. population) represent the second largest minority group in our society. Their origins may vary and include Mexico, Puerto Rico, and Cuba (Tienda and Ortiz, 1986). Although Mexican Americans (9 million or 4 percent of the U.S. population) represent the largest portion of the Spanish sector, the term "Mexican American" is problematic:

> In addition to the term Mexican American, the terms Chicano, Mexicano, Latin American, Hispano, Spanish surname, and La Raza are among the identifiers that have been prominently used to designate this group. Each of these terms is preferred by certain group members and is considered inaccurate or offensive by others. Each of them also has a fairly specific connotation that sets it apart from the others. The term Chicano, for instance, frequently is preferred by the younger or more politically active members of the group. (McLemore and Romo, 1985, p. 4)

Asian Americans (3.6 million, including Chinese, Japanese, Korean, Filipino, and Korean Americans) comprise only 1.6 percent of the U.S. population but represent 20 percent of college and university student enrollments. The families of these students place a premium on ambition, persistence, deferred gratification, and intergenerational mobility (Hirschman and Wong, 1986). Where possible, we will refer not only to white but also to black, Hispanic, and Asian American spouses, marriages, and families.

Self-Assessment Inventories

To be consistent with the theme of making decisions, every chapter includes an inventory or scale to enhance decision making in various areas of marriage and the family. Examples include the Love Attitudes Scale, the Sexual Attitudes Scale, and the Relationship Involvement Scale. You might want to complete these self-assessment inventories to learn more about yourself.

Considerations

Sprinkled throughout the text are short paragraphs that also could be labeled "What this may mean for you" or "The point is . . . if you haven't thought of this." These considerations encourage you to relate what you have been reading to your life and your interpersonal relationships.

Data

Because the study of marriage and the family (also referred to as "family science") is a social science, we present data on who does what as reported in various professional journals. These data help us to gather as much information as possible with which to make decisions. For example, the fact that those who marry after having known each other for only a short time have a higher divorce rate than those who marry after having known each other for at least two years may be important in deciding when to marry a person you are very much in love with but have known for only a short time.

Exhibits

The exhibits offer practical illustrations (and sometimes suggestions) in reference to particular issues. Examples are "How to Meet Anyone on Your Campus" and "Two Views of One Dual-Career Marriage."

Acknowledgments

The second edition of *Choices in Relationships: An Introduction to Marriage and the Family* is a result of the work of many people. Peter Marshall provided the vision for expanding the demographics of the text to include black, Mexican American, and Asian American marriages and families. Delene Rhea suggested emphasizing how social forces influence decisions. Maralene Bates orchestrated the review process and provided numerous suggestions for changes in this edition. Jane Bacon secured permissions, Mary George copyedited the manuscript, and Jean Cook served as production manager who ensured that every detail in reference to the manuscript was handled appropriately and punctually. A number of professors who teach the course for which this text is written read the manuscript and provided valuable insights and suggestions:

Carol Campbell California State University—Long Beach
Karen Conner Drake University
Clifton Harrell City University of New York
Delbert and Ellen Hayden Western Kentucky University
Thomas Holman Brigham Young University
David Hollindrake Utah Valley Regional Medical Center
Hadley Klug University of Wisconsin—Whitewater
Sandra Latham Panhandle State University
Sam Mayhall Indiana University—Southeast
Carol K. Oyster Goldey Beacon College
Elliott Robins University of North Carolina—Greensboro
Lucille Sansing Northern Virginia Community College
Melton Strozier Houston Baptist University
Marilyn Stuber Meredith College
Sim Swindall Oklahoma State University Technical Institute
Joel Tate Germanna Community College
Andrew Weber Catonsville Community College

Finally, Christa Reiser and Ken Wilson have once again developed a superb Instructor's Manual and Study Guide to accompany the text. Their fine products will facilitate teaching and learning.

David Knox

PART ONE

PERSPECTIVES

THERE IS AN old joke among professors who teach marriage and family courses that they can use the same tests year after year because even though the questions remain the same, the answers keep changing. The percentages of women and men who choose to remain single, who enter marriage as virgins, and who have a dual-career marriage change continually. Heraclitus said, "Nothing endures but change." This is certainly true of marriage and the family.

Women no longer look to marriage and the family for total fulfillment. Although these relationships continue to be a major source of enjoyment, they are supplemented by success in the work world and by interactions with coworkers and friends. Likewise, although the job remains a primary source of satisfaction for most men, it is being supplemented by an increased interest in the family unit. In particular, some men are becoming more involved in their role as father.

CHAPTER 1

Choices in Marriage and the Family: A First View

Contents

Is It True?*

1. By the year 2000, most people will be choosing to remain single rather than to get married.
2. Blacks are more likely to be married than whites.
3. When it comes to making choices about marriage, most people don't care what other people think.
4. Marriage and the family are basically the same concept.
5. Most research in marriage and the family has flaws.

*1 = F; 2 = F; 3 = F; 4 = F; 5 = T.

> BUT I THINK the simple reality that we all have to face is that you can't do everything in life. There really are genuine forks in the road, where in order to do one thing, you give up the opportunity to do something else.
>
> —Pete Dawkins

These words by a former winner of the Heisman Trophy in college football emphasize the importance of making choices. Making choices in your relationships—particularly in regard to marriage and the family—is the most important set of decisions you will make in your life, and will involve your greatest joys and sorrows. In no other area of life will choices be so crucial.

Five Basic Choices

Although you will make an array of interpersonal choices (see Exhibit 1.1) throughout your life, five basic "forks in the road" will have an impact on your other choices.

Singlehood or Marriage?

Although more than 90 percent of us eventually marry (Norton and Moorman, 1987), whether to remain single or to marry remains a choice. Some people who do not marry are homosexuals. Some heterosexuals are not suited to marriage and should not marry just because they feel society expects them to. According to one person:

I would be married, but I'd have no wife. I would be married to a single life.
—Richard Crashaw

> I can't stand living with other people. I need my own place with no one else there. Sure, I enjoy other people and they come over to my place, but I don't want anyone living there but me. Marriage means that you are burdened with having to interact and to consider another person in everything you do. I'm simply not cut out for that kind of life.

Other people enjoy the intimacy of marriage. One spouse said, "If you've got a good marriage, you've got the best there is." The "best" this spouse is referring to not only includes the intimacy but the companionship and mutual support that marriage may provide.

Just what percent of adult men and women in our society are married?

Data – Among American males, 68 percent of white, and 51 percent of blacks, are married. Among females, 63 percent of white, and 43 percent of blacks are married. (*Statistical Abstract of the United States*, 1987)

Children—Yes or No?

Just as most people marry, most people express a desire for and eventually have children. However, some people do not want children. Children take time and are a drain on financial and emotional resources. Individuals who are not anxious to share their lives with an infant, child, and teenager may decide not to have children.

Exhibit 1.1

FIFTY CHOICES IN RELATIONSHIPS

Life style
Marriage?
Singlehood?
Live together?

Marriage
Premarital counseling?
Premarital agreement?
Traditional or egalitarian relationship?
Who manages the money?
Live with parents?
Partner's night out?
Separate or joint vacations?

Communication and Conflict
How much should you tell?
Talk about issues or avoid them?
Consult a therapist?
Marriage enrichment weekends?

Sex
Intercourse before marriage?
Infidelity?
Open marriage?
Heterosexual, homosexual, bisexual?
Consult sex therapist if problems?

Employment
Job or career?
Part-time or full-time work?
One- or two-income marriage?
Move if one career requires?
Who does what chores at home?
Hire outside help?

Birth Control
Use of a contraceptive?
Which contraceptive?
Sterilization?
If become pregnant, keep child, abort, or give up for adoption?

Children
Have children?
Number of children?
Single parent by choice?
Artificial insemination by husband?
Artificial insemination by donor?
Ovum transfer?
Test-tube fertilization?
Surrogate mother?
Home or hospital birth?
Day care for child?
Public or private school?

Divorce
Stay married or divorce?
Custody to one parent?
Joint custody?
When and how to tell parents?
What to tell children?
Relationship with ex-spouse?
Amount of child support?
Remarry?
Remarry person with children?
Remarry person against your children's wishes?

ONE- OR TWO-CAREER MARRIAGE?

I'm learning that the twice we're earning doesn't mean it's twice the fun.

—A dual-career spouse

The fact that about 65 percent of all married couples have two incomes illustrates their involvement in employment and their need for money. One partner, more often the wife, has a job that permits easy entrance and exit from the labor force to accommodate the needs of the family. Couples who decide to pursue joint careers may enjoy personal and economic advantages but may also have less time for each other, particularly if they have children. For the child-free couple, two careers are easier to manage.

Fidelity

Two flavors confuse the palate.
—Chinese proverb

Most of us expect emotional and sexual fidelity from our partner. Yet 50 percent of all husbands and almost as high a percentage of all wives have sexual relationships with someone other than their spouse. Although most couples remain married after such involvements occur, each spouse must continually decide whether to be monogamous. "Someone is always available if you want to have an affair," said one spouse. "It's really up to you whether you do or not."

Positive or Negative View?

A final—and perhaps the most important—basic choice is deciding how you wish to view something. Life has positive and negative aspects. Your choice of whether to focus on the positives or on the negatives is of critical importance to your personal and interpersonal happiness.

Most people are about as happy as they have made up their minds to be.
—Unknown

When you look at your partner, you can focus on his or her loving eyes or on facial pimples. Similarly, you can focus on the times your partner did something you liked or on the times he or she did something that offended or hurt you. You can focus on your partner preparing a meal rather than forgetting to put the ketchup on the table. In dissolving a relationship, you can view it as the end of a life or as the beginning of a life.

In other words, how you choose to view a situation will often have more to do with your happiness than the situation itself. A positive perception affects not only your psychological health but also your physical health (Trotter, 1987).

Some Facts about Choices

When you make choices, it is important to keep several issues in mind.

Not to Decide Is to Decide

What is not possible is not to choose, but I ought to know that if I do not choose, I am still choosing.
—Jean-Paul Sartre

It is important to recognize that to not make a decision *is* a decision. The act of not deciding for something is to decide against something. For example, if you are sexually active and do not use birth control, you have decided for pregnancy. As a child-free career woman, if you don't decide to have a baby, you may be deciding not to have one forever. Choosing—through action or through inaction—means taking responsibility for the consequences of your decisions.

Choices Are Only Probabilities

Chance favors only the mind that is prepared.
—Louis Pasteur

The outcome of any choice is at best a probability, because it is difficult, if not impossible, to know exactly what the best choice is for all time. We can only make decisions based on the information available to us at the time of the decision. Later we may become aware of new information which, had we known it initially, may have influenced us to have made a different decision. For example, one woman decided on the basis of a two-year courtship to marry a man with whom she was deeply in love. He was suave, attractive, and considerate. Not until their honeymoon did she discover that he was an alcoholic. "He literally passed out and his face hit the fish he was eating on our first dinner out after we were married," she said. "He had been hiding his alcoholism from me throughout our courtship." This is an extreme but true example.

Choices often require deliberate thought.

Choices Are Continual

Life is what happens while you are making other plans.
—John Lennon

Making choices is a continual process. Life is not one or two BIG decisions. It is a series of some big decisions and a constant stream of smaller ones. For example, if you choose to be single, you can live alone, with another partner in a heterosexual or homosexual relationship, or with a roommate. You can live in a one-room apartment or on a communal farm with 1,600 others (as on the Farm in Tennessee). If you choose to marry, you can select from a variety of marital styles (traditional, open, dual-career, child-free). If you decide to separate and eventually to divorce (as most of us visualize "somebody else" doing), you will be making an additional choice to remain single or to remarry. Remarriage will involve still other choices, including whether to marry a person with children or to be child-free.

Consideration

Whereas the single person makes a decision to get married, the married person makes a decision to stay married. "I think sometimes I would be better off if I were single . . . but then again I think marriage isn't so bad," said one spouse. We do not "decide"; we continue to decide.

Choices Involve Trade-offs

Any choice you make involves gains and losses. Barbra Streisand once considered having her nose altered by a plastic surgeon, but she was told that to do so might also alter the nasal sound and timbre of her voice. The trade-off was not worth the risk for her.

Interpersonal choices also involve trade-offs. For example, one spouse said:

> Everything is a trade-off. If you get married, you are less free; if you don't get married, you may be more lonely. If you have kids, they cost money, make noise, and tear up the house; if you don't have kids, you may miss them. If you have an affair, you feel guilty and may lose your marriage; if you don't have sex with others, you wonder what it would be like. So what's the answer?

Most Choices Are Revocable

Whether your choices involve a philosophy of life, a career, or selecting a mate, most of them are revocable. Although the emotional or financial price is higher for certain choices than for others (for example, backing out of the role of spouse is somewhat less difficult than backing out of the role of parent), you can change your mind. Most choices can be modified or changed. However, once you decide to get married, you can never return to your previous status (single); if you dissolve the marriage, you will acquire a new status (divorced).

Choices Are Influenced by Social Context and Social Forces

You do not make choices in a vacuum. Your choices are influenced by the social context in which they occur. *Social context* refers to what significant others (people you care about) are saying and doing. Their behavior provides a model that guides your own behavior. If all of your friends are married and have children, you are much more likely to choose both marriage and parenthood. Significant others also reward and punish your choices. If you elect to marry a person twice your age, your peers may question your choice, which may influence your eventual decision to marry that person.

Social variables that influence your choices also operate at the larger societal level (see Exhibit 1.2 for recent changes in marriage and the family). Examples of such social forces include inflation, unemployment, and war. Inflation influences your choices by dictating what you can afford. Unemployment will dramatically affect the feelings you have about yourself and your spouse. And even though U.S. involvement in a new war is not imminent, couples are still reeling from Vietnam and military couples continue to experience the impact of separation.

Both the social variables in your immediate social context (the micro perspective) and in the larger society (the macro perspective) influence your choices in relationships. Although social influence is not the only explanation for why we make a particular choice, it is often an overlooked explanation (in preference for individual determinism). We will emphasize social influences in the Choices section in the back of each chapter.

What Is Marriage?

Choices in marriage and the family are the two major categories of relationships that we will consider in this text. To begin, let's define and examine the various types of marriage.

Exhibit 1.2

RECENT CHANGES IN MARRIAGE AND THE FAMILY

Our society provides the social backdrop against which choices in marriage and the family are made—and our society is undergoing rapid change. The following changes or events that are commonplace in your life were not true when your parents were growing up.

Contraception

Your generation is the first to grow up while the contraceptive pill is readily available. Abortion (Roe v. Wade) is also legally available if contraception fails.

Singlehood

Although most people eventually marry, increasing numbers are delaying marriage to enjoy singlehood and to establish careers. Some people will never marry, which is in part a function of musical chairs; there are more women than there are men to marry. Too few men is a particular problem for black women; there is only one eligible black man for every five black unmarried women.

Living Together

Living together is regarded by some as an extension of courtship. Unmarried couples who cohabit represent about 4 percent of all couples (married and unmarried). A high divorce rate, a delay in women having their first child, and an increasing acceptance of the behavior have all contributed to the rise in the frequency of cohabitation among unmarrieds. Once considered a lower-class practice, living together has become an accepted middle-class custom.

Employed Wives

Increasingly, spouses are choosing a two-income marriage. Although some couples need two incomes to survive, other couples have two incomes to afford a plush standard of living. In addition, more mothers with infants are working outside the home. The wife who stays at home to be with her children is becoming less frequent. Only 6 percent of all households include a bread-winning husband, a homemaking wife, and two children (Hewlett, 1986).

Children

Children are no longer viewed as essential to marital fulfillment. Although most couples continue to have children, having a child-free marriage is an option. For the single person, marriage is no longer considered a prerequisite to having children. Single Mothers by Choice is an organization for women who are tired of waiting for a husband to come along and who want to have a baby now.

Divorce

One in two marriages ends in divorce. Today, unhappy spouses are less willing to stay married for the sake of the children or what others may say.

Technology

Technology influences your life every day. Riding in a car to withdraw cash from a banking machine to buy food that has been heated in a microwave at a restaurant involves three technological innovations. Technology also influences your choices in relationships. Some examples include computers for computer dating, VCRs for the home viewing of video cassettes, video cameras to store your memories, satellite dishes for unlimited television home viewing, the separation of X and Y sperm to select a girl or a boy baby, artificial insemination for infertile couples, and penile implants for impotent males.

Definition of Marriage

Marriage in the United States is an arrangement in which two adults of the opposite sex have an emotional relationship and a legal commitment to each other according to the laws of the state in which they reside. Most marriages involve a public announcement and a public ceremony. All require a marriage license, which provides for the transfer of property and legitimizes offspring.

Emotional Relationship

Most people say they want to get married because they are "in love." This motivation reflects that marriage is a relationship sought by two people who care a great deal for each other, who enjoy being together, and who want to share their lives permanently. They want a lover, a friend, a buddy, a person they can trust and talk to in an otherwise competitive and often impersonal world. A 27-year-old single person said, "Marriage is one way of expressing your ultimate love for a person by wanting to spend the rest of your life with that person."

It is as absurd to say that a man can't love one woman all the time as it is to say that a violinist needs several violins to play the same piece of music.
—Honoré De Balzac

Your movement toward marriage may be measured in terms of the seriousness of a relationship. The Relationship Involvement Scale is designed to help you assess the degree to which you are drifting toward marriage.

Sexual Monogamy

In a marriage, the emotional commitment to each other is often thought to imply that each partner will be sexually faithful to the other. Although 50

Intimacy is an important human experience.

Self-Assessment

The Relationship Involvement Scale

This scale is designed to measure the degree to which you are involved with your partner. There are no right or wrong answers.

Directions: After reading each sentence carefully, circle the number that best represents your feelings.

1 Strongly disagree
2 Mildly disagree
3 Undecided
4 Mildly agree
5 Strongly agree

	SD	MD	U	MA	SA
1. I have made it clear to my partner that I love her or him.	1	2	3	4	5
2. I feel that I know my partner's parents.	1	2	3	4	5
3. I feel that my partner knows my parents.	1	2	3	4	5
4. Our relationship is exclusive. We do not date other people.	1	2	3	4	5
5. We spend most of our free time together.	1	2	3	4	5
6. We have talked about getting married.	1	2	3	4	5
7. Our close friends know that we are very involved with each other.	1	2	3	4	5
8. My partner and I would like to be engaged.	1	2	3	4	5
9. I have borrowed some things that belong to my partner.	1	2	3	4	5
10. My partner and I have told each other a great deal about ourselves.	1	2	3	4	5

Score ________

Scoring: Add the numbers you circled. The response that suggests the least involvement is 1 (strongly disagree), and the response that suggests the greatest involvement is 5 (strongly agree). Therefore, the lower your total score is (10 is the lowest possible score), the more likely you are to remain single for now; the higher your total score is (50 is the highest possible score), the closer you are to getting married. A score of 30 places you at the midpoint between singlehood and marriage.

percent of all husbands and almost as many wives eventually have intercourse with someone other than their partner during the marriage, they usually hide their extramarital encounters from the spouse. With the exception of couples who agree that extramarital partners are acceptable, sexual fidelity is expected.

Legal Commitment

Marriage is also a legal commitment that only those of the opposite sex (one female, one male), age (usually 18 or older), and marital status (neither partner may be married to someone else) may contract. The marriage license certifies that the individuals were married by a legally empowered representative of the state with two witnesses present.

Data – Between 2,400,000 and 2,500,000 marriage licenses are issued annually in the United States. (*Statistical Abstract of the United States*, 1987)

The license entitles each partner to share in the estate of the other. In most states, whatever the deceased spouse owns is legally transferred to the remaining spouse at the time of death.

Consideration

The marriage license also verifies the legal relationship between the woman and the man. Insurance companies that provide life and health protection pay claims for deceased and hospitalized spouses. They do not recognize girlfriends, boyfriends, and live-ins as beneficiaries. If your partner says, "The real marriage is in the heart, and the license doesn't make our marriage a real marriage," remember that the law generally does not see it this way. The exception is common-law marriage (possible in some states), which means that if a couple cohabit and present themselves as married, they will be regarded as legally married. Blacks are much more likely to cohabit and have common-law marriages than whites.

Legitimacy of Children

Although laws are changing, the marriage license deems any child born to the marrying couple as legitimate and makes the parents legally responsible for the care of their offspring. Although individuals marry for love, fun, and companionship, the *real* reason (from the viewpoint of the state) for marriage is the legal obligation of a woman and man to nurture and support any children they may have. In our society, childrearing is the primary responsibility of the family, not of the state.

Marriage is a relatively stable unit that helps to ensure that children will have adequate care and protection, will be socialized for productive roles in society, and will not become the burden of those who did not conceive them. Thus, there is tremendous social pressure for individuals to be married at the time they have children. Even at divorce, the legal obligation of the father and mother to the child is theoretically maintained through child-support payments.

Public Ceremony

The legal bonding of a couple is often preceded by an announcement in the local newspaper and a public ceremony in a church or synagogue. Of their announcement one groom-to-be said, "The fact that Barbara and I were actually getting married was not real to me until I saw her picture in the paper and read the sentence that we were to be married on June third." The newspaper is not the only means of publicly announcing the private commitment. Telling parents, siblings, and friends about wedding plans helps to verify the commitment of the partners and also helps to marshal the social and economic support to launch the couple into marital orbit.

Types of Marriage

There are two major types of marriage—monogamy and polygamy. In *monogamy,* one wife and one husband have an exclusive sexual relationship. Monogamy is the only legal type of marriage in the United States. Although people in group and homosexual relationships may regard themselves as married, legally they are not. But as one man from Nigeria said, "Some men in my country have three wives at once; in your country, you have three wives but not all at the same time." With 50 percent of all U.S. marriages ending in divorce and 80 percent of these resulting in remarriage, we have a system of *serial monogamy* (individuals having several successive monogamous relationships).

Polygamy is a general term that refers to having several spouses. One form of polygamy is *polygyny,* in which one husband has several wives. Although illegal, polygyny is practiced by a few religious fundamentalist groups in the western United States (Arizona, New Mexico, Utah) that have splintered off from the Church of Jesus Christ of Latterday Saints. Officially, any member of this church who practices polygyny is excommunicated.

I'd rather have three husbands than one. I should have married more.
—Ingrid Bergman

Albert Barlow, now 84, lives in Utah with his three wives, 34 children, 270 grandchildren, and 70 great-great grandchildren. These fundamentalists believe that they must create large earthly families so they will have large heavenly families. They also believe that polygyny is ordained and sanctioned by God as evidenced in Biblical history. From a worldwide perspective, all societies south of the Sahara Desert in Africa practice polygyny. Specific examples are the Yoruba of Nigeria and the Pokomo of Kenya.

Consideration

Although most American males view polygyny solely in terms of sexual pleasure with a variety of women, the reality in other societies is quite different. Additional wives are sought to produce heirs and to help with housework and are often encouraged by first wives, who view several wives as a symbol of their husband's success (not to mention as helpers with domestic chores and childrearing). Much as a wife may encourage her husband to buy a new car or house to elevate her own status among her peers, so the wife in certain polygynous societies will want her husband to acquire additional wives. Such wives may also relieve first wives of sexual duty, and the husband of many wives is expected—indeed, obligated—to have sex with each wife on a regular basis.

Even though polygyny is permitted in a number of societies, most marriages in these societies are monogamous. Although additional wives produce heirs, they may also cost money—and only wealthy men can afford to support several wives and children. If a Pokomo man in Kenya has more than one wife, he must supply each with a house and help each cultivate a separate field.

In another form of polygamy, *polyandry*, one wife has several husbands, as do the Buddhist Tibetans. In some cases, these husbands may be brothers. Polyandry is functional economically. Several men can pool their resources and support one wife, which not only distributes the economic burden but also benefits the wife who may want several children. Polyandry also helps keep the birthrate low; each woman usually produces only one child every nine months, regardless of the number of husbands she has. In contrast, if all the husbands were married to different women, more babies would be born.

What Is Family?

As with marriage, family may be similarly defined and typed.

Definition of Family

One definition of *family* is a social group characterized by common residence (the spouses live together), economic cooperation (the spouses share their money and chores), and sexual reproduction (the spouses have or adopt children). This definition does not cover all families: some dual-career couples live apart, some spouses keep their money separate, and some spouses are child-free. Indeed, not all definitions of the family require the presence of children or spouses. The U.S. Census Bureau defines "family" as a group of two or more persons related by blood, marriage, or adoption. According to this definition, two siblings or two spouses may constitute a family.

Data – There are over 60 million families in America. (*Statistical Abstract of the United States*, 1987)

Call it a clan, call it a network, call it a tribe, call it a family. Whatever you call it, whoever you are, you need one.
—Jane Howard

Types of Family

Families may be typed according to an individual's function within the family and according to member inclusiveness.

Family of Orientation

The *family of orientation* is the family into which you were born. This represents you, your parents, and your siblings. When you go to your parents' home for the holidays, you return to your family of orientation.

Data – Among whites, 80 percent of all children live with both parents, compared to 40 percent among blacks. (*Statistical Abstract of the United States*, 1987)

Family of Procreation

The *family of procreation* represents the family you will begin if you marry and have children. More than 90 percent of us marry and establish our own family of procreation. We travel through time from the family of orientation to the family of procreation (see Figure 1.1).

Nuclear Family

The *nuclear family* may refer to either your family of orientation or procreation. Your nuclear family consists of you, your parents (or parent), and siblings or of you, your spouse, and your children (or just of you and your children). During the transition from your family of orientation to your family of procreation, you are in two nuclear families.

Extended Family

The *extended family* includes not only your nuclear family but other relatives as well. In practical terms, if you live with your extended family, your spouse, children, parents, and siblings all live with you. Blacks, Mexican Americans, and Asian Americans are much more likely to live with their extended families than whites. The problems and solutions of living in extended families is not new. Writing in the twelfth century about Chinese family life, Yuan Ts'ai observed:

FIGURE 1.1 MOVEMENT FROM FAMILY OF ORIENTATION TO FAMILY OF PROCREATION

The specific number of children a family has will vary from zero to many, depending on the parents' choices.

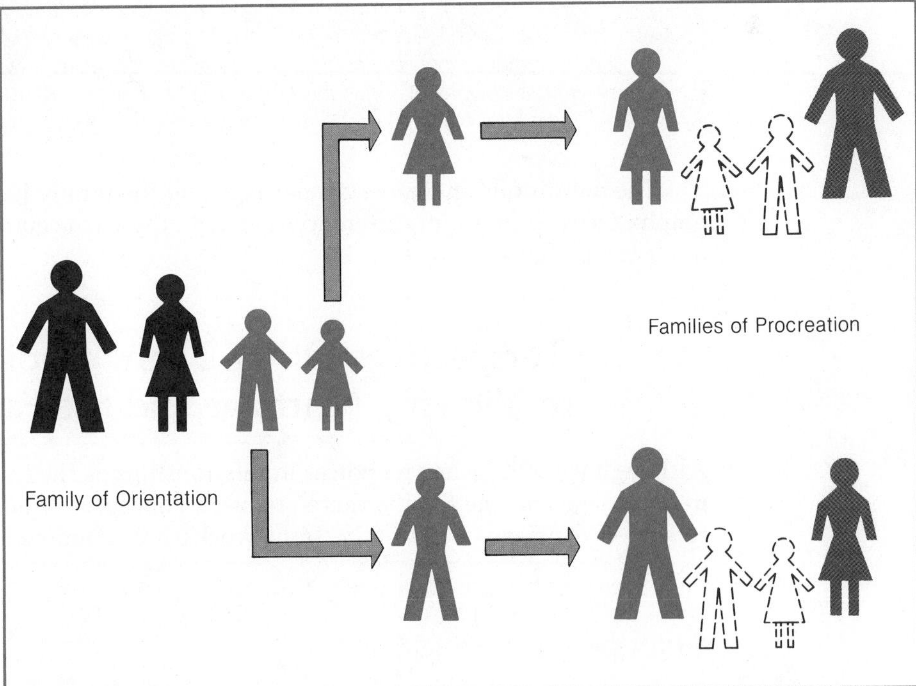

TABLE 1.1 SOME DIFFERENCES BETWEEN MARRIAGE AND THE FAMILY

Marriage	*Family*
Usually initiated by a public ceremony.	Public ceremony not essential.
Involves two people.	Can be as few as two.
Ages of the individuals tend to be similar.	The individuals represent more than one generation.
Individuals usually choose each other.	Members are born or adopted into the family.
Ends when spouse dies or is divorced.	Continues beyond the life of the individual.
Sex between spouses is expected and approved.	Sex between near kin is neither expected nor approved.
Requires a license.	No license needed to become a parent.
Procreation expected.	Consequence of procreation.
Spouses are focused on each other.	Focus is diluted with the addition of children.
Spouses can voluntarily withdraw from marriage with approval from the state.	Spouses/parents cannot voluntarily withdraw from obligations to children.

Source: Axelson, 1987

Dislike among blood relatives may start from a very minor incident but end up ingrained. It is just that once two people take a dislike to each other they become irascible, and neither is willing to be the first to cool off. When they are in each other's company day in and day out, they cannot help but irritate each other. If having reached this state, one of them would be willing to take the initiative in cooling off and would talk to the other, then the other would reciprocate, and the situation would return to normal. This point is worth deep consideration. (1984, pp. 186–87)

Consideration

There are numerous variations of these and other types of families that we discuss later in the text. Single-parent families headed by either a woman or a man, child-free families, communal families, and stepfamilies are examples. Awareness of these alternative family types expands the range of your choices.

The definitions and types of marriage and the family just described do not emphasize the important differences between these concepts. These differences are listed in Table 1.1.

Perspectives Other Than "Choices" in Viewing Marriage and the Family

Although we will focus on choices in relationships as the framework for viewing marriage and the family, there are other conceptual frameworks. These alternative marriage and family frameworks are examined in the following sections.

Structure and Function

The *structure-function view* of marriage and the family emphasizes the functions these institutions serve for the rest of our society. Just as the religious institu-

Socialization, a major function of the family, involves teaching children specific skills.

tion helps to explain the unknown, the economic institution ensures the production and distribution of goods and services, and the legal institution provides social control, so the institutions of marriage and the family have two major functions.

First, marriage and the family serve to replenish society with socialized members. Our society cannot continue to exist without new members, so we must have some way of ensuring a continuing supply. But just having new members is not enough. We need socialized members—those who can speak our language and know the norms and roles of our society. The legal bond of marriage and the obligation to nurture and socialize offspring help to assure that this socialization will occur.

Second, marriage and the family promote the emotional stability of the adult partners and give children a place to belong. Society cannot afford enough counselors to help settle us down whenever we have problems. Marriage provides an in-residence counselor who is, theoretically, a loving and caring partner. To have someone who loves and cares about us helps to keep us stable, so that we can adequately perform our work roles in society. Children also need people to love them and to give them a sense of belonging. The affective function of marriage and the family is one of its major strengths. No other institutions focus so completely on fulfilling our emotional needs as do marriage and the family.

TABLE 1.2 ALTERNATIVE FAMILY LIFE CYCLES

*(A) FAMILY LIFE CYCLE OF THOSE WHO MARRY ONLY ONCE**

Life Stage	*Average Age*
Marriage	Males: 26 Females: 23
First child born	Males: 28 Females: 26
Last child born	Males: 34 Females: 32
Last child leaves	Males: 52 Females: 50
Grandparent	Males: 53 Females: 51
Widowhood	Females: 71
Death	Males: 72 Females: 79

*(B) FAMILY LIFE CYCLE OF THOSE WHO MARRY AND DIVORCE**

Life Stage	*Average Age*
Marriage	Males: 26 Females: 23
Divorce	Males: 32 Females: 30
Remarriage	Males: 35 Females: 34
Widowhood	Females: 71
Death	Males: 72 Females: 79

*Ages are for white males and females and are taken from 1987 U.S. Vital Statistics data.

Family Life Cycles

That we are all moving forward in time is illustrated by the *family life cycle view* of marriage and the family. Examples of family life cycles (see Table 1.2) reveal what is happening to us at various ages. Cycle (A) is for people who marry only once and have two children. Cycle (B) is for people who get divorced and who remarry. Racial origin, family income, and education affect the timing of marital events as people proceed through the life course. For example, being black, having a lower income, and having completed less than 12 years of education increase a person's chance of divorce. Other factors associated with divorce are discussed in Chapter 18.

Social-Psychological

The *social-psychological view* emphasizes the importance of social variables as they act on the individual in marriage and the family. Examples of these variables are self-concept and the self-fulfilling prophecy.

To love oneself is the beginning of a life-long romance.
—Oscar Wilde

The *self-concept* is affected by family members who are social mirrors into which we look for information about who we are and how others feel about us. If we see approval in our parents and spouses, we develop and maintain a positive feeling about ourselves. One wife displayed her very positive self-concept in the birthday card she gave her husband. It read: "I don't know what to get you for your birthday . . . you've got everything . . . you've got me!"

The *self-fulfilling prophecy* implies that we behave according to the expectations of others. If our spouses expect us to be on time, faithful, and productive, we are likely to behave to make those expectations come true. On the other hand, if they expect us to be late, unfaithful, and lazy, we are likely not to disappoint them.

Consideration

What expectations do you have of your partner and what expectations does your partner have of you in regard to punctuality, faithfulness, and productivity? If these expectations are positive, then the behavior is also likely to be positive. In a sense, you find what you look for in your partner and your partner finds what he or she looks for in you.

Social Class

Stratification, a term that has been borrowed from geology, refers to the differential ranking of people into higher or lower horizontal layers or strata. When individuals who occupy similar social positions on the scale of prestige are stratified, we say they are in the same *social class.* Students on your campus have been stratified into the academic classes of freshmen, sophomores, juniors, and seniors.

Marriages and families are also stratified into different social classes. The criteria used to define "social class" dictates whether marriage and family are regarded as belonging to the upper, middle, or lower classes. Although family background, values, and goals may help to identify an individual's social class, the most frequently used criteria are income, occupation, and education. Table 1.3 reflects the percentages of white families in the United States at different income levels. Black families earn 58 percent and Hispanic families earn 65 percent of the median income of white families (*Statistical Abstract of the United States,* 1987). Whites typically have higher-paying, more prestigious occupations than blacks or Hispanics. Data regarding education follows.

TABLE 1.3 INCOME OF WHITE FAMILIES IN THE UNITED STATES

Amount	*Percentage*
$10,000 or less	20%
$10,000–14,999	12%
$15,000–24,999	21%
$25,000–49,999	33%
$50,000 and more	15%

Source: *Statistical Abstract of the United States,* 1987.

Data – Of those completing four years or more of college education, 20 percent are white, 11.1 percent are black, and 8.5 percent are of Spanish origin. (*Statistical Abstract of the United States*, 1987)

Consideration

One way to assess social class is to define it in terms of acceptance—for example, who asks whom to dinner. If you want to know who your social-class equals are, look across the table at your next meal.

RACE

There are racial differences in the ways in which blacks, Mexican Americans, Asian Americans, and whites experience marriage and the family. Blacks and Chicanos are more economically disadvantaged than whites, which increases marital stress and results in a higher divorce rate. Asian Americans also have lower incomes than whites but are less likely to divorce than blacks or Chicanos due to a profamily and antidivorce value.

Black females are more likely than white females to be without a husband and to rear their children alone. A shortage of black males is a result of a lower life expectancy, a greater number of homicides, and a greater tendency to be in prison, mental institutions, or on drugs than is characteristic of whites. Black males also have fewer positive role models (many grow up without a father) and are stereotyped in the media as "irresponsible, hustling fathers who avoid gainful employment and sexually exploit women" (Poussaint, 1986). Such stereotypes belie employed, nurturing, caretaking black men who are devoted to their wives and children.

ROLE

Marriage and family relationships may also be viewed from a role perspective. *Roles* are behaviors in which individuals are expected to engage. The more common roles in marriage and the family are those of wife, husband, and child. *Role theory* emphasizes that one role does not exist without another (there is no wife without a husband), that roles are interactive (you say "hello" and someone else responds in kind), and that the greatest predictor of what you will do is to know what role you are playing. (As a fianceé, you will sit close to your partner when riding in a car; as a spouse, you will rarely do so.)

CRISIS

Marriage and the family may also be viewed from a crisis perspective. A *crisis* may be defined as an event for which old patterns of adaptation are no longer helpful. Most individuals, spouses, and parents experience one or more crisis events in their lifetimes. Examples of crisis events include planned and unplanned pregnancy, divorce, widowhood, alcoholism, extramarital intercourse, incest, infertility, the birth of a child, unemployment, military separation, imprisonment of spouse, and spouse abuse. A crisis event may stem from an external source (for example, a recession may cause unemployment) or from an internal source (discovery of a spouse's affair may encourage alcoholism). Couples who successfully respond to crisis events have high degrees of *cohesion,* or emotional bonding, and *adaptability*—the ability of the marital system to change its power structure, role relationships, and rules in response to new situations. (Anderson, 1986).

Information Sources for Marriage and the Family

This text is based on a comprehensive review of studies in the area of marriage and the family that have been reported in professional journals. The most important journals in the marriage and family field include the following:

Family Relations
Family Process
Journal of Family Issues
Journal of Marriage and the Family
American Sociological Review
Journal of Family History
Journal of Family Therapy
Sex Roles
American Journal of Family Therapy
American Journal of Sociology
Journal of Divorce
Journal of Family Law
Family Planning Perspectives
Adolescence
Journal of Sex and Marital Therapy
Journal of Sex Research
Journal of Family Welfare
Journal of Marital and Family Therapy
Family Law Quarterly
Journal of Adolescence

Although not specific to marriage and the family, the following professional journals frequently include studies on interpersonal relationships, divorce, and sexuality:

Journal of Home Economics
Child Development
Journal of Gerontology
Studies in Family Planning
Journal of Social Issues
American Journal of Orthopsychiatry
SIECUS Report
Gerontologist

Two weekly newsletters report the latest information in the marriage and family field:

Marriage and Divorce Today
Sexuality Today

Some Cautions About Research

Although the findings of the various studies presented in the publications just listed do furnish a basis for making choices in the area of marriage and the family, it is wise to be cautious about research. Some research limitations to be aware of are discussed in the following sections.

Sampling

Most information about marriage and the family is based on *sampling*—studying a relatively small number of individuals randomly selected from an identified population and assuming that those studied are similar to that population.

My latest survey shows that people don't believe in surveys.
—Laurence Peter

For example, suppose you want to know the percentage of unmarried seniors (US) on your campus who are living together. Although the most accurate way to get this information is to secure an anonymous "yes" or "no" response from every US, doing so is not practical. To save yourself time, you could ask a few USs to complete your questionnaire and assume that the rest of the USs would say "yes" or "no" in the same proportion as those who did. To decide who those few USs would be, you could put the names of every US on campus on separate note cards, stir these cards in your bathtub, put on a blindfold, and draw 100 cards. Because each US would have an equal chance of having his or her card drawn from the tub, you would obtain what is known as a *random sample.* After administering the questionnaire to this sample and adding the "yes" and "no" answers, you would have a fairly accurate idea of the percentage of USs on your campus who are living together.

Due to the trouble and expense of obtaining random samples, most researchers study subjects to whom they have convenient access. This often means students in the researchers' classes. The result is an overabundance of research on "convenience" samples consisting of white, Protestant, middle-class college students.

Consideration

Because today's college students comprise only about 7 percent of all American adults, their attitudes, feelings, and behaviors cannot be assumed to be similar to those of their noncollege peers or older adults.

Although the data presented in this text include those obtained from young unmarried college students, they also refer to people of different ages, marital statuses, racial backgrounds, life styles, religions, and social classes.

Control Groups

Just as most samples are not representative, most marriage and family research is not experimental, because *control groups* (the groups that are not exposed to the factors being tested) are not used. The value of a control group is that it allows the researcher to draw more certain conclusions about the answers to particular questions. We could not conclude that taking a marriage and family course influenced reported desire to live together (which might be true in the experimental group) if those in the control group also reported an increased desire to live together even though they did not take a marriage and family class. Hence, it is essential to include a control group in marriage and family research if we want to know the effect that one factor has on another.

Terminology

In addition to being alert to potential shortcomings in sampling and control groups, you should consider how the phenomenon being researched is defined. For example, in the preceding illustration, how would you define *living together?* How many people, of what sex, spending what amount of time, in what place, engaging in what behaviors will constitute your definition?

Data – Researchers of living together have used more than 20 definitions.

What about other terms? What is meant by marital satisfaction, commitment, interpersonal violence, and sexual fulfillment? Before accepting that most people report a high degree of marital satisfaction or sexual fulfillment, be alert to the definition used by the researcher. Exactly what is the researcher trying to measure?

Researcher Bias

Even when the sample is random and the terms are carefully defined, two researchers can examine the same data and arrive at different conclusions. In your study of living together, suppose you find that 25 percent of the students on your campus are living together. In discussing your findings, would you emphasize that fact or the fact that the majority of the students (75 percent) are not living together? You can focus on either aspect of the data to make the point you want to make. Many researchers tend to focus on selected aspects of the data they are reporting.

Also, the answer a researcher gets is related to the question she or he asks. In one *New York Times*/CBS poll, 30 percent of the respondents answered "yes" when asked, "Do you think there should be an amendment to the Constitution prohibiting abortions, or shouldn't there be such an amendment?" But when the same people were asked, "Do you believe there should be an amendment to the Constitution protecting the life of the unborn child?," 50 percent answered "yes."

Time Lag

There is typically a two-year lag between the time a research study is completed and its appearance in a professional journal. Because textbooks are based on these journals and take from three to five years from writing to publication, by the time you read the results of a study, other studies may have been conducted that reveal different findings. Be aware that the research you read in this or any text may not reflect current reality. Many of the journals listed earlier will be in your library; you might compare the findings of recent studies with the studies reported in this text.

Distortion and Deception

Researchers in all fields may encounter problems of sampling, terminology, lack of a control group, researcher bias, and time lag, but other problems specific to social science research—particularly to marriage research—are distortion and deception. Marriage is a very private relationship that happens behind closed doors, and we have been socialized not to reveal to strangers the intimate details of our marriages. Therefore, we are prone to distort, omit, or exaggerate information, perhaps unconsciously, to cover up what we may feel is no one else's business. Thus, the researcher sometimes obtains inaccurate information. Marriage and family researchers only know what people say they do, not what they actually do.

You can fool some of the people all of the time, and all of the people some of the time, but you cannot fool all of the people all of the time.
—Abraham Lincoln

An unintentional and probably more frequent form of distortion is inaccurate recall. Sometimes researchers ask respondents to recall details of their relationships that occurred years ago. Time tends to blur some memories, and respondents may not relate what actually happened but only what they remember to have happened.

In addition to distortion on the part of the person being surveyed, outright deception on the part of the investigator is not unknown (Kohn, 1987). In response to pressures to publish or a desire for prestige and recognition, some researchers have doctored their data. For example, the late British psychologist Cyril Burt was renowned for his research designed to test the relative importance of heredity and environment on a person's development. Burt studied identical twins who had been reared in separate environments since birth and presented data that seemed to indicate clearly that heredity was more important. Five years after Burt's death, evidence came to light that he had altered his data, that his coauthors had never existed, and that the investigations had never been conducted.

Other Research Problems

Nonresponse on surveys and the discrepancy between attitudes and behaviors are other research problems. In regard to nonresponse, not all individuals who complete questionnaires or agree to participate in an interview are willing to provide information about such personal issues as money, spouse abuse, family violence, rape, sex, and alcohol abuse. They leave the questionnaire blank or tell the interviewer they would rather not respond. Others respond but give only socially desirable answers. The implications for research are that data gatherers do not know the nature or extent to which something may be a problem because people are reluctant to provide accurate information. In general, males are more likely to give less information than females.

The discrepancy between the attitudes people have and their behavior is another cause for concern about the validity of research data. It is sometimes assumed that if a person has a certain attitude (for example, extramarital sex is wrong), then his or her behavior will be consistent with that attitude (avoid extramarital sex). However, this assumption is not always accurate. People do indeed say one thing and do another. This potential discrepancy should be kept in mind when reading research on various attitudes.

Consideration

In view of the research problems outlined here, you might ask, "Why bother to report the findings?" The research picture is not as bleak as it may seem at first. A number of studies have been conducted that have none of these research drawbacks. The articles in *Journal of Marriage and the Family*, for example, illustrate the high level of methodologically sound articles that are being published. Even less sophisticated journals provide us with useful information about what is currently happening. The alternative to gathering data is relying on personal experience alone, and this is unacceptable to social scientists who study marriage and the family. (Brecher & Brecher, 1986)

Marriage and family courses are among the most popular on campus.

Trends

The farther backward you can look, the farther forward you are likely to see.
—Winston Churchill

Being married and having children will continue to be goals for most people due to the interpersonal satisfaction that these relationships provide. Regarding such satisfactions, in one of his movies, Woody Allen tells his psychiatrist about his uncle who thinks he is a chicken. The psychiatrist asks, "How long has he been thinking he is a chicken?" "Several years," Allen says. "But why haven't you reported this before now?," asks the psychiatrist. Allen replies, "It's because we need the eggs."

For all the problems that interpersonal relationships may cause, we continue to seek them. Marriage and family relationships in particular feed the emotional part of ourselves. These relationships involve primary groups of intimate individuals. In contrast, we more easily tire of impersonal, secondary group relationships with those with whom we interact during the business day (the person who serves you a burger at McDonald's is in a secondary group relationship to you) and look forward to more personal interaction with primary group members at the end of the day. Marriage is here to stay.

Functional (applied) courses in marriage and the family will be in ever-increasing demand by students. Concern over a high divorce rate coupled with a desire that their marriages will be different will compel more students to take such courses in the hope of finding out what they can learn to help them increase the chance of their own marriage or remarriage being a success.

Summary

Life is a series of choices. Deciding whether to marry, whether to have children, whether to have two careers in one marriage, whether to be monogamous, and whether to view a situation positively are among the more important choices you will ever make in your lifetime. This text examines the nature and consequences of these and more than 50 other choices.

Although we tend to think of choosing as an act, if you decide not to choose, you have already made a choice by default. The theme of this text is to take charge of your life by making deliberate choices in your interpersonal relationships. Such choices, particularly in marriage and the family, are continuous. While the single are contemplating whether to marry, the married are deciding whether to stay married and the divorced are considering whether to remarry.

As we will discuss in the choices section at the end of this chapter, the choices we make do not occur in a vacuum. Rather, they are influenced by the choices we see others make and the degree to which they approve of our choices. Such societal events as inflation, unemployment, and legislation also influence our choices.

Perspectives other than "choices" of marriage and the family include the structure–function, family life cycle, social–psychological, social class, race, role, and crisis views. The structure–function perspective emphasizes the benefits to society of the institutions of marriage and family. Marriage bonds a female and a male together in a legal relationship that obligates them to nurture and socialize any offspring they may have. Because society and its institutions depend on marriage and the family for new members, marriage will continue to be a valuable institution in our society.

Marriage in the United States is both an emotional relationship and a legal commitment. It usually includes a public announcement, a public ceremony, and sexual monogamy. It always provides for the transfer of property and the legitimizing of children. Marriage in other societies may be monogamous or polygamous. Polygamy may be polygynous when one man has several wives or polyandrous when one wife has several husbands. The latter is rare.

Family in the United States refers to a group of people who live together, cooperate economically, and reproduce. A wife, husband, and children represent the usual American family, although several variations (two spouses or two siblings or one parent and one child) also qualify as a family. The family of orientation is the one into which we are born; the family of procreation is the one we begin with our own spouse.

The research reported in this text should be viewed cautiously. Inherent in most research may be such methodological problems as the use of a small, nonrandom sample, lack of a control group, vague terminology, researcher bias, and distortion. These cautions do not imply that all research is problematic. Indeed, journals that report studies of marriage and family are becoming more sophisticated in their methodology and reflect some excellent research.

Although the form of marriage and the family will continue to change (for example, dual-income marriages and single-parent households will increase), the importance of marriage and the family as a set of relationships that meets our emotional needs for love and support will continue.

Questions for Reflection

1. What is the most significant choice you have made in reference to your interpersonal relationships?

2. If you knew that studying marriage and the family as a personal search would contribute to the break up of your relationship with your partner, would you still choose to study the subject from this perspective? (Questions 2 and 3 will become meaningful after reading the choices section that follows.)
3. Describe several decisions you have made by deciding not to decide.

CHOICES

CHOOSING TO STUDY marriage and the family as an academic exercise or a personal search, consciously choosing between two alternatives or choosing by default, and choosing to be tolerant or condemnatory about the decisions of others are basic choices to be made in a marriage and family course.

MARRIAGE AND FAMILY: AN ACADEMIC OR PERSONAL SEARCH?

Until your final grade for this course is posted, you will be involved in the systematic study of marriage and the family. One way to regard this course and the content of this text is as an academic exercise in which you come to class, take notes, skim the book, take tests, and go to the next course without ever becoming involved with the content. This is a legitimate choice. People take marriage and family courses for a variety of reasons and may do so to complete a social science requirement, to fill a transcript, or out of intellectual curiosity.

An alternative reason for studying marriage and the family is to explore the intimate relationship between you and your lover, spouse, or parents with the goal of making better decisions in your own life about marriage and family issues. As one student said:

> A lot of people I know, including my parents and brother, are divorced or running around on their partners. I want to know all I can about why people do these things so I can help avoid similar things happening to me. My partner and I are taking this course together in hopes that we can beat the odds.

You may choose to regard the study of marriage and the family as an academic or personal search, or as both. Some people have mixed feelings:

> Somehow I feel that some things should remain a mystery and maybe marriage, love, and sex are things you shouldn't "study"—it might take the spontaneity out of them if you do. On the other hand, I think of marriage the same way I do a garden. Some things make it flourish, and some things make it wither. Knowing what those things are could make the differences in being happily married and being divorced three times.

CHOOSING CAREFULLY OR CHOOSING BY DEFAULT

Some of us believe we can avoid making decisions about marriage and the family. We cannot, because not to decide is to decide by default. Some examples follow:

- If we don't make a decision to pursue a relationship with a particular person, then we have made a decision (by default) to let that person drift out of our lives.
- If we don't decide to do these things that are necessary to keep or improve the relationships we have, then we have made a decision to let them slowly disintegrate.
- If we don't make a decision to be faithful to our dating partner or spouse, then we have made a decision to be open to situations and relationships in which we are likely to be unfaithful.
- If we don't make a decision to avoid having intercourse with a new partner early in the relationship, then we have made a decision to let intercourse occur.
- If we are sexually active and don't make a decision to use some form of birth control, then we have made a decision to become a parent.
- If we don't make a decision to break up with our dating partner or spouse, then we

(Continued)

have made a decision to continue the relationship with him or her.

Throughout the text, we consider various choices with which we are confronted in the area of marriage and the family. It will be helpful for us to keep in mind that we cannot avoid making choices—that not to make a choice is to make one.

Tolerance or Condemnation for the Choices of Others?

Regardless of the choices we make about our own behavior and life styles, we must also make a choice about the rights of others to make choices that are different from ours. Most people are relatively tolerant of the choices others make. According to one woman:

> One of my closest friends has started living with her partner. While I wouldn't want to do this myself, I feel it is okay for her to do what she wants.

Some people find it more difficult to be tolerant about homosexuality. The same woman remarked of another friend:

> I couldn't believe she was gay when she told me. I can't handle her being gay and told her so. My tolerance stops when my friends want to be or do something that is unnatural. I guess I'd feel the same way if my boyfriend said he wanted to tie me up to have sex.

Impact of Social Influences on Choices

Earlier in this chapter, we noted that the decisions you make are influenced by the social context and social forces of those decisions. The degree to which you view the study of marriage and the family as an academic or a personal search may be influenced by the marriages of your parents, siblings, and friends, by a current partner, and by your level of involvement. For example, if your parents, siblings and most of your close friends are divorced, you may be more cautious about marrying and you may view the study of marriage and the family as more than a course on a transcript. Your awareness that 50 percent of all marriages end in divorce may further influence your study of marriage and the family.

Your perception of this course may also be influenced by a current partner. If she or he feels that the study of marriage and the family is silly because "you can't learn about real life from books," then she or he may not be interested in discussing these issues with you. Such lack of support for the study of marriage and the family may influence you to treat it only as "another course" and not to discuss it with your partner. Hence, the event of taking a marriage and family course will be perceived in reference to the marriages of those close to you and the opinions of those important to you.

Finally, your consideration of various personal choices may be related to the family in which you have been reared. For example, Asian American families are more likely than white families to believe in the importance of the family unit at the expense of the individual. Hence, the consideration of divorce and the subsequent decision to do so are much less likely to happen among Asian Americans than among whites (Staples & Mirandé, 1980).

CHAPTER 2

Love Relationships

Contents

Is It True?*

1. Women are more romantic than men.
2. Being in love is good for your health.
3. A person in love is expected to suffer and endure pain.
4. Love is more important than sex for human happiness.
5. Men are more likely to be jealous than women.

*1 = researchers disagree; 2 = T; 3 = T; 4 = T; 5 = F.

"BECAUSE WE'RE IN love" is the reason most Americans give for wanting to get married. "Loss of love" is also the reason many couples give for wanting to get a divorce. Due to the importance of love in our (western) decision to marry and divorce, it is imperative that we try to understand the dynamics of love—how it develops, how it dies, and how to keep it alive and flourishing.

Although parent–child, sibling–sibling, and friend–friend relationships (same or opposite gender) often involve love, heterosexual and homosexual love feelings are the focus of this chapter. Here, we will explore various definitions of love, the importance of love, and the relationship scripts men and women learn. We will conclude with an examination of the similarities and differences between love and sex.

Definitions and Dilemmas of Love

Love is the only thing I know that hurts so good.
—Dennis Rogers

La Rochefoucauld said, "True love is like ghosts which everyone has talked about but few have seen." His definition suggests that love feelings are mysterious and that the individual alone has access to what she or he experiences. Because the experience is personal, the definitions of love are varied.

When students in the author's classes were asked to "define the meaning of love," some listed various qualities like "caring," "compassion," "respect," "sharing," and "commitment." One student said that "love is sacrificing because you want to;" another said that "love is being in a crowded room full of beautiful people of the opposite gender and wishing you were alone with your partner."

Consideration

The one element these definitions have in common is that they are different. Love is a private emotional experience; no single definition can cover all its variety.

The worst of having a romance of any kind is that it leaves one so unromantic.
—Oscar Wilde

Love may not only be defined differently; it may also be expressed in complicated ways that create dilemmas for us. One dilemma includes being in love with two people at the same time. "I know I love my husband," said one woman, "but I also love the man I work with." Such a dilemma is not unusual. The feelings are a consequence of being in two relationships at the same time that have engendered these feelings. It is possible to be involved in several relationships at the same time and to have love feelings for each of the people. But although it is possible to love two or more people at the same time, it is not possible to love them to the same degree at any particular moment because an individual must make a choice in terms of how to spend his or her time. If you choose to spend time with person X, then you value that person more than others—at least for that moment in time.

Consideration

Some people do not like the feeling of being in love with two people at once and try to reduce their feelings for one of them. This is often accomplished by deciding to see only one of the persons and by thinking negative things about the other. For example, Jan, who was in love with both her husband and her colleague, decided to stop seeing her colleague socially. When she did think of him, she made herself think only of the negative aspects of being involved with him—he was married, he drank heavily, he was 12 years older than she, and he had three children.

Another dilemma of love is being in love with a totally inappropriate person. Someone who is radically different in age, who has severe problems (alcoholism, drug addiction), who values nothing you value, who criticizes you continually, and who lies to you may not be a good partner for you. Nevertheless, you might love that person and feel that everything will turn out all right in the end. Most marriage therapists would empathize with your love feelings and suggest that you look at the payoffs for your loving this person. Does it upset your parents? Do you feel this is what you deserve because you are "no good"? Do you feel pity for the person and want to be her or his therapist? These questions imply that the love relationship is based on some motivations that should be carefully examined.

Importance of Love

Although people disagree about the definition of love, they rarely disagree about its importance. In a study of 224 husband–wife couples, "love and affection" were more important for marital satisfaction than sex or open communication (Rettig & Bubolz, 1983).

Health Significance

Health may be adversely affected by unfulfilled love needs. A specialist in psychosomatic disease (Lynch, 1977) reported that being lonely and unloved often leads to heart disease and premature death for the single, widowed, and divorced. Also, in a study on love and health (Kemper & Bologh, 1981), the respondents who had recently ended a love relationship had the most negative health status. The authors concluded, "A relationship of long duration that is going well appears to have a positive effect on one's health status" (p. 86).

Emotional Significance

In a nationwide study on happiness, the researchers concluded that the presence of a love relationship was essential for many people if they were to be happy (Freedman, 1978). Diana Ross remarked on the Johnny Carson show, "I want to be in love again," partly echoing Tennyson's

O that 'twere possible
After long grief and pain
To find the arms of my true love
Round me once again!

The world is a comedy to those that think, a tragedy to those who feel.

—Horace Walpole

Love is important for our physical and emotional health.

For some people, love is addictive (Peele & Brodsky, 1976). It produces a feeling of euphoria that a person learns to enjoy and depend on. Once we get accustomed to the euphoria of love, we need to be with our partner to feel the heightened sense of contentment and happiness. Withdrawal symptoms—depression, unhappiness, even somatic complaints—may begin when the love relationship is broken. According to these writers, the person suffering from a broken love relationship goes through withdrawal in much the same way as an alcoholic who has given up alcohol.

Consideration

Although love may be important for our emotional well-being, we all differ in the degree to which we need love relationships. For some of us, our support system of friends satisfies our need for connectedness. An intense one-on-one love relationship may not be necessary or desirable. "I don't like the obligations that creep into a love relationship," said one woman. "I have a lot of friends and enjoy being with them, but I don't need to be 'deeply in love' with a particular person to be happy or productive in my work." Other people may only feel content when in a love relationship and inordinately depressed if not.

Conditions of Love

Love sometimes develops under various social, psychological, physiological, and cognitive conditions.

Social Conditions

Our society provides a basic context for love feelings to develop by emphasizing the importance of love. Through popular music, movies, television, and novels, the message is clear: love is an experience to enjoy and to pursue; you are missing something if you are not in love.

Peer influence is also important in creating the conditions for love to develop. Many of our peers establish love relationships and pair off. Their doing so makes love relationships normative and encourages us to seek the same experience. "All but one of my closest friends are involved in a steady love relationship," said one math major. "I'm wondering when I'm going to fall in love and be involved with someone."

Our society also links love and marriage. Couples who are about to get married are expected to be in love. If they are not, they would be ashamed to admit it. The fact that more than 90 percent of all Americans marry suggests that few escape the love feelings that are supposed to accompany courtship and marriage.

Psychological Conditions

Two psychological conditions are sometimes associated with falling in love: a positive self-concept and the ability to self-disclose.

Positive Self-Concept/Self Love

The way you feel about yourself is your self-concept. If you have a positive self-concept, you like yourself and enjoy being who you are.

A positive self-concept is important to the development of love; once you accept yourself, you can believe that others are capable of doing so too. In contrast, a negative self-concept has devastating consequences for the individual and the people with whom he or she becomes involved. Individuals who cannot accept themselves tend to reject others. "My daddy always told me I was no good and would never amount to anything," said one man. "I guess I have always believed him, have never liked myself, and can't think of why someone else would either." Woody Allen has become famous for exploiting a negative self-concept. Groucho Marx once said, "I would never want to belong to an organization that would have me as a member."

I am larger, better than I thought. I did not know I held so much goodness.
—Walt Whitman

The way we feel about ourselves and our ability to relate intimately to others are learned behaviors. Our first potential love relationships were with our parents or the person who cared for us in infancy. As babies we were helpless. When we were hungry, cold, or wet, we cried until someone came to take care of us. Our parents became associated with reducing our discomfort.

If we were well cared for as infants, we were helped to establish a good self-concept by being taught two things: (1) we were somebody that someone else cared about, and (2) other people were good because they did things that made us feel good. When people learn as young children to love and trust those around them, they can generalize this experience to others and eventually establish loving adult relationships.

Self-Disclosure

In addition to feeling good about yourself, it is helpful to disclose your feelings to others if you want to love and be loved. Disclosing yourself is a way of

Being loved is important for a positive self-concept.

investing yourself in another. Once the other person knows some of the intimate details of your life, you will tend to feel more positively about that person because a part of you is now a part of them.

In a study (Rubin et al., 1980) of 231 couples who defined themselves as "going together," the researchers observed that the more the partners disclosed themselves to each other, the greater their love feelings for each other and the closer they regarded their relationship. As for what they disclosed, 70 percent of the women and men reported they had disclosed "fully" their feelings about their sexual relationship, and six in 10 had given full information about their previous sexual experiences. "Even in an area in which one would expect the greatest degree of reserve, 38 percent of the women and 35 percent of the men reported that they had revealed fully to their partners the things about themselves they were most ashamed of" (p. 313).

It is not easy for some people to let others know who they are, what they feel, or what they think. They may fear that if others really know them, they may be rejected as a friend or lover. To guard against this possibility, they may protect themselves and their relationships by allowing only limited access to their thoughts and feelings.

Trust is the condition under which people are willing to disclose themselves. To feel comfortable about letting someone else inside their head, they must feel that whatever feelings or information they share will not be judged and will be kept safe with that person. If trust is betrayed, a person may become bitterly resentful and vow never to disclose herself or himself again.

One woman said, "After I told my partner that I had had an abortion, he told me that I was a murderer and he never wanted to see me again. I was hurt and felt I had made a mistake telling him about my intimate life. You can bet I'll be careful before I disclose myself to someone else."

Partners who are successful in disclosing to each other tend to feel better about their relationship—not only in courtship, but also in marriage. In a study of 120 couples (Jorgensen & Gaudy, 1980), those reporting the highest levels of satisfaction also reported the highest levels of self-disclosure. "Being open about fears, problems, self-doubts, feelings of anger or depression, and aspects of marriage perceived to be bothersome to one or both partners, as well as openly sharing positive feelings about the self and other" (p. 286) contributed to the happiness of the respective spouses.

But disclosure must be equal to benefit the relationship. In one study (Davidson et al., 1983), the researchers found that those partners who were similar in affective disclosure had better adjustment than those who were dissimilar.

> "We both love each other at the same level," said one woman. "I tell him that I love him about as often as he tells me. I was once in a relationship where the guy loved me more than I loved him. He would always be telling me that he loved me. I got tired of hearing him say that, and it made me feel guilty when he did."

Consideration

Although it helps to have a positive self-concept at the beginning of a love relationship, sometimes this develops after becoming involved in a love relationship. "I've always felt like an ugly duckling," said one woman. "But once I fell in love with him and he with me, I felt very different. I felt very good about myself then because I knew that I was somebody that someone else could love."

Other partners keep their disclosure at a very low level until after they define themselves as being in love. "I can't tell anybody anything that matters until after I feel that I can trust them," said one man. "When I start to love them, I usually tell them more than they want to know."

Physiological and Cognitive Conditions

There are many people who would never have been in love if they had never heard love spoken of.
—La Rochefoucauld

After the social and psychological conditions of love are operative, the physiological and cognitive components of love become important. The individual must be physiologically aroused and interpret this stirred-up state as love (Schacter, 1964; Walster & Walster, 1978). For example, Carol was beginning her first year at a midwestern university. Being three states away from home in an unfamiliar environment, she felt lonely and bored. During registration, she met a good-looking junior. They exchanged pleasant glances and small talk and planned to go out together that night around 8:00. Carol became anxious when Brad had not shown up by 8:45. When he finally arrived at 9:00 (car trouble had delayed him), they went to a concert, drank some beer, and played video games at a local pub. Carol had a terrific time.

Two days went by before Carol heard from Brad again. He called to ask if she wanted to go home with him for the weekend. By the end of that weekend, Carol felt she was in love. Her loneliness, the fun they had when they were together, frustration (she never knew when Brad would call or come by), and sexual arousal (they had petted but had not yet had intercourse) were enough to induce an agitated, stirred-up state. Both her roommates were "in love," so Carol identified herself as being in the same condition.

Consideration

Social, psychological, physiological, and cognitive conditions are not the only factors important for the development of love feelings. The timing must also be right. There are only certain times in your life when you are in the "market" for a love relationship. When those times occur, you are likely to fall in love with the person who is there and also "in the market." Hence, many love pairings exist because each of the individuals is available to the other—not because they are particularly suited for each other.

The Lover Role

When all of the foregoing conditions are met, an individual may assume the role of lover. Like all roles, the role of lover suggests that the person will engage in certain behavior. First, the lover can be expected to idealize the partner. The lover will see qualities that are not there (perhaps the person is "never" selfish) and avoid seeing qualities that are there (such as the beginning of a drinking problem). Such idealization is functional. It enhances the lover's self-esteem ("I must be a terrific person if I am in a love relationship with such a terrific person").

Another consequence of the lover role is that of suffering. The lover expects to endure a certain amount of pain, from either longing, unrequited love, or outright rejection.

> The suffering element of the lover role has an additional consequence: the lover is allowed to continue suffering because he is in love. If one regularly absorbs abuse from his neighbor and takes no action, his behavior is considered foolish; it is expected that one take immediate action to avoid further pain. However, if one is suffering rejection from his lover, it is expected that he endure the pain while attempting to establish mutual love. (Buehler & Wells, 1981, p. 454)

A final element of the lover role is fantasy. The lover is allowed to spend a great deal of time envisioning a future that may be unrealistic. "The two of us together in a cottage by the sea" is a visual image of how some lovers think of marriage. The demands of working until 10:30 p.m. on the job or getting up three times a night with an infant who has colic is rarely part of the fantasy.

A Triangular Theory of Love

Love may be viewed as consisting of three central elements—intimacy, passion, and commitment (Sternberg, 1986). *Intimacy* (the top vertex of the triangle) is the emotional connectedness that two people feel for each other. The partners feel bonded to each other in a context of emotional warmth.

Lovers sometimes idealize each other.

Passion (the left-hand vertex of the triangle) refers to the romantic and physical aspects of the relationship. The partners are physiologically aroused in reference to each other.

Commitment (the right-hand vertex of the triangle) is the desire to maintain the relationship. This is the cognitive aspect of the relationship over which the partners exercise the greatest conscious control.

Various kinds of love can be described on the basis of these three elements.

1. *Nonlove:* The absence of all three components in reference to another person.
2. *Liking:* The intimacy element of the relationship is present, but passion and commitment in the future are lacking.
3. *Infatuation:* The experience of passion without intimacy or commitment.
4. *Empty love:* The absence of both intimacy and passion but a commitment to love another.
5. *Consummate love:* A love resulting from a full combination of intimacy, passion, and commitment.

Consideration

To what degree are intimacy, passion, and commitment elements of the love relationship you have or have had? How important are each of these elements in terms of your satisfaction in a love relationship?

Romantic and Realistic Love

Emotion has taught mankind to reason.
—Marquis de Vauvenargues

For some people, love is romantic; for others, it is realistic. *Romantic love* (sometimes referred to as *infatuation*) is characterized by such beliefs as "love at first sight," "there is only one true love," and "love conquers all." The symptoms of romantic love include drastic mood swings, palpitations of the heart, and intrusive thinking about the partner. Romantic love is a combination of intimacy and passion (Trotter, 1986).

In contrast to romantic love, *realistic love,* or *conjugal love,* tends to be characteristic of people who have been in love with each other for several years. Partners who know all about each other yet still love each other are said to have a realistic view of love.

It is impossible to love and be wise.
—Francis Bacon

The following Self-Assessment—the Love Attitudes Scale—is a way for you to measure the degree to which you are romantic or realistic. You might want to take the inventory and sum up your numbered responses into a total score. 1 (strongly agree) is the most romantic response, and 5 (strongly disagree) is the most realistic response. Thus, the lower your total score (30 is the lowest possible score), the more romantic you are about love, and the higher your score (150 is the highest possible score), the more realistic you are about love. A score of 90 places you at the midpoint on the scale of romantic–realistic love.

Consideration

When you determine your score on the Love Attitudes Scale, be aware that you are merely assessing the degree to which you are a romantic or a realist. Your tendency to be one or the other is not good or bad. Both romantics and realists may be happy, mature people.

Some of the beliefs and comments of people who have completed the Love Attitudes Scale follow.

Love at First Sight? (Self-Assessment Statement 11)

"To love someone 'at first sight,' " said one woman "means that you are only physically attracted to that person. This is usually infatuation, not love." She disagrees that love happens quickly and feels that the longer it takes for love to develop, the longer it will last.

One spouse said that love "at first sight" had happened to him and his wife:

> I spotted her in the auditorium in high school when she was reading a part for a school play. I was in love with her before she finished her lines. I asked a friend to introduce us, and we started dating. That was 23 years ago; today, we have three children. For me, just like the song says, "Just one look, that's all it took."

Love Conquers All? (Self-Assessment Statement 13)

Realists disagree that you can work out all your problems if you have enough love. "Loving a person does not come with a guarantee of a problem-free life,"

Self-Assessment

The Love Attitudes Scale*

Directions: Read each sentence carefully and circle the number that you believe best represents your opinion. Be sure to respond to all statements.

1 Strongly agree
2 Mildly agree
3 Undecided
4 Mildly disagree
5 Strongly disagree

	SA	MA	U	MD	SD
1. Love doesn't make sense. It just is.	1	2	3	4	5
2. When you fall "head over heels" in love, it's sure to be the real thing.	1	2	3	4	5
3. To be in love with someone you would like to marry but can't is a tragedy.	1	2	3	4	5
4. When love hits, you know it.	1	2	3	4	5
5. Common interests are really unimportant; as long as each of you is truly in love, you will adjust.	1	2	3	4	5
6. It doesn't matter if you marry after you have known your partner for only a short time as long as you know you are in love.	1	2	3	4	5
7. If you are going to love a person, you will "know" after a short time.	1	2	3	4	5
8. As long as two people love each other, the educational differences they have really do not matter.	1	2	3	4	5
9. You can love someone even though you do not like any of that person's friends.	1	2	3	4	5
10. When you are in love, you are usually in a daze.	1	2	3	4	5
11. Love "at first sight" is often the deepest and most enduring type of love.	1	2	3	4	5
12. When you are in love, it really does not matter what your partner does because you will love him or her anyway.	1	2	3	4	5

(Continued)

Self-Assessment

13. As long as you really love a person, you will be able to solve the problems you have with that person.	1	2	3	4	5
14. Usually you can really love and be happy with only one or two people in the world.	1	2	3	4	5
15. Regardless of other factors, if you truly love another person, that is a good enough reason to marry that person.	1	2	3	4	5
16. It is necessary to be in love with the one you marry to be happy.	1	2	3	4	5
17. Love is more of a feeling than a relationship.	1	2	3	4	5
18. People should not get married unless they are in love.	1	2	3	4	5
19. Most people truly love only once during their lives.	1	2	3	4	5
20. Somewhere there is an ideal mate for most people.	1	2	3	4	5
21. In most cases, you will "know it" when you meet the right partner.	1	2	3	4	5
22. Jealously usually varies directly with love; that is, the more you are in love, the greater your tendency to become jealous will be.	1	2	3	4	5
23. When you are in love, you are motivated by what you feel rather than by what you think.	1	2	3	4	5
24. Love is best described as an exciting rather than a calm thing.	1	2	3	4	5
25. Most divorces probably result from falling out of love rather than failing to adjust.	1	2	3	4	5
26. When you are in love, your judgment is usually not too clear.	1	2	3	4	5
27. Love often comes only once in a lifetime.	1	2	3	4	5
28. Love is often a violent and uncontrollable emotion.	1	2	3	4	5
29. When selecting a marriage partner, differences in social class and religion are of small importance compared with love.	1	2	3	4	5
30. No matter what anyone says, love cannot be understood.	1	2	3	4	5

*From D. Knox, *The love attitudes inventory,* rev.ed. (Saluda, N.C.: Family Life Publications, 1983). Reprinted by permission.

said one dual-career wife in Denver. "The spouses can have different personalities and priorities, and love won't be able to resolve everything."

But sometimes love does conquer all. Karen is engaged to a graduate student who lives in another state. She says of their relationship, "Had it not been for the deep love we have for each other, our relationship would never have survived the separations and abortion we had to go through. Love was the glue that kept our relationship together."

One True Love? (Self-Assessment Statement 14)

The magic of first love is our ignorance that it can never end.
—Disraeli

The romantic believes that he or she will love only one person completely. "While you may love more than one person in your lifetime," said one wife of 18 years, "you will have only *one true love.* This is the person who has a special place in your heart and mind even though you can't be with that particular individual."

Sometimes a person believes there is only "one true love" until that true love is replaced. This happened to one husband, who said, "I fell in love with a girl in high school and dated her through two years of college. I was deeply in love with her. But she moved away when her dad was transferred to another state. I thought the end of the world had come until I met the woman who became my wife."

Ideal Mate? (Self-Assessment Statement 20)

One husband said he believed in ideal mates because the way his wife talked about her first husband, he must have been one. Romantics feel there is one special person for each person. Realists disagree, saying that any one person can meet, fall in love with, and be happy with numerous people. "I'd better tell you that my wife is the only person I could be happy with," said one husband, "because if I didn't, she'd whop me on my bald head with a skillet."

Love Comes Once, Twice, Three Times? (Self-Assessment Statement 27)

"He's the only one I've ever really loved" reflects the feelings of the romantic. Such was the experience of Lauren Bacall. She spoke of Humphrey Bogart as her one great love, and while emphasizing that life goes on and that she had adjusted, she remarked that the specialness they shared would never come again. Dionne Warwick sings in one of her songs, "I'll never love this way again."

Realists don't buy that view. They believe that each person can enjoy a great love relationship with numerous people. "I've loved many men," said one woman, "and while I've loved each one in a different way, it doesn't mean that I've loved any one of them less than the others." The song "For All The Girls I've Loved Before" reflects the theme of various loves.

Who Is Romantic? Who Is Realistic?

Using the Love Attitudes Scale, several studies have been conducted to find out the degree to which various categories of people are romantic or realistic.

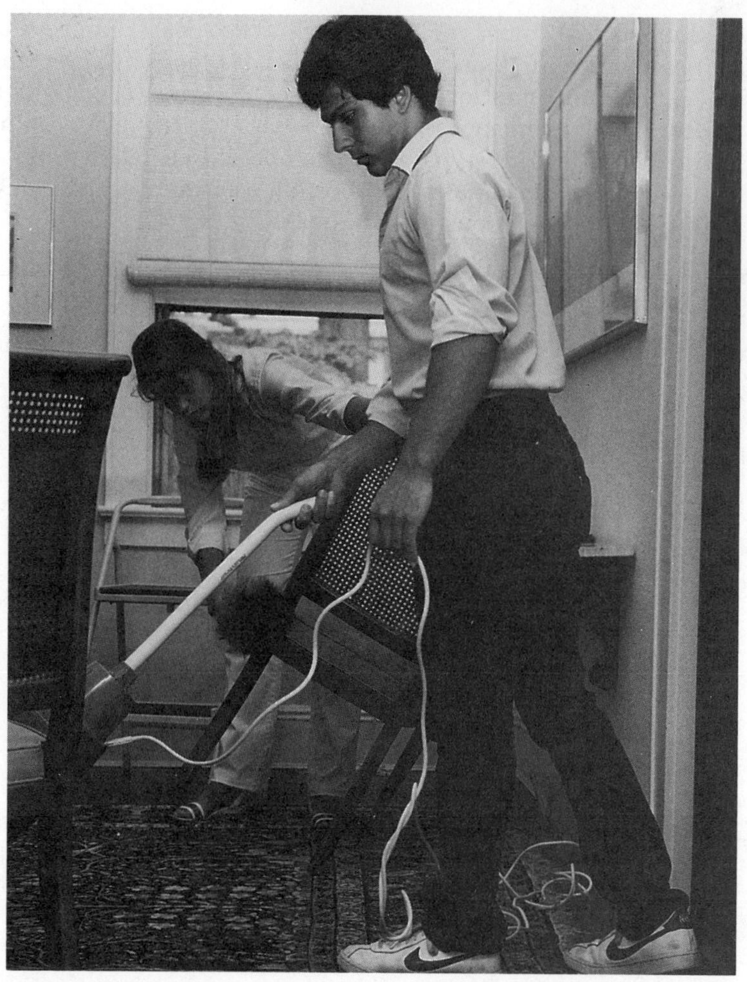

Spouses are more realistic in their attitudes toward love than are single people.

When 100 unmarried men and 100 unmarried women college students completed the inventory, the results revealed that men were more romantic than women and that freshmen were more romantic than seniors (Knox & Sporakowski, 1968). Comparable results were found in a similar study (Knox, 1982) in which 94 was the average score of 97 students; men and freshmen had more romantic scores, and women and seniors had more realistic scores. However, after analyzing the results of a romance survey of slightly less than 12,000 *Psychology Today* readers, the researcher concluded that "more women than men say that romance is important, and men rate their partners as being more romantic" (Rubenstein 1983, p. 49).

I don't want realism, I want magic.
—Tennessee Williams

Another study (Knox, 1970) compared the love attitudes of 50 men and 50 women high-school seniors with 50 husbands and 50 wives who had been married more than 20 years. Both the unmarried and married groups revealed a romantic attitude toward love. These findings were expected for the high-school seniors but not for the older marrieds. It may be that partners who have been married for 20 years adopt attitudes that are consistent with such a long-term investment of their time and energy; that is, the belief that there is only one person with whom an individual can really fall in love and marry justifies those who have done so. Also, some older marrieds grow to love each other. One wife said:

> I knew when I married him I didn't love him. I was pregnant, and since you didn't get an abortion back then, I went through with the wedding. Our first years were rough, but we hung on to each other and have had a good marriage. My love for him is now stronger than I would have ever imagined. Love is something you grow into—not something that just happens.

When the high-school seniors and older marrieds were compared with 100 couples who had been married less than five years, the last group proved to be very realistic. For them, moonlight and roses had become daylight and dishes. This is not to suggest that recently married spouses do not love each other. However, their feelings about each other may change as a result of their movement from the role of lover to spouse. Lovers spend all of their time together and orient their day around each other. Spouses spend most of their time earning money and orient their day around their work. One husband said:

> My wife and I have been married for almost 10 months. The first six months were extremely gratifying, sexually and in all other aspects. Since then, we have begun working up to 10 or 12 hours per day, six days a week, trying to accumulate enough money to buy a new mobile home. This has put a lot of strain on us. Our sexual activities have been cut drastically to approximately once a week. We are more irritable toward each other, and we are overlooking some of each others' needs. I realize that we are losing our "romantic love," and I hope things will improve after I graduate and start working on a less demanding and more stable schedule.

From a racial and cross-cultural perspective, black and Japanese students view love differently from white students. When 327 black high-school and college students completed the Love Attitudes Scale, the results revealed that black students had more romantic attitudes toward love than white students (Mirchandani, 1973). One explanation suggests that because black students are more likely to come from divorced and economically disadvantaged homes, they may seek romantic love relationships as an escape.

Japanese students are more realistic than American students in their attitudes toward love. Japanese students are more likely to have been taught that love may follow rather than precede marriage. In addition, their parents are more involved in the selection and approval of the people they date than the parents of American students (Simmons et al., 1986).

Consideration

Is romantic love a sound basis for marriage? If the love you have for your partner is based primarily on physical attraction, little time together, and few shared experiences, marrying on this basis may be taking an unnecessary risk. To marry someone without spending a great deal of time with him or her (the minimum is one year) in a variety of situations (your home, your partner's home, four- or five-day camping trips, and so on) may be like buying a Christmas present without knowing what is inside.

Greek Views of Love

In addition to viewing love on a romantic–realistic continuum, love may be conceptualized as *phileo, agape,* and *eros.* Introduced by the Greeks and reflected in the New Testament, *phileo,* or friendship love, may be in reference to siblings *(philadelphia)* or people in general *(philanthropia).*

Agape means a love of self-sacrifice that is spontaneous and unmotivated. This type of love is altruistic and requires nothing in return. The love of parents for their children is reflective of *agape* love.

Eros is a type of selfish love designed to get from another person what is valuable to the "taker." Exploiting someone sexually is reflective of *eros* love.

Relationship Scripts

A social script defines the roles of the people in a situation and predicts their behavior. For example, the social script of your marriage and family class dictates the situation (an academic learning experience), the roles (students and teacher), and the behavior (students are to attend class, take notes, and score well on exams; the teacher is to lecture, prepare tests, and give feedback on test performances). Relationship scripts identify how women and men are to view each other, what their roles are, and what they are to do. These scripts are learned from parents, peers, novels, television, and movies, among other sources. Exposure to these influences allows people to develop a way of thinking and behaving in reference to romance. But the relationship scripts are different for women and for men, and they do not ensure a meaningful and lasting relationship:

> During the course of the courtship, the couples collectively manage to overcome a plethora of obstacles to their love and achieve the goal of making a lifetime commitment to each other. Abruptly, once the pair has been established as a couple, the story ends. The extent of the script provided for how to weather the remaining course of the relationship is a parsimonious "happily ever after." (Rose, 1985, p. 251)

The Relationship Script for Females

Females are taught to be passive, to exchange sexual favors for commitment, and to prolong the arousal phase of an encounter. Although there are exceptions, females typically do not call men for dates. They are more likely to react rather than to be the acting agent. The relationship script for the female is to "be" not to "do." In the classic fairy tale, Rapunzel uses her long hair as a ladder so that her prince can climb up to see her in the tower.

Females have also learned that males want to have sex with them and that they can use sex to bargain for what they want—commitment. "I want a love that lasts past Saturday night," is the lyric from *A Sunday Kind of Love,* which emphasizes the desire on the part of the woman to have sex only if it leads to a stable relationship.

Because women are in the most control before they deliver sexual favors, they are taught to prolong the encounter and to pace the male. To stretch out the distance from what the male wants to when he gets it ensures that the female is getting the bargain she wants. In the romantic novel *Seaswept,* the heroine, Monica, kisses her partner once in a nine-page span but "also tells him 14 times that she isn't interested in him. In the interim, vivid descriptions of her passionate thoughts about him are detailed. What is symbolically satisfied here is the power to prolong and control the arousal phase of the sexual encounter" (Rose, 1985, p. 265).

THE RELATIONSHIP SCRIPT FOR MALES

While females are being socialized to use one script in courtship, males are learning another script. The primary themes of this script are activity, conquest, and variety. Activity may be physical (lifting weights) or career success. Either produces the same outcome—approval from male peers and admiration from females. "There is no shortage of women for men at the top," notes one famous golfer.

Males are taught that success can occur independently, without regard to a relationship. Men view women as objects of conquest—as trophies or entities to obtain. Even though "getting a woman" (a phrase used in male peer groups) may have only a sexual connotation, it can also result in "getting a mate," due primarily to the skills of the female in prolonging sex to obtain commitment.

There is no greater or keener pleasure than that of bodily love—and none which is more irrational.
—Plato

The relationship script for males also involves variety. Because males view females as sexual conquests, men believe that the more women they can conquest, the better.

> A steady stream of interchangeably beautiful women grace the pages of *Playboy, Penthouse,* and other magazines. The antidote for boredom in either pictorials or fiction is variety in sexual partners, positions, or practices. Intimacy and commitment have no place in the hedonistic pursuit of immediate sexual gratification (Rose, 1985, p. 260)

Black males may be particularly vulnerable to the variety issue, because there are 141,000 more single black females than single black males (*Statistical Abstract of the United States,* 1987). The sheer number of females competing for his attention may nudge the black male into a variety motif.

RELATIONSHIP CONSEQUENCES FOR THE RESPECTIVE SCRIPTS

Both the female and the male are likely to experience negative consequences for internalizing the relationship scripts offered by our culture.

Consideration

For the female, disappointments that are likely to occur after the courtship include a loss of influence over the male, exposure to male frailty, and a lack of erotic anticipation preceding sexual encounters. Because she has already obtained the marital commitment, the female has no script to incite her sexual interest when there is nothing to bargain for. One wife said to her husband, "I took care of you in courtship, but now sex is your problem."

The male is likely to feel cheated because he no longer feels admired, to tire of his conquest and look for another, and to resent still having to court his wife for sexual favors.

What is lacking in the relationship script for females is that they should take charge of their lives, enjoy sex rather than bargain with it, and consider the possibility that they can be happy and fulfilled with or without a male partner.

What is lacking in the relationship script for males is that they should recognize that there may be more enjoyment in relationships than in work, that women are adult peers, not trophies, and that there are benefits to monogamy.

Homosexual Love Relationships

Although we have been discussing heterosexual love relationships, lovers may also be homosexual. The love feelings of two homosexual men or homosexual women are the same as the love feelings experienced by two heterosexuals, but the expression of these feelings—the behavior—is different. Here, we will examine the definition and prevalence of homosexuality and explore male–male relationships and female–female relationships.

Definition and Incidence

Homosexuality refers to both emotional attachment and sexual attraction to those of one's own gender. Homosexual people, who are also called "gay" people, may be either men or women. When most people use the term *homosexual,* they mean a man who has an emotional and sexual preference for other men. The term *lesbian* refers to a woman who has an emotional and sexual preference for other women.

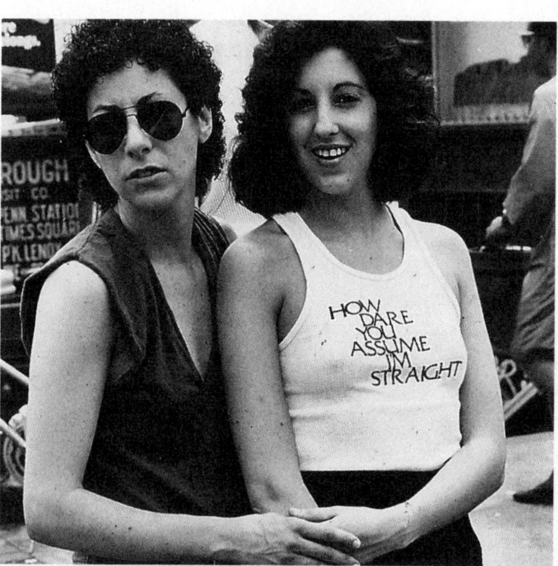

The emotions homosexual lovers experience are identical to those heterosexual lovers experience.

Data – In a study of 100 undergraduate University of Northern Iowa students, 22 percent reported having had a homosexual experience as an adolescent. Eight percent of the women and 10 percent of the men reported having had a homosexual experience as an adult. (Story, 1985)

Rarely is anyone entirely homosexual or heterosexual in both attitudes and behavior. Rather, our sexual orientation can be placed on a continuum devised by Kinsey et al. (1953) and illustrated in Figure 2.1. Gay people cannot be stereotyped or pigeonholed. They are young and old, white and black, single and married, and from all social classes, occupations, and religions. The idea that a homosexual person is instantly recognizable is false. Although some effeminate men are homosexual, others are not.

Gay Male Relationships

Prior to public awareness of the fact that AIDS (acquired immune deficiency syndrome) kills and anyone who has sex with others is a potential victim, gay male relationships were often casual.

Data – In a study of 50 AIDS victims, the Center for Disease Control in Atlanta found that the median number of lifetime sexual partners for these men was 1,100, with a few of the men reporting as many as 20,000. The median number of different partners for a homosexual control group without the disease was 550. (Meredith, 1984)

Cruising is the term in the gay subculture for going to a bar, bathhouse, or party to pick up a sexual partner. Since people have become aware that contracting AIDS occurs primarily through sexual contact with gay men, the extent of cruising has diminished (Meredith, 1984).

It [homosexuality] is not a new life style—just a more public one.
—Vern L. Bullough

The sexual activities of gay male partners, even when they are intensely enjoyable, are usually not enough to keep the couple together. Many of their relationships are short-lived. Some gay men do establish lasting emotional and sexual relationships. One man said the relationship with his partner had lasted longer and was considerably happier than either of his sisters' marriages. However, although stable relationships based on sexual fidelity and emotional intimacy are desired by most gay men (Harry & Lovely, 1979), such relationships are the exception, not the rule.

FIGURE 2.1
THE HETEROSEXUAL–HOMOSEXUAL RATING SCALE

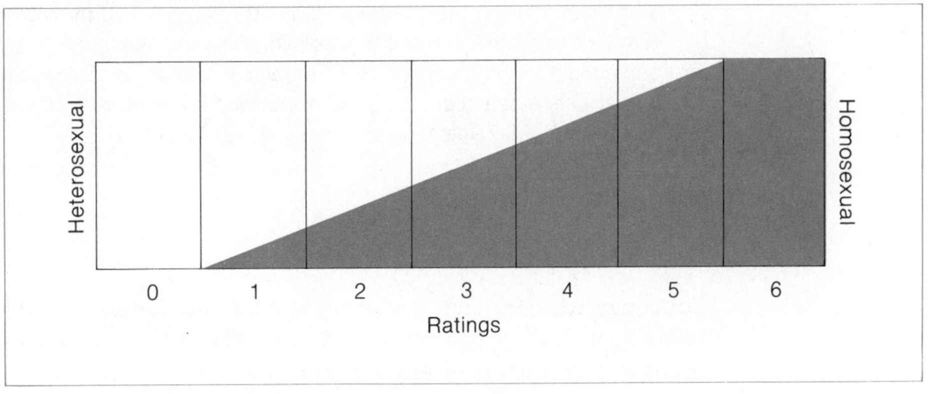

Source Kinsey, et al., 1953.

Several reasons may account for the transitory nature of gay male relationships. Because men have been socialized to be sexually focused in their relationships, gay men, as well as heterosexual men, may prefer the variety that transitory relationships provide. However, most heterosexual men marry and make a commitment to their wives that they will be monogamous. Women help channel the male's sexual expression into marriage. Homosexual males do not have a partner's expectation of fidelity and their own expectation of punishment if they stray. One gay man said, "If I wanted monogamy, I'd get me a wife and stay at home. But being gay means that I can have men—as many as I want, as often as I want—with no 'wife' telling me who I can and can't sleep with."

Gay relationships also have few social and economic supports. When a heterosexual couple are in love, they can be public about their feelings and expect others to approve of their relationship. Many gay couples feel they must hide their love, their "marriage" is illegal, and their living together is suspect. They cannot file joint tax returns, collect Social Security widowhood benefits (even though they may have lived as a couple for 50 years), or be granted the favorable insurance rates given to married people.

The lack of social support for homosexuals is illustrated in the 1983 Family Protection Act, which was submitted to the House of Representatives for consideration. The Act states:

> No federal funds may be made available under any provision of federal law to any public or private individual, group, foundation, commission, corporation, association, or other entity for the purpose of advocating, promoting, or suggesting homosexuality, male or female, as a life style. (p. 9)

In short, our society does not approve of homosexual relationships and gives same-sex couples no help in establishing or maintaining such relationships.

Gay relationships are also very intense. Often excluded by the larger society, gay men try to satisfy all needs for each other. In the midst of a hostile social environment, this goal may be unrealistic.

Consideration

Although many gay male relationships are short-lived, they may be very satisfying. In a study of 128 gay men (Peplau, 1981), 80 percent said they were currently in love with their partner and rated their relationships as "best friendships" with the added component of romance and erotic attraction. Some gay male relationships are committed. One researcher studied 50 males who had lived with their respective partners an average of 3.7 years. (Lewis et al., 1981)

Gay Female Relationships

Some gay women have transitory sexual encounters, but this is unusual. Most women, including gay women, have learned that sexual expression "should" occur in the context of emotional or romantic involvement.

Consideration

For gay women, the formula is love first and sex second; for gay men, it is sex first and the emotional relationship second. This pattern is also characteristic of heterosexual women and men.

The feelings of love in gay female relationships are almost identical to the love feelings that females express in heterosexual relationships. In one study comparing the two feelings, the researcher said:

> It is interesting, therefore, to point out that the respondents feelings and comments about their lesbian love were indistinguishable from their emotions about heterosexual love, if personal pronouns were eliminated. There are the same expressions of ecstasy, joy, anguish, and suffering, regardless of the gender of the love object. Each of the comments made by the exclusively lesbian women about their passions could be matched by a similar comment made by a straight woman about a heterosexual passion. (Loewenstein, 1985, p. 21)

Although gay female relationships normally last longer than gay male relationships, long-term relationships (20 years or more) are rare. Serial monogamy (one relationship at a time) seems to be the dominant lesbian life pattern. Loss of romantic love or the inability to sustain feelings across time seem to be major reasons for the breakup of gay female relationships. Just as strong love feelings brought them together, their absence makes each person in a relationship question why they stay together. "I don't know what happened," said one woman. "I just wasn't in love with her anymore. And I couldn't fake my feelings any longer, so I left her."

Gay women also are typically denied the experience of rearing children, which (being parents) can have a stabilizing effect on relationships. Prejudice against homosexuals being parents springs from the belief that their children will also become homosexual. But 36 of 37 children reared by lesbian or transsexual parents had heterosexual gender-role preferences (Green, 1978).

When homosexual and heterosexual relationships are compared, which couples exhibit the greatest degree of satisfaction and commitment? In a comparison of the relationships of 25 lesbians, 25 homosexual males, 25 heterosexual females, and 25 heterosexual males, the researchers (Duffy & Rusbult, 1985/86) found that gender was more important than sexual preference in predicting relationship satisfaction. Both lesbians and heterosexual women reported investing more in their relationships and being more committed to maintaining their relationships than homosexual or heterosexual men. Greater commitment was also associated with greater satisfaction.

The more we learn about people's true private lives, the less do we find that their most intimate personal behavior conforms to conventional societal images.

—Sophie Loewenstein

Bisexuality

Bisexuality may be defined by three criteria:

1. Eroticizing or being sexually aroused by both females and males.
2. Engaging in (or desiring) sexual activity with both females and males.

3. Adopting "bisexual" as a sexual identity label (as opposed to the labels "heterosexual" or "homosexual").

Data – About 25 million Americans exhibit some combination of homosexual and heterosexual behavior. However, it is not known if these individuals define themselves as bisexual. (Zinik, 1985)

At one time in a bisexual's life, he or she may be primarily drawn to one gender but still open to encounters with the other. Or the bisexual may be exclusively attracted to one gender at one point in his or her life and be exclusively attracted to the other gender later in life. That human love and sexuality may be a fluid variable that is not fixed in infancy or adolescence is the suggestion of one researcher (Loewenstein, 1985), who studied seven women who had their first lesbian experience after the age of 30. Each of these women had already lived though "important heterosexual passions before they assumed the identity of lesbian" (p. 22).

> Today's protean [changing] men and women respond to the rapid cultural changes by adopting more fluid identities. Women and men no longer expect that marriage will necessarily last a lifetime. Careers are now changed in midlife, and sometimes more than once. People take advantage, either deliberately or inadvertently, of new options and opportunities for self-expression and life styles that a more diverse society makes available to them. The apparent greater fluidity of love-object orientation that has formerly been assumed challenges early deterministic theories. (p. 23)

Love and Sex

Sex without love is an empty experience.
—Diane Keaton

Yes, but as empty experiences go, it's one of the best.
—Woody Allen

Whether lovers are homosexual or heterosexual, there are similarities and differences between love and sex. We will compare these concepts now.

Similarities between Love and Sex

In general, love and sex are more similar than they are different. These similarities include the following:

Both love and sex represent intense feelings. To be involved in a love relationship is one of the most exciting experiences an individual ever has. To know that another person loves us engenders feelings of happiness and joy. "No one ever really loved me until now," remarked one man, "and because of this love, I have a very good feeling inside."

Sex has the same capability to generate intense excitement and happiness. Although sex is more than orgasm, the latter is the epitome of intense pleasure.

Both love and sex involve physiological changes. When a person is in an intense love relationship, his or her brain produces phenylethylamine, a chemical correlate of amphetamine, which may result in a giddy feeling similar to an amphetamine high (Liebowitz, 1983). When the love affair breaks up, the person seems to crash and go through withdrawal because there is less phenylethylamine in his or her system. Some heartbroken lovers reach for chocolate, which contains phenylethylamine.

O love, thy kiss would wake the dead!
—Tennyson

Further support for the idea that love has a physiological component has been suggested by Money (1980), who studied patients who had undergone brain surgery or suffered from a pituitary deficiency. Although they were able to experience various emotions, passionate love was not one of them.

The physiological changes the body experiences during sexual excitement have been well documented by Masters and Johnson (1966) in their observations of more than 10,000 orgasms. Such changes include increased heart rate, blood pressure, and breathing.

Both love and sex have a cognitive component. To experience the maximum pleasure from both love and sex, the person must label or interpret what is happening in positive terms. For love to develop, each person in the relationship must define their meetings, glances, talks, and the like as enjoyable. The significance of labeling is illustrated by the experience of two women who dated the same man. Although they spent similar evenings, the first woman said, "I love him—he's great," but the other woman said, "He is a jerk."

Positive labeling is also important in sex. Each person's touch, kiss, caress, and body type are different; sexual pleasure depends on labeling sexual interaction with that person as enjoyable. "I can't stand the way he French kisses" and "I love the way he French kisses" are two interpretations of kissing the same person. But only one of these interpretations will make the event pleasurable.

Both love and sex may be expressed in various ways. The expression of love may include words ("I love you"), gifts (flowers or candy), behaviors (being on time, a surprise phone call or visit), and touch (holding hands, tickling). Similarly, sex as well as love may be expressed through a glance, embracing, kissing, fondling, and intercourse.

The need for love and sex increases with deprivation. The more we get, the less we feel we need; the less we get, the more we feel we need. The all-consuming passion of Romeo and Juliet, perhaps the most celebrated love story of all time, undoubtedly was fed by their enforced separation. The following reflects a similar love-from-afar experience:

> I feel the thing that has affected me the most about love is that we broke up over a year and a half ago and I still think of him every day. I feel that if he walked in the door tomorrow we would start up where we left off—but that will never happen. A month after we became involved, he got a girl pregnant in his home town and married her. This destroyed me completely, and for a long time I wouldn't go out with anyone. The thing that bothered me most was when I saw him recently at a bar, he told me that he still loved me but that he had to marry her because his parents found out she was pregnant.

Sex alleviates tension and love causes it.
—Woody Allen

Deprivation has the same effect on the need for sex. Statements of people who have been separated from their lover for several weeks may be similar to "I'm horny as a mountain goat," "We're going to spend the weekend in bed," and "The second thing we're going to do when we get together is take a drive out in the country."

Basic Differences between Love and Sex

There are several differences between love and sex. These include the following:

Love is crucial for human happiness; sex is important but not crucial. After analyzing the data from a study of more than 100,000 people about what makes them happy, one researcher concluded:

> Many people are unhappy with their sex lives, and many think this is an important lack, but almost no one seems to think that sex alone will bring happiness. Romance and love were often listed as crucial missing ingredients, but not sex; it was simply not mentioned. (Freedman, 1978, p. 56)

Barbara Lockhart (1983), a competitive speed skater on the U.S. Olympic team, commented on sex and love:

> To me, channeling my energies in training was positive, exciting, and rewarding, and so is the channeling of sexual energy. I do not feel sorry for myself, nor do I feel deprived or depraved, not having any "outlet" for sexual feelings. I really enjoy not having sex in my life. It would be wonderful to be able to enjoy sexual intimacy, but as long as I am single, I am experiencing a far greater joy in my life by not having sex be a part of it. (p. 38)

Love is pervasive whereas sex tends to be localized. Love is felt all over, but sexual feeling is most often associated with various body parts (lips, breasts, or genitals). People do not say of love as they do of sex, "It feels good here."

Love tends to be more selective than sex. The standards people have for a love partner are generally higher than those they have for a sex partner. Expressions like "I'll take anything that wears pants," "Just show me a room full of skirts," and "I wouldn't kick him out of bed" reflect the desire to have sex with someone—anyone. Love wants *the* person rather than *a* person.

The standards for a love partner may also be different from those for a sexual partner. For example, some people form relationships with others to meet emotional intimacy needs that are not met by their sexual partners. A sexual component need not be a part of the love relationship they have with these people.

Gender Differences in Love and Sex

Although there are individual differences, women tend to be more interested in the emotional aspects of a relationship and men tend to focus more on the sexual aspects. Harlequin romance novels reflect this theme. One researcher has observed:

> A surprising number of Harlequins employ the same vocabulary to describe the inner conflict of the heroine as she struggles against the hero on his own grounds where he has all the weapons. His main weapon in this idealized world is his powerful sexual attraction; her main weakness is her susceptibility to that attraction, which quickly becomes total love. Her struggle aims to prevent the hero from exploiting her love for his own sexual desires . . . (Rabine, 1985, p. 48)

Jealousy

The jealous are troublesome to others but a torment to themselves.
—William Penn

Feelings of jealousy are not uncommon in love relationships. *Jealousy* is a set of emotional feelings that results when an individual perceives that the love relationship he or she has with a person is being threatened. The specific feelings are those of fear of loss or abandonment, anxiety, pain, anger, vulnerability, and hopelessness.

Data – Of 103 women and men of varying ages and involvements in relationships, 75 percent reported feeling jealous. One-half of the respondents described themselves as "jealous" people. (Pines & Aronson, 1983)

Individuals who are more likely to be jealous are women (who have more reason to be jealous due to the higher infidelity rate among men), those who are not in a monogamous relationship, those who are dissatisfied with the sexual relationship with their partner, and those who are dissatisfied with their relationship in general (Hansen, 1983; Pines & Aronson, 1983).

CAUSES

Jealousy feeds on suspicion, and it turns into fury or it ends as soon as we pass from suspicion to certainty.
—La Rochefoucauld

Jealousy may be caused by external or internal factors. An external factor is the behavior of the partner that elicits jealousy. In the Pines and Aronson (1983) study of 103 respondents, most said they became jealous when they were at a party with their partner and their partner spent a great deal of time talking, dancing, and flirting with someone of the opposite gender. "I get to feeling very uncomfortable when I see him enjoying himself and putting his hands all over another woman," remarked one woman. Other behaviors of the partner that create jealousy include the partner expressing appreciation of and interest in someone else, having a close friend of the opposite gender, and involvement in a love or sexual relationship with someone else.

Jealousy may also be triggered by thoughts of the individual who has learned to be distrustful in previous situations. "I know my husband is faithful to me," said one wife, "but my ex-husband wasn't, and it's hard for me to trust men again."

Jealous feelings may also result from low self-esteem and self-confidence (De Moja, 1986). People who feel inadequate in looks or personality may doubt their ability to get another person to love them and be faithful to them, so they are continually jealous of others whom they fear may take their partner away.

Finally, jealousy is more likely to exist when an individual has no perceived alternatives. In a study of jealousy among spouses, the most jealous were those that felt that they could not get anyone else if their partner became attracted to someone else (Hansen, 1985).

Consideration

It is not unusual that the interaction of two people in a relationship encourages the development of jealous feelings. Suppose John accuses Mary of being interested in someone else, and Mary denies the accusation and responds by saying "I love you" and being very affectionate. If this pattern continues, Mary will teach John the rewards of jealousy. John learns that when he acts jealous, good things happen to him—Mary showers him with love and physical affection. Inadvertently, Mary is reinforcing John for exhibiting jealous behavior. To break the cycle, Mary should tell John of her love for him and be affectionate when he is not exhibiting jealous behavior. When he does act jealous, she should say that she feels badly when he accuses her of something she isn't doing and to please stop. If he does not stop, she should terminate the interaction until John can be around her and not act jealous.

Consequences

Low levels of jealousy are functional for a couple's relationship. Not only does jealousy keep the partner aware that he or she is cared for (the implied message is "I love you and don't want to lose you to someone else"), but also the partner learns that the development of romantic and sexual relationships "on the side" is unacceptable. One wife said:

> When I started spending extra time with this guy at the office my husband got jealous and told me he thought I was getting in over my head and asked me to cut back on the relationship because it was "tearing him up" and he couldn't stay married to me with these feelings. I felt really loved when he told me this and drifted out of the relationship I was developing with the guy at the office.

Jealousy may improve a relationship in yet another way. When the partners begin to take each other for granted, involvement of one or both partners outside the relationship can encourage them to reevaluate how important the relationship is and can help recharge it.

In its extreme form, jealousy may have devastating consequences, including murder, suicide, spouse beating, and severe depression. "I turned into an alcoholic overnight," said one male. "I just didn't want to be sober because I would think about her and this other fellow. I almost drank myself into oblivion."

Trends

The most predictable trend in love relationships is that there will be little change. The excitement of love will still characterize each new love relationship. Although a person may have been disappointed in previous relationships, love feelings help to create the illusion that the current love relationship will be different. One person cannot convince another that love is something more than illusion, deception, and idealization. Such a perception is grounded in experience. Even those with extensive interpersonal experience are not immune to "falling in love" and riding the love wave.

Prejudice against homosexual men and women will also continue. Like a robin among snakes, gay people live in a hostile environment. They are called pejorative names ("queer," "dyke," "faggot"), labeled as having negative characteristics ("sick," "dangerous"), and legally prohibited from marrying each other. Although being a homosexual is not a psychiatric disorder, being *homophobic* (having an unrealistic fear of homosexuals) is. Because heterosexuals (to their knowledge) have limited interaction with homosexuals, they do not have an opportunity to form more positive feelings about gay men and women. Without more positive experiences, negative stereotypes will continue to guide the perceptions and feelings of many heterosexuals.

Social acceptance of homosexual love relationships will be slow. Just as resistance to full participation by blacks in society was first muted by legislative changes, followed by much slower attitudinal changes, so will the breakdown of negative feelings against gay people follow legal change. Such changes include the right of homosexuals to legally adopt their lovers, which gives legal recognition to their relationship and provides for inheritance.

Summary

Love is a crucial element in human happiness. It is also the feeling most western people have when they say they want to get married. Most people agree on its importance, but they do not agree on the definition of love. Love is a feeling that people experience individually and privately.

Love occurs under certain conditions. Social conditions include a society that promotes the pursuit of love, peers who enjoy it, and a set of norms that link love and marriage. Psychological conditions involve a positive self-concept and a willingness to disclose one's self to others. Physiological and cognitive conditions imply that the individual experiences a stirred-up state and labels it "love." All of these conditions are important but not essential. What is essential is a high frequency of positive verbal and nonverbal behavior from the partner to furnish the basis on which love feelings may develop. It is easy for us to fall in love with someone who compliments us, is affectionate, and shares our value system. We rarely develop love feelings for those who criticize us, do not enjoy touching us, and do not respect our values.

A person who accepts the role of lover engages in predictable behaviors. Not only will the person idealize the partner, but she or he will also endure suffering and fantasize about the future with the beloved.

Three basic components of love are intimacy, passion, and commitment. Consummate love consists of all three components; infatuation consists of passion only.

Love may be viewed on a continuum from romanticism to realism. Men, college freshmen, and never-marrieds tend to be more romantic than women, college seniors, and young marrieds.

Relationship scripts specify how women and men view each other, what their roles are, and what they are to do. Females are taught to be passive, to exchange sexual favors for commitment, and to prolong the arousal phase of an encounter (the condition of greatest control for the female). Men are taught to be active, to view women as objects of conquest, and to seek sexual variety. What is lacking in both scripts is the perception of each partner as a friend and companion.

Intense love feelings also occur between members of the same gender. All homosexual relationships tend to be less stable than heterosexual relationships, but gay male relationships are less stable than gay female relationships.

Love and sex are similar and different. Both love and sex represent intense feelings, involve physiological changes, have a cognitive component, are expressed in various ways, and increase with deprivation. The differences suggest that love is crucial for happiness but that sex is not. Love is pervasive, whereas sex is localized; also, love tends to be more selective than sexual desire.

Jealousy is a common feeling that results from the fear of losing a valued love partner. It may be external or internal. Jealousy may have been learned in previous situations and also may result from low self-esteem.

Trends in love relationships include little change in the romance component in new love relationships, continued prejudice against homosexual people, and slow social acceptance of gay love relationships.

Questions for Reflection

1. To what degree are you comfortable disclosing yourself to others? How did you develop this level of comfort or discomfort?
2. To what degree do you feel the opposite gender is consistent with the relationship script discussed in this chapter?
3. To what degree are your decisions dominated by rational versus emotional concerns? (This questional concerns? (This question applies to the choices section that follows.)

CHOOSING TO LISTEN to one's heart or head when making decisions and choosing to have sex with or without love are two important decisions about love relationships. We will examine the consequences of each choice here.

HEART OR HEAD: WHICH SHOULD YOU LISTEN TO?

Lovers are frequently confronted with the need to make decisions about their relationships, but they are divided on whether to let their heart or head rule in such decisions. In a marriage and family class, 120 students were asked whether they used their hearts or their heads in making such decisions. Some of their answers follow.

Heart

Those who relied on their heart (females more likely) for making decisions felt that emotions were more important than logic and that listening to your heart made you happier. One woman said:

> In deciding on a mate, my heart should rule because my heart has reasons to cry and my head doesn't. My heart knows what I want, what would make me most happy. My head tells me what is best for me. But I would rather have something that makes me happy than something that is good for me.

Some men also agreed that your heart should rule. One said:

> I went with my heart in a situation, and I'm glad I did. I had been dating a girl for two years when I decided she was not the one I wanted and that my present girlfriend was. My heart was saying to go for the one I loved, but my head was telling me not to because if I broke up with the first girl, it would hurt her, her parents, and my parents. But I decided I had to make myself happy and went with the feelings in my heart and started dating the girl who is now my fiancée.

Relying on one's emotions does not always have a positive outcome, as the following experience illustrates:

> Last semester, I was dating a guy I felt more for than he did for me. Despite that, I wanted to spend any opportunity I could with him when he asked me to go somewhere with him. One day he had no classes, and he asked me to go to the park by the river for a picnic. I had four classes that day and exams in two of them. I let my heart rule and went with him. Nothing ever came of the relationship and I didn't do well in those classes.

Head

Most of the respondents (males more likely) felt that it was better to be rational than emotional.

> In deciding on a mate, I feel my head should rule because you have to choose someone that you can get along with after the new wears off. If you follow your heart solely, you may not look deep enough into a person to see what it is that you really like. Is it just a pretty face or a nice body? Or is it deeper than that, such as common interests and attitudes? After the new wears off, it's the person inside the body that you're going to have to live with. The "heart" sometimes can fog up this picture of the true person and distort reality into a fairy tale.

> Love is blind and can play tricks on you. Two years ago, I fell in love with a man whom I later found out was married. Although my heart had learned to love this man, my mind knew the consequences and told me to stop seeing him. My heart said, "Maybe he'll leave her for me," but my mind said, "If he cheated on her, he'll cheat on you." I got out and am glad that I listened to my head.

(Continued)

Some feel that both the head and the heart should rule when making relationship decisions.

When you really love someone, your heart rules in most of the situations. But if you don't keep your head in some matters, then you risk losing the love that you feel in your heart. I think that we should find a way to let our heads and hearts rule together.

Sex With and Without Love

Some individuals feel that sex is best in the context of a love relationship. Of 12,000 respondents in the *Psychology Today* survey on romance, 30 percent of the men and more than 40 percent of the women said that sex without love was either unenjoyable or unacceptable. Half of those under the age of 22 felt this way (Rubenstein, 1983).

Here is an example of what some men and women have said about the importance of an emotional relationship as a context for sexual expression:

Sex is good and beautiful when both parties want it, but when one person wants sex only, that's bad. I love sex, but I like to feel that the man cares about me. I can't handle the type of sexual relationship where one night I spend the night with him and the next night he spends the night with someone else. I feel like I am being used. There are still a few women around like me who *need* the commitment before sex means what it should.

Other people feel that love is not necessary for sexual expression. Indeed, the theme of the book *Sex without Love* (Vannoy, 1980) is that sex should be enjoyed for its own sake. One person said:

You choose a lover according to how you wish to be loved, and you choose a sex partner according to how you wish to be laid. There is no guarantee whatever that the person you love and the person whom you find most sexually desirable are one and the same. There are just certain things a lover may not be able to give you, and it may be good sex. (p. 24).

The idea that sex with love is wholesome and sex without love is exploitive is a fallacious dualism. Two strangers can meet, share each other sexually, have a deep mutual admiration for each other's sensuous qualities, and go their separate ways in the morning. Their parting is not evidence that their sexual encounter was exploitation. Rather, it is a sign of their preference for independence and singlehood rather than permanent emotional involvement and marriage. (Vannoy, 1980, p. 26)

Each person in a sexual encounter will undoubtedly experience different degrees of love feelings; and the experience of each may differ across time. One woman reported that the first time she had intercourse with her future husband was shortly after they had met in a bar. She described their first sexual encounter as "raw naked sex" with no emotional feelings. But they continued to see each other over a period of months, an emotional relationship developed, and "sex took on a love meaning for us."

Sex with love can also drift into sex without love. One man said he had been deeply in love with his wife but that they had gradually drifted apart. Sex between them was no longer sex with love.

Both love and sex can be viewed on a continuum. Love feelings may range from nonexistent to intense, and relationships can range from limited sexual interaction to intense interaction. Hence, rarely are sexual encounters with or without love. Rather, they will exhibit varying degrees of emotional involvement. Also, rarely are romantic love relationships with or without sex. Rather, they display varying degrees of sexual expression. Where on the continuum one chooses to be—at what degree of emotional and sexual involvement—will vary from person to person and from time to time.

Impact of Social Influences on Choices

The degree to which you feel that sex and love always go together will be influenced by your gender. As a male, you have been socialized to be more concerned with intercourse and orgasm than the person with whom you have a sexual encounter. Male sexuality is often *homosocial* in that males engage in sex with females so that they can have something to tell their male peers about.

Females have been socialized to focus more on the relationship aspect of a sexual encounter. Some females only have intercourse in the context of a love relationship because they fear being used and/or dropped. Hence, the event of intercourse is perceived differently by men and women because each reports to and is evaluated by a different gender group. Male friends will want to know if their male peer "got any;" female friends will want to know, "Will you see him again" ("Does he care about you?").

CHAPTER 3

Gender Roles

Contents

Is It True?*

1. Women have more health problems than men.
2. Even before birth, parents relate to their children on the basis of gender.
3. Women tend to evaluate their appearance more negatively than men evaluate their own appearance.
4. Men are more likely to express their emotions than women.
5. Spouses who share the power in their relationship have the least amount of depression and the greatest amount of marital satisfaction.

*1=T; 2=T; 3=T; 4=F; 5=T.

AMERICAN MEN ARE self-reliant and strong; they rarely, if ever, cry. They have full-time careers and support their families; they are not especially interested in changing diapers, planning a meal, or buying clothes for their children. In contrast, American women need husbands to protect and support them; they are emotional, and they cry when they are unhappy. They have a special talent that men lack for nurturing babies, preparing gourmet meals, and finding good buys on food, clothes, and household items.

Do these descriptions sound familiar? If they do, it is not necessarily because they accurately depict the people we know. Instead, we recognize the stereotypes (simplified beliefs, often inaccurate, about members of a particular group) because we have all learned in varying degrees what the traditional roles of men and women are supposed to be in our society. In this chapter, we will explore the biological and social origins of gender roles, the consequences for the individuals who assume these roles, the trends regarding such roles, and the decisions we can make in reference to them. We all occupy various social roles; because most of us eventually assume the roles of spouse and parent, it is important for us to be aware of their implications. We begin by defining some basic terms.

Terminology

Sociologists, family specialists, home economists, and other family-life educators often have different definitions and connotations for the terms sex, gender, gender identity, and gender role. We use these terms in the following ways.

Sex refers to the biological distinction of being female or male. The primary sex characteristics that differentiate women and men include external genitalia (vulva and penis), gonads (ovaries and testes), sex chromosomes (XX and XY), and hormones (estrogen, progesterone, and testosterone). Secondary sex characteristics like the female's larger breasts and the male's beard are additional distinctions.

In contrast to the biological distinctions, *gender* refers to the social expectations that a social group imposes on its members because one is either male or female. Traditionally, men are expected to earn money; women are expected to take care of children. Sex is a biological term; gender is a social term.

Gender identity is the psychological state of viewing one's self as a girl or a boy and later as a woman or a man. Such identity is learned and is a reflection of the society's conceptions of masculinity and femininity. A person's gender identity is usually formed at about age 3.

Gender role, also called *sex role,* refers to the socially accepted characteristics and behaviors typically associated with a person's gender identity. In our society, the traditional concept of being female includes being emotional, dependent, and family-oriented, whereas the traditional concept of being male includes being nonemotional, independent, and career-oriented. These gender-role stereotypes are changing. Today, more parents are encouraging a wider range of behaviors in their children. Increasingly, women are being encouraged to be assertive and men are being encouraged to be nurturant.

Whether gender roles are primarily a function of biological or social influences is a continuing controversy (to be examined later in this chapter).

Most researchers acknowledge that biological and social factors interact to produce an individual's personality. Although children are born female and male, they learn culturally defined feminine or masculine characteristics. In the following sections, we will review the biological beginnings of women and men and examine the ways in which the sexes are socialized.

FIGURE 3.1
FERTILIZATION

Fertilization occurs when a sperm penetrates an egg in a Fallopian tube.

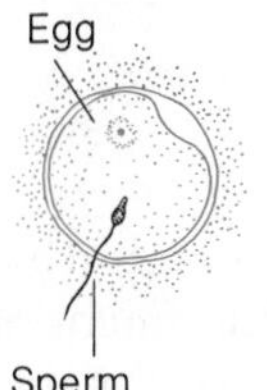

Biological Beginnings

Although all human life begins with a *zygote*—a fertilized egg (Figure 3.1)—all zygotes are not alike. They carry different *chromosomes* and *hormones* that result in women and men being housed in different bodies.

Chromosomes

Women and men have different genetic makeups. Every normal human *ovum* (egg) contains 22 "regular" chromosomes or *autosomes* (Figure 3.2) and one sex chromosome. Every normal human sperm contains 22 "regular" chromosomes and one X *or* Y chromosome. The autosomes contain various genes that determine the individual's eye color, hair color and body type; the sex chromo-

FIGURE 3.2
CHROMOSOME PAIRS

Within each cell of a person's body are 23 chromosome pairs.

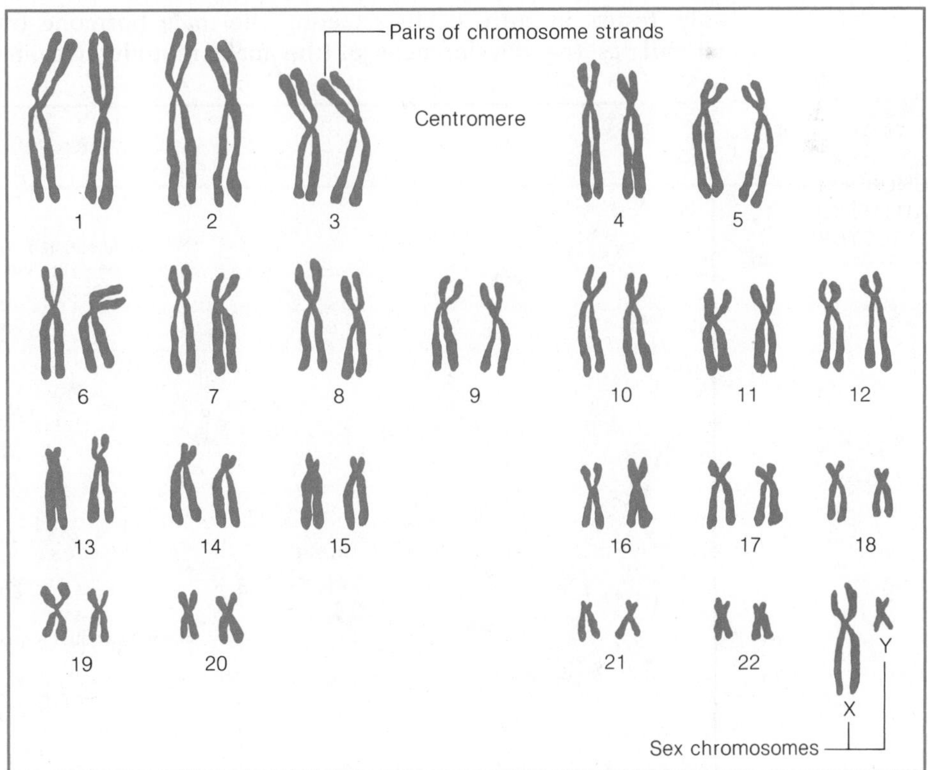

some determines the biological sex of the individual. Because the sex chromosome in the ovum is *always* X (the female chromosome), the sex chromosome in the male sperm determines the gender of the child. If the sperm contains an X chromosome, the match with the female chromosome will be XX, and a female will result. If the sperm contains a Y chromosome, the male chromosome, the match with the female chromosome will be XY, and a male will result. Hence, the normal female has 44 regular chromosomes (22 from each parent) plus an X chromosome from her mother and an X chromosome from her father. The normal male also has 44 regular chromosomes and an X chromosome from his mother but a Y chromosome from his father.

HORMONES

Although the same hormones are in each sex, the release of these and other hormones into the bloodstream in varying amounts causes the development of a female or a male *embryo* (the human organism from conception until the end of the eighth week). Male and female embryos are indistinguishable from one another during the first several weeks of intrauterine life. In both, two primitive gonads and two paired duct systems form during the fifth or sixth week of development (Figures 3.3 and 3.4). The reproductive system of the male develops from the Wolffian ducts, and the female reproductive system develops from the Müllerian ducts. However, both are present in the developing embryo at this stage.

If the embryo is genetically a male (XY), a chemical substance controlled by the Y chromosome stimulates the primitive gonads to develop into testes. The testes, in turn, begin secreting the male hormone testosterone, which stimulates the development of the male reproductive and external sexual

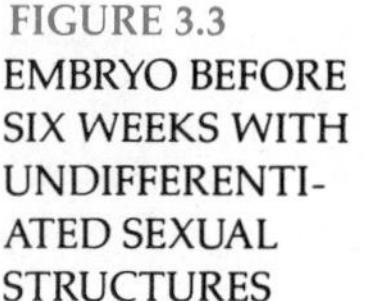

FIGURE 3.3
EMBRYO BEFORE SIX WEEKS WITH UNDIFFERENTIATED SEXUAL STRUCTURES

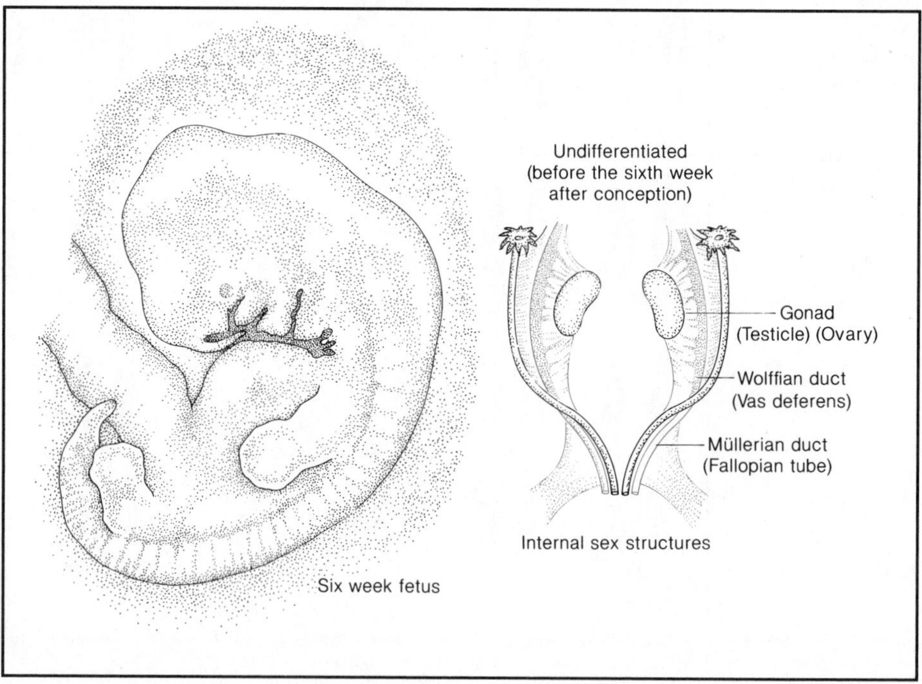

FIGURE 3.4
EMBRYO AT 12 WEEKS, SHOWING DIFFERENTIATED SEXUAL STRUCTURES

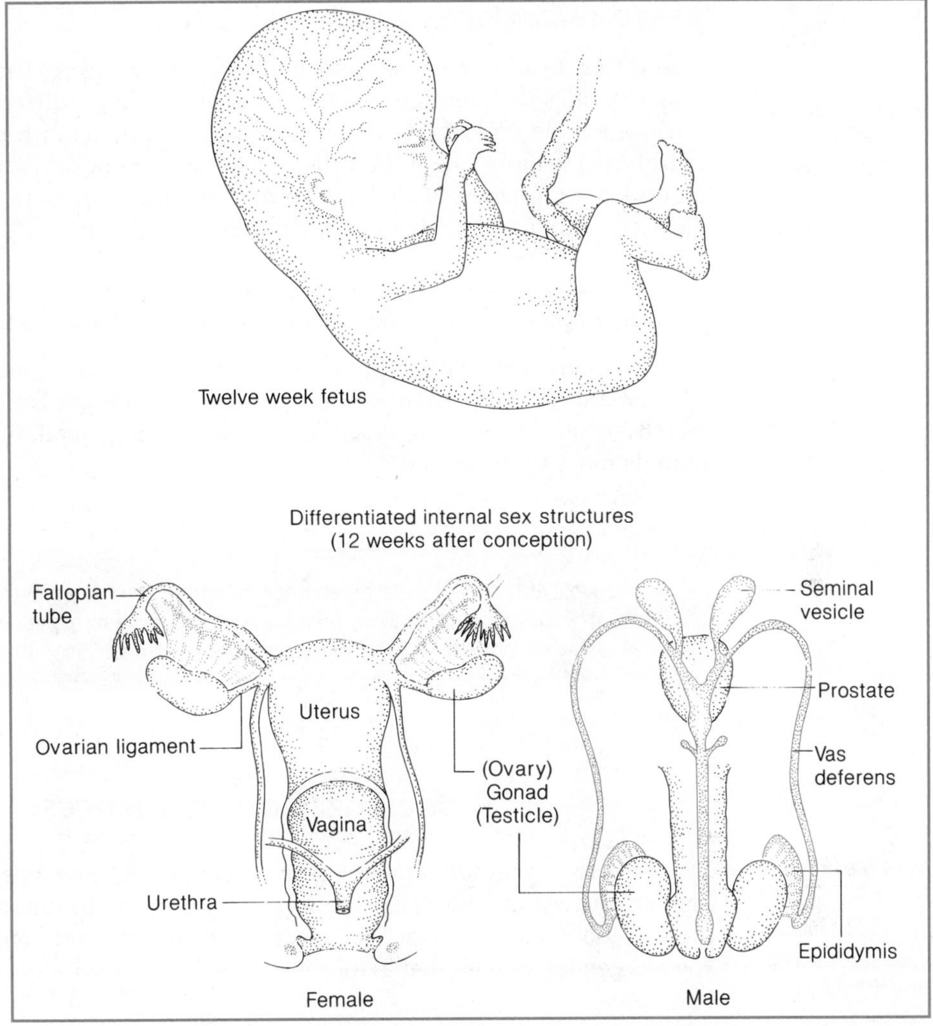

organs. The testes also secrete a Müllerian duct-inhibiting substance, which causes the potential female ducts to degenerate or become blind tubules. Thus development of male anatomical structures depends on the presence of male hormones at a critical stage of development.

The development of a female requires that no (or very little) male hormone be present. Without the controlling substance from the Y chromosome, the primitive gonads will develop into ovaries and the Müllerian duct system into the Fallopian tubes, uterus, and vagina. Also without testosterone, the Wolffian duct system (epididymis, vas deferens, and ejaculatory duct) will degenerate or become blind tubules.

The impact of hormones becomes even more evident at puberty. The testes and ovaries release hormones that are necessary for the development of secondary sex characteristics. Higher levels of testosterone account for the growth of facial hair in males and pubic and underarm hair in both males and females. Breast development, on the other hand, results from increasing levels of estrogen.

Anatomy and Physiology

If I told you you had a beautiful body, you wouldn't hold it against me would you?
—David Fisher

In addition to chromosomal and hormonal differences, a number of physical characteristics differentiate women from men. These differences begin before birth; the male *fetus* (the human organism from the eighth week of pregnancy until birth) is more likely than the female fetus to be stillborn during the early months of pregnancy. Male babies, children, and adults are also more likely to die each year than female babies, children, and adults.

Data – White females live seven years longer than white males; black females live eight years longer than black males. (*Statistical Abstract of the United States*, 1987)

Although men have higher mortality rates than women, they are taller, heavier, and stronger than women. The average height for the adult man is 5 feet, 8 inches; for women, it is 5 feet, 3 inches. In general, men weigh about 10 pounds more than women.

Consideration

Anatomical and physiological differences help to ensure different life experiences for the respective genders. Only women have the capacity to experience menstruation, pregnancy, and childbirth. Only men experience the ejaculation of semen.

Socialization Influences

Parents who have raised their child differently are finding that culture has an enormous influence. For example, there is the case of a woman physician whose child says that women can't be doctors.
—Carol Jacklin

We learn to engage in behavior that is socially defined as appropriate for our gender role. After reviewing the importance of environmental influences, we look at how parents, teachers, peers, the media, and religion influence us toward gender-specific behavior.

Significance of the Social Environment

The great majority of characteristics designated as feminine or masculine in any given culture are learned from the material and interpersonal environment in which we grow up. Gender-role prescriptions in our culture not only signal the color of the blanket in which an infant is to be wrapped but also dictate appropriate toys (doll or football), clothes (panties or briefs), and work roles (baby sitter or paper boy) for children. Gender roles also tell us whether to be aggressive or passive in interpersonal and sexual interactions.

That women's sexual aggressiveness or passivity is learned behavior is illustrated by a study of females attending male strip shows. In such a situation, women receive peer support for sexual aggressiveness and their passivity seems to disappear. After attending a male strip show weekly for eight months, Petersen and Dressel (1982) summarized their observations:

> A primary feature of the club is that it provides the opportunity for women to be assertive in sexual transactions with males. This takes several forms. Members of the audience initiate expressions of sexual interest, and they emulate male-typed courting behaviors by bringing gifts to, or doing favors for, their favorite dancers, as well as by

> propositioning strippers of their choice. This display of assertiveness by members of the audience is described by strippers as frequently being excessive, with women often becoming verbally and physically aggressive and sometimes engaging in behavior that dancers describe as lewd. (pp. 203–204)

The importance of the environment also impacts the health of an individual. When women and men are compared, women have more daily, annual, and lifetime health problems than men. When one researcher (Verbrugge, 1985) analyzed the relative importance of biological and environmental factors on health, she concluded that the difference between the physical conditions of men and women was primarily a result of the roles and stress imposed on women by our society.

Theories of Gender-Role Learning

Although most theorists agree that the environment has a profound effect on our gender-role development, they do not agree on the specific processes. There are three main explanations of how female and male gender roles are acquired.

Social Learning Theory

Derived from the school of behavioral psychology, *social learning theory* emphasizes that when gender-appropriate behaviors are rewarded and gender-inappropriate behaviors are punished, a child learns the behaviors appropriate to her or his gender. For example, two young brothers enjoyed playing "lady." Each of them would put on a dress, wear high-heeled shoes, and carry a pocketbook. Their father came home early one day and angrily demanded that they "take those clothes off and never put them on again. Those things are for women," he said. The boys were punished for playing "lady" but rewarded with their father's approval for playing "cowboys," with plastic guns and "Bang! You're dead!" dialogue.

Reward and punishment alone are not sufficient to account for the way in which children learn gender roles. Direct instruction ("girls wear dresses," "men walk on the outside when walking with a woman") is another way children learn through social interaction with others. But there are too many gender rules to learn. They require the use of other mechanisms like modeling.

The eye's a better pupil and more willing than the ear;
Fine counsel is confusing, but example's always clear.
—Edgar A. Guest

The concept of modeling is important in understanding gender-role acquisition from a social learning perspective. In *modeling,* the child observes another's behavior and imitates that behavior. On Monday afternoon, eight-year-old Bill helped his younger sister repair her tricycle. The Saturday before, Bill had observed his father putting spark plugs in their Dodge. His father was the "fix-it-man" in their home, and Bill, modeling after him, was the fix-it-man in his father's absence. Most parents are aware that their own roles were learned from their parents.

Data – Approximately two-thirds of all parents responding to a *Family Circle* survey say their roles in the family are similar to the roles of their own parents. (Rubenstein, 1985)

The impact of modeling on the development of gender-role behavior is controversial. For example, a modeling perspective implies that children will

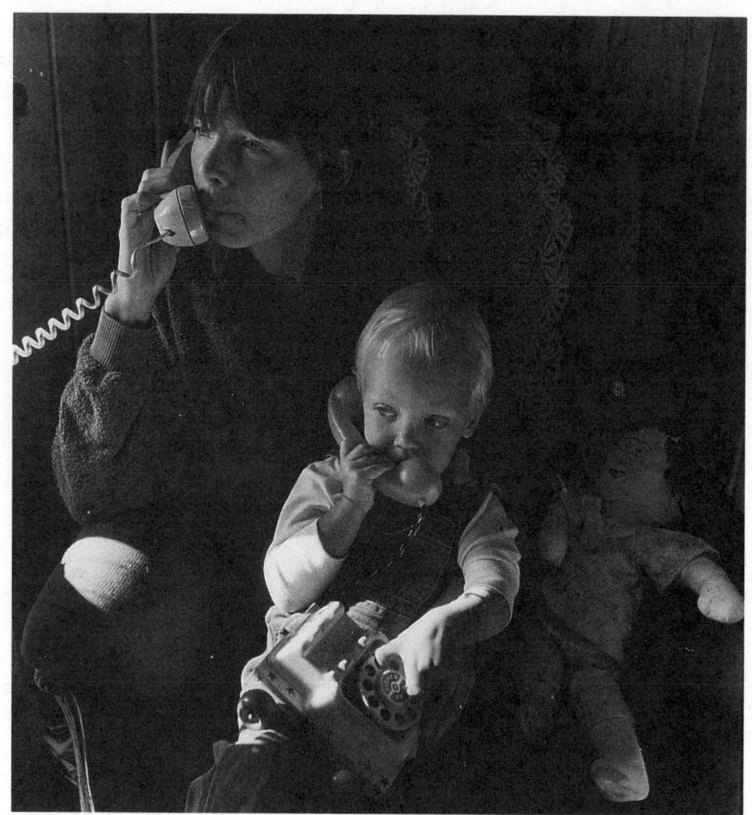

Children learn by observing their parents and modeling on their behavior.

tend to imitate the parent of the same gender, but children are usually reared mainly by the woman in all cultures. Yet this persistent female model does not seem to interfere with the male's development of the appropriate behavior for his gender. One explanation suggests that males learn early that they have more status and privileges in our society and therefore devalue the feminine and emphasize the masculine aspects of themselves.

Women also do not strictly model their mothers' behavior. Although women who work outside the home usually have mothers who did likewise, their mothers may also be traditional homemakers.

Cognitive-Developmental Theory

Male and female personalities are socially produced.
—Margaret Mead

The *cognitive-developmental theory* of gender-role acquisition suggests that the mental maturity of the child is a prerequisite to such acquisition (Kohlberg, 1969). Although 2-year-olds can label themselves and each other as "girl" or "boy," they have superficial criteria for doing so. People who wear long hair are girls, and those who never wear dresses are boys. Thus, 2-year-olds believe they can change their gender by altering their hair or changing clothes.

Not until age 6 or 7 does the child view gender as permanent (Kohlberg 1966, 1969). In Kohlberg's view, this cognitive understanding is not a result of rewards for appropriate, and punishments for inappropriate, gender-role behaviors. Rather, it involves the development of a specific mental ability to grasp the idea that certain basic characteristics of people do not change even though their hair style might. Once children learn that gender is permanent, they seek to become competent and proper members of their gender group. For example, a child standing on the edge of a school playground may observe one group of children jumping rope while another group is playing football. Her or his self-concept ("I am a girl" or "I am a boy") connects with the observed gender-appropriate behavior, and she or he joins one of the two groups. Once in the group, the child seeks to develop the behaviors appropriate to her or his gender.

Identification Theory

Identification results when the child takes on the demeanor, mannerisms, and attitudes of the same-gender parent. A child who identifies with her or his parent acts like that parent.

Sigmund Freud, the father of psychoanalysis, said that children identify with the same-gender parent out of fear (1925, 1933). Freud felt this fear could be one of two kinds: fear of loss of love or fear of retaliation. Fear of loss of love, which results in both girls and boys identifying with their mother, is caused by their deep dependence on her for love and nurturance. Fearful that she may withdraw her love, young children try to become like her to please her and to ensure the continuance of her love.

According to Freud, at about age 4, the child's identification with the mother begins to change, but in different ways for boys than for girls. Boys experience what Freud calls the "Oedipal complex." Based on the legend of the Greek youth Oedipus, who unknowingly killed his father and married his mother, the Oedipal complex involves the young boy's awakening sexual feelings for his mother as he becomes aware he has a penis and his mother does not. He unconsciously feels that if his father knew of the intense love feelings he has for his mother, the father would castrate him (which may be what happened to his mother, because she has no penis). The boy resolves the

Some learning is by direct instruction.

Oedipal struggle—feeling love for his father but wanting to kill him because he is a competitor for his mother's love—by becoming like his father, by identifying with him. In this way, the boy can keep his penis and take pride in being like his father. According to Freud, the successful resolution of this Oedipal situation marks the beginning of a boy's appropriate gender-role acquisition.

And here's the happy bounding flea—
You cannot tell the he from she.
The sexes look alike you see;
But she can tell, and so can he.
—Roland Young

While her brother is experiencing the Oedipal complex, the girl goes through her own identification process, known as the Electra complex. Around age 4, she recognizes that she has no penis, wishes she did (penis envy), and feels her mother is responsible for its absence. To retaliate, she takes her love away from her mother and begins to focus on her father as a love object. But her desire for a penis is gradually transformed into the need for a baby, and to get a baby from her father she recognizes that she must be more like her mother. So she identifies again with her mother. Her goal now is to be a woman like her mother and to be a mother herself. According to Freud, such gender-role identification is characteristic of a mature female.

Although Freud's identification theories are interesting to read, there is little scientific support for their validity as explanations for gender-role acquisition. Most 3- and 4-year-olds do not know the difference between males and females on the basis of their genitals. Also, it is possible that some women have status envy rather than penis envy. They may view the male role as offering more rewards, not because men have a penis, but because they tend to occupy social positions that are accorded status in our society (heads of corporations, senators, representatives).

Nevertheless, although verification for Freud's identification theories is weak, his belief in the biological basis of gender-role differences has had a significant impact. His dictum "biology is destiny" is still influential in research on gender differences.

Consideration

In reviewing the social learning, cognitive-developmental, and identification perspectives of how individuals become women and men, it is clear that no one explanation is adequate. Depending on the social situation, the age of the child, the frequency and nature of play interactions, and the attitudes of the child's parents, each process is influential at different times, in different ways, and to different degrees. Young children will at times be rewarded or punished for gender-appropriate or inappropriate behaviors, cognitively choose to engage in gender-appropriate behaviors, learn gender roles through interaction with their peers, and identify with their parents.

Sources of Socialization

The preceding discussion implies that gender roles are learned through interaction with the environment. Parents, teachers, peers, mass media, and religion make up the social environment. What are the effects of each on gender differences? Researchers have suggested the following answers.

Parents

Gender-role stereotypes begin early; children are able to identify gender-specific traits by age 4 (Albert & Porter, 1986). Parents are usually the first influence in a child's life. Even before the birth of their child, parents relate to their child on the basis of suspected or known gender. In one study of expectant parents, 22 out of 24 parents said that the way they related to their fetus depended on whether they thought or knew it was a girl or a boy. One father described the movements of his daughter inside his wife's uterus as "graceful and gentle." If the fetus was a male, the parents viewed its movement as "strong" (Stainton, 1985).

Although there is a trend toward giving children sex-role neutral toys (Robinson & Morris, 1986), parents tend to give their daughters dolls and their sons baseballs or footballs. They are also more protective of their daughters out of fear that they will be sexually molested. Such protectiveness often encourages girls to be less active in exploring their environment. Daughters, more than sons, are also socialized to be family-oriented, to be aware of who is having what birthday, and to want the family to be together for various holidays. Daughters are often expected to provide more care for ailing family members and relatives than their brothers. Finally, parents—particularly single fathers—expect their daughters to do more housework than their sons (Greif, 1985).

Teachers

Although parents have the earliest and most pervasive influence on their children, teachers are a major influence outside the home. Teachers may inadvertently respond to boys and girls differently in the classroom. As two researchers have observed:

> When boys call out comments without raising their hands, teachers accept their answers. However, when girls call out, teachers reprimand this "inappropriate" behavior with messages such as, "In this class, we don't shout out answers; we raise our hands." The message is subtle but powerful: boys should be academically assertive and grab teacher attention; girls should act like ladies and keep quiet (Sadker & Sadker, 1985, p. 56).

School courses also influence gender-role learning. Although American females can take whatever courses they choose, Korean females are required to take courses that stress family life, meal management, and clothing, among other subjects (Sun-Hee, 1985).

Peers

Peers become an important gender influence in the life of a child, beginning in grade school and continuing through adolescence. The individual looks to his or her peers to discover "the" appropriate language, dress, and interests. Recall your own high-school days when you spoke the same language, wore the same clothes, and pursued the same activities as those of your same-gender peers. Parents often recognize the significance of peer-group influence and encourage (sometimes by moving to a "better neighborhood") their children to have the "right friends."

Mass Media

Television also plays a significant role in gender socialization. It has been estimated that the typical child and teenager spends more time in front of the

The typical child spends more time watching television than attending school.

television than in school. There is also a difference in the amount of time that blacks and whites watch television.

Data – Blacks watch an average of one hour more of television each day than whites. (Bales, 1986)

On television, the child often sees characters in stereotypic roles with a male bias. News anchors are still predominately men, and narrators on special documentary programs are more often men than women. But changes are occurring. Women are increasingly seen as equals (Claire and Cliff in *The Cosby Show*) or as assertive and independent (*Cagney and Lacey*) in previously all-male roles.

Television also exposes youth to individuals who provide positive models. Jesse Jackson has emphasized that "black is beautiful," and Cesar Chavez of the United Farm Workers has encouraged Mexican Americans to have pride and dignity in their race.

Religion

Whether inadvertently or with purpose, some religions—particularly the more traditional and conservative religions—perpetuate the idea of a more dominant male gender. According to the Book of *Genesis*, women, as a group, fell when Eve was tempted by Satan to eat the forbidden fruit from the tree of knowledge.

Some traditionalists use this story of the Fall of Man to suggest that the man should be the dominant person in the home. "Wives be subject unto your husbands as unto your God." (Ephesians 5:22) However, more progressive religions steer clegions steer clear of the issue of the subjugation of women and emphasize role equality.

Consideration

Notice the degree to which your gender role in society has been influenced by your parents, teachers, peers, mass media, and religion. What jobs did you perform around the house when you were growing up? Were they gender-specific (for example, washing dishes for girls versus mowing the lawn for boys)? To what degree did your teachers encourage you to pursue gender-specific occupations (for example, nursing for women versus engineering for men)? How have the occupational choices of your peers influenced your career choice?

Nature versus Nurture: The Controversy

The relative importance of our biological heritage (nature) and our socialization experiences (nurture) in determining who we are continues to be one of the most controversial issues related to gender roles. In this section, we will examine both sides of this issue.

Gender-Role Behaviors Are Innate

Those on the "nature" side of the nature-nurture controversy contend that our biological inheritance programs us to be who we are. Women and men have different sex chromosomes (women-XX; men-XY) and hormones (women-more progesterone; men-more testosterone), which determine body type (females are usually smaller and shorter) and mortality expectations (females live an average of seven years longer than males.)

Studies of identical twins who were reared apart emphasize the impact of heredity on our development. Also known as *monozygotic twins,* identical twins develop from a single fertilized egg that divides to produce two embryos. These embryos develop into infants who, from a genetic viewpoint, are identical. If these individuals are exposed to different environments in their infancy and childhood but still show striking similarities as adults, heredity is the suggested cause.

A team of researchers at the University of Minnesota have studied 15 such pairs of twins, asking each twin about 15,000 questions. The researchers observed a striking tendency for the twins to show very similar physical and psychological characteristics. If one stuttered, had a phobia, had headaches, was shy, anxious, depressed, or had a particular interest, the other tended to have the same characteristic. Identical twins who were reared apart also tend to be similar in intelligence (Bouchard, 1983). Additional support for biological influence has been suggested in reference to criminological studies. Nine studies of criminality among twins all revealed that identical twins are approximately twice as likely as fraternal twins to be similar in regard to criminal behavior (Mednick, 1985).

Another way of assessing the importance of biological factors is to compare the lives of people who were adopted early in their childhood with the lives of their biological and adoptive parents to find out if genetic or environmental in-

Identical twins emphasize the influence of heredity on personality.

fluences are greater. The results of studying 1,800 cases revealed that subjects with alcohol or criminal problems had biological parents with similar problems, even though their adoptive parents had low frequencies of alcohol or criminal behavior (Cloninger, 1986). The conclusions of these studies suggest that genetic inheritance is an important but not a crucial variable in development.

Gender-Role Behaviors Are Learned

In contrast to the belief that biological influences determine who we are, other researchers state just as emphatically that we learn to be who we are. In one study, 26 couples were assigned to a problem-solving, skills-training program after taking the Bem Sex Role Inventory—a test designed to assess the degree to which each person views herself or himself as masculine or feminine. The training consisted of learning how to disclose themselves to each other and to express feelings to each other. After completing the eight-week program, both the men and the women took the Bem Sex Role Inventory again and scored higher on the feminine aspects. Similar changes were not observed in the control group of this experiment. Another study showed that men can learn empathy (Cleaver, 1987).

Both studies emphasize that self-disclosure and empathy—traits typically associated with women—can be learned. These traits are not innate but are acquired through social and cultural exposure to various learning experiences. Another study demonstrated that females display leadership skills similar to those of males when the situational context calls for such behavior (Koberg, 1985). Hence, the experiences a person is exposed to and the cues within a social context dictate the behavior that an individual expresses.

Consideration

Both heredity and the environment interact to produce society's members. You are a product not only of your genetic heritage but also of the experiences to which you have been exposed. As Tennyson said, in *Ulysses* "I am a part of all that I have met." The differences between women and men can be many.

Consequences of Becoming a Woman

The interaction of biological and learning factors results in a woman. Some of the consequences of becoming a woman in our society are discussed in the following sections.

A Negative Self-Concept?

Women may lack confidence in themselves, feel that there are more disadvantages associated with being a woman than with being a man, be prejudiced against other women, and view their bodies negatively. In a study in which women and men were told that they were not capable of performing a cognitive task, the women were more likely than the men to believe that they were incapable (Wagner et al., 1986).

Women also see more disadvantages associated with being a woman than with being a man (Fabes & Laner, 1986). Some of the disadvantages identified by 247 female college students included difficulty in getting a high-paying job, having to wait for someone to ask them for a date, being discriminated against, and having to deal with menstruation.

Regarding prejudice against themselves, when 180 females were asked to evaluate four academic articles, their opinions were less favorable if they thought the articles were written by a woman (Joan T.) than by a man (John T.) (Paludi & Bauer, 1983). Regardless of their actual weight, women also tend to see their bodies less positively than men see their bodies. Women view themselves as overweight or slightly overweight. Less positive attitudes toward one's body are related to lower levels of self-esteem (Mintz & Betz, 1986).

Disenchantment with being a woman may be related to *sexism,* which is defined as the systematic persecution and degradation of women based on the supposed inferiority of women and the supposed superiority of men. The Sexist Attitudes Scale given in the Self-Assessment section is a way to assess the degree to which you have prejudicial attitudes toward women.

An Unhappy Marriage?

Because the role of wife is closely related to adult feminine identity in our society, many women feel enormous pressure to get married. Yet there is evidence that wives are less happy in marriage than husbands. When asked about their marriages, more wives than husbands report frustration, dissatisfaction, problems, unhappiness, and a desire to divorce. About their mental health, more married women than married men feel that they are about to have a nervous breakdown, experience more psychological anxiety, and more often blame themselves for their own lack of adjustment (Caplan, 1985).

The explanation for the greater difficulty that women experience in marriage compared to men is that the wife is expected to make her husband, children, and employer happy, to keep the house clean and neat, and to correspond with her parents and her in-laws. To be "superwives," moms, and workers is a cultural expectation that is unrealistic for most women to accomplish. Yet few husbands are willing to change their expectations of what a wife should be or to help lessen the wife's work load. As a result, wives stay stressed and wonder what the satisfactions of marriage are.

A Brief Motherhood Role?

Wives and mothers who do not have a job or career that is meaningful to them can find it difficult to adjust to their children leaving home. Although much of her life has been spent in preparation for and investment in the role of mother, this role has usually ended by age 50, and the average woman has a remaining 30 years to live. Because men tend to be more involved in their careers, it is less difficult for them to adjust to the fact that their children have left home.

Marriage and Motherhood: Achievement Barriers?

Being a wife and a mother may limit a woman's achievements in such areas as education and employment.

Education

Women now constitute more than 50 percent of all entering college students. Although they earn more than one-half of all bachelor's and master's degrees, they earn only one-third of the Ph.D. degrees and fewer M.D. degrees. Whether the explanation is that women choose motherhood over long-term career preparation, lack educated female models, or believe there are not enough professional opportunities open to them, the result is the same—women tend to have other priorities than earning academic degrees.

One woman mused about education and her life:

> It seems to me that women in general don't look ahead and ask, "What will I be doing in ten years?" For example, even though I had talent in graduate school and worked for my master's, it never occurred to me to go ahead to a Ph.D. Once I married, I looked forward to having a family. In some ways, I'm glad that I didn't have the pressure of a career while my family was young. I loved that period and made the most of it. (Frankel & Rathvon, 1980, p. 91)

This picture may be changing. As external barriers to professional schools (law, medicine, business) are removed and dual-career marriages increase, more academic degrees will be awarded to women. However, a study of the effects of marriage on education confirms that women who marry early radically reduce their chances of getting additional education (Haggstrom et al., 1986).

Self-Assessment

The Sexist Attitudes Scale

Directions: Read each sentence carefully, and circle the number you feel best represents your opinion.

1 Strongly agree (definitely yes)
2 Mildly agree (I believe so)
3 Undecided (not sure)
4 Mildly disagree (probably not)
5 Strongly disagree (definitely not)

	SA	MA	U	MD	SD
1. Women are ruled by their hormones more than men.	1	2	3	4	5
2. Women tend to be less rational than men.	1	2	3	4	5
3. A man makes a better mechanic than a woman.	1	2	3	4	5
4. Women gossip more than men.	1	2	3	4	5
5. A man makes a better employer than a woman.	1	2	3	4	5
6. Women are better at taking care of a family than at any other role.	1	2	3	4	5
7. Women should take their husbands' name when they marry.	1	2	3	4	5
8. Women have become too independent and career-oriented.	1	2	3	4	5
9. Women should think more and talk less.	1	2	3	4	5
10. A woman will get more satisfaction from her family than from her career.	1	2	3	4	5

Scoring: Add the numbers you circled. 1 (strongly agree) is the most sexist response, and 5 (strongly disagree) is the most egalitarian response. The lower your total score (10 is the lowest possible score), the more sexist you are; the higher your total score (50 is the highest possible score), the more egalitarian you are about gender roles. A score of 30 places you at the midpoint on the sexist–egalitarian continuum.

Employment

Marriage and motherhood may also interfere with a woman's economic potential. Although most men (88 percent) and women (95 percent) prefer that the wife be employed if there are no children, employment preferences change when the children are born. In a national study of high-school seniors, almost one-half felt that the most preferred situation for the family with young children was for the husband to work full time and for the wife to work half time (Herzog et al., 1983).

A graduate student expresses how her interests were reoriented after she became involved in a relationship:

> It's not a choice between marriage and someone/anyone else. It's between singlehood and relationship. Mike is perfect for me, and I don't ever expect to meet anyone who can top him. But this relationship is affecting my career. As a graduate student, I am spending less time on schoolwork, doing poorer quality work, and enjoying it less because I'd rather be with Mike. Also because I'm in the relationship now, I am committed (and want to) spend time on it.

The fact that many women drop out of the labor force during their children's preschool years (compared with almost zero percent for men) has implications for the jobs women have and the money they earn. Two researchers (Kenkel & Gage, 1983) observed that women tend to select jobs on the basis of how enjoyable they might be rather than for their income-producing value. This may be accounted for by women's lack of job skills and work experience as well as by their expectation that work will be interrupted by childrearing.

I'm into hard work—not pretty dresses.
—Maria Shriver

The success of the Harlequin romance novels (14 million loyal readers) is based on the dissatisfaction of women with their jobs. Harlequin readers often have jobs as clerks, secretaries, waitresses, and teachers, but their heroines in the romance novels are musicians, painters, poets, Olympic athletes, photogra-

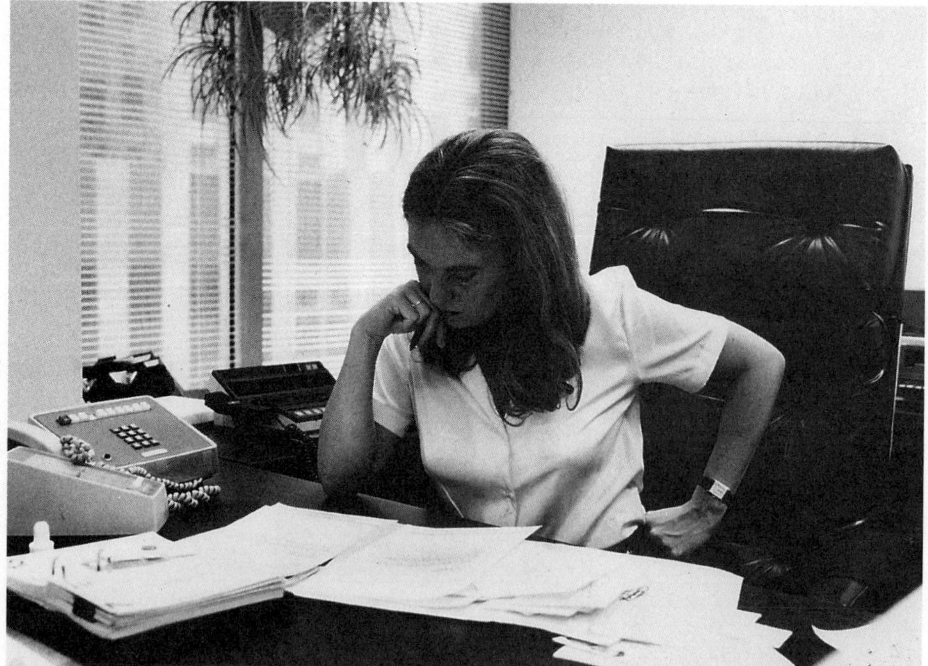

Only a few women hold managerial positions in large corporations.

phers, and female executives with glamorous jobs. The readers want the world of work to change to provide more money (and status) so that they can find happiness there (Rabine, 1985).

Not only am I angry, but I'm also angry at all the years I wasn't angry.
—Carol Kleinman

Women are also discriminated against in employment. They are given lower positions than men with equivalent qualifications, and they experience resistance when they seek jobs traditionally held by men (Riemer & Bridwell, 1982). Two researchers (Gerdes & Garber, 1983) asked 64 managers to review the job applications of men and women with equal experience, academic qualifications, and intellectual competence. The women were generally evaluated as being less suitable for the job than the men. The researchers concluded, "When the job description's stated requirements were not addressed by the applicant's materials, evaluators assumed that the male candidate possessed the required skills and the female candidate lacked these stereotypically masculine skills" (p. 314). The facts that women earn fewer academic degrees, work in lower-status jobs, and experience barriers to jobs traditionally held by men translate into a lower lifetime income than men achieve. Women still earn about 70 percent of what men earn (*Statistical Abstract of the United States,* 1987).

Consideration

With the 50 percent chance of divorce, the likelihood of being a widow for seven or more years, and the almost certain loss of her parenting role midway through her life, a woman without education and employment skills is often left high and dry. As one widowed mother of four said, "The shock of realizing you have children to support and no skills to do it with is a worse shock than learning your husband is dead." In the words of a divorced, 40-year-old mother of three, "If young women think it can't happen to them, they are foolish" (Crossman & Edmondson, 1985).

Marriage, Motherhood, Job: Who Has the Best of Everything?

Basically I want it all—but in manageable proportions.
—Meryl Streep

Some women view divorce as happening to someone else and the death of their husband as "too far off to worry about." For these women and others, the traditional gender roles of wife and mother offer more rewards than drawbacks. In contrast to many working mothers, full-time homemakers can more freely control and plan their own work and be their own bosses. They are more likely to see their children's first steps and to hear their first words than employed women, who must depend on reports about their child's achievements from a baby sitter or child-care worker. Women who enjoy the homemaker role find greater fulfillment in caring for those they most love than in working in a more impersonal setting toward more impersonal goals. They do not see the traditional role as an achievement barrier, because they define achievement as providing a good home life for their families and rearing their children successfully.

Although many women might prefer to stay at home with their children, especially when they are young, the 50 percent divorce rate and increased unmarried motherhood have created a number of female-headed households in which the woman is the sole wage earner. In addition, in couple households, inflation and high interest rates may require that both partners work outside

Exhibit 3.1

THE FEMININIZATION OF POVERTY

Women are more likely to have lower incomes than men—not only because they earn fewer advanced academic degrees but also because they tend to be employed fewer hours in order to be with and take care of their children. The femininization of poverty is yet another dimension of the same problem (Kniesner, 1986).

As women move into certain occupations, such as teaching and nursing, a tendency toward increased segregation of women develops in the marketplace (women in one occupation, men in another) and the salaries of women in these occupational roles increases at a slower rate. The salaries of the teaching and nursing professions, which are predominantly female occupations, have not kept pace with inflation, resulting in a concentration of segregated women in lower-paid occupations. Poverty is primarily a feminine issue because more women than men have inadequate incomes. One of the consequences of being a woman is to have an increased chance of feeling economic strain throughout life.

Women with children who have held low-income jobs and who are divorced or widowed often drift into poverty. If they are also older, their movement toward poverty is more swift. Unless women attend to the fact that they cannot depend on the income of a mate, they become economically vulnerable.

Single black females are particularly vulnerable to being economically disadvantaged. When black head-of-household women are compared with white head-of-household women, the former have 58 percent of the income of the latter (*Statistical Abstract of the United States,* 1987).

I do not love my career a fraction as much as I love my children. Never mind the tedium [of taking care of twin babies]; I would much rather be home with those babies.

—Jane Pauley

the home to achieve the standard of living desired by the couple or simply to make ends meet. Thus, many wives (as well as husbands) work in jobs that they do not enjoy. Part of this lack of enjoyment is the fact that some women don't want to feel so burdened with their jobs and careers that they cannot devote the desired amount of time to their families.

Data – Of 250 career women earning an average of $75,000, 70 percent said that they were "not very pleased" with their careers. (Gilson & Kane, 1987)

Originally, women fought to have an equal position in the marketplace. But the price has been higher than some had imagined. Some women who delayed having children to achieve professional careers now consider themselves too old to begin a family. One 39-year-old vice-president said:

> My job is exciting and gratifying, but I'm haunted by the fear that I'm missing out on the most meaningful part of life by not having children. Sometimes I imagine that if I died now, my tombstone would read: "Here lies Sharon Cohen. She read a lot of magazines." (Salholz et al., 1986, p. 59)

To summarize where women have been and where they want to go:

> Initially, women wanted a piece of the male pie; now they want a different pie. The ingredients: flexibility in their work, companionship in their lives, and recognition of their longing for children. (Salholz et al., 1986)

Some women are close to achieving the goal. They enjoy their work and are determined to integrate their careers with their personal and family life (Keown & Keown, 1985). The benefits that wives derive from such employment include increased interaction with a variety of individuals, a broader base for recognition, improved economic conditions for self and family, and greater equality between self and spouse.

Some Positive Consequences of Being a Woman

Although some of the foregoing may be viewed as negative aspects of being socialized as a woman, there are advantages to being a woman in our society. Among these are living longer, being able to express emotions more easily, having a closer bond with children, not having one's identity tied to employment, and being more likely to obtain custody of children in the event of a divorce. (Women are awarded custody in 90 percent of all custody cases.)

Consideration

In an effort to eliminate the potential negative consequences of being socialized as a woman, parents might be alert to the societal bias against their daughters and attempt to minimize it. For example, parents might teach their daughters to view every occupation as an option for them, to regard being female as unique (the capacity to create a baby), and to supplement marital and family roles with a meaningful worker role that will provide an independent source of income and identity. In addition, should a daughter not evidence an interest in getting married or having children, the parents should consider supporting her interests completely.

Consequences of Becoming a Man

The role of men in our society has its own disadvantages and rewards. We will consider some of these in the following sections.

Required to Earn Money

A recent career advertisement in a national magazine showed a young wife looking at her husband while leaning on his shoulder. The man-to-man caption read, "One day, it suddenly strikes home that we're going to be working for a living the rest of our lives." Just as the woman is more often channeled into the roles of wife and mother, the man is channeled into the world of gainful employment to pay the basic bills of the family. He has little choice. He must work—his wife, children, parents, in-laws, and peers expect it.

A college senior responded to this observation by saying, "Baloney! I'm not getting caught in the work trap. I'm going to paint houses now and then—just enough to keep me going—and enjoy life." Three years after graduation, he reported, "I'm married now, and we need money for our child. It's easy to say you don't need money when you are single but when you've got a sick kid who's running up medical bills, you know it's time to get cooking."

A man's responsibility to earn an income and society's tendency to equate income with success have implications for the male's self-esteem. Our society fosters the assumption that the man who makes $50,000 annually is more of a man than the one who makes $20,000 a year. Ultimately, a male in our society must earn money to feel good about himself.

Inadequate Development of Other Skills

The pressure to make money may also interfere with a man's development of other roles and skills. Most men were cared for by their mothers, and they expect similar nurturing and practical care from their wives. Some men have never learned how to cook, wash clothes, or take care of a home. As a result, they feel dependent on a woman for these domestic needs.

Some men stay married and others remarry because they feel unequipped to care for themselves. One divorced man said, "I can't cook. I need a woman to look after me."

Identity Equals Job

Ask a man who he is, and he will tell you what he does. His identity lies in his work. It is the principal means by which he confirms his masculinity. In studies of unemployment during the Great Depression, job loss was regarded as a greater shock to men than to women, although the loss of income affected both.

The importance of the relationship between work and male identity makes it particularly difficult for black males, who have a much higher unemployment rate than white males. The result of not being able to fulfill a suitable economic role is considerable psychological stress (Kessler & Neighbors, 1986).

Men get much of their identity from their work.

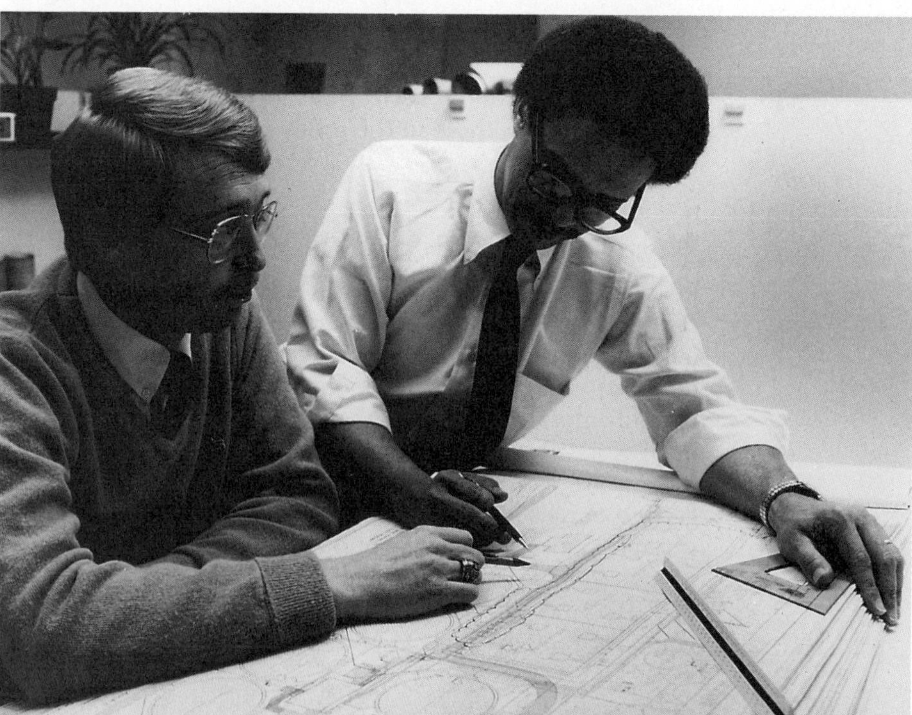

Exhibit 3.2

HEY MAN! CHICANO MACHISMO

Chicano men are stereotyped as being "macho" males. It is believed that they boss women around, beat them, and have numerous extramarital affairs. Although this image of *machismo* is widely held, it is not supported by consistent empirical data. Although some Chicano males do fit the stereotype, others are warm, nurturing, and egalitarian. The latter are more often found in marriages in which the wife is employed.

In cases in which Chicano males do display macho behavior, there are different interpretations as to why it occurs. A psychoanalytic interpretation views *machismo* as an *unconscious* attempt to overcompensate for feelings of inferiority, powerlessness, and inadequacy. According to this theory, the Chicano male unconsciously feels inferior because his Mexican forebearers were conquered by Spanish men who produced "the hybrid Mexican people having an inferiority complex based on the mentality of a conquered people" (Baca Zinn, 1980).

An alternative explanation—and a more acceptable one to sociologists—is that *machismo* behavior can be explained on the basis of the socially inferior position of the Chicano male and his *conscious* reaction to that position. As one researcher (Baca Zinn, 1982) notes:

> Men in certain social categories have had more roles and sources of identity open to them. However, this has not been the case for Chicanos or other men of color. Perhaps manhood takes on greater importance for those who do not have access to socially valued roles. Being male is one sure way to acquire status when other roles are systematically denied by the workings of society. This suggests that an emphasis on masculinity is not due to a collective internalized inferiority, rooted in a subcultural orientation. (p. 39)

Hence, not only is the existence of the "macho" Chicano male a disputed phenomenon, but there are also different interpretations for its presumed existence. The implication of this sociological explanation suggests that any male in a similar inferior social position with limited opportunities to express his masculinity may resort to a "Hey man, do as I say" routine.

Adapted from Maxine Baca Zinn. Chicano men and masculinity. *The Journal of Ethnic Studies*, 1982, 10(2), 29–44. Used by permission.

Mexican American men face a similar dilemma; they have a higher unemployment rate than whites, and they work in predominantly unskilled, blue-collar roles (see Exhibit 3.2). Moreover, access to education is more limited for Mexican Americans than it is for blacks or whites. In the United States, out of 25 million blacks, 2,200 have earned a Ph.D.; out of 9 million Mexican Americans, only 60 have earned a Ph.D. (Alvarez, 1985).

The identification of self with job also becomes a problem when it forces human concerns to become a low priority. One father told his 5-year-old daughter, who had asked him to play with her, "Don't bother Daddy. I'm busy. Please leave the study." Later that afternoon when he came into the child's room to play with her, she said, "Don't bother me. I'm busy. Please leave my room."

EMOTIONAL STEREOTYPES

Some men feel caught between society's expectations that they be competitive, aggressive, independent, and unemotional and their own desire to be more open, caring, and emotional. Not only are men less likely to cry than women, but they are also less able to express love, happiness, and sadness. The words "I love you," "I'm happy," or "I'm depressed" do not come easy for some men.

The inability to express feelings begins early in many males. A study of children of a median age of 9 years whose parents divorced revealed that the boys were 50 percent as likely as the girls to express their feelings about the event (Bonkowski et al., 1985). Males may also feel that it is unmanly to ask for help. Such reluctance is particularly true among Mexican American males, who have a strong sense of character and pride (Sanchez & King, 1986).

Adapting to the Modern Woman

As women change, so must men—and some are reluctant to do so. In a study of over 500 college students, 82 percent of the males (in contrast to 94 percent of the females) said that they would be interested in an egalitarian marriage (Billingham & Sack, 1986.)

But whether men like it or not, there is an emerging new equality in relationships between women and men. Modern women, in contrast to traditional women, are more likely to challenge their partners' rationale and to suggest alternative explanations and preferences. "Acquiescence" and "submission" are words that less often describe women in today's heterosexual relationships. Women who are married, who have a child, and who are employed are much more likely to have egalitarian expectations than women who are single and without a child or job (McBroom, 1986).

The egalitarian issue also expresses itself in the couple's attitudes toward higher education. The man no longer asks, "Where will you work to put me

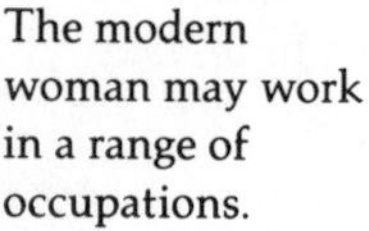
The modern woman may work in a range of occupations.

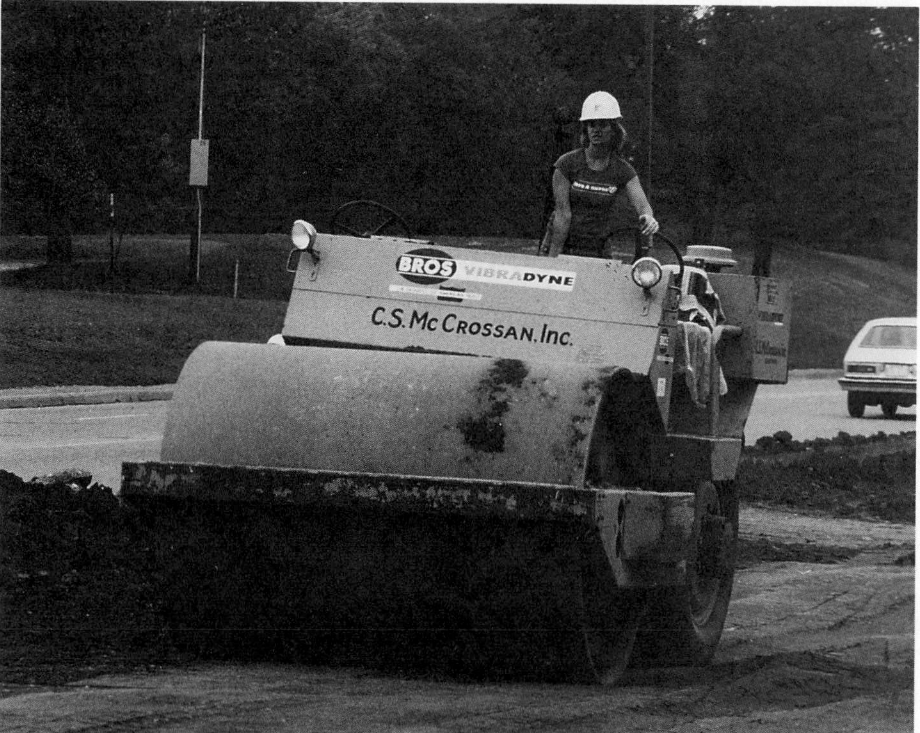

through school?" but "How will we finance our educations?" or "Do you want to finish your education before I finish mine?"

Any man today who returns from work, sinks into a chair, and calls for his pipe is a man with an appetite for danger.
—Bill Cosby

Due to women's increasing desire for education, career involvement, and economic independence, men today can expect women to be less interested in early marriage than the preceding generation. When women do marry, they are likely to expect more from their partners in terms of sharing child care and housekeeping responsibilities than changing a diaper and setting the table. Some feel that liberation for men is not only their freedom to cry but their willingness to share domestic work.

Finally, women have begun to assert their own sexual needs. Before Masters and Johnson's widespread influence, men could be concerned solely with their own sexual pleasure. Today, a man, after ejaculation, may hear his frustrated partner say, "I didn't have an orgasm." He can no longer be the great lover by satisfying only himself.

Some Benefits of Being a Man

Compared to females, males have more positive self-concepts, greater confidence in themselves, and more status (Wagner et al., 1986). Men also feel that they experience less discrimination and sexual harassment than women. Both males and females feel that more advantages are associated with being male than with being female (Fabes & Laner, 1986).

Consideration

> Males might consider the potential trap of focusing on making money and pursuing a career to the exclusion of being able to care for themselves independently and not developing relationships that provide meaning beyond work roles. "What is the value of making unlimited amounts of money if you have no one to share it with?," the male might ask.

The Ideal Man

A Man-of-the-Hour is the one whose wife told him to wait a minute.
—Laurence Peter

"Macho" does not prove mucho.
—Zsa Zsa Gabor

Women students in the author's marriage and family class of 120 students were asked to identify the qualities they most desired in a man. The characteristics most frequently mentioned were "loving," "loyal," "affectionate," "responsible," "intelligent," and "hard working." Here are some examples:

> My ideal man is a very loving and caring person who is not afraid to "feel" things or to show affection. He is very secure within himself and is not adversely affected or threatened by any of *my* achievements. He is very considerate of my feelings at all times and willing to solve problems by talking. He is a hard worker and very responsible and dependable in his "duties" as an employee, mate, and father. He can be trusted—I don't have to worry about whether or not he is loyal. He cares about his appearance and has a good self-concept.

> My ideal man is one who respects the new eighties woman, yet at the same time can open the car door for her. He is the man who surprises you by cooking dinner on the night you have to work late. He is the man who gives wonderful back rubs and foot massages (even when your feet stink). He also actually likes his in-laws. He can apologize when he's hurt your feelings and admit when he's wrong and you're right.

My ideal partner must be affectionate because I need positive attention in an intimate relationship. He must also be intelligent and open minded. Of course, physical attractiveness is important—my man can't be ugly! About 5′ 11″ or 6′, he would be dark-complected, with a mustache, hairy chest, and nice physique (but not too muscular). He must also be honest with me and teach me that I can trust him when I'm not around.

The Ideal Woman

Male students in the same class were asked to identify the characteristics of their ideal woman. "Physically attractive," "flexible," "trustworthy," "hard working," "intelligent," and "dependable" were the qualities most frequently mentioned by these males. Here are some examples:

I want not only a woman with a good head on her shoulders but also with a great body to support her head. In addition, she must be honest and sincere, so that I can trust her. A positive outlook toward religion and on life in general is also important to me. I basically want a good person who respects and is good to me and expects the same from me.

An ideal wife is any woman who has an ideal husband.
—Booth Tarkington

My ideal woman would first of all have to be attractive if I am to marry her. I also must be able to trust her. I would like her to be nice and have a good personality. Most important, we must be able to get along and have a good time together. When I'm with my friends, I want her to understand that there are other parts to my life than being a spouse.

I feel the ideal woman should be loyal and trusting, so there will be no misunderstandings about the time we spend apart from each other. I feel that she must be hard working and show incentive to make contributions to the relationship. She should be flexible and have a sense of humor that will alleviate tension. Dependability is important, because it shows a genuine concern and will to please.

Consideration

The respective ideal woman and man are very similar. Both are characterized by loyalty, dependability, and flexibility. The men tend to focus more on physical appearance, but the women also want a nice-looking man.

Trends

Although we continue to recognize that a person's biological heritage has a significant impact on her or his development, our society is becoming less rigid in its gender-role socialization. As a result, fewer roles will be closed to women and more androgynous people (those with both feminine and masculine characteristics).

As each gender begins to fill a wider range of roles, the trend toward androgyny will increase. For example, men will feel more free to be gentle and to express their emotions, whereas women will more often be assertive and competitive. Although cross-gender changes may be difficult for both women and men (Alperson & Friedman, 1983; Moore, 1985), movement toward these changes will be accelerated by women's greater participation in work outside the home and men's greater involvement in child care. Developing more of the qualities of the opposite gender is often viewed as having the best of both worlds—feminine and masculine—and may also be associated with better personal and marital adjustment (Kalin & Lloyd, 1985). In addition, spouses who share the power in their relationship evidence the least amount of depression (Mirowsky, 1985) and the greatest amount of marital satisfaction (Marshall, 1985).

In the past 10 years, a number of social barriers to women's participation in formerly all-male activities have been removed. No longer are women barred from being vice-presidential candidates, Supreme Court justices, West Point cadets, or astronauts, and girls now play baseball on Little League teams. Today's woman is not only a married housewife with two children living in surburbia. She also may be a never-married woman, a divorced woman, a married woman who works outside the home, or a child-free married woman. Stereotypes of who women are and what they do are fading.

The women's movement, which formerly focused on the passage of the Equal Rights Amendment (ERA) and abortion rights, will now turn its attention to the protection of working women who opt to become mothers. Because there is no government-sanctioned leave or child-care policy, a woman's income and job security nosedives when she has a child. Other countries (117 of them) have job-protected leaves of absence for pregnant women; the United States will move toward such protection. The 1987 Supreme Court decision requiring states to provide job protection for pregnant women is an example of such movement.

Finally, a new sexism is developing against men (Farrell, 1986). Increasingly, men are being viewed as wimps and jerks and as incapable of committing to a relationship. A recent cartoon featured a shopper saying, "I want a perfume that says to a man, 'Go to Hell'."

Summary

Sex refers to the biological distinction of being male or female. *Gender* refers to the social expectations that a group imposes on its members because one is either male or female.

A person's gender identity is her or his self-concept as a girl and later a woman or as a boy and later a man. Gender roles are the socially accepted characteristics and behaviors associated with a person's gender identity. In our society, the traditional female role is to be emotional, dependent, and home oriented and the traditional male role is to be unemotional, independent, and career oriented. Today, these stereotypes are breaking down under the impact of changes in family structure and job participation.

Gender-role behaviors of women and men result from the combined effects of biological inheritance and social environment. Biological inheritance includes the chromosomes and hormones that result in sexual differentiation. Only women menstruate, get pregnant, give birth, and nurse their infants. Only males have penile erections and ejaculate semen.

Biological inheritance is overlaid with environmental influences. Three explanations of how children learn appropriate gender-role behaviors are provided by social learning, cognitive-developmental, and identification theory. The social learning perspective states that children learn their roles by being rewarded for gender-appropriate behaviors and punished for inappropriate (opposite-gender) behaviors. According to the cognitive-developmental view of gender-role learning, children first reach the stage at which they understand that their gender is permanent and then actively seek to acquire masculine or feminine characteristics. Identification theory suggests that children take on the role of the same-gender parent either out of fear or love. Whereas biological development through chromosomes and hormones predisposes people to behave in certain ways, society (represented by parents, teachers, peers, mass media, and religion) guides the person's behavior into culturally approved channels (for example, girls playing with dolls and boys playing with cars and trucks). A long-standing controversy in gender-role development is the relative influence of heredity versus environment, but an interaction effect seems to account for most personal and social behaviors.

Being socialized as a woman or a man has varied consequences for the person. Women sometimes have less confidence in themselves than men do due to pervasive sexism. Marriage may be a disappointment if wives discover that husbands are more interested in work than in family. Women also pursue less education and earn less income than men. Those who do not develop an interest other than their husbands and children may feel a void when those roles terminate.

Men, on the other hand, feel an imperative to earn money and are looked down on by society if they do not. They are also less emotionally expressive and may place human relationships below their work in importance. Adapting to more assertive women and more egalitarian relationships is an increasing demand on the modern man.

The future of gender roles will include fewer barriers to women in pursuing various life options and a general movement toward androgyny. Some evidence suggests that androgyny is associated with good mental health.

Questions for Reflection

1. Why is there little agreement about the precise way in which gender roles are learned?
2. To what degree do you feel free to exhibit behaviors that are typically associated with the opposite sex?
3. To what degree do you feel comfortable about your partner engaging in behaviors that are typically associated with the opposite sex?

CHOICES

THE RESULT OF our society becoming less rigid in its gender-role expectations for women and men is a new array of choices of gender-role behavior. Such choices are becoming increasingly available in dating, marriage, parenting, and employment.

DATING: WOMEN ASKING MEN?

Traditionally, the only socially appropriate way for a woman and man to begin dating was for the man to call the woman up several days in advance and ask her if she would like to have dinner, see a movie, attend a concert, or whatever later in the week. Her role was passive. If she were asked, she could accept or reject. If a woman asked a man out for a first date, it implied that she was inappropriately aggressive: it was the man's role—not the woman's—to do the asking.

This pattern is still dominant. Most women are uncomfortable asking a new person for a date. Three women explain:

I just wouldn't feel right about it. I wouldn't want the guy to think I was too fast or pushy.

I couldn't take the rejection. Besides, nine out of 10 guys I would want are already involved with someone else. Even the guys I just find attractive and talk to have steady girlfriends, so I don't want to humiliate myself by asking them out and being turned down.

We always had a phone rule in my house: *Never call a guy unless he has called and is expecting you to call him back.* I have three older sisters, and my parents have always made sure that my sisters never called their boyfriends (unless it was a serious relationship). Their reason was "if he wants to go out, he'll call you."

But more and more women are questioning their socialization and asking the man out, and such a choice is becoming more acceptable.

I say "go for it" simply because there are more advantages than disadvantages. The only disadvantage I can think of is the possibility of coming over as pushy. But on the advantage side: (1) Maybe he doesn't know if you're interested. If you wait around for him to ask you and he doesn't, you may never get together. (2) Maybe he's shy. (3) Guys hate to say no to girls, so he'll probably go out with you and he may find that he likes you.

The boyfriend I have now I asked out over a year ago (he's shy). Things have been going great ever since. He told me about a month ago that if I had never asked him out, he would never have asked me out first because he thought I wasn't interested. I'm glad I let him know I was.

I wouldn't have much of a problem asking a guy out. Of course, I'd wait a little hoping that he would ask first. But some guys need a little push in the "right direction"—my direction.

Women are sometimes interested in what men think about women who call them up. Most men feel positive about being asked for a date and do not regard the woman as too forward. The following are examples of what men in the author's class said when they were asked, "How would you feel about a woman asking you out for a date if you have never dated her before?"

I'd love it. It makes me feel wanted, and I like for the female to be aggressive.

I prefer that the woman ask me out. I get tired of having to be the aggressor all the time.

I'm the traditional type. I'll do the asking.

Three girls have called me up for dates in the last year. I went out with two of them and had a terrif-

(Continued)

ic time. I made up some excuse for the one who looked like "Godzilla's sister."

If a woman decides to call a man for a date, what might she say? Does she call him up to borrow his class notebook or a record album and hope he will get the hint that she is interested in him? Or does she mention that there is a new movie in town that has had excellent reviews and wait for him to ask her? Both women who have asked men for dates and men who have accepted say that the direct approach is best. A woman might say "Hi! This is Jill. I'm in your English literature class and am calling to ask if you would like to go out Saturday evening to see the campus movie."

A woman who chooses to call a man for a date may experience what men experience who call a woman for a date—rejection. "She won't get turned down much," said one woman. "But it will happen, and she shouldn't feel bad about it when it does. I asked this one guy out who looked like Richard Gere, and he told me he was involved with someone and couldn't go—I wasn't surprised."

Marriage: Role Sharing

The choices available to spouses regarding their role behavior in marriage are also increasing. More egalitarian relationships mean that either spouse may now be employed, cook supper, clean the house, and call out spelling words to the children. Such role flexibility increases the potential for experientially sharing the work required in marriage and provides the basis for each partner to better understand the feelings of the other. In essence, role sharing allows a greater range of sharing in all aspects of the relationship.

When only the husband worked outside the home and the wife stayed home to take care of the house and children, each spouse had a set of experiences that was unknown to the partner. He would be tired at the end of the day from working at the office; she would be tired from cleaning the house, preparing food, and listening to the bickering of two young children. Each one was sure that he or she was more tired than the other partner and regarded their own role as the most difficult and the partner's role as "easy and nothing to complain about." One outcome of both spouses choosing to engage in a greater range of roles is the increased understanding of what the other partner is experiencing. "Since I have been employed and my husband has taken over the meals and child care, we both know what it is like to be tired for different reasons," said one wife.

Employment: Occupational Choices

The general trend toward gender-role flexibility is also having its impact on occupational role choices. Jobs traditionally occupied by one gender are now open to the other. Men may now become nurses and librarians, and women may become construction workers and lawyers. A match between personality needs and occupational choices is not overridden by arbitrary social restrictions regarding who can and can't have a particular job or career.

Impact of Social Influences on Choices

The degree to which you want an egualitarian or role-sharing relationship (which translates into sharing in earning the income and in caring for the house and children) will be influenced by the roles of your parents and peers, your exposure to role-sharing ideas, and your partner's expectations of your behavior. If your parents and peers assume traditional roles in their respective relationships with you and if you have had limited exposure to role relationships beyond traditional ones, your desire for a role-sharing relationship will be influenced by the partner with whom you are involved.

One woman living with her partner told him that she loved him and wanted to continue to live with him but that he could leave if he was not interested in doing his share of the work—washing dishes, doing laundry, and vacuuming the apartment. He stayed, and both report a very satisfactory relationship.

CHAPTER 4

Sexual Values and Behaviors

Contents

Is It True?*

1. Sexual behavior of blacks and whites is more similar than dissimilar.
2. Masturbation is not only approved but recommended in our society.
3. The sexual revolution has been primarily a female one.
4. Recently divorced individuals are more likely to engage in casual sex than those who have been divorced a long time.
5. The longer a couple has been married the less frequently they have intercourse.

*1=T; 2=T; 3=T; 4=T; 5=T.

OUR SEXUAL VALUES guide our sexual behavior. Think about the following situations.

> Two people are slow dancing to romantic music. Although they met only two hours ago, they feel a strong attraction to each other. Each is wondering how much sexual involvement is appropriate when they go back to one of their apartments later that evening. How much sexual involvement is appropriate in a new relationship?
>
> Two students have decided to live together, but they know their respective parents would disapprove. If they tell their parents, the parents will probably withdraw their financial support and both students will be forced to drop out of school. Should they tell?
>
> While Mary was away for a weekend visiting her parents, the man with whom she is living had intercourse with an old girlfriend. He says he is sorry and promises never to be unfaithful again. Should she take him back?
>
> A woman is married to a man whose career requires that he be away from home for extended periods of time. Although she loves her husband, she is lonely, bored, and sexually frustrated in his absence. She has been asked out by a colleague at work whose wife also travels. He too is in love with his wife but is lonely for emotional and sexual companionship. They are ambivalent about whether to see each other when their spouses are away. Should they see each other?

The individuals in these situations will all make decisions based on their personal value systems. Although we may not have experienced these particular encounters, we have confronted others that have required us to examine our own values. In this chapter, we will look at our sexual values and their behavioral expression in masturbation, petting, and sexual intercourse.

Types of Value Systems

Lord give me chastity—but not yet.
—Saint Augustine

Our sexual values become visible when we choose one course of action over another. This choice may be based on our feeling of what is right and wrong or moral and immoral or on a perception that one course of action will have more positive consequences than another. Sometimes a combination of factors affects our choice. A single woman who felt she was drifting into a love relationship with a married coworker stated:

> Although I felt strongly about him, I thought it was wrong and immoral for me to get involved with him. He also had three kids, and the hurt it would cause them and his wife wouldn't be worth it, so I stopped flirting with him and was very careful about what I said to him.

Several value systems may offer guidelines to people who are making decisions about their sexual behavior. These systems include legalism, situationism, hedonism, asceticism, and rationalism.

LEGALISM

Legalism—a legalistic view of sexual ethics—involves making decisions on the basis of a set of laws or codes of moral conduct. The term "legalism" does *not* refer to laws of the state. In the example of the single woman and her married coworker, part of the woman's reasoning was legalistic: it is "wrong" to become involved with a married person.

The official creeds of the Christian and Jewish religions reflect a legalistic view of sexual ethics. Intercourse between a man and a woman is a gift from God to be expressed only in marriage; violations (masturbation, homosexuality, and extramarital sex) are sins against God, self, and community. The person who adopts a legal set of sexual ethics is generally clear about what is appropriate, right, or moral. "I never wonder when I'm out with my fiancée if we're going to have intercourse or not—we won't," said a devoutly religious man.

Situation Ethics

One of the most prevalent forms of contemporary sexual ethics is *situation ethics.* This perspective suggests that sexual decisions should be made in the context of the particular situation. Genuine love and good will should be the core motives for each decision, and the prediction of positive consequences should be a basic guideline.

The situationist believes that to make all decisions on the basis of rules is to miss the point of human love and to do more harm than good. Whereas the legalist would say it is right for married people to have intercourse and wrong for the unmarried to do so, the situationist would say "it depends" and would ask, "What if the married people do not love each other and intercourse is an abusive, exploitative act? Also suppose that the unmarried people love each other, and their intercourse experience is an expression of mutual concern and respect. Which couple is being more loving or ethical?"

Consideration

It is sometimes difficult to make sexual decisions on a case-by-case basis, "I don't know what's right anymore" reflects the uncertainty of a situation ethics view. Once a person decides that mutual love is the context justifying intercourse, how often and how soon should the person fall in love? Can love develop after two hours of conversation? How does one know that her or his own love feelings and those of a partner are genuine? The freedom that situation ethics brings to sexual decision making requires responsibility, maturity, and judgment. In some cases, individuals may deceive themselves by believing they are in love so they will not feel guilty about having intercourse.

Hedonism

A third value perspective—*hedonism*—suggests that one need not be concerned with moral or contextual issues but only with pleasure. "If it feels good, do it" emphasizes the hedonistic ethic that sexual desire is an appropriate appetite and its expression is legitimate. Like hunger and thirst, the sexual urge need not be subject to moral constraints.

Too much has been made, says the hedonist, of the sexual act; it should be regarded as one of the many pleasures we are capable of experiencing. Some conservative individuals feel that the hedonist has the potential to become a sexual addict who relates to sex as a drug—needing more and taking risks to get it.

Asceticism

Puberty showed up and that was it: I knew Catholicism wasn't for me. We were told it was a sin to think about sex, and meanwhile, you'd have these hormones racing through your body at five times the speed of light.
—Kareem Abdul-Jabbar

Monks, nuns, and other celibates have adopted the sexual value of *asceticism.* The ascetic believes that giving into what he or she considers to be carnal lust is unnecessary and calls us to rise above the pursuit of sensual pleasure into a life of self-discipline and self-denial. Accordingly, the spiritual life is the highest good, and self-denial helps us to achieve it.

Rationalism

Rationalism, a fifth view of contemporary sexual ethics, refers to the use of reason in determining a course of sexual action. Rationalism is concerned with the intellect rather than with the emotions. The rationalist makes a decision on the basis of the facts and/or the consequences of that decision. A rational perspective is used to decide whether to have intercourse with a new partner. This perspective will be discussed in the "Choices" section at the end of this chapter.

Personal Sexual Values

You can clarify some of your own sexual values in several ways. One is a self-administered questionnaire, of which the following is an example.

Select one ending for each of the following statements, and consider why you chose that answer. You may wish to think of additional statements about sexual behavior that include a range of choices.

For me, it is most important that a sexual experience:

1. Be morally correct.
2. Be fun and pleasurable.
3. Increase the love feelings with my partner.
4. Improve my self-concept.
5. Result in orgasm.

The worst thing I could find out about my sexual partner is that she or he:

1. Has genital herpes.
2. Is homosexual.
3. Is unfaithful or has deceived me.
4. Is sterile.
5. Has been a prostitute.

In a sexual relationship, I would prefer that:

1. My partner be in love with me.
2. I be in love with my partner.
3. Sex means the same thing to both of us.
4. We are married to each other.
5. My partner is uninhibited.

If I am feeling the need for sexual release, I would rather:

1. Have intercourse.
2. Have my partner perform oral sex.
3. Engage in vigorous physical activity.
4. Masturbate.
5. Have a sexual dream resulting in orgasm.

Intercourse is appropriate under the following conditions:

1. The partners are married.
2. The partners are engaged.
3. The partners are in love.
4. The partners feel affection but not love for each other.
5. The partners feel no particular affection for each other.

Women and men differ in their relationship conditions for sexual behavior. Women require more love and commitment than men. Although this condition is becoming less evident, the tendency is still present (Earle & Perricone, 1986; Sherwin & Corbett, 1985).

Another way of clarifying sexual values is to think of the degree to which you regard sexual behaviors as acceptable. What category on the following continuum best reflects your sexual values about sex with love, sex without love, abortion, oral-genital sex, intercourse, masturbation, homosexuality, extramarital sex, and virginity at the time of marriage?

Idealism increases in direct proportion to one's distance from the problem.
—John Galsworthy

Still another exercise in values clarification is to develop an answer to a value dilemma. For example, Kathy and Bob are in love, and they plan to be married in June. Kathy is sterile and has been told by her physician that she can never have children. Bob has mentioned children, and Kathy knows he wants them. If she tells Bob of her sterility, she is certain that he will end the relationship with her. But she feels that he will not divorce her after they are married (although he could get an annulment) and that he will be willing to adopt. Should she tell him she cannot have children?

The goal in examining this and other value dilemmas is to explore our own sexual values. These values are influenced by the society in which we live, in which both liberal and conservative elements coexist. In the following section, we will examine the ways in which our society is both sexually permissive and conservative.

Society's Sexual Values

We live in a pluralistic society that contains both liberal and conservative elements. We sometimes make decisions about what works for us out of a synthesis of the societal perspectives to which we are exposed. What are these views, and what social outcomes result from each?

A Liberal View

We live in a sensate society, which seeks to excite the senses to their maximum potential. An experience like watching strobe lights flicker on an array of rock

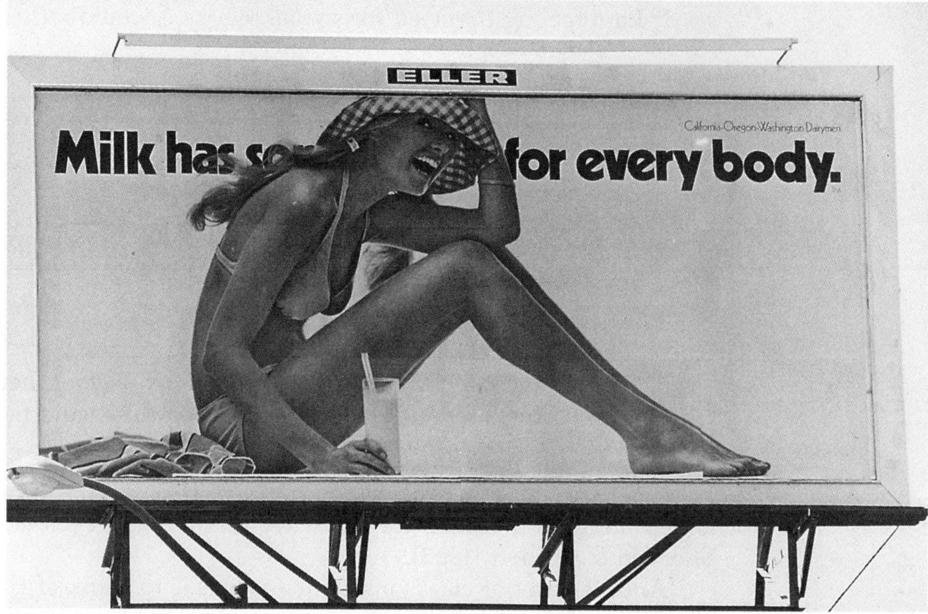

Sex is a frequent theme in advertising.

concert artists and listening to their amplified voices and blaring guitars feeds our visual and auditory senses to their limit. MTV (music television) specializes in stimulating our senses.

Orgasm, including the erotic feelings leading to it, is another sensation our society seeks to market. The first law of advertising is "sex sells." Our attention is grabbed by sexual appeals in advertising, such as Bruce Willis delivering "lines" to a female for Seagrams. Seminudity is a visual stimulus in countless ads in magazines and movies and on billboards and television.

We continually promote new media stars to personify our ideas of feminine and masculine sexuality. Femininity symbols like Vanna White, Grace Jones, and Sigourney Weaver are not to be outdone by masculinity symbols such as Billy Dee Williams, Julio Iglesias, and Tom Cruise.

In a sensate society, every member is affected by the pervasiveness of sex. From sex grafitti on restroom walls to the grinding hips on "Solid Gold" to the sensuous perfume commercials on television, we are reminded daily that we live in a sexually permissive society. Some of the effects of this sexual permissiveness are described in the following sections.

Sexual Openness

A promiscuous person is usually someone who is getting more sex than you are.
—Victor Lownes

Society's increased willingness to tolerate and even to encourage openness about sex has positive and negative aspects. Colleges and universities provide a responsible forum for open discussions about sexuality. The course in which you are enrolled is a forum for learning about interpersonal relationships and some aspects of your sexuality. Some universities sponsor conferences on sexuality, contraception, and sexually transmitted diseases. The results are a more systematic examination of human sexuality and a more informed public.

But such university-sponsored discussions on sexuality occur in the context of a media sex blitz. We are bombarded with stimuli from books (the best-seller list regularly features books on sex), magazines (even *Sports Illustrated* has an annual swimsuit issue), television (steamy soap operas and late-night cable TV), and music (with sexually explicit lyrics).

Sex as Recreation

Sex for the purpose of having children has been replaced largely by sex as recreation. Recreational (nonprocreative) sex is still preferred in the context of a love relationship. "I love sex," said one woman, "but I love it with someone I love and who loves me." Although emotional sex is the preferred norm, some feel that too much sexual freedom may not be good for the institution of marriage.

Data – In a Roper Poll, six out of 10 women and men believed that the new morality of greater sexual freedom will weaken the institution of marriage. (Roper Organization, 1985)

Less Virginity

Today, although some people remain virgins until marriage, most do not.

Data – In a study of unmarried students at an urban community college, 87 percent of 247 men and 85 percent of 318 women reported having had intercourse. (Belcastro, 1985)

Despite the trend toward more individuals having intercourse before marriage, virginity is still important to some individuals. One person said:

> I have been taught that sex before marriage is wrong, and I feel that it is. Besides, I think that waiting till you're married to have intercourse makes it special for you and your partner and gives the two of you a special beginning.

Most virgins are satisfied with the fact that they have not had intercourse.

Data – Of 114 male virgins, 76 percent were satisfied virgins and 24 percent were frustrated virgins. Of 119 female virgins, 95 percent were satisfied virgins and 5 percent were frustrated virgins. (Young, 1986)

Consideration

Women today have more freedom to have intercourse with less stigma than women of 20 years ago, but the price of this sexual freedom has been the loss of security. Men today feel less obligated to the women with whom they have sex than in previous times. In the past, men tended to feel more committed to such women. "I thought I should marry her since we had been having intercourse," said a traditional man.

It should also be understood that virginity is still highly valued in other societies and cultures. For example, among the people of Maltibog in the Philippines, the female is expected to be a virgin at marriage. If she is not, she ruins her own reputation and that of her family. (Asian Americans in general have more conservative sexual values than other minorities.)

The Slow Death of the Sexual Double Standard

The sexual double standard suggests that there are different standards of sexual behavior for men and women. Typically, fewer negative connotations are associated with men having sex with a variety of women than are associated with women having sex with a variety of men. The term *promiscuous* is used to describe women, not men, who have several sexual partners. However, attitudes toward which gender should have sex, when, with how many partners are changing, and women are seeking more sexual freedom.

Data – Eight out of 10 women believe that women should enjoy the same kind of sexual freedom as men. (Roper Organization, 1985)

A Conservative View

Although sexual themes permeate our society and the limit of what is sexually acceptable seems to be expanding, a strong and conservative religious element in our society is working to reverse this trend.

Data – The Moral Majority is composed of 72,000 ministers and 4 million laypersons. (Encyclopedia of Associations, 1986)

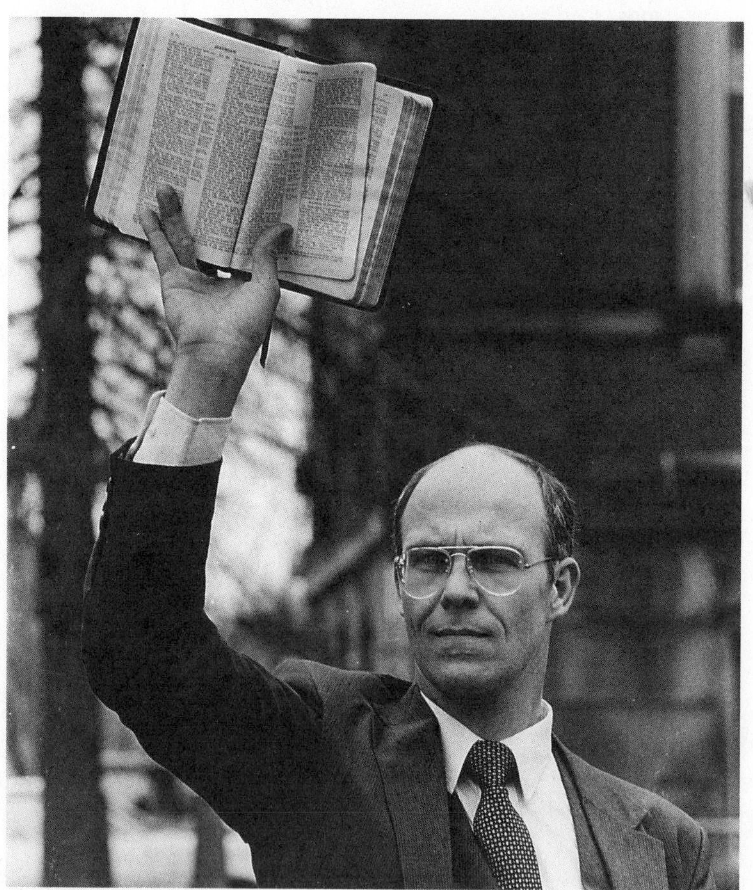

Members of the Moral Majority use the Bible as a basic guideline for sexual behavior.

Censors are people who know more than they think you ought to.
—Laurence Peter

Not all conservative or religious people support the Moral Majority, but those who do have mounted a vigorous opposition to permissive sexual values. The movement has identified a number of trends contributing to the country's moral decay: escalating divorce, the prohibition of school prayer, abortion on demand, pornography, homosexuality, drug use, and sex education in the public schools. In a nationally televised "Moral and Spiritual State of the Union" address Falwell said, that "For so long we have neglected to take stock in our moral standards as a nation that we have allowed the very foundation of our country to erode. Our forefathers were proud to bequeath us a government based on Biblical principles" (1984, p. s–1).

With the cooperation of a conservative administration, the Moral Majority has been instrumental in introducing several pieces of legislation into Congress for the following purposes:

Children should not be taught that premarital sex is a choice.
—Jerry Falwell

1. *Eliminate abortion.* The "Human Life" Bill defines life as beginning at conception, making all abortions a criminal offense.
2. *Encourage chastity.* The Adolescent Family Life Bill is a $30 million program to teach teenagers "self-discipline and chastity" and to discourage the use of birth control. The bill's definition of promiscuity is "a person under 21 having intercourse out of wedlock."
3. *Restrict sex education.* Schools receiving federal funds would be required to obtain parental approval of content and course material before providing sex-education courses.
4. *Penalize homosexuality.* Any agency or firm that advocates homosexuality as a viable life style should be denied federal funds. "We believe that homosexuality is moral perversion" (*Moral Majority Report,* 1984, p. 21).

These proposals testify to the current strength of the ultraconservative movement.

To assess the degree to which you are conservative or liberal, take the Sexual Attitude Scale (Hudson, Murphy, & Nurius, 1983) in the following Self-Assessment. According to the Sexual Attitude Scale, a liberal is one who feels that the expression of human sexuality should be open, free, and unrestrained; a conservative is one who feels that sexual expression should be considerably constrained and closely regulated. When 689 students (primarily seniors and graduate students) took the Sexual Attitude Scale, both genders tended to score from borderline-low to high-grade liberal (Nurius & Hudson, 1982).

Sexual Behavior of Blacks and Whites

Before we discuss the nature and frequency of various sexual behaviors, we will examine the extent to which black and white sexuality is similar. In general, the sexual behaviors of blacks and whites are similar. In one study (Belcastro, 1985) of 565 unmarried undergraduates that compared blacks and whites on 25 sexual behaviors, only a few differences occurred. Some of these differences are discussed in the following sections.

Self-Assessment

Sexual Attitude Scale

This questionnaire is designed to measure the way you feel about sexual behavior. It is not a test, so there are no right or wrong answers. Answer each item as carefully and accurately as you can by placing the most appropriate number beside each one as follows:

1 Strongly disagree
2 Disagree
3 Undecided
4 Agree
5 Strongly agree

	SD	D	U	A	SA
1. I think too much freedom is given to adults these days.	1	2	3	4	5
2. I think that the increased sexual freedom seen in the past several years has done much to undermine the American family.	1	2	3	4	5
3. I think that young people have been given too much information about sex.	1	2	3	4	5
4. Sex education should be restricted to the home.	1	2	3	4	5
5. Older people do not need to have sex.	1	2	3	4	5
6. Sex education should be provided only when people are ready for marriage.	1	2	3	4	5
7. Premarital sex may be a sign of a decaying social order.	1	2	3	4	5
8. Extramarital sex is never excusable.	1	2	3	4	5
9. I think there is too much sexual freedom given to teenagers these days.	1	2	3	4	5
10. I think there is not enough sexual restraint among young people.	1	2	3	4	5
11. I think people engage in sex too much.	1	2	3	4	5
12. I think the only proper way to have sex is through intercourse.	1	2	3	4	5
13. I think sex should be reserved for marriage.	1	2	3	4	5
14. Sex should be only for the young.	1	2	3	4	5
15. Too much social approval has been given to homosexuals.	1	2	3	4	5

(Continued)

Self-Assessment

16. Sex should be devoted to the business of procreation.	1	2	3	4	5
17. People should not masturbate.	1	2	3	4	5
18. Heavy sexual petting should be discouraged.	1	2	3	4	5
19. People should not discuss their sexual affairs or business with others.	1	2	3	4	5
20. Severely physically and mentally handicapped people should not have sex.	1	2	3	4	5
21. There should be no laws prohibiting sexual acts between consenting adults.	1	2	3	4	5
22. What two consenting adults do together sexually is their own business.	1	2	3	4	5
23. There is too much sex on television.	1	2	3	4	5
24. Movies today are too sexually explicit.	1	2	3	4	5
25. Pornography should be totally banned from our bookstores.	1	2	3	4	5

Scoring: Reverse the scores for statements 21 and 22 in the following way: 1 = 5, 2 = 4, 4 = 2, 5 = 1. For example, if you wrote 1 for statement 21 ("There should be no laws prohibiting sexual acts between consenting adults"), change that number to 5 for scoring purposes. Reverse score statement 22 similarly.

Add the numbers you assigned to each of the 25 statements. Your score may range from a low of 25 (strongly disagreed with all items: 1 × 25 = 25) to a high of 125 (strongly agreed with all items: 5 × 25 = 125). If you score between 25 and 50, you may be regarded as a high-grade liberal; if you score between 50 and 75, a low-grade liberal. If you score between 100 and 125, you may be regarded as a high-grade conservative; if you score between 75 and 100, a low-grade conservative.

Source: Hudson, W.W., Murphy, G.J., & Nurius, P.S. A short-form scale to measure liberal vs. conservative orientations toward human sexual expression. *Journal of Sex Research,* 1983, *19,* 258–272. A publication of the Society for the Scientific Study of Sex. Reprinted by permission.

Black Males Compared to White Males

When black males were compared to white males at the same midwestern university, black males were significantly more likely to have had interracial intercourse (40 percent versus 13 percent) and to have avoided masturbation (44 percent versus 17 percent). In addition, black males were more likely to have experienced intercourse with a partner who was on birth control or who used post-coital foam.

More frequent interracial intercourse may be a combination of black males socializing each other to try a "white woman" and white males socializing each other to avoid sex with a "black woman." Masturbation among black males has traditionally been viewed as an admission of not being able to seduce a woman for intercourse. Black males usually have sexual intercourse with more black females at younger ages than white males do with white females.

Black Females Compared to White Females

When black females were compared to white females, black females were significantly less likely to have performed fellatio (48 percent versus 82 percent) and less likely to have experienced coitus interruptus (48 percent versus 74 percent). However, black females were more likely to use birth control pills (77 percent versus 65 percent) than white females. (Belcastro, 1985)

The infrequent reporting of fellatio among black females is probably largely due to their socialization that fellatio is an unclean and demeaning sexual act. Black women may also feel that the best sex is "natural" (not oral or manual). Their slightly higher use of birth-control pills may be a reaction to the high incidence of pregnancy among black unmarried women.

Masturbation

Masturbation is defined as stimulating one's own body with the goal of experiencing sexual pleasure.

Data – In a study of 100 university undergraduates, 90 percent of the men and 44 percent of the women reported having masturbated. (Story, 1985)

In this section, we will review attitudes toward masturbation, who does it, and the benefits of masturbation.

Attitudes toward Masturbation

Masturbation has traditionally had "bad press." Historically, it is almost as though the fields of religion, medicine, and psychotherapy have "conspired" to give masturbation a bad name.

Religion

The Jewish and Catholic religions have been the most severe critics of masturbation, but Protestants have not been very positive about it either. Ancient Jews considered masturbation a sin so grave that it deserved the death penalty. Catholics once regarded masturbation as a mortal sin which, if not given up, would result in eternal damnation. Although Protestants felt that neither death nor eternal hellfire were appropriate consequences for masturbation, hell on earth (as a consequence of intense guilt) was.

Consideration

The historical basis for the negative view of religion toward masturbation is that masturbation is nonprocreative sex and that any sexual act that cannot produce children is a sin and an unnatural act. "Against nature" is a term that suggests an action is contrary to its essential purpose—or nature. For example, the essential purpose of eating is to sustain life. The essential purpose of sexual activity, according to Catholic thought, is to procreate.

Medicine

The medical community reinforced religion's prohibition of masturbation by bringing "scientific validity" to bear on the description of its physical and psychological hazards. In 1758, Samuel Tissot, a French physician, published a book in which he implied that the loss of too much semen, whether by intercourse or masturbation, was injurious to the body and would cause pimples, tumors, insanity, and early death (Tissot, 1766).

Adding to the medical bias against masturbation, American physician Sylvester Graham wrote in 1834 that the loss of an ounce of semen was equal to the loss of several ounces of blood. Graham believed that every time a man ejaculated, he ran the risk of contracting a disease of the nervous system. His solution was Graham crackers, which was supposed to help the individual control the release of sexual energy (Graham, 1848). By the mid-nineteenth century, Tissot's theories had made their way into medical textbooks and journals. In spite of a lack of data, physicians added loss of hair, weak eyes, and suicidal tendencies to the list of disorders resulting from masturbation.

Masturbation—it's sex with someone I love.

—Woody Allen

Psychotherapy

In the early twentieth century, psychotherapy "joined" religion and medicine to convince people of the negative effects of masturbation. Psychotherapists, led by Freud, suggested that masturbation was an infantile form of sexual gratification. People who masturbated "to excess" were fixating on themselves as sexual objects and would not be able to relate to others in a sexually mature way. The message was clear. If you want to be a good sexual partner in marriage, don't masturbate; if you do masturbate, don't do it too often. This view is outdated and no longer considered valid.

Consideration

The result of religion, medicine, and psychotherapy taking aim at masturbation was devastating. Those who masturbated felt the shame and guilt they were intended to feel. The burden of these feelings was particularly heavy because there was no one with whom to share the guilt. In the case of a premarital pregnancy, responsibility could be shared. The "crime" of masturbation was committed alone. In recent years, the fields of religion, medicine, and psychotherapy have been more tolerant and supportive of masturbation.

Benefits of Masturbation

Although shame, guilt, and anxiety continue to be feelings associated with masturbation in our society, new attitudes are emerging. Although the attitudes of some religious leaders are still negative, most physicians and therapists are clearly positive about the experience. Masturbation is not only approved but recommended. Specific benefits of masturbation include:

1. *Self-knowledge.* Masturbation gives you immediate feedback about what you enjoy during sexual stimulation. You can tell another what turns you on sexually by exploring your own feelings, rhythms, and responses in private.
2. *More likely orgasm.* Of a sample of more than 1,000 women, 92 percent said they achieved orgasm most of the time when they masturbated, but only 30 percent achieved orgasm regularly when they had intercourse (Hite, 1977). In another study of almost 15,000 women, masturbation was preferred among women who had difficulty climaxing during intercourse (Cook et al., 1983).
3. *Pressure off partner.* When one partner in a relationship does not want to have intercourse or other sexual involvement, masturbation is a way of experiencing sexual pleasure without obligating the partner.
4. *No partner necessary.* Masturbation provides a way to enjoy sexual feelings if no partner is available.
5. *Unique experience.* When combined with one's own fantasies, masturbation is a unique sexual experience. It is different from petting, intercourse, mutual stimulation of the genitals, and oral sex.
6. *Avoidance of sexual involvement.* Extramarital or extrapartner entanglements can be avoided by masturbation. Sexual tensions can be released by one's self without risking sexual involvement with a partner external to the primary relationship.

Consideration

In spite of the benefits of masturbation, it remains a private experience; the decision of whether to engage in the behavior is personal. Neither persons choosing not to masturbate nor those choosing to masturbate should feel guilty about their decision.

Petting

Petting is the term that traditionally has been used to describe interpersonal physical stimulation that does not include intercourse. (Although the term may seem out of date, no new one has replaced it.)

Data – Females (318) at a midwestern university reported having petted with an average of eight males; males (247) reported having petted with an average of 10 females. (Belcastro, 1985)

Whoever called it necking was a poor judge of anatomy.
—Groucho Marx

For some couples, petting acts as a substitute for intercourse. For example, a highly religious couple may engage in petting to orgasm and still see

A kiss is not just a kiss.

themselves as virgins. The following sections describe some of these petting behaviors from least to most involved.

Kissing

A kiss isn't just a kiss. There are different types of kissing. In one style of kissing, the partners gently touch their lips together for a short time with their mouths closed. In another, there is considerable pressure and movement for a prolonged time when the closed mouths meet. In still another, the partners kiss with their mouths open, using gentle or light pressure and variations in movement and time. Kinsey referred to the third style as "deep kissing" (also known as "soul kissing," "tongue kissing," or "French kissing").

One woman describes a good kiss:

> Variably soft and hard, but never rough. Tender touching of the lips, gentle parting—not too wide—playful archery and tactile explorations with the tongues. Letting emotions control the intensity of the contact—sucking, licking, and kissing.

Kissing may or may not have emotional or erotic connotations. A good-night kiss may be perfunctory or may symbolize in the mind of each partner the ultimate sense of caring and belonging. It may also mean different things to each partner.

Breast Stimulation

As the relationship becomes more involved, the man will usually stimulate the woman's breasts. "More involved" usually means by or after the sixth date for 60 percent of college women and by the fourth date for 60 percent of college men (Knox & Wilson, 1981). In our society, the female breasts are charged with erotic potential. A billion-dollar pornographic industry encourages the male to view the female's breasts in erotic terms. An array of adult magazines feature women with unusually large breasts in seductive poses.

Consideration

Not all women share men's erotic feelings about breasts. They rarely manually stimulate their own breasts and seem to neglect the breasts of their male partners. The latter may be unfortunate, as male breasts have the same potential for erotic stimulation as female breasts. For some males, breast stimulation by their partners is particularly important. Other males are not socialized to be aware of or receptive to that form of stimulation.

Manual Genital Stimulation

Manual genital stimulation may be done by either partner. When the woman stimulates the man's genitals, it is often the man who takes his partner's hand and moves it to his genitals. Other men use body language. Once manual caressing begins, it may result in ejaculation or be a prelude to oral stimulation, intercourse, or both. Sometimes the woman becomes aroused by observing her partner's erection and ejaculation as a result of her manual stimulation.

The man who stimulates the woman's genitals may be readying her for intercourse or doing so as an end in itself. Regardless of the motive, the style of stimulation may vary. Some partners rub the mons veneris area (see Sexual Anatomy and Physiology in Part Six), putting indirect pressure on the clitoris. Others may apply direct clitoral pressure. Still others may insert one or several fingers into the vagina, with gentle or rapid thrusting, at the same time they stimulate the clitoris. Orgasm sometimes results.

Data – In a study of 100 undergraduate University of Northern Iowa students, 74 percent of the women and 78 percent of the men said that they had experienced premarital petting to orgasm. (Story, 1985)

Not all women enjoy the insertion of the man's finger or fingers into their vaginas during petting. Some women permit it because their partners want to do it, and often the man wants to do it because he assumes that the woman wants something in her vagina. But the key to sexual pleasure for many women is pressure on and around the clitoris, not necessarily insertion.

CUNNILINGUS

Cunnilingus is the stimulation of the clitoris, labia, and vaginal opening of the woman by her partner's tongue and lips.

Data – Fifty percent of 258 white and 34 percent of 60 black female students said that they had been the recipients of cunnilingus by a male. (Belcastro, 1985)

Women who are most likely to have experienced cunnilingus have high self-esteem, masturbate, have intercourse, are emotionally involved, and are religious (Herold & Way, 1983). Regarding self-esteem, women who feel good about themselves are better able to assert themselves in their sexual lovemaking and are less concerned about being rejected or having their actions viewed negatively. Masturbation and intercourse are linked with cunnilingus, as those who are highly active in one sexual area are likely to be active in other areas. Greater emotional involvement and cunnilingus are associated because cunnilingus is regarded as a very intimate sexual behavior. "I can't let a guy do that to me if I don't care about him," reported one woman. Having a high frequency of church attendance is positively related to cunnilingus "perhaps because vaginal virginity is the prime concern among the highly religious, they might feel less guilty about oral sex than about coitus" (p. 335).

FELLATIO

In contrast to cunnilingus, *fellatio* is oral stimulation of the male's genitals by his partner. Although fellatio most often refers to the woman putting her partner's penis in her mouth and sucking it, fellatio may also include licking the shaft and glans, frenulum, and scrotum.

Data – Forty-five percent of 209 white and 43 percent of 38 black male students said that they had been the recipients of fellatio by a female. (Belcastro, 1985)

In spite of the reported high frequency of fellatio, it remains a relatively taboo subject. In many states, legal statutes prohibit fellatio as a "crime against nature." In this case, "nature" refers to reproduction and the "crime" is sex that does not produce babies.

People engage in fellatio for a number of reasons. Beyond the issues of pleasure and the desire to remain a technical virgin are motives of acceptance, dominance, and variety. One man said that his partner fellating him meant she really loved him and enjoyed his body. "It means total acceptance to me," he said. In one study (Blumstein & Schwartz, 1983), husbands who reported that their wives performed fellatio tended to be more happily married than husbands whose wives did not.

Dominance may be another reason for the enjoyment of fellatio. A common theme in pornographic movies is forcing the woman to perform fellatio.

In this context, the act implies sexual submission, which may give the male an ego boost. Aware of this motive, some women refuse to fellate their partners. One woman said her partner viewed her as a prostitute when she fellated him; she did not like such a perception and therefore had stopped doing so.

Variety is another motive for fellatio. Some lovers complain that penis-in-vagina intercourse is sometimes boring. Fellatio adds another dimension to a couple's sexual relationship. The greater the range of sexual behaviors a couple has to share, the less likely they are to define their relationship as routine and uninteresting.

Sexual Intercourse

Sexual intercourse, or *coitus,* refers to the sexual union of a man's penis in a woman's vagina. It is the event most people think of when the phrase "they had sex" is used.

Data – In a study of 220 undergraduate University of Minnesota at Minneapolis students, 72 percent of the men and 57 percent of the women reported having had intercourse. (Sheehan, 1986)

Sexual intercourse is also a means of communication that occurs for various reasons and in different contexts—before marriage, during marriage, outside marriage, and after marriage, as well as independently of marriage.

Intercourse is more than two bodies in motion. Each partner brings to the intercourse experience a motive (to express emotional intimacy, to have fun); a psychological state (contentment, excitement, hostility, boredom); and a physical state (aroused, relaxed, tense, exhausted).

Consideration

The combination of these motives and states may change from one sexual encounter to the next. Tonight, one partner may feel aroused and seek intercourse mainly for physical pleasure, but the other partner may feel tired and only have intercourse out of a sense of duty. Tomorrow night, both partners may feel relaxed and loving and have intercourse as a means of expressing their feelings for each other.

The verbal and nonverbal communication preceding intercourse may also give the partners information about how each feels about the other. One woman said:

> I can tell how we're doing by whether or not we have intercourse and how he approaches me when we do. Sometimes he just rolls over when the lights are out and starts to rub my back. Other times, he plays with my face and kisses me while we talk and waits till I reach for him. Still other times, we each stay on our side of the bed so that our legs don't even touch.

If intercourse occurs, the afterplay is also revealing. Some couples feel closest to each other after lovemaking.

Premarital Intercourse

In this section, we will review first intercourse experiences, the characteristics of those who have premarital intercourse (intercourse before marriage), and how many partners they have.

> *Data* – Of 38 unmarried black males, 95 percent reported having intercourse, in contrast to 80 percent of 209 unmarried white males. Of 60 unmarried black females, 90 percent reported having had intercourse, in contrast to 80 percent of 258 unmarried white females. (Belcastro, 1985)

First Intercourse Experiences

Because people attach a great deal of emotional and social significance to intercourse, the first experience is likely to be memorable. Some confusion, anxiety, and frustration about the when, who, why, and how of first intercourse are typical. The following statements reflect such feelings: "I'd like to get it over with"; "My closest friend has intercourse regularly. I wonder when I'll be doing it?"; "I feel that I should already have had intercourse by now, but I haven't." Compounding these concerns are those about the partner ("Will my partner respect me?"), pregnancy ("How lucky will I be?"), and genital herpes ("Will I get it?"). (See Exhibit 4.1 for reactions to first intercourse experiences). Some couples use contraceptive methods during the first intercourse experience.

Weiss (1983) collected data from 130 university women about their first intercourse experience. He found that women who perceived their first coital partners as gentle, loving, and considerate were also likely to experience pleasure and less likely to experience guilt or anxiety. These partner behaviors were more important in women reporting a positive first intercourse experience than whether they had just met their partner, were going steady, or were engaged. "Conversely, men who were seen as unloving, inconsiderate, and rough were associated with more negative affect even if the couple were engaged at the time of the woman's first intercourse" (p. 228).

> *Data* – One-half (52.3 percent) of 220 undergraduate University of Minnesota at Minneapolis students reported using effective birth-control methods (pill, condom, or diaphragm) the first time they had intercourse. The most frequently used contraception at first intercourse was the condom. (Sheehan et al., 1986)

Consideration

> A positive first intercourse experience was also more likely to be reported if the woman had previous experience with masturbation, kissing, petting, and oral-genital sex. Hence "rehearsal of sexual arousal itself may help shape affective reactions to the first intercourse." (Weiss, 1983, p. 24)

Who Approves of or Has Premarital Intercourse?

Some people are more likely to approve of or to have premarital intercourse than others. The factors most likely to influence intercourse before marriage include the following.

Exhibit 4.1

FIRST INTERCOURSE EXPERIENCES

Students in the author's marriage and family class were asked to describe their first intercourse experience. Although there was no typical description, elements of pain, fear, anxiety, and awkwardness were not unusual. The various experiences included the following:

My first intercourse was actually very nice—both physically and emotionally. I dated the same guy for four years in high school, and it wasn't until my senior year when we actually made love. I was nervous, and we did not use any contraception, which doubled my nervousness. Also, for years my mother preached, "Nice girls don't." My philosophy is that nice girls do, because they are the ones with the steady boyfriends.

I had been dating this guy for almost a year when we first made love. The first time was not the best. It was quite painful physically, and I couldn't understand how people could find such enjoyment from sex.

My first time I really felt nothing. I didn't know what to expect. I didn't feel guilty or sad or happy. I wasn't sorry it happened. I was not forced into the situation, and the guy was not in it just for sex because we are still dating.

My first intercourse experience was a disaster. Both the girl and I were virgins and had no idea what we were doing. Actually, we really didn't have intercourse the first time; she was so tight that I couldn't get inside of her. We gave up after 15 minutes.

I was 15, and my partner was 16. I had two fears. The first was my fear of getting her pregnant the first time. The second was of "parking" in dark and desolate areas. Therefore, once we decided to have intercourse, we spent a boring evening waiting for my parents to go to sleep so we could move to the station wagon in the driveway.

After near hyperventilation in an attempt to fog the windows (to prevent others from seeing in), we commenced to prepare for the long-awaited event. In recognition of my first fear, I wore four prophylactics. She, out of fear, was not lubricating well, and needless to say, I couldn't feel anything through the four layers of latex.

We were able to climax, which I attribute solely to sheer emotional excitement, yet both of us were later able to admit that the experience was disappointing. We knew it could only get better.

My first intercourse experience was simply terrible. There was no romance involved. He just came like a bull. He was the worst lover ever. I was very hurt when he left me, but now I'm glad he did.

Gender. In most studies, men report greater approval of premarital intercourse than women. In a national study, 64 percent of the men and 52 percent of the women said it was okay to have intercourse before marriage (*Gallup Report,* 1985). Virtually all studies also report that men are more likely to have actually had premarital intercourse than women (Earle & Perricone, 1986; Phillis & Gromko, 1985).

Egalitarian Gender-Role Orientation. The more egalitarian a woman is in her view of gender roles, the more likely she is to approve of premarital intercourse, to be assertive in sexual activities, and to instruct her partner in ways to enhance her own sexual pleasure (Koblinsky & Palmeter, 1984).

Education. Being educated is associated with an increased approval of intercourse before marriage. In one study of 1,000 women (Women's Views Survey, 1984), 60 percent of those who had attended college, compared with 40 percent of those who attended only high school, approved of premarital intercourse. In another study (Earle & Perricone, 1982), 46 percent of the freshmen women reported they had had intercourse, in contrast to 82 percent of the senior women.

Emotional Relationship. Those who are involved in a reciprocal love relationship are more likely to feel that intercourse is appropriate (Knox & Wilson, 1983).

Religious Affiliation. Protestant college women have a higher incidence of intercourse than either Catholic or Jewish women (Bell & Coughey, 1980).

Church Attendance. The less often a college student attends church or synagogue, the more likely that person is to have had intercourse (Diederen & Rorer, 1982). This is particularly true of women (Notzer et al., 1984).

Race. Black men and women are more likely to have premarital intercourse than white men and women (Belcastro, 1985).

> *Data* – In a national study, 91 percent of black women had intercourse before marriage, compared with 65 percent of white women. (Bachrach & Horn, 1985)

Peers Having Intercourse. Individuals, particularly men, who have close peers of the same gender who have had premarital intercourse are more likely to have premarital intercourse than those individuals whose close friends have not had premarital intercourse (Sack et al., 1984). Black females who have friends with permissive sexual attitudes also report higher rates of premarital intercourse than those who have friends who do not approve of premarital intercourse (Brown, 1985).

Age at First Intercourse. Today, both males and females have intercourse for the first time at surprisingly young ages. Blacks have intercourse at younger ages than whites.

> *Data* – In one study, the mean age at first intercourse was 13.6 for black males and 16.3 for white males. The mean age at first intercourse was 16.2 for black females and 16.8 for white females. The males had an average of 7.5 partners; the females, an average of 5.7 partners. (Belcastro, 1985)

Over 260,000 babies are born to pregnant teenagers between the ages of 15 and 19 each year. (National Center for Health Statistics, 1986)

Females have their first intercourse with a partner who is about three years older; males, with a partner who is about six months older. (Zelnik & Shah, 1983)

Divorced Parents. Individuals whose parents are divorced are more likely to have premarital intercourse than individuals whose parents are still married to each other (Kinnaird & Gerrard, 1986). This relationship may be a function of the norm-breaking model the parents provide by divorcing.

Very Strict Parents. Offspring who have very strict parents are more likely to have permissive sexual attitudes and to have intercourse than offspring who have parents who communicate concern but who are not overly strict (Miller et al., 1986).

Very Lenient Parents. Offspring who have very lenient parents who impose very few rules are also more likely to have intercourse than parents who are "middle of the road" and impose some restrictions (Miller et al., 1986).

Noncommunicative Parents. Female offspring whose parents are traditional and who have talked with their parents about sexuality are more likely to be virgins than female offspring whose parents are liberal and who have not talked with their parents about sex (Moore et al., 1986).

Consideration

These characteristics do not imply causation. Females, freshmen, Catholics, frequent church attenders, whites, offspring whose parents are married to each other, etc., or a person with all of these characteristics may also have intercourse before marriage.

Marital Intercourse

Marital intercourse (intercourse during marriage) is different from intercourse before marriage. Marriage is the traditional social context for most intercourse experiences.

Unique Aspects of Marital Intercourse

I wonder what Adam and Eve think of it [marriage] by this time.
—Marianne Moore

Marital intercourse is unique in terms of its social legitimacy, declining frequency over the course of the marriage, and varying importance to the partners.

Social Legitimacy. In our society, marital intercourse is the most legitimate form of sexual behavior. Homosexual, premarital, and extramarital intercourse do not enjoy society's approval, although attitudes and laws are changing. It is not only okay to have intercourse when married, it is expected. People assume that married couples make love and that something is "wrong" if they do not.

Declining Frequency. Marital intercourse is also characterized by declining frequency.

Data – For couples who have been married between one month and 25 years, the frequency of intercourse decreases as marital duration increases. (Jasso, 1985)

Typically, a couple starts out having intercourse three to four times a week; 25 years later, the frequency is less than once per week.

For some couples, it does not take long for the frequency of intercourse to diminish. (*Bill:* "How's married life?" *Phil:* "Same as before—only less often.")

Reasons for declining frequency are careers or jobs, children, and satiation. Regarding the impact of employment, one spouse said:

> Exhaustion is a very big problem. I never thought it could happen. When I'm working and running my business, it is totally absorbing and it takes me a long time to decompress at night, by which time Jerry is usually sound asleep! And I guess Jerry, unlike when we first got married, has a lot of responsibility in his position—so it's work that's taking its toll on our sex life! (Greenblat, 1983, p. 296)

Children also decrease the frequency of intercourse by their presence and by the toll they take on the caretaker's energy. "After taking care of a 3-year-old and a 9-month-old all day, I'm in no mood for sex. I'll tell you that straight out," said one mother. Also, the mere fact that children are in the house and can walk into the bedroom or knock on the door at any time translates into the couple having intercourse late at night when the children are asleep or early in the morning before they are awake. "It shoots spontaneity in the neck," said one husband.

Satiation in psychology means that repeated exposure to a stimulus results in the loss of its ability to reinforce. For example, the first time you listen to a new record album, you derive considerable enjoyment and satisfaction from it. You may play it over and over during the first few days. But after a week or so, listening to the album is no longer new and does not give you the same level of enjoyment that it first did. So it is with intercourse. The thousandth time that a person has intercourse with the same person is not as new and exciting as the first few times. "Everything gets old if you do it often enough," said one spouse.

Varying Importance. How important is intercourse to married couples? The range is very wide. Whether for physiological or psychological reasons, some married couples stop having intercourse. For them, sex is not a meaningful event. Yet they may love each other deeply and delight in the companionship they share.

Other couples regard sex as the only positive aspect of their relationship. One husband said that he and his wife had decided to separate, "and since we both knew that I would be moving out on Friday, we had intercourse twice a day that week." A year after the separation, he said, "Sex with us was the best there is. I don't miss the fights we had, but I do miss the sex." Some separated couples continue to have intercourse.

Between the extremes of "sex is nothing" and "sex is everything" is "sex is good but not everything." "It's the icing on the cake," said one man. "If you've got a good out-of-bed relationship, sex only makes things better. But sex can't make a bad marriage good."

EXTRAMARITAL INTERCOURSE

Extramarital intercourse refers to having intercourse with someone other than one's own spouse.

Data – Although it is difficult to know how many spouses have extramarital intercourse (there is a tendency to be dishonest about this very private aspect of one's life), various studies suggest that about 50 percent of husbands and almost a similar percentage of wives have at least one such encounter. (Thompson, 1983)

All extramarital encounters are not alike. The nature of the event, the participants, their motives, and the consequences for themselves and their marriages vary tremendously.

Types of Extramarital Encounters

Intercourse outside of marriage may be a brief encounter, a full-blown affair, or an event shared with the spouse.

The Brief Encounter. The lyrics to the song "Strangers in the Night" describe two people exchanging glances who end up having intercourse "before the night is through." Although the partners may see each other again, their sexual encounter is a "one-night stand" more often than not.

Data – In one study, 28 percent of the men and 5 percent of the women said their last extramarital encounter was a one-night stand. (Spanier & Margolis, 1983)

It's hard for an old rake to turn over a new leaf.
—Laurence Peter

The Affair. An *affair* implies a relationship with the partner that is beyond sexual involvement. The various combinations of pairs include married man–single woman, married man–married woman, and married woman–single man. Most relationships develop as a result of the partners meeting and interacting at work, because time away from the partner is usually time at work.

Intense reciprocal emotional feelings characterize most affairs. Such feelings are more a function of the conditions under which the relationship exists than any magical matching of the partners involved. For one thing, the time together is very limited. Like teenagers in love who are restricted by their parents, adult lovers are restricted by their spouses and other family responsibilities. Such limited access makes the time they spend together very special. In addition, the lover is not associated with the struggles of marriage—bills, children, house cleaning—and so is viewed in a more romantic setting.

Swinging. In the traditional affair, one or both of the spouses has intercourse with someone outside the marriage without the partner's knowledge. *Swinging,* also referred to as *comarital sex,* is another form of extramarital intercourse in which the spouses of one marriage or pair-bonded relationship have sexual relations with the spouses or partners of another relationship. Swinging differs from an affair in that it implies no deception (both partners are aware of the extramarital encounter) and both partners (rather than one) are usually involved. When 35 swinging couples were compared with 35 married couples who did not engage in swinging, the former group reported greater satisfaction with their marital sexual relationship. The researchers (Wheeler & Kilmann, 1983) commented:

> Thus, for comarital couples, engaging in recreational sexual activities with outside partners apparently does not interfere with each member's perception of a positive marital sexual relationship; for these couples, it may be that their marital sexual relationship is enhanced by agreed-on sexual contact with outside partners. This may not be the case for couple members who engage in covert extramarital sexual relationships, often as an "escape" from a dysfunctional marital relationship. (p. 304)

Who Has Extramarital Intercourse?

The factors most likely to influence a partner to have extramarital intercourse include the following.

Gender. The incidence of extramarital intercourse is somewhat higher for husbands than for wives. Reasons why wives are less likely to have affairs include more limited opportunities and social constraints. Businessmen have affairs with secretaries, pilots with flight attendants, physicians with nurses, and teachers with colleagues and students. Although married women are joining the work force in increasing numbers, about 30 percent still spend most of their time at home. Since an affair is dependent on knowing someone to have an affair with, the home-bound wife's contacts and opportunities are more limited.

Another reason husbands are more likely to have extramarital intercourse than wives is the greater availability of single women without partners. In *The New Other Woman,* the author (Richardson, 1985) points out that single women are increasingly more willing to have affairs with married men not only because single men are scarce but also because a relationship with a married man requires less commitment and leaves more time for the single woman to devote to her career. Single women who have affairs with married men are not out to marry them, are usually not guilty about the affair, and view the affair as time-bound (they don't see themselves having an affair forever).

Sexual Experience. Having had intercourse before marriage is also characteristic of those who have intercourse outside of marriage (Thompson, 1983). Most sexually experienced people not only have more than one sexual partner premaritally but also learn how to break norms. Both behaviors are involved in extramarital affairs.

Affairs sometimes result from having drinks after work.

Marriage Quality. Spouses who report low marital satisfaction, infrequent intercourse, and poor-quality intercourse are more susceptible to extramarital involvements (Thompson, 1983).

Marriage Commitment. Spouses who are less committed to their marriages are more likely to be involved in an extramarital relationship (Beach et al., 1985).

Urban Residence. Persons who live in urban areas are much more likely to engage in extramarital intercourse than persons who live in rural areas. Anonymity is much greater in urban areas than in rural areas.

> *Data* – Of those living in 12 of the largest metropolitan areas, 30 percent approved of extramarital intercourse, in contrast to six percent of those living in rural areas with no town of a population greater than 10,000. (Weiss & Jurich, 1985)

Peer Influence. Having a close married friend who has been sexually involved in an extramarital relationship is also related to whether an individual becomes involved in an affair (Atwater, 1982). Such a friend not only provides a role model for extramarital sex but also, in some cases, acts as a network link to other partners willing to have an affair.

Length of Marriage. How long a person has been married is also related to having an affair. Although some spouses report having had extramarital intercourse during their honeymoon, most report that several years of married life (seven or more) go by before their first experience (Petersen et al., 1983b).

Divorce. Spouses who have been married previously are more prone to having an extramarital relationship, possibly because they are less concerned about breaking social constraints. Some divorced and remarried spouses have sex with their ex-spouses.

Motives for Extramarital Involvements

I regret that I wasn't constituted, as some men are, to stay with one woman.
—John Huston

There are a number of reasons why spouses have intercourse with someone other than their mate. Some of these reasons are discussed here.

Variety. One of the characteristics of marital sex is the tendency for it to become boring and routine. Before marriage, the partners cannot seem to get enough of each other. But with constant availability, the attractiveness and excitement of intercourse seems to wane.

The Coolidge Effect helps to explain the need for sexual variety:

> One day the President and Mrs. Coolidge were visiting a government farm. Soon after their arrival, they were taken off on separate tours. When Mrs. Coolidge passed the chicken pens, she paused to ask the man in charge if the rooster copulates more than once each day. "Dozens of times" was the reply. "Please tell that to the President," Mrs. Coolidge requested. When the President passed the pens and was told about the rooster, he asked "Same hen every time?" "Oh no, Mr. President, a different one each time." The President nodded slowly and then said, "Tell that to Mrs. Coolidge." (Bermant, 1976)

Men seem more motivated by the need for sexual variety than women.

Data – Twice as many men have extramarital intercourse for sex only (without an emotional component) than women. (Thompson, 1984)

Although men typically have greater opportunities and fewer social constraints, their desire for sexual variety is difficult to overlook.

Consideration

One sociobiologist (Symons, 1979) suggests an evolutionary reason for men having a greater desire for sexual variety than women. The male who achieved the greatest reproductive success—who had the most surviving progeny—would be the one who impregnated the greatest number of females. On the other hand, reproductive success for the female depended on mating with the most fit male to ensure that her offspring would have the greatest possible chance of survival. She did not need a variety of partners.

Friendship. Some people view intercourse outside their marriage as a natural consequence of a developing relationship. "It's not that I'm crazy about sex; it's just that I enjoy relationships with other women, and sex is only a part of that," is an expression that typifies this feeling. Such relationships usually develop when people work together. They share the same world 8–10 hours a day and over a period of time may develop good feelings for each other that eventually lead to a sexual relationship. As the interaction between David and Maddie on the hit television series "Moonlighting" illustrates, flirting, friendship, and sometimes emotional attachment may develop out of a working relationship.

Apathetic or Uncooperative Spouse. Some spouses have affairs because their partner is not interested in sex. "He doesn't like sex and never has," remarked one wife. "And it frustrates me beyond description to have intercourse with him when I know it's just a duty to him. So I've found someone who likes sex and likes it with me."

Although a spouse's lack of interest in intercourse is often a reason for an affair, some go outside the marriage because their spouses will not engage in other sexual behaviors they want and enjoy. The unwillingness of the spouse to engage in oral sex, anal intercourse, or sexual positions like rear entry sometimes encourages the partner to look elsewhere for satisfaction.

Unhappy Marriage. It is commonly believed that people who have affairs are not happy in their marriage, but this is more likely to be true of wives than of husbands. Although husbands are more likely to have an affair than wives, they usually are not "dissatisfied with the quality of their marriage or their sex life with their wife" (Yablonsky, 1979, p. 15). Rather, men seem to seek extramarital relationships as an additional life experience.

Most wives "appear to seek extramarital sex when they experience some deficit—sexual, emotional, or, perhaps, economic—in their marriage, or perceive another man as being superior to (not merely different from) their husbands" (Symons, 1979, p. 238). Although trapped in a bad marriage, they may not want a divorce. "So they turn to an affair or a series of them as a means of treading water, keeping the marriage afloat for the time being until their children grow up or they (the wives) earn a degree, etc." (Schaefer, 1981)

You are only young once, but if you do it right—once is enough.
—Laurence Peter

Aging. A frequent motive for intercourse outside of marriage is the desire to reexperience the world of youth. Our society promotes the idea that it is good to be young and bad to be old. Sexual attractiveness is equated with youth, and having an affair may confirm to an older partner that he or she is still sexually desirable. Also, people may try to recapture the love, excitement, adventure, and romance associated with youth by having an affair. For some, it is viewed as the last opportunity to be young again.

One 47-year-old woman said she felt that life was passing her by and that "before long, it will all be over. To be in love is the most magical feeling I have ever experienced, and I want to have that feeling once more before I end up in a nursing home somewhere."

Absence from Spouse. Circumstances have more to do with some extramarital relationships than specific motives. One factor that predisposes a person to an extramarital encounter is prolonged separation from the spouse, which may make the partner particularly vulnerable to other involvements. Some wives whose husbands are away for military service report that the loneliness can become unbearable. Some husbands who are away say that it is difficult to be faithful. "You've almost got to be a saint to get through two years of not having intercourse if you're going to be faithful to your spouse," one air force captain said. "Most of the guys I'm stationed with don't even try."

Consideration

An extramarital sexual involvement will not occur because of these reasons alone. Other factors must be operative before an affair will actually take place. One factor is a value system that permits extramarital involvement under certain conditions. Some people have decided that extramarital sex is wrong and will not permit such involvement under any conditions. Others feel that extramarital sex is justified under certain conditions. "I didn't get married to be unhappy," said one spouse. "So if I can't find a responsive partner at home, I'll look somewhere else."

Other conditions under which extramarital sex is likely to occur include the availability of a willing partner and an opportunity to engage in the behavior without the spouse's knowledge. "When I was overseas, I had plenty of women," said one partner. "And there's no way my wife was going to find out." The reason some people do not have extramarital encounters is the lack of favorable conditions.

Postmarital Intercourse

Postmarital intercourse by the divorced and widowed is the last type of intercourse situation that we will consider in this chapter. First, we look at the situation of the formerly married.

Intercourse Among the Divorced

About 2.5 million people get divorced every year. Most will have intercourse within one year of being separated from their spouse. The meanings of intercourse for the separated or divorced vary. For many, intercourse is a way to reestablish—indeed, repair—their crippled self-esteem. Divorce is often a shattering emotional experience. The loss of a lover, the disruption of a daily routine, and the awareness of a new and negative label ("divorced person") all converge on the individual. Questions like "What did I do wrong?" "Am I a failure?" and "Is there anybody out there who will love me again?" loom in the minds of the divorced. One way to feel loved, at least temporarily, is through sex. Being held by another and being told that it feels good gives a person some evidence that he or she is desirable. Because divorced people may be particularly vulnerable, they may reach for intercourse as if for a lifeboat. "I felt that as long as someone was having sex with me, I wasn't dead and I did matter," said one recently divorced person.

Whereas some divorced people use intercourse to mend their self-esteem, others use it to test their sexual adequacy. The divorced person may have been told by the former spouse that he or she was an inept lover. One man said his wife used to make fun of him because he was occasionally impotent. Intercourse with a new partner who did not belittle him reassured him of his sexual adequacy and his impotence ceased to be a problem. A woman described how her husband would sneer at her body and say no man would ever want her because she was so fat. After the divorce, she found men who thought she was attractive and who did not consider her weight to be a problem. Other divorced men and women say that what their spouses did not like, their new partners view as turn-ons. The result is a renewed sense of sexual desirability.

Beyond these motives for intercourse, many divorced people simply enjoy the sexual freedom their divorced state offers. Freed from the guilt that spouses who have extramarital intercourse experience, the divorced can have

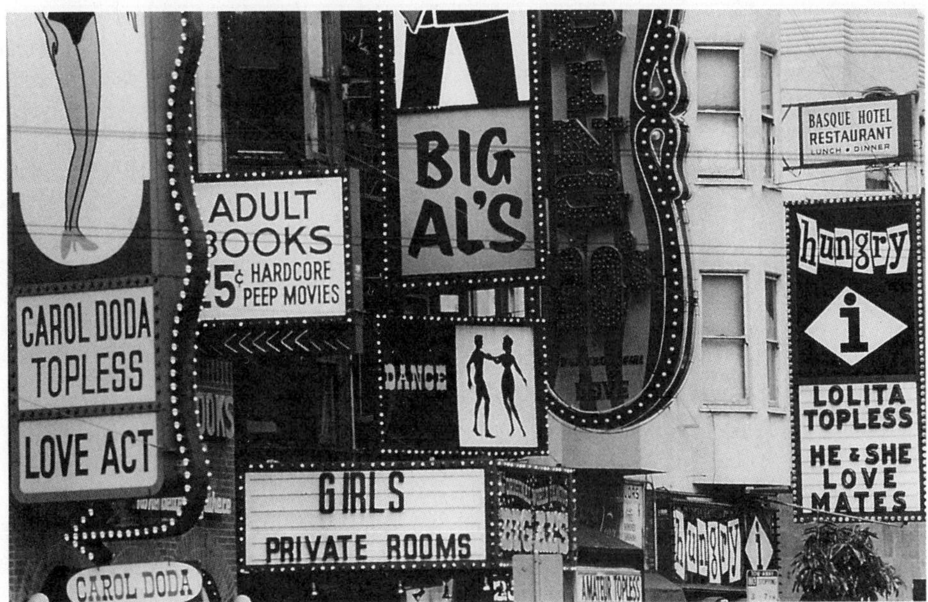

We live in a society that emphasizes the importance of sex.

intercourse with whomever they choose. Most choose to do so with a variety of partners.

Data – In one study, divorced men and women reported having an average of 30 and 22 sexual partners, respectively, since they were separated from their spouses. These averages were higher than those among singles, marrieds, remarrieds, and live-ins. (Petersen et al., 1983b)

Before getting remarried, most divorced people seem to go through predictable stages of sexual expression. The initial impact of the separation is followed by a variable period of emotional pain. During this time, the divorced often turn to intercourse for intimacy to soothe some of the pain, although this is rarely achieved.

This stage of looking for intimacy through intercourse overlaps with the divorced person's feeling of freedom and his or her desire to explore a wider range of sexual partners and behaviors than marriage provided. "I was a virgin at marriage and was married for 12 years. I've never had sex with anyone but my spouse, so I'm curious to know what other people are like sexually," one divorced person said.

But the divorced person soon tires of casual sex. One man said he had been through 22 partners since his divorce a year ago. He likened his situation to that of a person in a revolving door who is in motion but isn't going anywhere. "I want to get in a relationship with someone who cares about me and vice versa." The pattern is typical. Most divorced people initially use sex to restore their ailing self-esteem and to explore sexual parameters, but they soon drift toward sex within the context of an affectionate love relationship. "You get tired of screwing people or being screwed," said one person. "You get to where you want to love the person you're holding."

Intercourse Among the Widowed

In the long run we are all dead.
—John Maynard Keynes

The 13 million widowed in the United States differ from the divorced in their sexual behavior. In general, widowed men and women have intercourse less frequently than those who are divorced. A major reason is the lack of an available partner, but others have intercourse less frequently because they feel they are "cheating" on the deceased. "It's a guilty feeling I get," expressed one widower, "that I shouldn't want to get involved with someone else and that I shouldn't enjoy it."

Social expectations also do not support sexual expression among the widowed. Most are considered "too old" for sex. The lack of an available sexual partner, feelings of guilt at the idea of cheating on the deceased, and an unsupportive social context seem to conspire against the widowed. When a group of widows (ages 67–78) were asked how they coped with their sexual feelings when they had no partner, they responded:

> Only by keeping busy. Keep occupied with various activities and friends.
>
> Do physical exercise. Have many interests, hobbies.
>
> We just have to accept it and interest ourselves in other things.
>
> By turning to music or other arts, painting, dancing is excellent . . . using nurturant qualities, loving pets, the elderly, shut-ins. Reading, hiking . . . lots more. My mind controls my sex desires. (Starr & Weiner, 1982, pp. 165–167)

Other widows, particularly young widows, enjoy active sex lives with a new partner. "Just because your spouse is gone doesn't mean you're dead," said one 43-year-old widow. "I figure I've got half my life left, and I'm not about to give up sex yet."

Widowers have more access to sexual partners because there is an abundance of widows competing for a small number of men at later ages. Also, because our society supports male aggressiveness, widowers are more likely to initiate sexual contacts than widows.

Trends

The trend toward using a rational situation-ethics perspective in contrast to a rigid, legalistic one in making decisions about sexual behavior will continue. Individuals will rely more on their own judgment than on the rules of official religion.

However, our society wants to ensure that these individual decisions are not made at the expense of unwanted babies born to teenagers who cannot take care of them. The state of Wisconsin has passed a law that makes parents financially responsible for infants born to their unmarried children under age 18. Under this law, both sets of grandparents are required to support the infant if his or her parents cannot.

Masturbation will become a more accepted behavior and topic of discussion in the media, particularly on television. For example, on a segment of "The Tonight Show," Johnny Carson discussed masturbation with "Dr. Ruth." Because most people have been socialized to feel embarrassment and shame about masturbation, however, this trend will be slow.

The general trend toward sexual involvement with more partners before marriage will continue, but fear of AIDS will encourage people to be more selective in choosing and relating to a sex partner. In a survey of 999 students in 104 universities, more than one-third said that they would avoid casual sex due to the threat of AIDS (Stewart, 1986). One noted sex therapist (Crenshaw, 1986) said that "AIDS has had the greatest influence on the sex life of Americans since the introduction of the pill."

Extramarital sexual encounters will also increase, particularly among wives. As more wives join the labor force (close to 65 percent of all wives currently work), they will have more frequent contact with men and more freedom and opportunity to become involved in extramarital encounters.

Finally, since there will continue to be more single women than single men, more single women will opt to have brief affairs with married men. This option provides the freedom for the woman to pursue her career without the constraints of marriage.

Summary

Sexual values are moral guidelines for appropriate behavior. Legalism, situationism, hedonism, asceticism, and rationalism are basic value frameworks within which an individual makes decisions.

Both liberal and conservative elements are reflected in our society's attitude toward sexuality. On the one hand is the increased openness about sexual matters, especially in the media, and changing standards of sexual behavior for women. On the other hand is the reaction of the Moral Majority to increased liberalization, especially of abortion, gay rights, and pornography.

Masturbation is sexual self-stimulation. Traditionally, masturbation has been viewed as immoral and harmful in the communities of religion, medicine, and psychotherapy. However, attitudes toward masturbation are changing. Although religious leaders may still express disapproval, most physicians and therapists are clearly positive about masturbation.

Petting is a frequent sexual behavior involving any sexual contact that does not include intercourse. Examples include kissing, breast stimulation, cunnilingus, and fellatio. There are different types of kissing, and kissing may or may not have emotional or erotic connotations. Cunnilingus is oral contact with the female genitals; fellatio is oral contact with the male genitals.

Sexual intercourse is a method of communication. Intercourse also occurs in different interpersonal contexts before, during, outside, and after marriage. Premarital intercourse is significant because it represents first intercourse for most people and because it is not regarded as being as legitimate as marital intercourse. Most people who have premarital intercourse do so with relatively few partners and within the context of an affectionate love relationship. The effect of premarital intercourse on subsequent marital relationships is minimal.

In general, the sexual behaviors of blacks and whites are more similar than dissimilar. However, black males are more likely than white males to have interracial intercourse, to avoid masturbation, and to have intercourse with a partner who is on birth control. Black females are more likely than white females to avoid performing fellatio, to avoid manually stimulating their partner, and to use birth-control pills.

Marriage is the traditional social context for most intercourse experiences, and marital intercourse is the most socially approved form of sex. Its frequency declines the longer a couple is married.

Various studies suggest that about 50 percent of husbands and a similar percentage of wives have extramarital sex. Motivations include variety, absence of spouse, unhappiness in the marriage, and aging.

Intercourse among the divorced and widowed are two types of postmarital intercourse. The divorced typically have very active sex lives that include a number of sexual partners. After an initial period of casual sex, however, the divorced usually drift into monogamous relationships.

The widowed are usually more socially isolated and have more difficulty finding sexual partners than the divorced. Widows more than widowers often resign themselves to diverting their sexual energy to hobbies and other interests.

Questions for Reflection

1. How have your sexual values and behaviors changed in the last five years? To what degree are these changes related to your education, peers, and love relationships?
2. What impact do you think having a number of sexual partners has on the individual involved? Is it positive or negative? Why?
3. Why do you feel blacks and whites view some sexual behaviors differently?

CHOICES

DECIDING WHETHER TO have intercourse in a new relationship and whether to have extramarital sex are choices with which most people are confronted.

Deciding About Intercourse

In each new relationship, a decision about whether to have intercourse must be made. From the first meeting, each partner thinks about this. You might consider the following issues when making this decision.

Personal Consequences
How do you predict you will feel about yourself after you have intercourse? An increasing number of individuals feel that if they are in love and have considered their decision carefully, the outcome will be positive:

I believe intercourse before marriage is okay under certain circumstances. I believe that when a person falls in love with another, it is then appropriate. This should be thought about very carefully for a long time, so as not to regret engaging in intercourse. I do not think intercourse should be a one-night thing, a one-week thing, or a one-month thing. You should grow to love and care for the person very much before giving that "ultra" special part of you to your partner. These feelings should be felt by both partners; if this is not the case, then you are not in love and you are not "making love."

Those who are not in love and have sex in a casual context sometimes feel badly about the experience:

I viewed sex as a new toy—something to try as frequently as possible. I did my share of sleeping around, and all it did for me was to give me a total loss of self-respect and a bad reputation. Besides, guys talk. I have heard rumors that I sleep with guys I have never slept with.

The first couple of guys I had sex with pressured me, and I regret it. I don't believe in casual sex; it brings more heartache than pleasure. It means so much more when you truly love the partner and you know your love is returned.

However, not all people who have intercourse within the context of a love relationship feel good about it:

The first time I had intercourse, I was in love and I thought he loved me. But he didn't. He used me, and I have always hated him for it.

Some prefer to wait until marriage to have intercourse:

The person I marry will respect my wishes and wait until marriage. I don't want to sneak around and feel bad when I'm giving up an important part of myself. I want to be married, to be in our bed, and feel good that we have waited. I know that people have different values, and to each his own. But I feel that my decision to wait until I'm ready is as good as anybody else's.

The effect intercourse will have on you personally will be influenced by your religious values, your personal values, and the emotional involvement with your partner. Strong religious and personal values against intercourse plus a lack of emotional involvement usually mean guilt and regret following an intercourse experience. In contrast, values that regard intercourse as appropriate within the context of a love relationship are likely to result in feelings of satisfaction and contentment after intercourse.

Two researchers (Darling & Davidson, 1984) have compared the psychological and sexual satisfaction of 123 females who had had intercourse with 79 females who had not had intercourse. Among the sexually experi-

(Continued)

enced females, 75 percent were psychologically satisfied and 77 percent were physiologically satisfied with their sex lives. Among females who had not experienced coitus, only 46 percent reported psychological satisfaction and 47 percent reported physiological satisfaction with their sex lives.

Partner Consequences

Because a basic moral principle is to do no harm to others, it may be important to consider the effect of intercourse on your partner. Whereas intercourse may be a pleasurable experience with positive consequences for you, your partner may react differently. What are your partner's feelings about intercourse and her or his ability to handle the experience? If you suspect your partner will not feel good about it or be able to handle it psychologically, then you might reconsider whether intercourse would be appropriate with this person.

One man reported that after having intercourse with a woman he had just met, he awakened to the sound of her uncontrollable sobbing as she sat in the lotus position on the end of the bed. She was guilty, depressed, and regretted the experience. He said of the event, "If I had known how she was going to respond, we wouldn't have had intercourse."

Relationship Consequences

Does intercourse affect the stability of a couple's relationship? Apparently not. In a two-year follow-up on a study of the sexual behavior of 5,000 college sophomores and juniors who had ongoing sexual relationships (Hill et al., 1976), the researchers found that those who had had intercourse were no more likely to have broken up than those who had not. In another study (Ratcliff & Knox, 1982), less than 2 percent of 234 respondents said their relationship terminated as a result of their last intercourse. "Remained the same" was the most frequently chosen description of the effect intercourse had on the relationship.

Contraception

Another potential consequence of intercourse is pregnancy. Once a couple decides to have intercourse, a separate decision must be made as to whether intercourse should result in pregnancy. If the couple wants to avoid pregnancy, they must choose and effectively use a contraceptive method. But many do not. Among black women under age 20, 75% of all births are to unmarried women, compared to 25% of all births to young white women (Staples, 1986). In general, the interval between first intercourse and the use of a prescription method of birth control is about one year (Zelnik et al., 1984). Religiously devout individuals who have intercourse before marriage are particularly prone not to use contraceptives (Notzer et al., 1984). In most cases, the pregnancy was a surprise. One woman recalled:

> It was the first time I had had intercourse, so I didn't really think I would get pregnant my first time. But I did. And when I told him I was pregnant, he told me he didn't have any money and couldn't help me pay for the abortion. He really wanted nothing to do with me after that.

Sexually Transmitted Diseases

Avoiding sexually transmitted diseases (STDs) is an important consideration in deciding whether to have intercourse. The result of increasing numbers of people having more frequent intercourse with more partners has been the rapid spread of the bacteria and viruses responsible for numerous varieties of STDs.

For some, the fear of contracting a STD is a deterrent to having intercourse with someone they do not know. In a *USA TODAY* poll, 58 percent of the single men who responded said that men and women should avoid casual sexual relationships due to the threat of sexually transmitted disease (Peterson, 1986). One man said:

> A close friend got herpes on a one-night deal and has been plagued by it ever since. Intercourse isn't

worth getting herpes, so I've decided to be very careful about who I sleep with.

Some people are taking no chances. One woman told her new partner that she wouldn't sleep with him until he showed her a statement from a physician that he did not have a STD.

Although no method is completely safe, a sexually active person can reduce the chances of getting a STD by not having sex with someone who has multiple partners; by using a condom or a contraceptive, such as foam, cream, or jelly; by looking for sores or discharges and washing exposed areas after contact; and by urinating after contact.

Extramarital Sex? No

As noted earlier, about 50 percent of husbands and wives report they have had intercourse with someone other than their spouse. Conversely, about 50 percent of husbands and wives decide not to have an affair.

Some of those not having an affair feel that it causes more trouble to themselves and their partners than it is worth. "I can't say I don't think about having sex with other women, because I do—a lot," said one husband. "But I would feel guilty as hell, and if my wife found out, she would kill me."

Although his wife probably wouldn't "kill him," she probably would express her pain and disillusionment by asking, "How could you do this to me?". Extramarital intercourse is still regarded as adultery in an emotional sense. Like conspiring with a thief to rob their home, the adulterer is seen as conspiring with another to invade the privacy of the marriage. As a result, the partner may develop a deep sense of distrust, which often lingers in the marriage long after the affair is over. "I can forgive you," said one husband, "but I'll never forget what you've done." A wife said that whenever her husband is away on a business trip, she has visions of him being in bed with another woman. "I just don't trust him anymore."

In addition to guilt and distrust as outcomes of an affair, another danger is the development of a pattern of having affairs. "Once you've had an affair, it's easier the second time," said one spouse. "And the third time, you don't give it a thought." Increasingly, the spouse looks outside the marriage for sex and companionship.

A spouse who establishes a pattern of affairs also invests increasing amounts of time and energy in someone other than the marriage partner. Although this commitment of self to the new person helps to build the relationship with that person, it does nothing to improve the relationship with the spouse.

Of 108 marriages in which one of the spouses had an affair, 30 percent ended in divorce (Humphrey & Strong, 1978). One spouse said:

When you have an affair, you are playing with a ticking time bomb. I was able to hide mine for three years before she found out, but when she did, she threw me out of the house. When I think about what I actually did, I traded something good for something new. It was a terrible mistake.

Extramarital Sex? Yes

A small percentage of spouses who have an affair feel that it has positive consequences for them, their marriage, and their partners. One wife said, "I felt wanted, loved, desired, and sexually attractive. And every time I was with him, I felt I was someone special." In contrast to the spouse who has become familiar and inattentive, the lover is new and exciting—and makes the partner feel this way too.

Benefits to the marriage may also occur. Some partners become sensitive to the fact that they have a problem in their marriage. "For us," one spouse said, "the affair helped us to look at our marriage, to know that we were in trouble, and to seek help." Couples need not view the discovery of an affair as the end of their marriage; it can be a new beginning.

(Continued)

A final positive effect of a partner discovering an affair is that the partner may become more sensitive to the needs of the spouse and more motivated to satisfy them. The partner may realize that if spouses are not satisfied at home, they will go elsewhere. One husband said his wife had an affair because he was too busy with his work and did not spend enough time with her. Her affair taught him that she had alternatives—other men who would love her emotionally and sexually. To ensure that he did not lose her, he became intent on satisfying her.

Although an affair is dangerous for most marriages, one researcher (Britton, 1984) interviewed 276 spouses who had had an affair and identified the conditions under which an extramarital encounter is least likely to have negative consequences:

1. The spouses have a solid marriage relationship. The one who has the affair has a strong emotional commitment to the mate. The lover is viewed as short-term only—not as a potential replacement for the mate.
2. The spouses compartmentalize easily. The one who has the affair can keep the lover and the mate separated in time, place, and thought. Memories of the experiences with the lover are not allowed to blend into the relationship with the spouse so that behavior is adversely affected.
3. The spouses avoid disclosure. Disclosure is like a rattlesnake in the relationship; it strikes the spouse, and introduces a deadly venom. Few spouses can tolerate the information that their partner had or is having a sexual relationship with someone else.
4. The spouses limit contacts. Frequent contacts with one or more lovers take the energy away from the marriage and increase the chance of getting caught.
5. The spouses seek recreation only. Sexual experiences solely for spontaneous recreation do the least damage. Those that are carefully orchestrated for emotional impact take time and energy away from the mate.

Impact of Social Influences on Choices

Your willingness to engage in premarital and extramarital intercourse will largely depend on your friends and partners. If your friends engage in these behaviors and suggest that they tacitly approve of you doing so, then you are much more likely to do so than you would be if your friends do not have premarital or extramarital sex and would disapprove if you did.

Your partner is even more influential. If you are reluctant to engage in either premarital or extramarital sex, a partner who you care about, who is sexually attractive to you, and who is sexually aggressive can significantly impact your behavior. "I just couldn't resist," said one person. Those who do resist often have religious reasons (religious friends who support exclusive marital intercourse) for doing so or have had negative experiences in previous premarital or extramarital encounters.

PART TWO

DECISIONS

MORE THAN A century ago, young men and women faced great obstacles to spending time with each other. Not only were coeducational opportunities rare, but also the boy was expected to be introduced to the girl's parents before the partners could see each other socially. If her parents decided the boy was not suitable, no relationship would develop. If the partners did get together with their parents' approval, they were usually not alone. If they went out, the girl was often accompanied by a chaperone who would arrange the time, place, and events of the meetings between the partners. If they stayed inside, the boy would visit in the girl's house. They were expected to stay in the same room (usually the kitchen) with her parents. Private conversations were further limited because there were no telephones and no cars to escape adult monitors.

Today, dating and mate-selection decisions are made by the individual. While sitting in your marriage and family class, you might glance across the room and spot someone who is particularly attractive to you. You may envision developing a relationship with this person, including a number of dating events—dining together, going to parties, seeing movies, and attending concerts. The only obstacle to initiating the relationship is your instructor's lecture, which will be over in another 20 minutes. You may plan to approach this person after class and ask if you can borrow yesterday's class notes. If that person is not involved in another relationship and views you as a potential partner, your dating relationship will have begun.

The decision to initiate a dating relationship, consideration of a life-style preference, and selection of a spouse are the concerns of Part Two.

CHAPTER 5

Dating

Contents

Is It True?*

1. If your parents do not like someone you are dating, you will most likely avoid talking about that person with them.
2. Most women view men as very romantic on dates.
3. Over 25 percent of the respondents in one study who placed an ad to find a dating partner belonged to a dating services organization.
4. A primary motivation for dating is companionship.
5. Very shy people are less likely to get married.

*1=F; 2=F; 3=F; 4=T; 5=T.

YOU WILL RECALL that a central goal of marriage from the viewpoint of society is to bond two people together who will produce, protect, nurture, and socialize children to be productive members of society. To ensure that this goal is accomplished, society must make some provision for sexually mature females and males to meet, interact, and pair off in permanent unions for eventual parenthood. The dating process serves this function and guides woman–man interaction through an orderly process toward mate selection.

There are different patterns of dating—in groups and in nonexclusive or exclusive relationships. Some opposite-gender members date by "hanging around" and "getting together" in groups of various sizes; others prefer one-to-one relationships. The latter may be "open" (each partner may date others) or "closed" (the partners date each other exclusively). Such exclusive dating may or may not be oriented toward marriage.

Even pairings that lead to marriage are not permanent. Rather, individuals are likely to pair with a number of others over the course of their lifetime. Also, the criteria for choosing a partner at one stage in life may be different from the criteria at another time. One divorced man said:

> The first time around, I wanted someone who was a visual knockout. I married a real beauty, and because we argued all the time, she began to look like Cyclops to me. The next time, I will choose in reference to similar values and goals, because I've found that looks become much less important after you get the person home.

After reviewing how the Industrial Revolution changed the dating relationships of women and men, we will explore the various problems that women and men experience in dating. Because dating is the primary mechanism of mate selection, we will examine the various cultural, sociological, psychological, and sociobiological reasons you may be attracted to a particular person.

Dating in Historical Perspective

Having someone wonder where you are when you don't come home at night is a very old human need.
—Margaret Mead

In colonial America, a man who wanted to marry a woman had to ask the father's permission to do so. The following letter, written around 1705, is from William Byrd to Daniel Parke, asking his permission to marry his daughter (Woodfin & Tinling, 1942):

> Since my arrival in this country, I have had the honour to be acquainted with your daughters, and was infinitely surpriz'd to find young ladys with their accomplishments in Virginia. This surprize was soon improv'd into a passion for the youngest, for whom I have all the respect and tenderness in the world. However, I think it my duty to intreat your approbation before I proceed to give her the last testimony of my affection. And the young lady her self, whatever she may determine by your consent, will agree to nothing without it. If you can entertain a favourable opinion of my person, I dont question but my fortune may be sufficient to make her happy, especially after it has been assisted by your bounty. If you shall vouchsafe to approve of this undertaking, I shall indeavour to recommend myself by all the dutiful regards to your Excellency and all the marks of kindness to your daughter. Nobody knows better than your self how impatient lovers are, and for that reason I hope youll be as speedy as possible in your determination, which I passionately beg may be in favour of your & c.

The Industrial Revolution

The transition from a courtship system controlled by parents to the relative freedom of mate selection experienced today occurred in response to a number of social changes. The most basic change was the Industrial Revolution, which began in England in the middle of the eighteenth century. No longer were women needed exclusively in the home to spin yarn, make clothes, and process food from garden to table. Commercial industries had developed to provide these services, and women transferred their activities in these areas from the home to the factory. The result was to place them in more frequent contact with males.

Female involvement in factory work decreased parental control; parents were unable to dictate the extent to which their offspring could interact with those they met at work. Hence, values in mate selection shifted from the parents to the children. In the past, parents had approved or disapproved of a potential mate on the basis of their own values: Was the person from "good stock"? Did the man have property or a respectable trade? Did the woman have basic domestic skills? In contrast to these parental concerns, the partners focused more on love feelings. Finally, the Industrial Revolution created more leisure time for dating.

Parental Influence Today

As a result of the Industrial Revolution and the gradual loss of parental control, young American women not only became acquainted with young men outside the family circle but also felt free to consider them as possible mates. With the development of the automobile in the twentieth century came a radical change in the conditions of social interaction of unmarried men and women. Couples could now escape from their respective parents to do as they wished. Movies provided an additional place to share an evening away from friends. Within one generation, courtship had changed from parental to couple control.

Offspring of today are very careful in regard to what they tell their parents about their dating relationships. One researcher observed that they provide more information about persons they are more seriously involved with and try to change their parents mind if they feel their parents do not approve of their choice.

Data – Of 159 college students in one study, 85 percent reported having tried to influence their mothers in regard to their relationships; 77 percent reported having tried to influence their fathers. (Leslie et al., 1986)

These respondents said that with rare exception, their parents approved of their dating relationships. In general, the parents lived in areas and their offspring attended schools in which the pool of available dates from which the offspring selected was consistent with the parents' wishes.

American parents have a moderate influence on the mate choice of their offspring; Asian American parents often wield a heavy influence. Some Chinese, Japanese, Korean, and Philippine men and women will not marry someone if their parents disapprove of their choice of a mate.

Consideration

Parental interference sometimes drives dating partners to be together more often—even to marry. If your parents don't want you to date someone, try to separate the issue of why they disapprove of the person from the issue of whether you can see your partner. You can date and marry whomever you like. In a power struggle with your parents, you will win. The more important concern is why do they object? Your parents know you fairly well, love you, and probably have your best interests in mind. You may still decide to go against their wishes (it is your life), but do so because you genuinely disagree with their perceptions and concerns—not because you want to show them you can marry whomever you want whether they like it or not.

Contemporary Functions of Dating

Because most people regard dating or "getting together" as a natural part of getting to know someone else, the other functions of dating are sometimes overlooked. There are at least five of these—confirmation of a social self; recreation; companionship, intimacy, and sex; socialization; and mate selection.

Confirmation of a Social Self

It's what you learn after you know it all that counts.
—John Wooden

One of the ways we come to be who we are is through interaction with others who hold up social mirrors in which we see ourselves and get feedback on how we are doing. When you are on a first date with a person, you are continually trying to assess how that person sees you: Does he or she like me? Will he or she want to be with me again? When the person gives you positive feedback through speech and gesture, you feel good about yourself and tend to view yourself in positive terms. Dating provides a context for the confirmation of a strong self-concept in terms of how you perceive your effect on other people.

Recreation

Dating, hanging around, or getting together is fun. These are things we do with our peers, away from our parents, and we select the specific activities because we enjoy them. "I get tired of studying and being a student all day," a straight-A major in journalism said. "Going out at night with my friends to meet guys really clears my head. It's an exciting contrast to the drudgery of writing term papers."

Companionship/Intimacy/Sex

Major motivations for dating are companionship, intimacy, and sex. The impersonal environment of a large university makes a secure dating relationship very appealing. "My last two years have been the happiest ever," remarked a senior in interior design. "But it's because of the involvement with my fiancé. During my freshman and sophomore years, I felt alone. Now I feel loved, needed, and secure with my partner."

Some students prefer an exclusive relationship to casual dating. One physics major remarked, "I've had it with trying to get all the dates I can. They turn out to be like a revolving door; I have to tell the same stories, act the same superficial way, and read the same script for the first several dates. With one person, I can relate in a more open, relaxed way."

Socialization

Before puberty, boys and girls interact primarily with their own gender. A boy or girl may be laughed at if he or she shows an interest in someone of the opposite gender. Even when boy–girl interaction becomes the norm at puberty, neither gender may know what is expected of them. Dating offers the experiences of learning how to initiate conversation and developing an array of skills in human relationships, such as listening and expressing empathy. Dating also permits an individual to try out different role patterns, like dominance or submission, and to assess the "feel" and comfort level of each.

Sexual socialization is also a part of dating. Learning how to become physically close to another and to experience intimate encounters with different people is a typical pattern. "People make love differently. They hold you differently and have different preferences," said a drama major.

Mate Selection

Many a man has fallen in love with a girl in a light so dim he would not have chosen a suit by it.
—Maurice Chevalier

Finally, dating may serve to pair off two people for marriage. For those who want to get married, dating is a process of finding a person who has a similar agenda and the desired characteristics.

Consideration

Which dating function is most important will vary from person to person and for a particular person over time. "I've gone full circle," said one banking employee. "Dating used to be for fun, which led to companionship and marriage. But I'm recently divorced and am not interested in marriage. I'm dating just for the fun again, with no goal whatsoever of getting involved with anyone."

But another person said, "The big-time, have-a-party, get-drunk, fun aspect of dating is getting old to me. I'm bored being in crowded, smokey rooms listening to loud music. I want a relationship—a companion. I'm ready for marriage."

Dating Realities

Dating begins with finding a partner—not just any partner but the one that you want.

Data – There are 7.3 million more marriageable women than marriageable men in America. (Cassell, 1986)

After discussing various mechanisms for meeting someone, we will examine what people look for in the people they date and what they do on dates.

Finding a Partner

Just as people have a variety of motives for seeking a dating partner, there are a number of mechanisms for doing so—through friends, independently, through magazines or newspapers, computers, and video cassettes.

Friends

Table 5.1 shows how 482 single adults met others to date. Their responses emphasize the importance of the work or study environment as a place for meeting others. Many single adults also meet others while enjoying a favorite hobby or working out. Same-gender friends can play an important role in meeting new dating partners. The message seems to be "When you don't have a date (and want one), go with a friend." Both you and your friend are connections to dating partners for each other.

Independently

Based on the traditional assumption that the man initiates the dating relationship, 200 women in a courtship and marriage class were asked, "How would you go about getting a man to ask you out?" Most said they would either ask a friend to introduce him to her or engage him in a conversation. Others mentioned that "being friendly," "smiling at him," and "being where he'll be" were effective ways of encouraging a man to ask a woman for a date.

One researcher (Moore, 1985) identified 52 "flirting behaviors," including glance, gaze, head toss, hair flip, smile, and lip lick. Ten women were observed in four different contexts (singles' bar, snack bar, library, and women's meeting) during a 60-minute period to ascertain the degree to which these women exhibited these behaviors.

Data – Ten women in the singles' bar context exhibited 706 flirting behaviors within a one-hour period. During that time, each of the women were approached by an average of four men. (Moore, 1985)

The female's intent is more often to get the attention of the male, not to invite him to bed. Men usually misunderstand the intent of a woman's flirting.

TABLE 5.1 WHERE 482 UNMARRIED ADULTS MEET PEOPLE TO DATE (FEMALES = 337; MALES = 145)

Ways of Meeting	*Female*	*Male*
Work or place of study	53%	38%
Hobby or sport club	41	33
Mutual friends	38	34
Parties	34	36
Night classes	20	10
Singles' bars	18	24

Source: Austrom & Hanel, 1985.

Bars are utilized as places to meet dating partners.

Consideration

> The more often a woman evidenced her availability via flirting behavior, the more often she was approached. (Moore, 1985). Women who want to meet men should increase the frequency of their flirting behavior. Only if there is an approach do communication and intimacy become possible.

Some women feel that they do not have effective flirting skills but feel assertive enough to ask a man outright for a date. "I just call him up, tell him I'm in one of his classes, and ask him out to a concert," said a sports-medicine major. Exhibit 5.1 suggests a way you can meet anyone on your campus.

Magazines and Newspapers

Data – Of 482 single adults, 5 percent placed ads to find a dating partner. (Austrom & Hanel, 1985)

Because two people who are suited for each other may never meet by chance, personal ads have been developed to make such people aware of each other (Block, 1985). The following advertisements are typical of those designed to seek a particular type of partner or to offer one's self to someone who may be looking for a partner:

> MALE, 32, attractive professional looking for single, white, female for fun and frolic. Must be herpless but not hopeless, helpless, or hapless. Mike, P.O. Box 24, Arcola, IN 46704

> LADY, 28, seeks gentle Paul Bunyan for loving, working, the rest of my life. Nancy, Route 2, Box 54B, Republic, WA 99166

Exhibit 5.1

HOW TO MEET ANYONE ON YOUR CAMPUS

The following suggestion is a way for you to meet anyone on your campus.

Turn to page 41, on which you will see the Love Attitudes Scale. Hand the book to someone you are interested in meeting and say, "I'm enrolled in a marriage course on campus and have been requested to ask a person of the opposite sex to take this love test. Would you take a couple of minutes and complete it for me?"

Persons who are interested in some level of interaction with you will agree to complete the form. They may ask you questions about it ("What does the third statement mean?"), establish eye contact, and indicate (through smiles and gestures) a willingness to interact with you.

Not all persons will be receptive. The goal is to meet someone or to find out how others score on the Love Attitudes Scale—not for him or her to fall in love with you at first sight. If you ask 20 people to complete the inventory, expect only one to show an interest in you beyond the inventory. But you only need one. The dating world can be a very rejecting place; expect to meet some frogs before you find the prince or princess.

SINGLE mother, 34, 135, two biracial, adopted children, former model now technical writer, humorous, handy, desires correspondence with same type person. Mary Mitchener, 228 Culpepper Ave., Dothan, AL 35226

WANTED: One SWM [single white male] who (A) must be 35–50, bright, witty, articulate, interesting, tender, attractive, fun; (B) may be short, tall, handsome, mystical, earthy, mildly neurotic and/or reasonably obnoxious; (C) must not be macho, crazed, boring. Wanted by SWF [single white female] who is all of A, some of B, and none of C. Sally, Box 95, Chicago, IL 78764.

These ads might appear in such national magazines as *Intro, Mother Earth News,* or *Rural Singles of America* or in local newspapers. *The Washingtonian* features about 500 personals per issue; *The Village Voice* prints 200 personals a week. *Singles Register* (P.O. Box 567, Norwalk, CA 90650) advertises itself as the leading publication for singles.

The goal of placing a personal ad is to get a lot of responses and then select the best one. Personals provide a measure of control over the selection process. "I usually trash half the letters I get," said one person who took out an ad. "But the rest I respond to and see what happens next. It is really a great alternative to going to bars and taking a chance on who's there that night."

Dating Service Organizations

Data – Four percent of 482 single adults used dating services to find a dating partner. (Austrom & Hanel, 1985)

More than 5,000 organizations in the United States exist for the purpose of finding mates for their members. Although many of these organizations serve the general public, some are specialized. Examples include the Jewish Dating

Service (to match Jewish singles), Preferred Singles (to match singles who are overweight), Chocolate Singles (to match black singles), and Execumatch. The last, for a fee of $100,000, finds marriage partners for the wealthy. American Asian Worldwide Services in Orcutt, California, specializes in matching Asian women to American men; more than 6,000 such mail-order matches are made worldwide every year.

Singles' Clubs. Some cities have clubs that cater specifically to single people who are interested in meeting each other.

> *Data* – Ten percent of 482 single adults belonged to singles' clubs for the purpose of meeting dating partners. (Austrom & Hanel, 1985)

"I was very apprehensive about going to one of these singles' clubs," one single said, "I thought there would be only losers there. And while there were some duds (I'm not so sure I'm not one myself), I did meet some people and am very glad I joined."

Singles' Bars. One researcher (Murray, 1985) visited 50 singles' bars, collected 3,000 opening lines, and divided them into four categories:

Compliments: "I like your [article of clothing]."
Advertisements/declarations: "My name is . . ."
Questions: "Come here often?"
Propositions: "How about it?"

The researcher also kept a record of what type of opening line was used at what time of the evening. He found that between midnight and one o'clock, there were between 200 and 300 compliments, advertisements/declarations, and questions but close to 700 (674) direct propositions.

Computers

Computers can figure out all kinds of problems, except the things in the world that just don't add up.
—James Magary

The computer revolution has introduced another way of meeting a dating partner. Campus bulletin boards and newspapers often feature advertisements for computer-matched dates. Titles such as "Pick A Date," "Computer Match," and "Why Be Lonely?" are followed by the promise to find the "right" date for the person who completes the questionnaire. The information requested is designed to help the computer match respondents on the basis of social background, personal attitudes, and complementary needs. The individual's profile is matched with similar profiles in the computer, and he or she is given a list of several names, usually three.

The suitability of the partners will depend on how accurately each has completed the questionnaire. For example, individuals may indicate that they are more physically attractive than they actually are for fear that they may otherwise be paired with the son or daughter of Frankenstein's monster.

Computers may also serve as an initial contact between two people. Compuserve Information Services of Columbus, Ohio, offers the CB Simulator, which allows individuals with home computers to use any of its 36 channels to "talk" with another subscriber. In effect, individuals sit at their respective computer terminals and send written communications to each other.

(If more than two users at a time want to talk privately, they can scramble their messages by using a mutually agreed-on code.) "I first met my spouse by conversing with her through written messages on the computer," said a computer hacker. "Soon we set up a lunch date and were married about a year later. Some of my friends also talk with a girlfriend or boyfriend through their computer."

Video Cassettes

The newest method of finding a partner is to have yourself interviewed on videotape and let others watch your cassette in exchange for your watching those already on file. If you like what you see, you can contact the person directly for a date (and vice versa).

Great Expectations (Los Angeles), and People Network (Boston) offer to make a videotape of you and permit you to view the tapes of others. The price at People Network is $800.00 for unlimited viewing; one woman reported that she received 40 invitations and sent out nine in the six months she was a member.

Consideration

Although some people view finding dating partners through magazines, computers, or video services embarrassing, others regard it as an adventure. Some even feel it is easier than random dating, because such services permit members to prescreen a large number of individuals who have the desired qualities rather than spend money on dinner to find out that the person smokes or loves cats and you don't. These relatively new forms of finding a partner should be considered as viable alternatives. Of 4,000 marriages arranged through American Asian Worldwide Services, only 10 percent have ended in divorce. (Lawlor, 1986)

Dating Activities

There is considerable variation in the places people go on dates and in the degree to which their activities include sex and the use of drugs. In a survey of more than 65,000 women (Bowe, 1986), having dinner (26 percent), having coffee or a drink (24 percent), going to a movie, play, or concert (24 percent), and meeting for lunch (6 percent) were the most frequent activities. Regardless of the event, most men pay.

Cocaine is very attractive. And it's insidious. You think you're having a nice time, and in reality, you're on your way to the gallows. As in most cases with things like this, you don't see it until it's too late.

—Kareem Abdul-Jabbar

Data – Ninety-two percent of 65,000 women said that the man picks up the tab for the date. (Bowe, 1986)

Men do not seem to be too romantic on dates, at least as women perceive them to be. Only a quarter of the women in the survey said that their men were romantic on dates. One woman said, "In the beginning of a relationship, men try hard to be romantic. But once they get comfortable, you'll have to buy your own roses" (p. 265).

Drug use on dates is not unusual. Although alcohol remains the number one drug, marijuana and cocaine also have a following (Stewart, 1986b).

Some students have "study dates."

Consideration

> Choices made under the influence of drugs (alcohol included) may be different from choices made without drugs. If decisions are made independently of drugs, you avoid the "why did I do that?" or "I shouldn't have done that" feeling the next day. Just as drugs cannot stabilize or maintain relationships, they cannot be counted on to initiate them or to maximize making wise decisions. Individuals should also get to know each other under drug-free conditions.

Dating Problems

Dating can sometimes involve problems. One study sought to identify dating problems from the viewpoint of 227 college women and 107 men in a random sample (Knox & Wilson, 1983).

The Woman's View

Table 5.2 lists the most common problems that the college women in this study experienced on their dates.

Unwanted Sexual Pressure

Unwanted pressure to engage in sexual behavior was the most frequent problem reported by women students. Almost one-fourth felt that men wanted to move the relationship toward sex too quickly. "How quickly he can get his hand in my blouse and up my skirt is what every guy I date seems to have in the front of his brain," said one student. "Too quickly" is usually defined as before an emotional relationship has developed. "I can't get physical with a

TABLE 5.2 DATING PROBLEMS EXPERIENCED BY 227 UNIVERSITY WOMEN

PROBLEMS	*PERCENTAGE*
Unwanted pressure to engage in sexual behavior	23
Places to go	22
Communication with date	20
Sexual misunderstandings	13
Money	9

Source: Knox & Wilson, 1983.

guy unless I care about him and I know he cares about me," recalled another female. "It just doesn't feel right to do sex with a guy I'm not involved with."

The dilemma expressed by many of the women was not wanting to have too much sex too soon in the relationship but wanting to show enough interest in the man so that he would ask for another date. A related concern was getting the man to slow down his sexual advances without hurting his feelings. Margaret Kent (1986), who offers seminars on "How to Marry the Man of Your Choice" and has written a book by the same name, implies that women's fears are well founded: "Never deny sex, because that dooms any ideas of his marrying you."

Women in the study differed as to how they reacted to a sexually aggressive man on dates. Most told their date to "stop it," put their hands on his, and moved him away. "You have to be serious when you tell a guy to stop, or he'll keep right on," said one education major.

Other students went along with what their dates wanted to do sexually, even though it was not what they preferred. "It seemed important to him, and I knew it wouldn't kill me, so we left the party early and went back to his place. I wanted to stay at the party, but it wasn't worth fighting over." Date rape will be discussed in detail in Chapter 12.

Still other students kept their distance and ignored sexual advances. "I acted like I didn't know he was hustling me, and I kept away from him," recalled a parks and recreation major.

Communication

Regardless of where a couple spends time, talking with the partner was a problem for about one-fifth of the women. A major concern was trust. Honesty is the most important quality college women look for in their dating partners.

Knowing what to say and how to say it were other communication concerns. Part of the uneasiness grew out of the different levels of interest of the respective partners in the relationship. "I didn't want to get too involved with him, so I didn't tell him anything about myself. It was very awkward to keep the conversation on safe subjects like classes and his fraternity."

Jealousy was also a problem. "When I know he's out with someone else the nights he's not with me, I boil with anger," said one woman. "And when I see him having a beer with her at a local bar, I want to strangle him (and her)."

TABLE 5.3 DATING PROBLEMS EXPERIENCED BY 107 UNIVERSITY MEN

PROBLEMS	*PERCENTAGE*
Communication with date	35
Places to go	23
Shyness	20
Money	17
Honesty/openness	8

Source: Knox & Wilson, 1983.

Other Problems

Sometimes couples have a problem with places to go on dates. However, this is less a problem with emotionally involved couples than with those just beginning to date.

"Sexual misunderstandings" was a dating problem for 10 percent of the women students. Accidently leading a man on when you really don't want to have intercourse is an example. One woman explained that she had been very affectionate with her date throughout the evening: "We danced closely, and I was thoroughly enjoying being with him. But he interpreted my affection as a desire to have intercourse. I didn't, and the evening ended in a terrible argument."

Money was also viewed as a problem on dates by 10 percent of the women students. "Sometimes it gets so bad," said one sophomore, "we eat out of cans heated on the hot plate in my dorm room. We go to the free campus movies and drink a lot of beer at happy hour prices. Sometimes we would just like a few bucks so we could do something different."

Another aspect of the money problem on dates was who pays. The typical pattern was for the man to pay for everything on the first few dates. After that, from time to time, the woman would pick up the tab for both of them. "I know he has a lot of money at the first of the month when he gets paid. But by the second or third week, that's gone, so I start paying for things."

Some women said they would always pay for their own expenses on dates. "A guy buys you a beer, and he thinks he owns you. If he takes you out to eat, he expects sex later, so I just pay as I go and avoid feeling obligated."

Women also view the men they date as engaging in positive behaviors. More than 80 percent of the women in one study said that their dating partners displayed wit, industriousness, and humor (Laner, 1986).

THE MAN'S VIEW

The most common problems experienced by 107 college males on their dates are outlined in Table 5.3.

Communication

"Communication with date" was the major problem for one-third of the men. One man said:

> "I never know what to say. If I ask her a lot of questions, she tells me I am interrogating her. If I don't ask her questions, she says I'm not interested. If I talk a lot and tell stories, she thinks I don't care what she has to say. If I don't talk much, she says I'm boring—so what am I supposed to do?"

Communication will be discussed in detail in Chapter 11.

Others complained that they felt anxious and nervous when they knew the conversation was dragging. "After awhile, you run out of small talk about the weather and your classes. When the dialogue dies, its awful," expressed one senior. It is possible that men press for sex because they don't know what to say or how to communicate.

Some communication concerns decreased after the first few dates with the same person. "After I get to know a girl, I feel comfortable being with her and less self-conscious about what I say. The communication seems to flow more smoothly with someone you know," recalled an engaged male.

Shyness

A related problem is shyness, mentioned by 20 percent of the men. Some felt uncomfortable with what they perceived as responsibility for everything. One man said, "I'm supposed to call her up, think of intelligent or cute things to say, know how to read her mind, and ensure that she has a good time—give me a break!"

Other men said they did not meet people well and felt particularly shy during the first part of the first date. "I really get nervous and feel awkward," commented a basketball player.

Shyness can have long-lasting effects. One researcher (Gilmartin, 1985) identified 100 shy men over the age of 35 who said that they had never married due to chronic and severe shyness with women in informal social situations.

Other Problems

Like women, men also said places to go and money were dating problems. The men said they got tired of going to the same places. Also, although lack of money was a problem for almost one in 10 men, no man said that who pays was a problem. Although role relationships in our society are becoming more flexible and women are paying for expenses on dates more often, men still seem to accept paying for expenses as part of their role.

Honesty and openness were also problems for about one in 10 of the male respondents. How much to tell and how soon to tell it were concerns. One man said he did not want to get hurt, so he kept a close guard on what he said. There was also the feeling that neither partner knew what the other was thinking and that attempts to get the other to open up were frustrating. "She just sat there all night and didn't say a word unless I would ask a question," mused an anthropology major.

The reports of these college students suggest that women and men are experiencing the same dating event differently. Almost 25 percent of the females were frustrated by the necessity of warding off sexually aggressive males, but only 2 percent of the men were troubled by women being sexually aggressive.

While women are coping with unwanted sexual advances on dates, men are struggling to achieve and maintain communication on dates. Also, men feel much more shy than the women they date. Shyness was a problem on dates for 25 percent of the men, in contrast to only 5 percent of the women. This situation is a curious contrast in perceptions. University women view university men as sexually aggressive, but university men view themselves as shy.

Consideration

What is needed in dating is more openness about what the respective partners are feeling. The woman might let the man know she is turned off by sexual aggressiveness and turned on by behaviors that are more personally focused. The man might stop taking complete responsibility for "everything working out fine" and relax, which may reduce his expectation that communication flow in a certain way. Lowered anxiety and more realistic expectations would increase the probability of more relaxed communication.

Dating in the Middle Years

Dating during the middle years (defined by the U.S. Bureau of the Census as 45 to 65), which usually means dating after a divorce, is a very different dating experience than dating while in one's twenties and in reference to a first marriage. A neglected area of research (Rodgers & Conrad, 1986), courtship for remarriage differs from courtship for first marriage in terms of norms, sexual intimacy, children, and public disclosure. There are also fewer men in their middle years than there are men in their twenties for the available women in these age groups.

Data – Between the ages of 45 and 64, there are 54 unmarried men for every 100 unmarried women. (U.S. Bureau of the Census, 1986)

Fewer norms guide the dating behaviors of middle-age partners. In their twenties, it was usually clear who would call whom, how soon or late sexual intimacy would occur, and when parents would be involved. But in middle age, the norms are in flux. While one of the partners may be operating on the "old" norms, the other partner may be behaving in reference to a new set of dating norms. The latter imply that either sex calls the other, sexual intimacy usually occurs sooner than later, and parents are not consulted about involvement with the new partner.

Children are often an important consideration and influence in the courtship progress of remarriages, either through direct involvement (taking the kids to the beach) or through their opinions ("I don't like her/him"). Financial obligations to previous spouses and children can also have an impact on the decisions of the new couple. "He told me that he was going to send his paycheck to his first wife and their four kids because he felt guilty about leaving them," one woman said. "I knew I didn't want to continue dating him because there would be no money left for us if we were to get married."

Public disclosure in terms of announcements and a large wedding are more common in first than second marriages. The partners in a second marriage more often have a small wedding ceremony with a few selected friends. Announcements are less often sent out, and the couple are more likely to live together before getting married.

Dating in the Later Years

We have been discussing dating among college students, but senior citizens also date. In a study of 45 people, ranging in age from 60 to 92, who were divorced or widowed and dating again, two researchers observed that "when they fall in love, the older daters experience the same emotional somersaults, sweaty palms, and beating hearts as do younger couples" (Bulcroft & O'Conner-Roden, 1986, p. 68). Finding a partner is sometimes difficult because there are still more women than men in this age group.

Data – At age 65 and older, there are 26 unmarried men for every 100 unmarried women. (U.S. Bureau of the Census, 1986)

The older I grow, the more I listen to people who don't say much.
—Germain G. Glidden

The researchers also found that sexuality was an important part of dating in senior relationships, with a stronger emphasis on hugging, kissing, and touching. But not always. One 71-year-old widower said, "You can talk about candlelight dinners and sitting in front of a fireplace, but I still think the most romantic thing I've ever done is to go to bed with her" (p. 68).

These daters were also not too interested in marriage. They enjoyed their independence too much and wanted to avoid getting saddled with someone who might become ill and need a full-time caretaker. Nevertheless, dating relationships met an important emotional need in their lives that was not supplied by family or friends.

Mate Selection

The mutual selection of Prince Charles and Lady Diana, Johnny Cash and June Carter, Phil Donahue and Marlo Thomas, and Jane Fonda and Tom Hayden did not occur by chance. Various cultural, sociological, psychological, and—some sociobiologists say—biological factors combined to influence their meeting and marriage.

Cultural Aspects of Mate Selection

Cultural norms for mate selection vary. The degree of freedom an individual has in choosing a marriage partner depends on the culture in which he or she lives. In some cultures, arranged marriages predominate; in others, including our own, "free" choice is the rule. But some arranging takes place in all cultures. A great many American marriages have been arranged up to modern times, both in poor rural areas and in high society (for example, the marriage of Consuelo Vanderbilt to the Duke of Marlborough in 1895). The Reverend Sun Myung Moon of the Unification Church personally matched and married 2,075 couples in a mass Madison Square Garden ceremony in New York in the early eighties.

Endogamous–Exogamous Pressures

Whereas some societies exert specific pressure on individuals to marry predetermined mates, other societies apply more subtle pressure. The United States has a system of free choice that is not exactly free. Social approval and disapproval restrict your choices so that you do not marry just *anybody. Endogamous pressures* encourage you to marry those within your own social group (racial, religious, ethnic, educational, economic); *exogamous pressures* encourage you to marry outside your family group (to avoid marriage to a sibling or other close relative).

The pressure toward an endogamous mate choice is especially strong when race is concerned. One white woman said, "Some of my closest friends are black. But my parents would disown me if I were to openly date a black guy." In contrast, a black man said, "I would really like to date a girl in my introductory psychology class who's white. But my black brothers wouldn't like it, and while my parents wouldn't throw me out of the house, they would wonder why I wasn't dating a black girl."

These endogamous pressures are not operative on all people at the same level or may not work at all. Those who are older than 30, who have been married before, and/or who live in large urban centers are more likely to be color-blind in their dating and marrying. In Hawaii, interracial dating and marriage are normative, but interracial marriage occurs throughout our society.

Data - There are more than 700,000 interracial married couples in America. (*Statistical Abstract of the United States*, 1987)

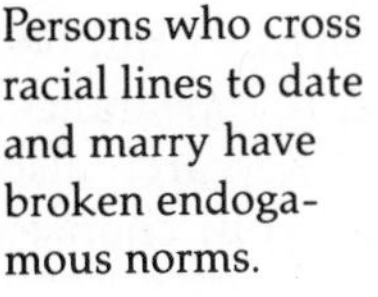

Persons who cross racial lines to date and marry have broken endogamous norms.

In contrast to endogamous marriage pressures, exogamous pressures are mainly designed to ensure that individuals who are perceived to have a close biological relationship do not marry each other. Incest taboos are universal. In no society are children permitted to marry the parent of the opposite gender. In the United States, siblings and first cousins (in some states) are also prohibited from marrying each other.

Consideration

Mate selection in the United States is free only to the extent that the individual is willing to marry as the laws of his or her state permit and is capable of withstanding the social pressures to make a choice that is not culturally sanctioned. The wife of an interracial couple remarked, "I married Reid because I loved him. I still do. But the cost has been high. My father wouldn't speak to me. My mother is heartbroken. Most of my friends approve of my marriage, but there is more grief than I thought."

The effect of the cultural influences just described is to narrow your choice of an "acceptable" mate from anybody to those outside your immediate family and to those of the same race, religion, and social class.

Sociological Aspects of Mate Selection

There are several sociological factors at work in the attraction of two people to each other. These concepts include homogamy, role compatibility, and propinquity.

Homogamy

The *homogamy* concept of mate selection states that you are attracted to and become involved with those who are similar to you in age, physical appearance, intelligence, education, social class, marital status, and religion. Research also suggests that the more similar you are to your partner, the better your chances are for achieving personal and marital happiness.

How old would you be if you didn't know how old you was?
—Satchel Paige

Age. When a friend gets you a date, you assume the person will be close to your age. Your peers are not likely to approve of your becoming involved with someone twice your age. A student who was dating one of her former teachers said, "He always comes over to my place, and I prepare dinner for us. I don't want to be seen in public with him. Although I love him, it doesn't feel right being with someone old enough to be my father." Such a concern for age homogamy is particularly characteristic of individuals who have never married. Those who have been married before are much more likely to become involved with someone who is less close to their age.

The tendency for men to marry down and women to marry up in age, social class, and education is referred to as the *mating gradient.*

Data – The median age at first marriage for American men is 25.5; for American women, it is 23. (U.S. Bureau of the Census, 1986)

As a result of such pairing, some high-status women and low-status men remain single. As a function of the mating gradient, the upper-class woman will receive approval from her parents and peers only if she marries someone of equal status. On the other hand, approval is usually forthcoming for the man who marries below himself in age and status. The educated, professional black female has a particularly difficult time finding a black male of equal status.

Consideration

> The mating gradient results in an oversupply of unmarried older, bright, attractive, educated, professional women. Men might consider the personal, social, and economic benefits of including such women in their pool of potential partners, and women might reconsider the idea that their mate must be older, educated, and professionally established. Solid happy relationships can result from a number of different pairings. The mating gradient may be an artificial restriction.

Beauty is altogether in the eye of the beholder.
—General Lew Wallace

Physical Appearance. Love may be blind, but it knows what the person looks like. In general, people tend to become involved with those who are similar in physical attractiveness. When you look in the mirror, you evaluate the degree to which you are physically attractive and assess the level of physical attractiveness of the person or persons whom you feel may be interested in you. A look at the various pairings on campus may illustrate this concept in operation. Are the "good-looking people" paired off with each other? Or are they mismatched? If they are mismatched, is the girl better looking than the boy? Some data suggest this would be the case (Janda et al., 1981).

Intelligence. Intelligence was the number-one characteristic that 122 male and 210 female undergraduates said they looked for in the opposite gender (Daniel et al., 1985). "There are plenty of bimbos on campus," said one student. "I need someone whose cortical cells are active and who thinks about things other than drinking Bud Lite." Another said, "I think intelligent guys are just more fun. They are never boring and seem to know what is coming down."

Education. The level of education you attain will also influence your selection of a mate. A sophomore who worked in a large urban department store during the Christmas holidays remarked, "The two weeks Todd and I spent selling record albums and tapes were great. But our relationship never gathered momentum. I was looking forward to my last two years of school, but Todd said college was a waste of time. I don't want to get tied to someone who thinks that way."

This student's experience suggests that you are likely to marry someone who has also attended college. Not only does college provide an opportunity to meet, date, and marry another college student, but it also increases the chance that only a college-educated person will be acceptable. Education affects not only what you know but also what you are aware of. The very pursuit of education becomes a value to be shared.

Social Class. You have been reared in a particular *social class* that reflects your parents' occupations, incomes, and educations as well as your residence, language, and values. If you were brought up in the home of a physician, you probably lived in a large house in a nice residential section of town. You were in a higher social class than you would have been if your parents were less educated and worked as clerks at K-Mart.

The social class in which you were reared will influence how comfortable you feel with a partner. "I never knew what a finger bowl was," recalled one man, "until I ate dinner with my girlfriend in her parents' Manhattan apartment. I knew then that while her life style was exciting, I was more comfortable with paper napkins and potato chips. We stopped dating."

Previous Marital Status. There is a tendency for the divorced to marry the divorced, the widowed to marry the widowed, and the never-married to marry the never-married. A divorced mother of twin boys remarked, "The only person who really understands me is a divorced father. He knows what a lonely experience divorce is and how important children are."

All religions must be tolerated . . . for . . . every man must get to heaven his own way.

—Frederick The Great

Religion. Some religious denominations socialize their members to seek mates of a similar religious orientation. Mormons, Jews, Catholics, and to some extent, fundamentalist Protestants encourage homogamous religious mate selection. "Don't date anyone you wouldn't marry, and don't marry anyone who is not of your faith," said one religious leader to his congregation.

Type T Personalities. Thrill-seeking or *Type T personalities* represent people who seek adventure, excitement, stimulation, and risk wherever they can find it. Shooting the rapids, climbing a steep cliff, racing a car, and performing daredevil stunts of the Evel Knievel variety are examples of such behavior. Persons who like to live on the edge of excitement tend to seek each other for spouses (Farley, 1986).

Propinquity

An American man married a woman who was born in Vienna, Austria but who had spent her senior year of high school in his parents' home as a foreign exchange student. Their marriage illustrates the concept of *residential propinquity,* which states that the probability that A and B will marry each other decreases as the distance between their residences increases.

It is obvious that we can only marry those with whom we interact, but the propinquity aspect of mate selection also includes convenience. Being in the same class, working at the same job, or living close to each other permits convenient interaction. Referring to his former fiancée, a library science major said:

> When I first transferred to State, I would drive the 300 miles each way to see her on weekends. I did that three times. Then I noticed a girl in one of my classes, and we began studying together. I soon stopped the ten hours of driving each weekend to see the other girl. It was only five minutes from my apartment to the new girl's place.

Psychological Aspects of Mate Selection

Beyond the cultural and sociological factors that restrain and guide your choice of a partner, various psychological variables are involved. These include complementary needs, exchange theory, and parental image. All of these psychological variables are concerned with the ways in which the individual, independent of his or her society, view the mate-selection process.

Complementary Needs

"In spite of the women's movement and a lot of assertive friends, I am a shy and dependent person," remarked a transfer student. "My need for dependency is met by Warren, who is the dominant, protective type." The tendency for a submissive person to become involved with a dominant person (one who likes to control the behavior of others) is an example of attraction based on *complementary needs.* Partners can also be drawn to each other on the basis of nurturance versus receptivity. These complementary needs suggest that one person likes to give and take care of another, while the other likes to be the benefactor of such care. Other examples of complementary needs may involve responsibility versus irresponsibility and peacemaker versus troublemaker.

That partners select each other on the basis of complementary needs has been suggested by Winch (1955), who notes that needs can be complementary if they are different (for example, dominant and submissive) or if the partners have the same need at different levels of intensity. As an example of the latter, two individuals may have a complementary relationship when they both want to do advanced graduate study, but both need not get Ph.D.s. The partners will complement each other if one is comfortable with his or her level of aspiration, represented by a master's degree, but still approves of the other's commitment to earn a Ph.D.

Winch's theory of complementary needs, commonly referred to as "opposites attract," is based on the observation of 25 undergraduate married couples at Northwestern University. The findings have been criticized by other researchers who have not been able to replicate Winch's study. Two researchers said, "It would now appear that Winch's findings may have been an artifact of either his methodology or his sample of married people" (Meyer & Pepper, 1977).

Two questions can be raised about the theory of complementary needs:

1. Couldn't personality needs be met just as easily outside the couple's relationship rather than through mate selection? For example, couldn't a person who has the need to be dominant find such fulfillment in a job that involved an authoritative role, such as head of a corporation or an academic department?
2. What is a complementary need as opposed to a similar value? For example, is desire to achieve at different levels a complementary need or a shared value?

Whether they are complementary or not, you expect your partner to meet some of your specific needs. The Needs Assessment Inventory (p. 154) is designed to help you identify the needs you expect your partner to fulfill and the degree to which she or he does so.

How much you respect someone is more often determined by the balance of giving and getting between you than by old-fashioned standards like honor, talent, virtue.
—Robert Karen

Exchange Theory

Your parents will not be haggling with your partner's parents over bride price or other such matters. You are your own broker, and your selection will involve various exchanges.

Self-Assessment

Needs Assessment Inventory*

Identify the needs you expect your partner to meet in column A by ranking them in importance from 1 to 16. Next, write in column B the degree to which you feel your partner can or does satisfy each of the needs you ranked (0 = low; 10 = high). You might also ask your partner to complete this exercise.

(A)	(B)		(A)	(B)	
______	______	Companionship	______	______	Makes me feel secure
______	______	Recreation	______	______	Provides direction
______	______	Affection	______	______	Desire to have children with
______	______	Good sex partner	______	______	Loves me
______	______	Good traveling partner	______	______	Has money
______	______	Supports my career	______	______	Accepts my values
______	______	Shares my values	______	______	Good communication
______	______	Takes care of me	______	______	Accepts my spending habits
______	______	Accepts my parents			
______	______	Intellectual exchange			

*This inventory was developed on the basis of an idea suggested by Lynda Harriman (1982).

Exchange theory suggests that you will marry the person who offers you the greatest rewards at the lowest cost of all the people who are available to you (Nye, 1980). Four concepts help to explain the exchange process in mate selection:

1. Rewards are the behaviors (your partner looking at you with the "eyes of love"), words (saying "I love you"), resources (being beautiful or handsome, having money), and services (driving you home, typing for you) your partner provides for you that you enjoy and that influence you to continue the relationship.
2. Costs are the unpleasant consequences of a relationship. One man said, "I have to drive across town to pick her up, listen to her nagging mother before we can leave, and be back at her house by midnight."
3. Profit is the excess reward when the costs are subtracted from the rewards.
4. Loss occurs when the costs exceed the rewards.

The Assets and Liabilities Inventory (p. 156) is a way for you to assess the profit you are experiencing in the relationship with your partner.

Exchange concepts operate at three levels of the dating relationship—who can date whom, the conditions of the dating relationship, and the decision to marry. As for whom you date, you are attracted to those who have something to exchange. If you are an attractive, self-confident senior with the social skills of Lady Diana, you will expect a lot in exchange from the partner you date. An unattractive, inept high-school student has little hope of becoming involved in a dating relationship with you, having little to exchange for your looks, status, and skills.

Once you identify a person who can offer the equivalent of what you have to exchange, other bargains are made about the conditions of your continued relationship. More than 35 years ago, two researchers (Waller & Hill, 1951) observed that the person who has the least interest in continuing the relationship can control the relationship. This "principle of least interest" is illustrated by the woman who said, "He wants to date me more than I want to date him, so we end up going where I want to go and doing what I want to do." In this case, the woman trades her company for the man's acquiescence to her choices.

Additional exchanges take place as the partners move toward marriage. They make a marital commitment when each person feels that he or she is getting the partner who offers the most rewards of all potential alternatives. A graduating senior and groom-to-be remarked, "It's easy. I've decided to marry Maria because sharing life with her is more fun than being with anyone else. And marriage is one way to help ensure that we will be together to share our lives across the years."

Consideration

Partners are more likely to continue their involvement in a relationship as long as they derive more profit from that relationship than from any other available to them (Lloyd et al., 1984). They discontinue relationships when the costs exceed the rewards, unless they have no alternative relationship. In this case, they may choose to suffer in an unhappy relationship rather than be alone or go through what they regard as the trauma of divorce.

Parental Image

Whereas the complementary and exchange theories of mate selection are relatively recent, Freud suggested earlier that the choice of a love object in adulthood represents a shift in libidinal energy from the first love objects—the parents. This means that a man looks for a wife like his mother and a woman looks for a husband like her father. In a study of almost 7,000 spouses, Jedlicka (1984) has observed that selecting a partner similar to the opposite-gender parent occurs more often than can be expected by chance.

Sociobiological Aspects of Mate Selection

Sociobiology suggests that there is a biological basis for all social behavior—including mate selection. Based on Charles Darwin's theory of natural selection,

Self-Assessment

Assets and Liabilities Inventory*

According to exchange theory, your partner brings both assets and liabilities to your relationship. The following inventory has been completed by a single woman who is contemplating marrying a divorced man:

Assets	*Liabilities*
1. Intelligent (5)	1. Divorced (3)
2. Sense of humor (4)	2. Has children (3)
3. Good looking (4)	3. Low self-esteem (2)
4. Ambitious (5)	4. In debt (4)
5. Educated (4)	5. Chain smoker (3)

The number to the right of each item is the relative importance (1 = not too significant; 5 = very significant) of each item. In this example, the sum of the assets (22) minus the sum of the liabilities (15) is +7. Higher inventory numbers indicate greater profits. The maximum profit in this case would be 25.

To evaluate the profit of continuing the relationship with your own partner, list her or his assets and liabilities and assign numbers to the relative importance of each characteristic, as in the example above.

Assets	*Liabilities*
1.	1.
2.	2.
3.	3.
4.	4.
5.	5.

*This inventory was developed on the basis of an idea suggested by Lynda Harriman (1982).

which states that the strongest of the species survive, sociobiologists contend that men and women select each other as mates on the basis of their concern for producing offspring who are most capable of surviving.

According to sociobiologists, men look for an attractive, bright, sexually conservative woman who will care for their offspring. Men also look for young women. "It is advantageous for males to have good form vision for females between the ages of 15 and 40. It serves no advantage for men to deposit their cheap sperm in matronly women, at least as far as procreation is concerned. Doing so increases the possibility of congenital aberrations (retardation, cleft palate, etc.)" (Knox & Daniel, 1986).

Women, in contrast, look for a strong, faithful, working man who will provide for their children. If a person ignores these variables, the sociobiologists say, his or her genes are likely to die off and not be perpetuated. (Buss, 1985).

The sociobiological explanation for mate selection is extremely controversial. Critics say that biological concerns are rarely conscious, if present at all, in mate selection. Men and women think more about their partners than about potential offspring when selecting a mate.

Trends

The future of dating relationships will include more people spending more time in a number of such relationships, a gradual shift away from traditional dating practices, increased interracial, interreligious, and interethnic dating, and increased confusion about roles in dating relationships. As noted in the last chapter, both women and men are marrying later than in previous years. The result of such delay is that each person will have more time to become involved with a variety of people before marriage. More time spent dating also has implications for how dating is perceived—initially, more for recreation than for mate selection.

As a result of this shift in dating focus from mate selection to recreation, the traditional dating pattern, which is geared toward early marriage, will become less functional. "Hanging out" and "getting together," whereby individuals go where they can meet members of the opposite gender in informal ways without an introduction, will increase. The women's movement has been instrumental in making some women feel more comfortable about initiating relationships.

The future of dating relationships will also include increased interracial, interreligious, and interethnic dating as desegregation continues and as endogamous pressures subside.

Differences in role expectations will also become more apparent. Whereas the women's movement has sensitized women to seek equalitarian relationships with men, the socialization of men to perceive women in other than traditional roles has been less extensive. As a result, there may be more confusion during first encounters when the modern woman and the traditional man meet. Also, because the women's movement has not influenced all women and because some men are nontraditional, the man seeking a woman who wants an equalitarian relationship may be surprised to find a traditional woman, and vice versa.

Other trends in dating will include greater use of mate-selection technology. As our society becomes more populated, urban, and industrial, there will be fewer personal networks within which to meet eligible mates. Increasingly, individuals who might not otherwise meet through traditional dating patterns will be linked through advertisements in newspapers or magazines and computer and videotape dating clubs.

Finally, as the liberal norms of western societies continue to spread, parents in other societies will come under increasing pressure from their offspring to let them participate in selecting the person with whom they will spend their life. The movement away from arranged marriages is already occurring in India, Africa, Israel, and Malaya.

Summary

Dating is the primary mechanism by which men and women pair off into exclusive, committed relationships. Contemporary functions of dating involve confirmation of a social self, recreation, companionship, intimacy, and sex, socialization, and mate selection.

Although dating may be in groups or in one-to-one relationships, finding a partner isn't always easy. Some meet at work, at a sports club, or through a friend; others establish contacts through newspaper advertisements, computer dating or video cassette clubs, or other dating service organizations.

The typical dating event involves going out to eat, having coffee or a drink, or seeing a movie, play, or concert. Conversation most often focuses on the couple's relationship.

Women view unwanted sexual pressure as the biggest problem on dates. Communication—not knowing what to say or do—is the most frequent problem reported by men.

As dating moves toward mate selection, the partners are influenced by various cultural, sociological, psychological, and perhaps biological factors. Although marriages in some cultures are arranged by parents or other relatives, our culture relies mainly on endogamous and exogamous pressures to guide mate choice.

Sociological aspects of mate selection include homogamy (people prefer someone like themselves) and propinquity (people prefer someone with whom it is convenient to interact).

Psychological aspects of mate selection include complementary needs, exchange theory, and parental image. Complementary needs theory suggests that people select others who have opposite characteristics to their own. They may also seek each other out if they both have the same need at different levels of intensity. Most researchers find little evidence for complementary needs theory.

Exchange theory posits that one individual selects another on the basis of rewards and costs. As long as an individual derives more profit from a relationship with one partner than another, the relationship will continue. Exchange concepts influence who dates whom, the conditions of the dating relationship, and the decision to marry.

The parental image theory of mate selection says that a man looks for a wife like his mother and a woman looks for a husband like her father.

The sociobiological view of mate selection suggests that men and women select each other on the basis of their biological capacity to produce and support healthy offspring. Men seek young women with healthy bodies, and women seek ambitious men who will provide economic support.

Trends in dating relationships include a longer period of dating, a gradual shift from the traditional dating pattern to a more informal one, increased interracial, interreligious, and interethnic dating, increased confusion over dating roles, greater reliance on technology in finding dates, and increased participation by offspring in other societies in their arranged marriages.

Questions for Reflection

1. How does exchange theory help to explain your involvement in your most recent relationship? What specifically are or were the rewards and costs of that relationship?
2. To what degree, if any, would you consider sociobiological factors when selecting a marriage partner?
3. What kinds of influence do your parents have on your dating relationships?

CHOICES

BEGINNING TO DATE someone involves a number of choices, including how interested you should appear to be, how available you should be, and whether to date one or several people.

How Interested Should I Appear to Be?

"If I let a man know I'm interested in him, I lose him," said one woman. "It happens every time. I'm learning to be very distant and cold with men." But her roommate said, "If you don't show your interest, he'll think you're not interested and he'll go away."

A frequent dilemma in dating is whether to let someone know you are interested in her or him. Like all decisions, looking at the positive and negative consequences of each course of action may suggest an answer.

One benefit of showing interest in someone is to give the person the feeling that he or she is attractive and desirable to you. Having the person reciprocate your feelings may not be your goal. "I just wanted her to know that I thought she was stunningly beautiful," said one guy. "If she never gives me another thought, it doesn't matter."

Another benefit is that by showing your interest, the other person doesn't have to guess whether you are interested. If you never get together, it won't be because the other person was unaware that at least one of you had an interest in the other. "A lot of men are shy," said one woman. "If you don't hit them between the eyes with a two by four, they don't know that it's time to ask you out."

The drawbacks of showing your interest in another are possible rejection, investment without profit, and social withdrawal. Since all people will not like you no matter who you are or what you look like, to extend yourself to another is to risk rejection. Some people handle rejection as a part of the dating game and are relatively unbothered by it. Others are devastated by rejection.

Another drawback is the fact that you may have invested your time and have nothing to show for it—time in which you could have done something else. "I spent a semester flirting with this girl, and when I finally called her up for a date, she didn't even know my name," said one man. "What a waste," he said.

A final problem with showing your interest in another is that if you are rejected, you may develop a pattern of avoidance and become depressed, withdrawn, and self-pitying. Such avoidance behavior may perpetuate itself. By being depressed and withdrawn you ensure that someone will not be interested in you, which further confirms your feelings of self-doubt.

Perhaps the best answer to whether to show your interest in another is yes—a little at a time. Being friendly by saying "hello" and smiling are sufficient expressions of your interest in another to stimulate a response if the other person is interested. Smiling back and being friendly might be met by further escalation of friendliness on your part. If the person does not reciprocate your overtures, you may conclude that he or she is not interested in you. But rather than decide that something is wrong with you, consider that something may be wrong with the other person (because he or she is not attracted to someone as terrific as you) and take your affections elsewhere.

How Available Should I Be?

Assuming that someone is showing an interest in you and wants to date you, how available should you be? If the person asks you

(Continued)

out on Thursday for Friday night, should you go? If you agree to go out Friday, will the person think you have nothing else to do but sit in your dorm all weekend because no one else wants you? If you don't go, will the person ask someone else and begin a dating relationship with her or him? The best answer might be to say, "I would really like to go out but cannot go tomorrow night. Please ask me another time." If the person is interested in you, your unavailability will more likely spur than deter interest. Making someone wait a week to get a date with you increases your value to that person and makes you both feel good about each other on the first date.

One suggestion to the person doing the asking. Rather than saying, "Are you doing anything next Friday?," say "Would you like to go out to dinner and see a movie next Friday?" The latter question avoids the possibility that people will feel bad by having to tell you that no one has asked them out and they aren't doing anything but watching paint dry.

Should I Date One or Several People?

Is it best to date one or several people? The answer will vary, depending on the person. One advantage of dating one person is to learn what it is like to manage a sustained relationship. If you date someone for a longer period of time, then you have a greater chance of experiencing and negotiating conflict. Being able to resolve conflict in an interpersonal relationship is a very valuable skill.

Dating one person will also prevent you from dating others. If you begin to date one person in your freshman year and continue to do so until your senior year, you will miss the experience of knowing a variety of people with different interests and values.

On the other hand, dating one person whom you enjoy may be more desirable than dating 50 others whom you don't enjoy. "Why should I date around, when all I want to do is be with Stan?" one woman asked.

A pattern some people adopt is first to date a wide variety of people. Then, around age 20, they begin to focus on the one person they might want to marry and date him or her exclusively for a period of several years.

Impact of Social Influences on Choices

Whether you date one or several people will be influenced by whether your peers are doing so and whether the person you most like to date will tolerate your seeing other people. If all of your friends actively avoid committed relationships and talk with you about avoiding "getting trapped," you are much more likely to "play the field" in your dating relationships. If the person you most enjoy dating says that he or she will not continue to date you if you are going to date others, your decision will depend on your alternative choices. If you have a number of other people whom you enjoy and who enjoy you, you are not likely to give them up for one person. However, if you have only a few others to date and you don't like them as much as the person asking you to give up others, you will probably agree to a monogamous relationship. Hence, whether you date many or one is really a decision based on your interactions with others in your life.

CHAPTER 6

Life-Style Alternatives

Contents

Is It True?*

1. The "real" reason that society requires a marriage license is the physical care and economic support of children.
2. Women view "loss of freedom" as a major disadvantage of marriage as much as men do.
3. Married people live longer and are more healthy than single people.
4. Most unmarried adults say that they are single by deliberate choice rather than by circumstances beyond their control.
5. Marriage will continue to be the dominant life-style choice for most Americans.

*1=T; 2=F; 3=T; 4=T; 5=T.

ONE WAY TO view your life is as a series of activities experienced alone or with other people. Eating, working, sleeping, seeing movies, attending concerts, and clipping coupons are all activities that occur within the context of a life-style choice. Although most people eventually opt for marriage, about 6 percent choose singlehood. An even smaller percentage choose to live in communal, contract cohabitation, or other alternative life styles.

Marriage

Data – Of all life styles, marriage is the option chosen by more than 94 percent of all Americans (white, black, Hispanic, and Asian). Every year, about 5 million people choose to tie the marital knot. (*Statistical Abstract of the United States*, 1987)

As we noted earlier, marriage and the family have traditionally served several main functions in our society: to replace old members with new, socialized members; to regulate sexual behavior; and to stabilize adult personalities by providing companionship.

Consideration

The companionship-intimacy function of marriage has become more important as the form of marriage has changed. Unlike the traditional marriage, which was formal and authoritarian, emphasizing ritual and discipline, the modern marriage pattern is delineated in terms of emotion, mutual affection, sympathetic understanding, and comradeship. The need for intimacy and companionship has become so strong that many couples consider divorce when they no longer feel "in love" or "able to communicate" with their partners. Other differences between the traditional and modern marriage are presented in Table 6.1.

Recently, the traditional justifications for marriage have been questioned. There is little concern now that our society would "disappear" if people stopped marrying. Children would continue to be born, and the increase in single-parent families suggests that the husband and wife team is not the only pattern for rearing children.

The argument that marriage tends to regulate sexual behavior is true, as most spouses have intercourse with each other most of the time. But again, the

TABLE 6.1 TRADITIONAL AND MODERN MARRIAGES COMPARED

Traditional Marriage	*Modern Marriage*
Emphasis on ritual and roles.	Emphasis on companionship.
Couples do not live together before marriage.	Couples may live together before marriage.
Wife takes husband's last name.	Wife may keep her maiden name.
Man dominant; woman submissive.	Neither spouse dominant.
Rigid roles for husband and wife.	Flexible roles for spouses.
One income (the husband's).	Two incomes.
Husband initiates sex; wife complies.	Sex initiated by either spouse.
Wife takes care of children.	Parents share childrearing.
Education important for husband, not for wife.	Education equally important for both.
Husband's career decides family residence.	Family residence decided by career of either spouse.

issue is children, and the development of contraceptive technology has made it possible for individuals to make love without making babies. It is the use of contraceptives, not marriage, that now prevents unwanted children.

The emotional support each spouse derives from the marital relationship remains one of the basic functions of marriage. In our social world, which consists mainly of impersonal, secondary relationships, a sense of belonging may be particularly important. But proponents of singlehood are quick to point out that soaring divorce rates suggest that marriage does not offer much emotional support for some people and that an array of intimate friendships may be superior to the one-to-one marital relationship. Still, most of us have been socialized to believe that it is better to have one relationship for 50 years than to have 25 relationships of two-year durations.

I think I'd be really great for a guy. If it happens, it happens. If it doesn't, I'll get a kitten.
—Ophrah Winfrey

Reasons for Marriage

Data – In a study of 999 college students on 104 campuses, 85 percent said that they wanted to get married. (Stewart, 1986)

Reasons for most of us being drawn to marriage include personal fulfillment, companionship, security, and parenthood.

Personal Fulfillment

We are socialized as children to believe that getting married is what adult men and women do. Even if our parents are divorced, we learn that being married is what they wanted, but it didn't work out. Marriage often becomes a goal to achieve. Achieving that goal is assumed to give us a sense of personal fulfillment.

To have and to hold from this day forward For better, for worse, for richer, for poorer In sickness and in health, to love and to cherish Till death do us part.
—Book of Common Prayer

Companionship

Many people marry primarily for companionship—for a *primary group relationship.* Primary groups are characterized by intimate, affectionate associations in which there is mutual love and caring. The family in which you grew up is a primary group. Your parents loved and cared for you more than anyone else.

Although marriage does not ensure it, companionship is the greatest expected benefit of marriage. Companionship is talking about and doing things with someone you love; it is creating a history with someone. "Only my husband and I know the things we've shared," said one wife. "The shrimp dinner at Ocean City, the walk down Bourbon Street, and the chipmunk in our backyard are part of our joint memory bank."

Just how many married people are there and what percent of our population do they represent?

Data – There are more than 107 million married people in our society. As a group, married people represent 63 percent of our population. (*Statistical Abstract of the United States,* 1987)

Data – Mexican Americans are more likely to be married than blacks; whites are more likely to be married than both groups. (*Statistical Abstract of the United States,* 1987)

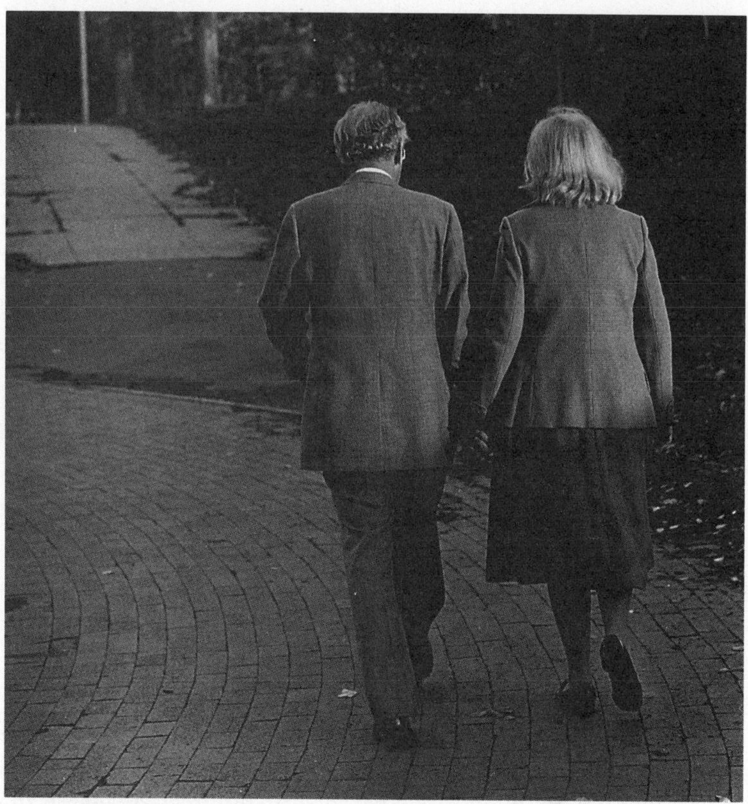

Companionship is a major benefit of marriage.

Security

People also marry for the emotional and legal security marriage can provide. A 32-year-old single person remarked, "I've been through three relationships in the past year, and it's getting old. I want security. I want to get in a relationship where my partner and I will let ourselves completely go and commit ourselves to each other for the full trip."

Parenthood

Some people marry to have children. Although some are willing to live with someone, it is rare that they express a desire for children outside of marriage. There is a strong presumption in our society that only spouses should have children. Role entry to parenthood is through marriage. One couple (both Ph.D.s) who had lived together for seven years said they decided to marry "so we could begin our family."

Other Benefits

There are also some side benefits to being married. From an economic viewpoint, two can definitely live together more cheaply than they can live apart. In addition, marrieds live longer, are more healthy, and report higher levels of social and psychological well-being than singles (Feinson, 1985).

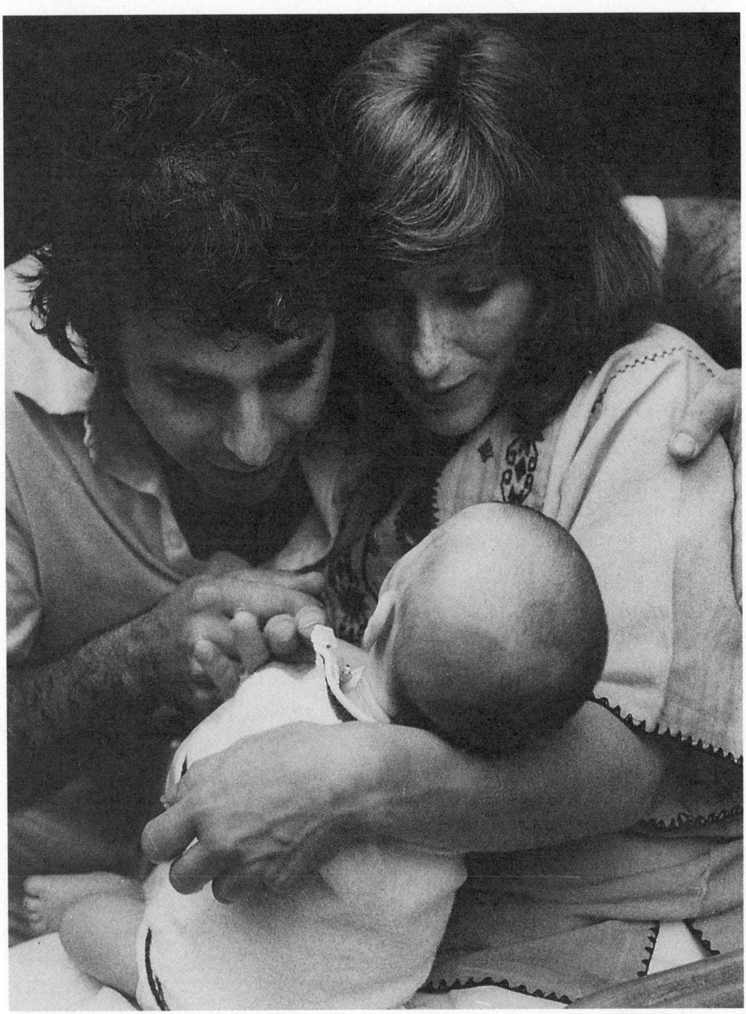

Marriage is often in reference to children.

Indeed, some people say that getting married might not be a bad idea because they don't want to grow old alone and have no one to care for or about them. One study of 76 older married couples in which one of the spouses was recuperating from being in the hospital supports this notion. The "well" spouse, regardless of gender, did provide physical care and psychological support for the sick spouse. The researcher (Johnson, 1985) concludes:

> The many years of shared experiences, of hardships as well as successes, are usually viewed as a source of cohesion. With the illness of one spouse, when additional demands are placed on the marriage, the interdependence that had developed over the years appears to provide the means to meet these needs, usually without reservations. (p. 171)

If a person divorces, the desire to remarry is high. Five out of six divorced men and three out of four divorced women remarry. Regardless of the reason, marriage seems to offer what most people want and miss once they have experienced it.

Data – In a study of 1,504 adults, 65 percent of the married subjects compared with 55 percent of the single subjects reported that their lives are satisfying. (Jankowski, 1985)

Consideration

Of course, it is possible that healthy, happy, satisfied people are more likely to marry (or are selected for marriage) rather than marriage creating such people.

Singlehood

We are witnessing a population explosion of "solos"—people who live alone, outside a family altogether.
—Alvin Toffler

The life-style choice being considered by an increasing number of Americans is singlehood. Law separates people into "marrieds" and "singles." No matter how married a couple may feel, if they are not legally married by ceremony or common law, they are two single individuals. Also, regardless of how single a married person may view himself or herself, unless the marriage has been dissolved by law or death of the spouse, that person is still married.

Categories of Singles

There are about 48 million single adults over the age of 18 in the United States, but they are not all alike. The different categories of singles include the never married, the separated or divorced, and the widowed.

Never-Married Singles

It is true that I never should have married, but I didn't want to live without a man. Brought up to respect the conventions, love had to end in marriage. I'm afraid it did.
—Bette Davis

Data – Never-married singles represent 20,543,000 men and 16,377,000 women over the age of 18. The total group constitutes 21.5 percent of our population. In the United States, 19 percent of all whites, 35 percent of all blacks, and 25 percent of all persons of other races (including Mexican Americans and Asian Americans) have never been married. (*Statistical Abstract of the United States*, 1987)

The never-marrieds represent the largest proportion of singles in the United States. Since 1970, there has been a dramatic increase in the percentage of men and women between the ages of 25 and 29 who are single. In 1970, 19 percent of the males and 11 percent of the females in these age ranges had never married; by 1985, these percentages had jumped to 39 percent and 26 percent, respectively (U.S. Bureau of the Census, 1986).

There is a larger percentage of single people at these ages now than in previous years for several reasons. These include a greater number of women in college, increased employment opportunities for women, more social support for singlehood (the woman's movement, peers), the availability of effective contraception, and no available partner.

Data – For every four unmarried men, there are five unmarried women. (U.S. Bureau of the Census, 1986)

Beyond the numbers, there is a new wave of youth who feel that their commitment is to themselves in early adulthood and to marriage only later. This translates into staying in school, establishing one's self in a career, and becoming economically and emotionally independent. The old pattern was to leap from school to marriage. The new pattern is to look, wait, and prepare before leaping.

Data – In a study of 999 college students at 104 campuses, 7 percent said that they wanted to remain single. (Stewart, 1986)

Separated and Divorced Singles

There is a tendency to think of single people as only those who have never married. But statistics show otherwise.

Data – There are 5,264,000 divorced men and 7,826,000 divorced women in our society who are "single again." As a group, the divorced represent 7.2 percent of our population. In the United States, 7 percent of all whites, 9 percent of all blacks, and 6 percent of all persons of other races are divorced. (*Statistical Abstract of the United States,* 1987)

For many of the divorced, the return to singlehood is not an easy transition. The recently separated and divorced are the least likely to say that they are satisfied with their life (28 percent of the divorced compared to 65 percent of the married) and with their health (46 percent versus 66 percent) (Jankowski, 1985).

After the initial impact of separation and divorce, most people remarry or adjust to and enjoy singlehood. One divorced man said, "I can stand being alone. Perhaps I even have a gift for it. What I can't stand is taking what's available until something better comes along."

Widowed Singles

Whereas some separated and divorced people choose to be single rather than remain in an unhappy marriage, the widowed are forced into singlehood.

Data – There are 2,109,000 widowed men and 11,375,000 widowed women in our society. As a group, the widowed represent 7.4 percent of our population. In the United States, 7 percent of all whites, 9 percent of all blacks, and 5 percent of all persons of other races are widowed. (*Statistical Abstract of the United States,* 1987)

The widowed exhibit higher rates of mortality and suicide and evaluate their health more negatively. Lacking money and feeling lonely may also be problems. But widowhood can have positive aspects. One widow said, "I miss my husband, but I'm not going to grieve about something I can't change. I've got friends and time to travel. I feel like I've been given a second life, and I'm going to make the most of it." Adjustment to widowhood will be discussed in Chapter 18.

Singlehood as a Life-Style Choice

Singlehood has different meanings to the never married, the separated, the divorced, and the widowed, but there are two basic ways of viewing it—as a life style or as a stage leading to marriage or remarriage. An increasing number of people are choosing singlehood as a life style.

TABLE 6.2 REASONS TO REMAIN SINGLE

Benefits of Singlehood	*Disadvantages of Marriage*
Freedom to have multiple sex partners.	Restriction to one sex partner.
Freedom to have a variety of interpersonal relationships.	Restriction to one basic relationship.
Freedom to move from city to city.	Restriction of career mobility.
Freedom to travel.	Travel restricted by spouse and children.
Responsibility for one.	Responsibility for spouse and children.
Not required to interact with others on an intimate basis.	Required to interact with others in household.
Spontaneous life style.	Life sometimes too routine.

Data – When 482 adults were asked why they were unmarried, 46 percent said by deliberate choice, 14 percent said by chance, 23 percent said by circumstances beyond their control, and 17 percent said that they did not know why. (Austrom & Hanel, 1985) In another study of over 500 college students, 19 percent of the men and 16 percent of the women said that they would be willing to remain single. (Billingham & Sack, 1986)

The reasons for remaining single include a desire to enjoy the benefits of singlehood and to avoid the entanglements of marriage. These reasons are detailed in Table 6.2.

The Benefits of Singlehood

I want to be alone.
—Greta Garbo

Benefits of deciding to remain single include freedom, autonomy, and spontaneity. Regarding freedom, being single permits the individual to pursue a range of activities with which marriage and children might interfere. Individuals who wish to establish themselves in a career without the interference of a spouse and babies might find singlehood particularly rewarding. Singlehood also permits a larger sense of freedom. "Being single allows me to do what I want to do, when I want to do it, and with the person or persons I choose," said a 27-year-old computer programmer. "There are no fences around what I want to do, and a spouse is the thickest, tallest fence I know of."

Freedom for the single person may also mean freedom to select different values, have sex with different people, travel more, and have no responsibility for others. The single person enjoys the freedom to change philosophies or life styles without considering the effects of his or her actions on another. "In the past two years since I've joined the health club, I've made many new friends," a graduate student said. "Just as I have changed friends, I think I would have needed to change spouses if my partner had not had the same experience." Behavioral psychologist, B.F. Skinner, said that one of the reasons he could not join the Twin Oaks commune (which used his book *Walden Two* as a model) is because he would have to get a divorce. "Communes are not my wife's cup of tea," he remarked.

The single person may also change sexual partners at will. The freedom to have a variety of sexual relationships is regarded as a major advantage of being single. "When you're married," remarked a divorced college teacher, "you have to act like you aren't sexually attracted to others, and you dare not put your thoughts into action. Although the sex life of the single person isn't what married people fantasize it is, it has its advantages."

Freedom from responsibility and freedom to travel are other advantages of the single life style (Harayda, 1986). Mates are responsible to each other and for any children they may have; the single person is responsible only to those he or she chooses. A recent graduate who is single said, "I don't have to use my

Singles who want to meet a wide variety of people may use video dating services.

paycheck to buy anything except what I want, nor do I need to spend my time cooking or running other people's errands."

Data – Men are much more concerned than women about the loss of freedom in marriage. In one study comparing 25 never-married men with 25 never-married women, 72 percent of the men cited "loss of freedom" as a drawback of marriage; only 8 percent of the women viewed this as a drawback. (Greenglass, 1985)

People who choose singlehood may be attracted by the spontaneity that the life style offers. The married person is probably better able to predict what he or she will be doing, when, than the single person. Some single people abhor regimentation. A friend may call, a new person may be met at work, or someone may drop by, and this will affect the activities for that evening or weekend. "I live not knowing what's going to happen next," observed a 32-year-old accountant, "and I like it that way."

Exhibit 6.1 reflects the insights of a 32-year-old woman in her first year of law school. She comments on both the positive and negative aspects of singlehood.

Most people remain single for a combination of the reasons we have discussed, but some do so out of a sense of responsibility for an ill or aging parent, or as a result of physical disability, homosexuality, or lack of an available partner. Some people also have a fear of marriage. One senior art student said:

Consideration

In making a decision to marry, it is important to be aware that the longer the decision is delayed, the more difficult it is to find a partner. This is particularly true for women. Because men marry women who are younger than they are, each year that a woman stays single, she reduces her chances of marriage the following year. A 25-year-old woman has a 50 percent chance of getting married; a 30-year-old, 20 percent; a 35-year-old, 5 percent; and a 40-year-old or older woman, 1 percent. One of every five females does not have a potential mate. (Richardson, 1985) The problem for single black females is even greater because there are fewer eligible black males for the number of black females.

Exhibit 6.1

A Single Woman's View

At this point in my life, I enjoy being single. Of course, there are disadvantages to singlehood, but I like the privacy and independence that it affords me.

Singlehood gives me a tremendous amount of freedom and time. Since I am responsible only for myself, I can decide to relocate and/or continue my education. This freedom allows me to change, grow, and develop as a person. Part of my growth is dependent on maintaining diverse relationships, including male friendships. Being single, I can consciously choose to become romantically involved with males who would not be threatened by my male friends. Singlehood permits all sorts of small but important freedoms. For example, I can sleep late, read in bed, travel, visit with friends after work, and eat odd meals at unusual times. I also have the option not to prepare meals, clean the house, or answer the phone.

Being single has made me more aware of the importance of developing a positive self-image and learning to "pat myself" on the back. It has been essential for my mental health to develop a good support system and to confide in close friends. I have also discovered the need to be competent in traditionally male areas of expertise, such as car and house repairs. Learning simple tasks like replacing a windowpane, repairing the lawn mower, and tuning the car engine increases my self-confidence and sense of independence.

I feel comfortable with my single status after listening to some of my married female friends discuss what is expected of them in terms of their role as a wife and mother. This is not a feeling of superiority because being comfortable with my choice does not prevent an occasional sense of ostracism for not being married. Also, feeling good about myself does not eliminate all the anxiety I have about singlehood. For example, I wonder if I am possibly missing something wonderful by not having children.

One of the most difficult aspects of singlehood to cope with is the attitude and behavior of a few of my peers. The belief that being single indicates a personality defect makes me defensive about my life style. Occasionally, I feel that I am viewed as a threat to married females, particularly if I have a professional relationship with their husbands. Also, my family is not completely supportive of my single status. Although my father was pleased and proud of my independence, his death removed much of my family support, and I believe that my mother and sisters would be relieved if I married.

The fact that I am single does not mean that I do not want a serious long-term relationship. However, being single is a challenge because, to be independent and to be comfortable enough to live alone, I have to like myself. So even though there are times I am lonely, overall I enjoy being single.

> My mom has been divorced three times. Marriage to me means nothing but arguments, misery, and grief. Why would anyone want to get married? I can't think of a reason.

Some people are single and don't want to be. For them, singlehood has little to do with fear of a commitment, alarm over the divorce rate, or not wanting children. Rather, not being able to meet people, not having met the right person, and having very high expectations of marriage are the primary reasons.

Whatever the reason, marriage does not attract everyone. Contemporary people who have never married (at the time of this writing) include Linda Ronstadt, Bruce Willis, Diane Sawyer, Steven Wright, Gloria Steinem, Ralph Nader, Barbara Jordan, Richard Chamberlain, Bernadette Peters, and Jacqueline Bisset. These individuals have chosen singlehood as a life style and view it as a positive experience.

The Disadvantages of Marriage

The land of marriage has this peculiarity, that strangers are desirous of inhabiting it, whilst its natural inhabitants would willingly be banished from thence.
—Montaigne

As Table 6.2 indicates, those who opt for singlehood may view marriage as restricting their potential for personal growth, trapping them in an undesirable role (spouse), or restricting their mobility. A single journalist wrote:

> I'm not the kind to be locked up in one room with one person for 50 years. I'd much rather take my chances with the singles who don't have stable relationships. I feel smothered by a one-to-one relationship and really don't like it. I need the space. And I would go nuts having to ask permission or consider someone else's needs every time I made a decision about something.

Related to the feeling that a person rarely maximizes his or her potential inside the marital relationship is the conviction that the specific roles of wife and husband are undesirable. Some women feel the role of the wife is to be a nurse and waitress to her husband. Some men feel their role as husband is a greater trap than the wife's. One middle-aged man remarked, "As a husband, I am expected to be economically responsible for everything, eat breakfast and dinner with my wife, stay in the house from six at night until morning, have sex only with my wife, and enjoy weekends with a two-year-old."

The spouse role can also isolate a person from other people. In a traditional marriage, the partners must carefully control the level of each new relationship for the sake of their marriage. Such control may result in feelings of isolation and loneliness. One woman remarked that she had been more lonely since she had married than when she was single. "My single friends don't call me anymore because they assume I have a built-in companion. I live in the same house with Rex, but companion isn't the word I would use to describe him. I'm terribly lonely."

Even those who have good marital relationships often feel it is unrealistic to expect their partner to satisfy all their emotional, social, physical, and sexual needs. "To be all things to one person is impossible," one married man concluded. "My wife and I love and care for each other, but we feel that we've got to find some way to take the heavy responsibility off each of us to be everything to the other. We haven't found the answer."

Some people also feel that marriage is no longer necessary. Society has encouraged marriage for the care and protection of children, but individuals may marry for different reasons. Men have traditionally married for sex; women, for economic security. In today's society, the idea that sex is justified within the context of a love relationship decreases the importance of marriage for sex, and the increasing economic independence of women is diminishing that particular reason for marriage. A divorced woman who recently received her Ph.D. remarked, "For the past 11 years, I needed my husband for food and shelter. Now I am economically self-sufficient. For the first time, getting married can be a choice for me. And although I may change, I doubt I'll choose to remarry."

Singlehood and Loneliness

It is sometimes assumed that most unmarried people are unhappy because they live alone—that to be alone is to be unhappy. But in one study, more than 400 older never-married men and women said that their happiness depends not on whether they interact with others but on their standard of living and level of activity (Keith, 1986). Those who had adequate enough incomes to avoid having to always worry about money and who had enough things to do that they enjoyed (either through employment or self-generated activity) were happy.

Data – About one-third of the men and women in this study reported never associating with neighbors or friends. (Keith, 1986)

However, other studies have demonstrated the importance of friendships among the never married for personal happiness. In one study, female singles were more satisfied with their friendships than male singles (Austrom & Hanel, 1985). Two other researchers (Cockrum & White, 1985) emphasize the importance of social relationships for those selecting the single life style:

> Perhaps the most important implication for practitioners involves the salience of social support for life satisfaction of never-married singles. Helping individuals develop skills that facilitate effective interpersonal relationships is possibly one of the most critical goals for enhancing life satisfaction. If individuals have the capability of establishing and maintaining effective social and personal relationships, they will have the social-support systems that can serve to strengthen their well-being and buffer them from the effects of loneliness. (p. 556)

Many singles are alone but not lonely.

One study of older (over age 60) unmarried persons revealed that dating was one of the most important activities in which they engaged. Respondents said that their dating partner was a "friend, confidant, lover, and caregiver." The researchers who interviewed the respondents said that dating provided a "buffer against loneliness" (Bulcroft & O'Connor, 1986). In general, the idea that single people are lonely and discontent is inaccurate (Rollins, 1986).

Singlehood as a Stage

For some people, singlehood is not a permanent choice but a stage between various life-style choices they make throughout their lives. A not unusual pattern is for a person to experience singlehood, marriage, divorce (return to singlehood), living together, and remarriage. The decision to opt for any of these at any given time may be complex. Contributing to the selection of one life-style alternative is the perception of the positive and negative consequences of doing so compared to those of the other alternatives. The single person may be free but lonely and perceive marriage as worth the cost of lost freedom to gain companionship. The married person may be secure but bored and view the variety of singlehood as worth the cost of security. The person who lives with another may enjoy the spontaneity of "a relationship based on love, not law" but not like the lack of permanence of the relationship. Legitimizing the relationship through marriage may be worth risking the loss of some spontaneity.

Consideration

Decisions to end or maintain a specific relationship can be explained in terms of exchange theory. People enter and remain in relationships or life styles only as long as the individuals evaluate these relationships and life styles as profitable (profit in exchange terms is rewards minus costs). "I know it sounds crazy," said one 40-year-old bachelor, "but I feel it's time for me to be married because the advantages of this freedom don't mean anything anymore."

Some Options Along the Way

Marriage or singlehood are the two predominant life-style choices (see the Life-Style Preference Inventory in the following Self-Assessment for a list of life styles). In addition, some people choose living together, contract cohabitation, or communal living. We will discuss living together in Chapter 7; here, we will focus on contract cohabitation, communes, and other life-style options.

Contract Cohabitation

Contract cohabitation involves hiring a companion. Edmund Van Deusen, a California writer, who did so, recalls, "My principal need was for someone to talk to . . .. Second, I needed a warm body to go to bed with." Van Deusen placed the following advertisement in the *Los Angeles Free Press,* interviewed several applicants, and selected the woman who best fit his job description:

> Freelance writer looking for woman who would be interested in room, board, and $500 a month. Send name, phone number, and photo to Tom Smith, Box 1251, Laguna Beach, Cal. 92652, (1974, p. 25).

Contract cohabitation is an eating, sleeping, and living arrangement between employer and employee, based on a written or unwritten employment contract. All contract items, including salary, are defined by the employer and accepted in advance by the employee. Free hours, annual vacations, and social or work activities outside the relationship are guaranteed by the terms of the contract. Sex is expected but cannot be demanded or denied. The employment contract can be canceled at any time by either party without reason or explanation.

An example of a job description for a contract cohabitation relationship follows:

> Specific Tasks—Light housekeeping, meal preparation, household shopping, estimated time per day: two hours. Companionship—Weekdays: 6:00 to 8:00 P.M.; Saturday: 3:00 P.M. on; Sunday: all day; Bedtime: normally 11:00 P.M.; Night off: Wednesday; Vacation: one week with pay per year; Client entertaining: optional; Social entertaining: required. (Van Deusen, 1974, p. 111)

The philosophy behind contract cohabitation is that the best way to get what you want from an interpersonal relationship is to specify your expectations in advance and pay for them. But beyond the specific exchange of money and services is the capacity to develop a caring relationship unencumbered by the roles of husband and wife. Van Deusen writes:

> This leaves me free to cherish Elaine [the first woman who became involved in Van Deusen's contract cohabitation], whom I have no need or desire to change. Why should I? In 30 days I may never see her again. I can enjoy her for who she is, and she can enjoy me in return. Neither of us is trying to force the other into a preconceived fantasy image. Neither of us feels possessive or possessed. Neither of us is depending on the other for self-image or identity. (p. 99)

Consideration

Van Deusen concludes that contract cohabitation, like all other life-style alternatives that involve another person, is something you have to work at: ". . . contract cohabitation has provided some very enriching experiences for me and the women who have lived here," says Van Deusen. "You get to know someone very well, and you avoid the entrapment of a love affair or marriage if you aren't ready for those types of commitments."

Historical analysis has shown communal movements are not randomly distributed across time and space but flourish only at points of relatively sharp social and cultural discontinuity.
—Angela Aidala

COMMUNES

Single individuals and married couples (with or without children) may choose a life style that includes an array of interpersonal relationships and join a *commune.* Also referred to as an *intentional community,* a *collective,* or a *cooperative,* a commune is a group of three or more adults with no legal or blood ties who live together by free choice. Many groups have about six members; the Farm in Summertown, Tennessee, has more than 1,600 members.

Self-Assessment

Life-Style Preference Inventory

Below is a list of life-style choices. To indicate your preference, assign a number from 0 to 10 for each life style (0 = no desire to experience this life style; 10 = a strong desire).

Life Style	Preference
Sexual	
Heterosexual	______
Homosexual	______
Bisexual	______
Singlehood	
Single until meet "right" person	______
Single until establish career	______
Single forever	______
Marriage	
Traditional roles	______
Shared roles	______
One income or career	______
Two incomes or careers	______
Sexually monogamous	______
Sexually open	______
Group marriage	______
Children	
None	______
One	______
Two	______
Three	______
Four or more	______
Live Together	
To further assess relationship	______
As a prelude to marriage	______
As a permanent alternative to marriage	______
For economic convenience	______
Housing	
Live alone	______
Live with someone of same gender	______
Live with someone of opposite gender	______
Live in commune	______
Live in contract cohabitation arrangement	______

Based on the preferences you selected, write a brief description of the life style you prefer. If you are involved in a relationship, also ask your partner to indicate her or his preferences for each of these life styles.

Data – There are over 1,000 communes in the United States, Canada, and other countries. (Directory of Intentional Communities, 1985)

Consideration

Specific information on communes in the United States, Canada, and other countries is detailed in the Directory of Intentional Communities, available from *Communities*, 126 Sun Street, Stelle, IL 60919. The most extensive library on communes has been collected by the Center for Communal Studies, Indiana State University, 8600 University Blvd., Evansville, IN 47712. These sources will be helpful in locating a commune with values and a life style consistent with your interests.

Types of Communes

Communes may be categorized as either rural or urban. Urban communes often cluster around universities. Membership tends to be more fluid in urban communes than in rural communes, which call for greater commitment. A commune member in Boston can move into a solo apartment at any time; moving out is harder for the communard of rural Twin Oaks, in Louisa, Virginia.

Data – In a study of more than 500 college students, 10 percent of the males and 3 percent of the females said they would be willing to live in an urban commune with shared sex. (Billingham & Sack, 1986).

In addition to the urban-rural dichotomy, there are a variety of other types of communes. Spiritual communes include such groups as the Amish, Abode of the Message, and the Agahpay Fellowship. People join religious communes to share a spiritual experience with others.

Ideological communes such as Twin Oaks in Louisa, Virginia are committed to a secular theme, such as behavioral psychology. Those who join an ideological commune wish to participate in planning and implementing a miniature society consistent with specific ideological principles. Youth communes that do not fall into the hip or ideological categories are usually composed of young people who simply want to share the economic or interpersonal advantages of group living. Group-marriage communes have the primary goal of working out new styles of interpersonal and family relationships. Finally, communes for the elderly include the Share-A-Home Association in Winter Park, Florida. This group has a manager who oversees the day-to-day operation of the home. Under this arrangement, seniors can enjoy the companionship of each other without being bothered by the details of running a home, planning meals, and other duties.

Motivations for Joining a Commune

Interpersonal and economic concerns are primary motivations in joining a commune. "I wanted to feel a connectedness to a variety of people, not just one," said one communard. "In marriage or in a living-together relationship, you're stuck with one other person. In a commune, you're not." Group living is

Communes provide an opportunity to enjoy multiple relationships.

also cheaper. Most communes have central dining facilities and large houses or dorms that provide inexpensive sleeping quarters.

Women often have another incentive for communal living—equality. Childrearing is often considered a community task and is assigned to men as well as to women. Household chores are also equally divided.

Stability of Communes

No matter how many communes anybody invents, the family always comes back.
—Margaret Mead

Most communes do not last longer than two years. Most people require more individual freedom and autonomy than communes can permit if they are to survive. There are exceptions, however. The Farm (Summertown, Tennessee) and Twin Oaks (Louisa, Virginia) are now in their second decade.

Serial Monogamy

Elizabeth Taylor, Mickey Rooney, and Walter Huston have all lived the life style of *serial monogamy*—marrying, divorcing, remarrying, divorcing, remarrying, etc. This life style results in an individual having a series of spouses, but only one at a time. Rarely do individuals plan a life style of serial monogamy. It is more of an emergent social fact, based on an individual's desire to have a satisfying marital relationship.

Data – Out of 526 college students, 9 percent of both males and females reported they would be willing to participate in serial monogamy. (Billingham & Sack, 1986)

Spouse Swapping

Going with your spouse to another couple's home and exchanging sexual partners is *spouse swapping* (also referred to as "swinging"). Those who spouse swap say that it is an honest form of adultery. "Rather than sneak around and have sex with someone my spouse does not know about," said one spouse, "we both do it at the same time and in the same place."

Data – Out of 526 college students, 13 percent of the males and 3 percent of the females reported that they would be willing to participate in spouse swapping. (Billingham & Sack, 1986)

Group Marriage

If you and your spouse lived with several other husband–wife couples and each of the men was married to each of the women and vice versa, you would be involved in a *group marriage.* Although such arrangements do exist, they are illegal.

Data – Out of 526 college students, 5 percent of the males and 1 percent of the females reported that they would be willing to participate in a group marriage. (Billingham & Sack, 1986)

In analyzing the questionnaires of the 526 students in the Billingham & Sack (1986) study, the researchers observed that although overall agreement exists between men and women in regard to their willingness to participate in alternative life styles, men generally are more interested in alternatives that "provide greater freedom and perhaps less responsibility" (p. 37).

Single Parenthood

Rarely do individuals choose to rear a child without a spouse. Those who do so feel that they want a baby even though no particular marriageable person is in their life at the time. Because this is more of a "biological clock" issue than a preference for the single parenthood life style, we will discuss this topic in Chapter 14 on "Planning Children." Also, because most single-parent families result from divorce, we will discuss the nature of these families in Chapter 18 on "Divorce, Widowhood, and Remarriage."

Trends

Marriage will continue to be the dominant life style choice for most Americans. Its lure of companionship, commitment, and economic security seems to offer more than alternate life styles. Although some people may delay getting married for educational or career reasons, there is no evidence of a major trend away from marriage.

Contract cohabitation has not attracted a large following and will probably continue to be a rare form of singlehood. Unlike contract cohabitation, communal living has historical precedents (the Shakers, Oneida, and Amish) and is the life style of about one-quarter of a million people. However, for an individual to be happy in a commune, she or he must reconcile personal and community goals. The existence of more than 1,000 communes worldwide suggests that a number of people are not only capable of but enjoy this merging of individual and group goals.

Summary

Traditionally, marriage has existed to replenish society with socialized members, to regulate sexual behavior, and to stabilize adult personalities. However, the problem of overpopulation and the availability of convenient, effective contraception have undermined the first two functions. Emotional support remains the primary function of marriage.

The decision to marry involves assessing the advantages and disadvantages of marriage compared to singlehood. Marriage offers a potentially intense primary relationship over time and avoids the potential loneliness associated with singlehood. But singlehood offers freedom to do as one wishes and avoids the obstacles to personal fulfillment associated with marriage. For many Americans, the decision to marry or to be single is not permanent. Many singles contemplate marriage, and many marrieds ponder whether they should stay married.

Older individuals (primarily men) who have the economic resources sometimes choose contract cohabitation. This arrangement is an employer–employee relationship in which behavioral expectations are specified, agreed to, and paid for.

Communal living is another infrequently chosen life-style option. There are hundreds of communes to select from, including those that emphasize religion, ideology, or group marriage. The advantages of communal arrangements include living with several people in an intimate environment and sharing expenses.

Spouse swapping and group marriage are also infrequently chosen alternatives to marriage. Generally, men are more willing than women to participate in these alternative life styles.

Marriage continues to be the dominant choice for most Americans.

Questions for Reflection

1. Which life style do you feel offers the most benefits? Why?
2. How would you defend your involvement in each life-style choice to your grandparents?
3. What do you think will be the dominant life style in the year 2000? Why?

CHOICES

BECAUSE OUR SOCIETY is becoming more tolerant of alternative life styles, a number of choices are realistic options for you. The basic choices and issues to consider follow.

Is Marriage for You?

The decision to marry or not might be based on the perceived consequences (positive and negative) of the respective life styles. The primary benefits of marriage include increased companionship, security, parenthood, and the development of a shared history. Although cohabitants may have made an emotional commitment to each other, spouses additionally have made a social and legal commitment. The blend of these commitments results in married people feeling more secure with each other and their relationship. "When your partner wants to marry you," said one male, "you know she is serious about you. Otherwise, she could disappear the next day, and you might never see her again."

Marriage also furnishes the socially appropriate context for children. Although some individuals opt for single parenthood, most want to be married when they become parents. Persons who are not married and who choose parenthood will have a more difficult time than those who are married.

The experience of parenthood is one of numerous events spouses share over the course of their life together. Partners who don't get divorced have 50 or so years of memories. One 40-year-old husband said:

> My wife and I have been seeing a movie a week since we began dating more than 20 years ago. We have already seen close to 1,000 movies together, and some of them have become a part of us. We still enjoy *Casablanca*.

In his play *Chapter Two*, Neil Simon likened a relationship to the alphabet. People who have just met are in the As and Bs; those who have known each other for years are in the Rs and Ss. One of the frustrating aspects of divorce is that we lose the shared history with a person and must begin at the As and Bs with a new person.

The disadvantages of marriage include loss of freedom, an increased risk of becoming divorced or widowed, and financial responsibility for others. The person who travels fastest, travels alone. If you have a career goal or want career success, the involvement of another person in your life can hinder your achievement of that goal. Not only may your career mobility be restricted, your freedom to become involved sexually with others will be eliminated. "If you want to be married, you have to give up other women," said one spouse. "You can't have it both ways."

At least 50 percent of all brides and grooms in the United States become divorced; by not marrying, individuals can avoid the traumatic experience of divorce. In addition, most women outlive their husbands by eight years or so, so most wives have inadvertently signed up for several years in the widow role.

Financial responsibility for children, for homes, and for all the things married people buy is part of the marital package. Some people don't like to get in debt or to be obligated to pay for things that someone else (the spouse) wants. If you marry, you will incur the financial obligations of your partner and vice versa.

The decision to marry may not be a one-time decision. Many of us will make the basic decision between marriage and singlehood many times throughout our lives. The single

(Continued)

decide whether to marry, and the married decide whether to stay married. For the divorced, the question is whether to remain single or to remarry.

Is Singlehood for You?

Singlehood is not a unidimensional concept. There are many styles of singlehood from which to choose. As a single person, you may devote your time and energy to career, travel, privacy, heterosexual or homosexual relationships, living together, communal living, or a combination of these experiences over time. The essential difference between traditional marriage and singlehood is the personal and legal freedom to do as you wish.

Although singlehood offers freedom, single people must deal with the issues of loneliness, money, education, and identity.

Loneliness

For some singles, being alone is a desirable and enjoyable experience. "The major advantage of being single," expressed one 29-year-old man, "is that I don't have to deal with another person all the time. I like my privacy." Henry David Thoreau, who never married, spent two years alone on 14 acres bordering Walden Pond. He said of the experience, "I love to be alone. I never found the companion that was so companionable as solitude."

Others view solitude as an opportunity to become deeply involved in their work. A single-by-choice woman artist remarked:

> Marriage would interfere with what I most enjoy—my work. I am most creative when I am alone. Fixing supper for someone else, changing a baby's diapers, or having to talk to someone else every night would be dreadful chores to me.

Steve Martin said in one of his talk-show interviews, "I like to be alone and to be private." (He has subsequently married.)

Economic Self-sufficiency

Having social relationships or developing an enjoyment for being alone are not the only prerequisites to successful single living. It takes money. Money is less likely to be a problem for a man who has been socialized to expect to work all of his life and who usually earns about one-third more than a woman. A woman who decides not to marry is giving up the potentially larger income her husband might earn. Also, both men and women who decide not to marry give up the possibility of a two-income family.

Education

Since higher incomes are often associated with higher education, the person who is considering singlehood as a life style might stay in school. Women and men who complete four years of high school can expect to earn about 30 percent less than those who complete four years of college. "It earns to learn" is a phrase that is used to promote the importance of education.

Personal Identity

Single people must establish an identity—a role—that helps to define who they are and what they do. Spouses eat together, sleep together, party together, and cooperate economically. They mesh their lives into a cooperative relationship that gives them the respective identity of being on their own marital team. On the basis of their spousal roles, we can predict what they will be doing most of the time. For example, at noon on Sunday, they are most likely to be having lunch together. Not only can we predict what they will be doing, their roles as spouses tell them what they will be doing—interacting with each other.

The single person must find other roles. A meaningful career is the avenue most singles pursue. A career provides structure, relationships with others, and a strong sense of identity ("I am an interior decorator"). To the degree that singles find meaning in their work, they are successful in establishing autonomous identities independent of the marital role.

(Continued)

In evaluating the single life style, to what degree, if any, do you feel that loneliness would be a problem for you? What are your educational and career plans to ensure that you will be employed in your chosen field and maintain the standard of living you desire?

The old idea that you can't be happy unless you are married is no longer credible. Whereas marriage will be the first option for some, it will be the last option for others. One 76-year-old single-by-choice said, "A husband would have to be very special to be better than no husband at all."

Impact of Social Influences on Choices

Your decision to remain single or to marry is significantly influenced by your relationships with others—your parents, friends, and peers—and by the presence of a person in your life who wants to marry you.

The scenario most predictive of your wanting to marry includes your parents having a happy marriage, close friends having happy marriages, no employer making heavy demands on your time, being in your early thirties (your society expects you to be married by then), and being in love with a person who wants to marry you.

Alternatively, the scenario most predictive of your remaining single includes your parents having an unhappy marriage, close friends being divorced or widowed and discussing the benefits of not marrying again, an employer making extensive demands on your time and leaving you little time for a relationship, and no one being currently available who wants to marry you and whom you want to marry.

Hence, whether you choose to remain single or to marry will very much depend on the social influences operative in your life.

CHAPTER 7

Living Together

Contents

Is It True?*

1. The number of individuals living together has remained the same in recent years.
2. Individuals who choose to live together have the same background characteristics as those who elect not to live together.
3. Most couples who live together eventually get married to each other.
4. Couples who live together have happier marriages than couples who don't live together before they are married.
5. In recent years, the courts have become increasingly involved in living-together relationships.

*1=T; 2=F; 3=F; 4=F; 5=T.

ONE OF THE major changes in our society has been the gradual acceptance of a couple's living together before marriage. This acceptance (in some cases, tolerance) has increased among people of all ages, races, and social classes. Some view living together as a necessary stage in a developing relationship before making a permanent commitment.

In this chapter, we will examine the characteristics of those who live together, their motivations for doing so, and how they evaluate the experience. In addition, we will assess the potential benefits and disadvantages of becoming involved in a living-together relationship. Finally, because the courts are indicating increased concern, we look at the legal implications of living together as a permanent alternative to marriage. The terms used to describe live-ins include *cohabitants* and *POSSLQ* (people of the opposite sex sharing living quarters), the latter used by the U.S. Bureau of the Census.

Definition and Types

We will define living together as two unrelated adults of the opposite sex living in the same household. An emotional and sexual relationship along with the sharing of a physical space (apartment or house) is an implied ingredient in the definition of living together.

Data – There are almost 2 million unmarried couples living together in the United States. This number is 5 percent of all couple households. (*Statistical Abstract of the United States*, 1987)

The various types of living-together relationships include individuals who are emotionally involved but are not ready for marriage, those who are waiting to get married, those who view living together as a permanent alternative to marriage, and those who live together for economic reasons (it is cheaper). Most individuals who live together have a strong affectionate relationship with their partners, but they have not yet made a commitment to marry each other. In traditional terms, they are "going steady," but they have also moved in together. As one student expressed this "involved but not committed to marriage" pattern of living together:

> The only thing I know about is today. And today I'm happy with my partner. Tomorrow? Who knows? While we both intend to get married someday, we're not sure that it will be to each other.

Other couples are committed to marry each other and are living together until the time is right. Although they may not be officially engaged, they plan to be married and are consciously assessing their compatibility. "The idea of agreeing to spend the rest of your life with someone you've never lived with is nonsense," said one live-in partner. "We love each other very much and feel very secure with each other. But we want to see if we can pull it off on a day-to-day basis."

A few people (about 1 percent) live together as a permanent alternative to marriage. Many of these individuals have been married and do not want to marry again but want a live-in lover relationship.

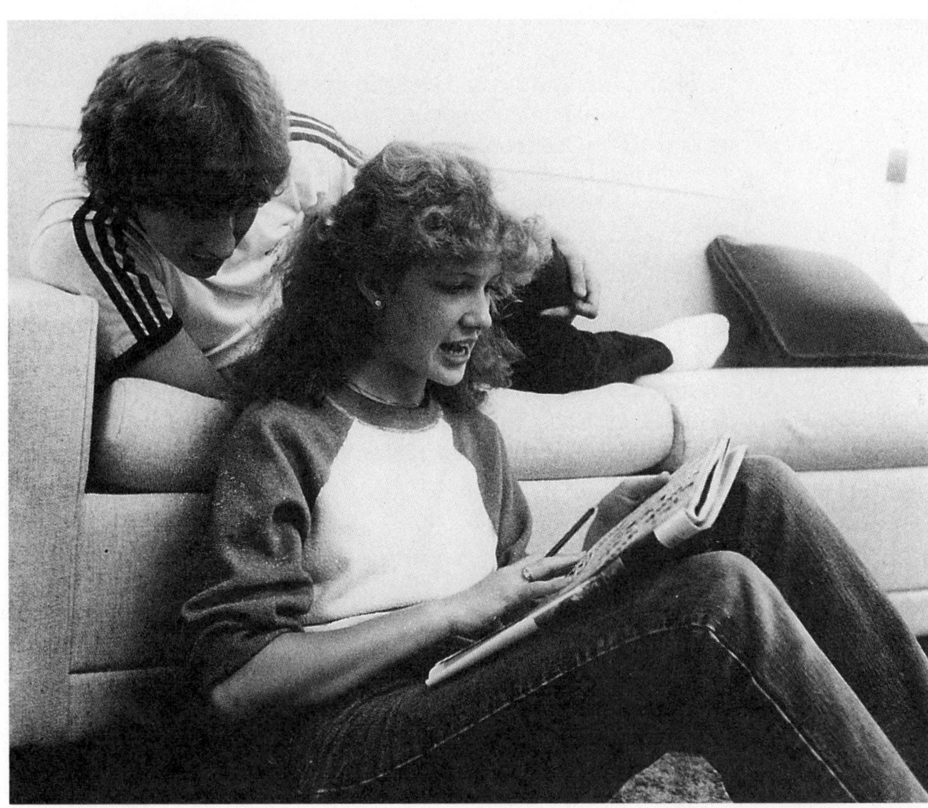

More than one-fourth of college students live together.

Living together is not a recent phenomenon. In the 1920s, Judge B. B. Lindsey suggested the living-together alternative out of his concern for the number of divorcing couples he saw in his court. He reasoned that if couples lived together before marriage, they might be better able to assess the degree to which they were compatible with each other. Similarly, Jessie Bernard suggested a "two-stage marriage." The first stage would involve living together without having children. If the partners felt that their relationship was stable and durable, they would get married and have a family.

The idea of living together did not catch on until the early sixties, when half a million couples were living together. By the late eighties, the number had increased four times. Reasons for the increase include fear of marriage; career or educational commitments; increased tolerance from society, parents, and peers; and the desire for a stable emotional and sexual relationship without legal ties. Although the number of couples who live together has leveled off, it still remains a life-style option for many individuals.

Data – Out of more than 500 college students, 43 percent of the men and 35 percent of the women said they would live together. (Billingham & Sack, 1986)

Characteristics of Live-In Partners

Although there are valid reasons for living together, most unmarrieds (single, divorced, or widowed) do not do so. What are the differences between those who live together and those who do not?

Age

Cohabitants tend to be over the age of 25.

> *Data* – Of all cohabitants, 25 percent are under 25, 50 percent are between the ages of 25 and 44, 15 percent are between the ages of 45 and 65, and 10 percent are over the age of 65. (*Statistical Abstract of the United States*, 1987)

Nonchurch Attenders

In a comparison of cohabitants and noncohabitants (Watson, 1983), 75 percent of the former in contrast to 25 percent of the latter reported never attending religious services. The cohabitors were also more likely not to be members of a church. Among those who were members, Catholics were the most likely to live together and fundamentalist Protestants were the least likely.

Drug Users

Couples who live together are more likely to have used marijuana and other illicit drugs than couples who do not live together. Two researchers who noted this tendency suggest that both living together and drug use are unconventional activities and that the latter predicts the former (Yamaguchi & Kandel, 1985).

Androgynous

When androgyny is defined as having both masculine and feminine characteristics, living-together partners are more likely to be androgynous than those who do not live together (Macklin, 1980). Such androgyny suggests that the partners are less rigid in their gender roles. "We don't see the house as his or her responsibility but ours," said one live-in partner. "If something needs to be done, the one who's there does it."

Formerly Married

> *Data* – More than 50 percent of those who live together have been divorced. (*Statistical Abstract of the United States*, 1987)

People who have been married before are more likely to live together than those who have not been married before (Watson, 1983). "I'm not about to marry a man without living with him first," said one woman. "My first husband was an alcoholic but I didn't find out until after the wedding." Another person said, "I'm just not interested in marriage anymore—I've done that. What I want is a close emotional relationship without the pressure of having to 'get along' that marriage creates."

Urban

That couples who live together tend to be grouped in large urban centers is not surprising. Cities offer anonymity and a context for liberal thinking and behavior that smaller towns do not.

Although most couples who live together do not have children, some do.

CHILDFREE

Most couples who live together do not have children living with them.

> *Data* – About 70 percent of all couples who live together do not have children under the age of 15 living with them. (*Statistical Abstract of the United States,* 1987)

BLACK

Blacks are more likely to live together than whites.

> *Data* – The rate of blacks living together is two times that of whites. (*Statistical Abstract of the United States,* 1987)

Not only are blacks more likely to be reared in homes where their parents were not married (modeling effect) but black females may feel more willing to have a man under any conditions (and not be committed to marriage) due to the scarce supply of black men. Also, black males—aware of the oversupply of black females—may feel less pressure to marry and prefer to keep their options open. Finally, if a woman with children is on welfare, her money may be stopped if she gets married. If her partner just lives with her (and is not discovered), then there is no economic penalty.

Cohabitants (at least those in Lane County, Oregon) tend to be more dissimilar to their partners in terms of age, previous marital status, and race than couples who do not live together (Gwartney-Gibbs, 1986).

The Experience of Living Together

What is living together like on a day-to-day basis? In this section, we will explore the issue of the decision to live together in terms of the commitment, intimacy, and problems involved in such a situation.

DECIDING TO MOVE IN TOGETHER

As anyone who lives together knows, there is rarely a time that a couple specifically discusses living together. Rather, the partners become emotionally involved with each other, spend increasingly larger amounts of time together, and gradually drift into a living-together arrangement. The typical pattern is to spend an occasional night together, then a weekend, then a night before or after the weekend, and so on. This escalation usually takes place over a period of months.

Data – In one study of 40 spouses who had previously lived together, 73 percent of the partners had known each other for at least six months prior to moving in together; almost 50 percent had known each other for more than one year. (Kotkin, 1985)

"We just enjoyed spending time together and the more, the better. We weren't aware that we were gradually moving in together—but that's what was happening," an English major recalls.

Another couple remember their experience:

> We were at his place fooling around when I said how nice it would be to have my stereo to listen to. We decided to go to my dorm and get it. Doing so was symbolic, because in the next few days we had moved my other stuff into his apartment. We never talked about living together, only "getting my stuff."

FEELINGS ABOUT MARRIAGE

What do couples who live together feel about marriage in general and about marriage to each other? When 40 college couples who were living together were asked these questions, 93 percent of the women and 85 percent of the men said they would eventually marry (Risman et al., 1981) "Just because we're living together doesn't mean we're anti-marriage," said one live-in partner.

Although most partners in living-together relationships plan to marry eventually, they are less certain about whether they will marry each other. They do not begin to live together with the idea that they will marry at some later date.

Data – In one study, 50 percent of the men and 65 percent of the women who were living together said they did not consider their doing so to be a trial marriage. (Kotkin, 1985)

In another study, termination—not marriage, was the most likely outcome of living together. (Yamaguchi & Kandel, 1985)

INTIMACY

When 40 couples who were living together were compared with 191 couples who were "going steady" (Risman et al., 1981), the living-together couples were more intimate—they disclosed more to each other, indicated greater love for each other, had sexual intercourse more often, and viewed their relationship as closer. Hence, although the living-together couples weren't sure about their future life together, they had drifted into very intimate relationships. Also, they were enjoying them. About 80 percent of both genders reported they were satisfied with their relationships. These percentages were slightly above the satisfaction levels of partners who were "going steady."

DIVISION OF LABOR

Who does the work in living-together relationships?

Data – In a survey of the readers of *Cosmopolitan* magazine, of women who were living with their partners, 25 percent did all of the housework, 51 percent did most of it, and 20 percent split the chores. (Bowe, 1986)

Although many couples share the work in their relationships, there seems to be a drift toward traditional roles, the woman doing more of the work. This traditional division of labor may be the unconscious replication of the role relationships the respective partners observed in their parents' marriages. One woman who cooks, cleans, and does the laundry said, "I really don't mind. I'd

Most couples who live together begin with a traditional division of labor.

rather be taking care of things around the apartment than just sitting around." One might predict that her mother also takes care of her father in a similar manner and feels guilty "just sitting around."

Some women feel frustrated and angry about the traditional drift toward conventional male-female roles in a living-together situation. One graduate student who had recently moved in with her partner said:

> Moving in together has caused some unanticipated problems. Things prior to that had been quite egalitarian, and I liked the way Bob treated me. After we moved in, the boxes had not even been unpacked and I became a *housewife*! I worked all day on *our* house while he went to school. It was horrible, and I was miserable. We talked about it, and two days later I was the housewife again. I'm hoping that since we're moved in and things are unpacked and cleaned, this problem will be gone.

PROBLEMS

Liberty is the one thing you can't have unless you give it to others.
—William Allen White

Partners who live together report certain problems regarding parents, jealousy, roles, and sex in their relationships.

Parents

Most college students are reluctant to tell their parents they are living together. They fear their parents' disapproval and, in some cases, retribution. "My dad would cut off my money if he knew Mark and I were living together," said one junior.

Some live-in partners do not care if their parents know they are living together. Those who do hide it feel guilty about the deception. "I don't feel good about being dishonest with my folks, but I tell myself it would hurt them more if they knew," one partner said.

Still others are sorry they can't share their feelings about their companion with their parents. "I've never been happier than since I moved into Carl's apartment. But the fact that my folks don't know and would be disappointed if they did bothers me. Carl is a very important part of my life, and I feel sad that I can't share him with my parents," observed a music major.

Older, noncollege, divorced people who live together also have parental concerns. "No matter how old I am," said one 36-year-old woman, "I'm still my mother's child, and she thinks living together is wrong." Not all parents disapprove of living together, however. Some prefer to see their offspring in a live-in situation than to see them marry too early or marry the wrong person.

Jealousy

About 50 percent of the partners who live together are not committed to marrying each other, so it is not surprising that jealousy sometimes occurs. "When she doesn't come in until late and I know she's been with another guy, it hurts me terribly," said one partner. "I know I don't own her, but I can't help being jealous."

Loss of Freedom

Some partners complain that a live-in relationship restricts their freedom. One woman said:

> Last week I hit a new low point. I felt very trapped and that all my independence and freedom were gone. I had earlier insisted that we have an open relationship (sex with others allowed), but it didn't occur to me until now that I am part of a *couple* and no one's going to be interested in me. Also, I felt I'd have no alone time except when I'm working (we do not have separate bedrooms and we use one car to go back and forth to school). I've had nightmares about being married and even awakened one night terrified because I had rolled over and felt someone in bed with me (guess I'd been dreaming I was "single" again).

Other Problems

Partners who live together experience many of the same problems that married couples experience. Lack of money, lack of space, and sexual problems are not uncommon. Differences over frequency of intercourse, lack of orgasm, premature ejaculation, and impotence may sometimes occur. A woman remarked how living together had changed her sex life with her partner:

> Before we started living together, we had intercourse less frequently because we weren't as available to each other. But when we were sleeping together every night, intercourse was always a possibility. It became a hassle because I wanted it more often, and he felt that only the male should be the aggressor.

Living Together as Preparation for Marriage?

Does living together result in happier marriages? Two researchers compared the marriages of 30 couples who lived together before they were married with 30 couples who never lived together. They concluded that ". . . cohabitation with a mate prior to marriage seemed neither to greatly benefit nor greatly harm the marriage relationship during the first year of marriage" (Markowski & Johnston, 1980, p. 125).

In another study (Jacques & Chason, 1979), 54 spouses who had lived together (not necessarily with each other) were compared with 30 spouses who had not experienced a live-in relationship. Each spouse was asked to indicate her or his marital satisfaction in reference to sexual satisfaction, need satisfaction, relationship stability, physical intimacy, sexual attractiveness, openness of communication, closeness to ideal partner, and the degree to which they worked on the relationship. Results revealed that those who had had living-together experiences did not describe their marriages as different from those who had not had such experiences.

In still another study of 309 spouses (DeMaris & Leslie, 1984), those who had lived together before they were married reported *lower* marital satisfaction than those who had not lived together. Of this unexpected finding, the researchers concluded that:

> Rather than acting as a filter that effectively screens out the less-compatible couples, cohabitation appears to select couples from the outset who are somewhat less likely to report high satisfaction once they are married. This may be due to the fact that those individuals expect more out of marriage from the beginning. Alternatively, these may be individuals who adapt less readily to the role expectations of conventional marriage than do the more traditional respondents. In either case, it is most probably the difference between the kinds of people who do and do not choose to cohabit before marriage, rather than the experience of cohabitation itself, that accounts for these findings. (p. 83)

Although the data derived from comparing couples who live together with couples who do not does indicate that living together is not necessarily a good way to prepare for marriage (Watson & De Meo, 1987), couples who live together seem to feel that doing so is good preparation for marriage.

Data – Of 40 spouses who had previously lived together, 95 percent said that doing so had prepared them for marriage. (Kotkin, 1985)

Consideration

These studies suggest that you should not live with a partner before marriage if your sole goal in doing so is to help to ensure a happy marriage with that partner. There is no data to support such a causal relationship.

Benefits of Living Together

Although having a successful marriage is not a predictable result of living with someone before marriage, some aspects of a living-together relationship may be beneficial to a marriage. The most pervasive benefit is that most couples who live together report it is an enjoyable, maturing experience. There are other potential benefits as well.

Delayed Marriage

Individuals who marry in their mid- and late twenties are more likely to stay married and to report higher levels of marital satisfaction than those who marry earlier. To the degree that living together functions to delay the age at which a person marries, it may therefore be considered beneficial. "I married when I was 20," remarked one woman, "because you just didn't live together in those days. I wish I had waited to get married and had had the option of living together in the meantime." Lana Turner, the blond Hollywood "sweater girl" of the forties, said one of the reasons she had seven marriages was that when two people became involved, they were not expected to live together—they were expected to marry.

Ending Unsatisfactory Relationships Before Marriage

When you are involved in a relationship before marriage and break up with the person, our society labels it a "broken engagement" at worst. After the wedding, the label changes to "divorce." Living together may clearly indicate that you and your partner are not suited for each other. "I love her, but know that we are incapable of living in the same house," said one man. Finding this out before tying the legal knot eliminates some unnecessary grief.

Consideration

A team of researchers studied the termination of various premarital relationships and concluded, "The best divorce you get is the one you get before you get married." (Hill et al., 1976)

Less Idealization

You have been to a dance and have seen a ball made up of small square glass mirrors that cast reflections from a light shining on it as it turns. Traditional courtship usually gives information about a person in small units much like the light reflected from a couple of these mirrors. In contrast, living together may give you more information; you will see more facets of the person by being around her or him more of the time. You may or may not like what you learn about your partner from this increased exposure.

Markowski & Johnston (1980) found that living together helps to break down idealization of the partner, at least for men. Men who had lived with their partners were much less likely to regard them as always composed, lighthearted, happy, and reasonable. Idealization was not reduced for women in the study.

Disadvantages of Living Together

"Never again" said a man who had formerly had a living-together relationship. "I invested myself completely and felt we would eventually get married. But she never had that in mind and just took me for a ride. The next time, I'll be married before moving in with someone." Living together does have negative consequences for some people.

Feeling Used

Desiring to be more than true, you are worse than false.
—Armand Baschet

When levels of commitment are uneven in a relationship, the partner who is most committed feels used. "I always felt I was giving more than I was getting," said one partner. "It's not a good feeling."

Feeling Tricked

Some partners feel they have been deceived. "I always felt we would be getting married, but it turns out that she was seeing someone else the whole time we were living together and had no intention of marrying me," recalled one partner.

Consideration

Since many living-together relationships do not end in marriage, if you agree to live together with the specific goal of marrying that person, you may be disappointed. By not requiring that the relationship end in marriage, you increase the chance that you can successfully emerge from the living-together arrangement, regardless of the outcome.

Developing Hostility

The feelings of being tricked and used often combine to create deep hostile feelings, not only against the live-in partner but also against others in general. Sometimes the person feels incapable of initiating or maintaining another relationship. "What's the use," remarked one partner who had recently terminated a relationship, "I'm burned out on investing myself in people."

Relationships to Avoid

A team of researchers identified the types of living-together relationships that had negative consequences for those involved (Ridley et al., 1978). These included the following.

The "Linus blanket" relationship. In this pattern, the individuals had an overwhelming need to be involved with someone—with anyone. The fear of breaking up caused the partners to defer to each other on almost every issue. As a result, the partners had no practice in problem solving and hid their real needs from each other. "We were always being nice to each other and never really disclosed ourselves to each other. . .. I guess that's why we broke up," said a business major.

The emancipation relationship. Often, one partner lives with someone to symbolize his or her independence from parents and rebellion against tradition. But feelings of guilt usually ensue, and the person soon withdraws from the relationship. Unless the person works out his or her ambivalent feelings about living together, the consequences of a live-in relationship are likely to be negative.

The one-sided convenience relationship. Although some live-in relationships involve mutual convenience, others do not. In the latter pattern, one partner manipulates the other to continue sexual, domestic, or other favors while withholding any semblance of commitment. There is little reciprocity, and the relationship becomes exploitive.

To assess the degree to which living together may have a positive or negative outcome for you and your partner, you can rate yourself according to the Living-Together Consequences Scale in the Self-Assessment.

Living Together as a Permanent Alternative

Whereas most people regard living together as a stage to a future marriage (although not necessarily with the person with whom they currently live), some people view living together as a permanent alternative to marriage. They enjoy living together, but they do not plan to marry anyone—ever.

Who Lives Together Permanently?

Those who select living together as a permanent alternative to marriage have usually been married before and don't want the entanglements of another marriage. Others feel that the "real" bond between two people is (or should be) emotional. They contend that many couples stay together because of the legal contract, even though they do not love each other any longer. "If you're staying married because of the contract," said one partner, "you're staying for the wrong reason."

Some women reject marriage for philosophical reasons:

> I have enough trouble with my identity as a woman starting her own business that I don't need to confuse it with __________'s business. I don't like the stigma. . . . I don't want to be a "Mrs." in any way. (Kotkin, 1985, p. 167)

Other individuals feel that living together permanently allows you to keep your own identity:

> . . . right now, we can take vacations separately; we can do things separately. It seems that once you're married, . . . the two of you become one identity—the way people look at you. (Kotkin, 1985, p. 167)

Legal Implications of Living Together

The law is reason free of passion.
—Aristotle

In recent years, the courts have become increasingly involved in living-together relationships (Freed & Walker, 1986), and a number of legal problems have surfaced.

Miscellaneous Problems

Unmarried couples who live together are sometimes refused apartments or homes by landlords and automobile or home coverage by insurance companies (or charged higher rates). One unmarried partner may be refused the other partner's family health-care or group-insurance coverage or denied United States citizenship; unmarrieds also cannot collect food stamps or Social Security survivors' benefits. A live-in partner cannot be listed as a dependent, which would provide a tax deduction.

Community Property and Inheritance

The couple who lives together for several years will probably accumulate considerable property in the form of a house, furniture, a car, stereo equipment, and so on. But it is no longer clear what belongs to whom if they separate. In the case of Michelle Triola Marvin and actor Lee Marvin, who lived together for almost seven years, the California Supreme Court ruled that "The fact that a man and woman live together without marriage, and have a sexual relationship, does not in itself invalidate agreements between them relating to their earnings, property, or expenses" (Myricks, 1980, p. 210). In essence, this case makes it possible for former live-in lovers to sue each other for a division of property.

Regarding inheritance, if an individual fails to make proper provision for the distribution of his or her estate (property) after death, the law of the state in which the death occurs will dictate the disposition of the property. In such cases, a legal spouse is usually automatically entitled to inherit between one-half and one-third of the mate's estate. But a living-together partner may get nothing; the next of kin to the deceased partner may be the benefactor of the estate.

Self-Assessment

Living-Together Consequences Scale

This inventory is designed to measure the degree to which living together will have positive or negative consequences for you and your partner. There are no right or wrong answers. After reading each sentence carefully, circle the number that best represents your feelings.

1 Strongly disagree
2 Mildly disagree
3 Undecided
4 Mildly agree
5 Strongly agree

	SD	D	U	A	SA
1. I have a fairly liberal background and living together is not against my values.	1	2	3	4	5
2. If we break up after living together without getting married, I will not be devastated.	1	2	3	4	5
3. I have thought a lot about the pros and cons of living together and feel that it is right for me and my partner.	1	2	3	4	5
4. I will not feel used if my partner breaks up with me and doesn't marry me.	1	2	3	4	5
5. I am not living with my partner so that I can get back at my parents.	1	2	3	4	5
6. I want to live with my partner out of love, not out of convenience.	1	2	3	4	5
7. My partner and I have known each other for a long time.	1	2	3	4	5
8. I am not counting on living together to help us have a stronger relationship.	1	2	3	4	5
9. My partner and I have discussed our future.	1	2	3	4	5
10. My parents would not disown me if they found out that I was living with my partner.	1	2	3	4	5

Scoring: Add the numbers you circled. 1 (strongly disagree) is the most negative response, and 5 (strongly agree) is the most positive response. The lower your total score (10 is the lowest possible score), the greater the negative consequences of living together; the higher your score (50 is the highest possible score), the greater the positive consequences of living together. A score of 25 places you at the midpoint between the positive and negative consequences of living together.

Palimony

A take-off on the word "alimony," *palimony* refers to the amount of money one "pal" who lives with another "pal" may have to pay if the pals split up. Lee Marvin was ordered to pay Michelle Marvin $104,000 by the Los Angeles Superior Court for "rehabilitative purposes." The amount was arrived at by taking the highest weekly amount she earned as a singer ($1,000) and computing it for a two-year period. Judge Arthur Marshall reasoned that Ms. Marvin acted as a companion and homemaker to Lee Marvin to the detriment of her career and should be given money to retool her skills.

In the past, partners in living-together relationships had no legal rights in reference to each other because the live-in arrangement was viewed as sexually illicit. Today, such arrangements are recognized as licit, and the parties can be held liable to each other and forced to pay money at the court's discretion. Exhibit 7.1 describes a number of court cases on living together.

But the courts may disagree. In 1982, the California Second District Court of Appeals overturned the $104,000 award to Ms. Marvin, saying there was no basis for the rehabilitative award—she had sustained no damages.

Consideration

If you and your partner decide to live together instead of marry, depending on the state, the judge, and the court, palimony is possible if there is a lawsuit after you separate. Division of property is not just possible, but likely.

Child Custody

If an unmarried couple has a child or children, the custody issue may arise if the parents decide to separate. The case of *Stanley v. Illinois* illustrates the legal consequences of having children without converting the living-together relationship into a legal marriage. Joan Stanley lived intermittently with Peter Stanley for 18 years. Although they were never married, they had three children. When Joan died, Peter lost custody of his three children. Under Illinois law, the children of unwed fathers become wards of the state on the mother's death. There was no hearing to determine the father's fitness as a parent; the presumption was that all unwed fathers are unfit to raise their children.

Consideration

If you have been married and do not plan to remarry (but want a sustained companionship relationship), permanent living together may meet your needs. Even if you have not been married but want to avoid marriage and children, a permanent live-in relationship may be for you. Obviously, the person you live with should also feel that never getting married is acceptable or preferable. It is not unusual for only one partner to view the relationship as a permanent alternative to marriage. "The biggest conflict we have," said one cohabitant, "is that he always wants to get married and I don't."

Exhibit 7.1

COURT CASES ON LIVING TOGETHER

Although the case of *Marvin v. Marvin* has been the most widely publicized, other live-ins have gone to court over palimony, child support, and division of property.

McHenry v. Smith

The Oregon Court of Appeals affirmed an award of $16,000 in damages to a woman who cohabited with a man for four years for breach of an oral agreement he made to "work and support" her in return for her supporting him while he was writing a book and was unemployed.

McCullon v. McCullon

A man who lived with a woman for 28 years was required to pay alimony and child support for her 18-year-old daughter. The New York Supreme Court said they had presented themselves as a married couple, filed joint tax returns, and held property in common.

Carlson v. Olsen

The Minnesota Supreme Court ruled that the property of a couple who had lived together for 21 years should be equally divided. The rationale was that the woman performed wifely and motherly services during the living-together years and was entitled to half of what the couple owned.

In other cases, the courts have viewed agreements between live-ins as illegal and unenforceable.

Warren v. Warren

A woman who sought a division of property with her former live-in lover was awarded nothing by the Nevada Supreme Court. The court did not recognize love letters as evidence of an implied contract to create a partnership.

Hewitt v. Hewitt

The parties began living together during college and told their parents they were married. The woman worked and put the man through professional training. They had three children, and were known as man and wife for 15 years. The Illinois Supreme Court denied the woman any money on the ground that her claims were against public policy.

Sources: McHenry v. Smith, *Family Law Quarterly,* 1986, *19,* 432; McCuilon v. McCullon, 410 New York Supp. 226 (1978); Carlson v. Olsen, 256 N.W.2d 249 (1977); Warren v. Warren 579 P.2d 722 (1978); Hewitt v. Hewitt, *Family Law Quarterly,* 1986, *19,* 433.

Trends

Due to the pressures of parents, married peers, and the societal norm that marriage precede parenthood, living together will never replace marriage. In the last two years, the number of individuals living together has remained the same. (*Statistical Abstract of the United States,* 1987)

Those who decide to live together will become more cautious about the legal implications of their relationships. This will be particularly true of those who live together for a considerable period of time. In such relationships, implied agreements between the partners may be enforceable. Rod Stewart,

Nick Nolte, Alice Cooper, and Rod Steiger have all been sued by their former live-in partners. The caution light is on for living-together relationships.

Parents will also become more accepting of the living-together relationships of their offspring. One parent said their first child was divorced after a year of marriage and "it would have been better if they had lived together rather than becoming legally tied." One young woman said, "My parents were very upset when my sisters lived with their boyfriends. But they've gotten used to it, and they think very little of me living with my boyfriend." In one study, 55 percent of the females and 72 percent of the males said their parents would approve of their living with a partner (Watson, 1983).

Summary

Living together may be defined as two unmarried adult lovers sharing a residence over an extended period of time. About 5 percent of all couples sharing a household are living together. Although most have a wait-and-see attitude about their relationships, others are committed to eventual marriage. A small number view living together as a permanent alternative to marriage.

Couples who live together are more likely to be over 25, not attend religious services, use drugs, be androgynous, be former marrieds, and be black. The last characteristic is related to parental modeling, the loss of welfare payments to the single-parent female, and a scarcity of black males.

Most live-ins drift into living-together relationships; few formally discuss living together first. Live-in partners report high levels of satisfaction in their relationships and divide housework along traditional lines. Many seem troubled that their parents do not know of their relationship but feel they would be disappointed if they did know. Some live-ins complain of jealousy, loss of freedom, and lack of money.

Living together before marriage does not seem to increase or decrease the chances of having a happy marriage. With one exception (DeMaris & Leslie, 1984), studies report that couples who lived together before they were married say basically the same things about their marriages in terms of sexual satisfaction, need satisfaction, openness of communication, and negotiation of conflict that couples who did not live together say. Potential benefits of living together include delaying marriage, ending unsatisfactory relationships before marriage, and reducing idealization. Disadvantages of living together include feeling used, tricked, and hostile toward the opposite gender.

Only a small percentage of unmarried-couple households consist of those who are living together as a permanent alternative to marriage. These relationships may cause legal problems if they terminate, because the courts are increasingly willing to enforce implied agreements made by live-ins.

Trends in living together include greater social tolerance for the pattern and increased parental tolerance for offspring living together.

Questions for Reflection

1. To what degree are any of the "relationships to avoid" mentioned in this chapter part of your background?

2. To what degree do you share the characteristics of those who live together, and how do you feel about your suitability for a live-in relationship?
3. How would you handle the issue of disclosure to parents if you lived with your partner?

CHOICES

CHOICES ABOUT LIVING together include whether to live together, whether to maintain two residences, whether to tell parents, and how long to live together. Careful decision making may help to make living together a more positive experience.

SHOULD I LIVE WITH MY PARTNER?

There are three conditions under which you should not live together. First, if your values are such that you believe living together is wrong, the arrangement will have only negative consequences for you. You will lose respect for yourself, your partner, and your relationship. Second, if you expect that marriage will result from living with your partner and you will be devastated if it does not, you should not live together. Living together is not equivalent to engagement, and it is not unusual for the partners who live together to have different goals about marriage. Even partners who view themselves as being engaged and who plan to marry may not do so after they have lived together. "I found out that I couldn't live with him," "I found out I didn't want to live with her," and "I found out I wasn't ready for marriage" are some of the comments made by those who live together but do not end up getting married. Third, it is unwise to live with someone you feel is exploiting you, regardless of the reason.

Aside from these three cautions, living together seems to have limited harmful effects and some beneficial ones. The primary benefit is that it may help partners to discover they are unsuited for marriage before they get married.

SHOULD WE HAVE ONE RESIDENCE OR TWO?

When partners drift into living together, they often end up living in the man's residence while the woman maintains her own place. The latter furnishes a cover story for both sets of parents, a place for her to get her mail, and a haven to retreat to when conflict erupts in the relationship. One woman who maintained her own apartment said:

> I needed a place I could go back to—to call my own—and to see my friends. Having a place of your own is expensive, but it gives you flexibility by not putting all your eggs into the living-together basket. I ended up breaking up with my partner, and I'm sure the adjustment was a lot easier because I had a place to retreat to when I needed it.

The disadvantage of maintaining a separate place may be the flip side of the advantages. If you have a place to retreat to, the skills of managing conflict with your partner may not be as easily learned. You can walk out when you want to, and your motivation for working things out may be lower. "I'm sure we would be apart," said one cohabitant "if I had not given up my dorm room. But because I had no place to escape to, we worked out our differences and have a stronger relationship for it."

SHOULD I TELL MY PARENTS I AM LIVING WITH MY PARTNER?

The decision to tell parents about the living-together relationship will depend on the parents, the relationship with them, the values of honesty and kindness, and the ability to hide the living-together experience.

Some parents are very conservative and are devastated to learn that their son or daughter is in a living-together relationship. One mother said:

> When we found out our daughter was living with her boyfriend, we were hurt more than we were shocked. We have a Christian home and always thought we had brought her up right. Her behav-

(Continued)

ior was a slap in the face at everything that we had taught her.

Other parents don't approve of their children living together but view their doing so as part of the liberalization of our whole society. One father said:

> We know that a lot of young folks are living together these days. Our son went to one of these liberal colleges and learned all sorts of things we don't approve of. But we trust his judgment and don't figure that living together will hurt him. Besides, we would rather he live with his girlfriend than get married as young as he is.

Just as some parents are conservative and others are more liberal, the relationships offspring have with their parents will vary. "I've always been fairly open with my parents no matter what it was," said one cohabitant. But another said, "I can't tell my parents anything without them criticizing me, so I've learned to live my life and let them know as little as possible." Whether you tell your parents about your living-together relationship will depend not only on who they are but also on your relationship with them.

The values of honesty and kindness are often in conflict when it comes to making a decision about telling parents about a living-together relationship. If you value being honest with your parents, you will tell them you are living with your partner. But doing so may hurt them and give them a problem to live with. As an alternative to being honest, you might choose to be kind and not tell them, sparing them the burden of living with such information.

Of course, your parents may already know of your living together or find out without your telling them. Keeping such a secret is difficult under the best of circumstances. The only way to ensure that your parents do not find out is to avoid the behavior. "I don't care whether my parents find out or not," said one person, "It's my life." But another said, "I couldn't do that to my parents."

How Long Should I Live With My Partner?

Are there good and bad periods of time to live together if your goal is to have a happy marriage? There is no evidence to suggest that living together before marriage for any length of time is predictive of a successful marriage relationship. However, it is known that any relationships in which the partners have known each other for at least a year have a higher chance of marital success than relationships of shorter duration.

Impact of Social Influences on Choices

Whether or not you live together with your partner will be influenced by your perception of the approval or disapproval of the persons you care about. If your primary group members (parents, siblings, children) would disapprove of your living together with a partner, then you will be less likely to do so.

Some partners want to live together very much, even though they know others will disapprove, so they hide their living-together relationship. Lest we think that sneaking around is unique to young people, a study of courtship couples in their sixties reported ducking the eyes of their children. One 63-year-old retiree said, "Yeah, my girlfriend (age 64) lives just down the hall from me . . . when she spends the night, she usually brings her cordless phone . . . just in case her daughter calls" (Bulcroft & O'Conner-Roden, 1986). Another 61-year-old woman reported that she has been unable to tell her family that her 68-year-old boyfriend spends three to four nights a week at her house. "I have a tendency to hide his shoes when my grandchildren are coming over" (p. 69).

CHAPTER 8

Commitment to Marriage

Contents

Is It True?*

1. Selecting someone very different from yourself usually results in a happy and exciting marriage.
2. Most people do not give their partners the real reason why they want to break up.
3. Individuals who delay marriage until they are in their thirties have a decreased risk of divorce.
4. Couples who date for about two years before getting married seem to report the highest degree of marital satisfaction.
5. Couples do not need an attorney when they draw up their premarital agreements.

*1=F; 2=F; 3=F; 4=T; 5=F.

AFTER A PERIOD of casual friendships, dating, and perhaps living together, individuals narrow their choice of a marriage partner to one. This chapter is about maximizing the chances for a successful marriage by selecting a compatible companion, rejecting those partners who are not compatible, and looking at the various issues that should be considered before marriage. To the degree that you use the premarital period to examine and evaluate your relationship, you can feel more secure in your choice of a marital partner.

Selecting a Compatible Partner

One of the most important topics of this text is identifying the person or persons with whom you will have the highest chance of a successful marriage. If you were to date 50 people, some of them would be more suitable mates for you than others—and you can't always depend on love to tell you the difference. Love feelings can alter your perception and judgment when it comes to choosing a marital partner. "I was so much in love with her, I knew we could work out any differences we might have," said one divorced man. "I was wrong."

A basic consideration in evaluating a potential partner is *compatibility*—the quality of being able to get along well with another person. Compatibility is important because it reduces conflict. Whatever your interests, they are shared by the people you choose as close friends. Consider the difficulty of being *married* to someone who does not like at least some of the things you like.

Of course, it is not necessary (nor is it possible) that you and your partner feel the same way about everything. However, it is important that you both feel the same way about issues the two of you regard as important. Achieving a compatible relationship means identifying those issues that are important to you and selecting a partner who shares your views. "The phrase to remember in choosing a mate," emphasizes one marriage and family teacher, "is 'know yourself and marry yourself.' " As a means of increasing your self-understanding and identifying a compatible partner, consider how important it is to you that you and your partner are compatible in each of the following areas.

RECREATIONAL COMPATIBILITY

When asked what he saw in his fiancée, an engaged man replied, "She's incredibly fun to be with." Since one of the reasons for your getting married may be the hope of continuing fun times with your partner, to what degree do you share recreational interests? What are your respective feelings about attending cultural events (opera, ballet, symphony, theater), watching sports (football, tennis, swimming), participating in sports (jogging, skiing, bowling, dancing, fishing, hunting, tennis, golf, racketball), or more sedentary activities (watching TV, going to movies, reading, listening to music). What is your idea of a good time? Some people like to go to parties and drink beer; others feel that a weekend of camping is fun. The degree to which you see humor in the same things is also important for your relationship. (Murstein & Brust, 1985)

Enjoying similar activities is an important aspect of recreational compatibility.

Consideration

It does not matter what recreational interests you enjoy. It only matters that your partner share those interests at a level that you mutually regard as desirable. It is also difficult to assess recreational interests in courtship because the enjoyment of being together is so intense that the partners could enjoy anything together.

Need-for-Partner Compatibility

Partners also vary in the degree to which they need each other. One partner said, "I need a great deal of freedom. I love Jim, but I don't want to be around him all the time and I certainly don't want him clinging to me." But Jim said, "I'm different. I need to be with Pam and am depressed when I'm not. I know she loves me, but sometimes I interpret her not wanting to be with me as rejection. Our different needs for each other's time has been a problem in our relationship." To what degree do you and your partner have similar needs for being with each other and how much does it matter?

Sexual Compatibility

For some partners, having a compatible sexual companion is essential to a happy relationship. Sexual compatibility most often refers to a mutually satisfactory sexual relationship that includes similar feelings about the frequency of intercourse and agreement on what is enjoyable and permissible. "We both love sex," said one student. "But she loves it more than I do, and it's been a problem for her that I just don't want to do it all the time."

Career and Family Goals Compatibility

The world is full of willing people; some willing to work, the rest willing to let them.
—Robert Frost

More important than recreational and sexual compatibility is the extent to which you and your partner agree on having a dual-income marriage and the number of children you want. Failure to discuss the issues of jobs and children is to assume that you and your partner have the same goals. "We were like two people in a bus station with tickets to different destinations," said a 26-year-old insurance adjuster. "I wanted her to stay home and for us to have a family. But she wanted a career in fashion merchandising and said that children would interfere with that."

Role Compatibility

I know a couple who got a divorce because they were incompatible—he had no income and she wasn't patable.
—Groucho Marx

Having compatible roles is as important as having similar goals. As a potential husband or wife, what do you expect to do and what do you want your spouse to do in each of the following areas? Who "should" pay the bills, cook the food, wash the dishes, do the laundry, mop the floor, vacuum the house, and clean the bathroom? If you have children, at what age is it appropriate to put them in a day-care center? Who is to care for the child when he or she is an infant? Who stays home from work when a child is sick? Who drives the kids to piano, ballet, and gymnastics lessons? The answers to these questions will help you to evaluate the degree to which you and your partner agree on your respective marital roles.

Consideration

Your role expectations are less important than you and your partner viewing your roles in the same way. Communicating about role expectations is important.

Data – The fact that 176 individuals who had been dating their partner for a year were no more likely to have role compatibility than when they first started dating indicates couples may pay little attention to role compatibility in courtship. Hence, other factors than role satisfaction (for example, love) were necessary to continue the relationship. (Leigh, et al., 1984)

Value Compatibility

Although concern for the compatibilities just discussed is critical to selecting the right partner, using a wide-angle lens on yourself and your partner may also be important. Your philosophy of life will influence many of your interests and activities. For example, a person with an intellectual philosophy of life is likely to read extensively, attend lectures, and pursue graduate study. Consider the degree to which each of the following orientations and its behavioral expression characterize you and how much you want them to characterize the person you marry.

Religious Values

How important is religion to you? How important should it be to your partner? If you are a religiously devout person, to what degree is it important that your partner participate in religious activities (go to church together, pray together) with you, provide a religious example for your children, and relate to your friends who are also religious? Some researchers feel that sharing a religious faith—being spiritually intimate—is positively related to marital satisfaction (Hatch et al., 1986).

Many religious doctrines view marriage as a permanent relationship. "Until death do us part" is a phrase from the traditional marriage ceremony. What is your concept of the permanence of marriage (Is divorce justifiable under any conditions?), and what is the concept held by your partner? Some people have a "let's see if the marriage works out" view; others regard marriage as a lifetime commitment. To what degree do you and your partner see marriage the same way, and how much does it matter to you if your views are different?

Life-Style Values

What is the sexual and economic life style you would like for your marriage? The concept of "open marriage" suggests that although married partners will regard each other as their primary partner, each may have emotional or sexual relationships outside the marriage. How do you and your partner feel about open marriage and about fidelity?

Consideration

It is not as important what your and your partner's values are as it is that you know what these values are and that you both agree (or agree to disagree) on them.

The economic life style that you expect in your relationship is also important. The social class in which you and your partner were reared will furnish a good index of what you are accustomed to. If your parents held high-status, high-income jobs (for example, if they were physicians or lawyers) you have been reared in an economic life style quite different from someone whose parents were laborers. Such rearing will have an influence on the economic expectations in your own relationship. Also, such expectations can have the reverse impact. One geology major said his parents were physicians and he had been "ignored while they did their careers." As a result, he did not want nor was he comfortable with the "things" his parents surrounded him with. He wanted the "simple life" and is now living in a commune.

Political Values

The women's movement, abortion legislation, nuclear armament, gun control, censorship, and the rights of gay people are all political concerns. Whereas some individuals are involved in these issues through thought, discussion, financial support, and organized effort, others are oblivious to their existence as problems. John Denver, for example, said that his ex-wife Annie did not share his concern for the hunger in Africa. Some feel that politics at any level on any issue is a colossal bore. Also, two people may have the same political concerns but different beliefs about the issues. To what degree do you and your partner share similar political orientations, and to what degree does the similarity or dissimilarity matter to you?

Self-Actualization Values

No man can completely know another but by knowing himself, which is the utmost extent of human wisdom.
—Samuel Johnson

A number of people are involved with "getting in touch with their feelings," increasing self-awareness, and actualizing their full potential. For some, this translates into transcendental meditation, yoga, and seeking inner peace. How much importance do you attach to these experiences, and how important is it to you that your partner share them with you?

Data – The fact that 176 individuals who had been dating their partner for a year were no more likely to have similar values than when they first started dating indicates that couples may pay little attention to value compatibility during courtship. Hence, value compatibility was not necessary for continuing the relationship. (Leigh et al., 1984)

COMMUNICATION

It was easier to share my deepest thoughts with 40,000 people than to talk with my wife.
—John Denver

All of the preceding issues are important in selecting a mate, but none takes precedence over the quality of good communication in your relationship. You will bring certain wants, needs, values, and expectations into the relationship with your partner. The probability that your partner's wants, needs, values, and expectations will be compatible with yours on every issue all the time is zero.

Consideration

Good communication not only helps to get the "hidden agendas" up front but also helps to negotiate differences, so that each partner continues to benefit from the relationship. Most couples drift into trouble when their needs are not expressed, go underground, and later resurface in a negative way. "I hated the way he treated me," said one woman, "but I never said anything. Finally, one day I just told him I was leaving. We never discussed why."

Communication between black women and black men is particularly important if negative stereotyping is to stop. (Norment, 1986) Black women sometimes stereotype black men as unreliable, interested only in sex, and less competent. Black men may stereotype black women as domineering, materialistic, and egotistical. Partners should talk to each other about what each is thinking, feeling, and experiencing.

FLEXIBILITY

Since you and your partner do have differences and will change in unpredictable ways throughout your relationship, it is highly desirable that you link yourself with someone who has the capacity to minimize the stress associated with the differences and change. In Chapter 12 on communication, we will

We rarely find that people have good sense unless they agree with us.
—La Rochefoucauld

discuss how you can negotiate differences with your partner. But your partner must be willing to negotiate! And negotiation requires flexibility.

Body-Clock Compatibility

Some of us are "morning people," and some of us are "night people." "If one partner rises early every morning ready for a hearty breakfast and the other cannot deal well with either early morning or breakfast, their rhythms do not match and they are said to exhibit assynchrony. On the other hand, synchrony is achieved, by the marriage of two larks or two owls, both of whom love to . . . "bound from the bed at 6 a.m. and go to sleep at sundown or do not truly awaken until mid-afternoon" (Darnley, 1981, p. 33).

To what degree does it matter if partners are matched or mismatched in terms of their body clocks? Two researchers (Adams and Cromwell, 1978), who studied 28 married graduate students, observed that some out-of-phase couples have less serious conversation, fewer shared activities, less sex, poorer marital adjustment, and more conflict.

Related to the body-clock issue is the issue of different energy levels. What is your energy level, and how does it compare with the energy level of your partner? If they are not similar, each of you will need to be able to tolerate the differences or define the differences as unimportant.

Love

We don't want to live with anyone unless there is love—not some silly idea of romantic love, but the sort of love that nourishes the soul and enables people to grow.
—Eda LeShan

"It don't mean a thing if it ain't got that swing," is the lyric to an old song from the big-band era. Its message points up the importance of love in a relationship. Even if all the compatibilities discussed were present in your relationship, it would probably be a mistake to marry someone you did not love. In the United States, we have been socialized to marry only those people for whom we feel a deep emotional attachment. To marry without love is to begin a relationship with a missing element, which may or may not develop.

In China, marriages are still arranged by a go-between on the basis of genealogical and horoscopic data. Love between the partners is of little concern (Freedman, 1970). In Japan, the actual parties are more involved in the decision to marry. Love is a variable, but still less so than for a person socialized in the United States (Pelzel, 1970).

In evaluating your total relationship, you might take the Relationship Assessment Inventory (see page 212).

Rejecting a Partner

Suppose that after evaluating your relationship with a particular person, you decide to terminate it. What do people give as the reasons for breaking up with their partners, and how might you go about breaking up with your partner?

Breaking Up: The Cover Story versus the Real Story

Most people who end a relationship give the partner a reason for doing so.

Self-Assessment

The Relationship Assessment Inventory

Assuming that you are involved in a relationship that is oriented toward marriage. The following questions are designed to increase your knowledge of how your partner thinks and feels about a variety of issues. You may want to read the questions to your partner and ask your partner to read them to you.

Careers and Money

1. What kind of job or career will you have? What are your feelings about "working in the evening" versus "being home with the family"? Where will your work require that we live? How often do you feel we will be moving? Where are the places you would refuse to move to? How much will your job require that you travel?
2. How much money will you make the first year we are married?
3. What are your feelings about joint versus separate checking accounts? Which of us do you want to pay the bills? How much money do you think we will have left over each month? How much of this do you think we should save?
4. When we disagree over whether to buy something, how do you suggest we resolve our conflict?
5. What "big ticket item" (washer, dryer, microwave, or whatever) do you think we should buy first when we have the money?
6. How often will you want to go on vacation? Where will you want to go? How will we travel? How much money do you feel we should spend on vacations each year?
7. How do you feel about my having a career? Do you expect me to earn an income? If so, how much annually? To what degree do you feel it is your responsibility to cook, clean, and take care of the children? When the children are under age 3, do you want me to stay at home with them or do you think they should be put in a day-care center? When they are sick and one of us has to stay home, who will that be?
8. What is your parents' annual income?
9. Do you want me to account to you for the money I spend?
10. How much money do you think we should give to charity each year?

Religion and Children

1. To what degree do you regard yourself as a religious person? What do you think about religion, a supreme being, prayer, and life after death?
2. Do you go to religious services? Where? How often? Do you pray? How often? What do you pray about? When we are married, how often would you want to go to religious services? In what religion would you want our children to be reared? What responsibility would you take to ensure that our children had the religious training you wanted them to have?
3. How do you feel about abortion? Under what conditions, if any, do you feel abortion is justified?
4. What do you think about children? How many do you want? Why? When do you want the first child? At what intervals would you want to have additional children? What do you see as your responsibility for child care—changing diapers, feeding, bathing, playing with children, and taking them to piano lessons? To what degree do you regard these responsibilities as mine?
5. Suppose I did not want to have children or couldn't have them, how would you feel? How do you feel about artificial insemination, surrogate motherhood, in-vitro fertilization (see Chapter 15), and adoption?

Self-Assessment

6. To your knowledge, can you have children? Are there any genetic problems in your family history that would prevent us from having normal children?
7. Do you want our children to go to public or private schools?
8. How should children be disciplined? How were you disciplined as a child?

Sex

1. How much sexual intimacy do you feel is appropriate in casual dating, involved dating, and engagement?
2. What do you think about masturbation, oral sex, homosexuality, S & M, and anal sex?
3. What type of contraception do you suggest? Why? If that method does not prove satisfactory, what method would you suggest next?
4. What are your values regarding sex outside of marriage? If I were to have an affair and later tell you, what would you do? Why? If I had an affair, would you want me to tell you? Why?
5. What sexual behaviors do you most and least enjoy? How often do you want to have intercourse? How do you want me to turn you down when I don't want to have intercourse? How do you want me to approach you for intercourse? How do you feel about just being physical together—hugging, rubbing, holding, but not having intercourse?
6. If we had a problem we couldn't work out, would you consider seeing a marriage counselor?
7. What does an orgasm feel like to you? By what method of stimulation do you experience an orgasm most easily?
8. What is pornography to you? How do you feel about it?

Partner Feelings

1. If you could change one thing about me, what would it be?
2. What would you like me to do to make you happier?
3. What would you like me to say or not say to make you happier?
4. What do you think of yourself? Describe yourself with three adjectives.
5. What do you think of me? Describe me with three adjectives.
6. What do you like best about me?
7. Do you think I get jealous easily? How will you cope with my jealousy?
8. How do you feel about me emotionally?

Feelings about Parents

1. How do you feel about your mother? Your father?
2. What do you like and dislike about my parents?
3. What is your feeling about living near our parents? How would you feel about my parents living with us? What will we do with our parents if they can't take care of themselves?
4. How do your parents get along? Rate their marriage on a 0–10 scale (0-unhappy; 10-happy). What are your parents' role responsibilities in their marriage?

Other Questions

1. If one of us has to make the final decision on an issue, who should that be?
2. What sports, interests, and hobbies do you enjoy?
3. How often do you like to drink beer, wine, or liquor? How often, if at all, do you like to smoke marijuana, snort coke, or take other drugs? Specify. To what degree do you want me to participate with you?
4. If we couldn't get along, would you be willing to get a divorce?
5. Would you sign a prenuptial contract if I asked you to?
6. After we are married, how often will you want to be away from home at night with your friends? How do you feel about me being out at night with my friends?

TABLE 8.1 CONTRAST BETWEEN THE COVER STORY VERSUS THE REAL STORY WHEN ENDING A RELATIONSHIP

Cover Story	*Real Story*
I'm going off to school and don't want to be tied down.	I wasn't attracted to him anymore.
I need some time to myself.	I was still involved with my old boyfriend.
Our relationship just won't work.	I started liking someone else.
I don't think we are right for each other.	I liked another girl more.
I don't want to get serious.	I liked him only as a friend.
I just want us to be friends.	He was a lousy kisser.
I told her it just wouldn't work.	She was ugly.
Things are confusing, and I need some time to think things out.	She was boring and we weren't compatible.
I'm going off to school, so let's date others.	There wasn't enough sex.
I'm tired of the games we are playing.	He didn't have enough money.
You're getting too involved.	He wasn't ambitious; he was lazy.
Things just won't work out.	He was a jerk.
We're not going anywhere.	We had different goals.
You're pressuring me.	She was lousy in bed.
It's time for us to disconnect.	He was too irresponsible.
I'm going off to school.	We couldn't communicate.
We would both be better off dating others.	I didn't trust him.
I didn't want to get too committed.	I was falling in love, and it scared me.

Source: Knox, 1985.

Data – Of 407 undergraduates, 85 percent reported that they gave their partners a reason for ending the relationship. (Knox, 1985)

However, the reason a partner gives for breaking up is sometimes not his or her "real" reason or motivation for ending the relationship. Table 8.1 illustrates the differences between the cover story and the real story.

Those partners (11 percent) who gave cover stories did so to protect the feelings of the person whom they were rejecting. The most frequent cover stories were designed to avoid telling the person that there was something wrong with him or her ("a lousy kisser, ugly, no ambition") or that they were to be replaced with someone else ("I met someone new"). Because being told either of these real reasons would cause emotional pain and anguish, it could be said that those who use cover stories usually do so out of a desire to prevent pain and to be humane. One woman explained "It would serve no purpose for me to tell him the real reason I didn't want to see him again. He was a nerd, and it was just easier for me to lie." Females were slightly more likely (55 percent compared to 45 percent for males) to give cover stories. (Knox, 1985)

STEPS IN BREAKING UP WITH YOUR PARTNER

Last night I wrote I loved you and your oatmeal cookies; tonight I write I hate you but I still love your oatmeal cookies.
—Hal J. Daniel III

Sometimes you are involved in a relationship that, for whatever reason, you feel the need to terminate. Some guidelines you might consider include the following:

1. Decide that terminating the relationship is what you want to do. In some cases, it may be easier to "fix" the relationship than to drop the partner and get another one. Negotiating differences, compromising,

changing expectations, and giving the relationship more time are alternatives to ending it. But in other cases, it may be wiser to terminate a wounded relationship than to try to keep it alive. As Rhett Butler says to Scarlett O'Hara in *Gone With The Wind:*

> I was never one to patiently pick up broken fragments and glue them together and tell myself that the mended whole was as good as new. What's broken is broken—I'd rather remember it as it was at its best than mend it and see the broken pieces as long as I lived. (Mitchell, 1977, p. 945)

2. Acknowledge and accept that the other person will probably be hurt when you terminate the relationship and that there may be no way you can stop the hurt. One person said, "I can't live with him any more, but I don't want to hurt him either." The two feelings are incompatible. To end a relationship with someone who loves you is usually to hurt him or her.

Consideration

But to continue a relationship with someone because you don't want to hurt him or her is to hurt yourself (you will continue to be frustrated and ask yourself "Why can't I get the nerve to end it?"), your partner (you are living with him or her out of pity), and your relationship (it only exists out of fear of what will happen if you do end it).

Breaking up is sometimes a very lonely experience.

3. Having decided that termination is the goal and that hurting the partner cannot be avoided, tell the partner that you do not want to continue the relationship for a reason that is specific to you ("I need more freedom," "I want to go to graduate school in another state," "I'm not ready to settle down," and the like). Don't blame your partner or give your partner a way to make things better. If you do, the relationship may continue because you may feel obligated to give your partner a second chance. By making the reason specific to yourself and your needs, you take the option of doing something to keep you away from your partner.

Although some people prefer to tell the partner in person, others feel that a letter is easier. "I know it's chicken," said one history major, "but I just can't tell her to her face. I've tried twice and she's talked me out of it both times." Still others prefer the phone. One person used a cassette tape. "I didn't want the coldness of a letter or to get trapped in a phone conversation and hear him start crying, so I made him a cassette tape and mailed it to him."

4. Cut off the relationship completely. If you are the person ending the relationship, you will be less involved in the relationship than your partner. Your lower level of involvement may make it possible for you to continue to see the other person without feeling too hurt when the evening is over. But the other person will have a more difficult time and will heal faster if you stay away completely. To let the person stay in your life is to keep his or her hurt alive. Once you have decided to terminate the relationship, you need to get it over with.
5. Start new relationships. By going out with others you force your ex-partner to acknowledge that you are serious about ending the relationship. You should also encourage your ex-partner to see others. Time usually heals all wounds, but meanwhile another partner is an alternative source of reinforcement.

Consideration

Although you may not feel like initiating contact with others, it will eventually heal the pain to get back into the stream of life by doing so. Don't wait until you feel like seeing others; do it immediately. But watch the level of involvement in a new relationship. Because you have just come from a terminated relationship, you may be particularly vulnerable or susceptible to a new love. For now, the goal should be to see others and have fun—not to fall in love or find a new partner.

Women seem to cope with terminations better than men. In a study of 231 involved couples, among those who ended their relationships, the women were less likely than men to be depressed, lonely, and unhappy afterward (Rubin et al., 1981).

When Your Partner Breaks Up with You

Now suppose that you are on the other end of the breakup and you are the one being dropped. What might you do to get over the terminated relationship and to ease the transition to a new relationship? Here are some possibilities:

1. Recognize that the pain is temporary. Although the hurt you feel when a partner withdraws from you will be intense, keep in mind that it will not last forever. You will get over it—in most cases, completely.
2. Focus on the negatives of the partner. When you think about your ex-partner, be careful not to dwell on the positives (how good the sex was, how much he or she once loved you, how you enjoyed a day at the beach or the Bruce Springsteen concert). These memories will only keep your hurt alive. Instead, focus on the negative aspects of your partner (he or she deceived you, saw someone else while still involved with you, was always late, drank too much, wanted too many or too few kids, or whatever you regard as the disadvantages of the relationship). You may not feel comfortable focusing only on the negative aspects of the relationship, but therapists recommend this technique to help someone get over being left by a partner.
3. Put away mementos of the person. If you have been involved with someone for a while, you may have various symbols of your relationship—gifts, pictures, stones you collected at the beach. If you put the things away that remind you of the person, you may minimize your pain—at least in the short run. Later you will be able to see the same items and perceive them differently. If they bother you, put them away. Shakespeare said, "Praising what is lost makes the remembrance dear."
4. Stay away. One of your greatest needs will be to make contact with the person and get your ex-partner to relate to you as he or she once did. Fight the need, and stay away. Don't call, drop by, or write. The best way to get over your feelings is cold turkey.
5. Initiate new relationships. The best antidote to a terminated relationship is a new one.

Consideration

Whether you terminate a relationship or it is terminated by your partner, take some time, become introspective, and try to learn from the experience. What can you apply to the next relationship as a consequence of having experienced the last relationship?

Timing Your Marital Commitment

Launching a communications satellite into space requires precise timing. If liftoff occurs at other than the exact moment, the satellite will miss its orbit and be lost in space. (RCA once lost a multimillion dollar satellite in space.) Getting into a successful marital orbit also requires timing. Issues to consider in timing your commitment to marriage are age, education, and career.

AGE

Your age and that of your partner at the time of marriage are predictive of your future happiness and stability. Individuals who get married in their early twenties (22–24) have the highest chance of being happy and staying together; those who marry in their teens or their late twenties (27–29) have the highest chance of divorce (Booth and Edwards, 1985). Very early marriages are associated with high rates of extramarital relationships, which are destructive to most marriages. Marriages in the late twenties may also be vulnerable to divorce because "later marriers may be wedding people who are quite different from themselves with respect to lifestyles and education" (p. 73). It is the fact of marrying someone different—not the fact of being "set in one's ways"—that contributes to marital instability in the twenties (Bitter, 1986). Another study found that those who delay first marriage until the age of 30 or beyond have an increased risk of getting divorced (Maneker and Rankin, 1985). Those who marry late must select from a smaller pool of partners.

Data – In a national survey of college students, women said that 25 was the ideal age for getting married; college men said 26 (Stewart, 1986). The actual age for women is 23.3; for men, 25.5. (*Statistical Abstract of the United States,* 1987)

Consideration

Waiting until you have completed college seems to be an ideal time to get married in terms of having a low chance of divorce. According to divorce statistics, marrying in your teens is something to avoid. The teen divorce rate is two to three times greater than the divorce rate among people who marry in their twenties.

Education

How much education you have, when you were educated, and whether you or your partner has more education may also affect your marital happiness and the stability of your relationship. Men who complete college have a lower rate of divorce than men who complete only high school or who leave college with-

Graduating from college helps to insure a higher income.

out graduating. If you marry before you complete college, you will be less likely to complete college. The reason for greater marital stability among college-educated men is not the education itself but the economic potential associated with increased education. The adage "The more you learn, the more you earn" is still true.

Data – The lifetime income of a male who completes high school is $861,000; of a male who completes college, $1,190,000. The lifetime income of a female who completes high school is $381,000; of a female who completes college, $523,000. (*Statistical Abstract of the United States,* 1987)

Increased education for women is predictive of marital stability, but not if a wife has more education than her husband. This is particularly true if the wife is a college graduate and her husband is not (Glick, 1984).

The more educated person may put more "thought" into the selection of a partner. Finally, increased education may also involve enhanced communication and problem-solving skills.

Career Plans

The timing of your marriage will also depend on your career plans. Some individuals feel that they want to be established in a career for a couple of years and be economically independent before they get married. "My sister married a guy in college and threw her career plans to the wind," said one woman. "She's now divorced and is on the job market for the first time at age 31. I'm not going to let that happen to me."

Other people feel they have to make a choice between their career and their partner and fear losing the partner if they choose the career. "I can't put my partner on hold for two years while I find out what it is like in the business world," said another woman. "I'm confident that I'll be a great success in my work, but I don't know how much it will mean if I'm not married to Bill. It is a real dilemma."

Becoming Engaged

Engagement has two meanings—in war, it's a battle; in courtship, it's a surrender.
—Laurence Peter

Having selected a partner after rejecting some partners—and perhaps having been rejected yourself—your mutual commitment to marriage with a compatible partner usually means an engagement. What are the implications of this stage, and how can you use it to increase future happiness?

Implications of an Engagement

The engagement period is usually regarded as serious, partner-exclusive, public, and a preparatory time for the wedding.

Serious

An engagement is a specific commitment to marry. Once the words "let's get married" are spoken and agreed to, the relationship assumes a different status.

The other person is no longer viewed as a casual partner but as a future spouse. Although a few regard engagement lightly, most take it seriously.

Partner-Exclusive

Engagements carry the expectation that all outside relationships (romantic and sexual) will terminate. Seeing other people during the engagement period is often regarded as a reason to break off the relationship. "After I found out he had been seeing his old girlfriend," said one fiancée, "I figured he would also be unfaithful to me when we were married. I confronted him, and he lied about it. We broke up."

Public

Before the announcement of a future wedding, the love relationship belongs solely to the partners. But although love is private, engagement is public. Parents and peers become involved in the event and communicate their evaluations of each partner's marital choice. One business major recalled, "When I was just dating Laura, my best friend said nothing about her one way or the other. But when I told him we were getting married after graduation, he told me she had a 'for rent' sign in her head and that I would be signing up for the nightmare of my life if I married her."

Preparations

Of first weddings, 80 percent take place in a traditional setting (a church or a synagogue) with bridesmaids and ushers. Such an event requires tremendous preparation and, for many couples, is a time of intense stress. "We were both

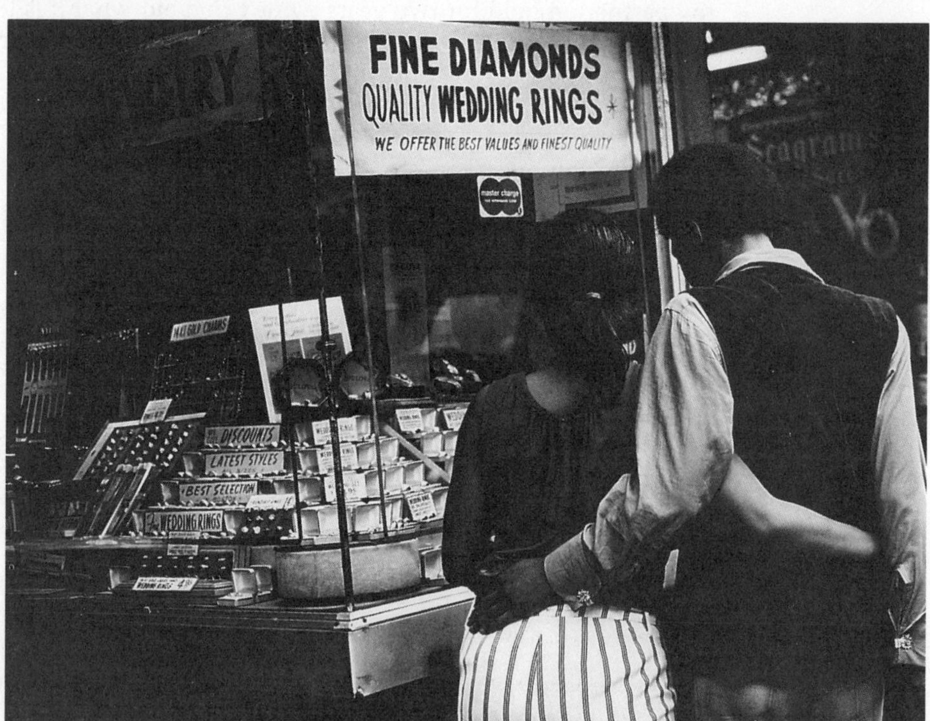

An engagement ring is a public announcement of a private relationship.

under so much pressure preparing for the wedding," recalled one bride, "at one time we considered calling it off. My daddy told us if it was going to be that big of a hassle, to elope and he would give us the $2,500."

Using Your Engagement Period Productively

Marriage is a great institution, but I'm not ready for an institution yet.
—Mae West

"He's not the man I married," said a spouse one year after her wedding. This is as often said of a wife. People frequently do not know the person they are marrying very well. "What you see is what you get" is not true of marriage partners. You really don't know what you have got until you relate to the person in the role of spouse over a period of time. But there are some things you can do to help minimize the surprises after marriage. These include systematically examining your relationship, recognizing dangerous patterns, visiting your future in-laws, and considering premarital counseling.

Examine Your Relationship

In a commercial for an oil filter, a mechanic says he has just completed a "ring job" on a car engine that will cost the owner over $400. He goes on to say that a $5.98 oil filter would have made the job unnecessary, and ends his soliloquy with, "Pay me now, or pay me later." The same idea applies to the consequences of using or not using your engagement period to examine your relationship. At some point, you will take a very close look at your partner and your relationship; but will you do it now—or later? Doing so now may be less costly than doing so after the wedding.

In examining your relationship, consider the compatibility issues discussed earlier in this chapter. To what degree are you and your partner compatible, similar, or dissimilar in terms of the issues that matter to each of you?

Recognize Dangerous Patterns

As you examine your relationship, you should be sensitive to issues that suggest you may be on a collision course. Three such issues are breaking the relationship frequently, constant arguing, and inequality resulting from differences in education, social class, and the like. A roller-coaster engagement is predictive of a marital relationship that will follow the same pattern. However, the psychic and social costs of separating during a marriage are higher.

The same is true of frequent arguments in a relationship.

Consideration

Lovers' arguments become the married couple's fights. Use the premarital period to develop a pattern of resolving differences. If this is not possible, consider the consequence of being married to someone with whom you will have a roller-coaster relationship punctuated by quarrels.

Relationships in which the partners are regarded as being unequal to each other are precarious. Consider the case of Bill and Susan. He was a divorced physician with two children. She was a nurses' aide, and although she held him in awe, they had little in common. Although lovers may view each other with awe, spouses rarely do. Eventually, Bill may feel cheated because he does not have a companion equal to his life and educational experience. Susan may feel stress at continually trying to be what she is not to appease Bill. So persons who are radically different in age, education, social class, and values should be cautious about marrying. Friends select each other because they have something in common and will maintain their relationship for the same reason. Lovers may select each other on the basis of love feelings, but when these feelings dissipate, what they have in common is likely to maintain their interest in each other.

Observe Your Future In-Laws

Don't let your in-laws become out-laws.
—Ed Hartz

Engagements often mean more frequent getting together with each partner's parents, so you might seize the opportunity to assess the type of family your partner was reared in and the implications for your marriage. When visiting your in-laws-to-be, observe their standard of living, the way they relate to each other, and the degree to which your partner is like the parent of the same gender. How does their standard of living compare with that of your own family? How does the emotional closeness (or distance) of your partner's family compare with that of your family? Such comparisons are significant because both you and your partner will reflect your respective home environments to some degree. If you want to know what your partner may be like in 20 years, look at his or her parent of the same gender. There is a tendency for a man to become like his father and a woman to become like her mother.

Consider Premarital Counseling

Most clergy offer three premarital sessions before marrying a couple. These sessions may consist of information about marriage, an assessment of the couple's relationship, or resolving conflicts that have surfaced in the relationship. Those who do not plan to be married in a church or a synagogue or who do not choose to see a clergyman for premarital counseling sometimes see a marriage counselor. A third party can be helpful in assisting a couple to assess their relationship. Although the couple might deny the existence of a problem for fear that looking at it will break up the relationship, the counselor can help them examine the problem and work toward the goal of solving it.

The Premarital Assessment Program (Buckner and Salts, 1985) involves one introductory session and six assessment sessions held over a period of 12 weeks. During this time, the counselor explores with the partners their dating history and wedding plans, expectations of each other, financial situation, parents, values and sexuality, and communication patterns. The Relationship Assessment Inventory on page 212 covers similar concerns.

Premarital counselors make it clear that the goal of the sessions is to explore the relationship between the partners with the partners—not to find something wrong with the relationship. Specifying this goal is important because some persons fear that premarital sessions will break them up and want nothing to stand between them and the wedding.

Prolong Your Engagement If . . .

Even though you and your partner may have examined your relationship, seen a counselor, and feel confident about your impending marriage, there are four conditions under which you might consider prolonging your engagement. In combination, these conditions argue against getting married at this time.

Short Courtship

Couples usually do not date too long before they decide to get married.

Data – In a study of how long 51 spouses dated each other before making a marriage commitment, 29.4 percent dated 0–5 months, 23.5 percent dated 6–11 months, 31.4 percent dated 12–24 months, and 15.7 percent dated 25 months or longer. (Grover et al., 1985)

An extended period of time before the wedding provides an opportunity for each partner to observe the other in a variety of settings. Although we all know happily married people who married soon after they met, the probability of marital success is low for such couples. In general, the longer the partners know each other before they marry, the better chance they have of staying married and having a happy relationship. Even partners who are separated by physical distance can continue to get to know each other as long as they visit frequently and are committed to the future (Carpenter & Knox, 1986).

Consideration

Spouses who date each other for more than two years before making a marriage commitment report the highest degree of marital satisfaction (Grover et al., 1985). While it is possible to date for shorter periods of time and have a happy marriage, the odds are in favor of more time. For dating time to be productive, partners should consider spending time with each other, with their respective future in-laws, and with friends of both partners. Taking the Relationship Assessment Inventory (page 212) will help partners to address some of the important issues in their future marriage.

Lack of Money

A divorced woman listened intently as her lover explained the details of his finances: "Since I too am divorced, I pay alimony and child support. The money that's left barely pays for my food and rent. I'm writing a novel now and will be financially okay if it sells. If it doesn't, my money situation will be tight." The woman refused to see this man again, saying, "I love him, but I loved my first husband too. We literally ate soup, bologna, and peaches for most of our meals. I'm tired of being poor. People who say that love is all you need to make a marriage work must have money." Two researchers (Rosenblatt and Keller, 1983) observe that couples who experience economic distress also tend to blame each other more often.

Data – According to a recent national survey of college students, graduating seniors expect to earn an average of $23,200 annually. (Stewart, 1986)

Parental Disapproval

A parent recalled, "I knew when I met the guy it wouldn't work out. I told my daughter and pleaded that she not marry him. She did, and they are divorced." Such parental predictions (whether positive or negative) often come true. If the predictions are negative, they may contribute to stress and conflict once the couple marries.

Even though parents who reject the commitment choice of their offspring are often regarded as unfair, their opinions should not be taken lightly. The parents' own experience in marriage and their intimate knowledge of their offspring combine to help them assess how their child might get along with a particular mate. If the parents of either partner disapprove of the marital choice, the partners should try to evaluate these concerns objectively. The insights may prove valuable.

Premarital Pregnancy

Of unmarried women who become pregnant, what percent get married?

Data – Of the unmarried women who become pregnant, 48 percent of all unmarried white women and 10 percent of all unmarried black women marry before the birth of the child. (*Statistical Abstract of the United States*, 1987)

The spouses of such marriages have a higher risk of marital unhappiness and divorce than those who do not conceive children before marriage. Combined with a short premarital period, lack of money, and parental or in-law hostility, premarital pregnancy represents an ominous beginning for newlyweds.

Consideration

Should you call off the wedding? If you are having second thoughts about getting married to the person to whom you have made a commitment, you are not alone. About one-third of all engagements are broken. Although some anxiety about getting married is normal (you are entering a new role), constant questions to yourself, such as "Am I doing the right thing?," or thoughts, such as "This doesn't feel right," are definite caution signals that suggest it might be best to call off the wedding. Before marriage, you will be breaking an engagement; after marriage, you will be getting a divorce. Although calling off the wedding will create more anxiety, calling off the marriage (divorce) will create even more. "When in doubt, don't go through with the wedding," says one marriage counselor.

Negative Reasons for Getting Married

In addition to premarital pregnancy, other questionable reasons for getting married include rebound, escape, and pity.

Data – In a survey of over 56,000 *Woman's Day* readers, 41 percent said that they married for the wrong reasons. (Lear, 1986)

Rebound. A rebound marriage results when you marry someone immediately after another person has terminated a relationship with you. It is a frantic attempt to reestablish your desirability in your own eyes and in the eyes of the partner who just dropped you. One man said:

> After she told me she wouldn't marry me, I became desperate. I called up an old girlfriend to see if I could get the relationship going again. We were married within a month. I know it was foolish, but I was very hurt and couldn't stop myself.

Consideration

> To marry on the rebound is questionable because the marriage is made in reference to the previous partner and not to the partner being married. In reality, you are using the person you intend to marry to establish yourself as the winner in the previous relationship. To avoid the negative consequences of marrying on the rebound, you might wait until the negative memories of your past relationship have been replaced by positive aspects of your current relationship. In other words, marry when the satisfactions of being with your current partner outweigh any feelings of revenge.

Escape. A partner may marry to escape an unhappy home situation in which the parents are often seen as oppressive and overbearing and their marriage as discordant. Their continued bickering may be highly aversive, causing the partner to marry to flee the home. A family with an alcoholic parent may create an escape situation. One woman said:

> I couldn't wait to get away from home. Ever since my dad died, my mother has been drinking and watching me like a hawk. "Be home early, don't drink, and watch out for those horrible men," she would always say. I admit it. I married the first guy that would have me. Marriage was my ticket away from that woman.

Consideration

> Marriage for escape is a poor idea. It is far better to continue the relationship with the partner until mutual love and respect, rather than the desire to escape an unhappy situation, become the dominant forces propelling you toward marriage. In this way you can evaluate the marital relationship in terms of its own potential and not solely as an alternative to an unhappy situation.

Pity. Some partners marry because they feel guilty about terminating a relationship with someone who has undergone a radical physical change. The boyfriend of one woman got drunk one Halloween evening and began to light fireworks on the roof of his fraternity house. As he was running away from a Roman candle he had just ignited, he tripped and fell off the roof. He landed on his head and was in a coma for three weeks. A year after the accident his speech and muscle coordination were still adversely affected. The woman said she did not love him any more but felt guilty about terminating a relationship now that he had become physically afflicted. She was ambivalent. She felt it was her duty to marry her fiancée, but her feelings were no longer love feelings.

Pity may also have a social basis. Consider the spouse who fails to achieve a lifetime career goal (for example, flunks out of medical school). The partner may feel badly for the person who has failed but continue to value getting married to someone who is a professional (or successful) in a career or an occupational sense.

Consideration

If one partner loses a limb, becomes brain damaged, or fails in the pursuit of a major goal, it is important to keep the issue of pity separate from the advisability of contracting the marriage. The decision to marry should be based on factors other than pity or gratitude to the partner. This is a value judgment based on the potential long-term negative consequences of contracting a relationship in which one partner has become afflicted late in the courtship process. Although the short-term consequences of marrying an afflicted fiancé may be positive (the partner can avoid the guilt of withdrawal and be steadied by the idea that "I did the responsible thing"), the long-term consequences may have a debilitating effect on the relationship. Negative consequences may be thoughts such as "I married only half a person" or the difficulties of continuing to cope with living with an afflicted person. It is very important to accurately assess the way you feel about your partner if she or he has experienced a physical impairment.

Delaying marriage until all of the "right" conditions are met may be extremely difficult. Most of us assume that *our* marriage will be different, that it will not end in divorce, and that love is enough to compensate for such factors as premarital pregnancy or lack of money. But is this a reasonable assumption in the light of factors suggesting that the wedding be delayed?

Even though all of the indications for a successful marriage are present, either you or your partner may be reluctant to make a commitment. Reluctance may be related to a negative experience in a previous relationship or to the perception that making a commitment may be followed by the other person losing interest or beginning to date others. One student said, "As long as you don't make a commitment, you've got them. Once they know they've got you, they don't want you."

Writing a Premarital Agreement

The primary purpose of a *premarital agreement* (also referred to as an *antenuptial, prenuptial,* or *marriage contract*) is to specify ahead of time how property will be divided and who will be responsible for paying what amounts if there is a divorce. Regarding the popularity of the premarital agreement, two researchers (Freed and Walker, 1986) observed:

> . . . antenuptial agreements are no longer merely concessions used by senior citizens who wish to leave their estate to children of a former marriage. Instead, they have acquired a new appeal for younger working couples or parties seeking to enter into a second marriage, who realize that their nuptials can end in divorce. With the recent expansion of the notion of freedom of contract, crowded court calenders, and the high divorce rate, it has become increasingly attractive for prenuptial spouses to write, within limits, their own ticket by setting the duration and amount of alimony or maintenance, and to make their own equitable distribution of property. (p. 438)

Persons who have been married before are often concerned that money and property be kept separate in a second marriage. One established widowed physician wanted his property and assets to go to his children. The woman he was to marry was also a widow and wanted her estate to go to her daughter.

Those who write a premarital agreement often have children from a previous marriage.

They drew up an agreement stating that whatever property and assets they had would not become the spouse's in the event of death or divorce.

When only one party has assets, a prenuptial contract can have negative consequences for the other party. Sherry, a never-married 22-year-old, signed such an agreement:

> Paul was adamant about my signing the contract. He said he loved me but would never consider marrying anyone unless we signed a prenuptial agreement stating that he would never be responsible for alimony in case of a divorce. I was so much in love, it didn't seem to matter. I didn't realize that basically he was and is a selfish person. Now, five years later, after a divorce, I go to the court begging for alimony while he lives in a big house overlooking the lake with his new wife.

Although most people who are marrying for the first time do not opt for a prenuptial agreement, a higher proportion of people in their second marriages do. Some agreements are designed to keep property separate. Other agreements are informal and designed to clarify expectations in the relationship. Exhibit 8.1 is a marriage agreement of spouses who have been married before. Most of the items in the agreement are about relationship issues and are not enforceable.

Consideration

When the goal of a personal marital contract is to keep property separate, contact an attorney. The laws regulating marriage and divorce vary by state, and only an attorney can ensure that the document that is drawn up will be honored.

Second, a premarital agreement has value beyond the legal commitment. Such an agreement is a form of self-counseling in that many of the topics are the same as those a counselor would discuss with the couple.

Exhibit 8.1

MARRIAGE AGREEMENT

Pam and Mark are of sound mind and body, have a clear understanding of the terms of this contract and of the binding nature of the agreements contained herein; they freely and in good faith choose to enter into this PRENUPTIAL AGREEMENT and MARRIAGE CONTRACT and fully intend it to be binding upon themselves.

Now, therefore, in consideration of their love and esteem for each other and in consideration of the mutual promises herein expressed, the sufficiency of which is hereby acknowledged, Pam and Mark agree as follows:

Names

Pam and Mark affirm their individuality and equality in this relationship. The parties believe in and accept the convention of the wife accepting the husband's name, while rejecting any implied ownership.

Therefore, the parties agree that they will be known as husband and wife and will henceforth employ the titles of address: Mr. and Mrs. Mark Stafford, and will use the full names of Pam Hayes Stafford and Mark Robert Stafford.

Relationships with Others

Pam and Mark believe that their commitment to each other is strong enough that no restrictions are necessary with regard to relationships with others.

Therefore, the parties agree to allow each other freedom to choose and define their relationships outside this contract, and the parties further agree to maintain sexual fidelity each to the other.

Religion

Pam and Mark reaffirm their belief in God and recognize He is the source of their love. Each of the parties have their own religious beliefs.

Therefore, the parties agree to respect their individual preferences with respect to religion and to make no demands on each other to change such preferences.

Children

Pam and Mark both have children. Although no minor children will be involved, there are two (2) children still at home and in school and in need of financial and emotional support.

Therefore, the parties agree that they will maintain a home for and support these children as long as is needed and reasonable. They further agree that all children of both parties will be treated as one family unit, and each will be given emotional and financial support to the extent feasible and necessary as determined mutually by both parties.

Careers and Domicile

Pam and Mark value the importance and integrity of their respective careers and acknowledge the demands that their jobs place on them as individuals and on their partnership. Both parties are well established in their respective careers and do not foresee any change or move in the future.

The parties agree, however, that if the need or desire for a move should arise, the decision to move shall be mutual and based on the following factors:

1. The overall advantage gained by one of the parties in pursuing a new opportunity shall be weighed against the disadvantages, economic and otherwise, incurred by the other.
2. The amount of income or other incentive derived from the move shall not be controlling.
3. Short-term separations as a result of such moves may be necessary.

Exhibit 8.1

Mark hereby waives whatever right he may have to solely determine the legal domicile of the parties.

Care and Use of Living Spaces

Pam and Mark recognize the need for autonomy and equality within the home in terms of the use of available space and allocation of household tasks. The parties reject the concept that the responsibility for housework rests with the woman in a marriage relationship while the duties of home maintenance and repair rest with the man.

Therefore, the parties agree, to share equally in the performance of all household tasks, taking into consideration individual schedules, preferences, and abilities of each.

The parties agree that decisions about the use of living space in the home shall be mutually made, regardless of the parties' relative financial interests in the ownership or rental of the home, and the parties further agree to honor all requests for privacy from the other party.

Property; Debts; Living Expenses

Pam and Mark intend that the individual autonomy sought in the partnership shall be reflected in the ownership of existing and future-acquired property, in the characterization and control of income, and in the responsibility for living expenses. Pam and Mark also recognize the right of patrimony of children of their previous marriages.

Therefore, the parties agree that all things of value now held singly and/or acquired singly in the future shall be the property of the party making such acquisition. In the event that one party to this agreement shall predecease the other, property and/or other valuables shall be disposed of in accordance with an existing will or other instrument of disposal that reflects the intent of the deceased party.

Property or valuables acquired jointly shall be the property of the partnership and shall be divided, if necessary, according to the contribution of each party. If one party shall predecease the other, jointly owned property or valuables shall become the property of the surviving spouse.

Pam and Mark feel that each of the parties to this agreement should have access to monies that are not accountable to the partnership.

Therefore, the parties agree that each shall retain a mutually agreeable portion of their total income and the remainder shall be deposited in a mutually agreeable banking institution and shall be used to satisfy all jointly acquired expenses and debts.

The parties agree that beneficiaries of life insurance policies they now own shall remain as named on each policy. Future changes in beneficiaries shall be mutually agreed on after the dependency of the children of each party has been terminated. Any other benefits of any retirement plan or insurance benefits that accrue to a spouse only shall not be affected by the foregoing.

The parties recognize that in the absence of income by one of the parties, resulting from any reason, living expenses may become the sole responsibility of the employed party and in such a situation, the employed party shall assume responsibility for the personal expenses of the other.

Both Pam and Mark intend their marriage to last as long as both shall live.

Therefore the parties agree that should it become necessary, due to the death of either party, the surviving spouse shall assume any last expenses in the event that no insurance exists for that purpose.

Pam hereby waives whatever right she may have to rely on Mark to provide the sole economic support for the family unit.

Evaluation of the Partnership

Pam and Mark recognize the importance of change in their relationship and intend that

(Continued)

Exhibit 8.1

this CONTRACT shall be a living document and a focus for periodic evaluations of the partnership.

The parties agree that either party can initiate a review of any article of the CONTRACT at any time for amendment to reflect changes in the relationship. The parties agree to honor such requests for review with negotiations and discussions at a mutually convenient time.

The parties agree that, in any event, there shall be an annual reaffirmation of the CONTRACT on or about the anniversary date of the CONTRACT.

The parties agree that, in the case of unresolved conflicts between them over any provisions of the CONTRACT, they will seek mediation, professional or otherwise, by a third party.

Termination of the Contract

Pam and Mark believe in the sanctity of marriage; however, in the unlikely event of a decision to terminate this CONTRACT, the parties agree that neither shall contest the application for a divorce decree or the entry of such decree in the county in which the parties are both residing at the time of such application.

In the event of termination of the CONTRACT and divorce of the parties, the provisions of this and the section on "Property; Debts; Living Expenses" of the CONTRACT as amended shall serve as the final property settlement agreement between the parties. In such event, this CONTRACT is intended to affect a complete settlement of any and all claims that either party may have against the other, and a complete settlement of their respective rights as to property rights, homestead rights, inheritance rights, and all other rights of property otherwise arising out of their partnership. The parties further agree that in the event of termination of this contract and divorce of the parties, neither party shall require the other to pay maintenance costs or alimony.

Decision Making

Pam and Mark share a commitment to a process of negotiations and compromise that will strengthen their equality in the partnership. Decisions will be made with respect for individual needs. The parties hope to maintain such mutual decision making so that the daily decisions affecting their lives will not become a struggle between the parties for power, authority, and dominance. The parties agree that such a process, while sometimes time consuming and fatiguing, is a good investment in the future of their relationship and their continued esteem for each other.

Now, therefore, Pam and Mark make the following declarations:

1. They are responsible adults.
2. They freely adopt the spirit and the material terms of this prenuptial and marriage contract.
3. The marriage contract, entered into in conjunction with a marriage license of the State of Illinois, County of Wayne, on this 12th day of June, 1988, hereby manifests their intent to define the rights and obligations of their marriage relationship as distinct from those rights and obligations defined by the laws of the State of Illinois, and affirms their right to do so.
4. They intend to be bound by this prenuptial and marriage contract and to uphold its provisions before any Court of Law in the Land.

Therefore, comes now, Pam Hayes Carraway, who applauds her development which allows her to enter into this partnership of trust, and she agrees to go forward with this marriage in the spirit of the foregoing PRENUPTIAL and MARRIAGE CONTRACT.

Exhibit 8.1

Therefore, comes now, Mark Robert Stafford, who celebrates his growth and independence with the signing of this contract, and he agrees to accept the responsibilities of this marriage, as set forth in the foregoing PRENUPTIAL and MARRIAGE CONTRACT.

This contract and covenant has been received and reviewed by the Reverend Ralph James, officiating.

Finally, comes Karen James and Bill Dunn, who certify that Pam and Mark did freely read and sign this marriage contract in their presence, on the occasion of their entry into a marriage relationship by the signing of a marriage license of the State of Illinois, County of Wayne, at which they acted as official witnesses. Further, they declare that the marriage license of the parties bears the date of the signing of this PRENUPTIAL and MARRIAGE CONTRACT.

Predicting Your Marital Happiness

Whether or not you develop a marriage contract with your partner, you will make a prediction about the success of your marriage. But how can you be sure you are right? You can't. It is not possible to predict with 100 percent accuracy what your level of marital satisfaction will be even three days after your wedding. There are several reasons why.

Illusion of the Perfect Mate

The illusion that you have found the perfect partner—one who will be all things to you, and vice versa—will carry you through courtship. However, the reality is very different. You have not found the perfect mate—there isn't one. Anyone you marry will come with a minus quality, and the one quality that is lacking may become the only one you regard as important (Sammons, 1987). When some people discover that their partner lacks something they think is essential ("the ability to communicate," "being faithful," "loves me"), they may consider a divorce.

Data – Of 56,000 women responding to a *Woman's Day* survey, one-half said that they would not marry the same man again. (Lear, 1986)

Marital happiness is hard to predict because the drug of the premarital period—love—alters your view of the partner; but this view is only an illusion.

Deception During the Premarital Period

Your illusion of the perfect mate is helped along by some deception on the part of your partner. At the same time, you are presenting only favorable aspects of yourself to the other person. These deceptions are often not deliberate but are merely attempts to withhold the undesirable aspects of yourself for fear that your partner may not like them. One male student said he knew he drank too much, but that if his date found out, she would be disappointed and might drop him. He kept his drinking hidden throughout their courtship. They married and are now divorced. She said of him, "I never knew he drank whiskey until our honeymoon. He never drank like this before we were married."

Courtship elicits only the most positive aspects of an individual. Marriage elicits more (and sometimes less positive) aspects of the individual.

Confinement of Marriage

Life is like a dog-sled team. If you ain't the lead dog, the scenery never changes.
—Lewis Grizzard

Another factor that makes it impossible to predict your continued happiness is the different circumstances of the premarital period and marriage. Although premarital norms permit relative freedom to move in and out of relationships, marriage involves a legal contract. One recently married person described marriage as an iron gate that clangs shut behind you, and "getting it open is almost impossible." One's freedom to leave a relationship is transformed by the wedding ceremony. Thereafter, there is tremendous social pressure to work things out and a feeling of obligation to do so that was not previously present. The new sense of confinement often brings out the worst in partners who seemed very cooperative before marriage.

Balancing Work and Relationship Demands

Predicting marital happiness is also difficult because the partners must necessarily shift their focus from each other to the business of life. Careers and children emerge as concerns that often take precedence over spending time with each other, going to parties, and seeing movies. Time and energy spent on jobs and childrearing often leave marriage partners too tired to interact with each other. "I never see my partner" is a statement often heard by marriage counselors. Also, the more abrasive communication encouraged by conditions of stress has negative consequences for the way partners feel about each other. "Whenever we do get together, we fight," said one partner.

Inevitability of Change

One of the major themes of this text is that you are continually changing. Just as you are not the same person you were 10 years ago, you will be different 10 years from now. The direction and intensity of these changes are not predictable for you or for your partner. You, your partner, and your relationship will not be the same two years (or two days) in a row. Reflecting on change in her marriage, one woman recalled:

Though we were still happy with each other, we were growing in different ways.
—Cybill Sheperd of her ex-spouse

> When we were married we were very active in politics. Now I have my law degree and am enjoying my practice. But Jerry is totally immersed in meditating and taking health-food nutrients. He also spends four nights a week playing racketball. I never imagined that we'd have nothing to say to each other after only three years of marriage.

Other spouses may maintain similar interests across years of marriage, but either or both may undergo a dramatic change in mental functioning. In recent years, Alzheimer's disease and its attendent problems for interpersonal relationships has been featured in the media (Wasow, 1986). One spouse said:

> We've lived together for 36 years, and now she has Alzheimer's disease. It means that the last of life we were looking forward to sharing has become a nightmare. She

sometimes forgets my name and resents it when I try to help dress her. But if I don't she'll put her bra on backwards and she literally forgets where the bathroom is. I know that her brain has deteriorated and that the person I once knew is no longer inside, but it hurts me so much.

Consideration

Whether or not you will be happily married after your wedding cannot be predicted. Although selecting a compatible partner is basic, other factors that are crucial to a successful marriage include giving up any illusions of finding a perfect mate, minimizing premarital deception, accepting (and enjoying) the confinement of marriage, balancing work and relationship demands, and adapting to whatever changes occur.

Trends

With more than 50 percent of all marriages ending in divorce, some couples are becoming more cautious about entering into marriage. The growing possibility that "divorce may happen to me too" may reduce the number of hasty, ill-conceived marriages. The fact that age at marriage is inching upward may reflect a greater determination to marry when the conditions are right, not when the emotions are ready. Also, the use of marriage agreements reflects a concern that each partner be aware of the other's expectations to prevent misunderstandings.

It appears to me that finding someone one can truly enjoy is, to some extent, a happy accident.
—James Walters

In addition to exercising greater caution in entering into marriage, alternatives to the traditional formal engagement are becoming more acceptable. Although the engagement ring and wedding announcement will continue to be the script for most people, a growing number, particularly those who live together, will bypass the formality of an engagement period.

Summary

In selecting a marital partner, you might consider the degree to which you are compatible in the areas of recreation, sex, career and family goals, roles, and values (religion, life style, politics, self-actualization).

Communication, flexibility, and body-clock compatibility are also critical issues to assess in selecting a partner. Being able to talk about your feelings, needs, and expectations and being able to negotiate differences when they occur are probably the most essential characteristics in selecting a partner. Flexibility is important because life continually involves change. Body-clock compatibility, although less significant than the ability to communicate with a flexible partner, will make day-to-day living, working, and playing with your spouse a little easier.

The process of selecting a partner may involve rejecting some partners. This usually cannot be done without hurting the partner, but giving reasons specific to yourself, not blaming the partner, and dating others will help to heal the hurt in a shorter period of time. When you are rejected, as we all are, the adjustment can be enhanced by recognizing that the pain is temporary, focusing on the negative aspects of the terminated relationship, and instigating new relationships immediately. The only caveat of new relationships is to avoid any immediate new commitments.

You can use the engagement period productively by systematically examining your relationship, observing your future in-laws for clues about your partner's background and character, and going for premarital counseling. Conditions under which you might want to prolong your engagement include having known each other for less than two years, having an inadequate or unstable source of income, having parents who disapprove of your marriage, and being pregnant.

Some couples decide to write a marriage agreement to specify the understandings of their relationship. If these involve the disposition of property and assets, a lawyer should be asked to draw up the agreement. Otherwise, the document may not be in legal terms recognized by the courts.

Regardless of what you do, you will not be able to guarantee yourself and your partner a happy marriage. The illusion of the perfect mate, deception during the premarital period, the confinement of marriage, the demands of careers and children, and the inevitability of change make prediction of future marital happiness impossible.

Trends in marital commitments include the possibility of greater caution in entering marriage (the fact that people are marrying later is some evidence for this) and the bypassing of some formal aspects of the engagement period.

Questions for Reflection

1. Most people in marriage feel that if the partners love each other enough, a personal marriage agreement is unnecessary and is a violation of the spirit of marriage. How do you feel? Would you develop an agreement for your marriage or agree to do so if your partner asked you to?
2. Why is it difficult to terminate a relationship that an individual knows is not a good one?
3. What are the conditions under which you would terminate a relationship before making a marital commitment?

CHOICES

SEVENTY STUDENTS IN a marriage and family class were asked if they would sign or ask their partners to sign a marriage agreement. About 40 percent said "yes."

Marriage Agreement: Yes

Those opting for a marriage agreement gave a variety of reasons:

I didn't have one in my previous relationship, and it caused a lot of problems because I didn't. I have a large inheritance, and my partner wanted to get his hooks into it.

Such a contract will make a divorce settlement less complicated.

If I brought something into the marriage, such as a savings account, I wouldn't want my partner to have one cent of it if we got divorced.

You know what happened to Johnny Carson. If he had had such an agreement, he would have gotten off easier in the settlement.

Although we may marry for love, we divorce in a state of hate. A contract about who gets what would come in handy at that time.

Although you marry when you are in love, feelings change and it's hard to predict the future. I am a very independent person, and I would like my husband to be independent also. Although our relationship will be based on emotional dependence on each other, I want each of us to be financially independent.

I am an only child, and I would hate for the money that my parents and grandparents worked so hard for to go to somebody outside the family.

Marriage Agreement: No

An equal number of students (40 percent) said they would not sign a marriage agreement or ask their partner to do so. Their reasons follow:

Asking your future spouse to sign such an agreement would mean that you don't trust them. I wouldn't marry someone unless I was absolutely positive that he or she was the one for me and that we would be together for the rest of our lives.

Signing a prenuptial agreement implies that your marriage won't last. It's a bad way to start a marriage.

It [a marriage agreement] would weaken the marriage from the start by making it easier to get out if something goes wrong. It also doesn't show complete trust, which is a core issue in any successful marriage relationship.

I wouldn't have the nerve to bring up a prenuptial agreement. It would be like slapping my partner's face.

A prenuptial agreement in my opinion is like saying that I want as much as I can get, and I just don't like the feel of such an agreement. In a marriage relationship, there should be a special trust—and if you don't have that, you're in trouble.

Marriage is an emotional commitment of each partner to the other that results from the love each feels for the other. If either partner asks the other to sign such an agreement, this takes all the emotion out of the relationship and you're headed toward a divorce.

Marriage Agreement: It Depends

About 20 percent of the respondents in the marriage and family class said that they would sign or ask their partner to sign such an agreement under certain conditions:

I would definitely consider a prenuptial agreement if I were a widow or a divorcée with children and had a considerable estate or money. While a prenuptial agreement would take a lot of the "glitter" and "romance" out of a second marriage, my first priority would be to protect my money for my children.

(Continued)

> If I were making myself financially secure and found the girl of my dreams, I wouldn't ask her to sign such an agreement. But if I had already made my fortune and then found someone I loved, I would consider asking her to sign such an agreement.
>
> No matter how much in love a couple is, whenever one owns anything of monetary value and the other one does not, that person should think with his head about keeping what is rightfully his. Some people do marry for money, and you need to watch out for them.

One student emphasized the importance of open communication.

> I believe that both people must want a prenuptial agreement to alleviate some of the anxieties that might arise, such as distrust and misunderstanding. Moreover, I believe both people should communicate openly their fears, conceptions, and feelings about a prenuptial agreement. Further, I believe that if both have decided after lengthy dialogue that a prenuptial agreement is in order, both parties should sign on the dotted line. I want to emphasize that this must be a mutual decision with shared responsibility.

SHOULD THE WIFE KEEP HER MAIDEN NAME?

Although the U.S. Census Bureau does not keep records on the extent to which married women are keeping their maiden names, more and more women are and the trend is increasing. Reasons include the delay of marriage, during which time a woman establishes a professional identity she does not want to lose, pride in one's own family name, and an awareness of the high divorce rate and the desire to avoid having a name to remind you of a bad marriage if it ends. Options include the woman (for example, Mary Smith getting married to Mark Adams) keeping her last name (Ms. Mary Smith), hyphenating her last name (Ms. Mary Smith-Adams), or using her maiden name as her middle name (Ms. Mary S. Adams). Whatever the decision, it is important to use the same name consistently and to make sure that the name you are using is registered with the Social Security Administration and the Internal Revenue Service.

Impact of Social Influences on Choices

Whether or not the respective partners insist on a prenuptial agreement and/or the wife insists on keeping her maiden name are influenced by the social forces that operate on the man and the woman. Regarding a marriage agreement, if each partner has been married before and has children who will inherit from him or her, there is an increased probability that each partner will develop a marriage agreement. The social context of offspring has more to do with whether or not a couple has a prenuptial agreement than with whether or not the partners feel that such an agreement connotes a lack of love or commitment.

A woman who insists on keeping her own name after marriage has also probably been strongly influenced by peers who have done the same and/or by parents who support her doing so. Such decisions are rarely made independently of what others think.

Finally, the timing of your commitment to marriage is often related to completing a particular phase of education (for example, graduation) or establishing yourself in a career or some other goal or "rite of passage." Hence, a person becomes "ripe" and seeks a mate in reference to something external to the partner. He or she marries one person from a pool of potential partners who are available at the time the selection occurs. Sometimes two people are very compatible, but one or both of them is not ready to get married. They break up, years go by, and each marries someone else when he or she is ready. Social forces of readiness—not the occasion of actually finding a compatible and loving partner—often dictate when a person gets married.

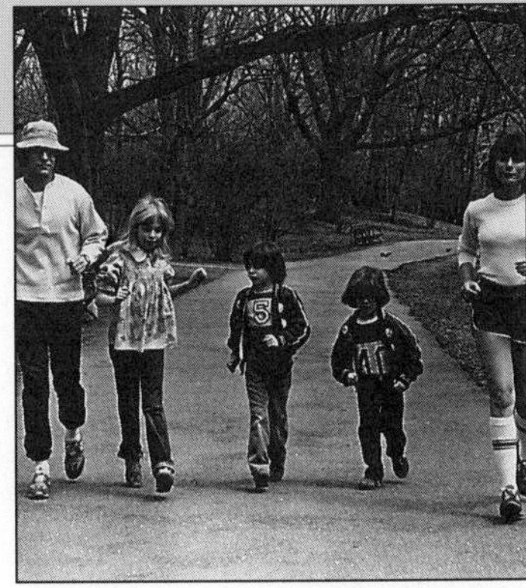

PART THREE

REALITIES

WHEN THE UNITED States was primarily rural, family members looked to each other to fulfill a variety of their needs—religious, recreational, educational, economic, and protective. Although people went to church, family members would gather around the open fire in the evening while father read from the Bible. Instruction in honesty, faithfulness, and obedience was part of the family's religious ritual. Education was also home-generated; although there was much work to do on the farm (milking cows, repairing fences, and tending crops), the family was the recreational unit, too. Finally, the rifle over the mantle was a symbol of family protection and sometimes a practical necessity.

Today, all of these needs can be met outside the family. Churches and synagogues compete for membership. The state has taken over the education function. Recreation is no longer home-oriented; family members look to events outside the family for fun and to people outside the family to have fun with. Family members also earn their living outside the family by working for the government or for private industry or business. The spirit generated from working together as a family is gone. Finally, public police protection has replaced the need for a rifle over the mantle.

Although most of the needs of family members can be met outside the family, the need to feel emotionally connected to others, to be a part of others' lives, continues to be a major aspect that marriage and the family offer. Other realities of marriage involve work, sex, communication, and abuse.

CHAPTER 9

Marriage Relationships

Contents

Is It True?*

1. Married students tend to have more friends than single students.
2. The wedding ceremony involves an exchange of property.
3. Black marriages tend to be less happy than white marriages.
4. In black marriages, the mother-child relationship tends to take precedence over the wife-husband relationship.
5. Wives of retired husbands tend to be happier than wives whose husbands are going to work every day.

*1=F; 2=T; 3=T; 4=T; 5=F.

After making the final choice of a marriage partner, two people make a marital commitment, get married, and move into their new roles as spouses. Such a transition involves various rites of passage and personal, social, and legal consequences. In this chapter, we will examine these changes as well as an array of marriages of different groups and types—college, mixed (interfaith, interracial, age-discrepant), black, Mexican American, "very happy," and elderly marriages. The prevailing theme of this chapter is that there is no one marriage relationship. There are only marriage relationships, which differ by social class, ethnicity, religion, physical ability (or disability), presence or absence of children, degree of freedom or intimacy, and education of spouses, among other variables. These differences imply that your marriage will be unique—special to you and your partner.

Marriage as a Commitment

Maxim Gorky said, "When a woman gets married, it's like jumping into a hole in the ice in the middle of winter; you do it once, and you remember it for the rest of your days." One of the reasons getting married leaves such an indelible memory is the significance of the commitment. Marriage represents a multilevel commitment—person to person, family to family, and couple to state.

Person to Person

Marital happiness is the most important determinant of overall happiness.

—Mary Benin & Barbara Nienstedt

Commitment may be defined as an intent to maintain a relationship. Saying "I do" in a marriage ceremony implies that you and your partner are making a personal commitment to love, support, and negotiate differences with each other. You are establishing a primary relationship with your partner. All other relationships become secondary.

Family to Family

Marriage also involves commitments by each of the marriage partners to the family members of the spouse. Recently married couples are often expected to divide their holiday visits between both sets of parents. In addition, each spouse becomes committed to help his or her in-laws when appropriate and to regard family ties as part of marital ties. For some older couples, this means caring for disabled parents who may live in their home. "We always said that no parent was ever going to live with us," said one spouse. "But my wife's father died, and her mother had no place to go. Her living here was an initial strain, but we've learned to cope with the situation quite well."

Not all couples accept the family to family commitment. Some spouses have limited contact with their respective parents. "I haven't seen my folks in years and don't want to," said one woman in her second marriage.

Couple to State

Finally, the spouses become legally committed to each other according to the laws of the state in which they reside. This means they cannot arbitrarily decide to terminate their own marital agreement.

Families represent a commitment across generations.

Data – Around 2½ million marriage licenses are issued to couples every year. These represent a legal bond—not only between the individuals, but also between the couple and the state. (*Statistical Abstract of the United States*, 1987)

Just as the state says who can marry (not close relatives, the insane, or the mentally deficient) and when (usually at age 18 or older), legal procedures must be instituted if the couple want to divorce. The state's interest is that a couple stay married, have children, and take care of them.

Rites of Passage

The transition from one social status to another that is marked by some specific event is referred to as a *rite of passage.* The first day in school, getting a driver's license, and graduating from college are all events that mark major role transitions (to student, driver, and graduate). For two people in love, the marriage ceremony is a rite of passage to the role of spouse.

WEDDINGS

I hope you will be as happy as we all thought we would be.
—Said to a bride at her wedding reception.

In preparation for the wedding, some states require each partner to have a blood test to certify that neither has a sexually transmitted disease in the communicable stage. (The American Medical Association and the Centers for Disease Control in Atlanta have also recommended requiring an AIDS antibody test before marriage.) This document is then taken to the county courthouse, where the couple applies for a marriage license. Two-thirds of the states require a waiting period between the issuance of the license and the wedding. (Table 9.1 details state laws on marriage.) Eighty percent of the couples are married by a clergyman; 20 percent (primarily remarriages) go to a justice of the peace.

TABLE 9.1 MARRIAGE LAWS

Revised by Gary N. Skoloff, lecturer on Matrimonial Law, Institute for Continuing Legal Education, Newark, N.J., as of September 17, 1986.

State	Age with parental consent		Age without consent		Physical exam and blood test for male and female: Maximum period between exam and license (in days)	Scope of medical exam	Waiting period (in days)	
	Male	Female	Male	Female			Before license	After license
Alabama*	14a	14a	18	18	30	b	—	s
Alaska	16c, z	16c, z	18	18	30	b	3 w	—
Arizona	16c, z	16c, z	18	18	30	—	—	—
Arkansas	17c	16c	18	18	—	—	v	—
California	aa	aa	18	18	30	bb	—	h
Colorado*	16z	16z	18	18	30	bb	—	s
Connecticut	16z	16z	18	18	35 w	b	4 w	ttt
Delaware	18c	16c	18	18	—	—	—	e, s
Florida	16a, c	16a, c	18	18	60	b	3	s
Georgia*	16c, f	16c, f	16	16	30	b	3g	—
Hawaii	16d	16d	18	18	—	b	3 w	—
Idaho*	16z	16z	18	18	—	bb	—	—
Illinois	16c	16c	18	18	15	b, n	—	ee
Indiana	17c	17c	18	18	60	bb, n	3	t
Iowa*	aa	aa	18	18	20	b	3	tt
Kansas*[y]	18z	18z	18	18	30	b	3 w	—
Kentucky	18a, c	18a, c	18	18	—	—	3	—
Louisiana	18d	16d	18	18	10	b	—	3 w
Maine	16d	16d	18	18	60	—	3 v, w	f
Maryland	16c	16c	18	18	—	—	2 w	ff
Massachusetts	18d	18d	18	18	33	bb	3 v	t
Michigan	16c	16c	18	18	30	b	3	—
Minnesota	16z	16z	18	18	—	—	5 w	—
Mississippi	17d	15d	17	15	30	b	3 w	—
Missouri	15d	15d	18	18	—	—	3 w	—
Montana*[yy]	15d	15d	18	18	20	bb	3	ff, 3 w
Nebraska[yy]	18c	16c	17	17	30	bb	2	—
Nevada	16z	16z	18	18	—	—	—	—
New Hampshire	14k	13k	18	18	30	b, l	5 v	h
New Jersey	16z, c	16z, c	18	18	30	b	3 w	s
New Mexico[y]	16c	16c	18	18	30	b	—	—
New York	16j	14j	18	18	30	nn	10	1 w, t
North Carolina	16c	16c	18	18	30	m	—	—
North Dakota	16	16	18	18	—	b	—	—
Ohio*	18c, z	16c, z	18	18	30	b	5	t
Oklahoma	16c	16c	18	18	30	b	p	—
Oregon	17	17	18	18	—	—	3 w	t
Pennsylvania*	16d	16d	18	18	30	b	3 w	t
Puerto Rico[y]	18d	16d	21	21	—	b	—	—
Rhode Island*	18d	16d	21	21	40 w	bb	—	—
South Carolina*	16c	14c	18	18	—	—	1	—
South Dakota	16c	16c	18	18	—	—	—	tt
Tennessee	16d	16d	18	18	30	—	3 cc	s
Texas*[y]	14j	14j	18	18	21	b	—	s
Utah	14	14	18x	18x	30	b	—	s
Vermont	16z	16z	18	18	30	b	—	3 w
Virginia	16a, c	16a, c	18	18	30	b	—	t

Washington 17d	17d	18	18	—	—	3	t
West Virginia 18c	16c	18	18	30	b	3 w	—
Wisconsin 16	16	18	18	20	b	5 w	s
Wyoming 16d	16d	18	18	30	b	—	—
Dist. of Columbia* 16a	16a	18	18	30 w	b	3 w	—

*Indicates 1987 common-law marriage recognized; in many states, such marriages are only recognized if entered into many years before. (a) Parental consent not required if minor was previously married. (aa) No age limits. (b) Venereal diseases. (bb) Venereal diseases and Rubella (for female). In Colorado, Rubella for female under 45 and Rh type. (c) Younger parties may obtain license in case of pregnancy or birth of child. (cc) Unless parties are over 17 years of age. (d) Younger parties may obtain license in special circumstances. (e) Residents before expiration of 24-hour waiting period; nonresidents formerly residents, before expiration of 96-hour waiting period; others 96 hours. (ee) License effective 1 day after issuance, unless court orders otherwise; valid for 60 days only. (f) If parties are under 16 years of age, proof of age and the consent of parents in person is required. If a parent is ill, an affidavit by the incapacitated parent and a physician's affidavit to that effect required. (ff) License valid for 180 days only. (g) Unless parties are 18 years of age or more, or female is pregnant, or applicants are the parents of a living hcild born out of wedlock. (h) License valid for 90 days only. (i) Age of consent for common-law marriage male 14, female 12. (j) Parental consent and permission of judge required. (k) Below age of consent parties need parental consent and permission of judge. (l) With each certificate issued to couples, a list of family planning agencies and services available to them is provided. (m) Mental incompetence, infectious tuberculosis, venereal diseases, and Rubella (certain counties only). (n) Venereal diseases; test for sickle cell anemia given at request of examining physician. (nn) Tests for sickle cell anemia may be required for certain applicants. (o) Feeblemindedness, imbecility, insanity, chronic alcoholism, and venereal diseases. In Washington, also advanced tuberculosis and, if male, contagious venereal disease. Marriage prohibited unless it is established that procreation is not possible. (p) If one or both parties are below the age for marriage without parental consent, (3 day waiting period). (r) Judge may waive requirements if religious beliefs conflict or emergency exists. (s) License valid for 30 days only. (t) License valid for 60 days only. (tt) License valid for 20 days only. (ttt) License valid for 65 days. (v) Parties must file notice of intention to marry with local clerk. (w) Waiting period may be avoided. (x) Authorizes counties to provide for pre-marital counseling as a requisite to issuance of license to persons under 19 and persons previously divorced. (y) Marriages by proxy are valid. (yy) Proxy marriages are valid under certain conditions. (z) Younger parties may marry with parental consent and/or permission of judge. In Connecticut, judicial approval.

World Almanac & Book of Facts 1987, p. 106. © Newspaper Enterprise Association, Inc.; 200 Park Avenue; New York, NY 10166. Used by permission.

Although some couples may agree to a religious ceremony and perfunctorily participate to abide by their parents' wishes, others accept the emphasis in traditional religious weddings that marriage is a sacred relationship ordained by God. The religious representative, the setting, the music, and the words of the ceremony ("holy matrimony") take marriage from the secular into the spiritual realm. Indeed, the ending of the traditional ceremony emphasizes God's presence and approval: "Therefore, whom God hath joined together, let no man put asunder." The solemnity of the ceremony is designed to impress the couple with the seriousness of the responsibilities they are undertaking to each other, to their future children, and to their respective families.

It is no longer unusual for couples to have weddings that are neither religious nor traditional. Only friends of the couple and members of the immediate families may gather in the bride-to-be's back yard. Rather than the traditional white gown, the bride may wear her favorite dress. The groom may wear a suit (he just as well may not), and everyone else wears whatever they think is appropriate. In the exchange of vows, neither partner promises to obey the other, and their relationship is spelled out by the partners rather than by tradition. Vows often include the couple's feelings about equality, individualism, humanism, and openness to change (see Exhibit 9.1).

Part of the preference for less lavish, less traditional weddings is economic. A couple can easily spend $10,000 on a wedding for the reception, rings, clothes, photographer, clergyman or woman, and other related expenses. This amount does not include the honeymoon.

Exhibit 9.1

A Modern Exchange of Vows

I love you and want to be with you. I do not belong to you nor do I want you to belong to me, but rather I want us to have a relationship in which we will want to be with each other and in which we will nurture each other's growth while maintaining our own separateness and individuality. In that interest, I express the following goals, promises, and commitments.

First of all, I accept responsibility for myself. I will not depend on you for my fulfillment as a person. I will accept my ultimate aloneness in life and the responsibility for my own happiness. But out of my aloneness, I desire to share time and space with you. I will be with you while intimately sharing past and present experiences along with hopes, dreams, and plans for the future.

I will be reliable and open to you so that we will maintain a basis of trust between us. I will love and trust myself in order to continually become a more trustworthy person to you and add fidelity, security, and depth to our relationship. I will grow and change, but through honest dialogue I will maintain your trust in me.

I will respect you as an individual person and will cherish your uniqueness. I will strive to help you become more of yourself, even though that may differ from what I would like for you to be. I will take pride in you and your differences from me. I will consistently remember those qualities and traits that are beautiful about you and consistently communicate my love by recognizing your inner and outer beauty through words and actions.

In times of need, I will care for you and for myself. I understand that there will be times of pain as well as joy in our relationship. In troubled times, I will try to be considerate, compassionate, caring, nonjudgmental, and forgiving. I understand that you and I, in our humanness, have limitations and will make mistakes. I will accept those limitations in myself and in you and will not expect either of us to be perfect. I understand that in your love you have exposed your human vulnerabilities. I will respond with consideration—to cherish and invite you to feel protected without undue pain.

I will not take you for granted. I will consistently be aware of and emotionally present to you. I will listen to you when you speak, and I will encourage you whenever I possibly can.

In giving myself to you, I will give from my inner joy and not from duty. I will consistently enjoy sharing those parts of myself that you enjoy. I will enrich and preserve my body, mind, and spirit for you and me. I will continue to change, striving to become a more mature and stimulating person. I will accept changes in you as well as in myself. I will gracefully accept the limitations of aging for both of us. As I grow older, I will try to develop wisdom and integrity of character, and I will encourage and appreciate similar growth in you.

I will consistently make time available for being together, for communication, for work, for fun, and for love. No matter how many demands or enticements I experience for success or childrearing, I will set aside and give the highest priority to our time together.

I will share in the parenting experience of providing care, setting limits, and giving opportunities for Megan Carol and any other children born to us. I will share in helping them to grow as persons and achieve their own wishes, hopes, and dreams. With you, I will give them roots and stability, but I will also let them go to develop their own wings.

Exhibit 9.1

I will share with you in the development of a community of friends and family. I will share with you in contributing to our larger community around us.

As much as possible, I will try to be aware of a sense of values, of eternal values. I will try to consider those things that are of real consequence, as well as respond to the cares of the moment.

Most of all, I will try to be a real person to you. I will try to give you the kind of love that will encourage the realness in you. Let our lives be filled with effort, expectation, and desire and something evermore about to be.

Hal and Sherry

Reprinted by permission of Hal G. Gillespie, M.D., and Cheryl L. Gillespie, R.N., M.S.

Consideration

The alternative to spending such large sums on a wedding is elopement. Some couples make a deal with their parents either to elope or to have a small wedding in the back yard. One bride said, "The marriage license cost us $10, and we're using the $4,000 my dad gave us as a down payment on a mobile home." However, other couples want the experience of a big wedding. "I'm only going to get married once," said one bride-to-be. "And I want it to be a big church wedding with a horse-drawn carriage to take us away after the reception."

Honeymoons

Couples who live together before marriage are less likely to go on a honeymoon following their wedding. After brunch, dinner, or a party, they may return to their apartment or house, much as they would at the end of a normal day. "The newness is gone once you've lived with someone," remarked a new husband. "And while being married is supposed to be different, it doesn't *feel* that way."

For honeymooners, their first week or 10 days as a married couple are often spent in one resort location, traveling each day to a new place or loafing for several days with no schedule of places to be or things to do. Disneyland, the Bahamas, and camping are favorite honeymoons for many couples.

Regardless of where the couple goes, the honeymoon serves various social and personal functions. The social function of the honeymoon is to make it normative for the couple to isolate themselves from others. Although a few people will play pranks like tampering with the couple's car, hiding the luggage just after the wedding, or handcuffing the new husband to a doorknob, most people are socialized to view honeymooners as deserving of privacy.

This period of undisturbed privacy provides a personal function of the honeymoon—recuperation. Traditional weddings may include bridal showers, a rehearsal, a rehearsal dinner, and a long reception; the bride and groom often feel exhausted by the time they reach their first night's destination. The bride is usually more fatigued, since she has assumed greater responsibility for the wedding than her partner. "I was sick when we got to the motel room," recalled an exhausted bride. "I hadn't slept soundly in three days and had

A honeymoon is a time to be alone.

eaten only peanuts and cookies. I was a wreck." But the honeymoon dictates no responsibilities, plenty of sleep, and good food—the physician's prescription for fatigue.

Consideration

When deciding whether to go on a honeymoon, remember that there is only one honeymoon for each marriage and it can only take place right after the wedding. Although a couple may take subsequent trips, their first days following the wedding (particularly if they have not lived together) are unique. You can't have a honeymoon later.

Changes After Marriage

Whether a couple go on a honeymoon or not, they will become aware of various changes—personal, social, legal, and sexual—that occur as a result of getting married.

Personal Changes

An initial enhanced self-concept is a predictable consequence of getting married. Your parents and closest friends will arrange their schedules to participate in your wedding and will give you gifts to express their approval. In contrast, there is no rite of passage if you decide to remain single, cohabit, or live in a commune. There is no ceremony, no fussing and excited parents or friends, no gifts—only the implied question, "Is something wrong with you?" As a married person, you are assumed to be "normal" and to have made the right decision. The strong evidence that your spouse approves of you and is willing to spend a lifetime with you also tells you that you are okay.

The married person also begins adopting new values and behaviors consistent with the married role. Although new spouses often vow that "marriage won't change me," it does. For example, rather than stay out all night at a party, which is not uncommon for singles who may be looking for someone to bed, spouses (who are already paired off) tend to go home early. Their roles of spouse, employee, and parent, force them to adopt more regular hours. The role of married person implies a different set of behaviors than the role of single person. Although there is an initial resistance to "becoming like old married folks," the resistance soon gives way to the realities of the role.

Almost all newlyweds like sex in the beginning.
—Ellen Frank & Carol Anderson

Another result of getting married is disenchantment. It may not happen in the first few weeks or months of marriage, but it is almost inevitable. Farrah Fawcett once said, "Marriage—that's when the blazing torch of love slowly turns into a pilot light." Whereas courtship is the anticipation of a life together, marriage is the day-to-day reality of that life together—and reality does not always fit the dream. Daily marital interaction exposes both partners as they really are: human beings who get tired and irritable. "Burt never snapped at me about anything when we were dating, but I never acted like a mean bitch (his term) before we were married either," expressed a wife of six months.

The disenchantment is also related to shifting the partners' focus of interest away from each other and toward their work. When children come, their focus extends to the children. If the woman is not home-oriented, she may shift her interest into her career. In any case, each partner gives and gets less attention in marriage than in courtship.

The speed of the disenchantment process may be related to the number of other changes going on in the partners' lives. As an example, Bob and Louise, a newly married couple, moved to another city and bought a house. Louise wrote her dissertation for her Ph.D. while Bob changed careers and enrolled in medical school. They also decided to begin their family, and Louise became pregnant.

Consideration

Disenchantment is balanced by more positive aspects of the new relationship. Compared with singles, married people are happier, healthier, more satisfied with their relationships, earn higher incomes, and are less lonely. (Feinson, 1985)

"I've been single, and I've been married," said one spouse. "Marriage is better." Most people agree.

Parents, In-Laws, and Friendship Changes

Marriage affects relationships with parents, in-laws, and the friends of both partners. Parents are likely to be more accepting of the partner following the wedding. "I encouraged her not to marry him," said the father of a recent bride, "but once they were married, he was her husband and my son-in-law, so I did my best to get along with him."

Just as acceptance of the mate by the partner's parents is likely to increase, interaction with the partner's parents is likely to decrease. This is particularly true when the newly married couple moves to a distant town. "I still love my parents a great deal," said a new husband, "but I just don't get to see them very often." Parents whose lives have revolved around their children may feel particularly saddened at the marriage of their last child and may be reluctant to accept the reduced contacts. Frequent phone calls, visits, invitations, and gifts may be their way of trying to ensure a meaningful place in the life of their married son or daughter. Such insistence by the parents and in-laws may be the basis of the first major conflict between the spouses. There is no problem if both spouses agree on which set of in-laws or parents they enjoy visiting and the frequency of such get-togethers. But when one spouse wants his or her parents around more often than the partner does, frustration will be felt by everyone.

Consideration

Most marriage counselors believe that when the spouses must choose between their partner and parents, more long-term positive consequences are associated with choosing the partner than vice versa. Ideally, of course, such choices should be avoided. For partners to try to deny their mate access to the mate's parents is risky. When an individual marries, he or she inherits an already existing family; parent and in-law relationships come with the marriage.

Marriage also affects relationships with friends of the same and opposite genders.

Data – In a study of 419 students at Pennsylvania State University, students who were married reported having the fewest friends of all. (Johnson & Leslie, 1982)

Once I found the woman [Yoko], the boys became of no interest.
—John Lennon

Less time will be spent with friends of the same gender because of new role demands from the spouse. In addition, friends will assume that the newly married person now has a built-in companion and is not interested in (or would be punished by the spouse for) going barhopping, to movies, or whatever. More time will be spent with other married couples, who will become powerful influences on the new couple's relationship.

Opposite-gender relationships also change. The single person is free to seek and become involved in new sexual relationships. But unless married people have an open marriage and agree that outside sexual partners are appropriate, each spouse is expected to carefully monitor the level of interaction with people of the opposite gender to ensure that an affair does not develop. Although, as we have noted, 50 percent of all husbands and wives do have intercourse outside their marriage at least once, it is clearly a violation of their agreement not to do so.

Consideration

What spouses give up in same- and opposite-gender friendships they gain in developing a close relationship with each other. "We still enjoy our friends, but we end up spending more time with each other than with anyone else. We like it that way," said an elementary-school teacher.

However, it is a mistake to abandon friendships after getting married. The spouse cannot be expected to satisfy all social needs, and friends can often relieve some of the spouse's burden. Also, since 50 percent of all marriages end in divorce, friends who have been maintained throughout the marriage can become vital support systems when adjusting to a divorce.

Legal Changes

Unless the partners have signed a prenuptial agreement specifying that their earnings and property will remain separate, the wedding ceremony involves an exchange of property. Once the words "I do" are spoken, each spouse is entitled to inherit a portion of the other's estate. Although the amount varies by state, many states permit between one-third and one-half of the estate to be inherited. Also, the husband becomes legally responsible for the economic support of any children produced in the marriage. Even if the couple divorce, he cannot arbitrarily decide that he no longer wants to support his children. The law says it is his responsibility.

Sexual Changes

Sex will also undergo some changes during the first year of marriage. The frequency declines for most married couples, but the quality improves. According to one wife:

> The urgency to have sex disappears after you're married. After a while you discover that your husband isn't going to vanish back to his apartment at midnight. He's going to be with you all night, every night. You don't have to have sex every minute because you know you've got plenty of time. Also, you've got work and other responsibilities, so sex takes a lower priority than before you were married.

Even though the constant availability of a sexual companion and increased responsibilities may reduce the frequency of sex, such a decline does not imply that sex becomes less meaningful. Rather, sex in marriage takes on a richer and deeper quality. You are now a committed couple—not only in a personal but also in a legal sense. You have extended yourself to each other to the fullest, and your sexual relationship will express itself in the context of that commitment. "Jim and I enjoyed sex before we were married," recalls one bride of 11 months. "And it was good then. But it feels better or closer now, and I'm not talking about the physical part."

Quality improves not only because you feel more comfortable with each other but also because you become more aware of each other's preferences. "I thought I knew what she liked before we were married," shares one new husband. "But now she's more comfortable telling and showing me what turns her on. And I'm still learning." A quality sexual relationship results from such feedback and time. Like the Boston Pops orchestra—it sounds good because the musicians have been practicing.

Division of Labor Changes

One result of the feminist and woman's movement is that an increasing number of couples share the domestic work in their relationship. In one study of 95 engaged couples, the men who accepted a feminist ideology anticipated they would be helpful and cooperative in the home, splitting the grocery shopping, cooking, cleaning, ironing, and other domestic duties when they were married. However, after one year of marriage, the partners had drifted toward a more traditional relationship in which the woman did more of the domestic work than the man (Koopman-Boyden & Abbott, 1985).

Courtship is the preview of a marriage to come; marriage is the actual movie. It is not unusual for the preview to be different from the reality in terms of the division of labor, sex, friendships, and other factors.

College Marriages

Data – Sixteen percent of all white, 15 percent of all black, and 11 percent of all Spanish Americans complete between one and three years of college. (*Statistical Abstract of the United States*, 1987) In general, about 20 percent of all college students are married.

This proportion of married college students is radically different from the proportions of earlier years. Before 1940, it was not uncommon for a college or university to deny admission to married students or to require enrolled students to drop out if they married. It was believed that married students would have an undesirable influence on other students. After World War II, the return of married veterans to college established the social legitimacy of the college marriage. (Even high-school marrieds are acceptable now.)

In general, married college students make good grades.

Data – In a study of 600 full-time juniors and seniors attending a southwestern university, students who were married and who had children had the highest grade point averages; those who were married and had no children had intermediate averages; and those who were unmarried had the lowest averages. (Ma, 1983)

Young Married College Students

Although most college students prefer to finish their degrees before getting married, others seem compelled by the desire to be married while still attending college. A language major asked, "Why not marry? We're tired of waiting, don't believe in living together, and are miserable living in the dorms." Her fiancé said, "It's simple. I'm happiest with her, and she feels the same way about me. We talked to our parents during semester break, and while they would prefer that we wait until we graduate, they will support us if we decide to marry now. We've decided."

Marriage while in college seems to be related to completing college; at least this seems true for men. In a study of more than 200 males (Adler, 1982), those who married while in college were much more likely to complete college (65 percent) than those who did not marry (35 percent).

Role Changes

In addition to the role of spouse, the young married student may take on the additional roles of employee and parent. Unless their parents continue to support them, one of three patterns develop: both the husband and the wife get part-time jobs; the husband drops out of school while his wife continues; or the wife drops out of school while her husband continues. The first pattern may be especially stressful due to the difficulty of managing the respective roles. Some are surprised at the lack of control they have over the employee role. "As a student, you can miss a class or 'study later' if you need to. But when you're working for somebody, they expect you to do exactly what they want, when they want it, or you're fired," reflected a student working at a McDonald's near campus. "And if you've got a test that day, your boss doesn't care. Those hamburgers still have to be served."

Although most couples who marry in college plan to delay having children until after graduation, unwanted pregnancies may occur. An unplanned pregnancy after marriage is often handled differently from a premarital pregnancy. After marriage there is an increased chance the couple will have the baby. "I might have had an abortion had I gotten pregnant when we were living together," recalls a wife of three months. "But now it's different. We're going to have the baby, and I will finish school later."

Consideration

Although role strain is not unique to the college marriage, one role is more likely to be added to another without sufficient time to adjust to the previous role. Stacking the roles of student, spouse, employee, and possibly parent requires a greater degree of adaptation than is required of the single college student, who has fewer roles to juggle. Aware of the role-stacking effect, most students opt to delay marriage until after graduation.

Money Problems

Some parents disapprove of their offspring getting married while still in college and stop financial support after the wedding. Lack of money is not unique to the young and newly married college couple, but it introduces a variable that was not present when they were single and engaged. A sophomore who married in his freshman year writes:

> We began our marriage without any help from our parents. The result was a tremendous strain on our once happy relationship. Not having enough money put us both under tensions that neither of us had known before. We struggled to make rent, utilities, tuition, and other payments. We squeezed our budget for money to buy food with. Our recreational lifestyle had changed drastically because we rarely had money to eat out or to see a movie. We bought no new clothes—birthdays were the only times we got new ones. The result was unhappiness which we would not let others know about because of our pride. We were both from middle-class families, but we were poor.

Older Married College Students

A look around any college classroom reveals a number of older students, many of whom are married. In contrast to most of the younger college marrieds, many of these spouses have been or are employed in full-time jobs and have children.

College professor—someone who talks in other people's sleep.
—Bergen Evans

How does returning to school affect the marriage relationship? In a study of 361 women age 26 and older who were married and had at least one child, one-half of those who dropped out before completing their degree and one-third of those who did complete their degree reported that their return to school had resulted in some strain on the marriage (Berkove, 1979). This showed itself in the husbands' jealousy in competing with his wife's new interest and his annoyance over occasional late meals and a cluttered house. One student wife said of her husband:

> He mentions how much money my education is costing (even though I've worked part time off and on) and how much time I spend away from the family (he spends as much time away from the family as I do). He has stopped commenting on the state of the house, since I told him that if it was too dirty to suit him, he was welcome to clean it, because it suited me just fine.

Benefits also resulted from the wife's return to school. Most of the wives reported increased personal and intellectual development, and one-half reported that their husbands showed greater appreciation of, satisfaction with, and pride in the fact that their wives had returned to school (Berkove, 1979).

In another study (Van Meter & Agronow, 1982), married female students reported the least amount of role strain when they "placed the family role first" and did not allow the role of student to interfere with that of wife and mother. Under these conditions their husbands were very supportive of their wives going back to school. An additional finding was that husbands who had also attended college were much more supportive of their wives going to school. In general, wives are more supportive of the husband's return to school than husbands are supportive of the wife's return to school (Huston-Hoburg & Strange, 1986).

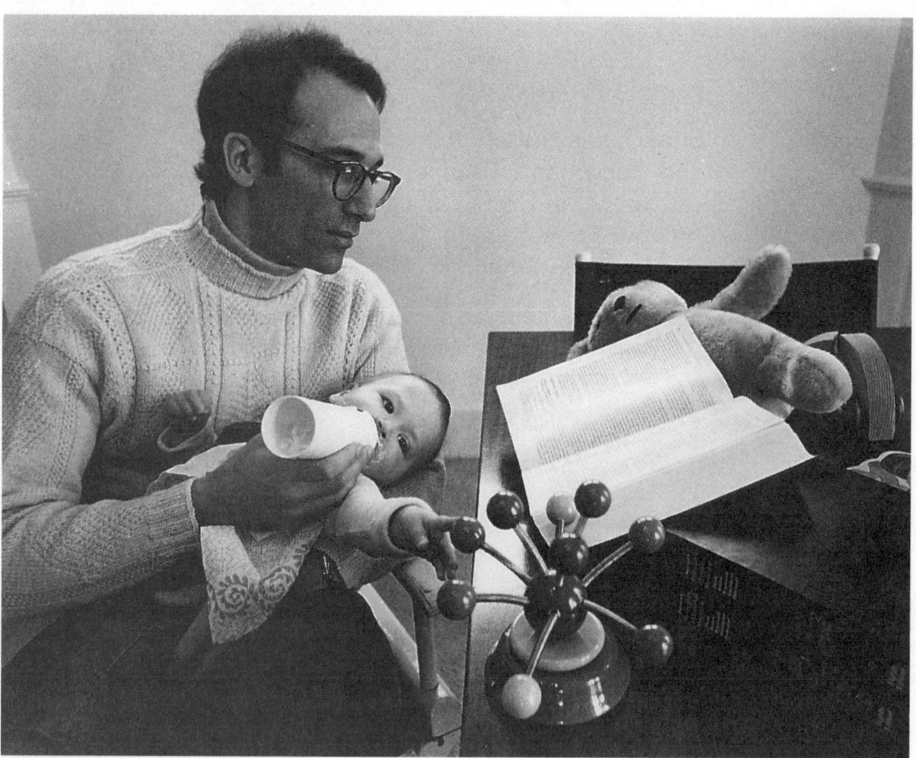

Many older college students have children.

Student wives who are also mothers report positive benefits for their children. In a study of 40 such women (Kelly, 1982), more than half said the relationships with their children had improved since they had returned to school. Their children showed an increased interest in their own schoolwork, and there was a new mutuality of interest—both mother and child would talk about "having to get homework done."

Making good grades and keeping their husbands and children happy is often accomplished at the expense of the student wife's sleep. In essence, the wife and mother "added her study (sometimes a full-time student load) to her existing program, and what she cut back on was sleep and leisure time. It is little wonder that one of the main problems cited by mature-age female students is chronic tiredness" (Kelly, 1982, p. 291).

Although the personal, marital, and parent-child relationships tend to improve when the wife returns to school (assuming she continues to put her family role first), what happens when the older married husband returns to school? McRoy & Fisher (1982) studied 20 couples in which only the husband was in graduate school and compared them with 20 couples in which only the wife was in graduate school and 20 couples in which both spouses were in graduate school. Results showed that the husband being in school was associated with less money and less marital satisfaction than either of the other two groups. It seems that when the husband does not contribute economically to the marriage and family, everyone suffers. "But that's not true of us," says one student husband who is being supported by his wife. "I put her through school, and now it's her turn to earn the money. We both agreed on this plan, and it hasn't been a problem for either of us."

Consideration

For those marriages in which one or both spouses are considering returning to school, it seems important for the wife to give her family priority to keep her husband's support high and conflict with him low. For husbands, it may be important to maintain some level of employment or economic contribution to the relationship.

Mixed Marriages

Interreligious, interracial, and age-discrepant marriages are examples of marriages in which the partners differ from each other in a particular way.

Interreligious Marriages

Data – Although most people marry those within their own faith, 18 percent of Catholics marry non-Catholics, 7 percent of Protestants marry non-Protestants, and 11 percent of Jews marry non-Jews. When the percentage of those who marry someone with "no religion" or from a religion other than Protestant, Catholic, or Jewish is calculated, 15–20 percent of existing marriages are between spouses with different religious preferences. (Glenn, 1982)

There has been a consistent trend in the willingness of people to marry someone who does not share their religious background. Even among Catholics, who have traditionally been socialized to seek a mate of the same faith, there seems little concern that their partner be Catholic. In a study of 162 Catholic students, only 8 (5 percent) said they were strongly opposed to interfaith marriages (Egelman & Berlage, 1982). This perspective might reflect "a continued secularization of the institution of marriage and a continued diminution of the influence of the church and the extended family on marital choice and on marriage relationships" (Glenn, 1982, p. 556).

Are people in interreligious marriages less satisfied with their marriages than those who marry someone of the same faith? The answer depends on a number of factors. First, people in marriages in which one or both spouses profess to "no religion" tend to report lower levels of marital satisfaction than those in which at least one spouse has a religious tie. Second, men in interreligious marriages tend to report less marital satisfaction than men in marriages in which the partners have the same religion. This may be due to the fact that children of interreligious marriages are typically reared in the faith of the mother, so that the father's influence is negligible whether he is or is not religious. Third, wives who marry outside their faith do not seem any less happier than wives who marry inside their faith (Glenn, 1982).

Consideration

The impact of a mixed religious marriage seems to depend on the degree of devoutness of the individual. If religion is a core value for you, to marry someone who does not share your faith may weaken your subsequent marital happiness. This may be particularly true if you are a man.

Interracial Marriages

Data – Of the more than 50 million married couples in the United States, 1.5 percent, are interracial marriages. (*Statistical Abstract of the United States*, 1987)

Although interracial marriages may involve many combinations, including American white, American black, Indian, Chinese, Japanese, Korean, Mexican, Malaysian, and Hindu mates, this section will focus on black-white marriages in the United States.

Data – Of the more than 50 million married couples in the United States, only 164,000, (less than 1 percent) are black-white couples. (*Statistical Abstract of the United States*, 1987)

Problems

Disapproval of parents and discrimination by employers and landlords is a problem for some black-white couples; such prejudices vary with the degree to which these who discriminate people have been socialized to perceive interracial unions as appropriate or inappropriate. Rural, conservative, dogmatic individuals are likely to look at such couples with hostile eyes. Liberal people who live in large metropolitan centers are more likely to have a "live and let live" philosophy and to regard such couples neutrally or with admiration.

We've not run into any problems. Some people may disagree, but we don't have to cope with them.
—Herschel Walker of his interracial marriage to Cindy Deangelis

Given the range of reactions, how are black-white couples actually treated by their parents, employers, and landlords? In general, although minority parents may be more accepting, both sets of parents tend to reject the interracial marriage of their son or daughter. One white husband says, "My parents have never accepted my marriage to a black woman. We have not visited or talked in nearly four years."

Such parental rejection springs from a concern about how the marriage will affect the parents' own status and their fear for the couple and the problems they must face. Hostility often disappears when the couple have a baby (the parents want access to their grandchild) or tragedy strikes (one partner becomes seriously ill). Difficulties with employers and landlords are less predictable. Some employers and landlords discriminate against an individual or a couple if they know that the marriage is interracial. Others, particularly those in larger cities, are indifferent to the marital status or choice of marriage partner of their employee or tenant.

The trend in interracial dating apparently is not only on the increase, but the secretiveness previously associated with it is also declining.
—Ernest Porterfield

Black-white spouses must also contend with problems concerning their children. Children of mixed marriages "will learn quickly that their lineage is a rarity that shapes friendships and futures, that white boys and white girls seldom date tan girls and tan boys, that color is not forgotten. That life in between is at once injustice and insight" (Harrington, 1982, p. 12). One resource for children of interracial parents is The Council on Interracial Books for Children (1841 Broadway, New York, NY 10023), which distributes a list of books designed to help the interracial child to develop a positive self-identity. At least one study of interracial offspring shows that they do not have more psychological problems than children born to parents of the same race (Johnson & Nagoshi, 1986).

Stability

In view of the problems experienced by some black-white couples, are they more likely to get divorced? Yes. When same-race and interracial marriages are compared, the latter are more likely to get divorced (Price-Bonham & Balswick, 1980). Lack of social support, overt hostility, and lack of similar backgrounds may contribute to a higher divorce rate for interracial couples. Black singer Lena Horne said of the divorce to her white husband, "We had a good life together and I loved him, but he didn't know what it meant to be black." Sammy Davis, Jr., and Mary Cunningham also divorced their respective spouses in earlier interracial marriages. The Interracial Family Alliance (P.O. Box 20290, Atlanta, GA 30325) is a support group for interracial couples. The group is particularly concerned about the social and psychological development of the children of interracial couples. Their unhappiness can affect the stability of interracial couples.

Consideration

Although individuals contemplating an interracial marriage might assess the degree to which different racial backgrounds will affect the relationship with their partners, divergent backgrounds are only one aspect of the decision-to-marry equation. Different racial backgrounds, in themselves, do not necessarily lead to subsequent divorce. Rather, this variable must be considered in the context of the total relationship.

Age-Discrepant Marriages

Although some women marry men who are younger than themselves (as examples, Olivia Newton-John is 11 years older than Matt Lattanz, and Debra Winger is five years older than Timothy Hutton), the most common age-discrepant marriage is between the younger woman and the older man. Celebrities and the number of years they are older than their spouses include, Johnny Carson, 26; Joe Namath, 19; Dustin Hoffman, 18; and Bruce Springsteen, 9.

Data – Of all married couples, 8 percent have an age difference of larger than ten years. (Vera et al., 1985)

Although there is an absence of hard data, the following observations have been made about May-December age-discrepant marriages.

Motives

Instead of marrying a middle-aged woman with three children, the man in the May-December marriage often marries a young woman with whom he can start life over. From the young woman's perspective, she is marrying a man who has already made his mark in the world. She begins her marriage with instant status and probably an ample bank account. U.S. Supreme Court Justice William O. Douglas was 68 when he married a 23–year-old bride. Cary Grant was 48 years older than his last wife; Fred Astaire was 43 years older than his wife.

Interests

Although partners of very different ages may develop mutual interests, there is a greater potential for their interests to be different. The younger partner might enjoy Van Halen; the older partner, Glenn Miller. The younger partner may feel that her mate is "showing his age" by such a preference.

Children

The May-December couple may experience several difficulties about children:

1. The wife may want children, but the husband may feel he is too old to be a father and may fear his wife's transition from lover to mother.
2. Children from a husband's previous marriage may require child-support payments, limiting the money available to the couple to start a new family. Or the current wife may resent not being able to take a family vacation because money is being drained off to send to her husband's children (in whom she may have little emotional investment).

3. Visits by the husband's children may be unwelcome because the wife resents playing the role of mother (preparing extra meals, doing extra laundry, making extra beds, and performing other such tasks).

Sex

A 60–year-old man may not be able to meet the sexual demands of a much younger woman. As a consequence, she may seek a sexual companion outside the marriage. The husband may be threatened by such competition, and the marriage relationship may be jeopardized.

Early Widow

American men die approximately seven years earlier than American women. The wife in the May-December marriage is therefore more likely to be a widow longer than the wife who is married to someone closer to her age. Reflecting on this concern, one woman said, "I'd rather have 15 years with this man than 50 with anybody else."

Consideration

None of these concerns is necessarily unique to the May-December marriage. Conflicts over sex, children, and recreation may occur in marriages in which the partners are the same age, and no newlywed is guaranteed that his or her spouse will be healthy and alive tomorrow. As for the success of such unions, three researchers who compared various couples in age-discrepant marriages found them to be no more likely to report problems regardless of how close or far apart the spouses were in age. (Vera et al., 1985)

Individuals who are considering marriage to someone who is much younger or older than they are do not seem to be taking an unnecessary divorce risk.

Black Marriages

For years, "The Jeffersons," a weekly television sitcom, was the only exposure many white people had to the internal dynamics of a happy and successful black marriage. George and Louise, a well-to-do business owner and his loving housewife, are portrayed as an upwardly mobile New York couple with a maid, a plush apartment, and interracial friends. More recently, another weekly TV sitcom, "The Bill Cosby Show," has captured the hearts of millions of white and black television viewers. As role-model parents, Dr. Cliff Huxtable, an obstetrician/gynecologist, and his wife Clare, a barrister, portray with tasteful humor the difficulties, values, and life style of a successful upper-middle-class black family.

Although black marriages similar to those portrayed in "The Jeffersons" and "The Bill Cosby Show" do exist—and both programs may serve as examples of what could or should exist in black families—these sitcoms tell us very little about the life styles, values, and choices available to the majority of black families. However, "Good Times," the TV show produced by Norman

Lear, comes close to dramatizing the hardships, frustration, love, joy, and humor of poor black families struggling to survive in an urban environment. Set in a Chicago public-housing apartment, amidst social deprivation and poverty, "Good Times" depicts with humor part of the emotional strain and suffering that many blacks are forced to endure in a society that discriminates against them. In spite of the disadvantages that this family experiences, it remains a close-knit and loving unit.

To better understand the difficulties confronting most black families today, we will examine some social and historical data that clarify some of the reasons why marriages such as those portrayed on "The Jeffersons" and "The Bill Cosby Show" are still unattainable for most black families.

Data – There are 6,778,000 black families in the United States, of which 3,469,000 (51 percent) are married couples. (*Statistical Abstract of the United States*, 1987)

The Crisis of Black Families

Current data on black Americans indicate that the incomes of 8.9 million black persons (31 percent) are below the poverty level, 44 percent of all black families are headed by females, 59 percent of all black children are born out of wedlock, and 54 percent of all black children are raised in one-parent families (*Statistical Abstract of the United States,* 1987). These statistics have caused many social scientists to use the term "crisis" to describe the status of the black family. They point out that slavery, racism, discrimination, and economic insufficiency are the direct causes of the present status of the black family.

Blame for the current "crisis" of the black family is placed primarily on the arbitrary, cruel, and inhuman practices of slaveowners—perpetuated after slavery by racism and discrimination against blacks, particularly in the areas of employment, education, housing, and other opportunities for social advance-

For black couples, marriage has the added stress of dealing with racism and discrimination.

ment. As a consequence, the self-esteem of the black male and female has been adversely affected and is often evidenced by behavior not conducive to the development of a stable family unit. Indeed, many social scientists point out that the feelings of inadequacy and self-hatred resulting from racial discrimination have led to distrust between black males and females.

The Context of Racism

A racially integrated community is a chronological term timed from the entrance of the first black family to the exit of the last white family.
—Saul Alinsky

As noted, black marriages occur in the context of continued racism, discrimination, and economic insufficiency. Blacks have higher levels of stress and die earlier than whites. Many feel powerless to defend themselves against racial pressures. One spouse said:

> They cut off expectations. I mean no matter how good you are, you will always be a nigger. Hey, that puts strains on people. I mean you can be smart, have a lot of bread, but you know that you will not be able to give your children or yourself an equal chance, and this takes its toll. A lot of really good people have a lot on the ball, end up on dope, alcohol, or one thing or another. I mean everyone that I know has one of these problems because of this racist society. Let me tell you, I do not have any hope for the future. (McAdoo, 1982, p. 484)

Much of the discrimination against blacks is economic. The median family income is about 40 percent less for blacks than for whites. Many black families live on the edge of poverty and are concerned with basic survival on a daily basis. Much of this economic strain is due to the unemployed black male and his lack of earning capacity (Schwartz, 1986).

Kinship Ties

Black America and black families can be understood only in the context of a white, racist America.
—Joyce E. Williams

Kinship was significantly important in the West African societies from which blacks were brought to be slaves in the United States. In these societies, an individual's social and economic status, as well as means of subsistence, depended on the maintenance of both nuclear and extended kinship ties. In spite of the efforts of slaveowners to sever kinship ties among blacks, the African pattern of family relationships, which consists of the cooperation and mutual support of mother, father, children, grandparents, brothers, nieces, nephews, and cousins, persisted and is regarded by scholars today as the major force contributing to the survival of black people in the United States.

As discrimination and economic insufficiency continued to plague black society, the need for kinship ties and community support became increasingly crucial and necessary to black survival. Today, black spouses continue to maintain close ties with their parents and kin after they are married. In some cases, they may live with their parents. Even if they do not, their parents continue to be important sources of emotional and economic support.

Data – In a national study of blacks, 65 percent said that they had daily or weekly contact with their extended kin. (Taylor, 1986)

The importance of kinship ties often supersedes that of the marital relationship. Two researchers (Aschenbrenner & Carr, 1980) who studied marriage relationships among blacks concluded:

> The black family is not primarily based on a conjugal relationship or a single household, as in the case of the idealized American family. Rather, it consists of a wide-reaching group of relatives involved in relationships of exchange and coparenting; and a collective and cooperative spirit prevails . . . (p. 469).

Marital Roles

The strong emphasis on ties to one's parents and the larger kinship system seems to affect the black marriage relationship. In many cases, the mother-child relationship seems to take precedence over the wife-husband relationship. It is uncertain whether this tie is maintained because the black wife feels that her economically disadvantaged husband will not be able to support her or that he will not stay around to do so (desertion rates among black males are higher than among white males). Not all black wives give allegiance to their kinship ties over their husbands.

Black Americans are still spatially segregated from the majority of the more affluent white citizenry, and certain cultural values distinguish their family life, in form and content, from the middle-class, white Anglo-Saxon model.
—Robert Staples

Just as role importance varies from couple to couple, so does the division of power. One researcher (Gray-Little, 1982) who interviewed 75 black urban couples found that 76 spouses described their marriage as "husband-led;" 53, as "egalitarian;" and 21 as "wife-led." The common assumption that black marriages are wife-dominated was not true for these couples.

Another aspect of marital roles among blacks is that both spouses are more likely than both white spouses to be employed. The black wife's employment is more often an economic necessity than the white wife's employment. In one study, 60 percent of black wives, compared with 40 percent of white wives, listed "financial necessity" as their reason for working (Landry & Jendrek, 1978).

Marital Satisfaction

Compared to white spouses, black spouses tend to be less happy. Reasons for their lower sense of marital satisfaction are primarily in reference to economic and social discrimination. Black wives may be particularly unhappy because, with fewer partners to select from, they may be forced to settle for husbands who have less education than they do. The sense of inadequacy the black husband may feel, coupled with the black wife's feeling that she has selected someone who is less than her ideal mate, may have a negative impact on both partners (Ball & Robbins, 1986b). Black husbands are also influenced by economic concerns: the higher the family income, the greater the satisfaction with family life (Ball & Robbins, 1986a).

Mexican American Marriages

Approximately 9 million Mexican Americans (about 4 percent of our population) live in the United States, primarily in the five southwestern states close to Mexico (California, Texas, New Mexico, Arizona, and Colorado). The term "Mexican American" refers to the white population of Mexican origin or descent living in America. The term has no specific referent; Chicanos, Spanish

Americans, Hispanics, Mexicanos, Californios, and Latin Americans may also regard themselves as Mexican Americans.

BACKGROUND

When America annexed Texas in 1845, Mexico became outraged and the Mexican War followed (1846–1848). In the Treaty of Guadalupe Hidalgo, Mexico recognized the loss of Texas and accepted the Rio Grande as the boundary between Mexico and the United States. Although the war was over, hostilities continued, and the negative stereotyping of Mexican Americans as a conquered and subsequently inferior people became entrenched. Such stereotyping and discrimination had implications for the stress to which Mexican American spouses were exposed. Compared to Anglos, Mexican Americans have less education, lower incomes, and work in lower-status occupations (Alvirez et al., 1981).

THE HUSBAND-WIFE RELATIONSHIP

There is great variability among Mexican American marriages, and any discussion of them should be viewed with caution. What is true in one relationship may not be true in another, and the same relationship may not resemble itself at two different points in time. Nevertheless, some "typical" characteristics of Mexican American relationships are detailed here.

Male Dominance

Although role relationships between women and men are changing in all segments of society, traditional role relationships between the Mexican American sexes are dominated by the male. He is responsible for making all major decisions, and his wife is responsible for carrying out his decisions. In the husband's absence, authority is delegated to the oldest son.

Machismo has both sexual and nonsexual interpretations. Sexually, *machismo* refers to the male's virility (his ability to be a smooth talker and have many sexual experiences with women). Adolescent males are socialized to tell stories of their "conquests"; extramarital relations are condoned and encouraged for males. The nonsexual component of *machismo* includes elements of courage, honor, and respect for others and also implies proper use of authority in a just and fair manner within the family (Alvirez et al., 1981).

Female Submissiveness

The complement to the male authority figure in the Mexican American marriage is the submissive female. Traditionally, she is subservient to her husband and devotes her time totally to the roles of homemaker and mother. Large Mexican American families are not only evidence of the husband's *machismo* but also of the wife's skill in managing and caring for a family. As more wives begin to work outside the home, the nature of the Mexican American husband-wife relationship is becoming more egalitarian (Staples & Mirande, 1980).

The divorce rate among Mexican Americans is lower than the rate for Anglos but higher than the rate for blacks. Intermarriage is increasing, as Mexican Americans move away from home to pursue lucrative jobs.

The Parent-Child Relationship

In the past, Mexican Americans have valued close relationships with both nuclear and extended family members (*familism*). Although members of the extended family (aunts, uncles, and grandparents) may still be regarded with great affection, Mexican Americans are becoming more Americanized and nuclear-oriented. In a study of 294 parents in which the *cohesion* (emotional bonding between family members) in Mexican American and Anglo (white population of non-Mexican origin) families was compared, the researchers found no significant differences (Vega et al., 1986).

The relationship between Mexican American children and their parents has traditionally been one of respect. In addition, it is common for the younger generation to pay great deference to the older generation. When children speak to their elders, they are expected to do so in a formal way.

Very Happy Marriages

The type of marriage most of us want is the happy marriage—not the "we-get-along" or "things-are-okay" marriage, but the type of marriage that continues the love feelings and fun in courtship. To find individuals in such marriages, two researchers studied 72 middle-aged, middle-class spouses who answered most of the following items positively (Ammons & Stinnett, 1980):

> My spouse and I enjoy doing many things together.
>
> I enjoy most of the activities I participate in more if my spouse is also involved.
>
> I receive more satisfaction from my marriage relationship than most other areas of my life.
>
> My spouse and I have a positive, strong, emotional involvement with each other.
>
> The companionship of my spouse is more enjoyable to me than most anything else in life.
>
> I would not hesitate to sacrifice an important goal in life if achievement of that goal would cause my marriage relationship to suffer.
>
> My spouse and I take an active interest in each other's work and hobbies. (p. 38)

These spouses also took a personality test (the Edwards Personal Preference Test), which revealed their various personality needs and characteristics. The goal was to find out what kind of people live in very happy marriages. The answers follow.

All marriages begin with the same hope—to be happy.

Sex

Almost nine in 10 of the spouses reported having a moderately high to a very high need for sexual activity. These partners saw sex as a way of expressing a very deep emotional involvement with each other—a meeting of their souls. Also their sexual needs were similar. Both partners enjoyed the sexual aspect of their relationship.

Empathy

The happily married spouses also had a need to be understanding and supportive of their partners. In contrast to a selfish, narcissistic orientation, they felt best when they were nurturing the needs of their partners. "I love to love her and do things for her," said one husband. The result was a relationship in which each spouse felt loved, supported, and cared for by the partner.

Commitment

The starting point in making a marriage work is working on ourselves.
—Sally Olds

These spouses were also deeply committed and determined to make their marriage work. "My marriage is the most important thing in the world to me, and I'm not going to let anything happen to it," said one spouse. "But as anyone who's married knows, the relationship won't spin by itself—you've got to work at it. This means that we work out problems as they come along and don't let things build up."

Another spouse said, "Most folks getting divorced today aren't committed to making their marriages work. You've got to want it to work before it will. Everything follows from your commitment and determination that it will succeed."

Two Strong Egos

Although a major focus of these very happily married spouses was each other, each partner was also an autonomous person, functioning independently of the other in her or his respective careers and roles. Their relationship was like a yardstick that can be best supported horizontally at each end. If the two supports are too close to the middle, the yardstick will topple. So it is with marriage. Two individuals standing independently provide the best support for the relationship. If they are immersed in each other to the exclusion of developing themselves and their interests, then their relationship will be less stable.

Other Characteristics

In a subsequent nationwide study of an additional 438 spouses, ranging in age from 20 to 78, who viewed themselves as having a strong family, the researchers identified communication, love, religion, and respect as contributing factors. When the respondents were asked what they did as a family that seemed to strengthen their relationship, enjoying the outdoors, taking vacations, going to church, and attending sporting events headed the list (Stinnett et al., 1982). Happy and strong families in Iraq seem to have similar characteristics (Brigman et al., 1986).

Consideration

The studies on very happy marriages suggest that these partners share four essential elements—commitment, communication, love, and shared activities. A strong commitment to each other to work out the problems in the relationship is basic, but this requires effective communication skills to negotiate differences. Motivation to talk out differences springs from an intense emotional connection between the partners. Their love feelings also propel them into sharing a wide range of activities. To assess your own marital satisfaction, determine your Marriage Happiness Scale score in the following Self-Assessment.

Elderly Marriages

Robert Browning said,

> Grow old along with me!
> The best is yet to be,
> The last of life,
> For which the first was made . . .

Self-Assessment

Marriage Happiness Scale

This inventory is designed to measure the way you feel about your spouse. There are no right or wrong answers. After reading each sentence carefully, circle the number that best represents your feelings.

1 Strongly disagree
2 Mildly disagree
3 Undecided
4 Mildly agree
5 Strongly agree

	SD	MD	U	MA	SA
1. My partner and I enjoy spending our free time together.	1	2	3	4	5
2. My partner and I have never discussed separation.	1	2	3	4	5
3. My partner lets me know that I am loved.	1	2	3	4	5
4. I let my partner know that I love her or him.	1	2	3	4	5
5. My partner and I have a lot in common.	1	2	3	4	5
6. My partner and I rarely argue.	1	2	3	4	5
7. My partner and I have a good sex life.	1	2	3	4	5
8. My partner and I are able to talk about anything.	1	2	3	4	5
9. My partner is supportive of my interests.	1	2	3	4	5
10. My partner and I are committed to make our marriage work.	1	2	3	4	5

Scoring: Add the numbers you circled. 1 (strongly disagree) is the most negative feeling you can have, and 5 (strongly agree) is the most positive feeling you can have. The lower your total score (10 is the lowest possible score), the less happy you are in your marriage; the higher your score (50 is the highest possible score), the more happy you are in your marriage. A score of 30 places you at the midpoint between an unhappy and a very happy marriage.

But is the best yet to be? What is marriage like for couples who have grown old together? After reviewing the concept of aging, we will look at several studies that have been conducted to provide information about elderly couples in marriage.

Data – At age 65 to 74, 62 percent of all persons living in the United States are married and living with their spouses. (U.S. Bureau of the Census, 1986)

Definitions of Elderly

Being elderly may be defined chronologically, physiologically, sexually, psychologically, sociologically, and culturally. Chronologically, an "elderly" or "old" person is defined as one who has lived a certain number of years. How many years it takes to be old varies with the perspective.

Consideration

Most people view anyone 15 years older than themselves as old.

Physiologically, the auditory, visual, and respiratory capabilities of an individual decline with age, but it is a myth that most elderly people become incapacitated. In a study of 68 elderly married couples (average age 70), over 60 percent rated their health as "good" or "excellent" and only 9 percent rated their health as "poor" or "very poor." Being in good health was the greatest predictor of life satisfaction in these couples (Sanders & Walters, 1985).

Psychologically, a person's own perception is important in defining how "old" that person is. Satchel Paige, the great black baseball player, said, "How old would you be if you didn't know how old you was?" Your answer is your self-concept of your age.

Sociologically, people age as they assume roles that have traditionally been defined as occupied by older people—grandparent, widow, retiree. A retired dentist recalls:

> After our daughter had her first child, it occurred to me that I would be sleeping with a grandmother. I kidded my wife about that, and she said, "Yes, grandpa, that's right, and I'll be sleeping with a grandfather." It made us feel old just to know that the word grandparents now meant us.

Culturally, the society in which an individual lives defines when or if a person becomes "old" and what it means to be old. In some cultures, as a person grows older, he or she gains prestige and status. For example, the oldest Navajo tribesman is a revered leader, commanding the respect of the less experienced members of the tribe. The Abkhasians in Russia, who often live into their 100s, have no phrase for "old people." In our society, we bestow our respect on certain individuals as they grow old; Walter Cronkite and Katharine Hepburn are good examples of such people.

Marital Happiness among the Elderly

A researcher who interviewed 21 elderly couples who had been married 30–50 years found that wives in two-income marriages were happier than wives who did not work outside the home (Tryban, 1985).

Data – Ninety percent of the working wives reported that they were happy with their marriages after their husbands retired in contrast to 60 percent of the wives who did not work outside the home. (Tryban, 1985)

Homemaker wives felt that their work loads increased when their husbands retired. They had to prepare more meals, had to keep their husbands company, and had less time to do what they wanted to do. As one woman expressed it, "What free time I do have, I still have to monkey around with things he wants to do." Another said that she resented her husband's attitude that she should be ready to go with him anywhere and anytime "at the drop of a hat" (p. 221).

In contrast, wives in dual-income marriages said that due to their own careers, their husbands had already become used to doing things for themselves, including fixing their own meals and keeping themselves occupied doing things that they found meaningful (outdoor work and a ham radio in the basement were two frequent activities for husbands). Older wives who earned their own income also enjoyed doing things with their husbands, including camping, traveling, dancing, golfing, and attending a health club.

In another study, the researcher found that couples who had been married for more than 40 years had worked out a good balance of separateness and togetherness that allowed each partner to have space. These partners also had many interests in common and basically valued the same things in life (Cole, 1985).

Consideration

Spouses who are autonomous yet interdependent may not be a burden to each other during the retirement years. However, such interactive patterns are established long before retirement occurs. Spouses—particularly husbands—might become more self-sufficient so that they do not burden their wives after retirement.

Another researcher studied the marriages of 79 couples living in a retirement community. Their average age was 74, and they had been married an average of 41 years. The results were clear. These respondents claimed to be happily married, to have high morale, and to have high levels of sexual interest. Of her respondents, the researcher said, "Marriage does seem to enhance the quality of life for those fortunate enough to survive to enjoy it" (Ade-Ridder, 1985, p. 235).

Household Tasks among the Elderly

One study of the allocation of household tasks among elderly couples revealed a division of labor along traditional lines. Wives typically cooked meals and washed dishes; husbands maintained the car, did yard work, and made house repairs. However, 30 percent of these couples shared washing the dishes, and 60 percent shared the shopping. The researchers concluded:

> These long-married couples have developed ways to accomplish tasks around the house in which they are responsible for gender-specific tasks *and* they share responsibility. In many ways, golden anniversary couples have negotiated elaborate, interdependent relationships. (Brubaker & Kinsel, 1985, p. 246)

Trends

Weddings will continue to take place in a variety of settings and to represent the desires of the spouses more than their parents. Because more couples are living together before marriage, fewer newlyweds will go on a traditional honeymoon. Also, due to changing male-female relationships, traditional marriages, which have been characterized by male dominance, will become less frequent. The trend toward egalitarian relationships will continue in white, black, and Mexican American relationships.

Asian intermarriage will continue to increase. The number of Asian Americans marrying non-Asians almost doubled between 1970 and 1980. Recent studies show that more than 50 percent of all Japanese Americans, 40 percent of all Chinese Americans, and 30 percent of all Korean Americans marry outside their ethnic group. The primary reason for these increasing intermarriages is increased acceptance by the larger society. However, Asian parents often disapprove and fear that their culture will disappear if their children intermarry. Some parents even disown their children if they intermarry (Kantrowitz, 1986).

Summary

All marriage relationships represent a commitment between the partners, the respective families, and the couple and the state.

The wedding is a rite of passage signifying the change from the courtship role to the spouse role. Although couples who have lived together are less likely to have a traditional wedding and honeymoon, most couples who get married for the first time have both.

Marriage results in various personal, social, and legal changes for the spouses. Personally, most spouses experience an enhanced self-concept because the people they are living with love and care for them to the extent that they have made a "permanent" commitment. Society also approves of a couple's marriage and encourages them to feel good about their decision. But the reality of marriage also involves disenchantment—the gradual process whereby each spouse becomes aware that the other person in courtship is not always the other person in marriage.

Marrying while still in college involves adding several roles in rapid succession. The transition from lover to spouse to employee and perhaps to parent may introduce strain in some relationships. Among older spouses returning to school, marital happiness seems highest if the wife student gives priority to her roles of wife and mother and if the husband student continues to earn a part-time income.

About 20 percent of all marriages occur between spouses with different religious preferences. Although mixed religious marriages do not necessarily imply a greater risk to marital happiness, marriages in which one or both spouses profess no religion are in the greatest jeopardy. Also, husbands in interreligious marriages seem less satisfied because children are usually reared in the faith (or nonfaith) of the wife.

The risk to marital stability is greater among black-white marriages, partly due to the social context of racism and economic insufficiency. Black marriages tend to include a larger and more involved kinship system than white marriages. In many cases, the mother-child relationship seems to take precedence over the wife-husband relationship. A higher divorce rate and a higher proportion of single-parent homes among blacks suggest that black marriages may be less happy than white marriages.

Very happy marriage relationships seem to be characteristic of spouses who have high sexual needs, who enjoy supporting and caring for each other, and who are committed to making their marriage work. These spouses also tend to be religious and to share common interests and activities.

Being happily married in the later years seems to be related to having independent interests, so that neither spouse feels burdened by the other. Having a balance of independent versus shared interests seems to work best.

One trend in marriage relationships is continued variation in the types of relationships. In addition, there will be an increased number of intermarriages.

Questions for Reflection

1. How do two strong individuals influence the probability of a strong marital relationship?
2. How do you feel about entering interreligious, interracial, and age-discrepant marriages?
3. How do the characteristics of your relationship compare with those of very happy marriages?

CHOICES

MARRIAGE PARTNERS MAY be confronted with decisions about the type of marriage relationship desired, the partner's "night out," parents as live-ins, and who manages the money.

Type of Marriage Relationship Desired

Two researchers (Cuber & Harroff, 1965) interviewed 211 spouses and identified five types of marriage relationships:

1. *Conflict-habituated.* The spouses have a basic incompatibility and argue about everything all the time. Their relationship is a constant quarrel.
2. *Devitalized.* The spouses don't argue; they are just bored. Their relationship is lifeless and apathetic.
3. *Passive-Congenial.* Whereas the devitalized spouses once shared good times together, the passive-congenial spouses have had a polite and stale relationship from the beginning. Their interests and energies are directed toward careers and children, not toward each other.
4. *Vital.* The mates share an emotional closeness and enjoy doing things together. Their central satisfactions in life are in their relationship.
5. *Total.* The total relationship is similar to the vital relationship except that it is more multifaceted. The "total" couple schedule their day around each other, meet for lunch, and anticipate every opportunity to be together.

It is not unusual for couples in courtship to begin with a total relationship and drift into a devitalized or conflict-habituated relationship after several years of marriage. If you choose to maintain a vital or total relationship, it will mean giving your relationship a high priority in terms of time and energy.

Partner's Night Out?

Although recently married individuals may want to spend all of their time together, this need diminishes over the years and the need to spend time without the spouse increases. Frequently one or both partners want to spend time with their friends. This may mean going to happy hour on Wednesdays with their coworkers, bowling, shopping, playing bridge, fishing, or golfing.

Some spouses have a policy of trust with each other. One wife said:

> I tell my husband to go anywhere he wants to with anyone he wants to just as long as he is emotionally and sexually faithful to me. I'm not going to try to restrict what my husband does. If he wants to be unfaithful to me, he will. But I have no reason to distrust him, and I'm sure he doesn't get involved with other women when we're apart.

Other spouses are very suspicious of each other. One husband said:

> I didn't want her having lunch or after-work drinks with her boss. I don't think it's a healthy situation. Before you know it they would be talking about getting together at the beach.

In general, most spouses have little problem with their partner being with a same-gender friend. Shopping, hunting, fishing, and drinking together are usually accepted. Some spouses have an unwritten "ticket" system. When one spouse wants to go out with friends, he or she tells the partner and the partner agrees; it is assumed that when the other spouse wants to do something with friends, that partner will also approve of him or her doing so (issue a "ticket").

For partner's night out to have a positive impact on the couple's relationship, it is important that the partners maintain emotional and sexual fidelity to each other, that each partner have a partner's night out, and that the partners spend some nights alone with each other. Friendships can enhance a marriage relationship by making the individual partners happier; but friendships cannot replace the marriage relationship. Spouses must spend time alone to nurture their relationship.

Parents as Live-Ins?

As the parents of the spouses get older, a decision must often be made by the spouses about whether to have the parents live with them. Usually it is the mother of either spouse; the father is the most likely to die first. One wife said:

> We didn't have a choice. His mother is 82 and has Alzheimer's disease. We couldn't afford to put her in a nursing home at $1,200 a month, and she couldn't stay by herself. So we took her in. It's been a real strain on our marriage, since I end up taking care of her all day. I can't even leave her alone to go to the grocery store.

Some elderly persons do have resources for nursing-home care or the spouses can afford it. But even in these circumstances, some spouses decide to have their parents live with them. "I couldn't live with myself if I knew my mother was propped up in a wheelchair eating Cheerios when I could be taking care of her," said one spouse.

When spouses disagree about parents in the home, the results can be devastating. According to one wife:

> I told my husband that mother was going to live with us. He told me she wasn't and that he would leave if she did. She moved in, and he moved out (we were divorced). Five months later, my mother died.

Who Will Manage the Money?

Marriage is a partnership of two people who cooperate economically. It is like a small business. Money comes in (income), and money goes out (expenses). Someone must be responsible for seeing that expenses do not consistently exceed income (to avoid going deeply into debt), bills are paid (to keep the lights and water on), and accurate records are kept (to pay taxes and for Internal Revenue Service audits). Couples differ in who manages the money. In some marriages, one spouse is responsible; in others, the partners may do so jointly. Joint bookkeeping works only if role responsibilities are clear and each person is disciplined enough to fulfill his or her responsibility.

How many checking and savings accounts to have is another issue. No pattern works best for all people. One couple may have one savings and one checking account; another may have three checking and three savings accounts. In an instance of the latter, the husband, wife, and child each had their own checking and savings accounts, and each was responsible for keeping the books for their accounts. "It is really easier if everyone keeps up with his or her own," said the wife.

Impact of Social Influences on Choices

The marriage relationship you develop with your spouse will be influenced by the marriage patterns the two of you have observed in your respective parents, friends, and other marital models. If you grew up in a home in which your parents demonstrated little affection toward each other, then you are likely to duplicate this pattern in your own marriage. Cartoons often picture marriage as a ball-and-chain, argumentative relationship. In the United States, the cultural image of courtship

(Continued)

is all love and fun, but marriage is depicted as all work and hassle—from moonlight and roses to daylight and dishes.

Chinese, Japanese, and other Asian marriages focus on the functioning of the family unit and less on the happiness of the individual members. Happy spouses are viewed as less important than happy children, and keeping the spouses together is a strong goal. American marriages tend to focus more on individual happiness. If the spouses are not happy with each other, divorce becomes a consideration. Hence, the degree to which there is affection in your marriage and whether you stay married may be influenced by social forces that are beyond the control of you and your partner.

CHAPTER 10

Two-Income Marriages

Contents

Is It True?*

1. Marriages in which the spouses have an equal say about how money is to be spent are more likely to remain intact than marriages in which one spouse dominates how money is to be spent.
2. Wives are as likely to have a career as husbands.
3. Spouses in commuter marriages spend little time, energy, and money trying to get together.
4. Wives who stay at home with their children report that they are personally more happy than wives who are employed outside the home.
5. Only a few countries have job-protected leaves of absence during pregnancy and birth.

*1=T; 2=F; 3=F; 4=researchers disagree; 5=F.

We MAY MARRY for love, but it is money that buys food, pays rent, and lets us have some of the other things we want. Because our very survival depends on it, money is a powerful determinant of how we feel about ourselves and how we interact with others. After examining the ways in which money is significant in our lives and in our relationships, we will look at the implications of having two earners in one marriage.

The Meanings of Money

Economists view money as the medium of exchange that makes possible the distribution of goods and services in our society. But money has more personal meanings, which relate to self-concept, power, security, freedom, social relationships, love—and to conflict in marriage.

Self-Concept

Money affects a person's self-concept because, in our society, human worth is often equated with financial achievement. A young husband and father mused:

You can be young without money but you can't be old without it.
—Tennessee Williams

> I've been working for seven years, and I've got nothing to show for it. I can't even pay the light bill, let alone buy the things we want. My two closest friends are making good money in their own businesses. It makes me feel bad when I know that I can't provide for my family the way they provide for theirs. I'm a failure.

Money also influences a person's self-concept in courtship. One 24–year-old said:

> I am not in school this semester because I had to drop out to earn some money. And finding a woman to date when you don't have any money is very difficult. Once a woman sees that I live in a trailer and that I'm broke, I never see her again. It has happened so many times I get depressed just thinking about asking someone out again. Money has a lot to do with the way a woman feels about you and the way you feel about yourself.

Power

There are a lot of things that money can't buy—for example, what it bought last year.
—Laurence Peter

Those who have money have a sense of power, a sense of control over things, events, and people. Whereas the average shopper may say to himself or herself, "I can't afford that," the person with great means may not have to consider the price of things and may buy as desires dictate. This ability to purchase goods and services at will results in a feeling of power; power means getting what we want when we want it.

Money provides not only the power to possess things but also the power to control events. For the poor, a combination of subzero temperatures and high fuel prices is almost certain to mean discomfort and may mean death. For the wealthy, the high prices caused by a shortage of fuel are not even an inconvenience. No matter how high the price or how low the temperature, the rich will be snug and warm.

Money also means power over people—employers over employees, parents over offspring, and employed spouses over unemployed spouses. Anyone who has worked for someone else knows the power of employers. Unless the employee complies with the wishes of the employer, the employer may terminate the worker's job. Parents exercise power over their offsprings' private lives. The parents of one student threatened to withdraw financial support of a daughter if she continued to live with her boyfriend. She was committed to pursuing a business career and would be unable to pay tuition without her parents' help, so she moved out. Money gave her parents power, and they used it.

Money used as shared power by the spouses has positive consequences for the marriage. In a study of how married couples managed the money in their relationships, two researchers observed that when the wife had equal or greater influence in deciding how much cash to keep on hand, paying bills, and keeping track of expenditures, there was a greater chance of the couple staying together. When the husband dominated how much money would be available to the wife, there was an increased chance for divorce (Schaninger & Buss, 1986).

Security

Oscar Wilde once said, "When I was young, I used to think that money was the most important thing in life; now that I am older, I know it is." Money represents security. People without money often feel that they live on the verge of disaster. "My car has four slick tires," said a single mother of two children who had returned to college, "and when one of those pops, I've had it. I don't have the money for new tires, and I can't walk to work."

Buying life insurance expresses the desire to provide a secure future for loved ones. "If something happens to me," one husband said, "my wife and children will need more than the sympathy they'll get at my funeral. They'll need money." Without money, there is no security—either present or future. Money also secures us against ill health. Because medical care often depends on the ability to pay for it, our health is directly related to our financial resources. Money buys visits to the physician, as well as food for a balanced diet and a well-heated home in winter.

It is life near the bone where it is sweetest.
—Thoreau

Freedom

Money gives us the freedom to do the things we like to do. One husband recalls:

> When we were in school, we didn't have money to eat out or to see a movie. It was a terrible feeling being cooped up all the time with no money to do anything. Now we've graduated, and both of us have good jobs. We've got money in the bank (a little) and some in our pockets. We're free to do what we want when we want. It's a nice feeling—very nice.

Social Relationships

Money affects the relationship between spouses, between spouses and their parents, and between spouses and their peers. People are more likely to stay married under conditions of financial stress. Although most studies indicate that increased income is associated with increased marital stability (there is less conflict over the lack of money), in the Gary Income Maintenance Experiment, the probability of a divorce increased when the income available to low-income couples increased. "The wives could afford to leave," said the principal investigator (Maiolo, 1982).

As for the effect of money on spouse-parent relationships, married partners who are financially dependent on their parents often discover that the use of their parents' money is not free. In exchange for parental support, the couple is expected to visit frequently and, in some cases, to consult the parents before making major decisions. "You bet," said one parent. "After sending them $500 a month, I expect them to appreciate what I'm doing. And that means before buying a new car or taking a job out of state, they should consult me." Money also affects relationships with peers. One wife said:

Money is like a sixth sense without which you cannot make the most of the other five.
—Somerset Maugham

> Our neighbors eat out every Friday night at an expensive restaurant and have asked us to join them. But we're on a tight budget and simply can't afford to spend $25 on a meal. We wave at them when we get the afternoon newspaper, but we haven't socialized with them in three months. If we had more money, it would be different.

Love

Money may also mean love. While admiring the engagement ring of her friend, a woman said, "What a big diamond! He must really love you." The assumption is that big diamond equals high price equals deep love feelings.

Similar assumptions are often made when gifts are given or received. People tend to spend more money on presents for the people they love, believing that the value of the gift symbolizes the depth of their emotion. People receiving gifts may make the same assumption. "She must love me more than I thought," mused one man. "I gave her a record album for Christmas, but she gave me a cassette tape deck. I felt embarrassed." His feeling of embarrassment is based on the idea that the woman loves him more than he loves her because she paid more for her gift to him than he did for his gift to her.

Similarly, the withdrawal of money may mean the absence of love. When two people get divorced, aside from what the court may order in alimony and child support, it is assumed that their economic sharing is over.

Consideration

One of the reasons we are motivated by money and tend to be despondent when we don't have it and comforted when we do is the powerful impact it has on so many aspects of our lives. Sophie Tucker's "I've been rich and I've been poor—and let me tell you, rich is better" reflects one view of the importance of money in our lives and in our relationships.

Conflict

Money may also be a source of conflict between spouses when one spouse wants to buy something that would prevent the other spouse from buying something else. For example, a husband wanted to buy a videotape recorder and camera that cost around $1,500. His wife wanted to buy a piano and furniture for their empty living room, which would cost around $2,000. The husband thought that spending money on "a sofa and piano that nobody

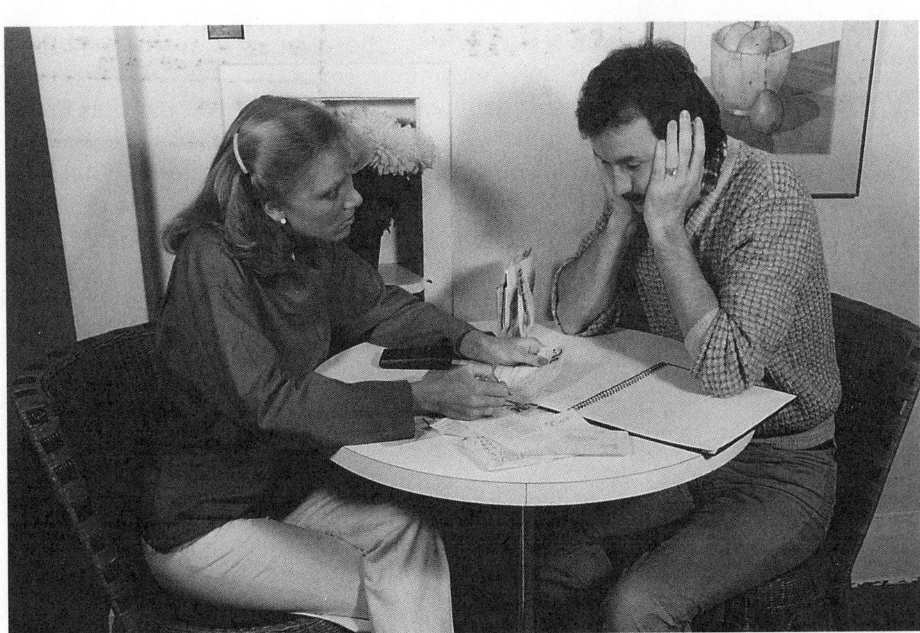

Money can be a source of conflict between spouses.

would play was foolish"; the wife thought that spending money on "movie stuff" was a "complete waste." Not all money conflicts in marriages may be over furniture and video recorders, but the issue is always the same—money spent for X can't be spent for Y.

Money can also be used to reduce marital conflict and stress. For example, partners who argue over who is to clean the house can hire a person to clean it for them once a week. Money also makes family vacations possible, allowing couples to escape day-to-day pressures and have fun together.

Consideration

To state the obvious, money is not the key to happiness. Although some assert that money helps, if you are rich but have nonexistent or negative relationships with your spouse and children, you can be emotionally bankrupt. Our society places a great deal of emphasis on making money and very little emphasis on meeting the human needs of love, intimacy, compassion for children, healthy home environments, and other important aspects of life. The relentless pursuit of money has its own price tag.

Dual-Income Marriages

In the past, the typical American family consisted of a husband who earned the income and a wife who stayed home and took care of their children. This pattern has changed.

Data – Both spouses work outside the home in 63 percent of all marriages. (*Statistical Abstract of the United States,* 1987)

Economic necessity is the primary reason for both spouses earning an income. It is not uncommon for a couple to pay $500 monthly on rent and utilities for an apartment and around $1,000 monthly for a home. Particularly for a home, only rarely can a young couple make such payments on one income. "We have the same dreams as everyone else," said one newlywed. "We want a place of our own. We know we could never afford what we want unless we were both earning an income."

Data – In a survey of 999 college students on 104 college campuses, 84 percent said that they wanted a marriage in which both spouses were employed. (Stewart, 1986)

Couples who think in terms of a two-income marriage are not limited to whites. Among Asian American families, at least two full-time workers are necessary to support their nuclear families (Glenn, 1983).

In the following sections, we will focus on the increasingly common pattern of the two-earner couple.

Employed Wives: Past and Present

We work to become, not to acquire.
—Elbert Hubbard

Before 1940, a married woman's place was in the home, and although she might sell her wares, sewing, laundry, and cooking skills (this work could be done without leaving home), she was not expected to earn an income working outside the home. The exception was the black, immigrant, rural woman, who has always tended to work outside the home out of economic necessity.

World War II marked the point at which female employment became acceptable for all classes of women. Their participation in the labor force became a national necessity rather than a social request. While most middle-class, wartime, employed women were expected to return to the roles of wife and mother after the war was over, a Women's Bureau survey conducted in 1944 and 1945 revealed that between 75 and 80 percent of all women war workers wanted to remain on the job after the fighting had stopped (Chafe, 1976). Although demobilization resulted in the loss of jobs for many women (and men), the trend toward increased participation of women in the labor force had been established.

Data – The proportion of employed married women increased from 20 percent just after World War II to 55 percent in 1986. (*Statistical Abstract of the United States,* 1987)

Today's Employed Wives

Among all married women, those more likely to be employed are black, have not completed college, do not have preschool children, and have fewer children. Of course, white college-educated wives with several children are also employed, but there are proportionally fewer of them. In the past, a wife's and mother's employment pattern followed the development of her children; her times of peak employment were before her children were born and after they left home. But this pattern has changed; more mothers with children of all ages now work outside the home.

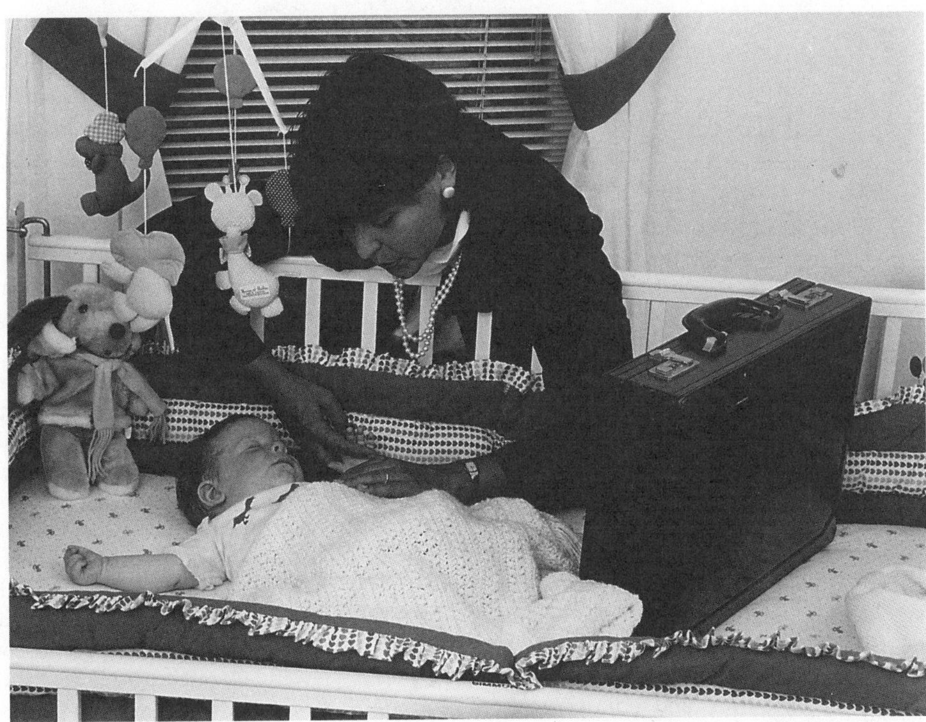

More than half of women with babies and young children are employed.

Data – Fifty-four percent of all wives with children under 6 years of age are in the labor force, in contrast to 68 percent of all wives with children aged 6 to 17. (*Statistical Abstract of the United States,* 1987)

Wives tend to have traditionally "female" jobs: food-service worker, secretary, teacher, cleaning-service worker, and sales clerk. These are often part-time jobs that provide flexibility in working times—an important benefit to women with children. Flexibility in work time is usually an irrelevant issue to Chinese Americans, who have to cope with another set of problems to keep their families together and to survive economically (see Exhibit 10.1).

Motivations For Employment

Women work for many of the same reasons that men work—money, personal independence, personal satisfaction, and expansion of a social network. Regarding money, one wife and mother said, "Money tends to dribble in and pour out. When you've got bills like we do (braces, tuition, car and house payments), you've got to do everything possible to get more money dribbling in." And the money is not equally distributed among families.

Data – The annual median income for whites is $24,908; for hispanics, $17,465; for blacks, $14,819. (*Statistical Abstract of the United States,* 1987)

Two can live as cheaply as one as long as one doesn't eat.
—A homemaker

Money also gives a sense of personal independence. "I like to have my own money," said one wife. "I don't like having to ask my husband for money every time I want to buy a pair of shoes. And it's a good feeling to know I could economically take care of myself if I had to."

Exhibit 10.1

CHINESE AMERICANS AND ECONOMIC SURVIVAL*

Chinese spouses and their children have experienced one of three patterns of family relationships since immigration to America began in 1850.

Split Household

The split-household pattern—husbands leaving their wives and children in China while they came to America to work in the railroad, mining, and agricultural industries—existed primarily between 1850 and 1920. Employers needed an abundance of inexpensive labor, which these young, able-bodied Chinese males were willing to provide. The husbands sent money back to China to provide support for their wives and children. (Actually, the husband sent money to his kin—usually his parents—with whom his wife and children lived. This arrangement ensured that the wife would stay chaste and subject to the ultimate control of her husband.)

The wives often preferred to stay in China—to live comfortably in their village on the money sent by their husbands. Some husbands had concubines in the United States. The marriage relationship lacked frequent nurturing, and the relationship between the father and his children was often formal and distant. The relationship between the mother and children was particularly strong, due to the husband's absence.

Small-Producer Family

As immigration laws were relaxed, more wives and children joined their husbands in America. From about 1920 to the mid–1960s, the typical Chinese American family functioned as a small producing unit:

> Some flavor of the close integration of work and family life is seen in this description of the daily routine in a family laundry, provided by a woman who grew up in Boston's Chinatown during the 1930s and 1940s. The household consisted of the parents and four children. The work day started at 7:00 in the morning and did not end until midnight, six days a week. Except for school and a short nap in the afternoon, the children worked the same hours as the parents, doing their homework between midnight and 2:00 a.m. Each day's routine was the same. All items were marked or tagged as they were brought in by customers. A commercial laundry picked up the laundry, washed it, and brought it back wet. The wet laundry was hung to dry in a back room heated by a coal burner. Next, items were taken down, sprinkled, starched, and rolled for ironing. Tasks were allocated by age and sex. Young children of 6 or 7 performed simple tasks, such as folding socks and wrapping parcels. At about age 10, they started ironing handkerchiefs and underwear. Mother operated the collar and cuff press, while father hand-ironed shirts and uniforms. Only on Sunday did the family relax its hectic regimen to attend church in the morning and relax in the afternoon (p. 40).

Dual-Income Family

Since 1965, over 20,000 Chinese have entered the United States each year. Unlike the earlier Chinese immigrants who came over one at a time, the new immigrants came to America in family groups—husband, wife, and children. At least 50 percent of these immigrants can be classified as working class. The husband usually works as a waiter, cook, or janitor; the wife, in a garment shop. Not unlike most American couples, Chinese American couples have come to consist of husbands and wives who work separate jobs. Chinese children are sometimes left unsupervised and complain that their parents are not around much to talk. One young student noted, "We can discuss things, but we don't talk that much. We don't have that much to say" (p. 42).

Exhibit 10.1

Our assumption that Chinese American families are always close-knit may not be true when we examine the degree to which the spouses are subjected to the strains of segregated employment and the children have limited interaction with their parents.

*Adapted from Evelyn N. Glenn. "Split Household, Small Producer, and Dual Wage Earner: An Analysis of Chinese American Family Strategies." *Journal of Marriage and the Family*, 1983, 45, 35–46. Used by permission of the National Council on Family Relations.

Many married women work for the personal satisfaction and self-actualization they derive from employment. A recently married college-educated woman said, "Housework bores me and so does staying home alone all day. I'm beginning my new job on Monday, and I'm excited about it." Another wife said, "As a journalist, I gain a sense of accomplishment from producing a first-class article that I don't get from cooking broccoli or making a lemon pie. My work is part of me, and I enjoy expressing that part of myself."

Employment also often means an expanded social network. Unlike the housewife, whose primary social contacts are her husband and children, the employed woman may interact with a variety of other people daily. One young mother said she needed adult interaction to keep her brain from atrophying. "I had spent so much time around our son, I began to talk 'baby talk' ('see the choo choo') to my husband. We agreed it was time for me to go back to my old job." Some women also have very positive feelings that they should be in the labor force (Greenstein, 1986).

For a variety of reasons, most wives want to have some type of employment outside the home. When a wife and husband disagree about whether the wife should be employed, the wife usually wins.

Job Versus Career

Regardless of the motives for involvement in the labor force, work doesn't mean the same thing to all employed wives. Some refer to their work as a "job"; others, as a "career." Let's examine what a career typically involves.

Criteria For A Career

Although there are many similarities between a job and a career, a career is more likely to require extensive training, commitment, continuity, and mobility. A clinical psychologist who is employed in a mental-health center said, "I didn't get where I am just because I like to work with people. I went to school for 20 years, read myself blind, and wrote a 230–page dissertation to get the Ph.D." A business major noted, "If you don't have your MBA [master's of business administration] degree, they won't talk to you."

In addition to formal training, a career also implies commitment in time and energy to pursue the goals of an organization or profession. An executive for a large insurance company observed, "The corporation wants your soul. If you are not willing to make phone calls in the evenings to your branch managers or to work on Saturdays—in general, work when the corporation needs you—you'll never be an executive and make $60,000 a year."

Consideration

Although corporations typically want the "souls" (the obligations are open-ended) of all of their employees at all levels, the career-minded person is more likely to meet their requests because the rewards are higher. In contrast, if too many demands (being asked to work overtime, cancel vacations) are made on the employee who views his or her work as a job, the person may conclude that the rewards are not worth the inconveniences and look for another job or quit working. "When my boss told me I would have to work on Saturday mornings, I said 'no way' " recalled one spouse. "That time belongs to me and my family." The fact that the obligations for both career and family are open-ended makes full investment in both difficult.

Related to career commitment is career continuity, which involves moving up the corporate ladder and remaining a full-time employee. In general, part-time workers tend to have jobs; full-time workers tend to have careers. Employed wives are more likely to have a job than a career; 75 percent do not work full time year-round. In addition, when employed wives are compared with employed husbands, the husbands more often are at the office on weekends, start their work earlier in the day, get off work later, work more hours per week, and hold second jobs (Pleck & Staines, 1985).

Data – Very few men work fewer than 40 hours per week; few women work more than 40 hours per week for paid employment. (Sorensen et al., 1985) One exception is a study of 21 successful female executives (annual salary = $25,000). The majority of these women said that they often worked 10–14 hours per day, skipped lunch, took work home, and worked on weekends. (Keown & Keown, 1985)

Mobility is a final element that helps to define a career. The trained, committed, full-time worker must be willing to move to another city as his or her career demands. An air-force officer observed, "Once you decide the air force is your career, you better decide to put up with the moving. We've moved 11 times in the last 20 years."

Some employers are reluctant to hire or promote women for fear they will give priority to their families and will not be willing to relocate if necessary. Their fears are well founded. In a Roper Poll (1985), more than 50 percent of the women said they would turn down a job in another city in order to stay with their husbands. Over 70 percent said they would quit their jobs and relocate if their husbands were transferred to another city. In another nationwide study, 43 percent of the working mothers said they had changed jobs or hours to spend more time with their family. Most preferred part-time work (Newsweek Poll, 1986). Few women are in executive positions.

Data – Only 7 percent of all women who work outside the home hold anything remotely approaching an executive position. (Hewlett, 1986)

Mobility is also related to income. If the wife is earning a high income—particularly if her income is higher than her husband's—there is an increased chance that the family (including the husband) will move in response to her promotion or transfer (Bird & Bird, 1985).

Consideration

Careers and jobs have their respective advantages. Careers may involve more money and higher status, but jobs provide more employment flexibility. Jobs are easier to enter and leave and to adjust to different personal and family needs.

Although there are numerous exceptions, husbands tend to have careers and wifes tend to have jobs (Straits, 1985). In the next section, we will examine why.

Obstacles to the Wife Pursuing a Career

There are at least three obstacles a wife may encounter as she pursues a career. These concern children, home, and husband.

Responsibility for Children

It's not difficult for a woman to combine a family and a career—if she knows how to put both of them first.
—Laurence Peter

More than 90 percent of all wives express a desire for children. Although there are exceptions, both wives and husbands tend to expect that the wife will be primarily responsible for child care—an expectation that may block the wife's career advancement (Rextoat, 1985). The demands of home and family life may make it more difficult for women to compete with male colleagues who are not encumbered with the daily responsibilities of homemaking and childrearing.

In general, wives tend to accommodate their work to their family rather than their family to their work. The needs of their children and husbands come before the requirements of a job (Sack & Liddell, 1985). An elementary-school teacher said:

> There is tremendous social pressure on me to be responsible for my children. I don't have to be with them personally to take care of them, but I end up being responsible for arranging that someone takes Sandy from school to piano lessons, that Sam starts his homework after baseball practice, and that Melanie is picked up at the nursery. My husband is very willing to help with the kids, but he's trying to build his practice as an attorney, and I can't see bothering him with the details. If I did, it would soon cut into his career, and neither of us wants that. Of course, my career suffers, but I have the psychological comfort that I am taking care of my family.

The commitment wives feel to their families is reflected in a national poll. Almost one-half (47 percent) of the wives polled said that they preferred to stay home and take care of the house and family (Roper Poll, 1985). Although there are exceptions, Hispanic females tend to have traditional sex-role attitudes about their place being in the home (Ortiz & Cooney, 1985). This is also true of Korean females, who are expected to give priority to their families over paid employment (Sawon, 1984). Career-oriented women find more reinforcement for their work outside the family and view children as less important (Reading & Amatea, 1986).

Data – According to one study of 250 career women who earn an average of $75,000 annually, the career women were 50 percent less likely to have children than the noncareer women. (Gilson & Kane, 1987)

Responsibility for Home

Careers are also difficult for the married woman because she has no "wife" at home to do those things the traditional wife typically does. (Aware of this need, two California entrepreneurs have begun to offer a "Rent-A-Wife" service to working women and bachelors.) Keeping milk in the refrigerator, the clothes clean, the children cared for, and the meals prepared are chores that must be done. In most families, a wife who has a full-time job still does most of the domestic work when she gets home.

Husbands of employed wives usually aren't much help. Most do not participate regularly in household and family tasks (Smith & Reid, 1986).

> *Data* – In one study of 113 university faculty wives, in no case did more than 3 percent of the husbands have a major responsibility for child care. Less than 10 percent of the husbands assumed a major responsibility for washing the laundry, scrubbing the bathroom, cleaning the kitchen, sewing, and preparing the meals. (Sack & Liddell, 1985)

In general, as the husband's income goes up, his participation in housework goes down. Likewise, as the wife's income goes up the husband's participation in housework increases. Indeed, when the husband helps more, the wife earns more (Statham & Larrick, 1986). However, he is more likely not to do housework unless specifically pressed into doing so and to grumble about it when he does. His dissatisfaction may be particularly great if he must help with very young children (Bird & Ford, 1985).

Husbands also don't do much worrying about household responsibilities. One lawyer wife said it occurred to her in court that she would need to stop at the store on her way home and get some toilet paper because the family was down to the last roll. "I bet my husband has never had a thought like that when he is at work," she remarked.

One way husbands can be supportive of their wives' employment is to do domestic work.

However, it is inaccurate to say that employed wives are always unhappy doing more than their share of the child-care and domestic work. In one study of university wives, 26 percent said they were dissatisfied with their husbands' participation in the work load; 69 percent reported that they were satisfied to some degree; and 5 percent were neutral (Sack & Liddell, 1985).

The Husband's Attitude

If the husband is not supportive of his wife's career, he can make it difficult for her to be successful and happy. Not only can he grumble about her working, but he can refuse to move if she has an opportunity for a promotion if she relocates to another city. However, few men want a wife who does not work outside the home.

Data – In a survey of 999 college students on 104 college campuses, only 15 percent of the men said that they wanted a marriage in which their wife does not work outside the home. (Stewart, 1986)

Consideration

Although an increasing number of American wives are demonstrating that it is possible to manage a job and a family, there is evidence to suggest that combining a career and a family is more difficult. Carol Orsborn says of the pressure:

> I began looking at ads and articles about working women, and it clicked. We all were expected to be wives, mothers, family providers, employees, and dynamic individuals—it was a complex trap we were falling for. I began talking about this with my friends, and they were as excited about it as I was. (Edmondson, 1986, p. 18)

In response, Orsborn founded Superwomen Anonymous, which encourages women to stop seeking gratification from others, turn inward, discover what is most important, and reorganize their lives. The group's motto is "Enough is enough." (More information is available from The Orsborn Group; 1275 Columbus; San Francisco, CA 94133.)

Dual-Career Marriages

Dual-career marriages are not all alike. In this section, we will look at some of the variations in this life style.

The wife of one famous tenor says her husband does not make love for two days before a performance and for two days after it. And he gives a performance every four days.
—Luciano Pavarotti

His/her Career

Stan is a lawyer who specializes in criminal law. Barbara is a therapist who works with adolescents in a mental-health center. Although each has a career, both Barbara and Stan regard his career as more important. Vacations, mealtimes, and social gatherings are more often scheduled around his work than hers. "It's not a problem for me," says Barbara. "He makes three times as much money as I do, so we feel it is more important to bend with his career than mine." This pattern in which the husband's career is given preeminence continues to be most common among dual-career couples.

Some careers are particularly devastating for marriage and family life. One researcher (Gerber, 1983) studied the lives and marriages of 60 physicians. As a group, they tended to be almost totally devoted to their careers to the exclusion of their wives and children. One medical intern said:

> When I come home, especially after I've been on call the night before, I just want to pour myself into bed. A lot of times, I'm not even hungry. When I am, I'd almost like somebody to feed it to me. I know it's not fair to Ellen, but I don't want to talk to her. I don't have the energy to talk to anyone. . . . and sex? Forget it. Last week she started to get undressed, and I fell asleep. . . . Doctors are really sexy, huh? (p. 104)

Her/his Career

In other dual-career marriages, husbands and wives see the wife's career as more important. "I'm in real estate," said the husband of a tenured college professor. "My income fluctuates from month to month; my wife's is stable. If she gets an attractive offer from another school, we wouldn't hesitate to move." But relationships in which the wife earns more are in the minority.

> *Data* – Only 12 percent of wives living with their husbands earn more money than their husbands. This represents about 6 million wives. Some of these wives may have outdistanced their husbands in their career aspirations, but it is more often the case that they are married to men who are temporarily having difficulty getting a job that pays a higher wage. (U.S. Bureau of the Census, 1983)

Whoever said "money can't buy happiness" just don't know where to shop.
—Jim Varney

Two researchers studied 46 spouses who were involved in marriages in which the wife's occupation was given priority over the husband's (Atkinson & Boles, 1984). Specific criteria for inclusion in the study included the husband's willingness to relocate to further his wife's career, the perception by the spouses that they would be more likely to move due to the wife's career, and the perception by the spouses that the family was organized around the wife's career. The spouses were in their forties and had been married an average of 12½ years. The men had flexible jobs; 42 percent were self-employed.

The wives and husbands in these marriages were asked to talk about the costs and rewards of this type of dual-career marriage. Wives said the costs included being responsible for the economic support of the family, being tired, feeling guilty over not being a good wife, lacking time to do things, and watching the husband suffer by comparison (for example, others viewing the husband as lazy, irresponsible, and unmasculine). "If he was any kind of a man, he wouldn't be moving just because of her job," said a father of his son.

The major costs of this arrangement from the viewpoint of the husbands were sacrifices in their own careers and their wives being away from home. Also, occasionally, the husband would have to deal with a cryptic remark like the question addressed to the husband of an office manager: "Does she manage you, too?"

Both spouses saw more rewards than costs. Wives talked of the opportunity to pursue their careers, financial gain, independence, freedom from household chores, enhanced self-esteem, having emotional support from husbands, giving husbands time to spend with the children, additional resources for the children, and flexible gender-role models for the children. One mother said:

> I think I show her (my daughter) that a woman can do things. I don't want my girl taking a back seat to a man. I know women who stayed home with their husbands because they were afraid to leave . . . to go out on their own. Those women are trapped—like slaves. I don't want that kind of life for my girl. If she's going to live with a man, it's going to be because she wants to.

For husbands, the rewards of the her/his career pattern included being relieved of the major responsibility for the economic support of the family and having the freedom and resources to pursue their own interests. One attorney said, "Her job has allowed me to pick and choose cases. I only handle cases in my area of specialization. Most lawyers have to take cases they don't find interesting or challenging."

As for the happiness of these marriages, more husbands than wives felt their marriages were "very happy" or "somewhat happy." In contrast to 77 percent of the wives, 95 percent of the husbands selected one of these phrases to describe their marriage.

Not all research on marriages in which the wife has a higher-status job and earns more than the husband reflects as positive a picture as the Atkinson & Boles research. In a summary of three studies made on these marriages, another researcher (Rubenstein, 1982) concludes:

> When a wife has a job that outshines her husband's, sex lives may suffer and feelings of love may diminish. In addition, these couples run a high risk of mutual psychological and physical abuse, which leads to a significantly higher rate of divorce. Finally, for some underachieving husbands whose wives are overachievers, premature death from heart disease is 11 times more frequent than normal. (p. 37)

A husband married to a physician may sometimes tire of the attention his wife gives to her career.

> Last night was the first night she was home before 7:30 in I don't know how long. Her schedule this rotation is incredible. The patients are really sick on her service, and I know she has to be there a lot. But last night I really wanted to be with her—to talk, to have sex, to enjoy ourselves. Well, she came home and said she just wanted to take a short nap first. Well, you can guess the rest. She didn't want to get up; she didn't want to talk; she didn't want sex. I tried to joke with her. I told her that I'm getting rusty, that I'm afraid I'll forget. So she yells "leave me alone" and gives me "the finger." (Gerber, 1983, pp. 106–107)

Some husbands who are married to career-oriented women become "househusbands." One researcher (Beer, 1984) observes that househusbands tend to have had fathers who were a positive role model in terms of doing housework, tend to have an extraordinary sense of fair play regarding domestic work roles, and tend to be professionals who can more easily control their own time. Few college students are interested in role-reversal relationships.

Data – Out of more than 500 respondents, 15 percent of the men and 20 percent of the women said they would be willing to participate in a role-reversal marriage. (Billingham & Sack, 1986)

Their Careers

Sometimes spouses view each other as equals and their careers as equally important. "We respect each other's career commitment, try to support each other, and feel that we mutually benefit from keeping two strong careers going," said one spouse. In Exhibit 10.2, two people share their views of their dual-career marriage. Although career commitment may be equal, in only a few cases do the spouses earn the same amount of money.

Data – In a survey of 65,000 women, 13 percent said they earned the same amount of income as their partner. (Bowe, 1986)

One researcher compared 81 marriages in which both spouses were in professional or managerial positions and worked full time (more than 35 hours each week) to the marriages of 1,500 other families. The study indicated that the dual-career couples were more educated, had higher incomes, were younger, were child-free (60 percent) or had fewer children (75 percent of those with children had one or two), and tended to live in urban areas. (Berardo, 1982)

Husbands in dual-career marriages did no more housework than other husbands. However, wives in dual-career marriages did less housework than wives in other marriages. In another study, the researchers observed that as the status of the wife's work and her income increased, the husband was more likely to help with meal preparation, house cleaning, and childrearing (Bird et al., 1984).

One researcher commenting on the phenomenon of physician–physician marriages noted that although the advantages include an affluent life style and a companion who understands the language and work stress of a physician's life, the disadvantages are not being able to find the work environment to satisfy both partners, little time together, and no one to be the "wife" at home. "I know of no reliable data, but my experience, socially and professionally, indicates that these marriages tend to be considerably above average in stability" (Mathis, 1984, p. 196).

Commuter Marriages*

Increased commitment on the part of wives to pursue a career and an increased willingness on the part of husbands to be pair bonded with and supportive of a wife who is pursuing a career have resulted in the emergence of *commuter marriages.* One of the most visible commuter marriages in our society was between Phil Donahue (in Chicago) and Marlo Thomas (in New York), who commuted to and from one another for four years until Donahue moved his program to New York.

Characteristics of Commuter Marriages

There are at least four characteristics of commuter marriages: equal career commitment, distance, permanence, and a preference for living together (Gerstel & Gross, 1984).

*Based on and reprinted by permission of the publisher of *Commuter Marriage* by N. Gerstel and H. Gross. Copyright © 1984 by The Guilford Press, New York.

Exhibit 10.2

TWO VIEWS OF ONE DUAL-CAREER MARRIAGE

Chris is a 40-year-old division chief at the New York Public Library in Manhattan. Janie is five years younger and is a full-time professional writer for national magazines. They have been married 14 years and have twins. They agree that the label "dual-career marriage" is an important part of their self-definition. Janie says:

> You know, it's like "tell me 10 words that describe you." . . . Dual-career couple is well up on the top of the list of phrases that describe us. A dual-career marriage is rigorous. It shapes everything.

But their feelings about their dual-career marriage are quite different.

Chris

We maintain this arrangement with my approval, but I have strong reservations. There are simply too many pieces in the puzzle. Our children live in a realm where time is beautifully unimportant. Parents with career lives are caught in time. Here we are, seeing ourselves as the radical left, institutionalizing our children in a nursery school from 9 to 3 and then farming them out to a sitter. Somebody else is raising our kids!

I would warn a couple contemplating a dual-career marriage in these terms: do you think your children are in a state of suspended animation from 8:00 a.m. to 7:00 p.m.? Look at my day outside the job. I wake everybody up, dress one child, and make the lunch boxes if I'm downstairs first. I try to leave Janie upstairs with the twins (age 4), so they can be relaxed together before she leaves. Then I drive the children to their school (50 minutes round trip) before taking the commuter train into Manhattan. I'm home just before 7:00 p.m. Also, we're forced into everything ready made: frozen foods and coloring books instead of a game of cards that involves interacting as a family.

What I see, principally, is that my wife is sharing in the goodies of a man's career world—her lunch friends, her college club in the city, her involvement in work that she finds exciting. I list all the negatives because Janie tends to see her job so rosily.

Janie

Our happiness is work, love, and children. I feel I have everything—more than most people, more than I knew married life could contain. The many roles—wife, mother, worker, friend, editor, family arranger—are invigorating. My perfectionism has diminished. The stages of life have softened. Motherhood doesn't have to replace a professional career.

I feel a very positive model to my 4-year-old daughter. She helps me choose clothes each day . . . her ideas are (honestly) better on sartorial matters than mine. She loves her French-American school, and we share our delight in each other's days. The ache I feel is more with her twin, my son. Beneath his quiet, fun-loving, busy nature, is there a mirror of the loneliness I feel for him during the day? Does he need more alone time than his day allows?

Our intimacy as a married couple certainly does not suffer. Once a week Chris and I meet for lunch—our Thursday tryst—between our places of work. We are happy, so it is easy to be affectionate and generous-spirited toward each other.

In her novel *Happy Marriages,* Laurie Colwin says to her old-fashioned, stay-at-home mother, "Stop hectoring me—my children are arranged for, coddled, and loved." That's what I feel. The guilt is only fretting. What childrearing situation is perfect?

Finally, the surprise to this dual working couple—when your income goes up so there is some discretionary income and each week you spend it.

Equal Career Commitment

In commuter marriages, both spouses are equally dedicated to the advancement and success of their respective careers. Her career is as important as his career. Like Brutus, who said of Caesar in Shakespeare's *Julius Caesar,* (Act III, Scene two) it's "not that I loved Caesar less, but that I loved Rome more," spouses in commuter marriages might say it's not that they love each other less but that they love their careers more.

The degree to which work represents a meaningful part of a commuter spouse's life is illustrated by a wife who said:

> I go to pieces when I don't work. I get bored when I am not working. We probably work too hard and occasionally feel guilty about it. But we're not the kind of people who can just relax. We think we have to do something. (Gerstel & Gross, 1984, p. 33)

Distance

It's a real managing kind of ballet to get us together.
—Marlo Thomas

In commuter marriages, the distance between the spouses is great enough to require the establishment of two separate households. Commuter spouses cannot live in the same place and commute to their separate work places. They must live near their work and commute to see each other. The distance can range to more than 1,000 miles.

Permanence

Spouses in commuter marriages view pursuing their careers while living apart as a permanent arrangement. There is no specific time that they plan to live together. They focus on their careers, not on living together.

People in commuter marriages work and live apart from their spouses during the week.

Preference For Living Together

Although separated in reference to their careers, spouses in commuter marriages wish they could be together. They are not separated because they are having marital problems or are drifting toward a divorce. They look forward to an undefined time in the future when they can have their careers and live together, too. In the meantime, they spend a lot of time, energy, and money traveling across the country so that they can be together.

Data – It is not unusual for commuter partners to spend about $6,000 per year traveling to be with each other. (Gerstel & Gross, 1984)

Commuters also recognize the costs of not living together. Each spouse feels as though both partners, individually and as a couple, would suffer if they did not pursue their career interests independently. One commuting wife said:

> I'd be miserable if I knew I gave up the opportunity to reach my career potential. I was reared in a home in which my mother had a career, and I was taught to pursue my career goals to the fullest. My dad was always supportive of my mother's career, so I always expected my husband to be supportive of my career.

Unique Problems in Commuter Marriages

Like all relationships, commuter marriages have their share of problems. Some of them will be examined in the following sections.

Fragmented Conversations

Because commuters don't return to the same house each evening, their spouse is not there to share the intimate details of life and work. Most miss the presence of their partner and use the telephone as a substitute for face-to-face interaction.

Data – In one study, 42 percent of commuter spouses phoned each other every day, and 30 percent called every other day. (Gerstel & Gross, 1984, p. 56)

But just as spouses who live together don't always view their communication positively, neither do commuters. One husband recalls:

> Sometimes she will call me, and I'll be really tired. I just won't have any life in me. And she'll want something more from the call. There's a clashing. Or it happens the other way around. I'll feel good, and she'll be focused on something she's doing. It's hard to shift gears to get into someone else's mood when there is no forewarning and the phone call will soon be over. (Gerstel & Gross, 1984, p. 58)

Lack of Shared Leisure

Each partner in a commuter marriage can talk with the other during the week, but going out to dinner, seeing a movie, or attending a concert or play with the spouse is not an option. Each spouse often misses not being able to spend leisure time with the other partner. Due to this high companionship need, most commuter spouses get together on weekends.

Data – More than 50 percent of 71 commuter couples got together every weekend. (Gerstel & Gross, 1984)

Marital Sex

Commuter spouses obviously are not sexually available to each other every evening. But even spouses who are rarely have intercourse every night. In commuter marriages, however, the partners' options of when they can have sex get compressed into smaller time periods. A partner who is not in the mood may feel that he or she should have sex because the weekend will soon be over. This places the unrealistic burden on the relationship that the limited time the couple does spend together should be perfect.

Some commuting women (although not commuting men) also experience the "stranger effect," reporting that they need a period of time to reacquaint themselves with their partner before they feel comfortable about having sex with him. "It takes me at least a day to feel close to him again," said one woman.

Feeling Unproductive

Because commuter spouses may feel disconnected, disjointed, and lonely, they may not be able to concentrate and get their work done. According to one spouse:

> I end up goofing off a lot. It's like I can't get motivated or focused on what I know I should be doing. When my partner is around, I have no trouble getting on-task. It's really crazy how the absence of my partner makes me feel like doing nothing.

Children

Children may be an additional problem for the commuter couple. In most cases, young children will stay in the home of one parent, in effect making a single parent out of one spouse. Although some spouses enjoy the role of primary caretaker, others feel resentful of the spouse who is able to pursue his or her career unhampered by the responsibilities of childrearing.

If the commuter couple are remarried and bring children from a previous marriage into the commuter marriage, then conflicts about how to spend holidays, with whom, and where may occur. Each spouse may want his or her own children and the partner to visit in his or her own home. There are only a limited number of holidays (there is only one Christmas Eve each year), so the competition for time can be enormous. One spouse said, "It would be nice if we liked each other's kids, but we don't. So vacation times always create real problems for us."

Benefits of Commuter Marriages

In spite of the problems, there are benefits to a commuter marriage. We will address some here.

Higher Highs

"I'd rather have two terrific evenings a week with my spouse than five average ones," illustrates the view that the time commuter spouses have for each other is, in some ways, like courtship time—more limited but definitely enjoyable. Each spouse makes a special effort to make the time they have together good time. Some commuter partners feel the periods of separation enhance the love feelings in their relationship. One woman said:

> It's added some romance. There are a lot of comings and goings. We give each other presents. When I come home, there's a huge welcome. And there are tears at parting. I usually arrive looking exhausted. Show up completely collapsed. And my husband has a bottle of wine, no kidding, with a bow around it and flowers or a bottle of Chanel. And he makes a bath for me. (Gerstel & Gross, 1984, p. 76)

Limited Bickering

To ensure that the limited time is positive, commuters often make a point of avoiding petty bickering that sometimes creeps into the relationships of spouses who see each other every day. "We just don't want to argue over the laundry when we're together. We don't want to spoil the time we have together," said one commuter.

In summarizing the rationale and benefits for living in a commuter marriage, one spouse said:

> I want it all. A husband and a career. And while I would prefer for us to be together, it turned out that he was already established in his work in one city and I got a job offer I have been training for all my life in another city. I'd say the benefits are that I can get my work done (I work very well in an empty house) and enjoy him on the weekends. The drawbacks are that I'd like to have dinner with him and talk with him face-to-face every night. Someone asked me, "Why not just be single?" The answer is I loathe the problem of looking for a stable companion in my life and someone to spend holidays with. This way, I have a booked flight with the man I love every weekend and all holidays and I can enjoy my work in the in-between times. I know a lot of spouses who live with each other all the time, and the only time they look forward to is being away from each other.

Consideration

Some of the conflict in living in a commuter marriage can be reduced by acknowledging to each other and to one's self that a career is important and that each partner values being married to a mate who has a high career commitment. The partners can focus on the benefits of their life-style decision and enjoy the very special times they have together.

Job-Sharing Marriages

Job sharing is defined as a situation in which a permanent, full-time position is restructured to provide part-time employment for two people. Instead of both partners working all day at a particular job, each partner works some of the time. Two researchers (Mikitka & Koblinsky, 1985) studied 20 married couples who were job sharing a university position.

The primary reason for the decision to job share was the inability to find two full-time positions. Each spouse preferred to have her or his own position but that was not possible. Not all couples selected job sharing as a last resort, however; 20 percent wanted a flexible life style, which job sharing provides. When neither partner has to work all the time, the partners can share child care and still have time for individual pursuits. Wives tend to work fewer hours than husbands in job-sharing marriages.

Data – Job-sharing wives reported averaging 45 hours of work per week; job-sharing husbands reported averaging 56 hours per week. (Mikitka & Koblinsky, 1985)

Both the husbands and the wives in this study expressed satisfaction with the emotional support they received from their spouses, child-care arrangements, and the division of domestic tasks. Spouses who job share may also share a common view of reality, which has been associated with marital satisfaction (Imig & Imig, 1986).

The disadvantages of job sharing were economic and political. The spouses earned less sharing one job than they would have earned if each spouse had had a separate job. About 50 percent of the sample felt exploited because they were given large amounts of committee work, received little economic support for research, and were expected to publish a greater volume of data because they had reduced work loads.

Data – Only one couple in 20 saw job sharing as a permanent life style; the other 19 found job-sharing salaries inadequate. (Mikitka & Koblinsky, 1985)

Consequences of Two Incomes in One Marriage

Regardless of the type of dual-income marriage that couples have, there are various consequences for the spouses and their marriage.

Consequences for the Wife

Researchers disagree on the degree to which a woman's happiness increases as a result of working outside the home. In one study comparing homemakers and women employed outside the home, the homemakers were more satisfied. The explanation suggested by the researchers (Stokes & Peyton, 1986) for women who work outside the home being more dissatisfied was in reference to working in stressful jobs with low pay and limited potential for advancement.

Other studies have shown that wives who work outside the home are happier than those who do not work outside the home (McLanahan & Glass, 1985) and that they feel happier about their marriages (Blumstein & Schwartz, 1983). Among the benefits that wives derive from outside employment are increased interaction with a variety of individuals, a broader base of recognition, enhanced self-esteem, and greater equality between self and spouse. One dual-income wife said:

> By having a career, you don't put all your eggs in the marriage-and-family basket. A career gives you another sphere of life to enjoy and in which to feel good about yourself. You can bring more to your husband and children when you're happy doing what you like.

Employed women who receive social support from coworkers and who feel socially integrated into their work environment also report feeling more healthy and spending fewer days in the hospital (Hibbard & Pope, 1985). Housewives who are not involved in community activities seem to be the least healthy.

One cost associated with being a dual-income wife is having less time for self due to the tendency of the wife to extend herself in both roles (career and wife-mother) as a way of coping with the conflict between the roles. Thus, the working wife's major coping strategy is to "do it all." The result is that she experiences more stress than her husband is aware of (White et al., 1986).

Another cost for the wife in a dual-income marriage involves self doubts about one's own femininity. The career wives studied by Atkinson & Boles (1984) said they were sometimes seen as unladylike, domineering, and manipulative. Some wives felt that their career changed the way they saw themselves, their spouses, and their marriages. Before a wife with small children decides to work outside the home, she should complete the self-assessment exercise. Sometimes her employment is not economically advantageous.

Consequences for the Husband

How do husbands feel about their wives being employed? In a study comparing 208 husbands whose wives were employed and 408 husbands whose wives were full-time housewives, the husbands of employed wives were less satisfied with their work and family lives than the husbands of women who stayed at home. These findings were true regardless of the husband's age, income bracket, or educational level. The researchers suggest that a husband's feeling about himself is related to his perception of his adequacy in the role of breadwinner. If his wife is employed, he feels he is not a good provider (Staines et al., 1986).

Husbands who grew up with a mother who worked outside the home are more supportive of their wives' occupational pursuits. Such an experience suggests that the wife's employment is normative.

Husbands whose wives have worked outside the home from the beginning of the marriage are more tolerant than husbands whose wives delay such employment. Husbands get accustomed to their wives preparing the meals, cleaning the house, and taking care of the children and miss these services when they stop. Husbands don't help much around the house, whether or not their wives work. True househusbands are rare (Beer, 1984). However, the husband of an employed wife does more than the husband of a full-time homemahomemaker. "Since women help bring home the bacon, they expect their husbands to help fry it," says Ann Landers. Also, husbands who have an egali-

Self-Assessment

Does It Pay for a Mother with Small Children to Work Away From Home?

Job satisfaction is certainly a worthwhile reason for a mother to seek employment. But will it pay to work full time while your children are young? Or in the long run, would you be better off acquiring and polishing skills at night school, during hours when your husband can baby-sit, and then stepping into a higher paying job—and probably a more satisfying one—after the children are more independent?

Sadly enough, from a financial standpoint, you will often find that when your children need care in your absence, a second family income is mostly illusory. You can sometimes save more money by serving two meatless dinners a week and sewing your own and the children's clothes than you can earn by going to work. In addition, staying at home with the children may create less of an emotional drain on the entire family.

Estimate your family's increases in spendable money if you take a job by filling in the following cost sheet. Remember, no matter how attractive your pay may seem, it is only what you get to keep that counts.

Daily transportation	________	x 250 =	$ ________
Lunches	________	x 250 =	$ ________
Baby sitter or day care per week	________	x 50 =	$ ________
Additional clothes			$ ________
Extra cost of convenience foods to substitute for your cooking	________	x 250 =	$ ________
Union or professional association dues	________	x number of payments per year	$ ________
Group life and health insurance (your share)	________	x number of payments per year	$ ________
Your share of pension plan contributions (this is really long-term savings, but it is not spendable cash now)			$ ________
		Subtotal of costs	$ ________
Add 10 percent of subtotal costs for office contributions, coffee breaks, and other inevitable and unexpected dollar dribbles.			$ ________
		Total costs	$ ________

Now subtract these total costs from your take-home pay (your net pay) after deductions for taxes, Social Security, and disability insurance. What is left is what you are actually going to earn. Is it worth it?

Staying home may turn out to make more economic sense due to the high cost of child care and other expenses. This does not mean you shouldn't work if you want to, however. Consider the kind of work you would really like to do. Then consider improving your skills with evening classes during your children's preschool years. Instead of starting as a file clerk, you could be a dental hygienist; instead of starting at assembly-line work, you could be a management supervisor. The early years of childrearing can be an opportunity—not only for your family but for yourself as well. One-half of all mothers with children under 6 do not work outside the home (Thornton & Freedman, 1983).

Source: *Parents Magazine,* September 1979, p. 24.

tarian view of gender roles are more likely to take responsibility for meal preparation, cleaning, and childrearing (Bird et al., 1984).

Although some husbands may complain about the extra housework they feel pressed into doing, most enjoy the economic benefits of the two-income marriage. "When you've got two people putting money in the kitty, it fills up faster and you can buy what you want now." Some couples who have adjusted to a standard of living based on two incomes feel dropping back to one income would have disastrous financial ramifications.

Data – The median income of a family with two earners is $31,707 compared to $20,291 when the husband is the sole earner. (*Statistical Abstract of the United States*, 1987)

A wife's career commitment may affect her husband's career. In a study of more than 300 husbands, the researchers found that the career mobility of a husband tends to be restricted when he is married to a wife in a high-status occupation (Sharda & Nangle, 1981). "Both husbands and wives tend to accommodate each other by restricting their own mobility" (p. 148).

A husband may also miss the emotional support of his wife:

> While homebound wives have traditionally depended on their husbands' achievements for much of their sense of worth, husbands have been at least as dependent on their wives—as listeners, consolers, and ego-builders—for their emotional sustenance. When the wife has a career of her own, however, the exchange is altered. The wife is less dependent on her husband for her own self-esteem, and she may also be less attentive to his needs and problems. (Rubin, 1983, p. 72)

Marital Consequences

What are the consequences for the marriage when the wife is employed? Results of studies differ. One study found that full-time employed mothers who had pre-school children were very unhappy in their marriages. They felt overwhelmed with the demands of their job and taking care of their preschooler after work. Although they viewed their husbands as caring and understanding, they did not have time to discuss daily matters with him (Schumm & Bugaighis, 1986). One wife said:

> By 9 o'clock at night, there is nothing left of me. I'm completely worn out by my job and my kid. I don't even feel like talking to my husband. I just want to be by myself and sleep. I'll tell you—it's no good for your marriage.

Another study confirms that working wives with children feel diminished sexual desire because they are physically and emotionally drained (Berg, 1986).

Other studies have found no effect of the wife's employment on the marriage. One researcher, who reviewed 27 studies covering a three-year period and involving 4,602 comparisons of marriages in which the wives did and did not work, concludes that "wife employment alone appears to have little or no effect on marital adjustment" (Smith, 1985).

Consideration

These different conclusions suggest that the wife's employment by itself does not determine whether a couple's marriage will be happy. Issues that do influence happiness in the dual-income marriage are more likely to include the husband's support of his wife's employment, flexibility of roles, and commitment by each spouse to allocate time to their relationship. "The bottom line of making a dual-income marriage work," said one spouse, "is to help your partner and be committed to your relationship."

Employment of the wife alters the traditional pattern of the marriage relationship in the direction of equality, as the money she earns increases her power in the marriage. An interior designer said:

> Now that I make a good income, my preferences are given equal weight by my husband. Whether we eat out or not, where we eat, and where we vacation are now joint decisions. Before, my husband would say, "We can't afford it . . ." and I would acquiesce.

The adage "He who pays the piper calls the tune" summarizes the relationship between money and power. In the dual-income marriage, there are two pipers and two potential tunes.

Consequences for the Children

Most husbands and wives feel the wife's employment has more positive than negative personal and marital consequences, but they are more ambivalent about the consequences for their children. Most parents think it is best for their children for the mother to be with them when they are small.

Negative effects of a mother's employment on her children's self-concept, school achievement, and vocational development have not been verified. Rath-

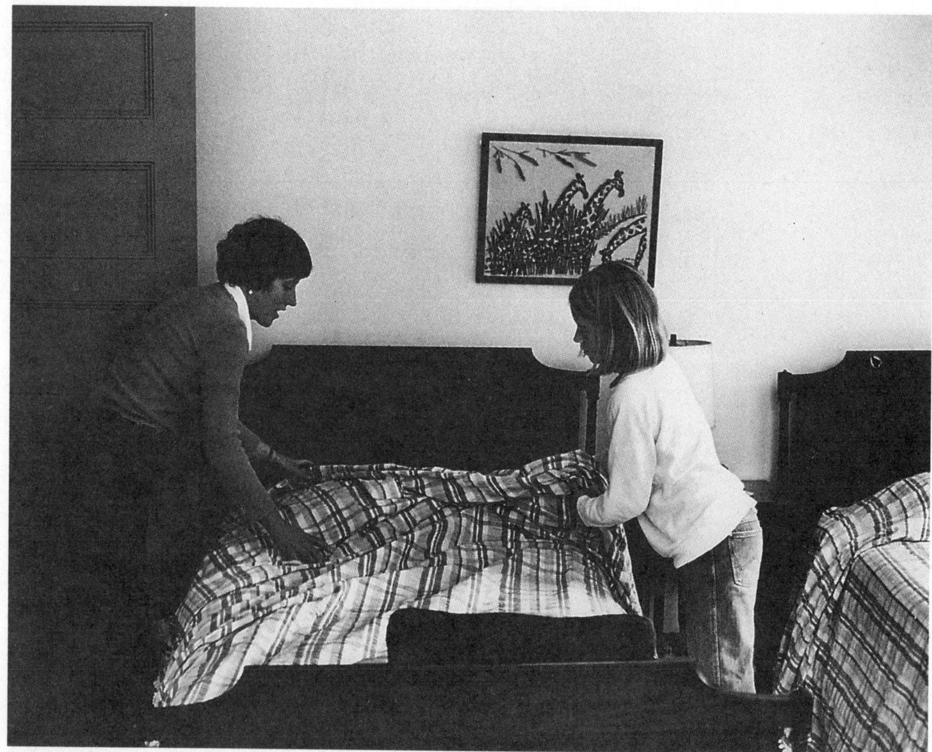

Children in two-income marriages do more domestic work than children in one-income marriages.

er, research shows that children of working mothers develop just as well emotionally, intellectually, and socially as children whose mothers stay at home (Berg, 1986). In addition, daughters of employed mothers also feel that women have much more career options than daughters of mothers who are not employed (Selkow, 1985). When children are asked about their parents' dual-career marriages, they are approving.

Data – Out of 93 children, 96 percent said they were "satisfied" with the fact that both of their parents have careers. (Knaub, 1986)

But when mothers are asked the degree to which they feel their working outside the home is good for their children, only a few feel that it is.

Data – In a *Redbook* survey of almost 1,000 women, only 8 percent of the working mothers agreed children are better off when the mother works outside the home. (Gaylin, 1986)

Mothers who work outside the home often feel guilty about doing so. One mother said:

> I'm very tired when I get home from teaching third grade all day, and I don't feel like going to Parents Night at my child's school. But I ask myself, "What kind of a parent am I if I don't go to my own child's school functions?" and the guilt is usually enough to get me there.

Although most children are not harmed by their mother's employment, "latch-key" or "self-care" children may be.

Data – About 7 million self-care children from 6 to 12 years of age come home after school to an empty house (they let themselves in with a "latch key") and remain there alone until their working parents get home. (Meredith, 1986)

With no one to supervise them until after 5:00 p.m., it is possible that these self-care children are more likely to experiment with sex and drugs, to be victims of crime, and to have accidents. But there are exceptions. Some self-care children respond to being left at home alone by developing a sense of independence and by using the time productively without getting into trouble (Meredith, 1986). The data on self-care children is still not available to the extent that it is possible to say it is "bad" for these children to be left unsupervised. (Rodman & Cole, 1987)

To help allay children's fears, PhoneFriend is available in State College, Pennsylvania, and other areas such as Boston and Houston. By calling a specified number, the children have someone they can talk to in times of stress. Other cities have extended school hours, provide supervised sports activities, or provide after-school activities through local churches (Robinson et al., 1986).

Consideration

Children who must spend time alone at home should know the following:

1. How to reach their parents at work (the phone number, extension number, and name of the person to talk to if the parent is not there).

2. Their home address and phone number in case information must be given to the fire department or an ambulance service.
3. How to call emergency services, such as the police and fire departments.
4. The name and number of a relative or neighbor to call if the parent is unavailable.
5. To keep the door locked and not let anyone in.
6. Not to tell callers their parents are not at home. (They are busy or can't come to the phone.)
7. Not to play with appliances, matches, or the fireplace.

A unique book for latch-key children is *Alone After School* by Helen Swan and Victoria Houston (1985).

Other Consequences

Couples in two-income marriages note that household chores, childrearing responsibilities, and time priorities are potential problems. Because each spouse's occupational role makes considerable demands on that partner, each spouse needs a "backup." In the traditional marriage, this is the nonworking wife. In the dual-income marriage, there is no backup.

Patterns of response to the "no wife at home" problem vary. As already noted, wives typically extend themselves and do much of the domestic labor and child care in addition to their paid employment. Some husbands share the work. Other couples hire substitutes. One couple hires a person to come to the home Monday through Friday from 7:30 a.m. to 5:30 p.m. to take care of the couple's infant, clean the house, and prepare dinner.

Regardless of how the work gets done, two-income couples complain that they have little time for each other. "We have to schedule Saturday from five till midnight for ourselves. If it weren't for the Saturday nights alone together, we would be divorced. If you don't spend time with each other, you grow away from your partner," remarked a real estate broker.

Because they have limited leisure time and that is usually allocated to the children and each other, two-income couples may feel isolated from others. They have fewer friends. The friendships that do develop tend to be with other dual-income couples, which helps to validate the life style.

Trends

The number of married women employed in the labor force will continue to increase. Most working women will continue to have jobs, but an increasing number will become involved in careers. For some brides, the understanding that they will pursue a career during their marriage is a nonnegotiable issue. "I want to be married," said one woman, "but I won't let it interfere with my career."

The percentage of husbands with supportive attitudes toward a wife's employment will also increase. Economic necessity, male peers with working wives, and being reared by mothers who were employed outside the home will all contribute to this increase. Whether this support translates into an equal sharing of domestic and child-care tasks remains to be seen. Unless men take on more of the work load at home, women will continue to be burdened with the two major roles of worker and homemaker.

More mothers with young children will enter the work force. To encourage young parents to continue working, more companies will offer flextime (25 percent currently do so)—a system that permits a worker to select the eight hours she or he will work. At Forecasting International in Arlington, Virginia, 50 percent of the employees work from 7:00 a.m. to 3 p.m. and 50 percent work from 9 a.m. to 5 p.m. Other accommodations by industry to family needs include the four-day workweek (four 10½-hour days), job sharing (two workers share one full-time job), and on-premise day care (about 2,000 companies provide day care where the mothers of small children work). All of these alternatives allow parents to continue to work by ensuring care for their infants and young children.

For the working parent with a sick child, a new industry is emerging. About 40 day-care programs for sick kids are available. One such program—Sniffles 'N Sneezes at AMI Southeastern Medical Center in North Miami Beach, Florida—provides nursing care and a visit by a pediatrician for $30 per day.

Although the U.S. government is not likely to get into the day-care business, federal policy may move toward protecting the jobs of parents who must take temporary leaves of absence from work due to their children.

Data – Job-protected leaves of absence at the time of childbirth are a matter of course in 117 countries. The United States is not one of these. (Hewlett, 1986)

In general, the more a company is supportive of family values, the more committed an employee is to work for that company. (Orthner & Pittman, 1986)

Summary

Employed wives are becoming increasingly common, particularly in the middle class. Before 1940, female workers were primarily poor, black, and immigrant, but with World War II, middle-class wives flooded the labor force. At the end of the war, about 20 percent of all married women were employed; by 1988, that figure had jumped to almost 70 percent.

In general, although wives are motivated by money and the desire for adult interaction, their labor force participation is related to the stage of their families' development. Wives with no children are the most likely to be employed, and those with preschool children are the least likely to work outside the home. Almost 50 percent of mothers with children under the age of 6 are not employed.

When a career is defined in terms of training, commitment, continuity, and mobility, most wives seem to have jobs rather than a career. Responsibility for the children and having no "wife" at home are among the obstacles married women must overcome in pursuing a career.

Dual-career marriages may be described as "his", "hers," or "theirs." When working wives are asked to evaluate the effect of their employment on themselves, their marriages, and their children, most report being happier individuals and happier in their marriages. Husbands report mixed feelings about their wives' employment. Although many husbands are delighted that their wives are happier and enjoy the economic benefits of a two-income marriage, they may miss the personal and domestic attentions of their wives and feel pressed into doing more housework themselves. Trends in two-income marriages include more two-income marriages, more mothers of small children working outside the home, and more companies offering flextime, leaves of absence, and day-care facilities to working parents.

Questions for Reflection

1. Does the work role you foresee for yourself approximate a career or a job?
2. How much do you want the person you might marry to be involved in a career? In a job?
3. How does having or not having money influence your mood, your feelings about yourself, and your interaction with others?

CHOICES

MAKING DECISIONS ABOUT a dual-income marriage involves different issues for the wife and the husband. How much to spend and how much to save may also become issues.

As a Wife, Do I Want a Dual-Career Marriage?

As a current or potential wife, personal needs, your husband's support, and your desire for children are issues you might consider in making a decision to pursue a career during your marriage. It is clear that some women are miserable in the sole roles of wife and mother. A newswoman for a television station said:

> My employment offers me the chance to stay alive. When my children leave home or if my husband dies, I will still be a journalist. Otherwise I'd be nothing.

The husband's emotional support for his wife's employment is another important consideration. "I've got the best husband you could imagine," said one university professor. "He has always encouraged my involvement in whatever I wanted to do, and he struggled through the grind of a Ph.D. program with me." Not all husbands are this supportive. Your husband's enthusiastic support is critical if your goal is to pursue a meaningful career and be a wife.

Finally, think about your desire for children. Unless your husband is willing to share the responsibility of rearing children fully (he takes the children to piano lessons or sees that someone else does; he calls out the spelling words; he helps with the math homework), your career advancement may suffer. It is common for wives to reduce the conflict between children and job demands by reducing job demands to meet family needs. This strategy will work as long as you are involved in a job, not in a career. If a career is your goal, consider the consequences of having children and a husband who does not support your career.

As a Husband, Do I Want a Dual-Career Marriage?

As a current or potential husband, you might assess the degree to which you want your wife to pursue a career. In general, husbands point to the empathy aspects, more money, and the knowledge that their wives are happier working than being at home as the primary benefits of a wife's employment. One husband said:

> When your wife has a career, she understands what the stress of the work world is like. She knows what it is to meet deadlines, to have conferences that are boring, and to be exhausted by traveling. The empathy that each of you have for the other's work stress is a major benefit.

Increased money is also an advantage of a dual-income marriage from the husband's perspective. More money not only improves the couple's immediate life style (Home Box Office, new cars, a swimming pool), but it may also prolong the life of the man. One husband said:

> My dad died of a coronary when he was 46. I'm sure that one of the reasons for his early death was the fact that he was totally responsible for earning all the money. Since my mother did not work outside the home, he worked himself crazy with the stress of two jobs. Since my wife earns a terrific income, I don't worry as much about money and certainly don't feel that I am responsible for sending our three kids to college on the money that I earn.

(Continued)

A final benefit to the husband of the wife's career involvement is her happiness. According to one husband:

> I'm living with a happy woman. Although she is very busy and exhausted half the time, she loves her work. She's not the kind that can sit home and cut out orange-juice coupons all day long.

Husbands also point to several disadvantages of being married to a woman who has a career, especially missing the services of a domestic wife, feeling obligated to help more around the house, and feeling threatened by the wife's own income, increased power, and independence. Missing the services of the domestic wife is more characteristic of husbands whose wives were first homemakers and then career wives. Husbands who began marriage with the career wife don't know what they are missing.

The domestic obligation husbands feel increases as the career demands of the wife escalate. Some husbands respond to this feeling in a cooperative spirit and take over the cooking, cleaning, shopping, and laundry. Other husbands negotiate with their wives to hire a person to come in once or twice a week to take care of the house. Some dual-career spouses hire a full-time, live-in helper so that neither is burdened with housework.

The wife's economic independence is a problem for some husbands. Suddenly they recognize they are no longer needed economically. For the husband who has a low sense of self-esteem and needs his wife's constant adulation, her independence may be a problem.

In evaluating these advantages and disadvantages, questions husbands might ask include "Is the loss of domestic services counterbalanced by more income?," "Is my wife's absence from the home made up for by her greater fulfillment?," and "Am I willing to share the responsibility of parenting?"

Do Children Want Both Parents to Work Outside the Home?

As a result of the value parents place on money (in the case of the single parent, money is often necessary for survival), increasing numbers of preschool children are being reared in homes where they are taken to day-care centers by day and live with parents who are too tired or irritable to spend time with them at night. When they reach school age, many of these children come home to an empty house to fend for themselves (self-care children) until their parents return from work. One child-development expert asked, "Can American Families Afford the Luxury of Childhood?" (Garbarino, 1986) and commented:

> The economic facts of the matter predict that parents will believe that young children are capable of assuming early responsibility for self-care and that early demands for maturity are in the child's best interests (and, by implication, there is something wrong with children if they cannot meet those demands). . . . it seems that many adults are taking the position that their families cannot afford to subsidize the child's experience of childhood as it has evolved in western culture as a desirable stage in life. (p. 126)

Suppose preschool children were asked if they wanted a parent (father or mother) to stay home with them rather than have their parent work outside the home while the child is in day care. And suppose self-care children were asked to express their preference for being at home with a parent versus being home alone. Would the predictable answers influence the choices parents are making in reference to their employment and parenting?

Impact of Social Influences on Choices

As a woman, your desire to work outside the home in a job or career will be influenced by your mother's role, the degree to which your married female peers are employed, the presence of children, and the preference of your partner. If your mother worked outside the home, your peers work, you have no children, and your husband expects you to earn an income, the chance of your working is very high. However, if your mother did not work outside the home, your peers don't work, you have children, and your husband prefers that you stay at home, the likelihood of your working outside the home may be equally strong. In effect, economic necessity may dictate whether you are employed outside the home—but always within the context of your relationships with others.

As a man, the issue of your working outside the home has such a strong cultural bias that you probably do not even consider staying home as an alternative. The employment patterns of your father and your male peers establish the norm that you are to have a career. Although some husbands and fathers are househusbands, they are still an extremely rare phenomenon. Social influences currently lock the performance of various roles into position.

CHAPTER 11

Sexual Fulfillment

Contents

Is It True?*

1. Wives report lower sexual fulfillment than husbands.
2. The most common problem sex therapists treat is premature ejaculation.
3. Most impotent men who have had penile implant surgery wish they had not had the operation.
4. Individuals who participated in a sexual-enrichment program said satisfaction with their sexual partners decreased after the workshop.
5. About 50 percent of all couples who have been married for more than 50 years say they no longer have intercourse.

*1=T; 2=F; 3=F; 4=F; 5=T.

"SEXUAL FULFILLMENT FOR me," said a 26–year–old woman "is having sex with someone I love. He accepts my sexuality and is not turned off to my strong responses. In addition, he is responsive to my needs and is willing to invest the time it takes to excite me. Good sex takes love, time, patience, caring, and experimentation."

In this chapter, we will look at the meanings, prerequisites, and facts related to sexual fulfillment. We will also examine sexual dysfunctions common to women and men. Finally, because growing older is something we all do, we look at sexuality in the middle and later years.

The Meanings of Sexual Fulfillment

Sexual fulfillment means different things to different people at different times.

INDIVIDUAL DEFINITIONS

When wives and husbands are asked about the degree to which they are sexually fulfilled in their relationships, wives report lower sexual fulfillment than husbands. Wives also tend to view sexual fulfillment in the context of marital intimacy. If a wife feels emotionally close to her partner, she is more likely to view herself as sexually fulfilled. Husbands, on the other hand, are more likely to evaluate their sexual relationship separately from their marital relationship. Husbands can report a good sex life with their wives but a bad marriage with them (Patton & Waring, 1985).

Sexual fulfillment depends in part on having a good sexual partner. In a survey conducted by the author, 100 respondents were asked to specify the characteristics of a good sexual partner. The most frequent characteristic mentioned by both genders was being loved or cared for by their sexual partner. "Having sex with someone is easy," said one person. "It's the person behind the genitals who cares about you that makes it special." But other respondents did not mention the emotional relationship with a partner. Rather, they focused on such characteristics as variety, aggressiveness, patience, and endurance (see Figure 11.1).

SEXUAL FULFILLMENT AND INTERCOURSE

The variety of definitions associated with sexual fulfillment make it clear that there is no specific element, including intercourse, in a sexual relationship that must be present to achieve sexual fulfillment.

I have steak and sex the same way—very rare.

—Rodney Dangerfield

A couple who never has intercourse may be sexually fulfilled. One couple reported:

> We've been married for 43 years and haven't had intercourse in 10 years or so. The idea that you need to have intercourse with your spouse to be sexually and emotionally happy is nonsense. We love each other, go everywhere together, and have three beautiful grandchildren. There is more to life than intercourse.

There are a number of reasons why intercourse is not necessary for some couples who define themselves as sexually fulfilled and happy:

FIGURE 11.1
CHARACTERISTICS OF PEOPLE WHO SAY A SEXUALLY FULFILLING RELATIONSHIP IS IMPORTANT

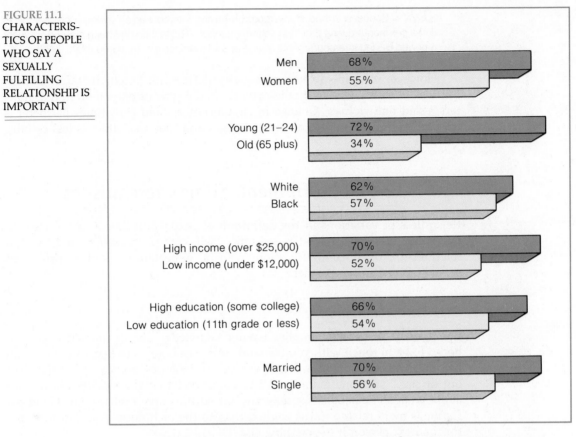

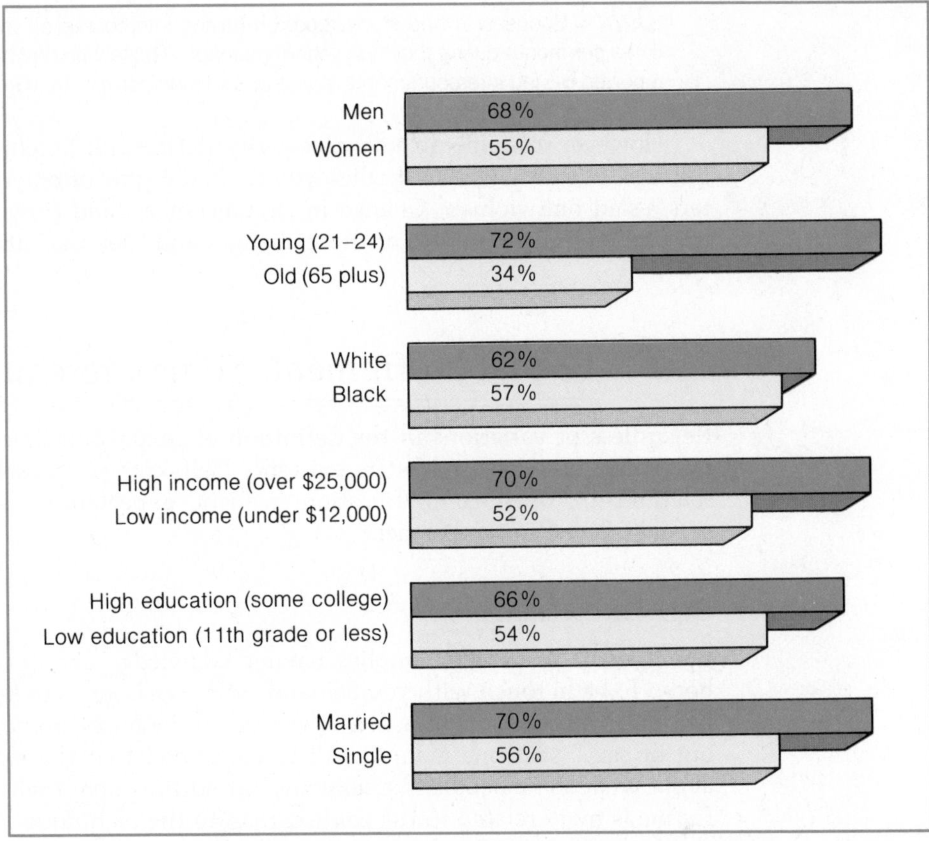

1. There is little peer pressure for spouses to have intercourse.
2. Sexual experiences may not have been particularly enjoyable. Perhaps the man ejaculated prematurely or the woman did not climax.
3. Masturbation may be preferred over intercourse.
4. Other shared interests are more enjoyable than sexual involvement.
5. Physical problems (arthritis, slipped disc, or the like) may make sexual participation painful or unpleasant.
6. Definitions such as "we're too old for that" or "that part of our life is over" may be adopted by the couple who feel that sex should diminish with age.
7. Mutual playful physical affection (hugging, holding, kissing) may have become a substitute rather than a prelude to intercourse.
8. One partner may initially be more disinterested in sex than the mate and discourage sexual advances; over time, the mate learns not to expect sex from the partner.

Sexual Fulfillment over Time

The degree of sexual fulfillment also varies with time. After conducting interviews with 80 spouses about the frequency of intercourse in their marriages, one researcher concluded that from the first year on "almost everything—children, jobs, commuting, housework, financial worries—that happens to a couple conspires to *reduce* the degree of sexual interaction and almost nothing leads to increasing it" (Greenblatt, 1983, p. 294).

Data – Spouses in one study reported having intercourse an average number of 15 times per month during their first year of marriage. Those who had been married six years reported having intercourse an average of six times per month. (Greenblatt, 1983)

However, couples do not necessarily define fulfillment in terms of frequency. "It's how you do it when you do it, not how often you do it, that matters," said one woman. Change in circumstances (and sometimes partners) is inevitable. But the impact of those changes and their definition is less certain.

Sexual Fulfillment: Some Prerequisites

Regardless of variations in the definition of sexual fulfillment, there seem to be several prerequisites for its existence: self-knowledge, self-esteem, a good relationship, open communication, realistic expectations, and a display of sexual interest in the partner.

Self-Knowledge

Being sexually fulfilled implies having knowledge about yourself and your body. To be in touch with yourself and your own body is to know how you can best experience sexual pleasure. "I've read all the books on how to get the most out of sex," said one man, "and I've concluded that the experts know a lot about what some people like sexually, but nothing about what *I* like. Good sex for me is more related to the context than to the technique. And I'm sure that for the next person it's something else."

Self-Esteem

Sexual fulfillment also implies having a positive self-concept. To the degree that you have good feelings about yourself, you will regard yourself as a person someone else would enjoy touching, being close to, and making love with. If you do not like yourself, you may wonder how anyone else would either.

A Good Relationship

Is not the true romantic feeling—not the desire to escape life, but to prevent life from escaping you?
—Thomas Clayton Wolfe

A rule among therapists who work with couples who have sexual problems is "Treat the relationship before focusing on the sexual issue." The sexual relationship is part of the larger relationship between the partners, and what happens outside the bedroom in day-to-day interaction has a tremendous influence on what happens inside the bedroom. The statement "I can't fight with you all day and want to have sex with you at night" illustrates the social context of the sexual experience.

A good out-of-bed relationship includes spending time together, being affectionate, communicating, and sharing similar values. Also, the nature of a couple's economic relationship can affect their sex life. In a study of dual-career marriages, the researchers reported that the wives became much more assertive and sexually demanding after they were employed. This was viewed as a function of the wife's increased economic power and self-esteem once she began to bring money into the marriage (Johnson et al., 1979). "Many wives

A good out-of-bed relationship is conducive to a good in-bed relationship.

seemed less likely to accept the blame for unsatisfactory sexual performance. . . . Some attempted to get their husbands to read sex manuals or were more vocal about the staleness of their sexual relationship" (p. 7).

The type of relationship may also be important. One study, comprised of separate interviews with the spouses of 53 newlywed couples, was designed to assess the degree to which having an equitable relationship contributed to sexual satisfaction. The researchers concluded that equitably treated men and women were more satisfied with their sexual relationships overall than those who felt they were getting more or less out of the relationship than their partners were (Hatfield et al., 1982).

So the effects of a couple's overall and sexual relationships are intertwined. According to an old adage, when sex goes well, it is 15 percent of a relationship; when it goes badly, it is 85 percent. Undoubtedly, many partners agree. The sexual relationship positively influences the couple's overall relationship in several ways: (1) as a shared pleasure, a positively reinforcing event; (2) by facilitating intimacy, as many couples feel closer and share their feelings before or after a sexual experience; and (3) by reducing tension generated by the stresses of everyday living and couple interaction (McCarthy, 1982).

Consideration

Intercourse communicates how the partners are feeling and acts as a barometer for the relationship. Each partner brings to intercourse, sometimes unconsciously, a motive (pleasure, reconciliation, procreation, duty); a psychological state (love, hostility, boredom, excitement); and a physical state (tense, exhausted, relaxed, turned on). The combination of these factors will change from one encounter to another. Tonight the wife may feel aroused and loving and seek pleasure, but her husband may feel exhausted and hostile and only have intercourse out of a sense of duty. Tomorrow night, both partners may feel relaxed and have intercourse as a means of expressing their love for each other.

The verbal and nonverbal communication preceding, during, and after intercourse also may act as a barometer for the relationship. One wife said:

> I can tell how we're doing by whether or not we have intercourse and how he approaches me when we do. Sometimes he just rolls over when the lights are out and starts to rub my back. Other times, he plays with my face while we talk and kisses me and waits till I reach for him. And still other times, we each stay on our side of the bed so that our legs don't even touch.

Open Sexual Communication

Good communication is as stimulating as black coffee, and just as hard to sleep after.
—Anne Morrow Lindbergh

Sexually fulfilled partners are comfortable expressing what they enjoy and do not enjoy in the sexual experience. Unless both partners communicate their needs, preferences, and expectations to each other, neither is ever sure what the other wants. A classic example of the uncertain lover is the man who picks up a copy of *The Erotic Lover* in a bookstore and leafs through the pages until the topic on how to please a woman catches his eye. He reads that women enjoy having their breasts stimulated by their partner's tongue and teeth. Later that night in bed, he rolls over and begins to nibble on his partner's breasts. Meanwhile, she wonders what has possessed him and is unsure what to make of this new (possibly unpleasant) behavior. Sexually fulfilled partners take the guesswork out of their relationship by communicating preferences and giving feedback. This means using what some therapists call the touch-and-ask rule. Each touch and caress may include the question "How does that feel?" It is then the partner's responsibility to give feedback. If the caress does not feel good, she or he can say what does feel good. Guiding and moving the partner's hand or body are also ways of giving feedback.

If it weren't for pickpockets, I'd have no sex life at all.
—Rodney Dangerfield

But open sexual communication is more than expressing sexual preferences and giving feedback. Women wish that men were more aware of a number of sexual issues. Some comments from students in the author's classes follow:

- It does not impress women to hear about other women in the man's past.
- If men knew what it is like to be pregnant, they would not be so apathetic about birth control.
- Most women want more caressing, gentleness, kissing, and talking *before* and *after* intercourse.
- The loss of a woman's virginity may have negative psychological effects.
- Sometimes the woman wants sex even if the man does not. Sometimes she wants to be aggressive without being made to feel that she shouldn't be.
- Intercourse can be enjoyable without a climax.

- Many women do not have an orgasm from penetration only; they need direct stimulation of their clitoris by their partner's tongue or finger. Men should be interested in fulfilling their partner's sexual needs.
- Most women prefer to have sex in a monogamous love relationship.
- When a woman says "no," she means it. Women do not want men to expect sex every time they are alone with their partner.
- Many women enjoy sex in the morning, not just at night.
- Sex is *not* everything.
- Women need to be lubricated before penetration.
- Men should know more about menstruation.
- Many women are no more inhibited about sex than men.
- Women do not like men to roll over, go to sleep, or leave right after orgasm.
- Intercourse is more of a love relationship than a sex act for some women.
- The woman should not always be expected to supply a method of contraception. It is also the man's responsibility.
- Women tend to like a loving, gentle, patient, tender, and understanding partner. Rough sexual play can hurt and be a turn-off.
- Men should know that all women are not alike. Not all women are ready to jump in bed the same night you meet them, nor are they all as cold as a deep freeze. Each one is different.

Men also have a list of things they wish women knew about sex:

- Men do not always want to be the dominant partner; women should be aggressive.
- Men want women to enjoy sex totally and not be inhibited.
- Women should learn how to kiss passionately.
- Women need to return love while in bed. They should know how to give pleasurable fellatio.
- Women need to know a man's erogenous zones.
- Oral sex is good and enjoyable, not bad and unpleasant.
- Many men enjoy a lot of romantic foreplay and slow, aggressive sex. One man says, "I hate a dead screw."
- Men cannot keep up intercourse forever. Most men tire more easily than women.
- Looks are not everything.
- Women should know how to enjoy sex in different ways and different positions.
- Women should not expect a man to get a second erection right away.
- Many men enjoy sex in the morning.
- Pulling the hair on a man's body can hurt.
- Many men enjoy sex in a caring, loving, exclusive relationship.
- It is frustrating to stop sex play once it has started.
- Women should know that all men are not out to have intercourse with them. Some men like to talk and become friends.

Realistic Expectations

To achieve sexual fulfillment, expectations must be realistic. A couple's sexual needs, preferences, and expectations may not coincide. Women and men not only have different biological makeups, but they also have been socialized differently. It is unrealistic to assume that your partner will want to have sex with the same frequency and in the same way that you do on all occasions.

Consideration

Sexual fulfillment means not asking things of the sexual relationship that it cannot deliver. Failure to develop realistic expectations will result in frustration and resentment.

A Healthy Attitude toward Sex

The best way to hold a man is in your arms.

—Mae West

Sexual fulfillment also depends on having a positive attitude toward sex. Incestuous or traumatic sexual experiences may create an intense negative attitude toward sex. Any sexual advance or contact can cause the individual to become anxious and engender the desire to escape or avoid the situation. Such negative reactions to sex are best dealt with through therapy.

Sexual Fulfillment: Some Facts

Sexual fulfillment also requires an awareness of some basic facts about human sexuality. In addition to the information about anatomy and physiology given in Part Six (pages 603–611), other facts important to sexual fulfillment relate to learned attitudes and behaviors, sex as a natural function, the development of sexual communication, "spectatoring" as an interference with sexual functioning, the sexual response cycles of women and men, and the effects of health and drugs on sexual performance.

Sexual Attitudes and Behaviors Are Learned

Whether you believe that "Sex is sinful" or "If it feels good, do it," your sexual attitudes have been learned. Your parents and peers have had a major impact on your sexual attitudes, but there have been other influences as well: school, church or synagogue, and the media. Your attitudes about sex would have been different if the influences you were exposed to had been different.

The same is true of sexual behavior. The words you say, the sequence of events in lovemaking, the specific behaviors you engage in, and the positions you adopt during intercourse are a product of your and your partner's learning history. The fact that learning accounts for most sexual attitudes and behaviors is important because negative patterns can be unlearned and positive patterns can be learned.

It is also important to be aware that you have been reared in American society and that your thoughts, feelings, attitudes, and behaviors are consistent with those of this culture. Had you been reared in another culture, your perceptions of sexuality would be different. For example, whereas having intercourse with a brother or sister is likely to induce feelings of shame or disgust in our society, the Dahomey of West Africa and the Inca of Peru have viewed such a relationship as natural and desirable (Stephens, 1982).

Also, from a cross-cultural perspective, sexual behavior that is punished in one society may be tolerated in a second and rewarded in a third. In the Gilbert Islands, virginity until marriage is an exalted sexual value and violations are not tolerated; premarital couples who are discovered to have had intercourse before their wedding are put to death. Our society tolerates premarital intercourse, particularly if the partners are "in love." In contrast, the Lepcha people of India believe that intercourse helps young girls mature; by the age of 12, most Lepcha women are engaging in regular intercourse.

There are also cultural variations in the frequency of intercourse. Although most couples throughout the world have intercourse between two and five times a week (Gebhard, 1972), the Basongye in the Kasai province of the former Belgian Congo, have intercourse every night even when they are in their fifties and sixties (Merriam, 1972). In contrast, a Cayapa man may go for several years without having intercourse; their Cayapan term for intercourse, *medio trabajo,* means "a little like work."

Sex Is a Natural Function

Although your sexual attitudes and behaviors are learned, your genital reflexes are innate. Males cannot be taught to have an erection, and females cannot be taught to lubricate vaginally. These are natural processes (Kolodny et al., 1986). Sex therapy is often aimed at minimizing the impact of negative learning experiences so that the natural physical processes can take over.

Effective Sexual Communication Takes Time and Effort

Most of us who have been reared in homes in which discussions about sex were infrequent or nonexistent may have developed relatively few skills to employ in talking about sex. Shifting to sex talk with our partner from, say, talking about current events may seem awkward. Overcoming our awkward feelings requires retraining ourselves so that sex becomes as easy for us to talk about as what we had for lunch. Some suggestions that may be helpful in developing effective sexual communication follow.

Say Sex Words

Develop a list with your partner that contains all of the technical and slang words you can think of about sex. Then alternate with your partner, reading one word after the other from the list. Laughter, embarrassed or otherwise, usually accompanies the first few readings, but repeat the readings until each of you is as comfortable with the words on the sex list as with those on a grocery list. It usually takes several readings over a period of weeks before you will develop a neutral reaction to the sex words. This reaction is important for you to feel comfortable talking about sex with your partner.

Ask Open-Ended Questions

To learn more about your partner, ask specific questions that cannot be answered with a yes or no. Examples include "What does orgasm feel like to you?," "Tell me about the sexual activities you like best," and "How often do you feel the need for sex?"

Give Reflective Feedback

When your partner shares a very intimate aspect of herself or himself, it is important to respond in a nonjudgmental way. One way to do this is to reflect back what your partner tells you.

Suppose Mary tells Jim that the best sex for her is when he is holding and caressing her, not when they are actually having intercourse. An inappropriate response by Jim to her disclosure would be "Something must be the matter with you." This would undoubtedly stop Mary from telling Jim anything more about her feelings. But Jim's reflective statement, "Our being close is what you like best in our relationship," confirms for Mary that he understands how she feels and that her feelings are accepted.

"Spectatoring" Interferes with Sexual Functioning

One of the obstacles to sexual functioning is spectatoring. When the researchers in one extensive study observed how individuals actually behave during sexual intercourse, they reported a tendency for sexually dysfunctional partners to act as spectators by mentally observing their own and their partners' sexual performance. The man would focus on whether he was having an erection, how complete it was, and whether it would last. He might also watch to see whether his partner was having an orgasm. His partner would ask corresponding questions about herself and him (Masters & Johnson, 1970).

Consideration

Spectatoring as Masters and Johnson conceived it, interferes with each partner's sexual enjoyment because it creates anxiety about performance; and anxiety blocks performance. A man who worries about getting an erection reduces his chance of doing so. A woman who is anxious about achieving an orgasm probably will not. The desirable alternative to spectatoring is to relax, focus on and enjoy your own pleasure, and permit your body's natural sexual responsiveness to take over.

Spectatoring is not limited to sexually dysfunctional couples and is not necessarily associated with psychopathology. Spectatoring is a reaction to the concern that the performance of the sexual partners is consistent with their expectations. We all probably have engaged in spectatoring to some degree. It is when spectatoring is continual that performance is impaired.

Women and Men Have Different Sexual Response Cycles

As the spectatoring problem reveals, human sexuality has a psychosocial component. The other major component of human sexuality, the biophysical, includes the sexual response cycle. Masters & Johnson, who observed the sexual response cycles of more than 10,000 individuals, reported that women and men do not necessarily progress through the cycle in the same way (see Figures 11.2 and 11.3).

The four phases of the sexual response cycle are excitement, plateau, orgasm, and resolution. These phases represent what people report they experience when they have sexual intercourse. First, there is the period when sexual activity is about to begin (excitement); then the partners give pleasure to each

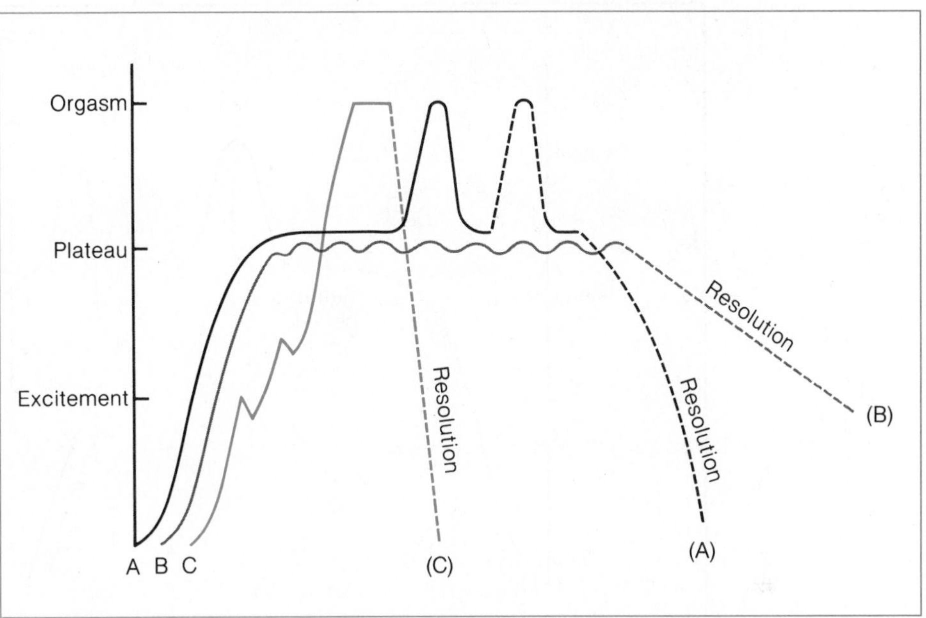

FIGURE 11.2
FEMALE ALTERNATIVE SEXUAL RESPONSE CYCLES

The female may experience one of three patterns in her response to sexual stimulation: Pattern C, the typical response, involves moving from excitement to plateau to one orgasm to resolution. Pattern B involves becoming excited, stabilizing at the plateau phase, and moving toward resolution. Pattern A involves having an orgasm, returning to the plateau phase, and then back to another orgasm; this pattern may be repeated again and is referred to as multiple orgasm.

Source: William H. Masters & Virginia E. Johnson, *Human sexual response.* Boston: Little, Brown, 1966. P. 5. Copyright© by Masters & Johnson, 1966.

other for some time but not to the point of orgasm (plateau); then one or both partners have a climax (orgasm); and this is followed by a period of relaxation and a return to the state that preceded sexual excitement (resolution).

The female alternative sexual response cycles are illustrated in Figure 11.2. Once sexual excitement begins, there may be three outcomes: (1) progression from excitement to plateau to one orgasm to resolution (line C); (2) progression from excitement to plateau to orgasm to plateau to orgasm (or to a number of additional orgasms) to resolution (line A); or (3) progression from excitement to plateau to resolution without experiencing an orgasm (line B).

The male alternative sexual response cycles are illustrated in Figure 11.3. Once sexual response begins and assuming that both partners are willing for the male to complete the cycle, there is essentially only one outcome—progressing through plateau to orgasm to resolution. Although men may have additional orgasms, there is usually a considerable refractory (or recovery) period before doing so.

Physical and Mental Health Affect Sexual Performance

Effective sexual functioning requires good physical and mental health. Physically, this means regular exercise, good nutrition, lack of disease, and lack of

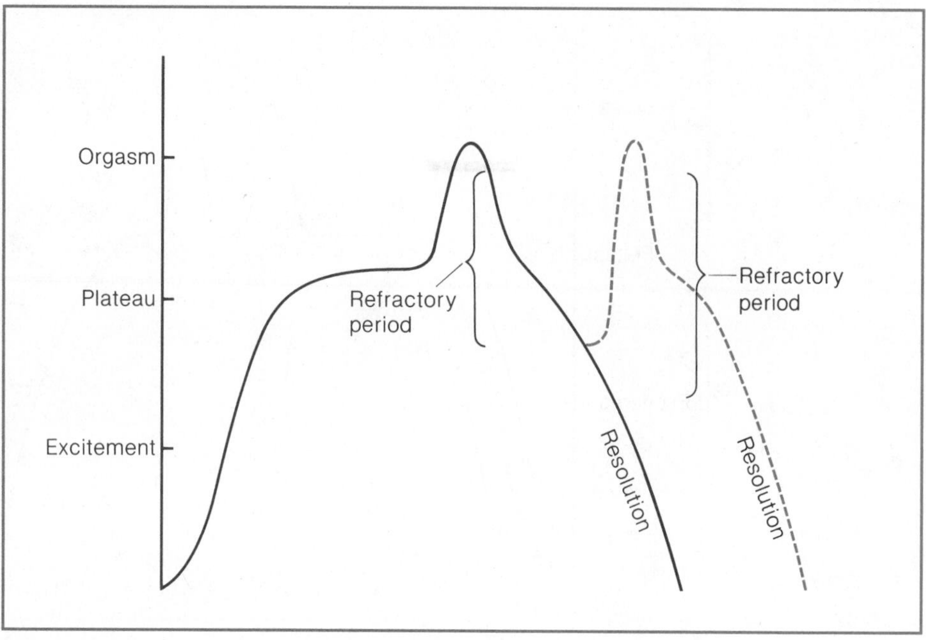

FIGURE 11.3
MALE ALTERNATIVE SEXUAL RESPONSE CYCLES

The male typically experiences the pattern indicated by the solid line in his response to sexual stimulation. He becomes excited and moves through the plateau, orgasm, and resolution phases of the sexual response cycle. The dashed line describes the pattern in which, after a brief refractory period during which the male does not want additional stimulation, he enters the cycle at the plateau phase and has another orgasm, which is followed by another refractory period and resolution.

Source: William H. Masters & Virginia E. Johnson, *Human sexual response.* Boston: Little, Brown, 1966. P. 5. Copyright © by Masters & Johnson, 1966.

fatigue. Regular exercise, whether walking, jogging, swimming, or bicycling, is related to higher libido, sexual desire, and intimacy (Ash, 1986).

Consideration

Observation of the sexual cycles of the two genders reveals two essential differences. (1) The male usually climaxes once during sexual intercourse, but the female may not climax at all or may climax several times. (2) When the female does experience several climaxes, she is capable of doing so with only a brief time (seconds) between climaxes. In contrast, the male needs a considerable refractory period (minutes to hours) before he is capable of additional orgasms.

Drugs Interfere with Sexual Performance

Alcohol is the most frequently used drug by American adults. Although a moderate amount of alcohol can help a person become aroused through a lowering of inhibitions, too much alcohol can slow the physiological processes and deaden the senses. Shakespeare may have said it best: "it [alcohol] pro-

People who exercise regularly report high levels of intimacy and sexual desire.

vokes the desire but it takes away the performance" (Macbeth, Act II, Scene three) The result of the excessive intake of alcohol for women is a reduced chance of orgasm; for men, it is an increased chance of impotence.

The reactions to marijuana—a drug also used during sexual arousal—are less predictable than the reactions to alcohol. Some individuals report a short-term enhancment effect; others say that marijuana just makes them sleepy. In men, chronic use may decrease sex drive because marijuana may lower testosterone levels.

Cocaine is sniffed into the nostrils or injected into the vein. The latter method of administration results in an erect penis that may last for 24 hours or longer. Even when this does not occur, users report that cocaine increases their sensory awareness and enhances their enjoyment of the sexual experience. However, high doses may result in impotence.

Female Sexual Dysfunctions

It is not uncommon for couples who are very satisfied with their relationship to have one or more sexual problems (Heiman et al., 1986). Sex therapists refer to such problems as *sexual dysfunctions.* The existence of a sexual dysfunction implies that the partners want something to happen that is not happening (for

Exhibit 11.1

PREMENSTRUAL SYNDROME

Also known as PMS, premenstrual syndrome refers to the physical and psychological problems a woman experiences from the time of ovulation to the beginning of, and sometimes during, menstruation. There are a number of symptoms, which may include the following:

Psychological
Tension
Depression
Irritability
Lethargy

Excessive energy
Altered sex drive

Neurological
Migraine
Epilepsy

Respiratory
Asthma
Rhinitis

Dermatological
Acne
Herpes

Orthopedic
Joint pains
Backaches

But it is the experience of the woman that makes the syndrome real. Alice A., a 35–year–old housewife and mother, is usually a friendly and productive person, but two weeks out of each month she is overwhelmed by extreme irritability, tension, and depression.

> It's as if my mind can't keep up with my body. I cook things to put in the freezer, clean, wash windows, work in the yard—anything to keep busy. My mind is saying slow down, but my body won't quit. When I go to bed at night, I'm exhausted. And everything gets on my nerves—the phone ringing, birds singing—everything! My skin feels prickly, my back hurts, and my face feels so tight that it's painful. I scream at my husband over ridiculous things like asking for a clean pair of socks. I hate myself even when I'm doing it, but I have no control. I can't stand being around people, and the only way I can even be civil at parties is to have several drinks.
>
> This lasts for about a week, and then I wake up one morning feeling as if the bottom has dropped out of my life. It's as if something awful is going to happen, but I don't know what it is and don't know how to stop it. I don't even have the energy to make the beds. Every movement is an effort. I burst out crying for no reason at crazy times, like when I'm fixing breakfast or grocery shopping. My husband thinks I'm angry with him, and I can't explain what's wrong because I don't know myself. After about four days of fighting off the depression, I just give up, take the phone off the hook, and stay in bed. It's terrifying. I feel panicky—trapped.
>
> Then one morning I wake up and suddenly feel like myself. The sun is shining, and I like life again.*

Between 5 and 10 percent of women experience PMS to the degree that Alice does. Some people have attributed instances of child abuse, alcoholism, divorce, and suicide to PMS. Recently, two British women introduced PMS as part of their legal defense for murder.

Other women experience a milder form of PMS, including different symptoms in varying degrees. But because more than 150 symptoms have been associated with PMS, there is little agreement about when a person is experiencing the phenomenon. The only

(Continued)

Exhibit 11.1

agreement on premenstrual syndrome seems to be that the individual's specific symptoms occur together at regular intervals.

There also is no agreement on the causes of PMS and even less agreement on the cure. Hormones, diet, and culture are among the suggested causes. Some physicians treat the woman with PMS as though it is all in her head and will go away in a few days. Others view the problem as an imbalance of hormones and prescribe progesterone. Still others focus on nutrition and exercise. Diet changes include eliminating alcohol, sugar, salt, and caffeine. Eating several small meals every two to four hours is also suggested.

Increasingly, PMS is being recognized as a legitimate set of symptoms that require treatment. The Premenstrual Syndrome Clinic in Reading, Massachusetts, has treated more than 1,000 women. The clinic's approach to therapy is multidimensional, including diet, exercise, vitamins, and progesterone (if necessary). The clinic also assists women in diagnosing PMS and demonstrating its impact on their lives. Such diagnosis is facilitated by getting women to chart their physiological and psychological reactions as they progress through their cycles.

The National PMS Society (1106 West Cornwallis Road, Office 105; Durham, NC 27705; phone: 919–489–6577) may be contacted for further information and help.

example, orgasm) or want to stop something from happening that is happening (for example, vaginismus). In this section, we will examine lack of sexual desire, inability to achieve orgasm, pain during intercourse (dyspareunia), and inability to control constrictions of the vagina (vaginismus) as the major sexual dysfunctions among women.

Consideration

Although we will discuss treatments for both female and male sexual dysfunctions in this chapter, sex therapy is usually indicated. The name of a certified sex therapist in your area can be located by calling 202–462–1171 or by writing to the American Association of Sex Educators, Counselors, and Therapists (11 Dupont Circle, N.W., Suite 220; Washington, D.C. 20036). A sex therapist will usually ask you to complete a form similar to the Personal Sex History Inventory given in the Self-Assessment section.

Lack of Sexual Desire

The person who lacks sexual desire—a problem also referred to as *inhibited sexual desire*—never initiates sexual activity and is rarely receptive to another who does. Sex is a bore and a chore. Although women more frequently experience lack of sexual desire, men may also lack such interest.

Data – In a study comparing the reported sexual desire of 75 women with 45 men, the women consistently reported lower sexual desire. (Mehrabian & Stanton-Mohr, 1985)

When 289 sex therapists were asked to identify the most common problem brought to them, 31 percent said discrepancies in sexual desire between partners. (Kilmann et al., 1986)

Lack of sexual desire may be primary (the person has never been interested in sex) or secondary (the person has demonstrated interest in sex with the same or a different partner in the past, but does not do so presently). Several reasons may account for a lack of sexual desire or low libido in women.

Relationship Dissatisfaction. It is important that the woman feel an emotional bond with her sex partner if she is to enjoy a satisfactory sex life with that person (Talmadge & Talmadge, 1986). Women who do not love or who have hostile feelings for their partners often are aversive to any sexual encounter with their partners. One woman said that it was "horrible having to make love to a man I didn't love."

Restrictive Child Rearing. The unresponsive woman was usually told as a child that sexual stimulation and sexual pleasure were sinful and dirty. As a result, she has learned to feel guilty and ashamed about her sexual feelings.

Passive Sexual Role. The woman with low libido has often been taught to be a passive and dependent sexual partner. The silent message of her socialization has been that it is not feminine to lose herself in sexual ecstasy. Because such abandonment is incompatible with the passive feminine role, she does not permit herself to become sexually excited.

Physical Factors. Disease, drugs, fatigue, and infection may also erase a person's sexual responsiveness. A nurse said, "After I take care of the kids all day and work the night shift at the hospital, sex is the last thing in the world I'm interested in. And when my partner touches me, I just have to tell him the truth—I'm not interested."

Data – Out of 1,207 wives, 80 percent reported that "feeling tired" was their most common reason for lack of sexual desire. (Grosskopf, 1983)

Sex therapy for low libido in a woman may involve rest and relaxation, reeducation, improving the relationship with her partner, the use of sensate focus, and masturbation or hormones. Reeducation includes systematically examining the thoughts, feelings, and attitudes the woman was taught as a child and reevaluating them. The goal is to redefine sexual involvement, so that it is viewed as a positive, desirable, pleasurable experience. Reeducation also means discarding the belief that one must feel interest in sex before one can enjoy it. Rather, the therapist recommends that the woman become involved in sexual activity first. The premise is that "you can act yourself into a new way of thinking quicker than you can think your way into a new way of acting."

Consideration

The woman's relationship with her partner is central to her sexual enjoyment with him. Does she love him? Does she trust him? Does she feel emotionally close to him? Unless the relationship with her partner is loving and reciprocal, gains in increasing sexual responsiveness may be minimal.

The woman and her partner are also encouraged to practice sensate focus exercises (see Figure 11.4). Introduced more than 20 years ago by Masters &

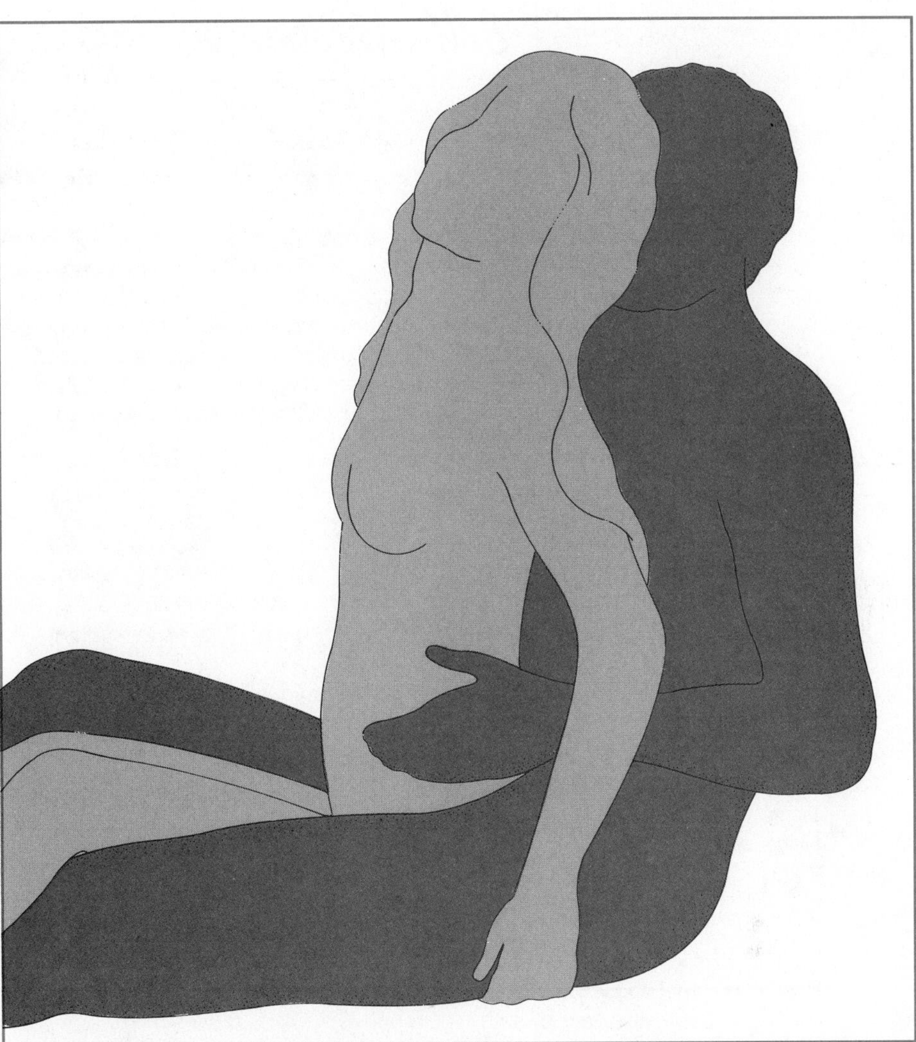

FIGURE 11.4
SENSATE FOCUS

Source: Human Sexual Inadequacy by William H. Masters and Virginia E. Johnson. Published by Little, Brown, and Company, Boston, Mass.: 1966, p. 300. Reprinted by permission.

Johnson, sensate focus is the mutual exploration and discovery of the partners through touch, massage, fondling, or tracing. Specific guidelines for the exercises include the following: (1) Both partners are nude. (2) The partners are not to have intercourse or touch each other's genitals, and the man is not to touch the woman's breasts. (3) One partner is to give pleasure by touching and gently massaging the other. (4) The other partner is to pay attention to the pleasurable feelings of being touched and gently massaged and to let the first partner know when he or she does something that is or is not pleasurable. (5) The partners are to switch roles, so that each gives and gets sensual pleasure. Sensate focus creates an environment in which the woman is permitted to explore her sexual feelings without having to perform for her partner.

The woman may be encouraged to masturbate—a suggestion also made to women who have difficulty climaxing. Some physicians recommend testosterone to increase a woman's interest in sex. Although unwanted facial hair may occur in 10–15 percent of the cases, it may heighten a woman's libido.

Self-Assessment

Personal Sex History Inventory

The purpose of this inventory is to obtain information about your sexual self. By answering these questions as completely and as accurately as you can, you will facilitate your therapeutic program. Please complete this history when you are alone and do not discuss your answers with your partner. It is understandable that you might be concerned about what happens to this form. Because much or all of this information is highly personal, your inventory is strictly confidential. No outsider is permitted to see your answers without your written permission.

I. General Date ______

Name ______

Address ______

Telephone numbers: Office ______

Home ______

Relationship status: Married ______; Divorced ______; Separated ______; Single ______; Living together ______; Widowed ______.

Are you currently living with a partner? ______ How long? ______

How do you feel about the person with whom you are currently involved or with whom you have been most recently involved? ______

______.

Is your sexual orientation Heterosexual ______? Homosexual ______? Bisexual ______?

II. Background

1. What did you learn about sex from your parents? Your teachers? Your church? Your peers?
2. What sexual behaviors make you feel guilty?
3. How much emotional involvement have you had with your sexual partners? How have you felt about this level of involvement?
4. What sexual fantasies do you have? How do you feel about your fantasies?
5. What is the content of your sexual dreams? How do you feel about your sexual dreams?
6. How do you feel about your mother? Your father?
7. When you use the word *"sex"*, what do you mean? List five adjectives for sex.
8. What are your feelings about your body? The body of someone of the opposite gender? The same gender?
9. List the various sexual experiences you have had, your age at the time of first occurrence, how you felt about each experience then, and how you feel about having similar experiences now. Use a form like the following:

   Experience

   Age ______

   Feelings then ______

   Feelings now ______
10. Describe any sexual experiences you would label "negative."
11. Have you or any of your sexual partners ever had a sexually transmitted disease? Name or describe these diseases. What were the outcomes?
12. What are your feelings about oral sex?
13. What drugs do you take? How often?
14. When did you first masturbate? What is your current frequency? How do you feel about masturbation?
15. Describe any specific sexual problem you are having. How long have you had this problem? What has your partner's response been to this problem?

Self-Assessment

16. What have you done to try and resolve the problem? What was the result?
17. Have you consulted a therapist before? Who? When?
18. What is the state of your physical health? Are your menstrual periods regular? Do you have menstrual cramps or premenstrual tension? How severe are these problems?
19. Have you experienced what you define to be an orgasm?
20. On a scale from 0 to 10, how would you describe your level of interest in sex?

INABILITY TO ACHIEVE ORGASM

Data – Out of 365 college-educated women, 13 percent said they had never experienced orgasm. (Coleman et al., 1983)

Masters & Johnson characterize women who have never had an orgasm as having *primary orgasmic dysfunction* (also known as *primary anorgasmia* or *preorgasm*). Those who have had an orgasm by any other means at any time in the past but who are unable to do so currently are regarded as having *secondary orgasmic dysfunction* (also known as *secondary anorgasmia*).

Some of the causes of inability to achieve orgasm are similar to the causes of lack of sexual interest (restrictive childrearing, passive sexual role, and so on). Other causes include the following.

Focusing on Partner. Many women have been taught to feel it is their duty to satisfy their partners sexually. But having an orgasm requires that a woman focus on the sexual sensations she is experiencing. If a woman is overly intent on pleasing her partner, she may do so at the expense of her own orgasm.

Too much of a good thing can be wonderful.
—Mae West

Negative Feelings about Mate. If the woman is angry at her partner or feels that he is using her sexually, she may "withhold" having an orgasm. "If I have an orgasm, he'll think I'm having a good time and really enjoying him," said one woman. "I wouldn't give him that kind of pleasure. I'm very mad at my partner now because I just found out he has been seeing other women when I'm not around."

Too Little Stimulation. The duration of stimulation is associated with whether a woman climaxes. In a study of about 1,000 wives, two-fifths reported climaxing after one to 10 minutes of foreplay. When foreplay lasted 21 minutes or more, three-fifths reported climaxing almost every time (Brewer, 1981). Similarly, the longer her husband's penis stayed erect and inside her, the greater the wife's chance of having an orgasm during intercourse. If penetration was one minute, 25 percent reported orgasm; between one and 11 minutes, 50 percent reported climax. If penetration lasted more than 15 minutes, two-thirds reported climax. A woman's orgasm is also related to how accurately her partner is aware of what he does that gives her sexual pleasure (Kilmann et al., 1984).

Fear of Letting Go. Some women feel it would be too embarrassing to lose control in an orgasmic experience, so they deliberately block their sexual arousal.

Having positive feelings about each other is related to a good sexual relationship.

Too Much Alcohol. While moderate drinking of alcohol (one or two mixed drinks) induces relaxation and increases sexual arousal, heavy drinking has a depressant effect on the woman's orgasmic response.

Too Little Self-Knowledge. Some women have not discovered the kinds of stimulation that produce orgasm either through masturbation or with a partner. Most women report that stimulation on or around the clitoris is necessary for them to achieve orgasm.

Too High Expectations. Some women feel they should have an orgasm during every sexual encounter and that not doing so is evidence that they are not normal. Such expectations produce a great deal of anxiety, which blocks the ability of these women to have an orgasm even though they may try desperately to do so.

Because the causes for primary and secondary orgasmic dysfunction are extremely variable, the treatment must be tailored to the particular woman. We have already discussed the use of sensate focus exercises to encourage a woman to explore her sexual feelings and to increase her comfort with her partner. In addition, the therapist may recommend that the woman masturbate to orgasm. Such self-stimulation provides direct feedback to the woman of the type of stimulation she enjoys, eliminates the distraction of a partner, and gives her complete control of the stimulation.

Sex therapists are reasonably successful in treating secondary orgasmic dysfunctions.

Data – A total of 289 sex therapists in the United States say they have successfully treated 56 percent of their secondary orgasmic dysfunction cases. (Kilmann et al., 1986)

After the woman has learned how to bring herself to orgasm through masturbation, she is encouraged to teach her partner how to stimulate her manually to orgasm, first while not having intercourse. Finally, if the partners prefer, the woman is taught how to have an orgasm during intercourse by using the "bridge method":

> The couple make love until the woman is aroused. Then the man penetrates, either in the female superior position or one of the variations of the side-to-side position. Then, with the penis contained, the man (or the woman) stimulates the woman's clitoris. When she nears orgasm, clitoral stimulation ceases at her signal, and the couple commence thrusting actively to bring about her orgasm. (Kaplan, 1974, p. 138)

Pain During Intercourse

Pain during intercourse, or *dyspareunia,* occurs in about 10 percent of gynecological patients and may be caused by vaginal infection, lack of lubrication, a rigid hymen, or an improperly positioned uterus or ovary. Because the causes of dyspareunia are often medical, a physician should be consulted. Sometimes surgery is recommended to remove the hymen.

Dyspareunia may also be psychologically caused. Guilt, anxiety, or unresolved feelings about a previous trauma, such as rape or childhood molestation, may be operative. Therapy may be indicated.

Vaginismus

A less common sexual dysfunction in which the vaginal opening and outer third of the canal constricts involuntarily, making penetration impossible, is known as *vaginismus.* Like anorgasmia, vaginismus may be primary or secondary (Shortle & Jewelewicz, 1986). Primary vaginismus means that the vaginal muscles have always constricted to prevent penetration of any object, including tampons. Secondary vaginismus, the more usual variety, suggests that the vagina has permitted penetration in the past but currently constricts when penetration is imminent.

Vaginismus is most often found in women whose background has included traditional religious teachings suggesting that intercourse is dirty and shameful. Other background factors include rape, incest, repeated childhood molestation, or organic difficulties. Examples of the last are a poorly healed episiotomy (an incision in the perineum to prevent injury to the vagina during childbirth), a poorly stretched hymen, infections or sores near the vaginal opening, or a sexually transmitted disease. The woman who fears pain during penetration will try to avoid it, sometimes unconsciously.

Assuming that vaginismus is not caused by an organic or physical problem (for which a physician should be consulted), the treatment is first to have the woman introduce her index finger into her vagina while she relaxes. Then two fingers are introduced into the vagina, and this exercise is repeated until she feels relaxed enough to contain the penis. Once the woman learns that she is capable of vaginal containment of the penis, she is usually able to have intercourse without difficulty. Of course, therapy focusing on the woman's cognitions and perceptions about sex and sexuality with her particular partner precedes the finger exercises.

Male Sexual Dysfunctions

Sexual dysfunctions among women are only one side of the bed. Men may be troubled by sexual apathy, inability to achieve and maintain an erection (erectile dysfunction), inability to delay ejaculation as long as they or their partners would like (premature ejaculation), or inability to ejaculate at all (ejaculatory incompetence).

Sexual Apathy

It is a myth that men are always ready for sex. Some are apathetic or completely uninterested. "I just don't have any desire for sex," said one man. "And if I never have to do it again, I'll feel relieved."

There are many causes for a low sex drive in men: negative feelings about the partner, hormonal insufficiency, career fatigue, fear of parenthood, terror of intimacy, guilt over extrapartner relationships, drugs, and a "too aggressive partner." In addition, the cultural expectation that men are always interested in sex may threaten a man's feelings of masculinity. Treatment for sexual apathy among men often begins with giving them permission not to be interested in sex. The therapist tells the male client not to masturbate or have intercourse until the next session. Then the contributing factors are explored.

Sexual apathy can result from couple conflict.

Erectile Dysfunction

Erectile dysfunction, also known as *impotence,* is the lack or loss of an erection firm enough for intercourse, which may occur during foreplay, the moment of penetration, or intercourse. Generally, a man who cannot get an erection feels humiliated and embarrassed. Few problems are as devastating to the man as a penis that will not become and remain erect.

Like some female sexual dysfunctions, erectile dysfunction may be primary (the man has never been able to have intercourse) or secondary (he is currently unable to have intercourse). Erectile dysfunction may also be situational: the man can get an erection in one situation (say, through masturbation) but not in another (such as intercourse). Occasional, isolated episodes of the inability to get an erection do not warrant the label of erectile dysfunction, nor is treatment necessary.

Primary or secondary impotence may be caused by organic or psychosocial (psychogenic) factors. Organic factors include endocrine malfunctions like diabetes, low testosterone levels, neurological disorders like multiple sclerosis, and medications, such as those for high blood pressure. If organic causes are suspected, a neurological examination by a physician is indicated (Appell, 1986).

If there is an organic problem, one alternative is a penile implant, which consists of either semirigid rods of silicone rubber that are surgically inserted into the penis to make it hard, resulting in a permanent semierection, or inflatable cylinders implanted in the penis. Most males are satisfied with the result.

Data – Of 35 males who had penile implant surgery, only one said he would not do it again. The others reported a high degree of satisfaction and increased self-esteem. (Coleman et al., 1985)

Consideration

More often, erectile dysfunction is caused by psychosocial factors, and anxiety heads the list. The anxious man cannot get an erection because an erection depends on a state of relaxation. For example, as a male, assume you are in a classroom and a platoon of Russian soldiers walks through the door, putting a gun to the head of each male student. Their leader announces, "You guys have 30 seconds to get an erection, or we'll blow your heads off." The demand for such a performance will create intense anxiety, and no man in the class will be capable of getting an erection.

A similar situation may happen in the bedroom. The woman makes it clear to the man that she expects him to have an erection and to have intercourse with her. Whereas such an expectation is a welcome situation for some men, the man who has been impotent in the past begins to fear that he will not be able to get an erection and satisfy her. His anxiety about performing and his fear of her disapproval if he fails help to ensure that he will not get an erection. What follows is a devastating cycle of negative experiences locking the man into impotence at each sexual encounter: anxiety, impotence, embarrassment, followed by anxiety, impotence, and so on.

The man also has his own ideas of how he is supposed to perform as a male. Even if the partner is sympathetic and supportive, it may be his own self-imposed performance demands that create the anxiety that interferes with achieving an erection.

Anxiety may also be related to alcohol use. After more than the usual number of drinks, the man may initiate sex but fail to achieve an erection. He becomes anxious and struggles even more to get an erection, ensuring that he will not. Although alcohol may be responsible for his initial failure, his impotence continues because of his anxiety.

Treatment for erectile dysfunction of psychosocial origin begins with the instruction that the couple not have intercourse. If there is no expectation for intercourse, the associated anxiety is minimized. The therapist then discusses with the couple how anxiety (and alcohol, if this is an issue) inhibits erection. The purpose of this information is to help the partners understand the man's erectile dysfunction rather than continue to be mystified by its occurrence.

The partners are also instructed to begin sensate focus exercises, and the man is encouraged to give pleasure to his partner through manual or oral stimulation. After several sensate focus sessions, during which there is no pressure to perform and the man learns alternative ways to pleasure his partner, he is more likely to have an erection.

But suppose the man cannot get and maintain an erection because he is anxious and has no sexual partner with whom to work on the problem? Or suppose the man has organically caused impotence and does not want a penile implant? One new alternative suggested by some sex therapists is Papavarine, a drug injected into the base of the penis to increase blood flow. Papavarine produces a sustained erection of from 45 minutes to three hours (Sidi et al., 1986). The primary side effects are risk of infection and dependency on the shot to perform. The Northwest Center for Impotence (1201 116th Avenue, N.E., Suite I; Bellevue, WA 98004) may be contacted for additional information.

Premature Ejaculation

Premature ejaculation, also known as *rapid ejaculation,* is the man's inability to control the ejaculatory reflex.

Data – Out of more than 65,000 men in one survey, 81 percent reported times when they ejaculate too quickly, and 7 percent of these men said it happened frequently. (Petersen et al., 1983a)

Whether a man ejaculates too soon is a matter of definition, depending on his and his partner's desires. Some partners define a rapid ejaculation in positive terms. One woman said she felt pleased that her partner was so excited by her that he "couldn't control himself." Another said, "The sooner we get it over with, the better."

The cause of premature ejaculation lies in early learning experiences. Some men who ejaculate sooner than they want to report that their early masturbation and intercourse experiences were hurried. They felt pressure to ejaculate as soon as they could. One example is the male who had to masturbate quickly before his parents could discover what he was doing; another is the man whose prostitute partners would try to make him climax quickly so they could get to the next customer. Regardless of the reason, most males ejaculate relatively quickly.

Data – The average duration of intercourse before ejaculation in men is two minutes. (Hong, 1984)

Use of the squeeze technique developed by Masters & Johnson, is the most effective procedure for treating premature ejaculation. The woman stimulates her partner's penis manually until he signals her that he feels the urge to ejaculate. At his signal, she places her thumb on the underside of his penis and squeezes hard for three to four seconds. The man will lose his urge to ejaculate. After 30 seconds, she resumes stimulation, applying the squeeze technique again when her partner signals. The important rule to remember is that the woman should apply the squeeze technique whenever the man gives the slightest hint of readiness to ejaculate. (The squeeze technique can also be used by the man during masturbation to teach himself to delay his ejaculation.)

Other techniques are sometimes used in treating premature ejaculation but are generally not effective. These include the use of several condoms (one man used six), ointments such as Detane that anesthetize the head of the penis, and distraction (counting, playing tennis in one's head). One-half of the more than 65,000 men in a study who reported premature ejaculation said they deal with the problem by stimulating their partner in another way; one-fourth of these men said they simply wait and start again (Petersen et al., 1983a).

Ejaculatory Incompetence

In contrast to the man who experiences rapid ejaculation, the man who experiences *ejaculatory incompetence* cannot ejaculate at all, even after prolonged intercourse. Also referred to as *retarded ejaculation, absence of ejaculation,* or *inhibited ejaculation,* ejaculatory incompetence may be primary or secondary. Primary ejaculatory incompetence describes the man who has never ejaculated inside a woman's vagina. Secondary ejaculatory incompetence, the more common form, refers to the man's current inability to ejaculate inside the woman. It is not unusual for ejaculatory incompetence to be situational; it may occur with one partner but not another or with the same partner on one occasion but not on another.

Consideration

Most causes of ejaculatory incompetence are psychological. For example, one husband reported that for 33 years his wife would not let him ejaculate inside of her because she did not want to get pregnant. As a result, he learned to prolong his orgasm and to take his penis out of her vagina before ejaculating. After his wife's menopause, she wanted him to ejaculate inside of her but he could not.

Lack of sexual excitement and feeling that the vagina is a disgusting place to ejaculate are other psychological causes of ejaculatory incompetence.

In treating this condition, the therapist discusses the psychological issues and recommends sensate focus exercises. Following these exercises, the woman manually stimulates the man to ejaculate. After they are confident that he can be brought to orgasm manually, she stimulates him to a high level of sexual excitement and, at the moment of orgasm, inserts his penis into her vagina so that he ejaculates inside her. After several sessions of first hand, then vaginal stimulation, the woman gradually reduces the amount of time she manually manipulates her partner and increases the amount of time she stimulates him with her vagina.

Sexual Enrichment Programs

It is not unusual for couples who have a good relationship and who are not experiencing any specific sexual dysfunctions to attend a sexual-enrichment program designed to further enhance their sexual relationship. One such program, Enhancing Marital Sexuality, consists of 11 hours (seven on Saturday and four on Sunday) during which the couples hear lectures, watch films regarding sexual enhancement, and participate in overnight "homework assignments."

Respondents who have participated in such programs reported that they felt better about themselves as sexual partners and more knowledgeable about what their partners wanted and that they derived increased pleasure from their sexual relationships. These benefits were maintained three months after they participated in the workshops. The researchers suggested that these results are a strong recommendation for similar couples (happy and not sexually dysfunctional) to participate in such programs. (Nathan & Joanning, 1985). Unhappy couples or those with sexual dysfunctions will be more likely to benefit from sessions with a therapist.

Sexual Fulfillment in Middle Age

The assumed focus of our discussion on sexual fulfillment has generally been on the sexuality of youthful partners. Although the same information is generally relevant to sexual partners in their middle years, we will now focus on some specific aspects of sexuality in the middle years.

When does a person become middle-aged? The U.S. Census Bureau regards you as middle-aged when you reach 45. Family-life specialists define middle age as beginning at the time when the last child leaves home and continuing until retirement or either spouse dies. Humorist Laurence Peter (1982) has provided a couple of additional definitions: "Middle age is when you can do just as much as you could ever do—but would rather not" (p. October 9), and "Middle age is when work is a lot less fun and fun is a lot more work" (p. May 4).

Regardless of how middle age is defined, it is a time of transition. Let's examine what happens to women, men, and their sexuality during this period.

Women in Middle Age

Women in middle age undergo a number of physiological and psychological changes.

Physiological Changes

Menopause—the primary physical event during this period—is defined as the permanent cessation of menstruation. Menopause is caused by the gradual decline of the hormone estrogen, which is produced by the ovaries. It occurs around age 50 for most women but may begin earlier or later. Signs that the woman may be nearing menopause include decreased menstrual flow and a less predictable cycle. After 12 months with no period, the woman is said to be through menopause.

The term *climacteric* is often used synonymously with menopause. However, menopause refers only to the time when the menstrual flow permanently stops; climacteric refers to the whole process of hormonal change induced by the ovaries, pituitary gland, and hypothalmus.

A typical reaction to such hormonal changes is the "hot flash."

Data – About 85 percent of all menopausal women report experiencing hot flashes. (Meeks, 1986)

The experience is a sudden rush of fiery heat from the waist up, increased reddening of the skin surface, and a drenching perspiration. Following the hot flash, there may be a very cold chill, whitening of the skin surface, and sudden shivers. Other symptoms experienced less often include heart palpitations, dizziness, irritability, headaches, weight gain, and backache.

Most women do not have these lesser experiences during menopause, but many women do report the following physiological and behavioral changes as a result of the aging process and of decreasing levels of estrogen: (1) a delay in the reaction of the clitoris to direct stimulation; (2) less lubrication during sexual excitement; (3) a less intense orgasm; (4) a smaller vaginal opening; and (5) perhaps increased sexual interest. Loss of bone mass is also a problem for some women during menopause.

Data – An estimated 25 percent of all white women over the age of 65 have osteoporosis manifested by vertebral body fractures. (Meeks, 1986)

Consideration

To minimize the effects of decreasing levels of estrogen, some physicians recommend estrogen-replacement therapy, or ERT. Not only does estrogen control hot flashes and atrophy of the genitals, but it also prevents loss of bone mass. However, ERT is also associated with an increase in uterine cancer. A woman and her physician must carefully weigh the relative benefits of taking or not taking estrogen during and after menopause.

Psychological Changes

The psychological reaction to menopause is mixed. Some women are elated that they do not have to worry about contraception or contend with the monthly blood flow. "I wish I had gone through menopause 10 years ago," reflected one woman. "My sex life has never been better."

But other women are saddened because they view menopause as the end of their childbearing capacity. At the extreme, some women view it not as the change of life but as the end of life. Their negative feelings about the menopausal years are related partly to the value our society places on the youthful appearance of women. To improve their self-esteem, some menopausal women seek a relationship with a younger man to affirm that they are still sexually desirable.

Consideration

A cross-cultural look at menopause suggests that a woman's reaction to this phase of her life may be related to the society in which she lives. For example, among Chinese women, fewer menopausal symptoms have been observed. One explanation for this phenomenon may be that older women in China are highly respected. In America, a woman's worth is viewed by some as declining with age, which may cause her to doubt her own value.

Some women in the middle years also feel stressed with the responsibility of caring for their widowed and aging parents. Although sons help financially, they usually do little to provide practical care, such as taking their widowed mother shopping, doing housework, and helping with baths. The employed woman who has an aging parent to care for may feel overwhelmed by the burden to be a "superdaughter" (Scharlach, 1986). She may be resentful of her situation ("Why doesn't someone help me?") and guilty about her feelings. With her children gone, she may find that she has none of the free time she expected to enjoy because she must care for an aging parent.

Men in Middle Age

While middle-aged women are adjusting to the consequences of menopause, men too are having problems in middle age.

Psychological Changes

Middle age requires that men adjust to change—or lack of change—in their jobs. Most men reach the top level of their earning power during middle age, and some find themselves well short of the peak they had hoped to attain. One man said, "I'm 45 and still selling socks at Sears—I'm never going to be president of anything."

Many middle-aged men feel they have reached a dead end. "Had I known this firm was never going to promote me," one man said, "I would have left 15 years ago. But now it's too late. Who wants to hire a 50–year-old when 30–year-olds are a dime a dozen?" Still others reach the top only to find that "success" is meaningless for them. One successful man said:

> I've been with the government since I left school, and now I'm the head of my division. But so what? I move papers around my desk and have conferences that are supposed to mean something but don't. I've always wanted to be a psychologist so I could work with people about something that matters, but now it's too late.

This middle-life thing has become a phobia; people think it's got to be a big problem, when it's simply not.
—Jack Nicholson

Whether they feel they have failed in the right career or succeeded in the wrong one, some middle-aged men respond to their disappointments and anxieties by having an affair. Love and sex with a young woman is often regarded as the last chance to experience youth. One middle-aged man said:

> I was surprised how easy it was to fall in love with another woman. She worked in my office, and it began with my just admiring the way she looked. She was 20 years younger than me and made me feel like I had been given a second chance at life. I wasn't going to let it pass me by.

The psychological changes American men experience in middle age seem to have little to do with their children or, with some exceptions, with being a grandparent. American men in middle age rank the grandparent role after worker, church participant, and leisure user in importance. They have low levels of interaction and assistance with their grandchildren (Kivett, 1985).

Physiological Changes

At midlife, men suddenly discover the value of intimacy, relationships, and care, the importance of which women have known from the beginning.
—Carol Gilligan

Physiological changes also accompany middle age in men. The production of testosterone usually begins to decline around age 40 and continues to decrease gradually until age 60, when it levels off. (The decline is not inevitable; it is related to general health status.)

The consequences of lowered testosterone include (1) more difficulty in getting and maintaining a firm erection; (2) greater ejaculatory control, with the possibility of more prolonged erections; (3) less consistency in achieving orgasm; (4) fewer genital spasms during orgasm; (5) a qualitative change from an intense, genitally focused sensation to a more diffused and generalized feeling of pleasure; and (6) an increase in the length of the refractory period, during which time the man is unable to ejaculate or to have another erection.

These physiological changes in the middle-aged man, along with the psychological changes, have sometimes been referred to as "male menopause." During this period, the man may experience nervousness, hot flashes, insomnia, and no interest in sex. But these changes most often occur over a long period of time, and the anxiety and depression some men experience seem to be as much related to their career perceptions as to hormonal alterations.

Consideration

A middle-aged man who is not successful in his career is often forced to recognize that he will never achieve what he had hoped and that he will carry his unfulfilled dreams to the grave. This knowledge may be coupled with his awareness of diminishing sexual vigor. For the man who has been taught that masculinity is measured by career success and sexual prowess, middle age may be particularly traumatic.

But middle age may also be the best of times. A character in William Hervey Allen's novel Anthony Adverse (1933) says, "Grow up as soon as you can. It pays. The only time you really live fully is from 30 to 60.. . . The young are slaves to dreams; the old, servants of regrets. Only the middle-aged have all their five senses in the keeping of their wits."

Sexual Fulfillment in the Later Years

Data – Twelve percent of all Americans (over 25 million whites; over 2 million blacks) are over the age of 65. By the year 2000, people over 65 will represent about 13 percent of our population (Statistical Abstract of the United States: 1987).

Love is the word used to label the sexual excitement of the young, the habituation of the middle-aged, and the mutual dependence of the old.

—John Ciardi

The way a society views the elderly influences the expression of their sexuality. Although our society tends to expect people to reduce their sexual activities as they age, this expectation is not characteristic of all societies. In one study 70 percent of one group of societies had expectations of continued sexual activity for their aging males (Winn & Newton, 1982). Among the Tiv in Africa, many older men "remain active and 'hot' for many years after they become gray-haired" (p. 288); among the Taoist sects of China, there are records of men retaining their sexual desires past 100 years of age. Similar reports of continued sexual activity and interest among aging women have been found in 84 percent of the societies for which data on this age group are available. The researchers conclude "that cultural as well as biological factors may be key determinants in sexual behavior in the later part of life" (p. 283).

Sexuality of the Elderly: Some Facts

Growing old need not mean an end to a person's sex life. To the contrary, it may improve. In a study of 800 elderly Americans (Starr & Weiner, 1982), three-fourths of those who were sexually active reported that their lovemaking had improved with the years. Let's take a more detailed look at sex among the elderly by reviewing some of the facts.

Data are Lacking

No nationwide random sample of the elderly has been interviewed or completed a questionnaire about sexual behavior. At this time, only scattered information, based on what some of the elderly have told us in various smallscale studies, is available.

Sexual Behavior Among the Elderly is Variable

As is true of the sexual behavior of other age groups, there are great differences in the sexual behavior among the elderly. Whereas some older people report frequent intercourse, masturbation, and oral sex experiences, others are disgusted with the implication that they would be interested in such activities. One elderly woman said to another, "I think that sex at my age is a waste of time." Her friend replied, "Speak for yourself."

Frequency of Intercourse Declines With Age

The longer a couple is married the less likely they are to engage in intercourse.

> *Data* – In a study of spouses who have been married for more than 50 years, 47 percent said they never have intercourse, 33 percent said they have intercourse once a month or less, and 92 percent said their sexual activity has decreased over the years. (Ade-Ridder, 1985)

Reasons for this decline include societal expectations, physical problems, and satiation. The elderly are sometimes forced into mandatory retirement from sexual activity; sexuality among the elderly in our society is not expected.

Sexuality does not end in the later years.

Physical problems also take their toll. In men, diabetes, malfunctions of the thyroid and pituitary glands, and alcoholism may impair the man's ability to get and keep an erection.

> *Data* – About 50 percent of all men 75 and older are impotent. For the elderly man who is not impotent, it is not unusual for him to require 30 to 40 minutes of stimulation before he gets an erection. (Rossman, 1978)

I'm not interested in age. People who tell their age are silly. You're as old as you feel.
—Elizabeth Arden

Although physical changes in older women result from a decrease in estrogen, the primary factor affecting the declining frequency of intercourse in an elderly woman is the waning interest or the absence of a sexual partner. The presence of a culturally approved sexual partner (husband) is often regarded as a prerequisite for heterosexual expression among elderly women—and many do not have a partner.

> *Data* – Fifty percent of all women over the age of 65 are widowed, compared to only 13 percent of all elderly men. (*Statistical Abstract of the United States,* 1987)

Masturbation Declines With Age

In a study of 1,000 males aged 51 to 95, there was a steady decline of reported masturbation with increasing age. Whereas 50 percent of the subjects in their early fifties reported they masturbated, less than 25 percent did so in their early nineties. Masturbation rates also declined with age among females. However, an upswing occurred in these rates following separation, divorce, and widowhood (Hegeler & Mortensen, 1977).

Lovemaking May Improve With Age

One definition of improvement in lovemaking is what two researchers call the "second language of sex." The first language is "involved largely with physical pleasure . . . but the second language of sex is emotional and communicative as well as physical" (Butler & Lewis, 1976, p. 140). One husband confided:

> At 65, I am having the best sex life I have ever had. My wife and I have few inhibitions and try anything we like. I'm usually the aggressor, but she likes to pull me into the bedroom and I don't struggle. We wander around our apartment naked, bathe together, and love each other's body and mind. Our love has been a developing one. First it was more sexual. Now it is that plus many other things. (Hite, 1981, p. 860)

Consideration

Lack of anxiety about pregnancy and more time and opportunity make it easier for people to experience the second language of sex. "When the kids aren't running about the house and you're both home all day, you've got time to do a lot of things, including sex," said a 76-year-old man.

Orgasm Remains an Important Experience

The golden years are supposed to be golden in other ways [than sexually].
—B.F. Skinner and M.E. Vaughan

Lest we think that sex for the elderly is confined to holding each other, orgasm was viewed by 75 percent of the 800 respondents in one study as important to a good sexual experience (Starr & Weiner, 1982). Many feel like Woody Allen, who said, "I've never had a bad orgasm."

Sex in General Remains an Important Experience

More important than orgasm is the whole idea of sex. More than 95 percent of the respondents in the study said they liked sex (Starr & Weiner, 1982). This finding contradicts the myth that the elderly never think of sex and certainly do not do anything about it. Indeed, for people who have had an active sex life throughout their youth, there is no time when they just stop being interested in sex any more than there is a time when they stop being interested in food or music or anything else they have enjoyed. Previous patterns of sexual behavior tend to continue.

Sexual Fulfillment among the Elderly

There are several things people can do to achieve sexual fulfillment in the later years: doing what they want to do sexually (including nothing), relabeling their "losses" as "transitions," and adapting as necessary. It is important that the elderly not view the publicity about sex in the later years as an obligation to enjoy an active sex life. Sexual fulfillment is individually defined. Each elderly person, like others, should decide what behaviors and frequencies make her or him feel comfortable. There are no normal or abnormal definitions.

Consideration

Rather than viewing partial erection, impotence, lack of vaginal lubrication, or pain during intercourse as sexual losses, the elderly might see them as inevitable transitions. We expect change in all other areas of life and should not be dismayed to discover that our bodies change too. (Olds, 1985). Adaptation to change is likely to be a more satisfying response.

Adaptation does not necessarily mean resignation. It may mean finding substitute techniques for sexual expression. For example, for partial erection or impotence, some couples use the "stuffing technique" (manually pushing the penis into the vagina). This often stimulates the penis to erection, which can be followed by intercourse. Another problem that can be helped is pain during intercourse, which was reported by slightly more than 10 percent of the women in the Starr & Weiner study (1982). Pain may be caused by decreased vaginal lubrication, a smaller vaginal opening, and friction against the thinner walls of the vagina. A liberal use of K–Y jelly, a sterile lubricant, is helpful in minimizing the pain. Applied to both the penis and vagina, it helps the penis slide in and out with less friction.

Trends

Trends in sexual fulfillment include greater access to information about sexual fulfillment, a wider range of expression of sexual fulfillment, and increased exploration of sexual alternatives. Magazines like *Cosmopolitan, Redbook, Ladies Home Journal, McCall's,* and *Family Circle* regularly feature articles on sexual aspects of the woman–man relationship. Masters & Johnson's research (1970) is available to every person who stands in line to pay for groceries. Such visibility of sexual topics is not limited to magazines but includes movies, television, and radio. The openness with which the media treats sex will continue.

One consequence of this visibility is an awareness of the widening range of sexual behaviors expressed by different people. "Donahue" once featured discussions on "safe" topics only; more recent programs have included such topics as polygamy, bisexual marriage, celibacy, and transsexuality. Exposure to media-mediated sex alerts us to the tremendous variations in sexual experience.

Because our population is gradually getting older, there will be a general trend away from a focus on sexuality in youth to sexuality in the middle and later years. A life-span focus on sexuality will replace the overconcern with teenage sexuality (Scales, 1986). A dominant theme of the television sitcom, "The Golden Girls," is sexuality in the middle and later years.

Psychological and sexual intimacy will continue to be an important experience.

Summary

Sexual fulfillment means different things to different people, and these meanings may vary over time. But there seem to be certain prerequisites for its existence, including self-knowledge, a good relationship, open communication, realistic expectations, and demonstration of sexual interest in the partner. Sexual fulfillment also requires an awareness of some basic facts about human sexuality, including the knowledge that sexual attitudes and behaviors are primarily learned, that sex is a natural function, that sexual communication takes effort, and that spectatoring interferes with sexual functioning.

Sexual dysfunctions are a concern in many relationships. Lack of sexual responsiveness, inability to achieve orgasm, pain during intercourse (dyspareunia), and involuntary constrictions of the vagina (vaginismus) are the main female sexual dysfunctions. Men may be troubled by sexual apathy or the inability to get and maintain an erection (erectile dysfunction), to delay ejaculation (premature ejaculation), or to ejaculate at all (ejaculatory incompetence).

Menopause and the woman's reaction to it are the primary physiological and psychological concerns of the woman during middle age. Men in their middle years may have to adapt to changes in career goals and lower testosterone levels.

Growing old need not lead to the end of a person's sex life. Although frequency of intercourse declines with age, orgasm and sex in general remain important. People can do several things to achieve sexual fulfillment in the later years, including doing what they want to do sexually (including nothing), relabeling their losses as transitions, and adapting as necessary.

Trends in sexual fulfillment include greater access to sexual information, increased visibility of sexual variations, and a greater concern for sexuality in the middle and later years.

Questions for Reflection

1. How do you define sexual fulfillment?
2. What physical changes, if any, are you experiencing that suggest to you that you are aging?
3. How willing would you be to consult a sex therapist for a sexual problem?

CHOICES

SOME COUPLES WHO are unable to resolve the sexual problems in their relationship become involved in sex therapy. Once the decision is made to consult a sex therapist (the issue of whether to see a sex therapist at all will be discussed in the Choices section of Chapter 12), several choices must be made, including whether one or both partners should attend sex therapy and whether to have private or group therapy.

Therapy: Alone or With a Partner?

Should just the person experiencing the sexual problem or the person and her or his sexual partner become involved in sex therapy? It depends. Some people prefer to go alone. One woman said:

> If I ask him to go to therapy with me, he'll think I'm more emotionally involved than I am. And since I don't want to encourage him, I'll just work out my problems without him.

Other reasons why a person might see a sex therapist alone are if no partner is available, if the partner won't come, or if the person feels more comfortable discussing sex in the partner's absence.

However, there are also several reasons why a person might want her or his partner to become involved in sex therapy: to work on the problem *with* someone, to share the experience, and to prevent one partner from being identified as the "one with the problem." Although there are exceptions, a greater proportion of sexual problems can be more effectively treated by engaging in sex therapy with a partner.

Therapy: Privately or in a Group Setting?

Once the decision to pursue therapy (with or without a partner) is made, another choice is whether to see the therapist in private or in groups with other people who are experiencing similar problems. There are advantages and disadvantages of each treatment pattern.

Although being seen privately helps to ensure that therapy will be tailored to fit the specific needs of the client, the cost is considerably higher for private therapy than it is if the client is treated in a group setting. Private therapy may cost $75 an hour; therapy in a group of five members may only cost $15 for the same amount of time.

Another advantage of group therapy is that being surrounded by others who have similar problems helps to reduce the feeling that "I'm the only one." One woman who had difficulty achieving orgasm said, "When I heard the other women discuss their difficulty with climaxing, I knew I wasn't abnormal." The empathy of a group of peers can be extremely effective in helping a person feel less isolated.

A group setting also furnishes the opportunity to try new behaviors. For example, some sexual problems may be part of a larger problem, such as the lack of social skills to attract and maintain a partner. Fear of rejection can perpetuate being alone. But group members, with the help of their therapist, can practice making requests of each other and getting turned down. Such an exercise helps to develop the social skill of approaching others while learning to deal with rejection. Practicing with other group members is safe and gives a person the necessary confidence to approach someone outside the group.

There are at least two disadvantages of group therapy. The first is the possibility that not enough time will be spent on the individual's own problem. The second is the risk to the relationship with the partner, who may not be involved in the group. In one study of women in group therapy for lack of orgasm, one in four reported a negative effect on their partner (Barbach & Flaherty, 1980).

Comparative Effectiveness

What is the comparative effectiveness of couples being treated in a group or in private therapy? In one study, when group-couple therapy for premature ejaculation and orgasmic dysfunction was compared with therapy for the same problems treated in private, there were no differences in outcome. Both treatment patterns were effective. Men reported satisfaction with their ability to prolong intercourse, and women reported satisfaction with their orgasmic ability. (Golden et al., 1978). Other researchers have found similar results: couples in groups are as successful in achieving their goals as couples in private therapy (Duddle & Ingram, 1980).

This suggests that *couples* can be treated effectively in either a private or a group setting. The selection of a therapy setting is therefore a matter of preference. But group therapy for *individuals* may not be as effective as therapy with a partner in private or in a couples group. However, most individuals in group sex therapy without a partner do benefit from the experience.

Impact of Social Influences on Choices

Your willingness to go public with your sexual problems is related to society's openness about sexuality, your having friends who have consulted a sex therapist, and your income. With the advent of Dr. Ruth Westheimer on television and radio and in newspapers, the discussion of sexuality has become normative. Problems of lack of orgasm, premature ejaculation, and impotence are now openly discussed by "Dr. Ruth" as well as "Dear Abby." As a result of such societal openness, you will be much more likely to consult a sex therapist than your parents were.

Having friends who consult a sex therapist increases the likelihood that you will if you and/or your partner need to do so. Individuals who live in large urban centers are more likely to be involved in sex therapy than people who live in small, rural areas. Also, sex therapy is expensive, so your income will influence whether you seek a sex therapist.

Therefore, although we might assume that involvement in sex therapy is an individual decision, contacting a sex therapist in reality is more related to societal openness about sexuality, to friendships, and to income.

CHAPTER 12

Communication

Contents

Is It True?*

1. Religion makes little difference in terms of reported marital happiness.
2. Researchers agree that women are happier in marriage than men.
3. Men and women have similar communication patterns.
4. Conflict in a relationship is sometimes productive.
5. Most psychologists have had extensive training in marriage therapy.

*1=F; 2=F; 3=F; 4=T; 5=F.

THE ROLE SHIFT from lover to spouse sometimes turns an exhilarating love relationship into one fraught with conflict. Part of the difficulty of this transition may be our unrealistic expectations about marriage. We need to communicate about our relationship and to learn to manage conflict with our partner. In this chapter, we will look at several myths about marriage and explore a systematic way to manage conflict. We will also review basic factors in communication, the differences between productive and nonproductive communication, and characteristics of spouses who communicate well with their partners. We will then explore marital therapy and marriage enrichment.

Myths about Marriage

In their classic book, *The Mirages of Marriage*, Lederer & Jackson (1968) wrote that marriage is

> like taking an airplane to Florida for a relaxing vacation in January, and when you get off the plane you find you're in the Swiss Alps. There is cold and snow instead of swimming and sunshine. . . . After you buy winter clothes and learn how to talk a new foreign language, you can have just as good a vacation in the Swiss Alps as you can in Florida. But . . . it's one big surprise when you get off that marital airplane . . ..'' (p. 39)

Marriage has a great deal to offer, but it is not a magic kingdom where the usual principles don't apply and where you get something for nothing.
—David and Vera Mace

One of the reasons we are surprised by the actual experience of marriage is that we have a poor idea of what day-to-day living together in marriage is real-

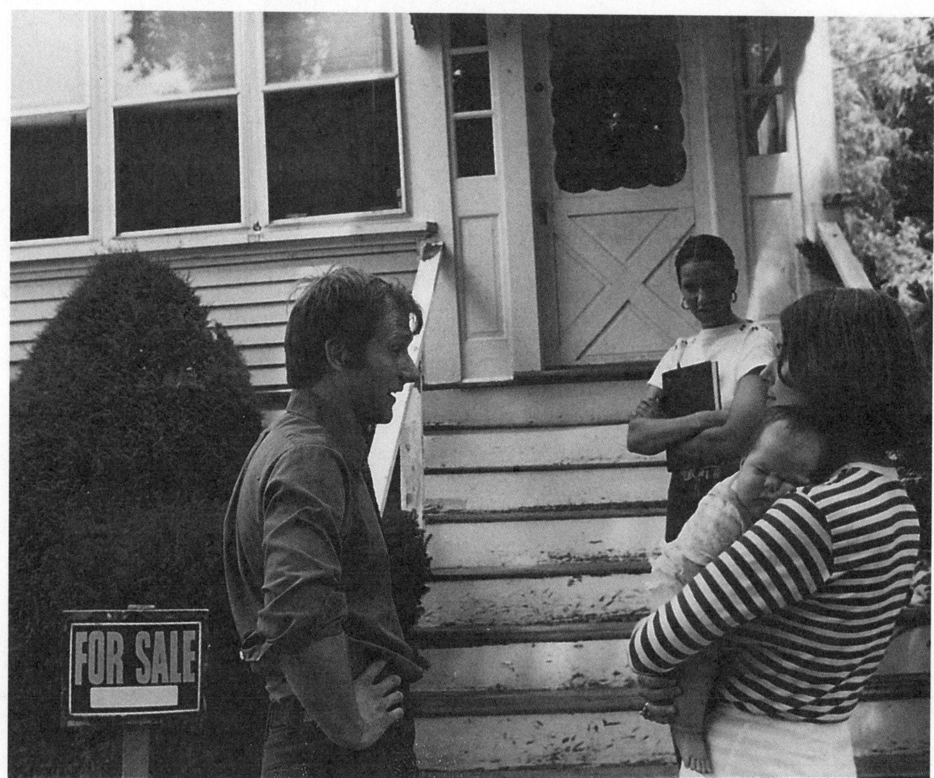

Marriage is not all romance. It is also about buying houses and rearing children.

ly like. Our assumptions are often distortions of reality. Some of the more unrealistic beliefs our society perpetuates about marriage are discussed here.

Myth 1: Our Marriage Will Be Different

All of us know married people who are bored, unhappy, and in conflict. Despite this, we assume our marriage will be different. The feeling before marriage that "it won't happen to us" reflects the deceptive nature of courtship. If we are determined that our marriage will be different, what steps are we taking to ensure that it is? This question is relevant because many of us who enter marriage believing that it will be different for us blindly imitate the marriage patterns of others instead of making a conscious effort to manage our own relationship to make it as fulfilling as we expect it to be.

Myth 2: We Will Make Each Other Happy

We also tend to believe that we are responsible for each other's happiness. One woman recalls:

> When my husband tried to commit suicide, I couldn't help but think that if I had been the right kind of wife he wouldn't have done such a thing. But I've come to accept that there was more to his depression than just me. He wasn't happy with his work, he drank heavily, and he never got over his twin brother's death.

Consideration

Although you and your partner will be a tremendous influence on each other's happiness, each of you has roles (employee, student, sibling, friend, son or daughter, parent, and so on) beyond the role of spouse. These role relationships will color the interaction with your mate. If you have lost your job or flunked out of school, your father has cancer, your closest friend moves away, or your mother, can no longer care for herself, but is resisting going to a retirement home, it will be difficult for your spouse to "make you happy." Similarly, although you may make every effort to ensure your spouse's happiness, circumstances can defeat you.

Myth 3: Our Disagreements Will Not Be Serious

Many couples acknowledge that they will have disagreements, but they assume theirs will be minor and "just part of being married." However, "insignificant" conflict that is not resolved can threaten any marriage. "All I wanted was for him to spend more time with me," recalls a divorced woman. "But he said he had to run the business because he couldn't trust anyone else. I got tired of spending my evenings alone and got involved with someone else."

Myth 4: My Spouse Is All I Need

All of us have needs that require the support of others. These needs range from wanting to see a movie with someone to needing someone to talk to about personal problems to needing the physical expression of a partner's love. Although it is encouraging to believe that our partner can satisfy all of our intellectual, physical, and emotional needs, it is not realistic.

Consideration

Perhaps a more accurate way to think of these four beliefs about marriage is to recognize that our marriage *may* be different, that we will be *one* important influence on our partner's happiness, that our disagreements *may* not be serious, and that we will be able to satisfy *some* of our partner's needs.

Marital Happiness

With or without a belief in various myths, most of us enter marriage expecting to be happy. But what does "being happy" mean? Let's examine the subjective and dynamic natures of marital happiness and the various factors that influence it.

What Influences the Perception of Happiness?

Happiness is a subjective term. The nature of happiness depends on an individual's point of view. One husband remarked that he had an incredible relationship with his wife because each of them was free to have sex with others. But another spouse said his relationship was "top of the line" because he and his wife were faithful to each other.

Data – Out of 27,000 wives, 78 percent reported they were happily married. (Greer, 1986)

In addition to being subjective, marital happiness is constantly changing. Marriage is a process, not a state. When one spouse was asked, "How happy are you in your marriage?" he replied:

> It depends on when you ask me. If you ask me when the kids are raising hell in the living room and when it's been 10 days since my wife and I had some good dialogue and sex, I'll tell you, 'Not too happy.' But if you ask me when the kids are with a sitter and my wife and I are enjoying a nice dinner by ourselves, I'll tell you, 'Terrific.'
>
> It's just that I'm not always happy or sad but have feelings every day based on what is happening. I think most spouses experience a range of feelings in their relationships.

Consideration

Most couples find that an essential ingredient in a happy relationship is spending time together sharing mutually enjoyable activities like dining or seeing a movie. Couples who don't spend time together gradually drift apart.

Other factors that affect how spouses rate their marriage include their relationships with other people, their fantasies about the happiness of other marriages, and their comparisons of their own marriage now with their marriage in earlier periods. One 25–year-old career woman explained how an outside friendship affected her feelings about her marriage:

> I guess I was happily married until I met Max. Since we worked together, we spent a lot of time together. I felt I could talk with him, and I began to compare the time with him with the time I spent with my husband. Within a few months, I defined my marriage as a failure and wanted out.

Even without a rewarding alternative relationship, imagining that other spouses are very happy may decrease a spouse's own marital happiness. "I feel like I'm caught in a bum marriage," observed one spouse. "My best friend and his wife have the kind of marriage I want. They are both professionals, like the same things, and seem to enjoy being with each other. They've got it made."

Comparing a marriage as it is now with the way it once was may be even more devastating. "Before the twins came," recalls a young mother, "Roger and I used to spend all our time together. Now we never go out to eat, see movies, or take vacations. I feel stuck, and life is no fun anymore."

Finally, marital satisfaction seems to be related to knowing what your partner wants you to do to please him or her. In a study of 152 couples, those who understood their partner's needs were more likely to be satisfied with their marriage than those who were oblivious to their partner's expectations (Tiggle et al., 1982).

Measuring Marital Satisfaction

The concept of marital satisfaction or happiness is somewhat elusive. One way of measuring it is to complete the Kansas Marital Satisfaction Scale, shown in the following Self-Assessment. One problem encountered in measuring marital satisfaction is that people tend to answer the way they think they should rather than to report the way things actually are (Schuum, Paff-Bergen et al., 1986). This tendency to give socially desirable answers (conventionalization) keeps the marriage experience hidden and makes it difficult to determine the degree of marital satisfaction spouses actually experience.

Keeping these cautions in mind, some of the characteristics of spouses who tend to score high on marital satisfaction and happiness scales include the following (Rao & Rao, 1986):

- High education
- High occupational prestige
- High income
- White
- Spend time together
- No children
- Flexibility
- Positive self-concepts
- Good communication/negotiation skills
- Frequent church attendance

Although conventionalization may be operative, religion is one of the strongest factors associated with marital satisfaction (Wilson & Filsinger, 1986). Persons who attend church frequently, give money to the church, and

Self-Assessment

Kansas Marital Satisfaction Scale

This scale may be taken by either husbands or wives, although it has been used more frequently with wives. Circle the number which best represents your feelings:

1 Extremely dissatisfied
2 Very dissatisfied
3 Somewhat dissatisfied
4 Mixed
5 Somewhat satisfied
6 Very satisfied
7 Extremely satisfied

	ED	VD	SD	M	SS	VS	ES
1. How satisfied are you with your marriage?	1	2	3	4	5	6	7
2. How satisfied are you with your husband or wife as a spouse?	1	2	3	4	5	6	7
3. How satisfied are you with your relationship with your husband or wife?	1	2	3	4	5	6	7

Add the numbers you circled. You can compare your scores with those of more than 450 wives in Kansas who completed this scale. The average total scores of the Kansas wives ranged from 17.3 to 18.3; however, among those wives who appeared to be giving the most *realistic answers on other related questions,* the scores were lower, ranging from 14.7 to 16.4 (Schumm, Paff-Bergen et al., 1986; Schumm, Scanlon et al., 1983; Schumm, Nichols et al., 1983; Schumm et al., 1985; Grover et al., 1984). By comparison, among a small group of wives who had recently separated from their husbands, the average total score was 10.1 and, among the most realistic, 7.8 (Schumm et al., 1985). On any given day, of course, a person might score lower or higher on the scale than usual. Scores on item 3 are lower than scores on items 1 and 2 on the average.

agree with such statements as "I know what it feels like to repent and experience forgiveness of sin" score higher on marital adjustment scales than those who do not evidence these behaviors and feelings. High religious commitment, particularly among Jews, is also associated with a low divorce rate (Brodbar-Nemzer, 1986). Such a low divorce rate is a result of the values Jews have for family stability and the social integration which occurs as religious involvement increases.

Good communication skills are also strongly related to marital happiness. In a study of 33 couples who had been married 2–46 years, being a "good communicator" was associated with high levels of marital satisfaction (Moffitt et al., 1986). "If you can't talk to your partner, you won't have one long," expressed one spouse. In another study, the ability to resolve disagreements was the best predictor of marital adjustment (Meeks et al., 1986).

Exhibit 12.1

MARRIAGE: AS TIME GOES BY

One wife rated her marriage (0 = very unhappy; 10 = very happy) and wrote a brief summary on the anniversary of her marriage for the first seven years.

First Year (10)

Marriage, surprisingly enough, turned out to be much more satisfying than I anticipated. We have worked things out well and established a good, positive relationship and understanding of each other. Hopefully, as the years pass, we will continue to be as happy and in touch with each other as we have been during our first year of marriage. It has really been a fantastic year.

Second Year (10)

Believe it or not, Melanie's birth has enriched our marriage, as we have both shared in the joy of the experience and care of our new daughter together. Not only has the experience added new dimensions to our marriage, but it has enhanced our sexual relationship as well. During pregnancy, due to a mutual lack of interest, we failed to maintain much of a sexual relationship. So, after Melanie's birth we began to discover each other all over again sexually, and it has been the beginning of a new relationship. Marriage is continuing to be *most* satisfying! (P.S. Having a baby has undoubtedly been the ultimate high of my life!)

Third Year (6)

We experienced a major crisis this year—a toddler. As Melanie is increasingly becoming her own person, she is demanding our undivided time and attention. We are both enjoying her so much that we have neglected time for just ourselves. Mothering (and breastfeeding) is what is most satisfying to me at this point in my life.

My husband and I have recently come to realize just how out of touch with each other we've become. It seems like every minute of the day (and night!) my time is tied up with Melanie or some other household task. Usually by the end of the day, I'm completely worn out and have little energy or interest in sex. However, that has picked up recently! All in all, I'm still happy with marriage and even happier with Melanie.

Fourth Year (7)

My husband has gotten a promotion and is making more money now. We have gotten a house, so this is my ticket to stay home if I choose to do so. But family problems on my side have caused a lot of disagreements between us. My husband will barely speak to my father. The disagreements have caused a lot of strain in our relationship.

Melanie is 2 so we can leave her while we go out together. Sometime this fall, we will start "cooking up" another baby. This will put just the right spacing between our daughter and her sibling.

Fifth Year (5)

We are expecting our second child the middle of October. During this pregnancy (as with Melanie), we have had very little physical or sexual contact. My husband is completely turned off by a pregnant body. For the most part, I haven't really been interested anyhow, so I guess it is just as well. After our first child, we rediscovered each other sexually, and we are anxious for that experience again.

My husband has turned into a "work-a-holic." So while he is wrapped up in his work, I am involved with Melanie and getting ready for another baby. At this point,

(Continued)

Exhibit 12.1

mothering is providing me with much more satisfaction than my marriage itself. We do few things as a family and even less as a couple. When my husband has free time, he usually goes hunting. I'm looking forward to a new baby, another enjoyable nursing experience, and to reestablishing a sexual closeness with my husband.

Sixth Year (7)

Kathy is now 11 months, and Melanie has found it difficult sharing "her mommy." My husband claims to always come second to the children. He says everything we do centers around their needs. He is probably right to a certain extent, but he really has no room to talk, seeing how his work and leisures tend to be his priorities. When Melanie was a baby, he was involved in caring for her and helping out. But with Kathy, he is much less involved. Play seems to be his only interest (which is better than nothing!).

Sex is something quite irregular. We go through spurts. One week we manage to get together two or three times; then we'll go several weeks without even touching each other. Often we are both just exhausted. But when we find time and have the energy, it is pretty good.

Seventh Year (7)

Things are going pretty good. Our relationship is basically the same. My husband is the only one earning an income. I'm at home with the girls (Melanie, 5; Kathy, 21 months). They are lots of fun but keep me worn out as they are getting into more and more arguments.

I continue to put the children to bed early (7:30 or 8:00 P.M.), so that my husband and I have the evening time alone. This time is also the only break I get from the children. Sex has been great, and we've been making time for it. We've talked about another baby and will probably decide to have one in the next couple of years (it could actually be anytime, since the only birth control we are using is withdrawal). I suppose our reason for another child is quite old: my husband would like a BOY. The girls would also like a brother!

This is the happiest time of my life, and I enjoy it a great deal, but I am also working harder than ever, because I *always* have something to do!

Gender Differences in Marital Happiness?

Studies disagree on whether men or women are happier in marriage. In one study, both women and men report equal amounts of marital satisfaction (Schumm et al., 1985); in another study, husbands report greater happiness (Rao & Rao, 1986). One explanation for the greater unhappiness reported by some wives is the lack of control they feel they have over their lives. One wife said:

> Why shouldn't he be happier? He's got a career that he loves, and he makes good money. I've got a job I hate, and it's pitiful what they pay me. He also has the excuse that he can't take care of the kids because he's got to be at the office. The result is I'm stuck with the kids more and can't escape from them.

Two researchers (Rao & Rao, 1986) suggest that as a result of the women's movement, wives have been taught to look for benefits in employment and in the home (equal division of labor) that have not been realized unilaterally. The average working woman is still paid two-thirds of what a man is paid, and the wife still does the majority of the housework and childcare in most marriages.

This gap between what wives want and what they actually have contributes to lower satisfaction in marriage among women.

Communication: Some Facts

I Know You Believe You Understand What You Think I Said, But I Am Not Sure You Realize That What You Heard Is Not What I Meant.
—Unknown

As we have noted in several earlier contexts, communication is one of the most important aspects of marital happiness. "We can't communicate" is one of the most frequent complaints heard by marriage therapists. Such feelings are also expressed by dating couples. In a study of a random sample of 334 university students, "communication with date" was the top problem reported by males and one in five females (Knox & Wilson, 1983). Most students value good communication skills.

Data – Out of more than 5,000 students in four universities, 78 percent said they would like to learn better ways to express themselves in a relationship. (Martin & Martin, 1984)

What is communication, and how can we learn to communicate more effectively with our partners? Communication includes a number of basic elements.

Communication Is Symbolic

Silence gives consent or a horrible feeling that nobody is listening.
—Franklin P. Jones

Communication uses symbols (words) to transmit messages. When you write a letter, you are selecting symbols that refer to agreed-on meanings the receiver can understand. When you and your partner discuss where you would like to have dinner, you are using symbols that make it possible to convey your respective preferences.

Because we rely on words to express ideas and feelings, it is important that we attach common meanings to symbols in communicating with our partners. The result of not doing so may be merely comical, as in the following situation:

> One Sunday morning early in our marriage, my wife told me that every Sunday morning before the wedding she had coffee and peanuts to start the day off right. So, being a sensitive bridegroom, I trotted off to the kitchen and returned with coffee and a handful of peanuts to meet the (rather unusual) request of my bride. After a full minute of hilarious laughter, she calmed down enough to inform me that she expected coffee and the newspaper with the "Peanuts" cartoon strip. I went away feeling like Charlie Brown . . .. (Galvin & Brommel, 1982, p. 6)

Communication Is Interactive

Symbols alone do not constitute communication. They must be used by one person who is interacting with another. Each of us lives in a private world of our own thoughts. Direct communication requires being in the presence of another person or talking on the phone (a letter is a delayed one-way communication). Communication is interaction, expressing our thoughts, finding out about the thoughts of others, and reacting to the messages.

The interactive nature of communication means that the communication process is dynamic. As the psychological state (happy or energetic; sad or depressed) and physical state (healthy, hungry, tired, sick) of each partner changes, so will his or her communication patterns. "I had the flu, but Martin wanted to discuss our relationship," said a telephone employee. "I told him it was a bad time and to wait until I felt better. He thought I was trying to put him off, so we discussed it and broke up. If I had been feeling well, I'm sure we would still be together."

Consideration

Psychological and physical states change. It may be important to be sensitive to such things as mood and health before bringing up a difficult issue for discussion with your partner. As the preceding experience illustrates, the outcome of a discussion at time A may be very different from the outcome at time B.

Communication Affects Feelings and Behaviors

"Sticks and stones may break my bones, but words can never hurt me" is a familiar children's chant. But words can and do hurt us, just as they can fill us with joy. Recall the time someone complimented you or told you they loved you or the time you said similar things to someone else. Such occasions are usually accompanied by a swell of good feelings.

Consideration

During courtship, dating partners take time to be together, to compliment each other, and to share positive experiences. Their time and energy are directed toward each other, not toward work and children. In marriage, it is easy to drift into a pattern of not spending time together, of not complimenting, of not sharing positive experiences. But not to cultivate the relationship is to let it die. If your goal is to maintain good feelings about your partner and to have your partner feel good about you, it is important that you take the time to nurture your relationship as you did in courtship.

Words also affect behaviors. Physical violence in interpersonal relationships often follows name-calling or criticizing. "I told her she was a worthless slut, and the next thing I knew, she hit me with the lamp," one husband said.

My wife said I don't listen to her—at least that's what I think she said.
—Laurence Peter

Words also affect future behaviors. The self-fulfilling prophecy says we sometimes act to make the expectations of others come true. If your partner tells you he or she doesn't trust you and knows you will have an affair sooner or later, the chance that you will do so increases.

Communication Occurs in Context

All communication occurs in a previously understood context. When you stand in front of an elevator door that has just opened, the person inside (stranger, lover, friend, professor, spouse) will provide the context for the communication to follow. The interactions with each of these people will be different.

Part of the context is the social mirror each person holds up to you, reflecting her or his perception and feelings about you. If you feel that people have a positive image of you, your manner of interacting with them will be quite different than if you feel they see you negatively. Each person is a stimulus for the response of the other, and the cycle repeats itself. People in an established relationship also tend to have a better idea of what to expect from one another when they interact.

Communication Occurs at Two Levels

All communication operates at two levels—verbal and nonverbal (Alberts, 1986). The verbal communication is the literal content of the message (for example, "I'll see you"). The nonverbal communication, sometimes referred to as *metacommunication,* is the message about the message. It conveys to the receiver the "real" message through gesture, facial expression, tone, inflection, or body language. For example, "I'll see you" can be said to convey excitement and anticipation of the next meeting, or it can be said to convey lack of interest and the intention to never see the person again.

Other examples of discrepant messages include:

- Angrily saying "I'm fine."
- Avoiding eye contact when saying "I wouldn't lie to you."
- Saying "I'll write soon" and then not doing so for six months.
- Saying "I really want to be with you" but never making the time to do so.
- Saying "It was great!" but having a gloomy appearance.

Consideration

It is important that our verbal and nonverbal communication be consistent. Sending confused messages only confuses the receiver about what we mean.

Marital Communication Is Intense

German philosopher Schopenhauer told the story of two porcupines huddled together on a cold winter's night. As the temperature dropped, they moved closer together. But getting warmer through the closeness also meant getting "stuck" by the quills of the other. As the night wore on they shuffled and changed positions to receive the maximum amount of warmth with the least amount of sticking.

I can't express anger. That's one of the problems I have. I grow a tumor instead.
—Woody Allen

In some ways, marriage represents an attempt on the part of two people to achieve the maximum amount of emotional warmth with the least amount of discomfort. Having to deal with conflict is one source of discomfort that accompanies marriage. Alford (1982) identifies six styles of handling conflict:

1. *Avoidance:* Avoiding each other or the subject.
2. *Discussion:* Discussing the conflict without expressing anger or raising one's voice.
3. *Argument:* A more intense form of discussing the conflict, without yelling or making insulting remarks.
4. *Fight 1:* Raised voices, angry looks, mildly insulting remarks.
5. *Fight 2:* Yelling, screaming, and making personal insults.
6. *Fight 3:* Yelling, screaming, pushing, shoving, hitting, throwing things, and making extremely insulting personal references. (p. 365)

Communication is both verbal and nonverbal.

When the same researcher asked 455 respondents to identify which disputing style they used in what relationships, the closer the relationship was, the more violent the style of relating became. For example, a partner would avoid conflict with a neighbor but would argue with the spouse. Marriage—the most intimate relationship—generates intense interaction between spouses.

Gender Differences Exist in Communication Patterns

Wives typically display more emotion in communicating with their husbands than vice versa. In one study, wives and husbands were videotaped as they discussed a "salient relationship issue." The tapes were then watched and coded for various aspects of positive (warm, tender, affectionate, cheerful) and negative (cold, impatient, sarcastic, blaming) communication. Wives were much more likely to display emotion (positive or negative) than their husbands (Notarius & Johnson, 1982). This finding is consistent with previous research indicating that men are less expressive of love, happiness, and sadness (Balswick, 1980), compared to women. Also, when men do display their emotions, they often do so in a more "forceful," "dominating," and "authoritarian" way than women do (Kramarae, 1981).

Another study of 166 women and 110 men revealed similar gender-specific communication patterns. Women wanted empathy, and men wanted facts they could use when they were talking with someone. Women were also much more likely to call other women "just to talk" than were men likely to call other men (Sherman & Haas, 1984).

Data – In one study, 63 percent of the women, in contrast to 43 percent of the men, reported they called a person of their own gender "just to talk." (Sherman & Haas, 1984)

Consideration

Consider then the marriage of a man who has had most of his conversations with other men, to a woman who has had most of her conversations with other women, probably the typical situation. He is used to fast-paced conversations that typically stay on the surface with respect to emotions, that often enable him to get practical tips or offer them to others, and that are usually pragmatic or fun. She is used to conversations that, while practical and fun, too, are also a major source of emotional support, self-understanding, and the understanding of others. Becoming intimate with a man, the woman may finally start expressing her concerns to him as she might to a close friend. But she may find, to her dismay, that his responses are all wrong. Instead of making her feel better, he makes her feel worse. The problem is that he tends to be direct and practical, whereas what she wants more than anything else is an empathetic listener. (Sherman & Haas, 1984, p. 73.)

If the respective genders are to enjoy talking with each other, men might provide more empathy and reflective listening and women might get to the point.

Conflicts in Marriage

We sleep in separate rooms, we have dinner apart, we take separate vacations—we're doing everything we can to keep our marriage together.
—Rodney Dangerfield

One of the major functions of communication is to reduce conflict. As one professor in a marriage and family class said, "If you haven't had a disagreement with your partner, you haven't known him or her long enough." In this section, we will explore the inevitability, desirability, sources, and styles of conflict.

Inevitability of Conflict

If you are alone this Saturday evening from six o'clock until midnight, you are assured of six conflict-free hours. But if you plan to be with your partner, roommate, or spouse during that time, the potential for conflict exists. Whether you eat out, where you eat, where you go after dinner, and how long you stay must be negotiated. Although it is relatively easy for you and your companion to agree on one evening's agenda, marriage involves the meshing of desires on an array of issues for up to 60 years.

Although most men and women reach agreement on many issues before marriage, new needs and preferences will arise throughout the marriage. Changed circumstances sometimes call for the adjustment of old habits. A wife of three years recalls:

> I can honestly say that before we got married, we never disagreed about anything, but things were different then. Both my husband and I got money from our parents and never worried about how much we spent on anything. Now I'm pregnant and unem-

ployed, and Neal still acts like we've got someone to pick up the tab. He buys expensive toys like a computer and all the games and software he can carry. He thinks that because he uses VISA we can pay the monthly minimum and still live high. We're getting over our heads in debt, and we're always fighting about it.

Consideration

You and your spouse may not disagree on who spends how much on what, but the probability is zero that you will agree throughout your marriage on every issue related to sex, in-laws, recreation, religion, and children. Marital conflict is inevitable.

Desirability of Conflict

Not all conflict is bad (Altschuler & Krueger, 1986). One study found that confronting an issue may be healthy for the couple's marriage. When 138 divorced people were asked to talk about the communication patterns in their previous marriages, almost half of them said they seldom quarreled and only two in 10 said they constantly quarreled. The researchers concluded that "conflict was not an important variable because there often was no communication whatsoever occurring between the couple" (Hayes et al., 1981, p. 23).

In another study of how spouses cope with marital distress, ignoring and resigning one's self to a problem actually increased the stress level experienced by the spouses. Although negotiating differences may not reduce immediate stress (it is often upsetting and uncomfortable to discuss a conflict in the relationship), such discussions were associated with fewer problems at a later time among the 758 interviewed spouses (Menaghan, 1982).

Consideration

When you or your partner are concerned about an issue in your relationship, discussing it may have more positive consequences than avoiding it. You may not like what your partner has to say about the reason you are upset (and vice versa), but resolving the conflict becomes a possibility. Brooding over an unresolved issue may lead to further conflict.

By expressing your dissatisfactions, you alert each other to the need for changes in your relationship to keep your satisfactions high. One wife with a full-time job said she was "sick and tired of picking up her husband's clothes and wet towels from the bathroom floor." He, on the other hand, was angered by his wife talking on the phone during mealtime. After discussing the issues, he agreed to take care of his clothes in exchange for her agreement to take the phone off the hook before meals. The payoff for their expressing their negative feelings about each other's behavior was the agreement to stop those behaviors. And confronting an issue may be good for your health. In one study, spouses with high blood pressure who suppressed their anger at their husbands or wives were twice as likely to die earlier than spouses who talked about what upset them (Julius, 1986).

SOURCES OF CONFLICT

There are numerous sources of conflict. Some of these are easily recognized; others are hidden inside the web of marital interaction.

Behavior

The preceding example in which one spouse left dirty clothes on the bathroom floor and the other talked on the phone during mealtime illustrates how the behavior of the partner can sometimes create negative feelings and set the stage for conflict. In your own relationship, you probably become upset when your partner does things you do not like (is late or tells lies). On the other hand, when your partner frequently does things that please you (is on time, is truthful), you tend to feel good about him or her and your relationship.

Perception

There are always flowers for those who want to see them.
—Henry Matisse

Aside from your partner's actual behavior, your *perception* of a behavior can be a source of satisfaction or dissatisfaction. One husband complained about the fact that his wife "was messy and always kept the house in a wreck." This same wife became interested in collecting coupons to get food discounts and began to stack boxes of various "proofs of purchase" all over the house. As a result, the house became even more messy. But because she was now saving more than $100 from their grocery bill each month, her husband saw money when he saw the array of boxes in their living room. The wife's "negative behavior" actually increased, but the husband's perception of that behavior became positive, so that a problem no longer existed.

Consideration

When dissatisfaction with your partner results from your partner engaging in behavior you do not like, consider if it may be easier for you to change your *perception* of the behavior rather than asking your partner to change the behavior.

Value Differences

Because you and your partner had years of socialization in different homes before you met, some of your values will be different. One wife, whose parents were both physicians, resented her mother not being home when she grew up. She vowed that when her own children were born she would stay home and take care of them. But she married a man who wanted his wife to actively pursue a career and contribute money to the marriage. This is only one value conflict a couple may have. Other major value differences may be about religion (one feels religion is a central part of life; the other does not), money (one feels uncomfortable being in debt; the other has the buy-now-and-pay-later philosophy), and in-laws (one feels responsible for parents when they are old; the other does not).

Consideration

Value differences in a relationship are not bad in and of themselves. What happens depends less on the degree of difference in what is valued than on the degree of rigidity with which each partner holds his or her values. Dogmatic and rigid thinkers, feeling threatened by value disagreement, try to eliminate varying viewpoints and typically produce more conflict. But partners who recognize the inevitability of difference usually try to accept in each other what they cannot successfully compromise. (Scoresby, 1977, p. 142)

Inconsistent Rules

Partners in all relationships develop a set of rules to help them function smoothly. These unwritten but mutually understood rules include what time you are supposed to be home after work, whether you should call if you are going to be late, how often you can see friends alone, and when and how you make love. Conflict results when the partners disagree on the rules or when inconsistent rules develop in the relationship. For example, one wife expected her husband to take a second job so they could afford a new car. But she also expected him to go out and party with her at night after he got off work at 10.

Leadership Ambiguity

Unless a couple has an understanding about which partner will make decisions in which area (for example, the husband will decide over which issues to "ground" teenage children; the wife will decide how much money to spend on vacations), each partner may continually try to "win" a disagreement. All conflict is seen as an "I win–you lose" encounter because each partner is struggling for dominance in the relationship. "In low-conflict marriages, leadership roles vary and are flexible, but they are definite. Each partner knows most of the time who will make certain decisions . . .." (Scoresby, 1977, p. 141).

Job Stress

When you are scheduled to take four exams on one day you are under a lot of pressure to prepare for them. The stress of such preparation may cause you to be irritable in interactions with your partner. A similar effect occurs when spouses are under job stress; they are less easy to get along with. When spouses are happy and satisfied with their employment, they are much more likely to report satisfaction in their marriages and in relationships with their children (Belsky et al., 1985). One husband said:

> If I've been on the road all week and haven't made any sales, I feel terrible. And I'm on edge when the wife wants to talk to me or touch me. I seem like I get obsessed with how things are at work, and if they aren't okay, nothing else seems okay either. But if I've made a lot of sales and the commission checks are rolling in, I'm a great husband and father.

When both spouses are employed outside the home and have children to care for when they return home, the stress level can be particularly high. Even if only one spouse is employed, a baby may alter the time the spouses have for each other. The career–baby drain reemphasizes the need for the spouses to spend time together if they are to avoid a drift toward divorce (Klagsbrun, 1985).

STYLES OF CONFLICT

Spouses develop various styles of conflict. If you were watching a videotape of various spouses disagreeing over the same issue, you would notice at least three styles of conflict. These styles are clarified in *The Marriage Dialogue* (Scoresby, 1977).

Complementary

In the *complementary style* of conflict, the wife and husband tend to behave in opposite ways: dominant–submissive, talkative–quiet, active–passive. Specifically, one person lectures the other about what should or should not occur. The other person says little or nothing and becomes increasingly unresponsive. For example, a husband was angry because his wife left the outside lights of their house on all night. He berated her the next morning, saying she was irresponsible. She retreated in silence. Each partner should talk about how he or she feels and what she or he wants the other partner to do.

Symmetrical

In the *symmetrical style* of conflict, both partners react to each other in the same way. If she yells, he yells back. If one attacks, so does the other. The partners try to "win" their positions without listening to the other's point of view. In the preceding incident, the wife would blast back at the husband, stating he lived there too and was equally responsible for seeing that the lights were out before going to bed. An alternative would be to decide who was responsible for what household duties and to have each partner make a commitment to do specific chores. Soft discussions should replace loud arguments.

Parallel

In the *parallel style* of conflict, both partners deny, ignore, and retreat from addressing a problem issue. "Don't talk about it, and it will go away" is the theme of this conflict style. Gaps begin to develop in the relationship, neither partner feels free to talk, and each gradually comes to believe that he or she is misunderstood. Both eventually become involved in separate activities, rather than spending time together. In the outside-light example, neither partner said anything about the lights being left on all night, but the husband resented the fact that they were. A better alternative is for each partner to talk about what he or she wants the other to do.

Every marriage probably uses all three styles to some degree. Nevertheless, knowing which style is characteristic of your relationship is a beginning for developing more effective communication.

Conflicts in Black Marriages

Black marriages may have some unique features that make marital conflict more likely. These features include more educated black women than educated black men, black women having higher occupational status than black men, and black women being much closer in income to black men than white women are to white men (Secord & Ghee, 1986).

More Educated Black Wives

The result of black wives being more educated than their husbands is that they are likely to expect their husbands to be "more sensitive, more emotionally nurturant, and more companionable" (Secord & Ghee, 1986, p. 27). Less-educated black males with a traditional male-dominant orientation may be less likely to fulfill the expectations of the black female. Conflict results when the black female expects behaviors from her partner that are not forthcoming. Although white women may also expect their husbands to be nurturant and companionable, the higher percentage of white educated husbands may result in more white males who meet the gender-role expectations of their partners.

Greater Occupational Status of the Wife

The fact that black wives tend to have greater occupational status than their husbands has implications for the marriage in that their husbands may feel threatened by this status. If the black male has been taught that his wife is to respect and admire him in his occupational role but he holds a lower-status job than his wife, then his self-concept may be negative. If he feels bad about himself, he may think that his wife shares his view. In an effort to deal with the discrepancy between what he is and what he thinks she wants him to be, the black husband may attempt to denigrate the black wife's status to make himself look better. Or he may want to disengage himself from her because she makes him feel bad by comparison.

Black Wife Almost an Equal Provider

The fact that black wives are likely to contribute a much larger share of the family income than white wives may result in some black wives being dissatisfied with the performances of their partners as providers. "Other working black wives who slaken their demands on their husband as a provider are apt to substitute new demands for more companionship, emotional support, and sharing of domestic and child-care duties" (Secord & Ghee, 1986, p. 27). Although some black males willingly meet these expectations, others resent them and lose their interest in staying married.

Whatever the reason, blacks divorce at a much higher rate than whites.

Data – In seven national surveys over a 10-year period, 37 percent of all black males and 42 percent of all black females surveyed have been divorced at least once, compared to 22 and 24 percent, respectively, of all whites surveyed. (U.S. Bureau of the Census, 1984)

Productive and Nonproductive Communication

Beyond the information-giving ("I got the milk"), information-getting ("Did you get the wine?"), and sharing ("Look at that.") functions, communication is essential for resolving difficulties as they crop up in a relationship. There are productive and nonproductive ways of communicating about conflict. Knowing which to use and which to avoid is one of the most valuable skills a spouse or couple can possess. In a study of almost 500 couples, the researcher noted that their marriage success had much more to do with their communication skills than with factors such as age at marriage or lack of money (Brandt, 1982).

Productive Communication

Productive communication increases the emotional closeness of the partners and brings their respective expectations and behaviors into alignment. Suppose one partner expects the other to be punctual, and the partners discuss the issue. Their communication will be productive to the degree that they feel closer as a result of the discussion and either one partner agrees to be more punctual or the other partner decides the issue isn't worth getting upset about and drops the expectation. Here is an example of productive communication:

> Mary and Bob have been living together for about six months. When they first moved in together, they agreed that because they were both in school and had part-time jobs, they would share the housekeeping chores—cooking, washing dishes, doing laundry, and keeping the apartment neat. It seemed to Mary that she was gradually drifting into the role of housewife, which she thought was counter to her agreement with Bob. She felt Bob wasn't going to start doing his share of the housework unless she brought it up, so she mentioned the subject one evening as she was preparing dinner.
>
> MARY: You know, I thought we agreed that we would do the cooking and other stuff together.
>
> BOB: Well, I guess we did . . . [feeling somewhat guilty for not living up to his part of the deal]. What do you want me to do?
>
> MARY: Since I've got classes Tuesday and Thursday nights, it would be nice for you to take care of the cooking and washing the dishes on those nights. I'll handle it Monday, Wednesday, and Friday, and we can worry about the weekend later."
>
> BOB: Okay. I guess I'm cooking Thursday night, eh? What would you like?

Nonproductive Communication

Nonproductive communication increases the emotional distance between the partners and leaves the discrepancy between their respective expectations and behaviors unchanged. An example follows:

> Alice and Jeff have the same problem as Mary and Bob. Jeff hasn't been helping around the apartment, and Alice is upset.
>
> ALICE: Jeff, I'm really fed up with your lying around the apartment while I do all the work. Didn't we agree to do this stuff together?
>
> JEFF: Maybe we did, but I've got all I can do with school and work, so you'll just have to do it yourself.

ALICE: You aren't being very sensitive to my needs—I go to school and work, too.
JEFF: What would you know about sensitivity?
ALICE: You're being hateful and mean.
JEFF: I guess you're being real sweet when you talk like that aren't you? I guess this means no sex again tonight.
ALICE: Right again, Sherlock. And besides, you're the lousiest lover I've ever had.
JEFF: And you've had plenty, so I must be real bad. You slut.
ALICE: I'm not listening to this crap.
JEFF: Yeah! What are you going to do about it?
ALICE: Leave—that's what.
JEFF: Go ahead.

An argument usually consists of two people each trying to get the last word—first.
—Laurence Peter

What began as a discussion about Jeff helping Alice around the apartment has escalated into a decision to terminate the relationship.

Productive and Nonproductive Communication Compared

Mary and Bob did everything right in handling the housework issue; Alice and Jeff did everything wrong. Table 12.1 compares the two styles.

In a study of 40 married couples, the researchers observed what styles of communication were associated with marital happiness (Honeycutt et al., 1982). Spouses who were relaxed, friendly, and empathetic in relating to each other were happier than those who were rigid, distant, and cold. Mary and Bob's communication patterns reflect these qualities.

Couples concerned about their relationships also establish unwritten rules about the parameters of communication and conflict in their relationships. Some of the rules identified by 33 couples include the following (Hennon, 1981):

1. Never go to bed mad.
2. Never hit each other.
3. Never fight in public.
4. Try not to "pick" arguments.
5. Do not let arguments affect sex life.
6. Never walk out when fighting.
7. Do not have sex when partner is angry.
8. Angry or not, do not avoid sleeping together; a good discussion might develop while just lying in bed.

Good communication patterns also imply that each partner will participate in stopping negative interaction from escalating, in focusing on issues rather than on personalities, and in responding to each other with supportive comments. The last implies that each partner creates the context of positive regard for the other (Schumm, Barnes et al., 1986).

Reflective listening—one of the most important aspects of effective communication—is the technique of paraphrasing how your partner feels about an issue rather than defending your own position. For example, suppose your partner wants the two of you to live together before you get married, but you are opposed to the idea. Rather than each of you becoming defensive and fixed in your own point of view, reflective listening implies that each of you explain to the other the other's point of view. Assuming that your partner has just told

TABLE 12.1 CHARACTERISTICS OF PRODUCTIVE AND NONPRODUCTIVE COMMUNICATION

PRODUCTIVE COMMUNICATION (Mary and Bob)	NONPRODUCTIVE COMMUNICATION (Alice and Jeff)
1. Avoidance of behaviors in column 2.	1. Blaming: ". . . your lying around the house while I do the work."
2. Neutral statement rather than accusation: "I thought we agreed. . . ."	2. Name calling: "lousy lover," "slut."
3. Acknowledgement of responsibility for partner's discomfort: "Well, I guess we did discuss my sharing the work."	3. Threatening: "I'm going to leave."
4. Expression of willingness to alleviate problem: "What do you want me to do?"	4. Using sarcasm: "What would you know about sensitivity?" "Right again, Sherlock."
5. Positive labeling of suggestion—"It would be nice if . . . ."	5. Being judgmental: "You're being hateful and mean."
6. Reciprocity: "I'll handle it Monday, Wednesday, and Friday."	6. Changing issues: ". . . no sex again tonight."
7. Positive expression at end of conflict: "Okay. I guess I'm on for Thursday night, eh?"	7. No attempt to stop escalation of conflict.
8. Brief: Mary and Bob took two turns each speaking.	8. Lengthy: Alice and Jeff took six turns each speaking.

you why he or she wants to live together, reflective listening would involve your saying something like the following in response:

> As I understand it, you feel that we should live together before we get married because it would give us an opportunity to find out about each other. You also feel that there is nothing wrong with living together and that we should not have any misgivings about doing so. You also love me very deeply and want me to know that you simply want to be with me more of the time.

At this point, your partner should give you feedback on the degree to which you accurately understand how he or she feels about living together.

Then you should express how you feel about living together (in this example, you are opposed to it) and your partner should reflect back to you how you feel. In this case, your partner might say something like the following:

> You feel that living together is something that we should not do. Although you love me, you feel that living together would make you feel uncomfortable and would have a negative impact on our relationship. You also feel that your parents would object to our living together and would blame our living together on me.

In each of these examples, the focus is on reflecting back what the partner has said. The next time you are in a disagreement with someone, you might try reflective listening rather than continuing to defend your own point of view. Although defense mechanisms should be avoided (see section to follow), reflective listening is most useful in the context of an overall plan to successfully resolve conflict. This context is discussed after defense mechanisms.

Avoid Use of Defense Mechanisms

Couples who have established good communication patterns avoid using *defense mechanisms* (any behavior that protects the psyche from anxiety). Defense mechanisms temporarily minimize anxiety and avoid emotional hurt, but they also interfere with conflict resolution.

Escapism

I drink to make other people interesting.
—George Jean Nathan

Escapism is the simultaneous denial and withdrawal from a problem. The usual form of escape is avoidance. The spouse becomes "busy" and "doesn't have time" to think about or deal with the problem, or he or she may escape into recreation, sleep, alcohol, marijuana, or work. The longer an unresolved conflict continues, the less time the spouses spend talking with each other, sharing sex, and going places together.

Rationalization

Rationalization is the cognitive justification for one's own behavior. For example, the wife who is having an affair may justify her involvement with another man on the basis that her husband is unwilling to have intercourse as often as she desires. "I'm tired of begging my husband to make love to me," one wife said. "The man I'm involved with makes it clear that he wants me."

Projection

Projection occurs when one spouse who is guilty of a particular behavior unconsciously accuses the other spouse of the same behavior. For example, the wife having the affair may accuse her husband of being unfaithful to her. Such blaming shifts the focus from her affair and puts her husband on the defensive.

Projection may be seen in statements like "You spend too much money" (projection for "I spend too much money") and "You want to break up" (projection for "I want to break up"). Projection interferes with conflict resolution by creating a mood of hostility and defensiveness in both partners. The issues to be resolved in the relationship remain unchanged and become more difficult to discuss.

Displacement

Displacement shifts the frustration one spouse may be experiencing in other role relationships to the other spouse. The wife who is turned down for a promotion and the husband who is driven to exhaustion by his boss may direct their hostilities (displace them) onto each other rather than toward their respective employers. The manager of a fast food chain expresses his own use of displacement:

> I hate to admit it, but our marital happiness is usually a reflection of how happy I am in my work. At the end of the month when the regional manager drops in to check the books, I get nervous. I am under pressure to increase profits, and I feel on edge by the time I get home. Last night my wife asked me to pass her the TV guide, and I blurted, "Get it yourself." My real problem is the regional manager, but there is no way I can vent my anger on him.

Emotional Insulation

Emotional insulation interferes with conflict resolution by reducing the commitment of the partner to the relationship. One married person said:

> I was emotionally devastated by my first marriage because I let myself be vulnerable. I hid nothing and loved as fully as possible. But my partner took advantage of my love

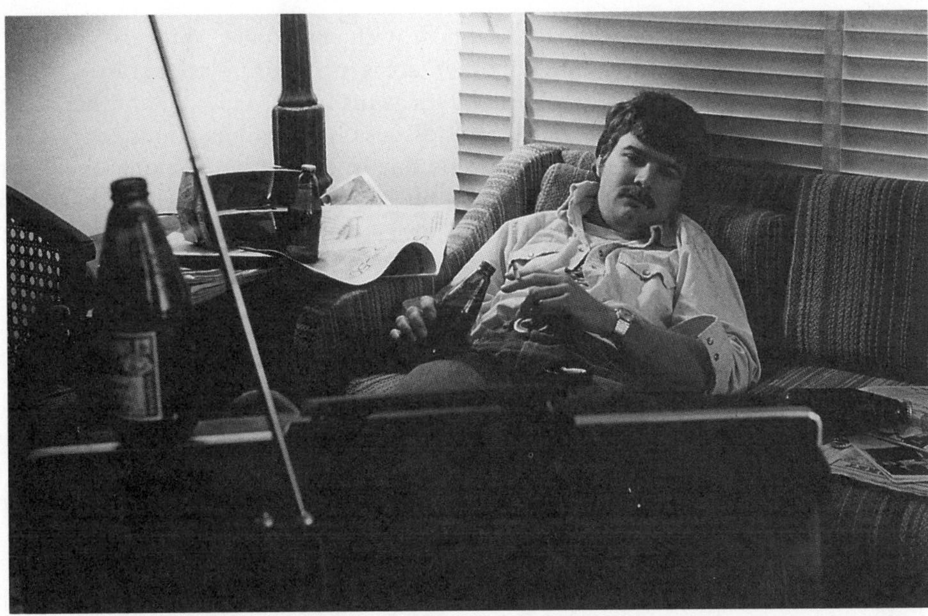

Alcohol is sometimes used to escape an unhappy relationship.

and did not reciprocate. I don't want it to happen again, so I am very guarded in my current relationship.

The partner has developed a protective posture to avoid being hurt. But the price of such protection may be high. A divorced person observed:

Getting hurt sometimes happens when you get involved. And if you take your resentments with you into the next relationship, you've had it. You can't make your new partner responsible for something your previous partner did (you can't shoot all the dogs because some of them have fleas). I know; I would not drop my guard, become vulnerable, and let my love feelings go, and it cost me my second marriage.

Consideration

By knowing about defense mechanisms and their negative impact on resolving conflict, you can be alert to their appearance in your own relationships. The essential characteristics of all defense mechanisms are the same: they are unconscious, and they distort reality. When a conflict continues without resolution, one or more defense mechanisms may be operating.

A Plan to Communicate Successfully about Conflicts

Being sure that defense mechanisms are not operative, it is helpful to have an overall plan to resolve a conflict. Such a plan might include at least six stages.

Address Recurring, Disturbing Issues

If you or your partner are upset about a recurring issue, talking about it may help. Pam was jealous that Mark seemed to spend more time with other people at parties than with her. "When we go someplace together," she blurted out,

Seldom, or perhaps never, does a marriage develop into an individual relationship smoothly and without crises; there is no coming to consciousness without pain.
—Carl Jung

"he drops me to disappear with someone else for two hours." Her jealousy was also spreading to other areas of their relationship. "When we are walking down the street and he turns his head to look at another woman, I get furious." If Pam and Mark don't discuss her feelings about Mark's behavior, their relationship may deteriorate due to a negative response cycle: he looks at another woman, she gets angry, he gets angry at her getting angry and finds that he is even more attracted to other women (who don't get angry), she gets angrier because he escalates his looking at other women, and so on.

Ask Your Partner for Help in Coping With an Issue

To bring the matter up, Pam might say something like "I feel jealous when you spend more time with other women at parties than me. I need some help in dealing with these feelings." By expressing her concern in this way, she has identified the problem from her perspective and asked her partner's cooperation in handling it.

Find Out Your Partner's View

We usually assume that we know what our partner thinks and why our partner does things. Sometimes we are wrong. Rather than assume how our partner feels about a particular issue, we might ask him or her to tell us how she or he sees a particular situation. Pam's words to Mark might be, "What is it like for you when we go to parties?" "How do you feel about my jealousy?" Notice that both of these sentences are open-ended: Mark is asked to generate his own thoughts about the situation. Such questions are preferable to closed-ended questions, such as "Do you still like me when I'm jealous?" "Do you want to go alone to parties?" These questions require the other person to answer yes or no and make elaboration difficult—if not useless—once a single-word response has been given.

Nonjudgmentally Summarize Your Partner's View

Once your partner has shared his or her thoughts about an issue with you, it is important for you to summarize your partner's perspective in a nonjudgmental way. Summarizing serves three functions:

1. It ensures that you understand the situation from your partner's point of view. (If you don't summarize correctly, your partner will correct you.)
2. It lets your partner know that you know what his or her perspective is.
3. It validates the partner's right to view the situation as she or he does.

After Mark told Pam how he felt about their being at parties together, she summarized his perspective by saying, "You feel that I cling to you more than I should and that you would like me to let you wander around without feeling like you're making me angry." (She may not agree with his view, but she knows exactly what it is—and Mark knows that she knows.)

Examine Alternative Solutions

After each partner has told the other how he or she views the situation and has nonjudgmentally summarized the other's perspective, both partners should make various suggestions about how the problem can be resolved. Such "brainstorming" is crucial to conflict resolution because partners often feel upset when they know how their partner sees a situation. Brainstorming shifts the focus from criticizing each other's perspective to working together to develop alternative solutions. The partners suggest as many alternatives as possible, and no suggestion is "put down."

Alternatives suggested by Pam and Mark included the following:

1. Pam should stop being jealous.
2. Mark should stop spending time away from Pam at parties and stop looking at other women.
3. They should break up.
4. They should stop going to parties together.
5. Pam should start spending time away from Mark at parties and begin dancing with other men.
6. Pam should start turning her head to look at other men while she walks down the street.
7. Pam and Mark should keep things as they are but not talk about the issue any more.
8. Pam and Mark should stop seeing each other for a week or two.

Select a Plan of Action

After generating a number of solutions, one or a combination of them should be selected. Pam and Mark, for example, selected aspects from several alternatives from which they derived specific actions. They agreed that they would spend 45 minutes of each hour at a party talking and dancing together; Mark would be responsible for initiating and maintaining their time together, and Pam would be responsible for initiating their time away from each other. They also agreed that Pam would say nothing about the time they were apart unless Mark brought it up. They further agreed that it was okay for each of them to look at members of the opposite sex when they were with each other but that neither was to say anything about the other partner's looking.

Consideration

Most of the agreements to resolve conflict that the partners feel good about are either compromises or contain elements of each partner's input. Each partner must be willing to assume responsibility for changing his or her own behavior first as a gesture of commitment and good faith toward the partner and the relationship.

Here are some other examples of agreements reached by partners in conflict:

She wanted a half-carat diamond for her engagement ring; he thought it would be silly to spend $2,000 for a "rock." She put up half the money for the diamond; he put $1,000 on a down payment for a car for her.

He wanted to snow ski in Vermont on their honeymoon; she wanted to go to the Bahamas. They went to Disney World.

He wanted to buy Carnation Instant Breakfast because he likes its taste; she wanted to buy cereal because it would save them money. They bought both and alternated what they had for breakfast each morning.

He wanted her to get a job to put him through school; she wanted him to get a job and put her through school. They decided to work part time and go to school part time.

She wanted a baby; he didn't (he had two children from a previous marriage). He agreed to have a baby in exchange for her agreeing to wait two years. (She waited, and they had their baby.)

You cannot do a kindness too soon, for you never know how soon it will be too late.
—Ralph Waldo Emerson

As we noted, some spouses view the resolution of their conflicts in win–lose terms rather than as compromises. In one study, 60 spouses (representing 30 marriages) were interviewed about relationship conflicts and their outcomes (Bell et al., 1982). The results showed that husbands "win most conflicts, regardless of the strategies they or their wives employ" (p. 111). Catholic and Mormon husbands were particularly likely to swing a disagreement their way. However, among couples in which the wife was a member of NOW (National Organization for Women), seven in 10 of the conflicts were "won" by the wife.

Marital Therapy

Sometimes it is impossible for spouses to resolve a conflict by themselves. Contacting a marriage therapist is an alternative. Examples of problems spouses bring to marriage therapy are described in Exhibit 12.2.

Questions about Marriage Therapy

If you decide to see a marriage therapist (see the Choices section at the end of this chapter), whom do you contact, how much will it cost, and what are the chances of a successful outcome? Your therapist should be a specialist with training in marriage therapy. She or he should also be a state-certified marriage and family therapist or a clinical member of the American Association for Marriage and Family Therapy (AAMFT). Only nine states (Utah, Connecticut, Georgia, South Carolina, Tennessee, California, New Jersey, North Carolina, and Florida) license or certify marriage therapists, so it is important to verify the training of your therapist. Don't be embarrassed to ask.

Data – Although psychologists devote a considerable percentage of their time to conducting marriage and family therapy, fewer than 10 training programs for psychologists offer specific training in marriage and family therapy. (Ganahl et al., 1985)

Exhibit 12.2

PROBLEMS COUPLES BRING TO MARRIAGE THERAPY

Sex
Lack of sexual desire
Infrequent or no orgasm
Pain during intercourse
Vagina too tight for penetration
Premature ejaculation
Impotence
No ejaculation
Differences over how sex occurs:
- Too little foreplay
- Spouse crude in approach
- Oral sex
- Positions
- Too little affection

Disagreement about frequency of intercourse
Disagreement about when sex occurs
Extramarital affair

In-laws
Talking over the phone to in-laws
How often in-laws visit
Borrowing money from in-laws
Living with in-laws
How often to visit in-laws
In-laws' dislike of spouse
In-laws' interference in children's lives
Loaning/giving money to in-laws

Recreation
No sharing of leisure time
Desire of spouse for separate vacations
Competition (egos may be hurt if one spouse is, say, more athletic than partner)
Disagreement over amount of money to allocate for vacation
Spouse doesn't like family vacations
Disagreement over what is fun
Where to spend vacation
How long to be on vacation

Children
Discipline of children
Care of children
Time with children
Number of children
Spacing of children
Infertility
Whether or not to adopt
Rivalry for children's love
Activities in which children should be involved
Sex education for children
Distress at children's behavior
Child abuse by one spouse
Retarded, autistic, or otherwise handicapped child
Stepchildren

Communication
Don't feel close to spouse
Rarely alone with spouse
Spouse complains/criticizes
Don't love spouse
Not loved by spouse
Spouse is impatient
Too little time spent communicating
Nothing to talk about
Intellectual gaps
Unhappiness with type of conversation
Spouse is unhappy and depressed
Arguments end in spouse abuse/violence

Money
Too little money
Wife's job
Husband's job
Conflict over who buys what
Gambling
Borrowing
Excessive debts

(Continued)

Exhibit 12.2

Religion
Which church to attend
Wife too devout
Husband too devout
Wife not devout enough
Husband not devout enough
Religion for children
Church donations
Observance of religious holidays and rituals, such as circumcision
Breaking of vows

Friends
Too few friends
Too many friends
Different friends
Confidences to friends
Time with friends

Alcohol or Drugs
Spouse drinks too much
Spouse smokes too much marijuana
Spouse takes too many pills
Amount of money spent on alcohol/drugs
Flirting as a consequence of drinking
Influence of drinking/drug habits on children
Violence as a consequence of drinking

The cost of private marriage therapy is between $35 and $100 per hour. You can obtain a list of AAMFT members in your area by looking in the Yellow Pages or by writing to AAMFT at 1717 K St., N.W., Suite 407; Washington, D.C. 20006; 202–429–1825. Members of AAMFT also conduct therapy in mental-health centers, where the fee is considerably less.

Most marital therapy sessions last about 50 minutes, during which the spouses are usually seen together in what is referred to as *conjoint marriage therapy.* Some therapists (Gurman & Kniskern, 1986) feel strongly that it is important to see the spouses together; others (Wells & Giannetti, 1986) feel it is not harmful to see a spouse alone.

Whether two married people remain together will depend on their motivation to do so, how long they have been in conflict, the severity of the problem, and whether one or both partners is/are involved in an extramarital affair. Two moderately motivated partners with numerous conflicts over several years are less likely to work out their problems than a highly motivated couple with minor conflicts of short duration.

The style of therapy is also important. Clients report greater improvement in marriage and family therapy if the therapy they become involved in is consistent with the way in which they view the problem and their conceptualization of how to correct it (Crane et al., 1986). For example, if you feel the problem in your relationship is your partner's behavior, then you will probably benefit from therapy with a behaviorist. However, if you feel the problem in your relationship is "deep-seated and of unknown origin, then you will probably be dissatisfied with behavioral therapy.

Consideration

Spouses most likely to benefit from marriage therapy come to therapy when they first begin to experience conflict or dissatisfaction in their relationships. Spouses who wait until they are ready to divorce to seek therapy have waited too long (except in the unusual case).

To what degree does involvement in marriage therapy pay off?

Data – A total of 102 clients who had been involved in marriage and family therapy reported the degree to which they felt therapy had been effective. Of their marriages, 73 percent said they had "improved," 20 percent said "no change," and 7 percent said they had "deteriorated" as a result of the therapy. (Crane et al., 1986)

Styles of Marriage Therapy

All marriage therapists are not alike. Primarily they differ in the ways in which they identify the causes of marital problems and the ways in which they attempt to resolve these problems. The various approaches to marriage therapy include the following.

Systems Therapy

Systems therapy suggests that marriage problems can best be viewed and treated by examining the spouses in the larger context of their relationships with their children, in-laws, and friends—how spouses are connected to other people in their interpersonal system. "Change in individuals who are embedded in contexts persists more significantly when confirmed and supported by the system." (Massey, 1986, p. 27).

Problem marital behaviors, such as chronic drinking, are viewed in terms of how they serve to keep the couple functioning at a stable level. For example, does the wife protect the husband from the consequences of his drinking so that she can play the role of nurse? If he gets well, will he need her? In systems therapy intervention, the therapist explains to the spouses what "rules" they have developed to perpetuate their problems. Spouses can then decide to adopt new rules to achieve new goals. For example, the wife of the alcoholic may decide to stop covering up her husband's alcoholism so that he may eventually seek treatment.

Behavior Therapy

Find out what a person will work for and what he or she will work to avoid, systematically manipulate these contingencies, and you can change behavior.

—Jack Turner

Behavioral therapy suggests that the cause of unhappiness between spouses is that each one engages in behavior that upsets the other. The behavioral therapist encourages each spouse to engage in behaviors of the kind and at a frequency desired by the partner and develops a behavior contract with each spouse to encourage new behavior. Exhibit 12.3 is an example of a behavior contract drawn up for a husband whose wife complained that he "leaves his clothes all over the house," "never helps me with meal preparation," "never says anything good about me," and "always criticizes me." Notice that the husband agrees to punish himself if he "forgets" to do what he agreed to do. By accepting a negative consequence, he teaches himself not to forget. A contract specifying what the wife will do for the husband (based on his requests) would also be developed. In this way, each spouse promises to change his or her behavior to be consistent with the expectations of the partner, so that each spouse will have a better behavioral basis for feeling positively about the other. Behavior contracts are one result of therapy, but a great deal of time is also spent on assisting the couple to develop positive communication and nego-

Exhibit 12.3

Behavior Contract

Name Tom Griffin Date October 18

Behaviors	M	T	W	T	F	S	S
1. Put clothes in closet or hamper by 8:30 a.m. every morning.							
2. Prepare and serve evening meal Monday and Thursday at 7:00 p.m.							
3. Compliment Theresa twice daily.							
4. Make no negative statements to Theresa.							
Terms If I fail to do any of the above as specified, I forfeit reading the newspaper and watching T.V. news.							

tiation skills. Two researchers reported that behavioral marriage therapy not only improved marital satisfaction but reduced depression (Beach & O'Leary, 1986).

Rational–Emotive Therapy

Despite our celebration of openness, in the power struggle, it's the person who's most vulnerable, most generous, most committed who loses.
—Robert Karen

Working from the theories of Albert Ellis, executive director of the Institute for the Advanced Study of Rational Psychotherapy, *rational–emotive therapy* suggests that spouses are unhappy as a result of irrational beliefs they have about themselves and each other. The rational–emotive therapist encourages partners to examine their beliefs and to change them if they have a negative impact on the marriage. For example, the belief that "My spouse should care more about me than anything or anyone else" would be examined for its potential negative consequences on the relationship. Other beliefs that interfere with marital happiness include "I should always be happy with my partner," "We should be as happy as we were in courtship," and "My spouse should never do anything that upsets me."

Transactional Analysis

Transactional analysis (TA) suggests that spouses are unhappy because one spouse is interacting with the other as though the other spouse were someone else. As examples, a wife may act as if her husband were her father or a husband may relate to his wife as though she were his mother. The TA therapist encourages spouses to examine the ways in which their role relationships with others have been problematic and how they may have introduced these unresolved conflicts into their marriage relationship.

Adlerian Therapy

Applying the theories of Austrian psychiatrist Alfred Adler, *Adlerian therapy* views marital discord as a result of power struggles between spouses. The individual is seen as trying to compensate for feelings of inferiority that began with the helplessness of infancy. The Alderian therapist seeks to improve marital relationships by helping couples to feel secure and to regard their power struggles as unnecessary.

Systems, behavioral, rational–emotive, transactional, and Adlerian therapy are only a few of the different approaches used by marriage therapists. Gestalt, psychoanalytic, humanistic, reality, and paradoxical therapy are others. Although systems therapy is currently attracting a new wave of therapists, no one therapy can be regarded as superior.

Consideration

All of the different styles of therapy can be placed into two basic categories—*directive* and *nondirective.* In behavioral, rational–emotive, and reality therapy, the therapist is more likely to be directive. He or she suggests specific ways in which the spouses can improve their marriage. Therapists of the systems, transactional, Adlerian, Gestalt, and psychoanalytic persuasions may or may not make specific recommendations. Whereas some clients want specific direction, others want to explore their relationships and develop insight into the dynamics of marital interaction. Should you decide to consult a therapist, you should seek the therapist who will offer the style of therapy you want. Regardless of particular orientation, the trained marriage therapist can be expected to express a genuine concern for your difficulty, to be nonjudgmental, and to regard all information as confidential.

Marriage Enrichment

Spouses who are having marital difficulties often see a marriage therapist as a last resort—their final choice before seeking a divorce. Marriage counselors are thought of as an emergency medical team at the bottom of a cliff that ministers to those who have fallen in the hope of reviving them—but why not a guardrail at the top to prevent couples from slipping off the edge? Such preventive intervention is the goal of marriage-enrichment programs. More than 50 of these programs are currently operative, including Marriage Encounter, International Marriage Encounter, the Minnesota Couple Communication

Program, Conjugal Relationship Enhancement (Pennsylvania), Training in Marriage Enrichment (TIME), and the Association of Couples for Marriage Enrichment (ACME).

One of the most well-known marriage-enrichment programs is Marriage Encounter. (There are two rival branches—National and Worldwide.) As originally conceived by Gabriel Calvo, a Roman Catholic priest, Marriage Encounter is a 44–hour weekend program that attempts to teach "God's plan for marriage." A team of laypeople and clergy present a series of talks designed to make couples aware that something is missing in their relationship. That something is *dialogue.* To correct the absence of dialogue, the group leader assigns the spouses a topic, asks them to write their respective feelings about the topic in a notebook, exchange their notebooks, and discuss the issue. The exercise focuses on sharing feelings, not on problem solving.

A number of couples have sought marriage enrichment through an encounter weekend.

Data – More than 1 million couples have participated in marriage encounter weekends. (Doherty et. al., 1986)

Most couples who attend marriage-enrichment or marriage-encounter weekends probably benefit from the experience. In one study, 80 percent of 200 couples who had attended a National Marriage Encounter weekend four years earlier reported they had a totally positive experience. The most positive aspect of the weekend was learning to express their feelings to each other. The most negative aspect was identifying needs during the weekend that were not subsequently fulfilled (Lester & Doherty, 1983).

For example, one wife said she wanted more frequent intercourse, which, at follow-up, had still not occurred. During this time, the husband had felt inadequate and the wife had felt frustrated.

Complete openness during an encounter weekend may be dysfunctional. One husband felt that to be honest he needed to disclose a previous affair to his wife. The encounter weekend was over before the effects of his disclosure were resolved by the couple. One respondent in a follow up study (Doherty et al., 1986) said:

> The reason I feel the Encounter had a negative effect was that my husband indicated that he was not interested in working on any of the areas. This really made me question the stability of our marriage. I felt very upset, because I began to wonder how I could survive knowing there would be no changes—and wondering if I could accept this and live this way. (p. 55)

Consideration

To minimize the negative effects of exposure to a marriage-enrichment program, the partners should not regard the experience as an opportunity to solve problems or to deal with difficult issues in their relationship. Such issues should be dealt with alone or in marriage therapy. Instead a marriage-enrichment program should be regarded as a place to improve communication skills between spouses who feel good about themselves and each other.

Couples who wish to experience a marriage-enrichment program might consider enrolling in one in which the spouses are permitted to question and discuss the ideas and recommendations presented by the leaders of the group. In Marriage Encounter, no such interaction is permitted during the sessions. (Doherty et al., 1986) Spouses should also feel comfortable contacting a therapist after an encounter weekend if they feel worse as a result of the experience.

Trends

The most significant trend regarding communication in marriage is the increased willingness of couples to "go public" with their problems. The realization that it is normal for couples to be faced with problems in their relationships is replacing the old idea that happy couples don't have conflicts. The continuing popularity of marriage-enrichment groups, encounter weekends, and marriage seminars reflects this trend.

A second trend concerns raising the standards that marriage and family therapists must meet. More states are enacting laws to create a classification of "certified marriage therapist" to denote that a counselor has the equivalent training and background required for admission to the American Association for Marriage and Family Therapy. This requires a minimum of a master's degree and specific training in marriage and family therapy, human sexuality, and ethics. Furthermore, the counselor must have conducted 1,500 hours of marriage and family therapy; at least 100 of these hours must be under the supervision of an approved supervisor. The hoped-for result will be a sufficient supply of highly trained and experienced marriage therapists to meet the growing demand for such services.

Summary

Our society perpetuates various myths about marriage. These include the notions that love will keep a couple together, that children increase marital happiness, and that each spouse can fulfill all of the other spouse's needs. A more realistic view of marriage is that love *may* help to keep spouses together, that children *may* improve a marriage, and that spouses will fulfill *some* of each other's needs.

Although being happily married is a major goal of most Americans, there is little agreement on what constitutes happiness. Marital happiness is subjective, constantly changing, and affected by multiple influences. Although marital adjustment may be assessed through the use of various scales, the results are often distorted by the desire of respondents to report a happy marriage whether they have one or not.

Communication is the core of any relationship. It involves the use of words and gestures to convey a message between two people. Productive uses of communication skills in conflict resolution include replacing accusations with neutral statements and sarcasm with positive labeling and not allowing a negative mutual-blame cycle to develop.

Marital conflict can erupt at any time. It is both inevitable and, under certain conditions, desirable. The causes of interpersonal conflict include behavior, perception, and value differences. Black spouses must also contend with discrepancies in education, status, and income. Spouses also develop various styles of conflict—complementary (one dominant, the other submissive); symmetrical (both partners react the same way to each other); and parallel (both partners avoid confronting the problem).

Having a plan to communicate about conflicts is essential. Such a plan includes deciding to address recurring issues rather than suppressing them, asking the partner for help in resolving the issue, finding out the partner's point of view, summarizing in a nonjudgmental way the partner's perspective, brainstorming for alternative solutions, and selecting a plan of action. To the degree that the plan of action includes suggestions made by each partner, the potential for success in resolving the problem is maximized. When we participate in a solution, we are more committed to seeing it work.

Some couples who can't resolve a conflict by themselves contact a marriage therapist. These therapists are not regulated by law in all states, so care should be exercised in selecting one. Also, there are many theoretical approaches; it is important to select a therapist who offers the style of therapy the couple wants. Most spouses report positive outcomes from their involvement in marriage therapy.

Marriage-enrichment programs are for couples who have good marriages and who want to keep them that way. However, some couples do report negative experiences from their involvement in these programs. Although such experiences are rare, couples should be careful about the type of marriage-encounter program they select.

Trends in conflict and communication include an increasing number of couples becoming involved in marriage enrichment or marriage therapy. Ensuring the adequate training of therapists who provide the latter service has become a priority for some state legislatures.

Questions for Reflection

1. How open have you been with your various partners? Do you feel the consequences have been positive or negative?
2. Which style of conflict (complementary, symmetrical, or parallel) tends to be characteristic of you and your partner? What changes can you make to improve your communication?
3. Would you be willing to become involved in marriage enrichment or marriage therapy? Why or why not?

CHOICES

A BASIC CHOICE OF individuals in a relationship is deciding how much of themselves they should share with the other person. After examining how much openness is productive for a relationship, we will consider the question of whether to consult a marriage therapist when relationship conflict becomes unmanageable.

How Much Should You Tell?

GOOD communication often implies open communication, but how much is good for a marital relationship? Does a "we tell each other everything" disclosure philosophy have more positive consequences then a "discreet disclosure" philosophy? One therapist feels that in spite of all the suggestions to "be open" and "let it all hang out," to "jump on the bandwagon for fully uncensored communication is a ride couples should not take" (Stuart, 1980, p. 218).

Adopting a "norm of measured honesty" in a relationship may be advisable for two reasons. First, negative information carries more weight than positive information. When partners disclose negatives, their partners may have difficulty keeping the disclosure in the context of other positives. A minister who said that he and his wife had the pattern of being completely open with each other disclosed:

> One night she told me that she didn't like my beard, which I had become very proud of. After I knew how she felt, I didn't want to kiss her or be near her because of what she had said. I know she loves me but I can't help feeling bad.

In his classic study of marital communication, Bienvenu (1970) found that the one item on his inventory that best discriminated well-communicating couples from poorly communicating couples was a negative answer to the question "Does your spouse have a tendency to say things that would be better left unsaid?"

The second reason for measured honesty is that all relationships may need some illusions to survive. Part of this perfectionistic thinking is that our partner loves and is sexually attracted to only us. When our partner tells us, "I am really attracted to this new person at work," we may appreciate the honesty but feel rejected at the content. The lyrics to an old song, "How many arms have held you, but I really don't want to know," aptly describe this ambivalence.

However, certain items that may be painful to the partner should probably be disclosed—particularly if the partners are dating and considering marriage. These issues include previous marriages and children, a sexual orientation different from what the partner expects, alcohol or drug addiction, having a sexually transmitted disease, such as genital herpes, and any known physical disabilities, such as sterility. Disclosures of this nature include anything that would have a significant impact on the relationship.

Should You Consult a Marriage Therapist?

Most people are reluctant to consult a marriage therapist. Most spouses have been taught that seeing a therapist about personal problems means they are mentally ill. "It's the crazy folks that see those counselors," said one woman. Other spouses feel that their marriage is private and nobody else's business. "You don't talk to strangers about

(Continued)

those kinds of things," said another spouse (Rothman et al., 1985). Still other spouses feel that if couples are really in love with each other, they will be able to work out anything. They assume it is only the people who don't love each other who can't work out their problems.

Each of these beliefs is a myth. Seeing a therapist does not mean that you are mentally ill. On the contrary, we are never more mentally and emotionally healthy than when we can acknowledge that we have a problem and seek help for it.

The fact that marriage is a personal and private affair does not mean we cannot discuss our concern with a specialist. Our bodies are also personal and private, but this does not stop us from seeing a physician when we have a physical problem. Our mental health is as important to our feeling good as is our physical health. Both physicians and marriage therapists can be expected to treat the information we share with them with strict confidentiality. This is required by their code of professional ethics.

Finally, as we have seen earlier in this chapter, love is not enough to ensure the resolution of all conflicts. Two people can love each other intensely and not be able to resolve their conflicts or to live together happily. "We loved each other," said one spouse, "but we just couldn't make a go of it together,"

Signs to look for in your own relationship that suggest you might consider seeing a therapist include feeling distant and not wanting or being able to communicate with your partner, avoiding each other, drinking heavily or taking drugs, privately contemplating separation, being involved in an affair, and feeling depressed.

If you are experiencing one or more of these concerns with your partner, it may be wise not to wait until it reaches a stage beyond which repair is impossible. Relationships are like boats. A small leak will not sink it. But if left unattended, the small leak may grow larger or new leaks may break through. Marriage therapy sometimes serves to mend relationship problems early by helping the partners to sort out values, make decisions, and begin new behaviors so that they can start feeling better about each other.

However, in spite of the potential benefits of marriage therapy, there are some valid reasons for not consulting a counselor.

Not all spouses who become involved in marriage therapy regard the experience positively. Some feel that their marriage is worse as a result. Saying things the spouse can't forget, feeling hopeless at not being able to resolve a problem "even with a counselor," and feeling resentment over new demands made by the spouse in therapy are reasons some spouses cite for negative outcomes. A husband said the result of therapy was that he did more housework because his wife was earning one-half of the income. "Before I came to therapy, I wasn't doing anything at home," he said. "Now I still don't do much but resent it when I do."

Therapists also may give clients an unrealistic picture of loving, cooperative, nonsexist, and growing relationships in which partners always treat each other with respect and understanding, share intimacy, and help each other become whomever each wants to be. Such expectations may encourage clients to focus on the shortcomings in their relationships and to feel discouraged about their marriages (Zilbergeld, 1983).

Impact of Social Influences on Choices

Feeling free to consult a marriage therapist is often related to knowing someone who has done so and who reports that the experience was positive. In the absence of a social learning experience such as this, we are left with the stereotype of lying on a couch while someone asks us about our relationship with our mother. For most of us, the fear of being in a situation like that makes us too anxious to actually call and make the appointment.

One marriage therapist tells couples who ask what they should tell their children about seeing a counselor that it is healthy and productive for children to know that their parents are seeking help for a marriage problem. This communicates to a child not only that married couples have problems but also that they can do something about them by seeing a therapist. The fact that children know that their parents are seeking marriage therapy will make it easier for them to ask for help when they grow up, marry, and must face their own problems.

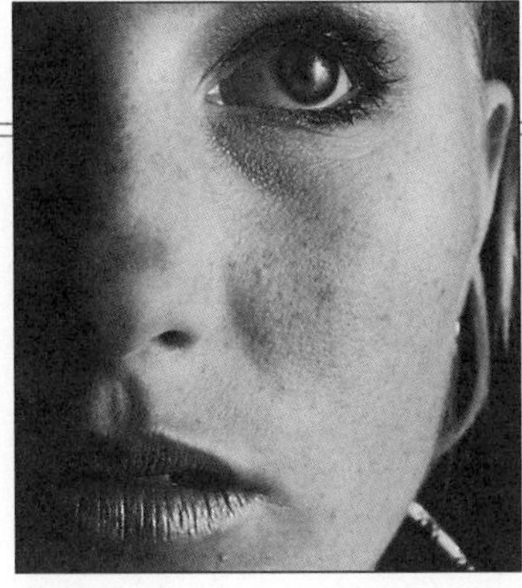

CHAPTER 13

Violence and Abuse

Contents

Is It True?*

1. Females are more likely to be victims of interpersonal violence than males.
2. Most individuals terminate a relationship after abuse occurs.
3. Violence is more prevalent among couples who are married than among couples who live together.
4. Having an abusive husband arrested results in less frequent future abuse.
5. Stepparents are more likely to abuse their stepchildren than biological parents are to abuse their biological children.

*1=T; 2=F; 3=F; 4=T; 5=T.

MOST PEOPLE MARRY for love. But things do not always seem to go right with those we love. Developing and maintaining a positive, enduring, committed relationship takes a great deal of energy and skill.

Although we expect there to be some difficulties in our relationships with those we care about, we are less likely to expect our partners to become violent with us. We may be even more surprised if we become violent toward them. In this chapter, we will examine violence among couples who are dating, living together, and married. We will also look at abuse among family members—parents abusing children, incest, and children abusing parents.

Violence in Dating Relationships

Shakespeare said "The course of true love never did run smooth" (A Midsummer Night's Dream, Act I Scene one). According to the type and amount of violence being expressed in dating relationships, his statement rings true. Violence between dating partners may be categorized as general or sexual.

General Violence

Dating partners sometimes become violent toward each other. *General violence* may be defined as throwing things at each other; hitting each other with objects; pushing, grabbing, and/or shoving each other; or slapping, kicking, biting, and/or punching each other. Notice that both partners are involved in the violence. Rarely is just one partner violent. Also, females seem to both receive and inflict more violence than males.

Data – In a sample of 325 college students, 40 percent of the females reported receiving and inflicting violence on their dating partners. In contrast, 30 percent of the males reported receiving and inflicting violence on their dating partners. (Lane & Gwartney-Gibbs, 1985)

In another study, 30 percent of the women and 25 percent of the men reported ever being victims of courtship violence. (McKinney, 1986)

In a third study, females experienced more violence than males. (Makepeace, 1987)

Violence also occurs in the context of an extended love relationship. Rarely does violence occur when the partners are getting to know each other. The experience of one female student follows:

> We had been engaged two months after a three-year courtship, and the subject came up about one of his old girlfriends. I said some bad things about her that we both knew were true, when all of a sudden he slapped me. I was really shocked because he had always been so gentle. He was shocked too and started crying and saying he didn't know why he did it because he loved me so much.
>
> Five months later he slapped me again. This time it was in front of six guys because I didn't want to go back to his apartment and drink beer. He apologized greatly and begged me not to leave him. I didn't, but I started to examine the wisdom of marrying this guy.
>
> The next four months he slapped me 11 more times, pushed me against a wall four times, and pulled my hair it seemed like 1,000 times. When I suggested that maybe we should break up, he said that since our parents had already spent $11,000 on the wedding I couldn't back out now. When I said, "I don't give a damn about the money," he

> went into a rage and blackened my eye, broke my nose, and fractured my collarbone. That was enough for me, so I broke the engagement. He begged me to take him back, saying he just couldn't live without me, but I didn't. I felt pity for him, and I'm glad I got out while the getting was good.

Violence usually occurs after people become angry. The partners have been arguing over an issue, and one or both of them erupt with a violent act. "She got right in my face and told me I was a liar," said one man. "The next thing I knew, I shoved her across the room and she hit her head on the refrigerator door." In many cases, the combination of alcohol and jealousy are predictive of an abusive event. One student revealed:

> He would always start pouring down the beers when he saw me dance with someone else. Then he would start trouble. First it was verbal, then physical. He would grab me and shove me or push me or yank on me or pull on me or throw me. He only hit me once, but the rest was pretty rough treatment.

Consideration

Because anger (sometimes jealous anger) and alcohol are two precipitating factors in the expression of violent behavior, partners who want to avoid such violence might be sensitive to the combined effects and carefully monitor not only their alcohol intake but also the escalation of their anger (and that of their partner's). By doing so, they can withdraw from each other before the violence erupts. One couple who had had problems with violence in their relationship agreed to withdraw from each other (one partner would leave the apartment) when either of them felt their anger had climbed above a level of 3 on a 10–point scale. If arguments over drinking alcohol are frequent, treatment by a substance-abuse counselor may be indicated. In some individuals, alcohol often creates the context for violence.

Once abuse occurs, it is not unusual for it to recur. When the abuse happens after the partners have become emotionally as well as sexually involved, the partners are less likely to view it as a reason for terminating the relationship.

Nothing multiplies more easily than force.
—Norman Cousins

Why do partners who experience abuse in a relationship stay together? Some stay because they see the violence as only a small part of the relationship. One woman said:

> Even though he slapped me around a lot, I never left him because when he wasn't hurting me he was so gentle and sweet. He would tell me that he loved me and that I was the only one in the world that really understood him. Besides, he never *really* hurt me, always told me he was sorry, and was good to me right after the violence.

Others continue the relationship because there is no perceived alternative. "If I leave him because he's rough with me now and then," said one woman, "I don't know what I would do. He's such a part of my world that I can't imagine life without him." Still others stay because they label the abusive acts as expressions of love. Much like children who were told when they were about to be punished, "I'm doing this because I love you; it hurts me more than you," so the dating partner interprets the violent acts as those only a person who loves him or her would engage in.

Some partners remain in an abusive relationship because they perceive violence to be a legitimate part of an intimate relationship. This is particularly

Anger sometimes leads to violence.

true if they grew up in homes in which their parents, whom they viewed as loving each other, abused each other. One person in an abusive relationship said:

> I grew up watching my dad get drunk and hit on my mother. I don't think it's right to hit a woman, but it happens and it's not the end of the world. Folks who live together are bound to hit each other sometime.

Finally, some courtship partners may continue a relationship after they have been abused because they feel they deserve such abuse ("I deserve to be pushed around and beaten; I'm no good") or they caused the abuse ("It was my fault he got angry and beat me . . . I was just asking for it"). Those who use this rationale for continuing to subject themselves to abuse often have negative self-concepts, which receive an additional blow with each violent episode. This inability to move away from an abusive relationship also suggests that some people are extremely psychologically dependent and will stay with an abuser rather than be alone.

Consideration

If you have experienced violence in the relationship with your dating partner, be aware that such expressions are likely to become a pattern in your relationship. Couples who do not make a conscious attempt to stop such violence are making an unwritten agreement that such behavior is going to be tolerated in their relationship. The Partner Abuse Scale in the Self-Assessment exercise is designed to help you predict the possibility of abuse becoming a part of your current relationship.

Self-Assessment

Partner Abuse Scale

This scale is designed to predict the potential for violence and abuse in your current relationship. There are no right or wrong answers. After reading each sentence carefully, circle the appropriate number:

1 Never
2 Rarely
3 Occasionally
4 Frequently
5 Very frequently

	N	R	O	F	VF
1. I get irritated easily.	1	2	3	4	5
2. At least one of my parents was abusive to the other.	1	2	3	4	5
3. I was abused as a child.	1	2	3	4	5
4. I have had the urge to hit my partner.	1	2	3	4	5
5. I sometimes feel out of control.	1	2	3	4	5
6. I am under a lot of pressure most of the time.	1	2	3	4	5
7. I drink a lot of alcohol.	1	2	3	4	5
8. I lose my temper when I drink.	1	2	3	4	5
9. I have felt the impulse to strike my partner.	1	2	3	4	5
10. It is hard for me to control my temper.	1	2	3	4	5

Scoring: Add the numbers you circled. 1 (never) represents the lowest probability for potential abuse; 5 (very frequently) represents the highest probability for potential abuse. The lower your total score (10 is the lowest possible score), the lower the chance of abuse in your relationship; the higher your total score (50 is the highest possible score), the higher the chance of abuse in your relationship. A score of 30 places you at the midpoint between a nonabusive and an abusive relationship.

SEXUAL VIOLENCE

Sometimes general violence leads to *sexual violence.* One female student said:

> I once dated a guy I was very much in love with. Our pattern was that when we argued about something, he would get real mad and slap me around. I would cry and he would beat me harder, and my crying would get him sexually aroused and he would want to make love.

Sexual aggression occurs when a person persists in forceful attempts to achieve a sexual goal, even though these actions are disagreeable and offensive to the other person. As noted in Chapter 6, "unwanted pressure to engage in sexual behavior" was the most frequent problem encountered on dates by a group of female university respondents (Knox & Wilson, 1983).

Sometimes sexual aggression toward women goes beyond forceful attempts and becomes rape. Such rapes are known as "acquaintance rapes" or "date rapes," because the rapist is someone the woman knows.

Data – Out of 325 undergraduate women in a northwestern university, 24 percent said they had had intercourse when they did not want to as a result of being pressured by continued arguments. (Lane and Gwartney-Gibbs, 1985)

One student described the experience of being raped by her boyfriend:

> Last spring, I met this boy and a relationship started, which was great. One year later, he raped me. The term was almost over, and we would not be able to spend much time together during the summer. So we decided to go out to eat and spend some time together.
>
> After dinner we drove to a park. I did not mind nor suspect anything, for we had done this many times. Then he asked me into the back seat. I got into the back seat with him because I trusted him and he said he wanted to be close to me as we talked.
>
> He began talking. He told me he was tired of always pleasing me and not getting a reward. Therefore, he was going to "make love to me" whether I wanted to or not. I thought he was joking so I asked him to stop playing. He told me he was serious, and after looking at him closely, I knew he was serious.
>
> I began to plead with him not to have sex with me. He did not listen. He began to tear my clothes off and confine me so that I could not move. All this time I was fighting him. At one time, I managed to open the door, but he threw me back into the seat, hit me, then he got on me and raped me. After he was satisfied, he stopped, told me to get dressed and to stop crying. He said he was sorry it had to happen that way.
>
> He brought me back to the dorm and expected me to kiss him good night. He didn't think he had done anything wrong.
>
> Before this happened, I loved him very much, but afterward, I felt great hatred for him. I wished that I had the courage to kill him.
>
> My life has not been the same since that night. I do not trust men as I once did, nor do I feel completely comfortable when I'm alone at night with my present boyfriend. Also my present boyfriend wants to know why I back off when he tries to be intimate with me. I can't tell him because he knows the guy who raped me.

The characteristics of men who force women they date to have sex include a background of being abused when they were growing up. Such abuse teaches a person to associate violence and intimate relationships. "It's okay to take sex from someone you love," said one man. Men also tend to deny and minimize the intensity of their abuse (Makepeace, 1986).

Acquaintance rapists also tend to believe certain myths about rape, female sexuality, legitimate victims, and male supremacy (Wilson & Faison, 1983; Lewin, 1985). For example, believing that rapists are strangers absolves the boyfriend from labeling himself as a rapist. He views his attempts at sexual intercourse as a natural part of the dating situation. Because female sexuality is often defined as passive and unresponsive, the boyfriend may see male aggressiveness as a necessary part of a sexual encounter. Further, legitimate victims for sexual aggression are women who deserve to be raped (so the myth goes) because they advertise their sexual availability by, say, going to a bar to pick up a man and then putting limits on the sexual relationship. "These women are really advertising lettuce [sex] but selling cabbage [date me awhile] and deserve what they get," said one man. By viewing the woman and his actions in this way, the man may feel he has done nothing wrong.

The ideology of male supremacy is also operative in date rape. One researcher (Lewin, 1985) observes:

> The ancient but flourishing ideology of male supremacy looks at sex as a relationship in which the man demonstrates his superiority and dominance by persuading the woman to agree and she demonstrates her inferiority, submission, and defeat by agreeing. This macho attitude finds voice in expressions such as, "He's putting another notch in his belt," "He's going to score," and "scalp hunting," as well as in the many euphemisms for sex which mean, "I took the female sexual role—that is, I was exploited, ill-used, or cheated." Of course, insofar as either partner accepts this belief, intercourse must be at least in part unwanted by the woman, who naturally does not wish to feel, or to be thought of as, defeated, exploited, or scalped. Men and women are still largely reared under the perhaps silent but influential societal ideology of male supremacy. It's harder to say no to a higher-status person. It's easier to be assertive with a subordinate. (pp. 190–191)

Violence in Living-Together Relationships

Violence may also occur between partners who live together.

Data – In a study comparing the violence of singles, cohabitants, and marrieds, cohabitants were more likely to experience and inflict violence than either singles or marrieds. (Lane & Gwartney-Gibbs, 1985)

One explanation for the greater violence among cohabitors is the lack of security in such relationships. Spouses have made a legal commitment to each other; singles don't expect much commitment from their dating partners. But cohabitors are in limbo. And when a partner is late or evidences interest in another relationship, jealousy, anger, and violence can follow. Alcohol and drug use also seems to be higher among cohabitors. They have reported being either drunk or stoned and having intercourse unknowingly more often than either singles or marrieds (Lane & Gwartney-Gibbs, 1985).

Violence in Marriage Relationships

The group to which most people look for love and gentleness is also the most violent civilian group in our society.
—Murray Straus

Violence also occurs in marriage.

Data – It is estimated that close to 2 million wives are beaten by their spouses each year. In families where beatings occur, over 50 percent of the husbands beat their wives three or more times per year. (Edelson et al., 1985)

Wives in second marriages are twice as likely to be abused as wives in first marriages. (Kalmuss & Seltzer, 1986)

Husbands tend to see relationships as mutually violent, whereas wives see relationships as husband-violent. (Browning & Dutton, 1986)

One wife said:

> My husband was usually violent toward me after he'd been out drinking with "the boys." When he got home, a simple "hello" would often trigger it. He'd start out yelling at me, and then slapping, punching, or kicking me, depending on his mood. On two different occasions, I ended up with broken bones.
>
> After the violence he was always very apologetic and swore he'd never do it again . . . but he always did.

The issues over which spouses argue and become violent can be anything. Jealousy, alcohol, money, children, and drugs were the top issues that triggered violence, according to 82 women who had been battered by their husbands (Roscoe & Benaske, 1985).

Violence can be psychological as well as physical. One woman said that she lived under constant fear that her husband was going to beat her. "Out of nowhere, he would come up and whop me," she said. Another woman said that her husband told her:

> . . . if I didn't do like I was supposed to, he'd see to it that I got punished, but I was never sure what I was "supposed" to do. He'd want his eggs one way one day and another way the next. I was a bundle of nerves.

Understanding Violence

It seems ironic that those individuals who care about each other are also the most likely to physically hurt each other. Why do people in marriage relationships behave violently toward each other?

Previous Family Learning

As noted earlier, being a participant in or an observer of violence in the home in which one was reared is associated with being violent toward one's own partner. "I grew up watching my dad slap my mother around," said one man. "And he beat on me a few times, too." In a study of more than 2,000 spouses, having observed hitting between one's parents was more strongly related to severe marital aggression than being hit as a teenager by one's parents, although both were factors (Kalmuss, 1984). This cycle of violence in which children observe, experience, and inflict violence in their own adult relationships is sometimes difficult to stop, as each generation tends to learn from the preceding one.

Low Self-Esteem

When 20 abusive husbands were compared with nonabusive husbands in both happy and unhappy marriages, the abusive husbands had lower self-esteem. Whether low self-esteem is a cause or an effect of spouse abuse is unknown. However, abusive husbands also reported that they viewed their wives as threatening to their self-esteem (Goldstein & Rosenbaum, 1985).

Argument is the worst sort of conversation.
—Jonathan Swift

Displacement of Tension

Sometimes being violent may have nothing to do with winning an argument or getting one's way. Rather, the partner may feel frustrated by unemployment or limited income, irritated by the bickering of children in a crowded house, or angered by the harassment of his or her boss. Any of these factors can produce a feeling of anxious tension, which is released on the spouse out of displacement (discussed in Chapter 12). The spouse may be blamed for the partner's unhappy, frustrated feelings, and the partner may see violence toward the spouse as a way of getting back.

Reinforcement of Violence

The law of *reinforcement* states that any behavior followed by a reward will increase the frequency of that behavior in the future. When spouses get their way as a result of being violent, the odds increase that they will use violence in the future. "I've found that I can control my wife by beating her up now and then," said one husband. "She's due for another licking soon."

No Referee

Marriage is private; there are no referees to intervene in cases of an escalating conflict. Spouses are judged to be in control of their own relationships without interference from the state. But this freedom is sometimes taken to an extreme; in some cases, the marriage license is regarded as a hitting license.

Violence in Society

Social models for violence on television and in movies create a norm of violence in our society.

> *Data* – Out of 1,600 television programs analyzed, 80 percent contained violence. (Matthews & Ellis, 1985)

When violence occurs in the home, our legal system—for the most part—looks the other way. Not only are the police reluctant to arrest a husband when the wife says he has abused her (police prefer to stay out of what they call "domestic trouble"), but when they do arrest him, he can be free to go home within one hour. It is extremely rare for a husband to be arrested, tried, found guilty, and sentenced to jail on the charge of assault and battery of his wife.

Rape in Marriage

Violence in marriage sometimes includes rape.

> *Data* – Of a random sample of 644 married women in San Francisco, 14 percent reported they had been sexually assaulted by their husbands. (Russell, 1982)

In the scale of the destinies, brawn will never weigh as much as brain.
—James Russell Lowell

Sexual assault may have included not only intercourse but also other types of sexual activities in which the wife did not want to engage, most often fellatio and anal intercourse.

Two researchers have identified several types of marital rape (Finkelhor & Yllo, 1983).

Battering Rape

These rapes occur in the context of a regular pattern of verbal and physical abuse. The husbands yell at their wives, call them names, slap, shove, and beat them. These husbands are angry, belligerent, and frequent alcohol abusers. An example follows:

> One afternoon she came home from school, changed into a housecoat, and started toward the bathroom. He got up from the couch where he had been lying, grabbed her, and pushed her down on the floor. With her face pressed into a pillow and his hand clamped over her mouth, he proceeded to have anal intercourse with her. She screamed and struggled to no avail. Her injuries were painful and extensive. She had a torn muscle in her rectum, so that for three months she had to go to the bathroom standing up. (p. 123)

Nonbattering Rape

These rapes occur in response to a long-standing conflict or disagreement about sex. The violence is not generalized to the rest of the relationship but specific to the sexual conflict. An example follows:

> Their love-making on this occasion started out pleasantly enough, but he tried to get her to have anal intercourse with him. She refused. He persisted. She kicked and pushed him away. Still, he persisted. They ended up having vaginal intercourse. The force he used was mostly that of his weight on top of her. At 220 pounds, he weighs twice as much as she. "It was horrible," she said. She was sick to her stomach afterward. She cried and felt angry and disgusted. He showed little guilt. "He felt like he'd won something." (p. 124)

Obsessive Rape

These rapes may also be categorized as bizzare. The woman is used as a sex object to satisfy an atypical need of the husband. An example follows:

> "I was really his masturbating machine," one woman recalled. He was very rough sexually and would hold a pillow over her face to stifle her screams. He would also tie her up and insert objects into her vagina and take pictures, which he shared with his friends. The interviewee later discovered a file card in her husband's desk which sickened her. On the card, he had written a list of dates—dates that corresponded to the forced sex episodes of the past months. Next to each date was a complicated coding system which seemed to indicate the type of sex act and a ranking of how much he enjoyed it. (pp. 124–125)

Impact of Marital Rape

Being raped by a husband can be more devastating than being attacked by a stranger. The primary effect is to destroy the woman's ability to trust a man in an intimate interpersonal relationship. In addition, the woman raped by her husband lives with her rapist and may be subjected to repeated assaults. Most of the women in the preceding study were raped on multiple occasions.

Consideration

The law is little help to most women who are raped by their husbands. In 36 of the 50 states and the District of Columbia, the law does not consider a situation in which a husband forces his wife to have intercourse to be rape. Historically, the penalties for rape were based on property-right laws designed to protect a man's property (wife or daughter) from forcible rape by other men. A husband "taking" his own property was not considered rape. Changing such laws has been opposed on the premise that there would be a rash of fabricated complaints.

Why Wives Stay Married to Husbands Who Rape and Abuse Them

Many wives who are raped by their husbands do not put up much of a fight. Some feel that it would not do any good no matter how hard they resisted because their husbands are bigger and stronger. In addition, some wives feel that if they resisted, their husbands would hurt them even more:

> I tried once to fight back, and he really flipped out and beat me worse than ever. He told me if I ever tried that again, he'd kill me. I never tried again. I believe he would.

Still other women feel they are to blame for their husbands' anger or frustration. "I've put him off so long, I guess men just go crazy when they don't have sex." Related to these reasons is that the women believe that they have no alternative—no place to go, nobody to go to. With no options, they take the view of "appeasement rather than massive resistance" (Finkelhor & Yllo, 1983, p. 126).

Furthermore, women (particularly those with young children) who do not have employment outside the home and who are not economically independent are more constrained to put up with their husbands' abusive behavior. The patriarchal structure of traditional, one-income marriages also helps to perpetuate the continued abuse of wives. Finally, wives who have remained married for several years because they feel committed to make the marriage work "no matter what" are likely to continue to stay in the relationship (Strube & Barbour, 1983). One woman who was abused weekly by her partner said, "I have always felt that 'you just don't get divorced.'"

He [Ike] tortured me with phones, shoes, and coat hangers.
—Tina Turner

Help for Spouse Abuse

Consideration

Wives who are abused by their husbands should consider calling the police and having their husbands arrested. Although there is the risk of making the husband angrier, there is some evidence that husbands may be less likely to be abusive if they know their wives will have them arrested if they are. Another alternative is to consider terminating the relationship if the spouse will not become involved in marriage therapy.

A study conducted by the Minneapolis Police Department revealed that of 314 cases in which the police were called because the husband was abusing the wife, arresting the husband was associated with fewer repeated incidences of spouse abuse than counseling both parties on the spot or separation (having the husband leave the residence for at least eight hours).

Data – Of the 314 men arrested by the Minneapolis Police Department for wife beating, 10 percent repeated the offense within six months, compared to 24 percent of those who were required to leave the residence for eight hours and 19 percent of those who were counseled by the officers. (Sherman & Berk, 1984)

Most of the wives who do decide to leave their abusing husbands go to their parents or relatives, an apartment of their own, a motel or car, or just wander. The fewest number go to shelters for battered women, which are available in more than 700 communities to furnish protection from further violence. These shelters provide individual assistance to help the woman decide what to do and give her a safe place to stay in the meantime. However, in some cases, by going to a shelter, the wife may inadvertently encourage retaliation on the part of the husband (Berk et al., 1986).

Child Abuse

Violence between parents and their children and between children and their parents is another abuse pattern. Such abuse, although often physical, may also include neglect.

Child abuse may be defined as any interaction or lack of interaction between a child and his or her parents or caregiver that results in nonaccidental harm to the child's physical or developmental well-being. The definition includes what a parent may do (beat, burn, scald) and may fail to do (feed the child, provide a caretaker for a young child, take the child to the doctor) to either bring physical harm to the child or negatively affect the child's development. The parents who refuse to take their ill and suffering children to the doctor are just as guilty of child abuse and neglect as the parents who poison their infant by

Child pornography is a hidden form of child abuse.

putting arsenic into the baby bottle. The number of abused children is staggering.

> *Data* – Estimates of child abuse occurring each year vary from 200,000 to 4 million cases. (Garbarino, 1986) In recent years, cases of reported child abuse have decreased. (Straus & Gelles, 1986)

There are twice as many cases of child neglect than of child abuse. Mothers are somewhat more likely to neglect their children; fathers, to abuse them. The children are most often normal (for example, not retarded, emotionally disturbed, or physically handicapped) and require some form of treatment for bruises, welts, lacerations, burns, and bone fractures in about 20 percent of the cases. In about 5 percent of the cases, skull fracture, bleeding within the skull, and severe burns require hospitalization. The long-term consequences for the child may be devastating—brain damage, mental retardation (as a result of improper nutrition), and physical deformities have been documented. In one study, 21 out of 134 battered children died (Smith & Hansen, 1983).

Characteristics of Child Abusers

Some research suggests that the less income and education parents have, the greater the chance that they will abuse and neglect their children. Being black has also been associated with higher incidences of child maltreatment (Downing, 1982). Other researchers have found income, education, and racial background to be unreliable predictors of child abuse (Schumm et al., 1982). For example, when blacks and whites of similar income were compared, the differences in child maltreatment were very small (Garbarino & Ebata, 1983). In addition, middle- and upper-class families are more able to hide abuse from professionals.

However, some factors are predictive of child abuse and include the following (Oates et al., 1983; Krugman et al., 1986):

1. The pregnancy is unplanned, and the father does not want the child.
2. The birth is complicated and unpleasant.
3. Mother-infant bonding is lacking.
4. Childrearing techniques are strict and harsh and include little positive reinforcement for the child.
5. The child is compared unfavorably with other children, and the parents have an unhappy relationship.
6. The parents are unemployed.

Causes of Child Abuse

There is little agreement on the cause or causes of child abuse. The best explanations point to a number of variables that, in combination, offer an explanation for some cases of child abuse.

Parent Psychopathology

Child abuse has been associated with parents who are anger-prone, rigid and domineering, and dependent on alcohol or drugs and who have low self-esteem and difficulty with self-control and handling stress (Burgess & Garbarino, 1983; Engfer & Schneewind, 1982). According to one social worker who specializes in child abuse:

> "Child abusers tend to get violently angry quickly." And they act on their impulses without thinking about what they are doing. All parents, whether they admit it or not, have had the urge to hit or harm their child in some way. What separates the nonabusers from the abusers is the ability to stop their impulses before they hurt the child.

Parents Modeling on Abusive Parents

Parents who were themselves abused or the victims of harsh physical punishment tend to duplicate these patterns in their own families (Herrenkohl et al., 1983). One father said:

> My father beat on me as long as I can remember. And for no reason at all. One time, it was because I walked over a newspaper in the living room and didn't pick it up. He got up from the couch and shoved me against the wall while yelling obscenities at me. Then he proceeded to sock me with his fists. He did that for years until I was finally old enough to leave home. I never want to go back. But when I had my own kids, I noticed that I had the impulse to do like my dad. I am able to control it most of the time, but at other times, it gets the best of me.

Displacement of Aggression

One cartoon shows several panels consisting of a boss yelling at his employee, the employee yelling at his wife, the wife yelling at their child, and the child kicking the dog who chases the cat up a tree. Some child abuse can be explained by our social norm that the strong dominate the weak. Both genders displace their anger. Of women's aggression, Washburne (1983) observes, "Women's abuse of children stems directly from their own oppression in society and within the family. . . . some women displace their frustration and anger on their children, the family members who are less powerful than they" (p. 291).

Parental Isolation

Unlike most societies of the world, we rear our children in closed and isolated nuclear units. In extended kinship societies, other relatives are always present to help with the task of childrearing. Our isolation means that there is no relief from the parenting role as well as no supervision by others who might interfere in child-abusing situations. One father who stayed with his 2–year-old all day when his wife was in the hospital having another child said, "I've never been so frustrated and will be glad to get back to work. Being with a kid all day is horrendous."

The Stepparenting Factor

Children are much more likely to be abused if they are being reared in a home where there is a stepparent.

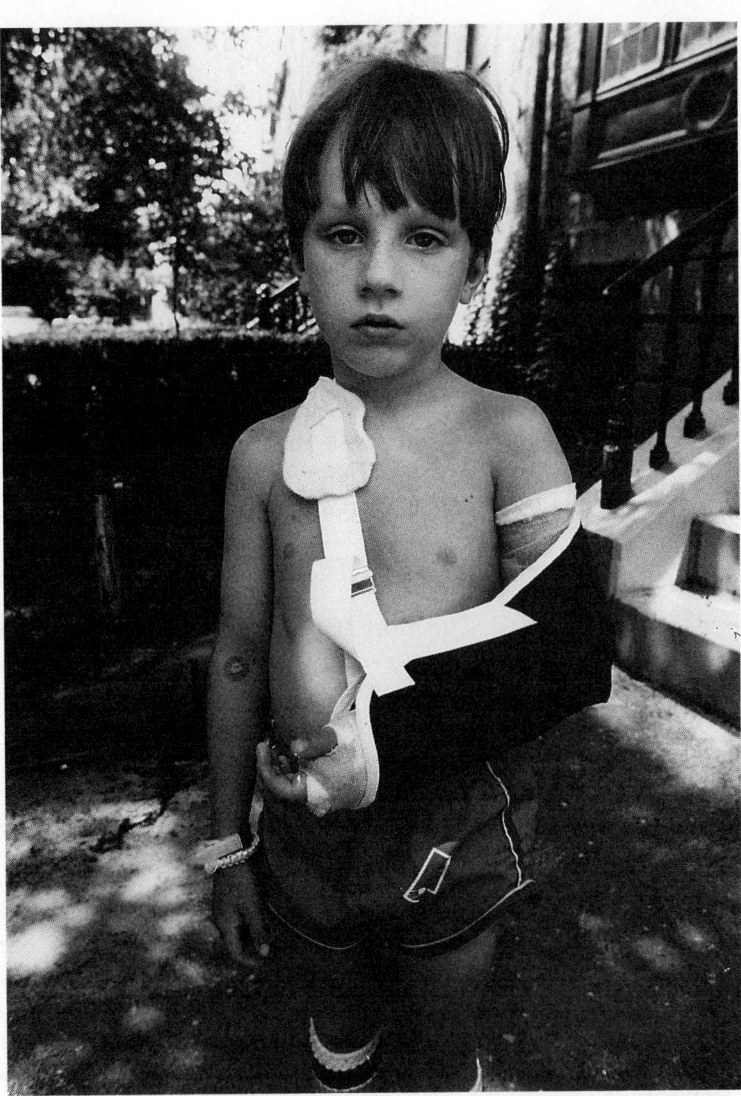

Children are often helpless victims of parental aggression.

Data – In one study, preschoolers living with one natural and one stepparent were 40 times more likely to become child-abuse cases than were like-aged children living with two natural parents. (Daly & Wilson, 1985)

The researchers suggest that because stepparents do not have a biological tie with their stepchildren, they are less tolerant and altruistic toward them. This lack of tolerance, when coupled with stress in the marital and parental relationship, often results in abuse (Daly & Wilson, 1985).

Consideration

No single factor is likely to result in child abuse, but several factors in combination do increase the likelihood of child abuse or neglect. An unemployed, alcoholic, stepparent with four stepchildren who was abused as a child is much more likely to abuse her or his stepchildren than an employed, chemically free, first-time married natural parent with one child who was not abused as a child.

Agency Response to Child Abuse

Social worker Patricia Capps has furnished the following information on how one state (North Carolina) responds to reported child abuse. Child abuse is normally discovered by a school counselor, neighbor, or physician who calls the local social service department, which is responsible for investigating the abuse. A social worker is required by law to visit the home of the alleged abused child within 24 hours if the abuse is physical and within 48 hours if the abuse is neglect. Parental response to these visits ranges from denial ("What are you talking about?") to anger ("Get off my porch!") to apology ("We're sorry it happened"). If the parents are cooperative, the caseworker discusses the nature and context of the abuse and ways to prevent it from recurring. Weekly visits are then made by the social worker to ensure that the abuse or neglect has been eliminated. If the parents are not cooperative, the social worker gets a court order to remove the child from the home temporarily. In rare cases, the child is placed in a foster home.

Treatment for the Child Abuser

Behavior is learned. The most effective way to treat child abuse is to train parents to behave more appropriately with their children. Several clinicians have observed that the best setting for such learning may be small groups of parents that meet for eight sessions twice weekly to examine self-control, alternative actions, and effective childrearing procedures (Barth et al., 1983).

Self-Control

Parents are shown a videotape of parental reactions to a child spilling milk. In one scene the reaction is volatile; in the other, self-controlled. After the first scene, parents identify factors that may have made the parent vulnerable to abuse—fatigue, frustration over work, hunger, and impending illness. The second tape shows the parent talking aloud to herself or himself to identify these factors and "recognize his vulnerability to provocation" (p. 317). After the child's accident, the parent stops, takes a deep breath, and consciously responds appropriately. After the video demonstration, first the group leader and then the members assume parent and child roles. "Initially guided by the script, then progressively without prompts, group members rehearse the use of self-talk, impulse delay, and relaxation to the 'spilled milk' situation" (p. 317).

Alternative Reactions

Group leaders and parents determine alternative behaviors to expressing anger aggressively—telephoning another parent, vacuuming the house, doing aerobic exercises, or looking in the mirror while smiling and saying positive things. Parents learn to yell "stop" subvocally and to engage in one of these behaviors overtly instead. An additional alternative is for parents to relax by means of deep-breathing exercises and tranquil fantasies.

Childrearing Procedures

Harsh physical punishment has negative consequences for children and their parents. It teaches children to fear and sometimes to hate their parents.

Although punishment may be effective in suppressing behavior temporarily, it does not teach the child appropriate behavior.

Positive reinforcement and time out are two alternative techniques parents can use to encourage the behavior they want in their children. "Catch the child doing good" and praise him or her—thus reinforcing positive behavior—rather than waiting until he or she drifts into expressing negative behavior that angers the parent. Parents are encouraged to systematically praise and compliment their children every day whenever the parents approve of the things their children do.

"Time out," also known as "time out from reinforcement," is an effective way of punishing children for negative behavior that avoids long-term negative consequences for the parent-child relationship. When the child misbehaves, the parent instructs the child to go to an isolated place in the home (for example, the bathroom) for about five minutes. Children usually do not like "time out;" it mildly punishes the behavior they were engaging in, so that the behavior is less likely to recur.

Consideration

If abusing parents learned self-control skills, alternatives to aggression, and "time out" as a childrearing tool, the problem of child abuse would be reduced. However, for any treatment program to be effective, the abusing parents must be motivated. One factor that predicts motivation for therapy is the degree to which parents are emotionally bonded with their children.

Prevention of Child Abuse

The ultimate solution to child abuse and neglect is the early socialization of parents. Three steps can be taken to execute this solution. First, educate the public, through the mass media, that child abuse and neglect do occur and that these behaviors are unacceptable. Second, provide community adult-education programs on marriage and family relationships, including interpersonal communication, coping with stress, and parent skills training. More one-on-one training might involve a health visitor program at home for *all* new parents for one to two years after the birth of their firstborn (Helfer, 1982). Such a program would be particularly valuable for new parents who were abused by their parents. Unless this high-risk group learns alternative ways of relating to infants and children, the cycle of abuse is likely to continue. Three, provide quality, low-cost day care to help alleviate adult stress in reference to rearing children.

For young parents who discover they are abusive, Parents Anonymous (6733 South Sepulveda Blvd. Suite 270; Los Angeles, CA 90045; 800–421–0353) is a national organization with 1,500 local chapters that will provide immediate help and support.

Incest

A variation of child abuse is incest. *Incest* is defined as sexual relations between close relatives, such as father and daughter, mother and son, and brother and sister. Although "sexual relations" may imply intercourse, it may also include fondling of the breasts and genitals and oral sex. "Relatives" usually implies biologically related individuals but may also include stepparents and stepsiblings. Sexual abuse is not unusual.

Data – As children, at least 25 percent of all women and 10 percent of all men in America have experienced some abuse, ranging from sexual fondling to intercourse. (Kohn, 1987)

Incest, particularly parent–child incest, is an abuse of power and authority. It is usually coercive and is therefore considered a form of family violence. A child is not in a position to consent to a sex act instigated by an adult. The experience of a black woman who, as a child, was forced to have sexual relations with her father is described here:

> I was around 6 years old when I was sexually abused by my father. He was not drinking at that time; therefore, he had a clear mind as to what he was doing. On looking back, it seemed so well planned. For some reason, my father wanted me to go with him to the woods behind our house to help him saw wood for the night. I went without any question. Once we got there, he looked around for a place to sit and wanted me to sit down with him. In doing so, he said, "Susan, I want you to do something for daddy." I said, "What's that daddy?" He went on to explain that "I want you to lie down, and we are going to play mama and daddy." Being a child, I said "okay," thinking it was going to be fun. I don't know what happened next because I can't remember if there was pain or whatever. I was threatened not to tell, and remembering how he beat my mother, I didn't want the same treatment. It happened approximately two other times. I remember not liking this at all. Since I couldn't tell mama, I came to the conclusion it was wrong and I was not going to let it happen again.
>
> But what could I do? Until age 18, I was constantly on the run, hiding from him when I had to stay home alone with him, staying out of his way so he wouldn't touch me by hiding in the corn fields all day long, under the house, in the barns, and so on, until my mother got back home, then getting punished by her for not doing the chores she had assigned to me that day. It was a miserable life growing up in that environment.

Although white women are sexually abused, too, it is not as unusual for a black woman to have had this kind of experience during her childhood.

Data – In a study of 60 sexually abusive families, 95 percent of the victims were female, 65 percent of the victims were black, and 80 percent of the offenders were the significant male in the household. (Estroff, 1986)

Father–Daughter Incest

Father–daughter incest has received the most attention in our society. Unlike the experience of the 6-year-old girl just described, incest may begin by affectionate cuddling between father and daughter. The father's motives may be sexual; his daughter's are typically nonsexual. More often, the daughter is innocent of the sexual connotations of her behavior; her motive is to feel acceptance and love from her father. Ambivalent feelings often result:

> My daddy never touched me unless he wanted to have me play with his genitals. I didn't like touching him there, but he was affectionate to me and told me how pretty I was. I was really mixed up about the whole thing.

Because of her ambivalence, the daughter may continue to participate in sexual activity with her father. Not only may she derive attention and affection from the relationship, but also she may develop a sense of power over her father. As she grows older, she may even demand gifts as the price of her silence. If her parents have an unhappy relationship (this is usually the case), she may enjoy her role as the "little wife." Father–daughter incest is rare.

Data – Only 1 percent of all adult women in five large cities reported sexual involvement with their natural father or stepfather. (Cameron et al., 1986)

Father–daughter incest may begin by force. There are a few cases of fathers having raped their daughters when they were very small—even as babies—injuring them badly. Baby incest is difficult for the wife to overlook, but she may sanction the sexual relations of her husband and her older daughter in her desire to preserve the family unit. One woman said that her "nerves" were about to "snap" because her husband and daughter were having sex. But she did not say anything about it because if she did, her husband, on whom she depended economically, might leave her alone with the children. "At least," she said, "his playing around is kept in the family."

What does the mother do when she finds out her husband has been molesting their daughter?

Data – In a study of 43 mothers whose daughters were sexually abused by their fathers, 56 percent sided with their daughters and rejected their mates, 9 percent denied the incest and took no action, and 35 percent sided with their mates at the expense of their daughters. (Myer, 1985)

Mother–Son Incest

Incest between mothers and sons occurs less frequently than father–daughter incest. It rarely includes intercourse but is usually confined to various stimulating behaviors. The mother may continue to bathe her son long after he is capable of caring for himself, during which time she stimulates him sexually. Later, she may stimulate her son to ejaculation.

The mother may also sleep with her son. Although no specific sexual contact may occur, she may sleep in the nude; this behavior is provocative as well as stimulating. In some cases, there is sexual contact; one mother had intercourse with her son two to three times a week from the time he was 13 until he left for college (Sarrel & Masters, 1982).

Brother–Sister Incest

One of the most common and least visible forms of incest occurs between siblings. Siblings are peers. Their incest may seem natural to them, and they may wonder why there is a taboo against it.

Whether brother–sister incest is a problem for siblings depends on a number of factors. If the siblings are young, of the same age, have an isolated sexual episode, engage only in exploratory, nonintercourse behavior, and both consent to the behavior, there may be little to no harm. But a change in any of these factors increases the chance that such incest will have negative consequences for future relationships.

If the siblings are young (age 4 to 8), they will have had less exposure to the idea that sexual behavior among siblings is inappropriate. Although they may have vague feelings that their parents would not approve of their sexual behavior, they will probably not feel the guilt usually associated with such behavior. As they grow older, they may relabel their former behavior as "child's play" to offset its impact.

Being of the same age will minimize the negative consequences of sibling incest. Although in most cases the siblings are of the same age, it is not uncommon for an older brother to seduce his younger sister into having intercourse with him. It is less common for an older sister to become sexually involved with a younger brother. A difference in age increases the chance that the sexual relationship will be exploitive.

A childhood sexual experience with a sibling that occurs once or twice is also less consequential than a series of such experiences that takes place over a number of years. Most incestuous experiences are limited, but some develop into a pattern and continue for years.

The nature of the sexual behavior is also important. Playing doctor, strip poker, or "you show me; I'll show you" probably has minimal impact on siblings. Siblings learn that these are common childhood experiences. But intercourse may increase the potential for negative effects.

Data – In one study, 18 percent of the brother–sister incest experiences in which the siblings were over the age of 13 involved intercourse. Half of the reactions to the experiences were positive; half were negative. (Finkelhor, 1980)

Consent is important if the negative consequences are to be minimal. Particularly when one sibling is older than the other, a brother or sister may use blackmail, bribery, or force to get the sibling to comply, as in the case of Jim, age 15, and his sister, Michelle, age 12:

> Michelle had stolen money from her mother to buy some marijuana. Jim threatened to tell their mother if Michelle did not let him fondle her when she was naked. After Michelle consented, Jim threatened her repeatedly over a period of three years. The parents never knew.

Impact of Incest

Since incest has become a more visible subject in the media, adult women who were sexually abused as children have begun to seek help. Their doing so has allowed researchers to become aware of the impact of incest years later. Although incest victims who do not seek help at mental-health centers may not have problems related to their incestuous experiences, in one study of 22 victims who sought help at a mental-health center, the researchers (Jehu et al., 1985) observed:

> Over three-quarters of these women appear to experience low self-esteem, guilt, and depression. Suicidal attempts and substance abuse are also likely to be prevalent in this client group. A similar proportion of the women have difficulties in their relationships with people generally and with men specifically. Those who are in a current partnership with a man report an even higher incidence of discord . . .. At least half the clients complain of some impairment in their sexual functioning. (p. 43)

Two other researchers reviewed the impact of child sexual abuse and concluded that the most negative consequences occur when the abuse is from the father in the form of forced genital contact (Browne & Finkelhor, 1986).

Consideration

> If you have been the victim of sexual abuse (particularly forced genital contact by your father) and the event or events have resulted in thoughts of suicide, drug abuse, or low self-esteem, you might contact your local mental-health center and schedule an appointment with a therapist to discuss these issues. To keep the feelings inside of you may be destructive.

Men may become impotent as a consequence of intimate, quasisexual relationships with their mothers. Having been confronted with a sexually inappropriate stimulus, they had to learn to turn themselves off sexually. Such negative learning can usually be reversed in therapy.

Not everyone who has an incestuous sexual encounter with a parent or sibling has difficulties as an adult. Indeed, many people learn to relabel what happened when they were younger, so that guilt or concern is minimal. For them, subsequent sexual relationships not only provide pleasurable experiences but also help to temper the effects of the earlier sexual encounters. Sometimes, in spite of the incest, a strong love bond can exist between a daughter and her father. In one case, a 16–year-old daughter who had been having sex with her father for two years told the judge that she loved her father and pleaded with him not to send her father to prison.

Treatment for Incest Abusers and Victims

More than 4,000 children and their families have been treated by the Child Sexual Abuse Treatment Program in Santa Clara County, California. In a typical case, a girl will tell a school nurse or counselor that she is being sexually molested by her father. The mother is called, apprised of the situation, and asked to come get the child. The police department is also called, and an officer is sent to obtain an initial statement from the girl. If the investigation suggests there is sufficient evidence to warrant an arrest and referral to the district attorney for prosecution, the father is arrested and placed in jail or released on his own recognizance. But he is not allowed to make contact with the daughter or to return to the home; if he does return home, the child is removed to a foster home or care shelter.

Counseling begins immediately. According to one therapist:

> Incestuous families are badly fragmented as a result of the original dysfunctional family dynamics, which are further exacerbated on disclosure to civil authorities. The child, mother, and father must be treated separately before family therapy becomes productive. (Giarretto, 1982, p. 263)

The mother and father are also contacted by telephone by a member of Parents United (P.O. Box 952; San Jose, CA 95108–0952; 408–280–5055) who has been through a similar experience and who becomes their "sponsor." In addition to personal contacts, the sponsor invites the clients to Parents United and prepares them for the initial group sessions in which other parents will discuss the incest that has occurred in their homes.

Their body belongs to them, and they can decide who touches it.
—Judith Hooper

Meanwhile, depending on the circumstances and the recommendation of the social worker, the father might face criminal proceedings. If he is charged with a felony (usually for child molestation or statutory rape), two court-appointed psychiatrists determine if he is a mentally disturbed sex offender. If he is, he is sent to the state psychiatric facility for chronic sex offenders. If he is not, he may be sent to prison or receive a suspended sentence if he agrees to participate in a treatment program of individual, group, and family counseling. The average length of treatment is about nine months.

Help for sex-abuse victims is available nationwide through Childhelp USA. Once a victim calls 1–800–422–4453, the counseling process begins immediately.

Prevention of Incest

The Committee for Children (P.O. Box 15190, Wedgewood Station; Seattle, WA 98115; 206–524–6020) is an organization that helps children acquire knowledge and skills to protect them from sexual abuse. Through various presentations in the elementary schools, children are taught how to differentiate between appropriate and inappropriate touching by adults or siblings, to understand that it is okay to feel uncomfortable if they do not like the way someone else is touching them, to say "no" in potentially exploitive situations, and to tell other adults if the offending behavior occurs.

Parent Abuse

Child abuse and incest focus on how the parent harms or exploits the child. Another form of family abuse is *parent abuse*—how children harm and exploit their parents, particularly older parents.

Therapy is part of the treatment for child abuse.

There are a number of ways in which children abuse their parents (O'Toole et al., 1983):

1. *Physical abuse:* Hitting parent with a fist or object.
2. *Emotional abuse:* Screaming at parent, ignoring parent, keeping parent locked in room.
3. *Nutritional neglect:* Failing to feed parent for 24 hours.
4. *Medical neglect:* Not giving parent medication; not keeping medical appointments.
5. *Cleanliness neglect:* Leaving parent on filthy mattress; leaving parent with infected sores; leaving dirty clothes on parent for days.

We will soon learn that the serious and complex problem of child abuse pales by comparison to the systematic familial abuse of elderly people.
—Scott Harshbarger

Data – It is estimated that the number of cases of abused, neglected, or exploited elderly ranges from 600,000 to 1 million, or 4 percent of the elderly population. (Eastman, 1984)

One 79-year-old woman testified before a joint hearing of the U.S. Senate Special Committee on Aging:

> The past three years have gotten worse. My daughter locked me in the garage and left me there for more than an hour. She always parked her car behind mine in the garage, so I could not get my car out except by her permission.
>
> If she found me using the electric toaster oven, my food was thrown on the floor and the toaster oven was removed and hidden for several days.
>
> Always hurting me physically and mentally; kicking me, pushing me, grappling with me, telling me to get out, at one time throwing a drawer down the stairs at me, calling me names, telling me I belonged in a nursing home and why didn't I go. (Eastman, 1984, p. 30)

Data – In all states but North Dakota and Pennsylvania and Puerto Rico statutes exist on elder abuse. (*Elder Abuse Report*, 1986)

Reasons for parent abuse vary. In some cases, parental abuse is one expression of a larger pattern of abuse (spouse and child abuse). In other cases, parent abusers are "getting back" for their parents' maltreatment of them as children. In still other cases, the children are frustrated with the burden of having to care for their elderly parents. For the last category of parent abusers, local agencies throughout the nation provide such services as Meals on Wheels and elderly day care to help children with their aging parents. The name of the agency nearest you may be obtained by writing the National Association of Area Agencies on Aging (600 Maryland Avenue, S.W., Suite 208; Washington, D.C. 20024). A newsletter, *Advice for Adults with Aging Parents,* is also available from Helpful Publications, Inc. (310 West Durham Street; Philadelphia, PA 19119–2901)

Trends

Trends in handling violent and abusive relationships include greater public awareness that such behavior occurs in intimate relationships, an increased number of shelters for battered women, and a less punitive approach to sexually abusive fathers.

Newspapers, magazines, and television often feature stories of violence and abuse in marriage and family relationships. "Sixty Minutes," the CBS news program, devoted a segment to the murder of a father by his son, who could no longer tolerate his father beating him and his sister. Previously, the news program had reported the case of a wife who took out a murder contract on her husband because he had been abusive. Violence is no longer known to only those behind closed doors.

Due to the increasing visibility of violence in intimate relationships, more shelters for battered women will be established. Although most battered women prefer to go to the home of a relative, those who have no place to go to escape violence will seek refuge in a shelter.

Prosecuting and jailing fathers who abuse their daughters is also abating. The current trend is toward putting the father on probation, thereby keeping the family together, and involving family members in individual and group counseling. Imprisonment only further loosens the family members' emotional ties and, in many cases, economically devastates the family. One social worker commented:

> Once you take the father out of the home, the breadwinner is gone. And although the mother may work, she can't produce the income two of them would produce. Also, it is assumed that every daughter wants her father to be sent to prison because of what he did to her. But that simply isn't so. I was in a courtroom when a judge sentenced a father to 15 years in prison for molesting his 15-year-old daughter. The daughter was in the courtroom at the time of the sentencing and went absolutely berzerk. After regaining her composure, she pleaded with the judge not to "send my daddy to prison."

The Institute for the Community as Extended Family (P.O. Box 952; San Jose, CA 95108–0952; 408–280–5055) will continue to train professionals to develop child sexual-abuse treatment programs like the one in Santa Clara County, California. The Institute has also developed another organization, Adults Molested as Children, to provide help to adults who are still adversely affected by earlier sexual-abuse experiences.

Summary

Violence occurs in about 30 percent of all dating relationships, usually after several months of dating. Such violence includes pushing, slapping, threatening, and punching. Either or both partners may be the abuser. It is not unusual for couples to continue their relationship after violence has occurred. For some individuals, violence is viewed as part of a love relationship. Others have no alternative to the primary relationship. Still others feel they deserve the abuse.

Courtship may also involve sexual aggression; about 25 percent of undergraduate women report that they had been pressured into having intercourse. Some men view women as legitimate victims and legitimize rape in their own mind.

Violence also occurs between partners who live together. Those who are younger, have lower incomes, and have not been previously married exhibit higher rates of violence in their relationships than older, more affluent, previously married cohabitants.

Violence extends into marriage. Marital violence may be explained by previous family learning, the perceived reinforcement following violence, the lack of controls in our society, and the modeling of violence in the larger society.

Rape occurs in marriage as well as outside of it. Marital rape may be part of a larger context of violence in the relationship or a specific conflict over sex. This type of rape is potentially more devastating than rape by a stranger because the woman lives with the rapist. Having the husband arrested for violence and abuse seems to reduce the frequency of such abuse. Therapy that focuses on communication and conflict resolution is the most desirable response to marital violence.

Child abuse is any action that results in nonaccidental harm to the child's physical or developmental well-being. Child abusers may be found in all races, and all income and educational levels. A primary predictive factor of the child abuser is a lack of emotional bonding with the child. Although there is no single cause of child abuse, the factors involved are lack of impulse control, parental experience of abuse as children, displacement of aggression, and environmental stressors. Successful treatment of child abuse includes teaching parents to exercise self-control and to use "time out" and positive reinforcement for good behavior as alternatives to harsh punishment for bad behavior.

Incest may be between father and daughter, mother and son, or brother and sister. Although brother–sister incest is probably most prevalent, parent–offspring incest is the most destructive. The parent or stepparent uses his or her authority to coerce the child into a pattern of sexual relations. The child often is not sure what is happening but senses it is wrong, as she or he is enjoined to secrecy and may even be threatened.

Treatment for incest should involve the whole family in individual, marital, and family therapy for several months. Teaching young children that it is not okay to let other adults touch them in ways that make them uncomfortable and to tell another adult if someone tries to do so is an incest-prevention technique.

Children may also abuse their parents. Examples of such abuse include yelling obscenities at aging parents, hitting them, and not taking food to invalid parents. Congressional hearings to assess the extent of such abuse and to recommend ways to alleviate it may have a positive effect.

Trends in handling violence and abuse are greater visibility of the subject, more shelters for abused wives, and a less punitive approach to parents who abuse their children.

Questions for Reflection

1. Have you experienced violence or abuse in your intimate relationships? If so, how has this behavior affected your relationships?
2. To what degree would you be willing to continue a relationship in which you were abused?
3. What are your feelings about criminally prosecuting a parent who has sex with his or her child versus putting the sexual abuser on probation and immersing him or her in individual, marital, and family therapy?

CHOICES

CHOICES ABOUT ABUSIVE relationships involve basically the decision to terminate or to continue such relationships.

Terminate an Abusive Dating Relationship?

People disagree on whether to terminate an abusive courtship relationship. In a marriage and family class, 70 students were asked if they would continue a relationship with someone they were dating who hit and kicked them. Their answers follow.

End Dating Relationship
Most said they would end the dating relationship, because such violence is intolerable in an intimate relationship, because they would lose respect for their partner, or because they would fear that the abuse would recur.

If my partner hit me out of anger or jealousy, it would be the first and last time. I would absolutely terminate the relationship—my reasoning being that if a person hits you once, he will more than likely hit you again and again. There is no acceptable reason whatsoever for a male to hit a female.

I would terminate the relationship immediately because I am totally against any type of violence. Striking anyone is an inhumane gesture, especially if it is done out of anger.

If a problem arises, I feel we should be able to discuss it in an adult manner. Hitting me would be uncalled for. If my partner hit me, I would hit him back and the relationship would be over.

If he feels that he could do it once and get away with it, he might do it again. If we were to marry, he would probably do it even more, so I would get out of such a relationship while I could.

I would have no desire to nurture a violent relationship and would leave the bum.

I would lose all respect for that person and couldn't trust him again. Besides, if he hit me, he might hit our child.

Continue Dating Relationship
A few said they would continue the dating relationship with the partner but that it would depend on the circumstances.

If the infraction was not severe and if the person was "sorry" for her actions and if she thought she had lost control for a split second, I would want us to continue our relationship. But if she hit and kicked me on a regular basis and showed no remorse, I would end the relationship.

I would not terminate a dating relationship if my partner hit or kicked me because I would want to find out my partner's rationale for her behavior. Maybe it was something that I did that provoked her anger . . . maybe I deserved it.

It would really depend on the situation or the severity of the blows. If it was for my own good and the violence was minimal, I would stick around. But violence is not the kind of thing I would put up with too often.

I would probably let it slide the first time, yet I would tell him that he had one and only one more chance. If it ever happened again, I would probably leave him. It also would depend on how long I had been dating him. If it was a second date, I'd leave him in a heartbeat, because there are other fish in the sea. If I had been dating him for a long time, I could tell if his outburst was intentional or emotional.

Terminate Abusive Marriage Relationship?

These students were also asked if they would end their marriage if the spouse hit and kicked them. Although some said they would seek a divorce, most felt that they should try to work it out.

(Continued)

Seek a Divorce
Those opting for divorce basically felt they couldn't live with someone who had or would abuse them.

I abhor violence of any kind, and since a marriage should be based on love, kicking is certainly out of the norm. I would lose all respect for my mate and I could never trust him again. It would be over.

Continue Marriage Relationship
Most felt that marriage was too strong a commitment to end if the abuse could be stopped.

I would not divorce my spouse if she hit or kicked me. I'm sure that there's always room for improvement in my behavior although I don't think it's necessary to assault me. I recognize that under certain circumstances, it's the quickest way to draw my attention to the problem at hand. I would try to work through our difficulties with my spouse.

The physical contact would lead to a separation. During that time, I would expect him to feel sorry for what he had done and to seek psychiatric help. My anger would be so great, it's quite hard to know exactly what I would do. I would feel like killing him.

I wouldn't leave him right off. I would try to get him to counseling. If we could not work through the problem, I would leave him. If there was no way we could live together, I guess divorce would be the answer.

I would not divorce my husband because I don't believe in breaking the sacred vows of marriage. But I would separate from him and let him suffer!

I would tell him I was leaving but that he could keep me if he would agree for us to see a counselor to ensure that the abuse never happened again.

Impact of Social Influences on Choices

Part of the reason people stay in or leave abusive relationships is their perception of how others view them. One woman said that she couldn't bring herself to tell her mother that her husband was beating her up, so she endured the beatings for five years. Finally, the beatings became so frequent and painful that she no longer cared how her mother would respond. She had reached the point at which she had to leave her husband to survive. She went to see a close girlfriend, who had also been abused by her husband and who had left him. The friend strongly encouraged her to leave and pointed out that there is a life beyond abuse. In this example, just as one social influence (the mother) kept this wife in an abusive relationship, another social influence (the friend) helped her to leave her abusive husband.

PART FOUR

FAMILIES

ONE HUNDRED YEARS ago, technology had very little impact on the family. The automobile and the television were nonexistent, and medical technology was relatively primitive. Family members spent most of their time working on the farm. Travel was by horse-drawn buggy, and information sources were limited to word of mouth and the printed page.

Today, automobiles of every color, style, and option are available to take courtship partners away from the watchful eyes of parents and families on extended, cross-country vacations. Television news provides instant exposure to the happenings of the day throughout the United States and the world. Situation comedies comment on a variety of life styles, values, and behaviors.

Medical advances such as artificial insemination, test-tube fertilization, ovum transfer, amniocentesis, and chorion biopsy offer infertile couples a way to increase the probability of pregnancy and help to ensure a healthy fetus and infant. In addition, new contraceptives (subdermal implants for women, a "pill" for men) are being developed to provide increased control over family size.

CHAPTER 14

Planning Children

Contents

Is It True?*

1. Child-free couples often go out at night and are frequently on vacation.
2. Middle-age couples whose children have left home are more satisfied than couples who never had children.
3. Only children have different personalities than children who have siblings.
4. About 25–30 percent of all women now in their twenties will probably never have children.
5. Most unmarried women who attend the "thinkers' group" sponsored by Single Mothers by Choice to contemplate whether to have a baby decide not to have a baby.

*1=F; 2=T; 3=F; 4=T; 5=T.

PARENTHOOD SHOULD BEGIN with planning. Before each academic term as a student, you decide how many courses you want to take and when you want to take them. You probably try to avoid overloading your schedule and feel pleased when you get the sequence of courses you want. Successful family planning means having the number of children you want when you want to have them. Although this seems to be a sensible and practical approach to parenthood, many couples leave the number and spacing of their children to chance.

Family planning has benefits for the mother and the child. Having several children at short intervals increases the chances of premature birth, infectious disease, and death for the mother or the baby. Parents can minimize such risks by planning fewer children at longer intervals.

Both parents may also benefit from family planning by pacing the financial demands of parenthood. "We spaced our three children every four years," said one father, "so we would have only one child in college at a time."

Conscientious family planning may also reduce the number of children born to parents who do not want them. A child born to rejecting parents is a tragic situation—but a preventable one.

Data – Eight percent of all white children and 22 percent of all black children were unwanted at conception. (*Statistical Abstract of the United States*, 1987)

Family planning also benefits society by enabling people to avoid having children they cannot feed and clothe adequately—children whose rearing may have to be subsidized by the taxpayer. Finally, family planning is essential to halting the continuing expansion of the world population and the consequent drain on limited environmental resources.

Data – In 1988, there will be 250,248,000 people in the United States. Worldwide, there will be 5,051,000,000 people. (*Population Today*, 1986)

Well over 90 percent of all human births are the byproduct of a moment of passion rather than of family planning per se.
—Roy Creep

In this chapter, you are encouraged to consider three basic questions: Do you want to be a parent? If so, how many children do you want? When is the best time to begin your family?

Do You Want to Have Children?

Most young adults say they want to have children "some day."

Data – According to a *USA Today* poll, 88 percent of 999 college students on 104 campuses want children. (Stewart, 1986)

In this section, we will examine the positive and negative consequences of having children, the social influences on the decision to have children, and the reasons people give for wanting children.

Playing with children is one of the delightful aspects of parenthood.

Positive Aspects of Parenthood

In their book *Parents in Contemporary America,* researchers LeMasters and DeFrain (1983) write that "rearing children is probably the hardest and most thankless job in the world" (p. 22). Yet most Americans express a desire to have this experience. Some of the benefits parents report from having children include the following.

Play

Children give you an excuse to express the child in yourself that society assumes you have outgrown. One parent said, "I like to ride an inner tube down a river with my kids in the summer and swing off a rope into the water, as I did when I was a kid. I can't ask my friends to play like that; they'd think I was nuts. With your own kids, you've got the chance to play, really play, again." It is also fun to observe and join in the spontaneity that children bring to their activities. Children have no internal schedule that tells them what they should do next. Being tickled, playing hide and seek, and flying a kite always have the potential of leading to another, perhaps more surprising, adventure.

Honesty

Children are honest. Unburdened by years of social programming, children express exactly what they feel. "When your 5-year-old wraps her or his arms around you and says 'I love you,' you know the feelings are real," one parent said. And every family therapist knows that a way to find out how mommy and daddy get along is to ask the kids. "She's always yelling at him because he drinks too much," said one 7-year-old.

Companionship

A mother of three children remarked, "After you finish school, all your friends scatter. The only relationships that really last are family relationships. Having children gives you the chance to be intimately involved in a family over a long period of time."

Parental Pride

"I can't describe the pleasure it gave me to see my daughter ride a horse for the first time," said a rancher. Pride in one's own children is a major reward of parenthood, and it is not dependent on the child's potential for becoming president. Parents feel pride when their children first roll over, walk, talk, ride a bike, and swim.

Spouse–Child Relationship

An additional delight for parents is to observe the interaction between their child and their spouse. A young father said, "Amy asks when she awakens from her nap, 'When's Mama coming home?' And when 'Mama' gets home, she lifts Amy in the air and they begin laughing with each other. As a result of watching them play together, I've developed a special love for my wife."

Parents also feel that they have a sense of immortality in their children, who continue the family line. "There will be a part of me left when I die," said one parent.

Negative Aspects of Parenthood

The positive aspects of parenthood have a flip side. The spontaneity children exhibit may erupt at the wrong time—when the parents are making love, reading, watching the evening news, or talking on the telephone or to each other. The honesty of children may also include telling a neighbor that mommy said daddy was a "pompous ass" or telling grandma that the oil painting she gave the family is hauled out only on the occasion of her annual visit. Parent–child companionship may also leave one spouse feeling excluded. Finally, parental pride can become parental grief when the child fails a grade, shoplifts, gets pregnant at 15, or takes drugs.

One woman who does not want children said, "They take the best years of your life and turn them into the best years of their life." Some of the negative aspects reported by parents about parenthood include the following.

Increased Expenses

The wife may drop out of the work force when she becomes a mother (about 45 percent of mothers with preschool children are at home with them).

Therefore, having a baby may mean that the couple's income is cut drastically. But whether or not the mother stops working, expenses will climb.

Data – About 20 percent of a couple's income will be spent on children. (Bloom & Bennett, 1986)

Restricted Social Life

"Before you have a baby," said one father, "you assume that you can always get a baby sitter when you want to and that your social life won't change. The reality is that when you spontaneously decide to go out, it's too late to find a sitter. You have to plan every social event at least three days ahead. The result—you go less often."

Another father who had been married 10 years before his child arrived expressed bitter resentment about the baby's interference with the sailing weekends he and his wife usually enjoyed from April through late fall each year. "You can't take a baby on a sailboat, and being with Carol was part of the fun. We fought it for three months but finally sold the boat. If we had known that a baby equals a blackout on our sailing together, we would have reconsidered having a child."

New Routines

Children influence the total life style of the couple, who must adjust to new routines. Changes include more frequent visits by and to parents and in-laws, less sleep (sometimes chronic exhaustion), family-focused entertainment (G-rated movies), and less lovemaking.

Consideration

Parents experience these aspects of parenthood to a different extent at different times throughout the family life cycle. Parenthood is neither positive nor negative all the time but is a mixture of these experiences over the years.

Social Influences on Deciding to Have Children

So I've realized there are other things grown-ups should be and need to be concerned with—such as kids.
—David Letterman

We live in a pronatalistic, or prochild, society. Unless the members of a society have children, the society will cease to exist. The Shakers, also called the United Society of Believers, provide an example of the consequences of a social deemphasis on procreation. Founded in New York in 1787, the Shakers were a religious community that grew to more than 5,000 members by winning others to their faith. Their doctrine included an emphasis on celibacy, which resulted in no marriage, no sexual intercourse, and no children. The effect of prohibiting reproduction was to ensure that the Shaker community would eventually cease to exist. Today, only a few members remain who were recruited into the community.

Aware of the importance of reproduction for its continued existence, our society tends to encourage childbearing, an attitude known as *pronatalism.* Our family, friends, religion, government, and schools help to develop positive attitudes toward parenthood. Cultural observances also function to reinforce these attitudes.

Family

The fact that we are reared in families encourages us to have families of our own. Our parents are our models. They married; we marry. They had children; we have children. Some parents exert a much more active influence. "I'm 73 and don't have much time. Will I ever see a grandchild?," asked the mother of an only child. Other remarks parents have made include "If you don't hurry up, your younger sister is going to have a baby before you do," "We're setting up a trust fund for your brother's child, and we'll do the same for yours," "Did you know that Nash and Marilyn (the child's contemporaries) just had a daughter?" "I think you'll regret not having children when you're old," and "Don't you want a son to carry on your name?"

Friends

Our friends who have children influence us to do likewise. After sharing an enjoyable weekend with friends who had a little girl, one husband wrote to the host and hostess, "Lucy and I are always affected by Karen—she is such a good child to have around. We haven't made up our minds yet, but our desire to have a child of our own always increases after we leave your home." This couple became parents 16 months later.

Religion

Religion may be a powerful influence on the decision to have children. Catholics are taught that having children is the basic purpose of marriage and gives meaning to the union. Although many Catholics use contraception and reject their church's emphasis on procreation, some internalize the church's message. One Catholic woman said, "My body was made by God, and I should use it to produce children for Him. Other people may not understand it, but that's how I feel." Judaism also has a strong family orientation. Couples who choose to be child-free are less likely than couples with children to adhere to any set of religious beliefs.

Government

The tax structures imposed by our federal and state governments support parenthood. Married couples without children pay higher taxes than couples with children, although the reduction in taxes is not large enough to be a primary inducement to have children.

Governments in other countries have encouraged or discouraged childbearing in different ways. In the 1930s, as a mark of status for women contributing to the so-called Aryan race, Adolf Hitler bestowed the German Mother's Cross on Nazi Germany's most fertile mothers—a gold cross for eight or more children, a silver cross for six or seven, and a bronze cross for four or five.

China has a set of incentives to encourage families to have a maximum of one child. Couples who have only one child are given a "one-child glory certificate," which entitles them to special priority housing, better salaries, a 5 percent supplementary pension, free medical care for the child, and an assured place for the child in school. If the couple has more than one child, they may lose their jobs, be assigned to less desirable housing, and be required to pay the government back for the benefits they have received.

Special Observances

Our society reaffirms its approval of parents every year by allocating special days for mom and dad. Each year on Mother's Day and Father's Day, parenthood is celebrated across the nation with gifts and embraces. There is no counterpart, such as a Child-free Day.

Consideration

Many pronatalism influences operate without our conscious awareness. For example, while growing up in a family, rarely are we told by our parents that children are a benefit and we should have them when we grow up. Rather, the experience of growing up in a family encourages us to duplicate the behavior of our adult models.

PERSONAL REASONS FOR HAVING CHILDREN

The impact of pronatalism influences is reflected in the reasons people give for having children. Some of these reasons follow.

Social Expectations

A sociologist and father of two daughters said, "Having children was never a deliberate decision. It was more of a feeling that one ought to have a family." A mother of two expressed a similar feeling: "All my friends were having babies, and I never questioned whether I would too." Our society expects its members to conform to certain conventions, not the least important of which is having children. Conforming to society's expectations assures a degree of acceptance from peers and places us in the mainstream of American life.

Personal Fulfillment

Some parents encourage their daughters to anticipate having children of their own. Giving them dolls and a dollhouse as playthings reinforces this. In some cases, the socialization is so strong that womanhood is equated with motherhood. "I suppose I felt I had to get pregnant to verify that I was a real woman," a young mother said.

Men also derive personal fulfillment from children. Paternalism—taking pride in meeting the needs of their offspring and showing affection for them—is a strong motive for some men. Men may also feel they affirm their masculinity by proving that they can conceive children.

You can learn many things from children. How much patience you have, for instance.

—Franklin P. Jones

Personal Identity

Related to the quest for personal fulfillment is the feeling that a baby gives the parent an identity. As one women explained, "Before my son, Benny, I had nothing. I was bored, I hated my job, and I didn't have any goals or focus to my life. Now I know who I am—a mother—and I feel that I am needed." Some fathers express the same feeling. "Having my child is the meaning of life," remarked the father of a newborn. "I am a lousy employee, but I'm a great father. For the first time in my life, I really feel like somebody."

Influence of Spouse

Some spouses have children primarily to please their mates. "I wasn't wild about the idea of having children but decided to go along with it because my husband wanted one. As it turns out, I'm glad we did," one mother said. When husband and wife feel differently about having children, the disagreement is not always resolved in favor of having them. The woman bears the child, and her preference is usually given more weight.

Accident

Many couples have children without intending to. "I was out of pills and we didn't have any condoms," recalls a young wife, "but we wanted to have intercourse and decided to take a chance. An eight-pound baby was the result." Such accidents are not unusual. They sometimes also occur before marriage.

Some people try to achieve immortality through their offspring or their works. I prefer to achieve immortality by not dying.

—Woody Allen

Data – In a national study, 25 percent of the married women polled became pregnant before the wedding. (Rogers & O'Connell, 1984)

Whatever reasons parents give for having children, the rewards of parenthood are basically intangible. Parents often speak of the delight of seeing children discover their world for the first time, the joy of holding a baby in their arms and realizing it is a part of them and their partner, and the pleasure of following their children's development through the years and of relating to them as adults. A clinical psychologist and mother of three said, "The real problem with children is not their coming but their going. My first daughter will soon be married and will move six states away. I used to feel that babies were not worth the trouble, but now I know the joy of an adult relationship with them. I'm not only losing a daughter but my best friend."

Consideration

Psychologist B. F. Skinner once said that if there were not two of us the question of why would never occur. The reasons for having children are basically explanations given to someone else to justify the person's own behavior. Often we do not know why we do what we do. We just know it is something we want to do and develop reasons when asked. As Freud said, "We do not want a thing because we have reasons for it; we find reasons for it because we want it."

The Child-Free Alternative

For all the happiness they may give, children also cause problems. For some couples, they tend to interfere with the marriage relationship, disrupt careers (particularly the mother's), cost money, and make noise. In addition, parenthood is a demanding role that not all people feel qualified to assume. For these and other reasons, some couples choose to remain child-free, particularly the college-educated.

Data – Of 500 college students, 23 percent of the males and 24 percent of the females said they would be willing to have a child-free marriage. (Billingham & Sack, 1986)

The reasons spouses give for remaining child-free include never having had a burning desire for children, wanting to pursue career commitments, desiring an intimate relationship unencumbered by children, having the freedom that comes with being child-free, and avoiding the expenses of childrearing. Spouses who want to remain child-free are also more likely to not have a practicing religion, to work full time, and to have more money and more education than spouses who do want children (Bloom & Bennett, 1986).

Wanting to remain child-free is also related to racial and ethnic background. Whites are most likely to consider marriage without children. Blacks and, in particular, Mexican Americans are more likely to be family-oriented and to consider children an important part of marital life (Rothman et al., 1985).

One of the stereotypes of child-free couples is that they are out every night and always on vacation. But a study (Ramu, 1985) comparing child-free couples with parents found very few differences. Although going out every night may have been a pattern early in the marriage, child-free spouses drift into staying home more often. One child-free husband said:

> There is something about life which is rotten. No matter how conscious you are to break routines, they have a grip on you like an octopus's tentacles. The year Jan and I got married, we used to go out all the time. But now, we sit home and watch TV most nights. (p. 139)

Of travel plans, one child-free wife said:

> Before we were married, I said to John, "I want to travel" and he said, "Sure, we will do that." For the last 5½ years we have been saying, "Sure we will do that." We are still procrastinating. (p. 141)

In summarizing the comparison between child-free and parental couples, the researcher said:

> Essentially, parents in this study lived in ways typically credited to child-free couples. In contrast, the voluntarily child-free couples have the potential and resources to pursue the same leisurely activities but seldom outdistance the parental couples in this regard . . .. Life for most child-free couples in this study is not marked by spontaneity and hedonism. (p. 144)

Being a housewife and a mother is the biggest job in the world, but if it doesn't interest you, don't do it. It didn't interest me, so I didn't do it. Anyway, I would have made a terrible parent. The first time my child didn't do what I wanted, I'd kill him.

—Katharine Hepburn

Some couples do not decide to remain child-free. They may be unable to have children and be forced to cope with involuntary childlessness (Matthews & Matthews, 1986). Billie Holiday, the blues singer of the 1930s, was devastated because she could not get pregnant and was turned down when she tried to adopt.

Other couples do not initially decide to be child-free. They put off having children ("we'll wait till we're out of school . . . until we get a house . . . until our careers are established . . . until we have more money") and become satisfied with the child-free life style and decide to continue it. However, those who never have children voluntarily are in the minority.

But how do couples who don't have children feel about their decision later in life? Two researchers (Bell & Eisenberg, 1985) have contrasted the life satisfaction of midlife, childless couples with empty-nest couples. Empty-nest individuals were more satisfied than childless persons with regard to their decisions regarding children; however, the childless individuals were not unhappy with their decisions. In another study comparing couples in their seventies who did and did not have children, the researcher (Rempel, 1985) concluded:

> . . . today's childless elderly have levels of well-being that match and sometimes exceed those of parent elderly . . .. It is erroneous to assume that the elderly have children who can and will look after them. We have learned from this examination that family is not necessarily the crucial element in determining high-quality life in old age. (pp. 346–347)

Consideration

Is the child-free life style for you? If you get your primary satisfactions from interacting with adults and from your career and if you require an atmosphere of freedom and privacy, perhaps the answer is yes. But if your desire for a child is at least equal to your desire for a satisfying adult relationship, career, and freedom, the answer is probably no. The child-free alternative is particularly valuable to persons who would find the demands of parenthood an unnecessary burden and strain. You can assess the degree to which you want to have children by completing the Attitudes Toward Children Scale.

How Many Children Do You Want?

If you decide to have children, how many children will you want? Table 14.1 indicates the number of children Americans say they want. Two children continues to be the ideal number for most Americans.

An Only Child

Many people who are hesitant about having an only child make statements like "It's not fair to the child," "Only children are lonely," "Only children are spoiled," and "One child doesn't make a real family."

Are these beliefs justified? Is the one-child family bad for the child and the parents? To find out, two researchers asked 105 only children and 168 parents

TABLE 14.1 IDEAL FAMILY SIZE

Number of Children Wanted	*Percent*
None	2
One	4
Two	56
Three	21
Four or more	11

Source: Gallup Organization, 1985. *Public Opinion* Dec/Jan 1986.

Self-Assessment

The Attitudes Toward Children Scale

This scale is designed to measure the way you feel about having and rearing children. There are no right or wrong answers. After reading each sentence carefully, circle the number that best represents your feelings.

1 Strongly disagree
2 Mildly disagree
3 Undecided
4 Mildly agree
5 Strongly agree

	SD	MD	U	MA	SA
1. I will be more fulfilled as a person if I have children.	1	2	3	4	5
2. I will be happier as a parent than just as a spouse.	1	2	3	4	5
3. Holding a baby is a very enjoyable experience.	1	2	3	4	5
4. Whatever children cost, they are worth it.	1	2	3	4	5
5. Children provide a type of satisfaction you get nowhere else in life.	1	2	3	4	5
6. Children may require a married couple to make more adjustments, but those adjustments are worth the experience of having children.	1	2	3	4	5
7. Child-free couples are really missing a worthwhile experience.	1	2	3	4	5
8. Most child-free couples will regret not having children when they are old.	1	2	3	4	5
9. Children may tie you down more, but they are worth it.	1	2	3	4	5
10. Children are worth sacrificing whatever career goals are necessary to have them and rear them properly.	1	2	3	4	5
11. Parenthood is more of an enriching experience than a burden.	1	2	3	4	5
12. Spending time with your spouse and children is more enjoyable than spending time alone with your spouse.	1	2	3	4	5

(Continued)

Self-Assessment

13. I wouldn't mind doing the work that taking care of a baby requires—feeding, changing diapers, giving baths, reading stories at bedtime.	1	2	3	4	5
14. Children make a lot of noise and tear up the house, but these are minor concerns in deciding to have children.	1	2	3	4	5
15. The happiest couples are those who have children.	1	2	3	4	5
16. When I see a baby in a department store, I want to hold her or him.	1	2	3	4	5
17. I enjoy the experience of taking care of a helpless infant.	1	2	3	4	5
18. Rearing children through the teen years would be a challenging experience rather than an experience to avoid.	1	2	3	4	5
19. Children usually appreciate what you do for them when they get older.	1	2	3	4	5
20. I can't imagine not having children.	1	2	3	4	5

Scoring: Add the numbers you circled. 1 (strongly disagree) is the most negative feeling you can have, and 5 (strongly agree) is the most positive feeling you can have. The lower your total score (20 is the lowest possible score), the more pessimistic you feel about parenthood; the higher your score (100 is the highest possible score), the more optimistic you feel about parenthood. A score of 60 places you at the midpoint between wanting and not wanting to become a parent.

of only children to describe the advantages and disadvantages of the one-child family pattern. When the parents of only children were asked how many children they would have if they were starting over, 23 percent said they would have one child, 40 percent would have two, and another 21 percent would have more than two (Hawke & Knox, 1977).

Although only children are often maligned, they do score higher on intelligence tests and make better grades than children with siblings. Their personality characteristics, social skills, and potential to be mentally ill are no different from individuals with siblings (Falbo & Polit-O'Harra, 1985).

When mothers who had only one child and wanted no more children were compared with mothers who wanted a second child, the mothers of only children were more likely to report higher career interests, to have husbands who helped less with child care, to feel bored with childrearing, and to evidence less enjoyment about the dependence of the child on them (Callan, 1985). In general, "mothers of one child by choice valued the experience of the first child less than other mothers did and they appeared to regard the costs as higher" (p. 162). Other mothers had their only child when they were in their late thirties (due to career commitments) and elected not to have additional children because of their age.

The number of children that couples want is also related to the society in which they live. America supports the stereotype that the ideal family is the two-child family. But China has adopted a one-child population policy and actively encourages its citizens to have an only child (Chen, 1985). This policy has resulted in a drop in that country's birth rate.

Two Children

One mother was asked the difference between having one and two children. She said that when her first child swallowed a quarter, they took him to the hospital to have his stomach pumped out. When the second child swallowed a coin, he was told, "It will come out of your allowance."
—Anonymous

The most preferred family size in the United States is the two-child family. How does having two children differ from having one? In one study, 144 mothers who had two children and whose second child was less than 5 years old revealed their motivations for having a second child and the consequences of doing so (Knox & Wilson, 1978). About one-half of these mothers said they enjoyed their first child and wanted to repeat the experience. More than one-quarter stated they wanted a companion for the first child. Other reasons included the husband wanting another child, personal fulfillment, and wanting a child of the opposite gender.

Data – Only 50 percent of parents who want one boy and one girl will achieve their desired sex combination with two births. (Bongaarts, 1984)

These mothers also commented on the consequences of having a second child. Almost half (49 percent) said the first child made a greater personal impact on them than the second child. Specific comments included "I lost my freedom to truly enjoy life and do what I wanted with the first child. Once I began forgetting myself, my second child had little effect;" "Childbirth and responsibility for a baby were new experiences with the first child. I felt more confident with the second child;" and "I got used to never being alone after my first child was born." (p. 24)

Although the second child had less personal impact than the first, the mothers reported that their marriages were more affected by their second child than by their first. One mother remarked, "The main difference I noticed with the second child was that I was more exhausted, since I had to relate emotionally to two children throughout the day." Another woman said:

> After I had listened to incessant pleading such as "I need a fork," "Can I have some more apple juice?" and "I don't like oatmeal," there was little left of me for my husband. And when the children were finally in bed, I needed to use the rest of the evening to catch up on the housework I was unable to do during the day because of the constant interruptions. (p. 15)

The sexes of the two children may also make a difference in the marital satisfaction of the wife. In a study comparing the marital adjustment of wives with no children, one child, and two children, the researchers concluded that only mothers with two young male children evidenced a decline in marital satisfaction (Abbott & Brody, 1985). The suspected reason is that young boys have been found to be more demanding temperamentally and behaviorally than young girls.

One of the motivations for having a second child is to have a companion for the first. While children may serve as companions for each other in their youth, what about when they become old? One researcher has studied the life satisfaction of the elderly as related to the presence of siblings living nearby and has found that sisters exert a more positive influence on the life satisfaction of each other than brothers (McGhee, 1985).

Three Children

Some couples want three children.

Data – In a national survey of college students, 24 percent of the men and 20 percent of the women wanted three children. (Stewart, 1986)

Having a third child creates a "middle child." This child may be neglected, because parents of three children may focus on "the baby" and the firstborn and only rarely on the one in between.

But some middle children see their position in the family in positive terms:

> I feel that being a middle child has turned out to be a great advantage for me. I received the love, but not the overattention, that was given my older brother and younger sister. Although I have at times been envious of my siblings, I am very close to them (even though they cannot get along with each other). I feel that I am capable of being responsive and caring for others when they need someone. All things considered, it's great to be a middle child!

About one in five couples choose to have three children.

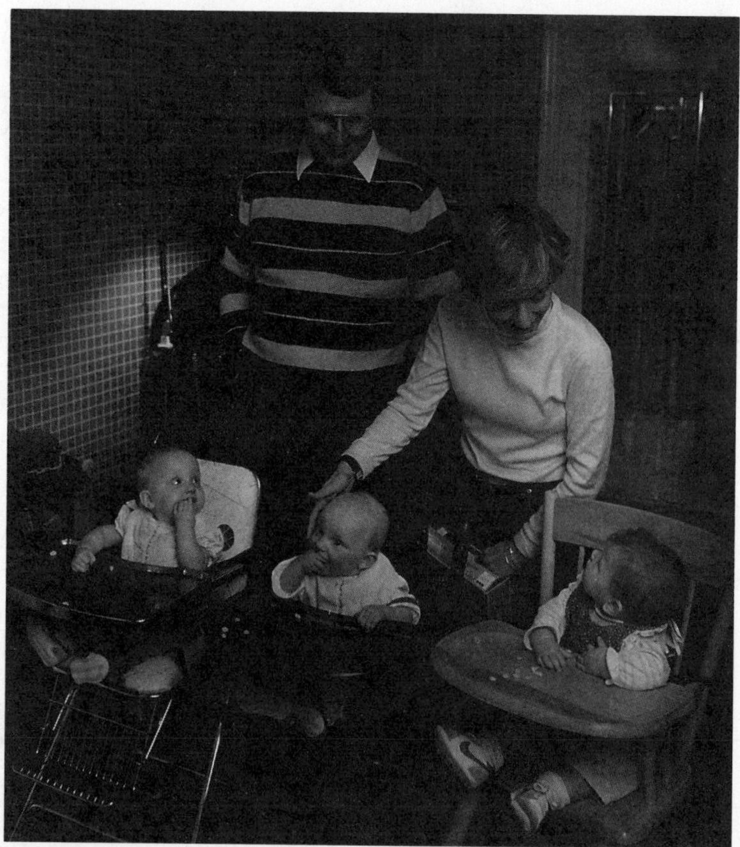

> I have one older brother and one younger sister, and they are loved very much along with myself. However, I am the one to be spoiled out of the three of us. I get whatever I want—not only from my parents, but also from my grandparents. (My grandparents gave me a new Ford Mustang for graduation.) At Christmas, I get very unhappy because I can see that my brother and sister resent me very much, and I have been told by their best friends that they resent me. But what can I do?

Four or More Children

In contrast to having only a few children or a child-free marriage, some couples want a child-full marriage.

> *Data* – In a national survey of college students, 12 percent of the men and 9 percent of the women wanted four children. (Stewart, 1986)

Men are more likely to want four or more children than women. Blacks and Mexican Americans are more likely to want larger families than whites (Rothman et al., 1985).

Larger families have complex interactional patterns and different values. The addition of each subsequent child dramatically increases the possible relationships in the family. For example, in the one-child family, four interpersonal relationships are possible: mother–father, mother–child, father–child, and father–mother–child. In a family of four, 11 relationships are possible; in a family of five, 26; and in a family of six, 57.

In addition to relationships, values change as families get larger. Whereas members of a small family tend to value independence and personal development, large-family members necessarily value cooperation, harmony, and sharing. A parent of nine children said, "Meals around our house are a cooperative endeavor. One child prepares the drinks, another the bread, and still another sets the table. You have to develop cooperation, or nobody gets fed."

Consideration

Assuming that you decide to have children, keep two issues in mind when choosing the number you want. First, each child will be different. One couple had decided to have only one child but because their daughter was beautiful, cooperative, and happy, they decided to have another. Their second child was born with a disfiguring birthmark on his face and was demanding and withdrawn. "We should have stopped while we were ahead," the mother said. Genetic differences, birth order, family economic situation, and parental experience ensure that each child will be different—often radically so.

Second, every family size has advantages and disadvantages. Only children may have more possessions, opportunities, and parental attention, but they may be lonely. Two or more children provide companionship for each other, but such interaction may turn into intense sibling rivalry, or the middle child may be neglected, or the parental resources of time and money may be spread too thin. In a large family, the individual needs of each child may be neglected.

Married women who prefer smaller families tend to be from small families and a higher social class, are currently employed, enjoy high-status careers, earn large incomes, and perceive themselves as equal partners with their husbands. Married women who prefer larger families tend to have the opposite characteristics.

Recent Demographics

In the 12 months ending March 1987, American women gave birth to 3,717,000 babies—a 2 percent decrease from 3,770,000 births for the previous 12 months. The birth rate (the number of live births per 1,000 general population) was 15.4, which was 3 percent below the rate of 15.8 for March one year ago. The fertility rate (the number of live births per 1,000 women aged 15–44) for this period was 65.1, which was 4 percent below the rate of 67.5 for March one year ago (National Center for Health Statistics, 1987).

Data – Out of all babies born annually, 20 percent are to unmarried mothers. (National Center for Health Statistics, 1986a)

Some couples want to select the sex of their babies. Exhibit 14.1 describes several controversial procedures for doing this.

Timing Your Children

People who say they sleep like a baby usually don't have one.
—Leo J. Burke

Having decided how many children you want to have, when is the best time to begin having them? There are at least three issues to consider in planning the first pregnancy.

Mother's Age

The age of the mother is related to the baby's birth weight. This weight is the greatest single predictor of the baby's current and future health. The more weight the woman gains during pregnancy (up to 35 pounds), the lower the risk of a low-weight baby.

Data – Babies born to mothers aged 25–34 tend to have the lowest risk of low birth weight. (National Center for Health Statistics, 1986b)

The median weight for all babies at birth is 7 pounds, 7 ounces. The median weight for white babies is 7 pounds, 9 ounces, for black babies, 7 pounds exactly.

Risks to the baby's life also increase with the mother's age. The chance of a chromosomal abnormality is 1 percent if the woman is in her early twenties, 2 percent at ages 35–39, 3 percent at 40, and 10 percent at 45 (Seashore, 1980). A higher proportion of babies born to older mothers die or have Down's syndrome (sometimes improperly called mongolism), a genetic defect caused by an extra chromosome. A Down's syndrome baby is physically deformed, mentally retarded, and has a shorter life span. Having a Down's syndrome baby is a particular concern of women who become pregnant after age 40. Many physicians recommend amniocentesis (described in Exhibit 14.1) for these women to determine the presence of this and other chromosomal abnormalities.

Amniocentesis is not without risks. In rare cases (about 2 percent of the time), the fetus may be damaged by the needle even though an ultrasound scan

Exhibit 14.1

SEX SELECTION

In addition to wanting a specific number of children, some couples are concerned about the gender of their children. In his desire to have a male heir, King Henry VIII discarded several wives because they delivered only female children. The hapless Anne Boleyn was beheaded. But only the third of his six wives, Jane Seymour, gave him a son, who died in childhood. Although few American men and women feel the same desperation to have a son, most express a slight preference for a male child.

Enter *gametrics*—the application of biological–mathematical theory to gamete separation. The biological part is the knowledge that Y chromosomes determine a male child and X chromosomes determine a female child. The mathematical part is increasing the probability of a male child by isolating the sperm carrying the Y chromosomes, putting them together, and artificially inseminating the woman.

The Y sperm are isolated by putting all of the sperm from an ejaculation on top of a thick substance in a test tube. Since Y sperm are stronger and swim faster, those sperm going through the substance and swimming to the bottom first are more often male sperm. These are collected from several ejaculations and are used for the artificial insemination procedure. The probability of conceiving a male child using the procedure is 80 percent. If left to chance, the probability is 50 percent. A list of Centers for Gender Selection in your area can be obtained from Gametrics Limited (475 Gate Five Road; Sausalito, CA 94965; 415–332–3141).

An alternative to the gametrics procedure is to separate the X sperm and Y sperm on the basis of their molecular properties. This process has also proved to be 80 percent effective in isolating X sperm to produce female offspring (Uzzell, 1985).

The method of amniocentesis and abortion may be used in gender selection. Fluid from the uterus in which the fetus floats contains fetal cells. These cells can be analyzed by inserting a needle into the pregnant woman's abdomen and withdrawing a sample of fluid to see if the cells carry XX (female) or XY (male) chromosomes. (This procedure is commonly used to test for certain genetic defects, such as Down's syndrome and sickle-cell anemia.) If the fetus is the gender desired by the parents, it is allowed to develop. Otherwise, it may be aborted. In one case, amniocentesis was used to preclude the possibility of a male birth because a lethal inherited disease was characteristic of male babies in that family.

Although amniocentesis has been used for the purpose of having a baby of the desired gender, it is unlikely to become routine. Not only are there moral objections to this procedure (some regard abortion as murder, and others see selecting males as sexist and biologically maladaptive), but there are also risks to the mother and the baby.

(sound waves beamed at the fetus which produce a detailed image) has been used to identify its position. Congenital orthopedic defects, such as clubfoot, and premature birth have been associated with amniocentesis. Also, if no specific abnormality is detected (as is the case 97.5 percent of the time), this does not guarantee that the baby will be normal and healthy otherwise (Hogge et al., 1986).

An alternative to amniocentesis is chorion villus sampling. Also risky, the procedure involves placing a tube through the vagina into the uterus.

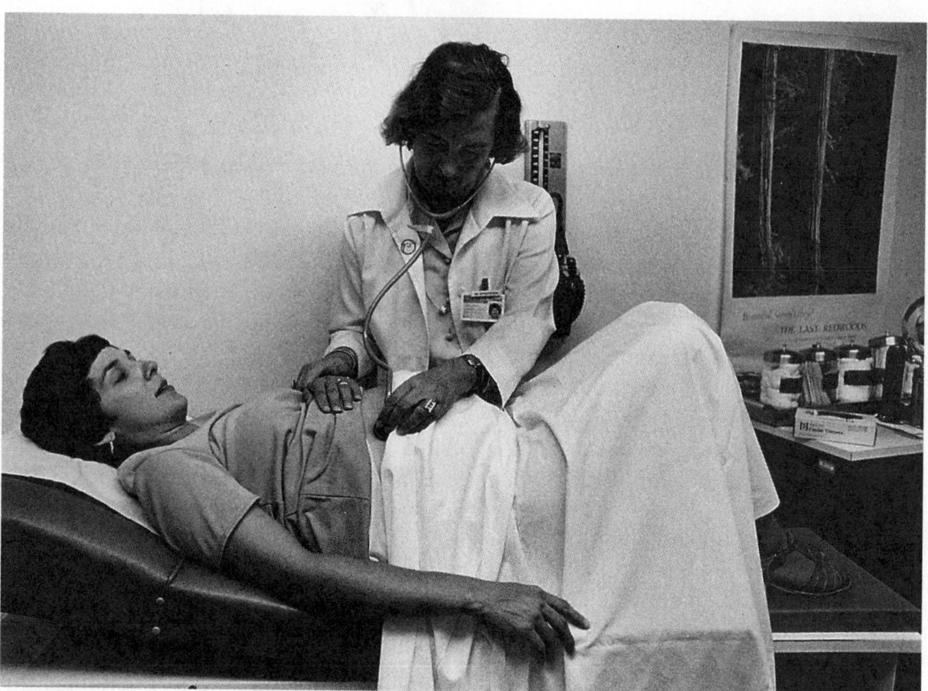

Women between ages 25 and 34 have the healthiest babies.

Chorionic tissue, which surrounds the developing embryo, is removed and analyzed in the laboratory to assess the presence of genetic defects. The procedure can be performed in a physician's office as early as the eighth week of pregnancy, and results are available in two to three weeks. (Amniocentesis is not performed until the sixteenth week, and results are not known for three to four weeks.)

There are also risks to the baby if the mother is too young. Studies have shown that mothers age 17 or younger are more likely to give birth to babies who are premature, have birth defects, and die before they are a year old. Teenage mothers are also likely to be less psychologically competent than older mothers. A nationwide study of 5,000 women aged 14 to 24 noted that women who have their first child before age 19 seem to have reduced personal efficacy; that is, they are more likely to feel they are not in control of their environment (McLaughlin & Micklin, 1983).

Most women have their first child in their early to mid-twenties; more educated women tend to wait a little longer. These ages have positive consequences for the mother and child and permit ample time for subsequent births. A woman who wants to become established in a career and waits until she is in her mid-thirties to become pregnant will have less time to work out fertility problems if they develop.

Consideration

An increasing number of women are waiting until their thirties and forties (examples include Victoria Principal, Farrah Fawcett, Bette Midler, and Meryl Streep) to have their children. For these women, the risks taken by delaying conception may be insignificant compared with the joy derived from motherhood. "I'm 38 and just had my first baby," said one professional woman. "I am absolutely thrilled with being a mother, and it frightens me that I might have thought it was too late to have a baby and missed this whole new terrific experience."

Father's Age

The father's age is also a consideration in deciding when to have the first child. Down's syndrome is associated with increased paternal as well as maternal age. Other abnormalities that may be related to the age of the father include achondroplasia (a type of dwarfism), Marfan syndrome (height, vision, and heart abnormalities), Apert syndrome (facial and limb deformities), and fibrodysplasia ossificans progressiva (bony growths). Such congenital defects are rare, however.

Data – Approximately 2 percent of all newborns have congenital defects that either result in an early death or are clinically significant because they require intensive or prolonged medical treatment. (Bongaarts, 1984)

To help reduce birth defects of genetic origin, older couples and those whose family histories show evidence of hereditary defect or disease should consider genetic counseling. Such counseling helps the potential parents to be aware of the chance of having a defective child.

Number of Years Married

Although most spouses are confident about their decision to have children when they are in their twenties or early thirties, they are somewhat ambivalent about how long it is best to be married before having a baby.

The mother's age affects the risks involved in first and subsequent births.

Data – The average length of time between marriage and the first birth is two years. (Bloom & Bennett, 1986)

One viewpoint suggests that newlyweds need time to adjust to each other as spouses before becoming parents. If the marriage is dissolved, at least there will not be problems of child custody, child-support payments, and single-parent status.

But if couples wait several years to have a baby, they may become so content with their child-free life style that parenthood is an unwelcome change. "We were married for seven wonderful years before Helen was born," recalls one mother. "The adjustment hasn't been easy. We resented her intrusion into our relationship."

Another parent said, "We wanted to begin our family shortly after we were married because we wanted to be young enough to be able to do things with our children. Both of our children were born by the time we were 23, and we have had a terrific time as a family."

In one study, more than 5,000 parents were interviewed on the effect of delaying children versus having them soon after the marriage. Results indicated that marital satisfaction after children was about the same regardless of the length of time the parents waited before having children (Marini, 1980).

Your degree of commitment to your career is also an issue to consider in timing your first child. Although couples have different agreements about child care, most couples prefer that the wife be primarily responsible for the child on a daily basis. Such allocation of responsibility will be a major barrier

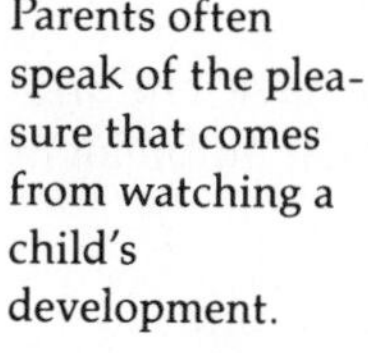

Parents often speak of the pleasure that comes from watching a child's development.

to the woman who wants to pursue a full-time career with its demands of training, commitment, mobility, and continuity. Career-oriented women often decide to get their career going before beginning their family or to have their children first and then launch a career. Unless the partners opt to truly coparent, having a child while pursuing a career will be difficult. An alternative is for the wife to have a job rather than a career.

Consideration

> Whether a couple conceives their first child a long or a short time after the wedding does not seem to positively or negatively affect their marriage, but being pregnant before the wedding and having the first child within a few months after the marriage does have a significant negative effect on the marriage. (Marini, 1980).

Timing Subsequent Births

Assuming you decide to have more than one child, what is the best interval between children? Most couples space their children within three years of each other. This interval allows parents to avoid being overwhelmed with the care of two infants, but is short enough so that the children can be companions. In addition, subsequent children conceived within a year of the last birth exhibit a much higher mortality rate than children conceived at greater intervals.

Trends

The future of family planning will include increased tolerance for the child-free alternative. Couples who decide not to have children will be viewed less often as selfish and immature. "You're no longer a sickie if you don't have kids," said one woman.

> *Data* – Of all women now in their twenties, 25–30 percent will probably never have children. (Bloom & Bennett, 1986)

The one-child family will also become more prevalent as current concerns about inflation, personal freedom and growth, and the woman's career influence young couples to limit family size. In addition, as more parents become aware that only children tend to be bright and career-oriented and to have high self-esteem, fewer couples will have a second child out of obligation to the first.

More single people will want to have babies without the entanglements of marriage. This issue is discussed in the Choices section.

A greater number of women will delay childbearing until their thirties due to later age at marriage and a desire to pursue their careers. Because the risks to the baby increase with the mother's age, amniocentesis and chorion biopsy will be used more often to diagnose genetic abnormalities.

Finally, researchers in the field of immunology will develop ways to accurately isolate and selectively destroy Y or X sperm cells to produce the child of the desired sex.

Summary

The decision whether to become a parent is one of the most important you will ever make. Unlike marriage, parenthood is a role from which there is no easy withdrawal. Individuals may try out marriage by living together, but there is no such trial run for would-be parents.

Spouses, children, and society all benefit from family planning. These benefits include less health risk to mother and child, fewer unwanted children, decreased economic burden for the parents and society, and population control.

Parenthood has both positive and negative aspects. The positive aspects include the opportunity to engage in spontaneous play, developing a close relationship with your own daughter or son, feeling pride in your child's accomplishments, and delighting in a close spouse–child relationship. Negative aspects include the expense, a restricted social life, and the necessity to adjust to a series of new routines.

The decision to become a parent is encouraged (sometimes unconsciously) by family, peers, religion, government, education, and cultural observances. The reasons people give for having children include social expectations, influence of spouse, accident, a sense of immortality, personal fulfillment and identity, and the desire for a close affiliative relationship.

Some couples opt for the child-free life style. Reasons wives give for wanting to be child-free are more personal freedom, greater time and intimacy with their spouses, and career demands. Husbands also are motivated by the desire for more personal freedom. They mention disinterest in being a parent and the desire to avoid the responsibilities of parenthood as reasons for choosing a child-free life style.

The most preferred family size in the United States is the two-child family. Some of the factors in a couple's decision to have more than one child are the desire to repeat a good experience, the feeling that two children provide companionship for each other, and the desire to have a child of each gender.

The timing of the birth of the first child and the intervals between children are important choices. Issues to consider in planning your first child include the ages of both spouses, the number of years you have been married, your career commitments, and your financial situation. The ability of the family to handle the expenses and the desire to have children far enough apart in age to ease the burden of infant care and expenses but close enough together to ensure their companionship usually influence the spacing of children. Typical American couples have their first child about three years after their marriage and subsequent children at three-year intervals. The greater the number of children, the shorter the intervals among them.

Trends in family planning include increased tolerance for the child-free alternative, more one-child families, and more people choosing single parenthood.

Questions for Reflection

1. Under what conditions do you regard the use of amniocentesis and chorion biopsy in sex selection appropriate?

2. What impact have your experiences in the family in which you were reared had on your desire for children? If you want children, how does the number of siblings you have influence the number of children you want?
3. To what degree do the only children you know fit the stereotype of being lonely and spoiled?

CHOICES

IN ADDITION TO the choices of whether to have children and, if so, how many, there is the choice on the part of some who are not married whether to have a child without a spouse. Because there are more men than women and because men marry women much younger than themselves, there are women in their thirties who want a baby but who have no husband. Other women are lesbians and do not want a husband. Still others, prefer to have a child without a spouse even though their sexual preference is heterosexual and potential marital partners are available. Regardless of the reason, the question remains the same.

Having a Child Without a Spouse?: The Biological-Clock Issue

Of the 9 million parents rearing children by themselves, 8 million are mothers and 1 million are fathers. Although most of these parents are separated or divorced, about one-quarter of them are never-married mothers (Hanson & Sporakowski, 1986). Most of the children born to these unmarried mothers were unplanned and were born when the mother was between the ages of 18 and 24. However, an increasing number of children are being conceived by single women over 30. Many older women feel that their biological clock doesn't allow them much more time. In a Roper Poll, four in ten women said that it is all right for adults to have children without getting married (1985). One woman said:

> I'm 37 and feel that I need to make a decision. I've always wanted a baby, and I always thought that someday I was going to meet the right guy and we would find a house and start our family. But each year, I meet fewer prospects, and the ones I'm dating aren't what you would call the pick of the litter. Because it looks like I may never get married, I'm looking seriously at getting pregnant and rearing a child on my own.

Jean Renvoize (1985) interviewed over 30 unmarried women who made the conscious decision to have a baby with the intent of rearing their baby alone. Of these women, the researcher said;

> I expected to find a group of tough-minded, militant women somewhat on the defensive; instead I found mostly happy, fulfilled, strong, but gentle individuals who gave out warmth and a readiness to share with others. These were women who had made their choice after much deliberation, mostly at a mature age, and who knew in advance that nothing in life comes free. (p. 5)

One single mother by choice said:

> I felt I could go through life without being married, I could be fulfilled without a man in my life, but I knew I couldn't be fulfilled without at least having experienced a pregnancy and raising a child. (p. 91)

In making the conscious decision to raise a child as a single parent, several issues might be considered:

1. *Satisfaction of the emotional needs of the child.* Perhaps the greatest challenge for single parents is to satisfy the emotional needs of their children—alone. Children need love, which a parent may express in a hundred ways—from hugs and kisses to help with homework. But the single parent who is tired from working all day and who has no one else with whom to share parenting at night may be unable to express her or his love fully.
2. *Satisfaction of adult emotional needs.* Single parents have emotional needs of their own that children are often incapable of satisfying. The unmet need to share an emotional relationship with an adult can weigh heavily on the single parent. Most single parents seek such a relationship.

3. *Satisfaction of adult sexual needs.* Most single parents regard their role as interfering with their sexual relationships. They may be concerned that their children will find out if they have a sexual encounter at home and frustrated if they have to go away from home to enjoy a sexual relationship. They may have asked themselves such questions as "Do I wait until my children are asleep and then ask my lover to leave before morning?," "Do I openly acknowledge my lover's presence in my life to my children and ask them not to tell anybody?," and "Suppose my kids get attached to my lover, who may not be a permanent part of our lives?"—and deal with the answers. (Most single parents hide their sexual relationships from their children and make them aware of another person in their life only if the other person is of significant emotional importance to the single parent.)
4. *Child care and supervision.* Because the single parent is likely to be employed, adequate child-care arrangements must be made. Using a relative or hiring a baby sitter are the most frequent arrangements for the preschool child of a single parent. Commercial day-care centers are also available, but paying for child-care services may take a large slice out of the single parent's often modest income.
5. *Money.* Lack of money is one of the most difficult aspects of single parenthood. The problem may be particularly acute when the single parent is a woman. The mean income for female-headed, single-parent families is less than half the mean income for two-parent families. Male-headed, single-parent families are less economically stressed because men typically make more money than women.
6. *Guardian.* The single mother needs to appoint a guardian to take care of her baby in the event of her death or disability.

An organization for women who want children and who may or may not marry is Single Mothers by Choice (P.O. Box 7788 F.D.R. Station; New York, NY 10150; 212–988–0993). The organization has more than 1,000 members and provides support for women who make this decision. The organization also has "thinkers' groups" for women who are contemplating whether to have a child outside of marriage. Most women attending these groups decide not to have children after they have been presented with all the facts. Other women can't envision a life without children even though they are aware of some of the difficulties:

> I knew that rearing my kids alone wasn't going to be easy. But I can also tell you that we have a wonderful, loving, sharing family that makes me swell with love. Yes, I am exhausted, and we don't have much money, and the kids get on my nerves. But we are a family unit and care about each other and that makes up for all the problems.

Impact of Social Influences on Choices

The combined factors of a shortage of men, peers who talk about having a child without a spouse, and social pressure to have a child account for the willingness of some women to have a child without being married. There are not enough single men for every woman who wants to get married and have a baby to do so. One alternative for a single woman who wants a baby is to get pregnant by a man she does not intend to marry. (Adoption is another alternative.) Women who do so are responding to one set of social pressures (have a baby) but resisting another (only married people should have babies). Those who discount the latter social pressures often develop friendship networks such as Single Mothers by Choice with other woman who have the same plan of action.

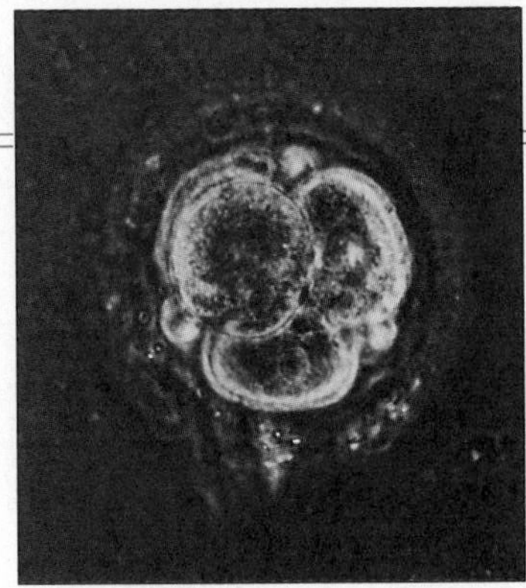

CHAPTER 15

Birth Control

Contents

Is It True?*

1. The sexually active females who are most likely to use contraception grew up in homes in which their parents were open about sex.
2. Undergraduate males tend to feel that it is the female's responsibility to ensure that contraception is used when a couple has intercourse.
3. There is only one type of IUD still prescribed by physicians.
4. A man who has had a vasectomy emits considerably less ejaculate than a man who has not had a vasectomy.
5. Women who have abortions have different personalities than women who have not had abortions.

*1=T; 2=F; 3=T; 4=F; 5=F.

HAVING DECIDED NOT to have children or to delay having them, the choice of which type of contraception to use becomes important. Prior to 1870 (when condoms were first mass-marketed), abstinence was the only way a couple could ensure that the woman would not get pregnant. Today, couples can separate their lovemaking from their babymaking with a variety of birth-control procedures. After reviewing the available array of contraceptives, we will examine sterilization and abortion as ways of controlling family size.

Contraception

Most women have no problem getting pregnant. But many get pregnant when they do not want to because they do not use contraception. "I was a freshman and unmarried. The last thing I wanted at that time in my life was a baby," recalls one woman. *Contraception*, the prevention of pregnancy by one of several methods, is an alternative to pregnancy.

All contraceptive practices have one of two common purposes—to prevent the male sperm from fertilizing the female egg or to keep the fertilized egg

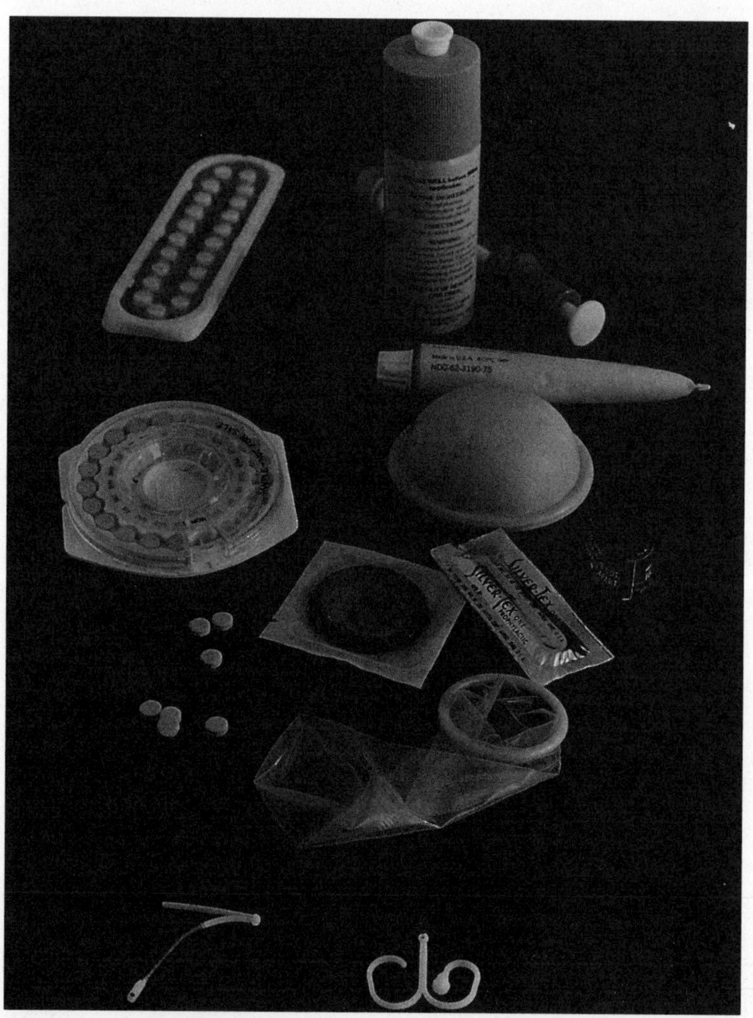

A variety of contraceptive choices are available.

from implanting itself in the uterus. In performing these functions, contraception permits couples to make love without making babies.

The sexually active females who are most likely to use contraception consistently have positive feelings about their sexuality, have high feelings of sexual self-awareness (as indicated by "currently masturbating" and "feeling good about self-masturbation"), grew up in homes in which their parents were open and nonjudgmental about their sexuality, and have low sex guilt (Hornick et al., 1985–1986; Berger et al., 1985).

However, resistance to using contraception may be strong; almost 40 percent of the undergraduates in one study said that they did not use contraception the first time they had intercourse (Sheehan et al., 1986). Reasons typically given for not using contraception include "I didn't want it to look like I was planning to have intercourse," "I thought I would be lucky and not get pregnant," "Sex should be spontaneous," and "It's against my religion to use birth control." You might want to assess the probability of your using birth control in your current relationship by completing the Contraceptive Use Scale in the Self-Assessment section.

Data – In a national survey of sexually active, never-married women between the ages of 20 and 29, 12 percent of the white women and 23 percent of the black women were not using contraception. (Tanfer & Rosenbaum, 1986)

When students in a marriage and family class were asked to describe their feelings when they had intercourse without using contraception, "worry," "anxiety," and "fear" were the most common descriptions. Specific comments follow:

> Each time I have done it [had intercourse without protection], I always feel extremely guilty and every day I prayed I would get my period. It's not a very secure feeling at all, since you know you can get pregnant.

> I feel stupid, and I talk to myself all month about how stupid I am. I always say, "This is the last time I'll ever have sex without contraceptives." I've been lucky so far, but it's not worth it—the entire month after having sex I worry and work myself into a frenzy. The tension is on.

Parents—the word for sexually active people who don't use contraceptives.
—Mary Elesha-Adams

> We had talked about sex for some time and had even talked about what type of contraceptive we would use if the need should arise. What happened, though, was we both got drunk, and without thinking about the consequences, one thing led to another. The next day she got scared, and then I got scared. That is when I started to think, "It couldn't happen to us. It was our first time; she was a virgin." But it did happen to us. She got pregnant.

Students were also asked to describe their feelings when they did use contraceptives while having intercourse. "Self-confident," "secure," and "safe" were common feelings:

> I feel good about myself knowing I'm on the pill. I tell myself that I'm not going to get pregnant. My boyfriend and I can enjoy sex so much better. It's a relief not having to sweat out the month wondering whether I'm pregnant.

> I have congratulated myself on gathering the courage to go to the infirmary and get the pill. I believe that if you are mature enough to have intercourse, you are mature enough to prevent mistakes. I find that now I feel more self-confident and that I don't worry during sex. It's having pleasure without the tension of worry.

Self-Assessment

The Contraceptive Use Scale

This scale is designed to measure the probability of your using birth control in a current relationship. After reading each sentence carefully, circle the number that best represents your feelings.

1 Strongly disagree
2 Mildly disagree
3 Undecided
4 Mildly agree
5 Strongly agree

	SD	MD	U	MA	SA
1. I feel comfortable with my body and my sexuality.	1	2	3	4	5
2. I am seriously involved with my partner.	1	2	3	4	5
3. I do not feel guilty about my sexual experiences.	1	2	3	4	5
4. It is easy for me to talk about sex with my partner.	1	2	3	4	5
5. I feel that I am responsible for seeing that I or my partner use some form of birth control if we decide to have intercourse.	1	2	3	4	5
6. I am aware of several methods of birth control.	1	2	3	4	5
7. I feel it is important that a couple use a contraceptive each time they have intercourse.	1	2	3	4	5
8. I have discussed contraceptives with my partner.	1	2	3	4	5
9. My partner feels positively about her or his sexuality.	1	2	3	4	5
10. I care about my partner and our relationship.	1	2	3	4	5

Scoring: Add the numbers you circled. 1 (strongly disagree) reflects the lowest probability of contraceptive use and 5 (strongly agree) reflects the highest probability of contraceptive use. The lower your total score (10 is the lowest possible score), the less likely you are to use contraceptives; the higher your total score (50 is the highest possible score), the more likely you will be to use contraceptives. A score of 30 places you at the midpoint between not using and using contraceptives.

I told myself when I had intercourse and used contraception that she would not get pregnant and we would not have to worry about having a baby. We were both more relaxed.

Although contraception is not always used, both sexes feel it is their responsibility to provide birth control.

Data – More than 91 percent of both male and female undergraduates in one study said that it was their independent responsibility to ensure that contraception was used when they had intercourse. (Sheehan et al., 1986)

For those who do decide to use contraception, the choices include the following.

Oral Contraceptives

Birth-control pills are the contraceptive preferred by most married and unmarried women.

Data – Of all married women between the ages of 15 and 44, 20 percent of the white women and 26 percent of the black women used the pill. (*Statistical Abstract of the United States,* 1987)

In a study of sexually active, unmarried women, 59 percent of the white women and 56 percent of the black women used the pill. (Tanfer & Rosenbaum, 1986)

Although there are more than 40 brands available in North America, there are basically two types of birth-control pills—the combination pill and the minipill.

The combination pill contains the hormones estrogen and progesterone (also known as progestin), which act to prevent ovulation and implantation. The estrogen inhibits the release of the follicle-stimulating hormone (FSH) from the pituitary gland, so that no follicle will develop. In effect, an egg will not mature. In other words, A (estrogen) blocks B (FSH), which would have produced C (egg).

The progesterone inhibits the release of luteinizing hormone (LH) from the pituitary gland, which during a normal cycle would cause the mature ovum to move to the periphery of the follicle and the follicle to rupture (ovulation). Hence, there is no ovulation. In this case, A (progestin) blocks B (LH), which would have caused C (ovulation).

The progesterone serves as a secondary protection by causing the composition of the cervical mucus to become thick and acidic, thereby creating a hostile environment for the sperm. So even if an egg were to mature and ovulation were to occur, the progesterone would ward off or destroy the sperm. Another function of progesterone is to make the lining of the uterus unsuitable for implantation.

The combination pill is taken for 21 days, beginning on the fifth day after the start of the menstrual flow. Three or four days after the last pill is taken, menstruation occurs, and the 28–day cycle begins again. To eliminate the problem of remembering when to begin taking the pill every month, some physicians prescribe a low-dose combination pill for the first 21 days and a placebo (sugar pill) or an iron pill for the next seven days. In this way, the woman takes a pill every day.

The second type of oral contraceptive, the minipill, contains the same progesterone found in the combination pill, but in much lower doses. The minipill contains no estrogen. Like the progesterone in the combination pill, the progesterone in the minipill provides a hostile environment for sperm and inhibits implantation of a fertilized egg in the uterus. In general, the minipill is somewhat less effective than other types of birth-control pills and has been associated with a higher incidence of irregular bleeding.

Either the combination pill or the minipill should be taken only when prescribed by a physician who has detailed information about the woman's previous medical history. Contraindications—reasons for not prescribing birth-control pills—include hypertension, impaired liver function, known or suspected tumors that are estrogen-dependent, undiagnosed abnormal genital bleeding, pregnancy at the time of the examination, and a history of poor blood circulation. The major complications associated with taking oral contraceptives are blood clots and high blood pressure. Also, the risk of heart attack is increased in women over age 30, particularly those who smoke or have other risk factors. Women over 40 should generally use other forms of contraception, because the side effects of contraceptive pills increase with the age of the user. Infertility problems have also been noted in women who have used the combination pill for several years without the breaks in pill use recommended by most physicians.

Although the long-term negative consequences of taking birth-control pills are still the subject of research, short-term negative effects are experienced by 25 percent of all women who use them. These mild side effects include increased susceptibility to vaginal infections, nausea, slight weight gain, vaginal bleeding between periods, breast tenderness, mild headaches, and mood changes (some women become depressed and experience a loss of sexual desire).

Consideration

In spite of the negative consequences associated with birth-control pill use, numerous studies involving hundreds of thousands of women show that the overall risk of pill use is less than the risk of full-term pregnancy and giving birth.

Immediate health benefits are also derived from taking birth-control pills. Oral contraceptives tend to protect the woman against breast tumors, ovarian cysts, rheumatoid arthritis, and inflammatory diseases of the pelvis. They also regularize the woman's menstrual cycle, reduce premenstrual tension, and may reduce menstrual cramps and blood loss during menstruation. Finally, oral contraceptives are convenient, do not interfere with intercourse, and most important, provide highly effective protection against pregnancy.

Whether to use birth-control pills remains a controversial issue. Some women feel it harms their body to take birth-control pills; others feel it harms their body not to take them. Whatever a woman's choice, it should be made in conjunction with the physician who knows her medical history.

Condom

Also referred to as a "rubber," "safe," or "prophylactic," the condom is currently the only form of male contraception. The condom is a thin sheath, usually made of synthetic material or lamb intestine, which is rolled over and down the shaft of the erect penis before intercourse. When the man ejaculates, the sperm are caught inside the condom. When used in combination with a spermicidal, or sperm-killing, agent, which the woman inserts in her vagina, the condom is a highly effective contraceptive. It is the second most frequently used contraceptive.

Data – Seven percent of married white women and 3 percent of married black women reported their partners used a condom. (*Statistical Abstract of the United States,* 1987) Twelve percent of all sexually active unmarried white women and 9 percent of all sexually active unmarried black women reported their partners used a condom. (Tanfer & Rosenbaum, 1986)

Consideration

The condom is the only contraceptive that provides some protection against sexually transmitted diseases.

Some men say they do not like to use a condom because it decreases sensation. Others say that having the woman put the condom on their penis is an erotic experience and that the condom actually enhances pleasurable feelings during intercourse.

Like any contraceptive, the condom is effective only when properly used. A space should be left at the top of the condom (some condoms already have a recessed tip) when it is rolled onto the penis to leave room for the semen to collect. Otherwise the condom may break. In addition, the penis should be withdrawn from the vagina soon after ejaculation. If the penis is not withdrawn and the erection subsides, the semen will leak from the base of the condom into the vaginal lips. The sperm can then travel up the vagina into the uterus and fertilize the egg.

In addition to furnishing extra protection, spermicides also provide lubrication, which permits easy entrance of the condom-covered penis into the vagina. If no spermicide is used and the condom is not of the prelubricated variety, K-Y jelly, a sterile lubricant, may be needed. Vaseline or other kinds of petroleum jelly should not be used because they may increase the risk of vaginal infection.

Condoms can be purchased in drugstores and most convenience stores. Among the brand names are Trojan, Ramses, Sheik, Naturalamb, and Fourex. The last two are made from lamb intestine and are considerably more expensive than condoms made from synthetic material.

Intrauterine Device (IUD)

The intrauterine device, or IUD, is a small object that is inserted by a physician into the women's uterus through the vagina and cervix. Due to problems (infertility, miscarriage) associated with IUDs and subsequent lawsuits, only one remains on the market—Progestasert T, which contains a slow-releasing progesterone and must be replaced every year by the physician. Although used most frequently by women who have had a child, some women who have never been pregnant may also use the IUD.

Data – Four percent of married white women and 5 percent of married black women use an IUD. (*Statistical Abstract of the United States,* 1987) Four percent of sexually active unmarried white women and 8 percent of sexually active unmarried black women report using an IUD. (Tanfer and Rosenbaum, 1986)

The IUD works by preventing implantation of the fertilized egg on the uterine wall. The exact chemistry is unknown, but one theory suggests that the IUD stimulates the entry of white blood cells into the uterus, which attack and destroy "invading" cells—in this case, the fertilized egg. Implantation may also be prevented by the IUD mechanically dislodging the egg from the uterine wall.

Whenever I hear people discussing birth control, I always remember that I was the fifth.
—Clarence Darrow

Side effects of the IUD include cramps, excessive menstrual bleeding, and irregular bleeding, or spotting, between menstrual periods. These effects may disappear after the first two months of use. Infection and perforation are more serious side effects. Users of the IUD have a higher incidence of pelvic inflammatory disease, which infects the uterus and Fallopian tubes and may lead to sterility. In addition, the IUD may cut or perforate the uterine walls or cervix, resulting in bleeding and pain.

Consideration

Due to these potential side effects, women who plan to have children should consider using a method of contraception other than the IUD.

Some women are unable to retain the IUD; it irritates the muscles of the uterus, causing them to contract and expel the device. To make sure that the IUD remains in place, a woman should check it at least once a month just after her period. The Progestasert T is particularly vulnerable to expulsion.

The fact that the IUD does not prevent conception is its greatest advantage and disadvantage. The advantage is that the IUD does not interfere with the body's normal hormonal and physiological responses. The disadvantage is that it permits conception and then destroys the fertilized egg, which is morally repugnant to some people. "It's the same as abortion," said one devout Catholic. Also, women who do get pregnant (tubal pregnancies with the Progestasert T do occur) while using the IUD must make a decision about whether to leave it in or remove it. There is a 50 percent chance of miscarriage if the IUD is left in and a 25 percent chance of miscarriage if the IUD is taken out. In most cases, the IUD is removed. However, there are no reports of birth defects if the IUD is left in and the baby is carried to a term delivery.

DIAPHRAGM

Data – Five percent of married white women and 2 percent of married black women use the diaphragm. (*Statistical Abstract of the United States,* 1987) Nine percent of sexually active unmarried white women and 3 percent of sexually active unmarried black women use the diaphragm. (Tanfer & Rosenbaum, 1986)

The diaphragm is a shallow rubber dome attached to a flexible, circular steel spring. Varying in diameter from 2 to 4 inches, the diaphragm covers the cervix and prevents sperm from moving beyond the vagina into the uterus. This device should always be used with a spermicidal jelly or cream.

To obtain a diaphragm, the woman must have an internal pelvic examination by a physician or nurse practitioner who will select the appropriate size of diaphragm and instruct the woman how to insert it. She will be told to apply one teaspoonful of spermicidal cream or jelly on the inside of the diaphragm and around the rim and to insert it into the vagina no more than two hours before intercourse. The diaphragm must also be left in place for 6 to 8 hours after intercourse to permit any lingering sperm to be killed by the spermicidal cream.

After the birth of a child, a miscarriage, abdominal surgery, or the gain or loss of 10 pounds, a woman who uses a diaphragm should consult her physician or health practitioner to ensure a continued good fit. In any case, the diaphragm should be checked every two years for fit.

A major advantage of the diaphragm is that it does not interfere with the woman's hormonal system and has few, if any, side effects. Also, for those couples who feel that menstruation diminishes their capacity to enjoy intercourse, the diaphragm may be used to catch the menstrual flow.

On the negative side, some women feel that use of the diaphragm with the spermicidal gel is messy and a nuisance. For some, the use of the gel may produce an allergic reaction. Furthermore, some partners feel that the gel makes oral–genital contact less enjoyable. Finally, if the diaphragm does not fit properly, pregnancy can result.

Vaginal Spermicides

Data – Less than 2 percent of both white and black married women use contraceptive foam. (*Statistical Abstract of the United States*, 1987) Three percent of sexually active unmarried white women and 4 percent of sexually active unmarried black women use spermacides. (Tanfer & Rosenbaum, 1986)

Spermicidal foam contains chemicals that kill sperm. The foam must be applied near the cervix (appropriate applicators are included when the product is purchased) no more than 20 minutes before intercourse. Each time intercourse is repeated, more foam must be applied. Spermicidal creams also kill sperm; each application comes individually packaged, and the packaging can be disposed of after use.

Foams are advantageous because they do not manipulate the woman's hormonal system and they have few side effects. These include allergic reactions in some men and women (their genitals may become irritated by the chemicals in the foam). The main disadvantage of contraceptive foam is that some regard its use as messy and its taste unpleasant if oral–genital contact is enjoyed.

Consideration

Contraceptive foams, such as Delfen and Emko, should not be confused with vaginal deodorants, such as Summer's Eve. The latter has no contraceptive value. Spermicidal foams should also not be confused with spermicidal gels that are used in conjunction with a diaphragm. These gels should never be used alone because they do not stick to the cervix as well as foam does.

Vaginal suppositories also contain spermicide. They are inserted about 30 minutes before intercourse. Also known as pessaries, vaginal suppositories provide protection by killing sperm and weakening sperm motility.

VAGINAL SPONGE

One of the newest contraceptives to win approval by the Food and Drug Administration is the vaginal sponge. The sponge is 2 inches in diameter, 1¼ inches thick, and contains spermicide that is activated when the sponge is immersed in water before insertion into the vagina. A small loop allows for easy removal of the sponge. Like condoms and spermicidal foams, the sponge is available in drugstores without a prescription. The brand name for the sponge is Today. It prevents fertilization, not only by releasing spermicide to kill sperm but also by blocking the cervix to prevent the sperm from entering and by absorbing sperm into the sponge.

Data – The Today sponge is the leading over-the-counter female contraceptive. (Collins, 1986)

A major advantage of the sponge is that it allows for spontaneity in lovemaking. It can be inserted early in the day, may be worn for up to 24 hours, and may be used for more than one act of intercourse without requiring additional applications of spermicide. According to FDA tests on 1,582 sponge users, the sponge is comparable to the diaphragm in effectiveness.

Consideration

Difficulty in removing the sponge and toxic shock syndrome when the sponge is used during the menstrual period have been reported by women using the sponge. The first problem has not been significant, but the second may be dangerous. The sponge should not be used during the menstrual period. (Greenberg et al., 1986)

RHYTHM METHOD

Data – Three percent of married women use the rhythm method. (*Statistical Abstract of the United States*, 1987)

The rhythm method is based on the premise that fertilization cannot occur unless live sperm are present when the egg is in the Fallopian tubes. Sperm usually live two to three days, whereas an egg lives 24 hours. Women who use the rhythm method must know their time of ovulation and avoid intercourse just before, during, and immediately after that time. There are four ways of predicting the presumed safe period: the calendar method, the basal body temperature method, the cervical mucus method, and the hormone-in-urine method.

Calendar Method

When using the calendar method to predict when the egg is ready to be fertilized, the woman keeps a record of the length of her menstrual cycles for eight months. The menstrual cycle is counted from day one of the menstrual period through the last day before the onset of the next period. She then calculates her fertile period by subtracting 18 days from the shortest cycle and 11 days from the longest cycle. The resulting figures indicate the range of her fertility period. It is during this time that the woman must avoid intercourse.

For example, suppose that during an eight-month period, a woman had cycle lengths of 26, 32, 27, 30, 28, 27, 28, and 29 days. Subtracting 18 from her shortest cycle (26) and 11 from her longest cycle (32), she knows the days that the egg is likely to be in the Fallopian tubes. To avoid getting pregnant, she must avoid intercourse on days 8 through 21 of her cycle.

Consideration

The calendar method of predicting the "safe" period is unreliable for two reasons. First, the next month the woman may ovulate at a different time from any of the previous eight months. Second, sperm life varies; they may live long enough to meet the next egg in the Fallopian tubes.

Basal Body Temperature (BBT) Method

This method is based on temperature changes that occur in the woman's body shortly after ovulation. The basal body temperature is the temperature of the body at rest on waking in the morning. To establish her BBT, the woman must take her temperature for three months at this time before she gets out of bed. Just before ovulation, her temperature will drop about 0.2° F. Between 24 and 72 hours later, there will be a rise in temperature of about 0.6–0.8° F above her normal BBT, signaling the time of ovulation. Intercourse must be avoided from the time the woman's temperature drops until her temperature has remained elevated for three consecutive days. Beginning on the night of the third day after the temperature shift is observed, she may resume having intercourse.

Cervical Mucus Method

The cervical mucus method is based on observations of changes in the mucus cycle from no perceptible mucus for several days after menstruation to sticky to very slippery mucus during ovulation to a cloudy discharge after ovulation ends. The mucus becomes thin and slippery, very similar to raw egg white, during ovulation to create a favorable environment for sperm. The woman should abstain from intercourse as soon as mucus appears before ovulation and continue to do so for four complete days after the peak of cervical mucus. A woman can check her cervical mucus by wiping herself with toilet paper several times a day before she urinates and observing the changes. This method requires the woman to distinguish between mucus and semen, spermicidal agents, lubrication, and infectious discharges. Also, the woman must not douche because she will wash away what she is trying to observe.

Other labels for the cervical mucus method are natural family planning and the Billings method (named after Evelyn and John Billings). Associated with the Billings method is the woman's observation of the *Mittelschmerz*—the mid-cycle abdominal pain or "ping" sometimes associated with ovulation.

Hormone-in-Urine Method

A hormone is released into the bloodstream of the ovulating female 12 to 24 hours prior to ovulation. Women can purchase First Response and Ovutime, two variations of the same test, in drugstores to ascertain if they have ovulated.

Nonmethods

Some people erroneously regard withdrawal and douching as effective methods of contraception. They are not.

Withdrawal

Withdrawal, also known as *coitus interruptus*, is the practice of the man taking his penis out of the vagina before he ejaculates. Not only does this technique interrupt sexual pleasure, but it is also an unreliable means of contraception. Even before ejaculation, the man can, without his awareness, emit a small amount of fluid from the Cowper's gland, which may contain sperm. In addition, the man may delay his withdrawal too long and inadvertently ejaculate some semen near the vaginal opening of his partner. Sperm deposited here can live in the moist vaginal lips and make their way up the vagina to the uterus.

Douching

Douching refers to rinsing or cleansing the vaginal canal. After intercourse, the woman fills a syringe with water or a spermicidal agent and flushes (so she assumes) the sperm from her vagina. But in some cases, the fluid will actually force sperm up through the cervix. In other cases, a large number of sperm may already have passed through the cervix to the uterus, so that the douche may do little good.

Consideration

In effect, a douche does little to deter conception and may encourage it. Also, most physicians question the advisability of douching. They feel that doing so may create chemical imbalances in the vagina that may lead to infection.

Postcoital Contraception

Some women who have engaged in unprotected intercourse in the middle of their cycle elect to take a morning-after pill, which contains high levels of estrogen to prevent implantation of the fertilized egg on the uterine wall. This is an emergency form of birth control, is potentially dangerous, and is available only by prescription from a physician.

Diethylstilbestrol (DES) is the most commonly used morning-after pill. The first of ten 25 milligram doses must be taken within 72 hours after intercourse (preferably, within 12 to 24 hours). Normally, the pills are taken twice a day for five days.

Consideration

Side effects of nausea, vomiting, bleeding abnormalities, and blood clots make routine use of this drug undesirable. In addition, studies indicate that the offspring of women who took DES (not knowing they were pregnant) were more likely to have birth defects and an increased risk of vaginal cancer and infertility. If the woman remains pregnant after taking DES, she might consider a therapeutic abortion.

A new drug—RW486—has no significant side effects and can end a pregnancy 85 percent of the time if taken within two weeks after a missed period. The drug is available in Europe but not in the United States.

Avoiding Sexually Transmitted Diseases and Pregnancy

A condom that is put on before the penis touches the other person's body will make it difficult for sexually transmitted diseases or STDs (including genital herpes and AIDS) to pass from one person to another.

It isn't very romantic to talk about STDs with a partner you are about to have sex with, but to ignore STDs one minute is to risk contracting one the next. Contraception should also be discussed before sexual intercourse. Not to do so involves the risk of unwanted pregnancy.

What might a person say about the issues of sexually transmitted diseases and protection from pregnancy before having a sexual experience with a new partner? Maggie Hayes at the University of Oklahoma asked her students how they would handle the situation if they were on an isolated moonlit beach with a person they wanted to have sex with. Some of their responses follow:

> In a situation like this, you have to be open and discuss the consequences. If this "messes up the mood," maybe that's the best thing—better than ending up diseased or pregnant. You can't let your feelings and your hormones [urges] control this situation. (a female)

> Even in the heat of passion, one still has to be concerned about herpes and pregnancy. I would first ask if he was going to share something with me that he knew I wouldn't want him to share. I would definitely clarify if necessary. I would also state that I am not ready to be a mother and that some sort of birth control is necessary to continue. (a female)

> The discussion of protection against pregnancy could be entwined into the romance of the evening, perhaps even made part of verbiage in sexual play. The discussion would probably not be purely sensual—rather one in which feelings of care and love are conveyed. The discussion of STD would not be nearly as simple. It would be next to impossible to keep this subject within the mood of the evening. One of the parties will probably be offended. Nonetheless, this topic is of vital importance to discuss—mind you, lightly, but it must be done. Perhaps after putting it into perspective for "our future," not to hurt each other, the ground lost can be recovered later in the evening. (a female)

> I would just have to come right out and question my partner point blank about the subjects. If she had no protection, I'd make a quick trip to the convenience store to buy

a condom if possible or abstain if not. If she had an STD, I would take her back to her place and ride off into the sunset as quickly as possible, never to return. (a male)

Bringing up a subject like herpes or contraception would seem to detract from the mood more than would abstinence. This fact, along with the guilt feelings I would have to deal with after the experience, with or without protection, has been enough incentive in this situation in the past to get me to stop short of intercourse, so that the beauty of the memory is as great as the beauty of the moment. I'll keep it that way. (a male)

Since this is a new experience for us, we would probably both be more comfortable if we completely leveled with each other about protection. This includes birth control as well as sexually transmitted disease. Is this agreeable with you? If the partner doesn't want to discuss it, I'd be wary of the partner. I'd also be aware that complete honesty is not always forthcoming in such situations. Open communication enhances any relationship—sexual or otherwise. (gender not specified)

The person most likely to discuss contraception with a potential sexual partner is usually involved in a relationship with that person, feels comfortable about his or her own body, and has had sufficient sex education to know about fertilization.

Data – In surveys over a 12-year period involving more than 8,000 students, fewer than 15 percent reported they received a meaningful sex education from their parents. (Gordon, 1986)

Students taking a sex-education course are more likely to use contraception. (Marsiglio & Mott, 1986; Dawson, 1986)

Teenage Pregnancy

Data – One in ten teenage girls becomes pregnant every year. Almost half of these pregnancies result in births—*30,000 of them* to girls under the age of 15. (Stark, 1986)

Teenage girls become pregnant for a number of reasons:

1. Not understanding the connection between their behavior and the consequences to follow.
2. Having a poor self-image that leads them to have a baby who will love them.
3. Being swept away by love into passionate sex.
4. Being a member of a society that does not adequately encourage the use of contraception.

For teenagers who want to get pregnant so that they can have a baby to love them, programs are now operative to teach them that they can be somebody without needing to be a mother or a father (Height, 1986).

Family acceptance of pregnancy is also a factor. Among black teenage fathers, teenage pregnancy is viewed as "common, accepted, and minimally disruptive to their lives now or in the future" (Rivara et al. 1985, p. 648).

The teenage pregnancy rate for the United States is almost twice that of France, England, and Canada, three times that of Sweden, and seven times that of the Netherlands. Teenagers in these countries are as sexually active as U.S. teenagers but have easier access to sex education and contraception (Stark, 1986).

Our approach to sex education should be the same as our approach to alcohol: Don't drink, but if you do drink, don't drive. Don't have intercourse as a teenager, but if you do have intercourse, use a reliable form of contraception (Gordon, 1986).

Sterilization

Unlike the temporary and reversible methods of contraception just discussed, sterilization is a permanent surgical procedure that prevents either gender from reproducing. Sterilization is losing its stigma as an extreme and undesirable method of birth control. It may be a contraceptive method of choice because the woman should not have more children for health reasons or because of a desire to have no more children or to remain child-free. Most couples complete their intended childbearing in their late twenties or early thirties, leaving more than 15 years of continued risk of unwanted pregnancy. Due to the risk of pill use at older ages and the lower reliability of alternative birth-control methods, sterilization has become the most popular method of contraception among married women who have completed their families.

Slightly more than half of all sterilizations are performed on women. Although male sterilization is easier and safer than female sterilization, women feel more certain they will not get pregnant if they are sterilized. "I'm the one that ends up being pregnant and having the baby," said one woman. "So I want to make sure that I never get pregnant again."

Female Sterilization

Data – Twenty-six percent of married white women and 22 percent of married black women have been sterilized. (*Statistical Abstract of the United States*, 1987)

Although a woman may be sterilized by removal of her ovaries (oophorectomy) or uterus (hysterectomy), these operations are not normally undertaken for the sole purpose of sterilization because the ovaries produce important hormones as well as eggs and because both procedures carry the risks of major surgery. But sometimes there is another medical problem requiring hysterectomy.

The usual procedures of female sterilization are the salpingectomy, or tubal ligation, and a variant of it, the laparoscopy. Salpingectomy, also known as "tubal ligation" or "tying the tubes," is often performed under a general anesthetic while the woman is in the hospital just after she has delivered a baby. An incision is made in the lower abdomen, just above the pubic line, and the Fallopian tubes are brought into view one at a time. A part of each tube is cut out, and the ends are tied, clamped, or cauterized (burned). The operation takes about 30 minutes. About 700,000 such procedures are performed annually. The cost is around $1,500.

A less expensive and quicker (about 15 minutes) form of salpingectomy, which is performed on an outpatient basis, is the laparoscopy. Often using local anesthesia, the surgeon inserts a small, lighted viewing instrument (laparoscope) through the woman's abdominal wall just below the navel through which the uterus and the Fallopian tubes can be seen. The surgeon then makes another small incision in the lower abdomen and inserts a special pair of forceps that carry electricity to cauterize the tubes. The laparoscope and forceps are then withdrawn, the small wounds are closed with a single stitch, and small bandages are placed over the closed incisions. (Laparoscopy is also known as "the band-aid operation").

As an alternative to reaching the Fallopian tubes through an opening below the navel, the surgeon may make a small incision in the back of the vaginal barrel (vaginal tubal ligation).

These procedures for female sterilization are highly effective, but sometimes there are complications. In rare cases, a blood vessel in the abdomen is torn open during the sterilization and bleeds into the abdominal cavity. When this happens, another operation is necessary to find the bleeding vessel and tie it closed. Occasionally, there is injury to the small or large intestine, which may cause nausea, vomiting, and loss of appetite. The fact that death may result, if only rarely, is a reminder that female sterilization is surgery and, like all surgery, involves some risks.

Male Sterilization

Data – Sixteen percent of married white women and 4 percent of married black women said their husbands had had a vasectomy. (*Statistical Abstract of the United States*, 1987)

The most frequent form of male sterilization is the vasectomy. About 750,000 are performed annually, usually in the physician's office under a local anesthetic. Vasectomy involves making two small incisions in the scrotum so that a small portion of each vas deferens (the sperm-carrying ducts) can be cut out and tied closed. Sperm are still produced in the testicles, but since there is no tube to the penis, they remain in the testicles and eventually dissolve. The operation takes about 15 minutes and costs about $300; the man can leave the physician's office within a short time. Most vasectomies are performed Friday afternoon so that an employed man will not have to miss work.

Since sperm do not disappear from the ejaculate immediately after a vasectomy, another method of contraception should be used until the man has had about 20 ejaculations. He is then asked to bring a sample of his ejaculate to the physician's office so that it can be examined under a microscope for a sperm count. In about 1 percent of the cases, the vas deferens grows back and the man becomes fertile again. In other cases, the man may have more than two tubes, which the physician was not aware of.

A vasectomy does not affect the man's desire for sex, ability to have an erection, orgasm, amount of ejaculate (sperm comprise only a minute portion of the seminal fluid), or health. Although a vasectomy may be reversed, a man should get a vasectomy only if he never wants to have a biological child.

Abortion

What if an unwanted pregnancy occurs? Keeping the baby or allowing the baby to be adopted are viable options. A more controversial alternative is an abortion—the removal of the fetus from the woman's uterus early in pregnancy before it can survive on its own (91 percent of all abortions are obtained within the first 12 weeks of gestation).

Data – Of the 1.6 million abortions performed annually in the United States, most are obtained by women who are young (63 percent are age 24 or younger), white (70 percent of all abortions), and unmarried (81 percent of all abortions), including the never-married, separated, divorced, and widowed. (*Statistical Abstract of the United States,* 1987) Women who have abortions and who carry their babies to term do not differ in terms of personality characteristics. (Baetsen et al., 1985)

The woman with an unwanted pregnancy may be beset by a number of strong feelings: fear ("What will I do now?"); self-anger ("How could I let this happen?"); guilt ("What would my parents think if they knew I was pregnant?"); ambivalence ("Will I be sorry if I have an abortion? Will I be sorry if I don't?"); and sometimes desperation ("Is suicide a way out?").

Consideration

One of the best decisions during this period of crisis is to talk with an abortion counselor or a counselor at a local mental-health center. These professionals are trained to help women look at alternatives to unwanted pregnancy and to help them decide what course of action is best for the individual woman. Perhaps most important, they can help the pregnant woman to make her decision with care and deliberation rather than under pressure.

Methods of Induced Abortion

An abortion may be spontaneous (by miscarriage) or induced. Methods of inducing an abortion include the following.

Suction Curettage

Data – Ninety-four percent of all abortions are performed using suction curettage. (National Center for Health Statistics, 1986)

In suction curettage, a hollow plastic rod attached to a suction aspirator is inserted into the woman's uterus through the cervix, which has been dilated and anesthetized. The device draws the fetal tissue and surrounding matter out of the uterus. Suction curettage can be performed in a physician's office and takes about 10 minutes. If done within eight weeks of the last menstrual period, the dilation and anesthesia may not be necessary and the procedure is referred to as a menstrual extraction.

Dilation and Curettage (D and C)

Data – One percent of all abortions are performed using the D and C method. (National Center for Health Statistics, 1986)

In place of the suction curettage, a metal surgical instrument is used to scrape the fetal tissue and placenta from the walls of the uterus. A general anesthetic is usually administered. This more traditional procedure is regarded as inferior to the suction curettage method.

Dilation and Evacuation (D and E)

Used in the second trimester, D and E is a combination of the vacuum curettage and D and C methods. However, greater dilation of the cervical opening is required.

Saline Injection

Data – Three percent of all abortions involve saline injection. (National Center for Health Statistics, 1986)

As pregnancy progresses, the fetus becomes too large to be removed safely by any of the preceding methods. Abortion by saline may be performed by inserting a long needle containing a concentrated salt solution through the abdominal and uterine walls into the amniotic cavity. This kills the fetus. From six to 48 hours later, the uterus contracts until the fetus is pushed out into the vagina.

Consideration

Because saline injection is a major surgical procedure, earlier termination of pregnancy is desirable.

A variation of the saline method of abortion is the use of prostaglandins—hormonelike substances that cause the uterus to contract. When introduced into the vagina as a suppository or injected into the amniotic sac, they induce labor and the fetus is aborted.

Data – Less than one percent of all abortions involve the use of prostaglandins. (National Center for Health Statistics, 1986)

Abortion is an experience that is different for each woman. Exhibit 15.1 describes three abortion experiences.

Abortion Legislation

In 1973, the U.S. Supreme Court ruled that during the first three months of pregnancy, a woman has the right to obtain an abortion from a licensed physician without interference by the state. From the fourth through the sixth month, the decision to have an abortion belongs to the woman and her physician, but because an abortion at this later stage of pregnancy is more dangerous, the state may require that the abortion be performed in a hospital. During the last three months of pregnancy, the state may prohibit abortion except in those cases where the life or health of the mother is in danger. Neither a woman's husband nor her parents may veto her decision. In effect, the Su-

Exhibit 15.1

THREE ABORTION EXPERIENCES

Mary found out that she was pregnant a week after she and her partner had broken their engagement.

> I had just begun the first quarter of my freshman year and did not know anyone on campus. At the time, I thought abortion was the only way out since none of my friends were close by. Little did I know I was about to go through what has been the most traumatic experience of my life.
>
> I became fast friends with a campus minister, and approximately one month after I found out I was pregnant I had an appointment to have the abortion. The "day" came, and my new friend drove me to the clinic. I went through the procedures of paying, talking with a therapist, and finally being taken to a small, white room where all the equipment was. I lay on a table with nothing but a hospital "robe" for nearly a half hour, during which I almost changed my mind. The doctor finally came in and the abortion was over in about 20 minutes—with some pain and the worst two needles I have ever received.
>
> After "it" was over, I lay there for another 15 to 20 minutes, feeling very scared and sick. I wanted to just burst out in tears, but I was afraid if I did, I would never stop crying. I remember how I wished I had been strong enough to change my mind before. I then got dressed and went to rest in a small room where my friend was waiting. I was amazed at how calm and unfeeling I seemed to be—at least as far as the doctor and nurse saw.
>
> But about a week later I found myself in bed one night crying . . .. I just kept thinking what I had done. It took several months before I could go an entire day without thinking about it. I felt like I had a constant pain way down deep in my stomach—the loss of a part of me. I began to appreciate my life in a very different way, realizing that I had no right to take another person's life—my baby's. One thing is for sure, I would never have another abortion.

Pam was involved in a four-year relationship with a man, during which time she had two abortions.

> The first pregnancy was an accident and happened when I was 18. It terrified me to know I was pregnant. Both of us were planning to go to college, so we knew the pregnancy had to be terminated. Neither of us was ready for a child. He paid for the abortion and went with me to the clinic. The abortion was a frightening and painful experience, but I kept my head straight and only thought about the realistic view of the situation.
>
> The second pregnancy was mostly my fault so we shared the expense of the abortion. As was true the first time, the abortion was painful but not as frightening because I knew what to expect. This time we gave the idea of keeping the baby more thought and it was through the process of pros and cons that we decided to terminate the pregnancy. I have no regrets about either abortion because I know it was the right thing for me and for the baby.

Joan was married and in her fifth month of pregnancy. Because of a genetic disorder that would prevent their baby from being born alive, the pregnancy had to be terminated.

> The physician induced labor, and I was in labor for 16 hours. The labor was followed by a very difficult breech birth. Each labor pain seemed to drive home the fact that the baby we had was lost. When the fetus was delivered, she was nearly the size of a newborn because of her genetic disorder. It was unreal to see them carry away our baby bundled in a blanket. There was no excitement or joy that went with the birth, only the realization that physically our ordeal was almost over. Emotionally, we would have a long way to go. One thing that stood out in our minds was the incredible feeling of death. One day I had been so enormously pregnant and the next day I wasn't—with no baby to show for it. All our hopes and expectations had been "terminated" with the pregnancy.

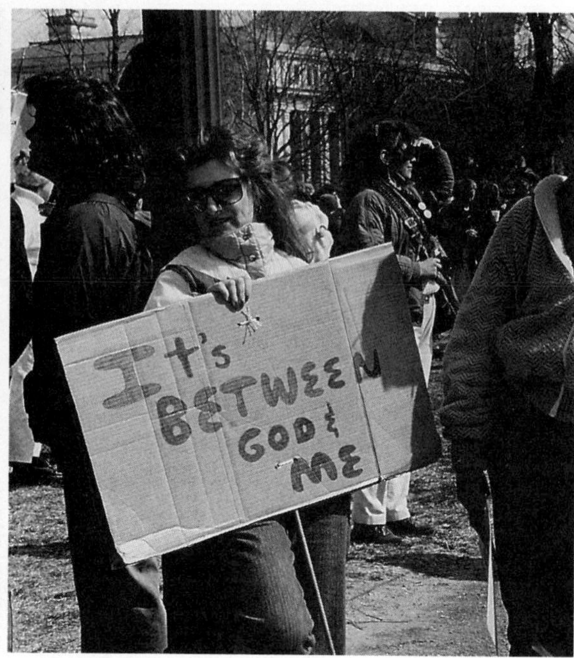

Abortion continues to be a highly debated issue.

preme Court ruled that the fetus is a *potential* life and not a "person." It is generally agreed that before six months there is little chance for the fetus to survive on its own.

In 1980, the Supreme Court ruled that federal funds could not be used to pay for abortions. This ruling upheld the Hyde Amendment (sponsored by U.S. Representative Henry Hyde), which restricted congressional spending of Medicaid funds for abortions when the mother's life was not in danger or when she was not impregnated by rape or incest. Although the decision has had little effect on abortion among affluent women, women with limited incomes who have an unwanted pregnancy—about half a million women per year—are seriously affected. Many of these women carry their pregnancies to term rather than resort to nonmedical abortions that are likely to be unsafe. But the cost of these babies to the American public is high—$339.6 million over a two-year period (Torres et al., 1986).

In 1983, the Supreme Court reaffirmed its position on abortion and struck down several state and local regulations designed to make obtaining an abortion more difficult. The court declared unconstitutional regulations requiring that (1) all abortions for women more than three months pregnant be performed in hospitals rather than clinics; (2) physicians tell women seeking abortions about possible birth-giving alternatives, abortion risks, and that the fetus is a human life; (3) there be at least a 24–hour waiting period between the time a woman signs a consent form and the abortion is performed; and (4) all pregnant, unwed girls under 15 must obtain a parent's consent or have a judge's approval before having an abortion.

In 1986, the Supreme Court struck down a Pennsylvania law requiring that detailed medical, financial, and counseling information be given to a patient 24 hours before an abortion. Justice Harry Blackmun wrote, "The state is not free, under the guise of protecting maternal health or potential life, to intimidate women into continuing pregnancies."

Trends

Trends in contraception are continued difficulty in reaching sexually active adolescents, more people who choose sterilization, and new contraceptive methods.

One new contraceptive method is a subdermal implant (Norplant 2) of levonorgestrel (a synthetic progestin) under the skin of the woman's arm. The procedure (minor surgery performed with a local anesthetic) takes about five minutes and furnishes protection against pregnancy for five years or more. Fertility returns after the implants are removed. Also being tested is an implant that is effective for one year and that is biodegradable and therefore does not require surgical removal.

A plastic ring placed in the vagina which would release contraceptive steroids and an antipregnancy vaccine to prevent the necessary hormonal changes for implantation of the egg in the uterus is also being tested.

Further, a pill is being tested that could be taken after sexual relations that occur in midcycle, when there is a likelihood of pregnancy. Such a pill would be useful to women who have intercourse sporadically and do not need continuous protection. This pill is currently not available (Atkinson et al., 1986).

For men, hormonal contraceptives such as MPA (medroxyprogesterone acetate) and TO (testosterone oenanthate) have been tested in Toronto, London, and Santiago, but have not received FDA approval for use in the United States. Gossypol, an extract of cottonseed oil, has also been tested in China as an oral contraceptive. U.S. research firms are now testing the long-term safety of gossypol. A major problem in male contraceptives has been to develop one that reduces sperm count without reducing sexual interest or making the man permanently sterile.

New forms of contraception are being researched and tested.

Finally, the Planned Parenthood Federation of America is putting pressure on the television networks to allow contraception to be advertised. They point out that each year there are 20,000 references to intercourse on television but not one to the responsible use of contraception. This pressure will result in the advertisement of condoms on television.

Summary

The primary methods of birth control are contraception, sterilization, and abortion. With contraception, the risk of becoming pregnant can be reduced to practically zero, depending on the method selected and how systematically it is used. Contraception includes birth-control pills, which prevent ovulation; the IUD, which prevents implantation of the fertilized egg; condoms and diaphragms, which are barrier methods; as well as vaginal spermicides and sponge, the rhythm method, withdrawal, and douching. These methods vary in effectiveness and safety.

Sterilization is a surgical procedure that prevents fertilization, usually by blocking the passage of eggs or sperm through the Fallopian tubes or vas deferens, respectively. The procedure for female sterilization is called salpingectomy, or tubal ligation. Laparoscopy is another method of tubal ligation. The most frequent form of male sterilization is vasectomy.

Abortion is one alternative if an unwanted pregnancy occurs. Methods of inducing abortion include suction curettage, dilation and curettage (D and C), and dilation and evacuation (D and E), all of which are used in the earlier stages of pregnancy; saline and prostaglandin injection are used when the pregnancy is more advanced. In 1973, the U.S. Supreme Court ruled that the abortion decision rests with the woman and her physician. Although the right to abortion has come under increasing legislative attack, the Supreme Court in 1983 and 1986 struck down a number of state and local regulations designed to restrict abortions.

TABLE 15.1 CONTRACEPTIVE EFFECTIVENESS

Methods	*Degree of Effectiveness*
Abstinence	100%
Abortion	100%
Female sterilization	99%
Male sterilization	99%
Birth-control pills	98%
IUD	95%
Condom	64–97%
Diaphragm with spermicide	80–98%
Spermicidal sponge	80–87%
Spermicial foam	70–80%
Basal body temperature (BBT) method	56–86%
Spermicidal suppositories	70–80%
Rhythm method	53–86%

Source: *FDA Consumer,* May 1985. FDA Pub. No. 85–1123. Washington, D.C.: Department of Health and Human Services, 1985.

QUESTIONS FOR REFLECTION

1. How do you feel about discussing contraception with a new sexual partner?
2. How do you feel about becoming sterilized?
3. To what degree are you prochoice or prolife regarding abortion? (This question will become more relevant after you read the Choices section that follows.)

CHOICES

THE AVAILABILITY OF contraception, sterilization, and abortion involves a number of personal and couple choices.

CONTRACEPTION: WHICH METHOD?

Although age, marital status, partner preference, and whether you want a child later will affect your choice of a contraceptive method, here we will discuss the issues of personal values, health, reliability, sexual fulfillment, and psychological contentment. Do your personal values permit you to use one of the more reliable forms of contraception (that is, a mechanical or chemical method)? "It's a sin to use anything but the rhythm method," one woman said, "I would feel immoral putting any of those devices in my body or contaminating my system with birth-control pills." But others feel it is immoral not to use one of the more effective contraceptive procedures.

Another major concern is your health. Some women are at risk using the pill or the IUD. If safety is the major concern, barrier methods, such as the condom plus spermicide or diaphragm plus spermicide, offer the greatest protection with the least risk to the woman's health. Some women whose values permit abortion choose one of these methods for health reasons and consider abortion as a backup contraceptive method.

The reliability of the contraceptive chosen is another crucial concern. Abstinence is, of course, the ultimate contraceptive, but the various nonsurgical contraceptives have varying rates of effectiveness. Table 15.1 indicates the failure rate of different contraceptive methods among one group of women. Other studies show that the pill and the IUD are identical in effectiveness and that the condom with spermicidal agent and diaphragm with spermicidal agent approximate the effectiveness of birth-control pills. The least effective method in all studies is the rhythm method.

Sexual fulfillment and psychological contentment are other issues. "It's important to me to have a good sex life," said one woman, "and fooling with a diaphragm every night is no fun. Yet I don't take the pill because I think it will harm my body." Her feelings emphasize that any decision about which contraceptive to use involves some trade-offs.

In choosing a contraceptive, it should be kept in mind that any contraceptive method carries a lower death risk than childbirth itself. Summarizing his findings on this issue, Ory (1983) said:

> Levels of mortality associated with all major methods of fertility control (tubal sterilization, the pill, IUD, condom, diaphragm, spermicides, rhythm, and abortion) are low in comparison with the risk of death associated with childbirth and ectopic pregnancy when no fertility-control method is used. The exceptions are the risks associated with pill use after the age of 40 for women who do not smoke, and with pill use after the age of 35 for smokers. The safest approach to fertility control is to use the condom and to back it up by abortion in case of method failure. (p. 62)

STERILIZATION: YES OR NO?

Most couples complete their intended childbearing in their late twenties or early thirties. This leaves more than 15 years of continued risk of unwanted pregnancy. In conjunction with the risk of pill use at older ages and the lower reliability of alternative methods, sterilization is being increasingly chosen as a primary method of fertility control. It is the most frequently used method of birth control for those 30 and over.

Among the issues to be considered for sterilization in either the man or the woman are the following:

1. *Permanence.* Sterilization should be considered permanent. Although microsurgery techniques do permit reversal of tubal ligations and vasectomies, the percentage of successful reversals that result in a baby is less than half.
2. *Self-image.* How do you predict you will feel about yourself following sterilization? As a woman, will you feel less feminine knowing that you are no longer capable of conceiving a child? As a man, will you feel less masculine because you can no longer father a child?
3. *Effect on Relationship.* How do you think sterilization will influence your relationship with your partner? Are you considering sterilization as a means of improving this relationship? No effect is the most common result of vasectomy on a couple's relationship.
4. *The Future.* There are a number of questions you might ask yourself about the future. Are you certain you will never want another child under any conditions? If you are child-free, is it possible that you will change your mind and decide you want to have a baby? If you have children, suppose they are killed by disease or accident? Would you then want to have another child? Suppose you were to get divorced (half of all married spouses do)? Might you want to have children with a new spouse? Suppose a new partner whom you love wouldn't marry you unless you could have a child?

There is also the possibility that your present spouse will die while you are still young enough to have children. One woman said:

> I was 29 and had my tubes tied after my second child was born. Brock and I had the boy and girl we wanted and saw no reason for me to continue with birth-control pills. But only a month after my laparoscopy, Brock had a heart attack and died. I'm now remarried, and my new husband and I want a child of our own.

To keep their options open, some men who decide to get a vasectomy deposit some of their sperm in a sperm vault. The largest sperm banks are Xytex in Augusta, Georgia; the Infertility-Sperm Bank Service at the University of Oregon Medical School, Portland; and Idant Corporation in New York City. Sperm storage the first year at Idant Corporation is $300. In subsequent years, the cost is $135. The probability of frozen sperm fertilizing an egg is somewhat less than that of fresh sperm.

In deciding about sterilization, it is important to balance considerations of its effect on you, your relationships and the future against the costs and benefits associated with less permanent forms of contraception.

Abortion: Prochoice or Prolife?

When faced with an unwanted pregnancy, some couples decide on abortion. These prochoice advocates believe that legislation prohibiting abortion is governmental intrusion into a woman's personal, private decision. "Keep your laws and your morality off my body" reflects the anger as well as the message women want to convey to those who try to pass laws that would require women to continue with a pregnancy whether they choose to or not. The slogan "A woman's life is a human life" is a vivid reminder that Senator Jesse Helms's Human Life Amendment would inflict tragedy and suffering on millions of women who would be forced to choose between having babies they did not want or seeking an illegal abortion with the

(Continued)

possibility of infection, permanent damage to the reproductive system, and even death.

Of all U.S. adults, 89 percent believe that a pregnant woman should be able to get a legal abortion if her health would be seriously endangered by the pregnancy; 79 percent support abortion if the baby is defective; 81 percent, if the pregnancy results from rape. Only 37 percent favor legal abortion for any reason (Smith, 1985).

For the majority of women, abortion is usually an unpleasant but necessary experience. For a smaller number of women, it can be a very emotional and stressful event. Postabortion support groups can help to alleviate such stress (Lodl et al., 1985).

Other couples who are faced with an unwanted pregnancy and who decide against abortion feel just as strongly that the unborn are defenseless human beings and that abortion is murder. "Choose life for your baby" and "Abortion is America's Holocaust" are two of the slogans on placards frequently carried by prolife advocates. They feel that legislation for the protection of the unborn is essential to prevent "helpless babies" from being killed without caution.

Some prolife advocates have become violent and set fire to or bombed abortion facilities in seven states and the District of Columbia. Others have joined with the Moral Majority's "Save the Baby" program, which provides free medical care for pregnant women anywhere in the United States, along with free room and board during the duration of their pregnancy and the use of adoption services if desired.

Impact of Social Influences on Choices

The degree to which you are prochoice or prolife is a reflection of the social groups in which you are immersed. Prochoice advocates are more likely to identify with the woman's movement; prolife, with conservative religions or Catholicism. Each group focuses on different aspects of the abortion issue. The women's movement focuses on the right of the woman to maintain control over her body; conservative religions focus on the right of the unborn baby to life.

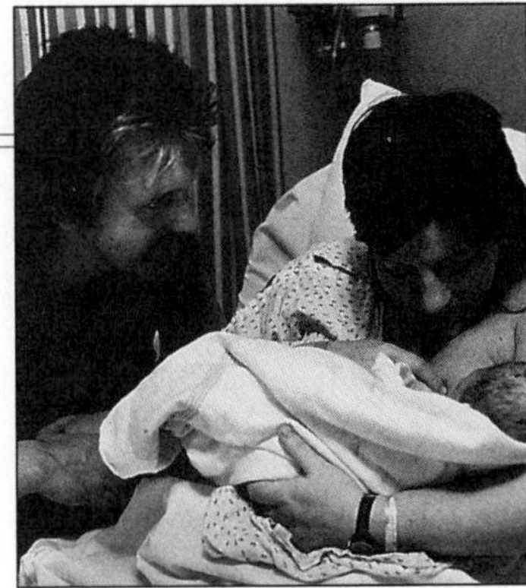

CHAPTER 16

Fertilization and Having Children

Contents

Is It True?*

1. Artificial insemination is more acceptable than adoption to college students if they are confronted with a problem of infertility.
2. Black students are more willing to use artificial insemination than whites.
3. If a couple adopts a child through a state agency, the biological mother can change her mind within 30 days and ask to have her baby back.
4. Black fathers have traditionally been absent from their homes—a pattern which began during slavery.
5. Studies agree on how children influence marital happiness.

*1=F; 2=F; 3=T; 4=F; 5=F.

WHEN A COUPLE or individual decides to have a child, getting pregnant becomes a goal. Recently, becoming pregnant through sexual intercourse has become one of several alternatives. Other alternatives include artificial insemination, in-vitro fertilization, and embryo transfer. Once a baby begins to develop, by whatever means, role transitions begin: wife to mother, husband to father, and couple to family. We will address these issues in this chapter.

Fertilization

Fertilization takes place when the female's egg, or ovum, unites with the male's sperm. This may occur through sexual intercourse or artificial insemination, or more recently, through the methods of test-tube or in-vitro fertilization and embryo transfer.

Sexual Intercourse

At orgasm, the man ejaculates a thick white substance called semen, which contains sperm.

Data – About 300 million sperm are expelled during the average ejaculation. (Greenberg et al., 1986)

Once the semen is deposited in or near the vagina, the sperm begin to travel up the vagina, through the opening of the cervix, up the uterus, and into the Fallopian tubes. If the woman has ovulated (released a mature egg from an ovary into a Fallopian tube) within eight hours, or if she ovulates during the two or three days the sperm may remain alive, a sperm may penetrate and fertilize the egg. About 30 percent of fertilized eggs die. Conception refers to a fertilized egg that survives through implantation on the uterine wall.

If the goal of an individual or a couple is to get pregnant, it is important to be patient about doing so, to time intercourse to coincide with ovulation, and to use the most efficient position during intercourse. In general, a woman in her twenties should allow herself about six months to conceive. A woman in her thirties should allow about a year, with the probability of conception dropping as the woman gets older.

Consideration

A woman who gives herself time to get pregnant will be less anxious about doing so. This is important because anxiety may affect ovulation. Social workers in adoption agencies have noted that women, frustrated and despairing over their attempts to get pregnant and seeking to adopt a child, frequently become pregnant soon after they obtain a child and their anxiety disappears. "It was only after we had completed all the red tape and finally had our adopted daughter in the bassinet that I became pregnant," recalls one mother. Stress may affect male fertility too. Testicle biopsies performed on men who were awaiting execution revealed that they had a lower sperm count than men not under such stress. The effect of ordinary levels of stress on sperm count is unknown.

When is the best time to have intercourse to maximize the chance of pregnancy? Since a woman is fertile for only about 48 hours each month, the timing of sexual intercourse is important. In general, 24 hours before ovulation is the best time. There are several ways to predict ovulation. Many women have breast tenderness, and some experience a "pinging" sensation at the time of ovulation. Also, a woman may record her basal body temperature and examine her cervical mucus. After menstruation, the vagina in most women is without noticeable discharge because the mucus is thick. As the time of ovulation nears, the mucus thins to the consistency of egg white, which may be experienced by the woman as increased vaginal discharge. Intercourse should occur during this time. In essence, the "technology" of the rhythm method to avoid pregnancy can be used to maximize the potential for pregnancy.

During intercourse, the woman should be on her back and a pillow should be placed under her buttocks after receiving the sperm so a pool of semen will collect near her cervix. She should remain in this position for about 30 minutes to allow the sperm to reach the Fallopian tubes. "She may get tired of lying there," said one woman, "but if she wants to get pregnant, it's the thing to do."

Some married couples are unable to get pregnant.

Data – About 15 percent of married couples in the United States are unable to conceive. (Greenberg et al., 1986)

Forty percent of the time, the male is infertile; 40 percent of the time, the female is infertile; 10 percent of the time, both partners are infertile; and 10 percent of the time, neither partner is infertile but the woman still cannot get pregnant. (Crooks & Bauer, 1984)

Some of the more common causes of infertility in men include low sperm production, poor sperm motility, effects of sexually transmitted diseases such as gonorrhea and syphilis, and interference with the passage of sperm through the genital ducts due to an enlarged prostate. The causes of infertility in women include blocked Fallopian tubes, endocrine imbalances that prevent ovulation, dysfunctional ovaries, chemically hostile cervical mucus that may kill sperm, and effects of sexually transmitted diseases. About half of all infertility problems can be successfully treated so that a pregnancy will result.

Artificial Insemination of Wife

When the sperm of the husband is low in count or motility, it sometimes helps to pool the sperm from several ejaculations and artificially inseminate the wife. This procedure is known as AIH (artificial insemination by husband). There is widespread acceptance of this method of fertilization.

Data – Out of more than 700 university students, 76 percent said artificial insemination of the wife with the husband's sperm was acceptable. (Dunn, et al., 1987)

In other cases, sperm from an unknown donor (AID, or artificial insemination by donor) is used. There is less acceptance for AID than for AIH.

Data – Out of more than 700 university students, 20 percent said artificial insemination of the wife by an unknown donor was acceptable. (Dunn et al., 1987)

Sometimes the donor's and the husband's sperm are mixed, so that the couple has the psychological benefit of knowing that the husband may be the biological father. "Our physician mixed my husband's sperm with a donor's sperm, so that we could always feel that maybe it was my husband's sperm that fertilized the egg," said one wife. One situation in which the husband's sperm is not mixed with the donor's sperm is when the husband is the carrier of a genetic disease, such as Tay-Sachs disease.

Some couples have sought sperm from the Repository for Germinal Choice. This controversial sperm bank in Escondido, California, specializes in providing sperm from men of known intellectual achievement. Among their donors have been three Nobel prize winners in science. No donor to the sperm bank has an IQ under 140.

In the procedure of artificial insemination, a physician or the husband who has been trained by the physician deposits the sperm through a syringe in the wife's cervix and places a cervical cap over her cervix, which remains in place for 24 hours. On the average, it takes about three such inseminations before fertilization occurs.

Data – In the United States, about 20,000 babies are born each year as a result of artificial insemination. (Greenberg et al., 1986)

One couple's experience with artificial insemination by donor follows:

Because of my need to get pregnant, my husband and I decided after long, hard thinking and sleepless nights to try artificial insemination. But I wasn't sure if that was what I wanted. I was very afraid that after the baby was born my husband would resent the child because it would be from another man's sperm. He tried to assure me that he would not feel that way. He wanted a baby almost as much as I did. So we began the procedures.

The first thing we had to do was to turn in my basal body temperature chart, so the physicians could determine the exact time I ovulated. Then we had to give them a picture of my husband and his personal and biological traits (they also categorize donors according to these characteristics). Then they tried to find a donor with the characteristics that matched those of my husband.

The injections of the donor semen cost $25 and were done the day before and the morning of ovulation. The actual procedure was very humiliating. I had to lay on the examination table after I received the injection with my feet up in the air at a 90° angle for 30 minutes.

I became pregnant after the first set of injections. It was really hard to believe that we were finally going to have a child. My husband was as excited as I was.

I carried the child full term and had no complications. It was hard to believe that after all those years of failing, some other man's sperm got me pregnant. Actually, I don't think about that now. We have a beautiful boy named Mark who is the joy of our lives. He is named after my husband, is very healthy, and we feel lucky to have him. As long as both parents agree, I feel that artificial insemination is the best answer to the problem of sterility. At least he is a part of one of us in flesh and bone! Our marriage is closer than ever now.

Consideration

Like this couple, most AID couples report having a positive experience. Although couples feel severe emotional pain when they learn of the husband's inability to impregnate the wife, they decide on AID because, as the wife in the narrative noted, it allows at least one-half of them as a couple to be biologically related to the prospective child. This fact is often kept secret, and neither their friends nor the child are told.

Data – The average cost for artificial insemination until conception is about $1,000. (Donovan, 1986)

Before AID is carried out, the parents-to-be agree that any child produced by this procedure will be their own and their legitimate heir. The potential legal problems with AID have not been worked out. Only 18 states have laws pertaining to artificial insemination. For example, a couple could charge a physician with negligence if the child was born with a severe defect.

Artificial Insemination of Surrogate Mother

I had very easy pregnancies, and I didn't think it would be a problem for me to carry another child. I figured maybe I could help someone.

—Valerie, a surrogate mother

Sometimes artificial insemination does not help a woman to get pregnant (for example, her Fallopian tubes may be blocked or her cervical mucus may be hostile to sperm). The couple who still wants a child and who has decided against adoption may consider parenthood through a surrogate mother—a woman who is impregnated with the husband's sperm and carries the child to term. As with AIH, the motivation of the prospective parents is to have a child that is genetically related to at least one of them. For the surrogate mother, the apparent motivation is to help involuntary childless couples achieve their aspirations of parenthood and to make money (the surrogate mother is paid about $10,000).

The concept of surrogate pregnancy is not new. The Bible reports that Abraham and his wife Sarah could not conceive a child. Their solution was for Abraham to have intercourse with Sarah's Egyptian maid, Hagar, who bore a child for them.

There is limited acceptance among university students for surrogate motherhood.

Data – Out of more than 700 University students, 15 percent said having a baby via a surrogate mother was acceptable. (Dunn et al., 1987)

One California firm (Harper, 1985), which screens surrogate mothers who will bear a child for an infertile couple, requires that the surrogate mother have children, a loving and stable relationship with her children, the complete support of her husband, a strong emotional, psychological, and genetic makeup, and no desire for more children of her own (her husband may have had a vasectomy).

Consideration

Legally, there are few guidelines to protect involuntary childless couples who engage a surrogate mother for procreative services. The surrogate could change her mind and decide to keep the child, as did a New Jersey surrogate mother. Mary Beth Whitehead decided she wanted to keep her baby, even though she had signed a contract to give up the baby for $10,000. William and Elizabeth Stern, the would-be parents, sued Whitehead for and eventually won custody of the child. Surrogate mothers who want to keep their babies are rare, however. Only 4 of 500 have sought custody. (Sharpe, 1987)

Engaging a surrogate mother is expensive.

Data – The surrogate mother is usually paid $10,000, and the legal and hospital fees usually cost another $10,000. To help would-be parents find surrogate mothers, John Stehura publishes a "Surrogate Mother Newsletter," which includes photographs of surrogate mothers and prices. (Greenberg et al., 1986)

IN-VITRO FERTILIZATION

About 2 million couples cannot have a baby because the woman's Fallopian tubes are blocked or damaged, preventing the passage of the eggs to the uterus. In-vitro or test-tube fertilization is an additional option to parenthood for infertile couples. Using a laparoscope (a narrow, telescopelike instrument inserted through an incision just below the woman's navel to view the tubes and ovaries), the physician is able to see a mature egg as it is released from the woman's ovary. The time of release can be predicted accurately to within two hours. When the egg emerges, the physician uses an aspirator to remove the egg, placing it in a small tube containing a stabilizing fluid. The egg is taken to the laboratory, put in a culture dish, kept at a certain temperature-acidity level, and surrounded by sperm from the husband. After one of these sperm fertilizes the egg, it divides and is implanted by the physician in the wall of the wife's uterus. Usually, several fertilized eggs are implanted in the hope that one will survive. Occasionally, some fertilized eggs are frozen and implanted at a later time, if necessary. This procedure is known as *cryopreservation.*

Student acceptance of in-vitro or test-tube fertilization is much greater than student acceptance of surrogate motherhood.

Data – Out of more than 700 university students, 55 percent said having a baby via in-vitro or test-tube fertilization was acceptable. (Dunn et al., 1987)

Louise Brown of Oldham, England, was the first baby to be born by in-vitro fertilization. After her birth in 1978, the first test-tube clinic in the United States opened at the Eastern Virginia Medical School in Norfolk, Virginia. Only women less than 35 years of age whose reproductive functions are normal (except for malfunctioning Fallopian tubes) are accepted. The procedure costs over $5,000, excluding hospitalization, and there is only a 23 percent chance of success. The Norfolk program has a waiting list of over 8,000 names (a 16–year backlog).

Other U.S. in-vitro fertilization clinics include those at the University of Texas, Duke University, and the University of North Carolina at Chapel Hill. As of this writing, eight "test-tube babies" have been born in the United States.

Consideration

There is considerable disagreement on the appropriateness of test-tube conception. Those who favor in-vitro fertilization feel that every couple should have the opportunity to have a child and view test-tube conception as the provision of that opportunity. Those who disapprove of this fertilization method often do so for religious reasons ("It's against God's plan") or out of fear that a baby so conceived will be deformed.

EMBRYO TRANSFER

An alternative to test-tube fertilization for the infertile couple when the woman's Fallopian tubes are blocked or damaged is embryo transfer.

> *Data* – Out of more than 700 university students, 26 percent said having a baby via embryo transfer was acceptable. (Dunn et al., 1987)

The husband allows his sperm to be artificially inseminated in a surrogate woman. After about five days, her uterus is flushed out (endometrial lavage) and the contents are analyzed under a microscope to identify the presence of a fertilized ovum, which is inserted into the uterus of the otherwise infertile partner. The embryo can be frozen and implanted at a later time.

Infertile couples opt for embryo transfer, also called ovum transfer, because the baby will be half theirs (the man is the biological father) and the partner will have the experience of pregnancy and childbirth. The surrogate woman participates out of her desire to help an infertile couple. Embryo transfers are being conducted at the Harbor–UCLA Medical Center (1000 West Carson Street; Torrance, CA 90509).

Adoption

> *Data* – Out of more than 700 university students, 86 percent said adopting a baby was acceptable. (Dunn et al., 1987)

Some parents choose not to have a baby by any of the ways discussed thus far. These couples want to adopt a child. If the parents are white, the child they have in mind is usually a white healthy infant. Less often do they think of adopting a black, retarded, handicapped, or older child. There are only a few of the former category but an abundance of the latter categories of children available for adoption.

> *Data* – Due to greater use of birth control, abortion, and pregnant women opting to keep their babies, there is only one child available for every 35 couples who want to adopt. (Edmondson, 1986)

Couples wanting to adopt a child have three options: state-agency adoption, private-agency adoption, and independent adoption. State agency adoptions are less expensive (only legal fees are involved) but they take longer (from nine months to forever) and have more stringent requirements about who can adopt. Spouses over 50 are usually considered too old; some agencies say that 25 is too young. Although unmarried heterosexual women and men are allowed to adopt, in most cases, homosexuals are prohibited from doing so.

Private-agency adoptions are more expensive, but there is a shorter waiting period for anxious would-be parents. Golden Cradle is a nonprofit adoption agency which connects mothers who want to give up their babies with couples who want to adopt babies. The program provides free room and board for a mother-to-be at the home of an adoptive couple (who will later adopt from

Adoption is a viable alternative to having children.

some other mother), free hospitalization, and free medical care. In exchange, the couple wanting a baby pays $10,000. The phone is 1–215–289–BABY.

Other private agencies may specialize in adoptions of babies from Korea, Colombia, India, and the Philippines. These are legal adoptions, and the couples are provided with either babies or young children.

Independent adoptions occur when a physician connects a couple who wants a baby with a pregnant woman who wants to give up her baby. Eighty percent of the adoptions in California are direct adoptions. In most cases, the pregnant teenager recognizes that she doesn't have the resources to take care of her baby so the mother gives up her baby in the hope that she or he will have a better life. In direct adoptions, the mother knows the spouses who adopt her baby; in agency adoptions, the mother does not know them. There are also two differences between state- and private-agency adoptions. In state-agency adoptions, the biological mother can change her mind within 30 days and get her baby back; this is usually not the case in private adoptions. Also, parents who adopt a child from a state agency can take her or him back if they are not satisfied; they usually cannot do so if the adoption is through a private agency.

Although we tend to think that most adoptions occur between children and would-be parents who don't know each other, over 60 percent of all U.S. adoptions aradoptions are by relatives. Most often, this involves a stepfather adopting stepchildren (Riche, 1986).

Adoption is not an "easy" alternative. Often, by the time a husband and wife realize they cannot conceive a child and adoption is their only parenting option, their age is a factor working against them. Not only must would-be parents locate a child, they must be evaluated as suitable parent material—a qualification not required of biological parents.

Childbirth Methods

Couples who give birth to a child have several methods from which to choose, including Lamaze, Dick-Read, Bradley, LeBoyer, regional anesthesia, and Cesarean births.

Lamaze Method

Preferred by an increasing number of couples, the Lamaze method of childbirth, often called "natural" or "prepared" childbirth, was developed by French obstetrician Fernand Lamaze. The method is essentially a preparation for childbirth, in which the woman and her partner take six one-and-a-half-hour classes during the last trimester of pregnancy, usually with several other couples. The goal of these sessions is to reduce the anxiety and pain of childbirth by viewing it as a natural process, by educating the couple about labor and delivery, and by giving them specific instructions to aid in the birth of their baby.

There are several aspects of the Lamaze method:

1. *Education about childbirth.* The instructor explains the physiology of pregnancy, stages of labor, and delivery.
2. *Timed breathing exercises.* Specific breathing exercises are recommended for each stage of labor to help with the contractions by refocusing the laboring woman's attention and keeping the pressure of the diaphragm off the uterus. These exercises are practiced between sessions, so that the couples will know when and how to use them when labor actually begins.

Lamaze continues to be one of the more popular methods of prepared childbirth.

3. *Pain control exercises.* The woman is taught to selectively tense and relax various muscle groups of her body (for example, her arm muscles). She then learns how to tense these muscle groups while relaxing the rest of her body, so that during labor she can relax the rest of her body while her uterus is contracting involuntarily.
4. *Husband's involvement.* A major advantage of the Lamaze method is the active involvement of the husband in the birthing event. His role (or that of a coach substitute if the father is not available) is to tell his wife when to start and stop the various breathing exercises, give her psychological support throughout labor, and take care of her in general (get ice, keep her warm, and so on).

Most husbands and wives report that the sharing of the labor and delivery is one of the most significant and memorable events of their lives. When the couple does not share the birth experience, the husband sits in the waiting room while his wife is in the labor room alone.

Dick-Read Method

Grantly Dick-Read introduced his concept of prepared childbirth in the 1930s, about a decade before Lamaze. He believed it was a woman's fear of childbirth that produced the physical pain during delivery and that pain could be avoided by teaching the woman to relax. Similar to the Lamaze method, Dick-Read classes emphasize breathing and relaxation exercises, basic information about the birth event, and the husband's support. In addition, they focus on preparation for parenthood.

Bradley Method

Another lesser known method of childbirth than the Lamaze method was developed by a Denver obstetrician, Robert Bradley. Also known as "husband-coached childbirth," the Bradley method focuses on the couple—their marital communication, sexual relationship, and parental roles—as well as on relaxation exercises and proper nutrition during pregnancy. An important aspect of the Bradley method is the couple's relationship with their physician. They are encouraged to deal with issues such as the kind of delivery they want (hospital or home birth) and breast feeding well in advance of the birth. The Bradley method emphasizes a couple's freedom to choose the type of birth experience that is desired. If the physician is reluctant to cooperate, the couple is encouraged to seek another physician.

LeBoyer Method

The LeBoyer method of childbirth is named after its French founder, Frederick LeBoyer, who has delivered more than 10,000 babies using his own method. The goal of a LeBoyer birth experience is to make the infant's transition to the outer world as nontraumatic as possible. The delivery room into which the baby is born is quiet and dimly lit. After emerging from its mother, the baby is placed on the mother's abdomen, where she gently strokes and rubs her child. The umbilical cord is cut only after it stops throbbing in the belief that this will help the newborn's respiratory system adjust to its new environment.

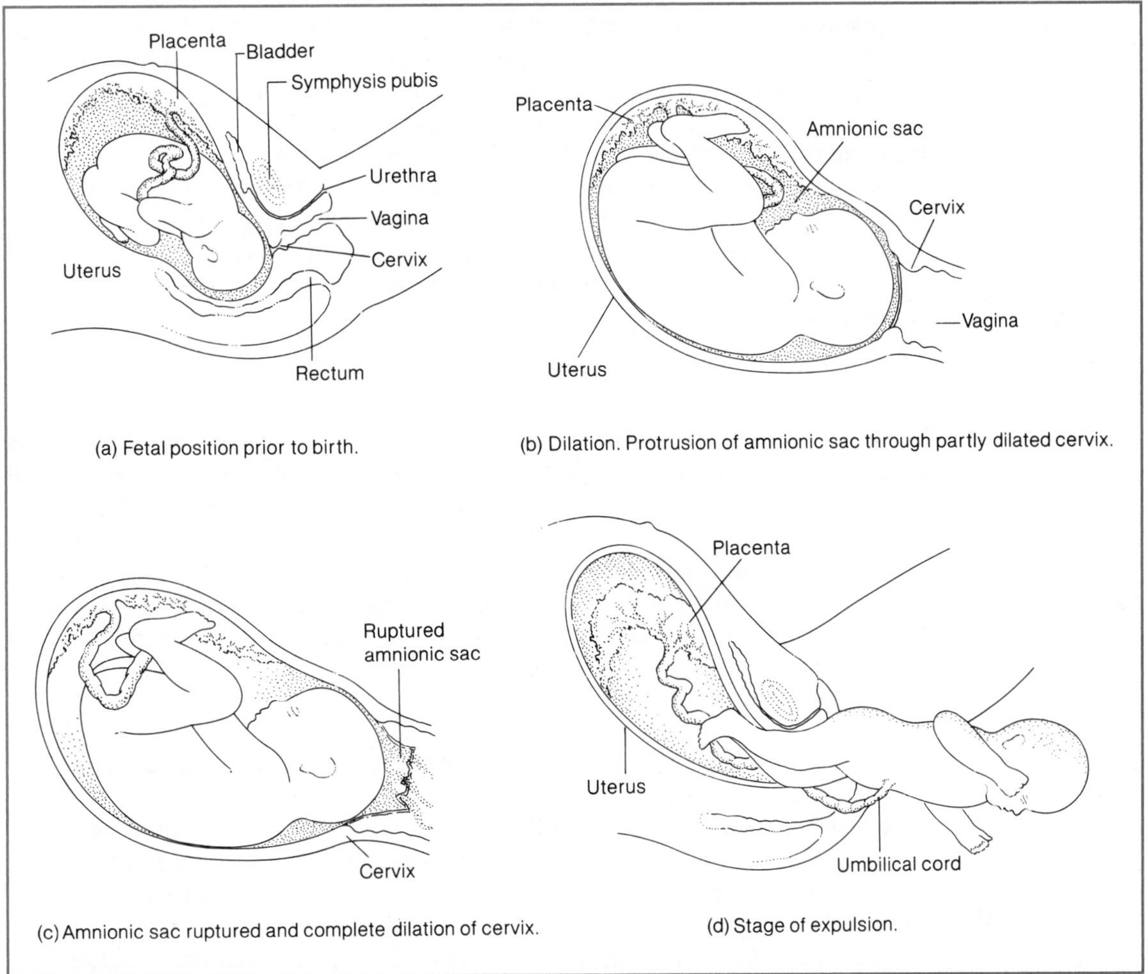

(a) Fetal position prior to birth.

(b) Dilation. Protrusion of amnionic sac through partly dilated cervix.

(c) Amnionic sac ruptured and complete dilation of cervix.

(d) Stage of expulsion.

FIGURE 16.1 THE BIRTH PROCESS

After a few moments, the baby is immersed in water that is the approximate temperature of the amniotic sac in which she or he has been floating for the past nine months. The infant is allowed to relax and enjoy the bath. Then the baby is wrapped in layers of cotton and wool and placed on her or his side next to the mother. Placing the child on its back is avoided because it is felt the spine should not be stressed this soon after birth.

To what degree is the LeBoyer method of childbirth beneficial to infants and mothers? A study comparing babies born LeBoyer style with babies born by conventional hospital procedures revealed no differences in responsiveness or irritability during the first three days of life (Nelson, 1979). Mothers delivering by the LeBoyer method did not see the experience any differently or make a different postnatal adjustment than mothers delivering by a conventional method.

The preceding methods emphasize drug-free deliveries. But not all pregnant women have the interest or the time to devote to childbirth preparation according to these methods and prefer to rely on more traditional methods of birthing their children with the least amount of pain. Two commonly used procedures for administering anesthesia are the caudal and epidural. Both involve introducing drugs into the spinal column, which eliminates the pain typically involved in childbirth. The caudal involves placing a needle at the base of the tailbone; the epidural involves placing the needle further up the backbone. The result—a pain-free delivery—is the same.

Other women prefer medications, which are usually administered intravenously, to alleviate labor pain at the onset of three to five contractions. These analgesics reduce the pain but allow the woman to be aware of the childbirth process. A woman should not view herself as a "failure" if she feels the need for medication.

Cesarean Births

Regardless of which method of childbirth a couple chooses, most anticipate that the baby will be born by passing through the vaginal canal. As a result they receive little information about cesarean births. In cesarean section, an incision is made in the woman's abdomen and uterus and the baby is removed. The term does not derive from the Roman emperor Caesar being delivered in this way but from a law passed during Caesar's reign that made it mandatory for women dying in the advanced stages of pregnancy to have their babies removed by surgical means.

Cesareans are not uncommon.

Data – Thirty percent of all births are by cesarean section. (Jensen & Bobak, 1985)

Cesarean deliveries are most often performed when there would be risk to the mother or baby through normal delivery; as examples, the fetus may be positioned abnormally, the head may be too large for the mother's pelvis, or the mother may have diabetes or develop toxemia during pregnancy. The woman is put to sleep with general anesthesia or given a spinal injection, enabling her to remain awake and aware of the delivery.

Although Cesareans are major surgery, the risk of death to the mother is less than 2 percent. When death occurs, it is usually the result of a preexisting condition, such as severe toxemia or heart disease—not a result of the surgery itself. The cesarean section is regarded as one of the safest of all abdominal surgeries and holds the record for the fewest postoperative problems.

Consideration

There has been considerable criticism of physicians who routinely perform cesarean surgery even when it is not medically indicated. Until recently, a woman who had had a C-section had to have all subsequent births by C-section, and these physicians were accused of creating a market for cesarean surgery. But due to advances in surgical techniques, the American College of Obstetricians and Gynecologists reversed its 75-year-old policy and said that some women who have a Cesarean delivery for their first child can have subsequent vaginal deliveries. More than 30,000 such deliveries have taken place. However, due to mothers being older when they give birth and to more conservative medical care in response to past litigation, the number of Cesarean deliveries is on the rise again.

When a Woman Becomes a Mother

A mother is not a person to lean on, but a person to make leaning unnecessary.
—Dorothy Canfield Fisher

About 3,730,000 babies are born each year in the United States. But this number does not reflect the individual experiences of the respective mothers. In general, motherhood results in a more profound change for the wife than fatherhood does for the husband (Wilkie & Ames, 1986). What are the nature of these changes and how do wives adjust to their new role as mothers?

Reaction to Childbirth

Although childbirth and the labor preceding it are sometimes thought of as a painful ordeal, some women describe the birthing experience as "fantastic," "joyful," and "unsurpassed." One woman said, "I would rather give birth every day than any other thing I can think of. Having that baby come out of me was literally the grandest experience I have ever had."

Once her baby is born, the mother often feels an enormous sense of pride. This pride is heightened as parents and friends come to view the baby, give gifts, and assure the new mother that she has accomplished a miracle. A mother of three days explained, "I love to hear people tell me how beautiful my baby is. I immediately project into the future and count them lucky to have seen a baby who is destined for greatness."

The strong emotional bond between mother and baby develops early, so that mother and infant resist separation. Sociobiologists suggest that there is a biological basis for the attachment between a mother and her offspring. The mother alone carries the fetus in her body for nine months, lactates to provide

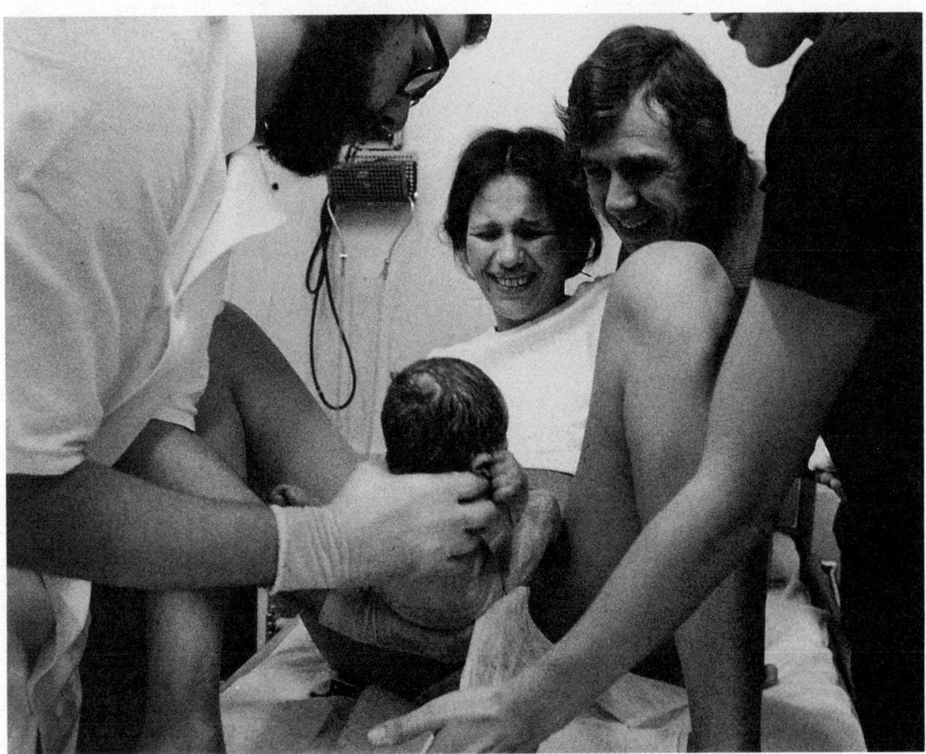

Most women report extreme joy in seeing their infant for the first time.

milk, and produces oxytocin—a hormone excreted by the pituitary gland during the expulsive stage of labor that has been associated with the onset of maternal behavior in lower animals.

Not all mothers feel immediate joy, however. Emotional bonding may be temporarily impeded by a mild depression, characterized by irritability, crying, loss of appetite, and difficulty in sleeping.

Data – From 50 to 70 percent of all new mothers experience the "maternity blues"—transitory symptoms of depression 24–48 hours after the baby is born. About 10 percent experience post-partum depression—a more severe reaction than "maternity blues." (Kraus & Redman, 1986)

Post-partum depression is believed to be a result of the numerous physiological and psychological changes occurring during pregnancy, labor, and delivery. Although the woman may become depressed in the hospital, she more often experiences these feelings within the first month after returning home with her baby. Most women recover within a short time; some (about 5 percent) seek therapy to speed their recovery.

Consideration

To minimize "maternity blues" and post-partum depression, it is important to recognize that having misgivings about the new infant is normal and appropriate. The danger in these thoughts is not that they occur but that they are labeled by others as inappropriate, so that the woman begins to feel like an awful person for having such thoughts. In addition, the woman who has negative feelings about her new role as mother should elicit help with the baby from her husband or mother so that she can continue to keep up her social contacts with friends.

Adjustments to Motherhood

"You can read about motherhood, watch your friends as they become mothers, and fantasize about having your own baby, but until you've done it, you can't really evaluate how you feel about motherhood," reflected a young mother. Whereas people can try out living together, they cannot try out being a parent.

Every woman goes into motherhood naively, and every woman has widely differing experiences in managing the role. For some women, motherhood is the ultimate fulfillment; for others, the ultimate frustration. Most women report mixed emotions during their mothering experience. Whatever a woman's attitude before the birth of her baby, she is not likely to take her role lightly. From the time she knows she is pregnant (or about to become an adoptive mother), no woman's life is ever the same (McKim, 1987).

Motherhood brings with it changes in a woman's daily routine, an increased feeling of responsibility, worry, and often a need to balance the demands of job or career and family. To adapt to all of these changes, she develops coping strategies. We will now examine each of these adjustments.

Routine Work

The new mother finds herself with a new set of tasks. Feeding, diapering, and bathing the infant are added to the responsibilities she already has. "Extra work to care for the baby" and "loss of sleep" are common problems mentioned by mothers of two-month-old infants. "Having less time for yourself" and "feeling physically tired and fatigued" are other common changes for first-time mothers. Mothers also feel less interested in sex and less sexually responsive during intercourse.

Responsibility

Most mothers contend that the actual day-to-day work of child care is not the factor that makes motherhood difficult; it is the incessant and unrelenting responsibility. Even when the husband and wife say they will share the responsibility for child care, this duty more often falls on the wife.

The responsibility of motherhood is long-term. A middle-class woman with two children observed:

Mother, I want you to be with me always.
—age 4, Tracy Ellis

I'll be with you always, and even when you don't want me to be with you.
—mother, Diana Ross

> People tend to think of having children only in terms of the baby period. While it may seem like an eternity, the baby-toddler stage of a child is short compared with the 12 or 16 years of the school-age child. Parents may not be legally responsible for a child beyond 21, but morally and emotionally, once a parent, always a parent.

Worry

"You can make them go to their rooms, but you can't get them out of your mind," said the mother of three daughters. Her observation reflects that children are an emotional as well as physical drain. First, a child's safety is a major concern. "I look at the clock at three and know that my child will soon be crossing the street from school," one mother said, "and although there is a policewoman there, I don't relax until I see her when I get home from work." When mothers do not worry about busy streets, it is money (Will there be enough for them to complete college?) or peer persecution (Will they make fun of her because she has one crossed eye?) or health (Does a sore throat warrant a trip to the doctor?) or her own employment (Will my children suffer because I'm too involved in my career?). "Confessions of a Supermom" in Exhibit 16.1 illustrates the frustration of worrying too much about being the best possible mother.

The Employed Woman as Mother

For the traditional housewife who stays at home, adding the role of mother may be relatively easy. She will have the time and resources (with her husband's economic support) to cope with her infant's demands. Indeed, being at home with her own baby is her dream come true. But more and more women are working outside the home and dropping out of the labor force only long enough to have their children.

> *Data* – Fifty-four percent of all mothers (husband present) with preschool children are employed outside the home. (*Statistical Abstract of the United States*, 1987)

To the demanding roles of employee and wife, she must add that of mother. Even with her husband's support, the employed woman must find ways to fit the demands of motherhood into her busy schedule.

Exhibit 16.1

CONFESSIONS OF A SUPERMOM*

I admit it. I did it. I broke the rules, the Supermom vows I held inviolate for so long. It all began when I started hiding my children's books. (The thought of reading aloud that same book, for the one hundredth time, made me break out in a cold sweat.) I even drastically reduced trips to the library, down to a few token visits a year. I confess, I allowed sugar into my home, processed cheese singlets, and refined flour. (Imagine, buying bread instead of assuring my children received the proper ratio of B-vitamins found in homemade whole-wheat bread.) And, as a means of survival, I began serving hot dogs (nitrates included), frozen pizza, and raviolios. I permitted the "Smurfs" (one of the most violently rated cartoons) to invade my living room on Saturday morning. Why? For the self-serving reason of affording myself the luxury of sleeping late. (Cardinal Rule # 5: *NEVER* use the TV as a baby sitter.)

For what it's worth, I did, and have held out against Count Chocula, Captain Crunch, and caffeine. This unfortunately, is countered by the fact that I confiscated the scissors from my first son at a time when the development of fine motor coordination was at its height. (I realize justifications aren't accepted, but he *had* cut his younger brother's hair. In fact, it was severe enough that my neighbors were convinced he had undergone brain surgery.)

Dare I confess to the times I relented and spanked my kids? I had done so well until then. I had maintained such control—the control only a Supermom could possess—even the time my second son tore my soft contact lens, the time he carved my living room sofa with the kitchen knife, or the time both boys, playing kamakazi pilots, dived through my sister-in-law's sliding glass door.

What kind of mother do you think I am? A reformed Supermom. A much more confident and self-assured mother. A mother who enjoys her children—in moderation—and actually laughs with them—occasionally. But it wasn't always this way. Two years ago I wouldn't have been able to admit to myself, much less to anyone else, that I had failed miserably at being a Supermom. Those were the days my self-worth was tied to my kids' performance. Those were the days that guilt pervaded my very being.

I did try. I embraced the ideal of the perfect mother with such zeal. I diligently prepared by faithfully attending childbirth classes and LaLeche League meetings. I read every child-care manual available. I was determined to succeed in every area my own parents had failed in. I was, unknowingly, setting myself up for failure. For you see, the standard I was measuring my success by was perfection. I discovered too late that Supermom is a myth—a fairy-tale mother who rarely exists except in our minds and on TV. She is the fantasy mother our society would have us believe was real. She is all-giving, all-loving, all of the time.

But, as so many other conscientious parents I believed it. I approached childrearing with high levels of caring, idealism, and enthusiasm. I was proud of my ability to do it all: to have a career and be a perfect mother too. I was driven by the delusion that I could equally "mother," cook, clean house, have sex, and pay bills (and not necessarily in that order). As the Enjoli commercial suggested, "I can bring home the bacon, fry it up in the pan, and never let him forget that he's a man."

The media, child-care experts, and our own parents constantly bombard us with

Exhibit 16.1

"good parent" criteria. And often, we unwittingly internalize their requirements, which later resurface as compulsions to be the best mother, striving dutifully to produce the best/brightest kid on the block, in the classroom, and on stage. We push, push, push, as if the child were a product whose worth was dependent solely upon performance. And the pressure is mounting. For now to be a *real* Supermom, one must produce a Superbaby. We are told we have but a few short years to determine our children's destinies. Intelligence and school performance can be determined by three years of age.

Alas, Supermom is on the move again. The prescription begins at conception: to create a Superbaby, and consequently a Superbeing, one must talk to the unborn child in utero. After birth, one must flash math and word cards before a baby's yet unfocused eyes. Then there's a rigorous gymnastics and swim program, and violin lessons by age 2. And lest we forget, the world of commercials will remind us: failure to present your daughter with a computer by her fourth birthday will ultimately make her a college reject.

The danger behind such expectations is that a mother's own sense of worth becomes dependent upon her child's achievements; her selfhood is as easily threatened as it is derived, in a large part, from the product she has so carefully and lovingly molded. The damage to the child can be equally disasterous. For when a child is made to feel that receiving his mother's love is contingent upon fulfilling certain rigid standards, his emotional development is jeopardized. For the young child, fear of losing a mother's love can be devastating.

Another danger to parent and child alike results when mother becomes disenchanted with her role and becomes a parent drop-out because she no longer has the physical and emotional energy to keep going, or giving. Dr. Joseph Procanccine of Loyola College in Baltimore terms this phenomenon, "Parent Burn-Out." He says, "Parents who burn-out have, in a sense, been 'on fire'. They have taken as a model for parenting a mythological ideal of the perfect parent." According to Dr. Procanccine, the greatest cause of parent burn-out is attempting to manage the anger—anger that results from "the guilt and frustration that occurs when these unrealistically high expectations for parenting (and for children's behavior) can't be met."

Preventing parent burn-out means reevaluating your expectations for yourself and your child. It means taking care of yourself and exerting control over how and where you expend your energy. It means stressing to your children that you love them unconditionally, even if they don't get a part in the school play, even if they break your favorite coffee mug.

Yes, I admit it. I was a Supermom, and I failed. I have, however, survived burn-out and by-passed a chronic state of disenchantment. And sure, it has been rough, but through it all I have gained a much greater understanding of myself. And it is comforting to hear my four-year-old daughter's words, as she assures me that my message to her has been clearly received: "Mommy, I love you *even* when you burp."

Suggested Reading:

The Growth and Development of Mothers
by Angela Barron McBride
Parent Burn-Out
by Dr. Joseph Procanccine
Parent Power, Child Power
by Dr. Helen De Rosis

* Published in *Becoming . . . American Society for Psychoprophylaxis in Obstetrics,* May/June 1984, 3(4), 1, 4. © by Martha D. Ogburn. Used by permission of author.

Consideration

Although most new mothers do return to the work force while their children are young, they are in conflict about doing so. Dr. T. Berry Brazelton thinks they should be. He recommends employers give parents six-month leaves of absence with partial pay to allow parents to bond with their babies and allow their babies to develop a sense of trust. Brazelton feels if the baby does not spend the early months of his or her life with a nurturing parent, the stage is set for problems later in life (1985).

Priorities must be established. When forced to choose between her job and family responsibilities (the baby sitter does not show up, the child is sick or hurt, or the like), the employed woman and mother generally responds to the latter role first. "Sarah, my 2–year-old, fell and cut her lip as I was about to leave for the office," remarked a young systems analyst. "Instead of dropping her at the day-care center, I took her to the doctor, who stitched her up. I didn't have to think about whether I was going to be late to work. My child is more important to me." Many employed women use their sick leave when their child is sick.

But other employed women have different priorities in a time of crisis. The managing editor for a local newspaper said, "My work comes first. I will see that my child is taken care of, but I'm not playing the role of resident nurse. Last week, my son got sick, but I took him to the sitter anyway. Of course, there are occasions I will let my work go, but they are rare."

Some employed women give up their work completely. "No job is so fulfilling, no experience so rich as that of being with my baby," said one woman. "Your employed friends with children don't like it. They think you are a traitor. But many of them feel guilty about not being with their children."

When a Man Becomes a Father

Whereas the woman may have dreamed of being a mother since early childhood and nourished that dream during pregnancy, her partner often has not fully considered the implications of fatherhood. In this section, we will examine how men view parenthood and their reactions to their new role.

How Men View Parenthood

Bill Cosby—in his role of father in his television series, *The Cosby Show,* and in his book (1986)—has re-emphasized the role of father in our society. Fathers often have different perceptions of their role, including provider, teacher, playmate, companion, caretaker, and nurturer.

Provider

Most fathers feel that one of their primary responsibilities is to make money for their families. Earning money to support a family is usually equated with responsibility to an employer. A salesman must face his field manager periodically with a report on the number of items he has sold. If he has performed poorly, he loses his job. The employer is not interested in knowing if the employee goes camping with his children or eats lunch with them or picks them up after school. "How many did you sell?" is the only question.

But this need to be the main economic provider, which many men have been taught to see as part of their masculine role, may conflict with other family needs. The conflict between family and career is particularly acute if the father chooses to climb the executive ladder in a large company. This requires taking work home at night, traveling extensively, and working more than the standard 40–hour week—all of which may interfere with spending time with the children and relaxing as a family together. For the man whose family comes first, there will be fewer promotions, smaller raises, and generally less in the way of career rewards of all types.

Because men are rewarded for putting their career above their family, they often justify their minimal parenthood contribution in economic terms. One father said:

> I've given them everything they ever wanted. They want me to go on camping trips with them, but they also expect me to pay the country-club dues so they can swim and to pay for their college educations. I'd really like to play, but somebody has to be responsible for the money.

However, fathers are often criticized because making money is all they do. One 27–year-old graduate student said, "Yes, my dad put me through school and bought me a car, but he is a stranger to me. I'll never get over his not spending time with me when I was younger."

Consideration

Because children are more likely to value being with their father than getting something from him, men might consider spending more time with their children than doing what employers reinforce, or reward, them for—staying away from home. (Some corporations approve of a man's divorce because it means he can throw himself into his work and not be encumbered by "external demands.") This change to a family orientation will not be easy for most men.

Teacher

Some fathers believe it is their responsibility to prepare their children for life in the outside world by teaching them to be independent, self-sufficient, and self-reliant. "I taught all my kids," said a father of three, "that there is always room at the top and the only way to get there is good morals and discipline."

Data – One myth of the black family is that black males have been absent from their homes since the days of slavery. An examination of black fathers in 13 American cities between 1850 and 1880 revealed that the proportion of black fathers present in families ranged from 70 to 90 percent. (McAdoo, 1985–1986)

Playmate

Fathers enjoy playing with their infants and children; they provide a different style of play than mothers. In general, fathers are more physical and vigorous when they play with their children (Ricks, 1985). As infants, they toss them in the air, swing them around in circles, and bounce them wildly on their knee. As the children grow, they ride them on their back, tickle them, and chase them. Some mothers engage in vigorous play with their children, but they are less likely to do so than fathers.

Companion

As children continue to mature, some fathers begin to relate to them on the level of companion. "Regardless of how busy my dad was, he always spent some time with me in the evening and on weekends. We would talk about everything from football to what really matters in life. I've always felt my dad cared about me, and I've tried to be the same kind of father to my children," said the father of two youngsters.

Some fathers like to think of themselves as a friend and companion to their offspring, although the relationship varies with the age and gender of the children. For example, a father may relate quite differently to his son and daughter during their childhood and adolescence. "I've always been closer to my son, even when he was a kid," observed one father. "We just had more in common. When he was an adolescent, we worked on cars together and did some hunting. Now we're in business together. I love my daughter but have never had much in common with her."

But a father of two daughters said, "I can't imagine what it would be like to have a son because I've always related to my two children as people, not girls. I have enjoyed them since they were babies, and while we had our differences when they were teenagers, we are friends."

Caretaker

In spite of a tendency toward more egalitarian roles in the home, most mothers still perform more work in taking care of the children than most fathers do.

> *Data* – In a study comparing first-time fathers and mothers, the fathers reported they were involved in child-care activities 25 percent of the time in contrast to 75 percent of the time for the mothers. (Goldberg et al., 1985)

However, there are exceptions. Some fathers do it all. "I enjoy taking care—feeding, bathing, singing to the baby—more than my wife," stated one husband.

Nurturer

Fathers are becoming increasingly visible in the new role of nurturer. Some men are excellent at providing warmth, affection, acceptance, and love for their children. When their child skins a knee, some males enjoy and are good at comforting the frightened child while washing and putting a bandaid on the open sore. Some evidence suggests that black fathers are more nurturing, warm, and loving toward their children than white fathers (McAdoo, 1985–1986).

Television is helping to provide a positive model for nurturing fathers. In a study of all family-oriented television programs shown on the three networks between 7:00 and 9:00 p.m., the researchers concluded, "Clearly, males are being portrayed as active, nurturant parents" (Dail & Way, 1985, p. 497).

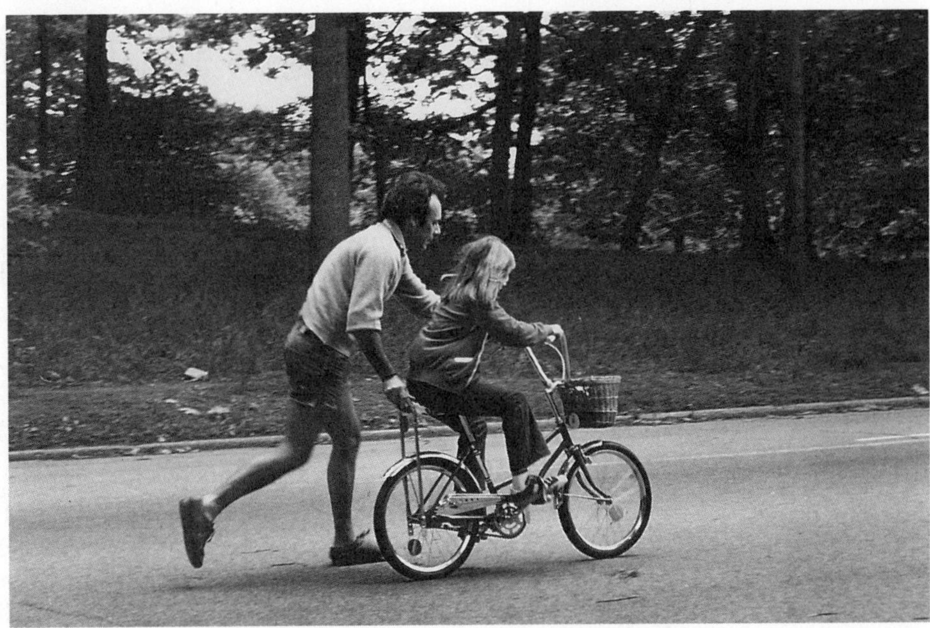

Increasingly, fathers are spending more time with their children.

Transition to Fatherhood

The fatherhood role begins with the woman's pregnancy as the husband relates to his wife as a mother-to-be. This means sharing her excitement about the pregnancy with parents and close friends. "It was like telling people that we were getting married," said one father. "We delighted in breaking the news to people who were as excited as we were."

Men who actively participate in caring for their newborns evidence a more favorable adjustment to parenthood than fathers who neglect or avoid changing diapers and feeding and bathing their babies. Not only do participating fathers feel better about their infants, they feel better about their wives and marriages, too (Goldberg et al., 1985).

Consideration

To ease the transition to fatherhood, new fathers might consider becoming actively involved in the care of their infants. Not to do so is to increase the chance of feeling more disgruntled and despondent about the entrance of a child into the marriage.

However, for fathers to become more actively involved in child care, they need to be encouraged by their wives. However, some women who desire more egalitarian relationships with their husbands may still feel conflict about giving up control of the house and child care and about their husband becoming less competitive and more family-oriented. Hence, a role shift of the husband into greater child-care responsibility will require a concomitant shift of the wife's role and perceptions.

When a Couple Becomes a Family

How does the prospect of having a child affect a couple's relationship, and what happens to their relationship after the baby is born? In this section, we will examine what happens when women/men have less time to be wives/husbands as they fit the demands of mother/father into their already busy schedules.

The Couple During Pregnancy

As soon as the woman becomes aware that she is pregnant, the future infant begins to influence the couple's relationship. One researcher observed that parents:

> . . . do form a relationship with their unborn baby during pregnancy and construct for themselves, as a couple, a perception of the infant as a separate other. . . . They referred to the real unborn baby as "the baby," "he," "she," or "it." (Stainton, 1985, p. 321)

In anticipating the birth of the baby, the couple will deal with matters that are entirely new to them—talking to parents and friends about the pregnancy, allocating existing space for the baby (or getting a larger house or apartment), furnishing a nursery, choosing names for the child, and deciding whether to attend parenthood classes.

Pregnancy may also be a time when husbands feel as though they are being moved into second place and react by reducing their emotional involvement in the relationship (Shapiro, 1987). Two researchers observed that wives are much more interested than husbands in satisfying the interpersonal needs of the spouse during the last trimester of the wife's pregnancy (Assor & Assor, 1985).

Pregnancy also affects the couple's sexual behavior. Most couples report a decreased frequency of intercourse throughout the pregnancy. Some view it as a time to explore alternatives to intimacy. Two researchers (Bryant & Collins, 1985) observed:

> Ed and Linda had had an active sex life together which primarily involved traditional lovemaking methods. During pregnancy, they found a decrease in their interest in intercourse but an increase in touching and holding each other. They found these activities to be satisfying which brought a closeness and unity that they had not felt in the pre-pregnancy state. (p. 109)

Consideration

Does having intercourse during pregnancy involve a risk to the baby? Generally not. Women who have had a previous miscarriage or who are experiencing vaginal bleeding, ruptured membranes, or threatened premature labor should consult their physician about intercourse during pregnancy. In the absence of these complications, most couples can continue intercourse as late in pregnancy as they desire.

After the baby's birth, when do couples resume having intercourse?

Data – Out of 328 women, 50 percent resumed having intercourse about five weeks after the birth of their baby; 40 percent of these women reported some pain during their first intercourse after the birth. (Grudzinskas & Atkinson, 1984)

Self-Assessment

Impact of Parenthood on Marriage Scale

This inventory is designed to measure how a new baby will affect your marital happiness. After reading each sentence carefully, circle the number that best represents your feelings.

1 Strongly disagree
2 Mildly disagree
3 Undecided
4 Mildly agree
5 Strongly agree

	SD	MD	U	MA	SA
1. I am not a jealous person and will not be upset if my partner gives a lot of time and affection to the new baby.	1	2	3	4	5
2. My spouse is not a jealous person and will not be upset if I give a lot of time and affection to the new baby.	1	2	3	4	5
3. I want this baby to be born.	1	2	3	4	5
4. My spouse wants this baby to be born.	1	2	3	4	5
5. My spouse and I agree on which partner is to do how much of the child care (feeding, changing diapers, getting up at night when the baby cries).	1	2	3	4	5
6. I am not a selfish person.	1	2	3	4	5
7. My spouse is not a selfish person.	1	2	3	4	5
8. The baby will not be an undue financial burden.	1	2	3	4	5
9. My spouse and I plan to arrange for a baby sitter to take care of our baby, so that we can leave the house and be alone some of the time after the baby is born.	1	2	3	4	5
10. My spouse and I agree about if and when the new mother will be employed after the baby is born.	1	2	3	4	5

Scoring: Add the numbers you circled. 1 (strongly disagree) reflects the potentially most negative impact on the marriage, and 5 (strongly agree) reflects the potentially most positive impact on the marriage. The lower your total score (10 is the lowest possible score), the greater the chance of reduced marital happiness; the higher your score (50 is the highest possible score), the greater the chance of increased marital happiness following the baby's birth. A score of 30 places you at the midpoint between decreased and increased marital happiness.

The Baby's Impact on the Couple's Marriage

After the baby is born and brought home from the hospital, how does his or her presence affect the marital happiness of the spouses, who are now mother and father? The answer is unclear. Some studies suggest that children increase marital happiness; others suggest the opposite.

Children Increase Marital Happiness

Some studies report that having a baby is associated with improving the marital relationship. Out of a total of 30,000 parents, 43 percent said they felt closer to their spouses after they had children (Greer, 1986). In another study of 75 fathers and 115 mothers, one researcher observed that couples who reported a high degree of marital satisfaction prior to the birth of their baby were more likely to experience positive changes as a result of the baby than spouses who reported a low degree of marital satisfaction prior to the birth (Harriman, 1986).

Consideration

The researcher said of the timing of one's children, "Adding the parenting role when there is stress in one's marital life may only compound the difficulties and the amount of stress experienced." (p. 238)

Research conclusions differ about the degree to which babies affect marital happiness.

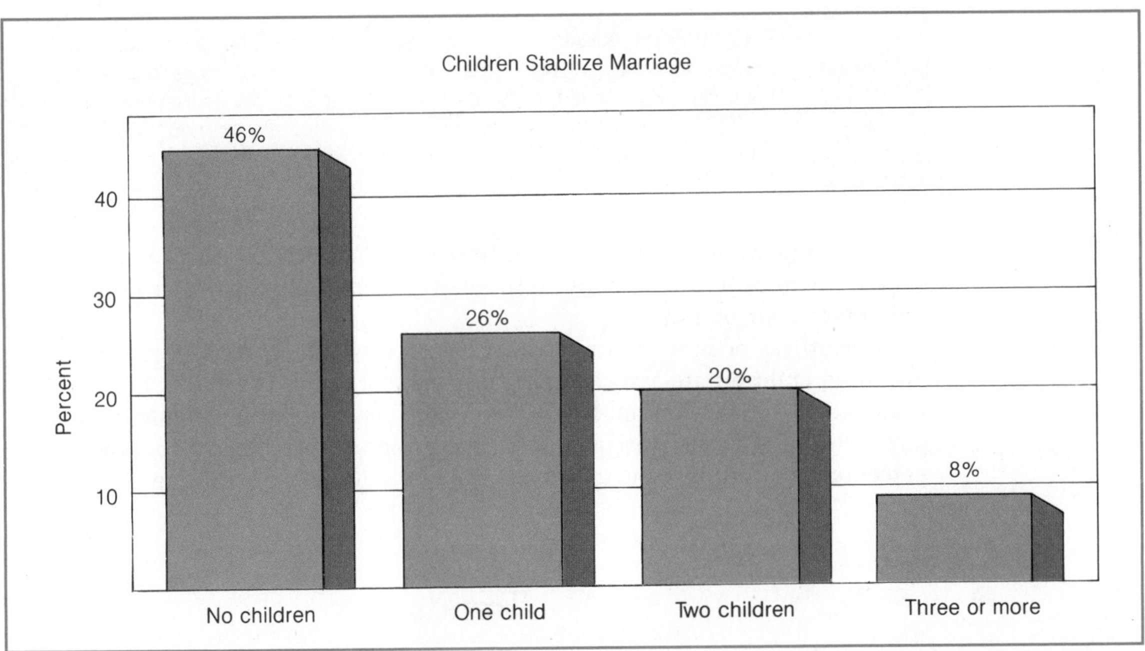

FIGURE 16.2 PERCENT OF COUPLES GETTING DIVORCED WHO HAVE CHILDREN

Children Decrease Marital Happiness

But other parents seem to feel just the opposite. In a study comparing couples expecting a first child with couples who had not yet decided about having children, those involved in the parenthood experience reported decreasing marital satisfaction and increasing marital conflict from pregnancy through 18 months after the baby was born (Cowen et al., 1985). "Who does what" was at the top of the list of conflicts, with each spouse feeling the other should do more. And although both spouses in the group who became parents reported that a larger part of their psychological self became parent and a smaller part became lover, husbands reported more unhappiness.

The energy that spouses spend on each other is limited after a baby is born. Even mustering the energy to talk becomes a problem. One husband said:

> But two or three nights in a row, we sat down, both dead tired, turned on the TV, and I really wanted to talk, but I was so tired. I couldn't motivate myself to start the conversation, knowing that it would get involved and would take time . . .. And every night, I'd say, "Well, tomorrow we're going, tomorrow night we'll do that." (LaRossa, 1983, p. 584)

Consideration

The answer to why children enhance satisfaction in some marriages but not others may lie in the different way spouses cope with having a new baby. Thinking about how things use to be may only prove frustrating; getting a babysitter and going out to eat with your spouse may provide the context for renewing the emotional communication between you and your partner.

> Keeping expectations realistic is also important. Marriages change from a recreational to a work focus beginning in the first year, whether or not a couple has children. Spouses reduce the extent to which they say and do things that bring each other pleasure by about one-third during the first year they are married. (McHale & Huston, 1985)

You may want to complete the Impact of Parenthood on Marriage Scale, shown in the Self-Assessment. Your answers may help to predict how a baby will affect your marriage.

Regardless of how children affect the feelings the spouses have about the marriage, children are associated with marital stability (White & Booth, 1985; Waite et al., 1985). "I'm not leaving my kids," is a common statement made by a parent who may be frustrated with his or her spouse. Figure 16.2 relates the percentage of couples who get divorced to the number of children.

Trends

Artificial insemination, in-vitro or test-tube fertilization, and embryo transfer will be used by an increasing number of people who cannot conceive a child through sexual intercourse. Some new reproductive technology is already in place. The development of cryogen, a refrigerant, permits the storage of human embryos for later implantation in the womb, so that couples may have children at desired intervals. (Zoe, a baby in Australia, has already been born from a frozen embryo.) Embryos will also be screened for desired gender and genetic and developmental defects. Before the twenty-first century, it may be possible to develop embryos in artificial wombs.

The legal issues raised by these developments will be numerous. Does a surrogate mother have a right to her baby if she changes her mind after delivery? If a deformed child results from an artificial insemination in a surrogate mother, do the parents who paid for the child have a right to reject it? What are the responsibilities of a sperm bank to provide sperm that is free of defects? Do frozen embryos have inheritance rights from the people who produced them?

Genetic engineering (also called biotechnology)—manipulating an organism's genes so that the "good" genes are passed on and the "bad" genes disappear—is not likely to be used on humans in the near future. Genetic engineering has been used to create plants that are resistant to frost, disease, and herbicides, leaner pigs, and cows that produce 25 percent more milk, but altering human genes is illegal.

The number of couples who want to share in the birth of their babies through some form of prepared, natural childbirth will also increase. In the past the mother was the only parent present at the birth of a couple's baby. Now the father may be part of the experience. This trend, coupled with more mothers working outside the home, will help the father assume a more active role in parenting.

More fathers will actively participate in the birth of their children, in taking care of their children and in taking off work to be with their children. The precedence for paternity leave has been established by the Equal Opportunity

Only a small percentage of births occur at home.

Employment Commission. Stephen Onera of Chicago was granted a six-month paternity leave to be with his new daughter.

Summary

Fertilization is the result of the union of an egg and a sperm. Pregnancy may occur through sexual intercourse, artificial insemination of the wife by husband (AIH) or donor (AID), artificial insemination of a surrogate mother by the husband, in-vitro or test-tube fertilization, or embryo transfer. Artificial methods of conception are being used increasingly by couples when one of the spouses cannot or should not conceive.

Some expectant parents, who are dissatisfied with traditional, hospital-managed deliveries, are choosing alternative childbirth methods, including the Lamaze, Dick-Read, Bradley, and LeBoyer methods. When there is a risk to the mother or baby through vaginal delivery, a cesarean section may be performed.

A woman's reactions to childbirth may include temporary feelings of depression as well as a developing emotional bond with her infant. Motherhood brings with it changes in the woman's daily routine, an increased feeling of responsibility, worry, and often the need to balance the demands of a job or career and family. For some women, motherhood is the ultimate fulfillment; for others, it is the ultimate frustration. Most women experience mixed emotions during their mothering experience.

The impact of becoming a parent is sometimes less profound for the man than for the woman because his daily routine doesn't change much after the baby is born. Most men are guided by certain impressions they have of the father's role. They tend to view the father as provider, teacher, playmate, companion, caretaker, and nurturer. Although fathers participate less in child care than mothers, they are interested and capable and, if given opportunity and encouragement, do become involved.

Having a baby affects the marriage relationship during as well as after pregnancy. During pregnancy, the couple may have to adjust to a new division of labor and an altered sexual relationship. After the baby is born, rosy expectations of parenthood give way to reality, as the couple begins to adjust to the new family constellation.

The future of fertilization includes the implantation of previously frozen human embryos and the legal unraveling of the complex issues involved in surrogate motherhood.

The future of parenthood includes a greater understanding of the parenting role, an increased sharing of spouses in childbirth and childrearing, and a questioning of traditional childbirth procedures (to be discussed in the Choices section that follows).

Questions for Reflection

1. To what degree are artificial insemination, surrogate mothers, in-vitro fertilization, and embryo transfers options you would consider if you and your partner were having difficulty becoming pregnant and wanted a baby?
2. As a woman, to what degree would you expect your husband to share the work of parenting if you had a baby?
3. As a man, to what degree would you want to share the work of parenting with your wife if you decided to have a baby?

CHOICES

SOME COUPLES WANT to have their baby at home. But should they? What issues need to be considered when deciding to have a child in the hospital or in the home? In addition, some fathers are making choices about the time they spend with their children. How should they allocate time to career and family?

Home or Hospital Birth?

At the turn of the century, about 95 percent of all babies were born at home. Because there were few physicians and fewer hospitals, a midwife was usually summoned to assist the laboring mother-to-be with her delivery. Birthing was a family event, with father, mother, and children competing to hold the new infant.

But because of infant and maternal mortality, the developing political strength of the medical profession, and the development of hospital facilities to handle difficult deliveries, home births became less common. Today more than 99 percent of all births take place in a hospital. When the woman experiences uterine contractions that are regular and intense, she checks into the hospital, is prepped (has her pubic hair shaved, an enema, and her vaginal area cleaned), and completes labor in a special room near the delivery room. Depending on whether the couple has taken preparation for parenthood classes and also on hospital policy, her husband may or may not be allowed to remain with her during labor and delivery.

Some expectant parents are concerned that traditional childbirth procedures are too impersonal, costly, and potentially dangerous. Those who opt for home birth are primarily concerned about avoiding separation from the new infant, maintaining control over who can be present at the delivery, and avoiding "excessive obstetrical management" (Sacks & Donnenfeld, 1984, p. 471).

Safety is a primary concern in deciding to have a baby at home. Most physicians view home births as unsafe and do not support the movement toward home births. However, some physicians feel that it is usually possible to predict a dangerous delivery because high-risk mothers (such as those with hypertension or diabetes) can be identified early in the pregnancy. Some proponents of the home-birth movement feel that for the mother without prenatal complications, there is greater risk in having a baby in the hospital than at home.

The nurse-midwife is most often asked to assist in home births. Some nurse-midwives are certified members of the American College of Nurse-Midwives and have successfully completed a master's degree in nurse-midwifery offered at various universities, including Georgetown, Emory, St. Louis, and Columbia. Two organizations—ACAH (Association for Childbirth at Home) and HOME (Home Oriented Maternity Experience)—help couples prepare for home births.

What is the relative safety of home versus hospital birth? A study designed to answer this question revealed that except in special cases, at home births involve no extra risks than births in hospitals. However, the researchers warned that in cases of delayed labor, breech birth, or fetal distress, a hospital is the safer environment (Hinds et al., 1985).

Sometimes preschool siblings observe the home births of their sisters and brothers. Some advocates of hospital births suggest that such observations have negative consequences for the children. But Lumley (1983)

(Continued)

compared the short-term effects on preschool siblings who observed their brothers and sisters being born with preschool siblings who were not allowed such observations and found no significant differences.

For Fathers: Career or Family?

Women have traditionally been socialized to give priority to their children over their careers, whereas men have been socialized to do the opposite. With the advent of preparation for parenthood classes, Lamaze births, and most wives working outside the home, men have been given the opportunity to rethink their socialization and make conscious choices on an individual basis. Some men still opt for their career. One man said:

> I love my children but I really am not happy being around them for more than a weekend. By Monday, I'm ready to go back to work and see them for a few minutes before bedtime during the week. I enjoy the competitive struggle of my work and making money is what I do best. I guess I'm lucky to be married to a woman who enjoys taking care of the kids.

But other men feel differently. One said:

> I make about all the money I need, and I've learned that it is a dead-end trail. Here I am at middle age— . . . my last child will be leaving for college in September, and I hardly know him. I've spent more time with the mailman that I have with him and now he's leaving. I've got money, but I don't have my boy. I think I've gotten my priorities mixed up.

Men might be aware that although they may be subject to enormous pressures to be successful in a career attaining such success without taking time to "smell the roses" with their children may be less than fulfilling.

Impact of Social Influences on Choices

Home births and the resocialization of men in the father role have only recently become issues in our society. The desire for home birth is a result of a general questioning of the medical profession and a feeling that prospective parents should be given all the data and allowed to make their own decision regarding where their baby will be born, rather than have the physician dictate the place of birth. "It's our baby," said one couple.

Industries reward males for career success—not for the time they spend with their children. Such an emphasis on male career achievement makes it difficult for a father to switch from external to internal reinforcers in reference to spending time with his children. To do so requires a conscious and deliberate choice.

CHAPTER 17

Rearing Children

Contents

Is It True?*

1. Your children will turn out right if you do everything right in rearing them.
2. Most parents are very knowledgeable about the basic stages of child development.
3. The Japanese father is more actively involved in the rearing of his children than the Japanese mother.
4. Taking urine samples of your own children is going too far to get your teenagers to stop using drugs.
5. Most parents are satisfied with the day care their children are receiving.

*1=F; 2=F; 3=F; 4=F; 5=T.

Most parents look forward to bringing up their children. They view childrearing as a process of teaching and instilling in their children the values and behaviors that will make the children happy. In this chapter, we will examine childrearing in perspective, the folklore that surrounds childrearing, various approaches to childrearing, and how parents might respond to teenage drug abuse, one of the most frightening problems parents can encounter in rearing children.

Childrearing in Perspective

Although rearing children is a major undertaking, it is helpful to keep it in perspective. In this section, we will make some generalizations about the realities of parenthood.

Parenthood Is Only One Stage in Life

Children are a great comfort in your old age—and they help you reach it faster, too.
—Lionel Kauffman

Parents of newly adult children often lament, "Before you know it, your children are grown and gone." Although parents of infants sometimes feel that the sleepless nights will never end, they do end. Unlike the marriage relationship, the parent-child relationship moves toward separation. Just as the marital partners were alone before their children came, they will be alone again after their children leave. Except for occasional visits with their children and possibly with grandchildren, the couple will return to the child-free life style.

Typical parents are in their early fifties when their last child leaves home. Since the average woman and man can expect to live until she is 78 and he is 70, spouses in a continuous marriage will have a minimum of about 20 years together after their children leave home. Hence, parenthood might be perceived for what it is—one stage in marriage and in life.

Data – Assuming an individual marries at age 24, has 2 children at 3 year intervals, and dies at age 77, children will live with the individual about 30 percent of her or his lifetime and 40 percent of her or his marriage.

One mother said:

> We had three kids, and I loved taking care of all of them. I think the happiest time in my life was when my husband and I would wake up in the morning and they would all be there. But that's changed now. They are married and have moved several states away. I know they still love me and they call to stay in touch, but I rarely see them anymore. I'm 55 and have at least 20 years left. I've gotten interested in Amway and am busy building my business. If I didn't have something to do, I would really be bored.

Parents Are Only One Influence in Their Children's Development

Although parents often take the credit—and the blame—for the way their children turn out, they are only one among many influences on child development. Peers, siblings (Abramovitch et al., 1986), teachers, relatives, and the mass media are also influential. Although parents are the first significant influence, peer influence becomes increasingly important and remains so into the college years. During this time, children are likely to mirror the values and behaviors of their friends and agemates.

Siblings are not necessarily peers, but they too have an important and sometimes lasting effect on each other's development. One adolescent said:

> I can remember walking up to my mother (I was about 5) after my little baby brother was born. My mother was nursing him while she was sitting in the chair in the den. I wanted to sit in her lap, but she said she couldn't hold both of us. I felt as though my mother had replaced me with my brother. It wasn't a good feeling; my brother and I have always been competitive.

Sibling influences may also be positive. "I've always been close to my sister," remarked one woman. "She's the best friend I have."

Relatives may be significant childrearing agents, especially grandmothers and aunts. One graduate student remarked, "My grandmother is the one that reared me. She was a very polite person, and although I resented her nagging me to be polite when I was a kid, I am very much the way she would have wanted me to turn out."

Teachers become influential once a child begins school, and they remain so as long as the child is exposed to the educational system. Most teachers are middle class and tend to stress the values of achievement and discipline. But teachers have another effect on their students. They may teach offspring things parents do not want them to know. One conservative parent told his son that he was more concerned about him getting a B.A. as a born-again Christian than a B.A. from the university he was attending. "You've got some liberal professors down there that are threatening your very soul," he said.

Parents are not really interested in justice. They just want quiet.
—Bill Cosby

Children don't need to go to school to be exposed to influences their parents may not approve of. Television is a major means of exhibiting language, values, and life styles to children that may be different from those of the parents. One father had Home Box Office and Showtime disconnected because he did not want his children seeing the movies and specials on those channels. Another parent went through the television guide each week and marked the

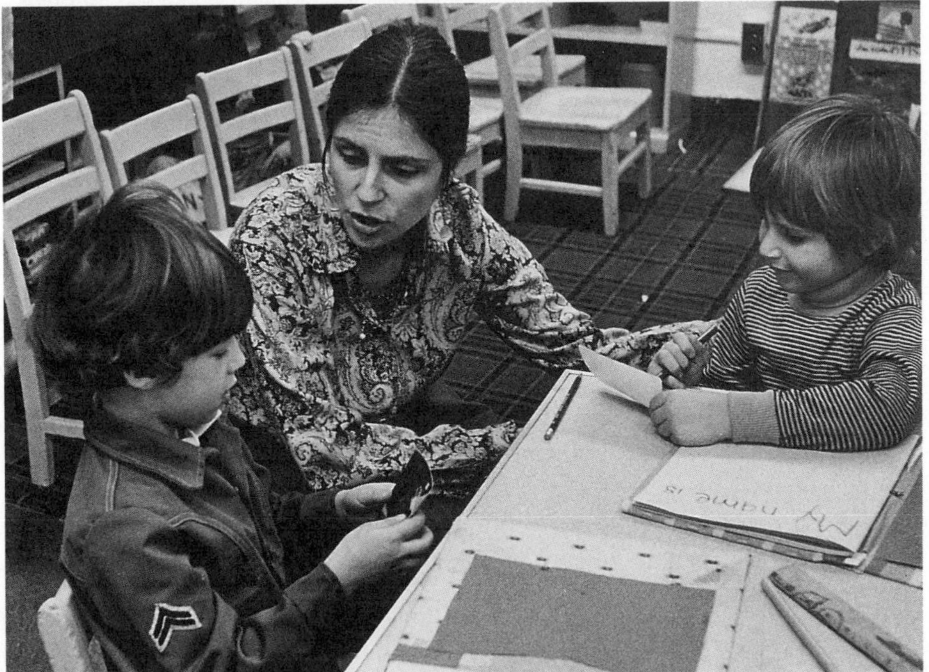

Teachers represent an important influence on our children.

programs he would not allow his children to watch. The guide was left on top of the television, and the children were to look at what programs had been approved before they turned it on.

Not all television viewing may have negative consequences.

Data – In a study of 116 households, the average amount of time spent viewing television together as a family unit was 2–3 hours daily Monday through Friday and 4–6 hours on the weekend. (Schroeder & Brocato, 1983)

These researchers concluded that the more time a family spent watching television together, the greater their interaction, discussion of individual problems, and feeling of having a "close, loving, and supportive family relationship" (p. 64).

In addition to being influenced by peers, siblings, relatives, teachers, and the mass media, children are affected by different environmental situations. An only daughter adopted into an urban, Catholic, upper-class family will be exposed to a different environment than a girl born into a rural, Southern Baptist, working-class family with three male children. Some of the potentially important environmental variables include geographic location, family size, how authoritarian or permissive the parents are, the family's social class, religion, and racial or ethnic background, and whether the children and parents are mentally and physically healthy.

Internal physiological happenings in the developing child will also influence the child's behavior. Particularly during pubertal development, hormones that influence social behavior (rebelliousness, disobedience, failure to follow rules) are released into the bloodstream of both genders.

Consideration

Because parents are only one of many influences on their children, they should be careful about taking the credit or the blame for the way they turn out. "It's not in the books," said a professor of psychology. "My wife and I have modeled a relatively conservative but ambitious life for our children and had hoped that they would want to become professionals. But they met a group in college and decided to drop out and join this commune. That was 10 years ago. It's not what we wanted for them, but they're happy."

Parenthood Demands Change as Children Grow Up

The best way to keep children home is to make the home atmosphere pleasant—and let the air out of the tires.
—Dorothy Parker

Parenthood is not the same in all of its innings. Enjoying children as infants and coping with the sleepless nights are characteristic of the first two years, but the issues change. The parent of a 10–year–old said, "It's getting my child to study, practice piano, and develop friends that keeps me frustrated." The parent of a 17–year–old said, "Wait till it's your turn to have a teenager . . . you'll know why it's the stage most parents wish they could skip."

Each Child Is Different

Children differ in their tolerance for stress, in their capacity to learn, in their comfort in social situations, in their interests, and in innumerable other ways.

Parents soon become aware of the specialness of each child—of her or his difference from every other child they know and from children they have read about. Parents of two or more children are often amazed at how children who have the same parents can be so different.

Most Parents Are Uninformed About Infants

Rearing a first baby is a new experience, and most parents don't know a great deal about child development.

> *Data* – When half of the new mothers and fathers in one study were asked basic child-development questions ("When is a child able to follow simple directions?," "When do babies begin to say their first words?"), less than half of the parents knew the right answers. (Kliman & Vukelich, 1985)

There are numerous books and university courses on child development. All soon-to-be parents should meet the parenting challenge by preparing themselves as much as possible in advance.

Parenting Styles Differ

Parenting styles differ—not only in America, but throughout the world. Two researchers studied four different types of parental units in America (unmarried parents, single mothers, commune parents, married parents) to see how children were turning out (physical, mental, academic, social development) as a result of being reared by parents representing different degrees of conventionality. The results showed that there were more similarities than differences and that the children of the single mothers were the most disadvantaged (Weisner & Eiduson, 1986). Apparently, most parents in America adhere to certain parental norms and scripts.

Looking at childrearing through a wide-angle lens, other societies provide still different contexts and styles. For example, Polynesian children learn to view not only their mother and father but also their grandparents and all relatives of equivalent age and gender as parents. In practice, multiple parenting in Polynesia means that a number of people will be involved in the life-transition ceremonies, that the children will have a number of houses they regard as home, and that they will have an array of adults who nurture them, love them, and protect them. Among Japanese mothers, the mother is the active parent and the father is virtually invisible at home (Bankart & Bankart, 1985). Among Mexican families, fathers are not aloof but playful and companionable with their children (Bronstein, 1984), exhibiting a pattern similar to that of American fathers.

The crux of parenthood is emotional grunt work. It's: No, you can't have a third cookie; no, you may not interrupt others while they're talking.
—Janet Barlow

Folklore About Childrearing

To encourage adults to rear children, certain folklore romanticizing the experience has arisen. Two researchers (LeMasters & DeFrain, 1983) have identified some widely held beliefs about parenting that are not supported by facts.

Myth 1: Rearing Children Is Always Fun

Would-be parents see television commercials of young parents and children and are led to believe that drinking Pepsi in the park with their 4-year–old is what childrearing is all about. Parenthood is portrayed as being a lot of fun. The truth is somewhat different than the folklore:

> The idea of something being fun implies that you can take it or leave it, whereas parents do not have this choice. Fathers and mothers must stay with the child and keep trying, whether it is fun, or whether they are enjoying it or not. Any comparison to bowling, listening to jazz records, or sex is strictly coincidental. . . . Rearing children is hard work; it is often nerve-racking work; it involves tremendous responsibility; it takes all the ability one has (and more); and once you have begun, you cannot quit when you feel like it. (pp. 22, 23)

Data – In one study, 47 percent of the parents polled said that rearing children was more difficult than they had imagined it would be. (Greer, 1986)

Myth 2: Good Parents Inevitably Produce Good Kids

Children are unpredictable. You never know what inconsistency they're going to catch you in next.
—Franklin P. Jones

It is assumed that children who turn out wrong—who abuse drugs, steal, and the like—have parents who really did not do their job. We tend to blame parents when children fail. But good parents have given both their emotional and material resources to their children and the children have not turned out well. One mother said:

> We live in one of the finer suburbs of our city, our children went to the best schools, and we spent a lot of time with them as a family (camping, going to the beach, skiing). But our son is now in prison. He held up a local grocery store one night and got shot in the leg. We've stopped asking ourselves what we did wrong. He was 23 and drifted into friendships with a group of guys who just decided they would pull a job one night.

A corollary to the belief that good parents will produce good kids is the idea that parents know what kind of kids they are producing. But a study com-

After divorce, children sometimes return home with their own children.

paring what parents thought their children's attitudes and values were on religion, drugs, and sex with what their children's beliefs actually were showed that parents had inaccurate perceptions (Thompson et al., 1985).

Myth 3: Love Is the Essential Key to Effective Childrearing

Parents are taught that if they love their children enough, they will turn out okay. Love is seen as the primary ingredient, which if present in sufficient quantities, will ensure a successful child. But most parents love their children dearly and want only the best for them. Love is not enough and does not guarantee desirable behavior. One parent said:

> We planned our children in courtship, loved them before they got here, and have never stopped loving them. But they are rude, have despicable table manners, and hardly speak to us. We are frustrated beyond description. We've done everything we know how to do in providing a loving home for them, but it hasn't worked.

Myth 4: Children Leave Home When They Are 18

Although 96 to 98 percent of all adults leave home to live independently of their parents (Goldscheider & LeBourdais, 1986), recent media attention has been given to those who delay leaving home or who return home after having left. The primary reason why children remain with their parents is unemployment (Grigsby & McGowan, 1986). Unmarried males who do not have a job are most likely to live with their parents. Some children who live with their parents are separated or divorced (2 percent).

> *Data* – Thirty-six percent of all white and 46 percent of all black children between the ages of 18 and 29 live with their parents. In the same age category, 33 percent of all children of Spanish origin live with their parents. (Glick & Lin, 1986)

Black males are the most likely to live with their parents due to their high rate of unemployment. Both males and females of Spanish origin are the least likely to live at home because they tend to marry early and move away from their parents.

Offspring who move back home after leaving it complain that they don't feel free to stay out late or bring friends home. In short, they feel they are living in someone else's house (which they are). Parents complain that their offspring make noise, treat the home like a motel, don't do their share of the work, and aren't developing the independent lives that they "should." Two researchers (Glick & Lin, 1986) have commented on the arrangement of adult offspring living in their parents' home:

> Young adults who do linger longer than their peers in the homes of their parents may risk thereby creating stressful relations to the extent that their more modern life styles tend to clash with those of older members of the family. Those who return after a period of absence also may find that personal relations in the family are not as cordial as they once were, especially if they bring a spouse and/or children with them. (p. 111)

Myth 5: Children Are Always Appreciative

Most parents think of childrearing in terms of love, care, and nurturing—and also in terms of giving their children things. These parents assume their children will appreciate their tender loving care and the material benefits, like stereos, computers, and cars they bestow. That assumption is wrong. Children think parents are supposed to love them and give them things. They view material benefits as their birthright.

Consideration

It is a mistake for would-be parents to embark on the adventure of having children with the expectation that they will always be appreciated. For the most part, parenting involves a lot of selfless giving with no thought of a return. One parent said, "The best part about being a parent is loving your children. If they love you back or appreciate what you are doing, you get a bonus. But don't expect it."

Data – In spite of the problems of parenting, 90 percent of 30,000 parents say having children is worth the sacrifice. (Greer, 1986)

Approaches to Childrearing

We will now explore five ways of viewing the childrearing process. Although socializing children may be viewed as teaching them the norms, roles, and values of society, there is no one or best way of accomplishing this goal. What works for one child may not work for another. It may not even work with the same child at two different times.

Developmental–Maturational Approach

For the past 60 years, Arnold Gesell and his colleagues at the Yale Clinic of Child Development have been known for their ages-and-stages approach to childrearing. Their *developmental–maturational approach* has been widely used in the United States. Let's examine the basic perspective of this approach, some considerations for childrearing, and some criticisms of the approach.

Basic Perspective

Gesell theorizes that what a child does, thinks, and feels is the result of her or his genetic inheritance. Although genes dictate the gradual unfolding of a unique person, every individual passes through the same basic pattern of growth. This pattern includes four aspects of development: motor behavior (sitting, crawling, walking); adaptive behavior (picking up objects and walking around objects); language behavior (words and gestures); and personal–social behavior (cooperativeness and helpfulness). Through the observation of hundreds of normal infants and children, Gesell and his coworkers have identified norms of development. Although there may be large variations, these norms suggest the ages at which an average child displays various behaviors.

Data – On the average, children begin to walk alone (although awkwardly) at age 13 months and use simple sentences between age 2 and 3.

Considerations for Childrearing

Gesell suggests that if parents are aware of their children's developmental clock, they will avoid unreasonable expectations. For example, a child cannot walk or talk until the neurological structures necessary for those behaviors have matured. "Parents who provide special educational lessons for their babies are wasting their time," because the infants are not developmentally ready to profit from the exposure (Scarr, 1984, p. 60). Also, the hunger of a 4–week–old must be immediately appeased by food, but at 16 to 28 weeks, the child has some capacity to wait because the hunger pangs are less intense. In view of this and other developmental patterns, Gesell suggests that the infant's needs be cared for on a demand schedule; instead of having to submit to a schedule imposed by parents, infants are fed, changed, put to bed, and allowed to play when they want. Children are likely to be resistant to a hard and fast schedule because they may be developmentally unable to cope with it.

In addition, Gesell alerts parents to the importance of the first years of a child's life. In Gesell's view, these early years assume the greatest significance because the child's first learning experiences occur during this period.

Criticisms of the Developmental–Maturational Approach

Gesell's work has been criticized because of (1) its overemphasis on the idea of a biological clock; (2) the deficiencies of the sample he used to develop maturational norms; (3) his insistence on the merits of a demand schedule; and (4) the idea that environmental influences are weak.

Most of the children who were studied to establish the developmental norms were from the upper-middle class. Children in other social classes are exposed to different environments, which influence their development. So norms established on upper-middle-class children may not adequately reflect the norms of children from other social classes.

Whereas parents may not be too concerned about the way in which developmental norms have been established, they may be quite concerned about the suggestion that they do everything for the infant when the infant wants them to. Rearing an infant on the demand schedule can drastically interfere with the parents' personal and marital interests. As a result, most American parents feed their infants on a demand schedule but put them to bed to accommodate the parents' schedule (Shea, 1984).

BEHAVIORAL APPROACH

In nature there are neither rewards nor punishments—there are consequences.
—Robert Green Ingersoll

The *behavioral approach* to childrearing, also known as the *social learning approach,* is based on the work of B.F. Skinner. We will now review the basic perspective, considerations, and criticisms of this approach to childrearing.

Basic Perspective

Behavior is learned through classical and operant conditioning. *Classical conditioning* involves presenting a stimulus with a reinforcer. For example, an infant comes to associate the faces of her or his parents with food, warmth, and comfort. Although initially only the food and feeling warm will satisfy the infant, later just the approach of the parent will soothe the infant. This may be observed when a father hands his infant to a stranger. The infant may cry because the stranger is not associated with pleasant events. But when the stranger hands the infant back to the parent, the crying may subside because the parent represents positive events and the stimulus of his or her face is associated with pleasurable feelings.

Other behaviors are learned through *operant conditioning,* which focuses on the consequences of behavior. Two principles of learning are basic to the operant explanation of behavior—reward and punishment. According to the reward principle behaviors that are followed by a positive consequence will increase. If the goal is to teach the child to say "please," doing something the child likes after he or she says "please" will increase the use of "please" by the child. Rewards may be in the form of attention, praise, desired activities, or privileges. Whatever consequence increases the frequency of something happening is, by definition, a reward. If a particular reward doesn't change the behavior in the desired way, a different reinforcer needs to be tried.

The punishment principle is the opposite of the reward principle. A negative consequence following a behavior will decrease the frequency of that behavior; for example, the child could be isolated for five or ten minutes following an undesirable behavior. The most effective way to change behavior is to use the reward and punishment principles together to influence a specific behavior. British psychiatrist Michael Rutter (1984) comments:

> Not just stopping children from doing things—that doesn't seem to me to be the way, and in any case it doesn't work in the long run. You have to provide children with alternatives, to teach them what they should be doing, rather than what they should not be doing. (p. 64)

If a child is rewarded (gets to watch television) every time she or he makes the bed and punished (can't watch television for 24 hours) every time she or he doesn't, it is likely that the bed will get made most of the time. In addition, children of parents who use a behavioral approach to discipline perceive their parents as being congruent—doing what they say they will do. This perception may result from parents backing up rules with consequences (Haffey & Levant, 1984).

Considerations for Childrearing

Parents often ask, "Why does my child act this way, and what can I do to change it?" The behavioral approach to childrearing suggests the answer to both questions. The child's behavior has been learned through his or her being rewarded for the behavior; the child's behavior can be changed by eliminating the reward for the undesirable behavior and rewarding the desirable behavior.

The child who cries when his or her parents are about to leave home to go to dinner or see a movie is often reinforced for crying by the parents' staying home longer. To teach the child not to cry when the parents leave, the parents should reward the child for not crying when they are gone for progressively longer periods of time. For example, they might initially tell the child they are going outside to walk around the house and they will give the child a treat when they get back if he or she plays until they return. The parents might then walk around the house and reward the child for not crying. If the child cries, they should be out of sight for only a few seconds and gradually increase the amount of time they are away. The essential point is that children learn to cry or not to cry depending on the consequences of crying. Because children learn what they are taught, parents might systematically structure learning experiences to achieve specific behavioral goals.

Criticisms of the Behavioral Approach

Professionals and parents have attacked the behavioral approach to childrearing on the basis that it is deceptively simple and does not take cognitive issues into account. Although the behavioral approach is often presented as an easy-to-use set of procedures for child management, many parents do not have the background or skill to implement the procedures effectively. What constitutes an effective reward or punishment, presented in what way, in what situation, with what child, to influence what behavior are all decisions that need to be made before attempting to increase or decrease the frequency of a behavior. Parents often do not know the questions to ask or lack the training to make appropriate decisions in the use of behavioral procedures. One parent locked her son in the closet for an hour to punish him for lying to her a week earlier—a gross misuse of learning principles.

Behavioral childrearing has also been said to be manipulative and controlling, thereby devaluing human dignity and individuality. Some professionals feel that humans should not be treated like rats in a cage and given food pellets for pressing a bar.

Finally, the behavioral approach has been criticized because it de-emphasizes the influence of thought processes on behavior. Too much attention, say the critics, has been given to rewarding and punishing behavior and not enough attention has been given to how the child perceives a situation. For example, parents might think they are rewarding a child by giving her or him a bicycle for good behavior. But the child may prefer to upset the parents by rejecting the bicycle and may be more rewarded by their anger than by the gift.

Parents who must cope with severe behavior problems may find practical help in Toughlove, described in Exhibit 17.1.

Parent Effectiveness Training Approach

As B.F. Skinner is to behavior modification, so Thomas Gordon is to parent effectiveness training (PET).

Basic Perspective

You can do anything with children if you only play with them.
—Prince Otto Von Bismarck

Parent effectiveness training focuses on what the child is feeling and experiencing in the here and now—how she or he sees the world. The method of trying to understand what the child is experiencing is active listening, in which the parent reflects the child's feelings. For example, the parent who is told by the child, "I want to quit taking piano lessons because I don't like to practice" would reflect, "You're really bored with practicing the piano and would rather have fun doing something else."

Exhibit 17.1

TOUGHLOVE

Although not based on a specific childrearing theory, TOUGHLOVE is a self-help organization of parents (none of whom profess to have "professional qualifications" other than experience) who have difficulty controlling severe problem behaviors of their teenage children, including drug abuse, physical abuse of parents, staying away from home without explanation, using obscene language to parents, and stealing from other family members. These parents feel overwhelmed with the magnitude of their child's unacceptable behavior and helpless to cope with it. They may have had "good kids" up until the teen years but are now experiencing behaviors in their children that they never imagined could occur.

TOUGHLOVE parents meet weekly with other parents in groups of about 10 to discuss their children and potential solutions to their behavior problems. The typical format is for each parent to tell what problems she or he is experiencing. Other group members will comment on having had a similar problem, what they did, and how it worked out. Although there is no pressure to talk about one's problems or to take action, once a parent decides to discuss a problem and becomes committed to a course of action, the group members will ask at the next meeting if the parent followed through and what the consequences were. TOUGHLOVE parents are very supportive of each other.

The group setting eliminates the parents' feeling that they are the only parents whose children have gotten out of control, that they are embarrassed at their inability to cope with the situation, and that they have something to be ashamed of. TOUGHLOVE parents take the position that they are people too and that they have a right to expect their children to behave appropriately. The TOUGH part becomes operative in the withdrawal of family resources when children consistently disregard parental requests. "The way you get cooperation from unruly young people is to withdraw the family resources that allow them to exploit their parents" (York et al., 1982, p. 114). For example, a child who says, "I am going to smoke dope whether you like it or not," may, as a last resort, be asked to find somewhere else to live. The child who is arrested for drunk driving for the third time is left in jail for three days even though his parents could bail him out.

The larger community consisting of teachers, probation officers, social workers, therapists, and citizens may also be involved in helping parents in TOUGHLOVE. For example, a child who takes drugs and has a history of lying about doing so may be taken to school by the parents, watched carefully at school by the teacher, have weekly meetings with a caseworker, and be taken home by another member of the TOUGHLOVE group. The community pulls together to try to help the parents control their child's negative behavior. The emphasis is not on blaming anyone but on correcting the behavior problem. There are more than 500 chapters of TOUGHLOVE in the United States (York & York, 1982). Information about a chapter in your community can be obtained from the cofounders of TOUGHLOVE, David and Phyllis York, (P.O. Box 70; Sellersville, PA 18960; 215–257–0421).

PET also focuses on the development of the child's positive self-concept. Such a self-concept is the result of other people reflecting positive images to the child—letting the child know he or she is liked, admired, and approved of.

Considerations for Childrearing

To assist in the development of a child's positive self-concept and in the self-actualization of both children and parents, Gordon makes a number of recommendations. These include managing the environment rather than the child, engaging in active listening, using "I messages," and resolving conflicts through mutual negotiation. An example of environmental management is putting breakables out of reach of young children but towel racks and toy boxes within reach. It is sometimes easier and safer to manage the environment—not just the child.

The use of active listening becomes increasingly important as the child gets older. When Joanna is upset with her teacher, it is better for the parent to reflect the child's thoughts than to take sides with her. Saying "You're angry that Mrs. Jones made the whole class miss play period because Becky was chewing gum," rather than saying "Mrs. Jones was unfair and should not have made the whole class miss play period," shows empathy with the child without blaming the teacher.

Gordon also suggests using "I" rather than "you" messages. Parents are encouraged to say "I get upset when you're late and don't call," rather than "You're an insensitive, irresponsible kid for not calling me when you said you would." The former avoids damaging the child's self-concept but still encourages the desired behavior.

Gordon's fourth suggestion for parenting is the no-lose method of resolving conflicts. He rejects the use of power by parent or child. In the authoritarian home, the parent dictates what the child is to do and the child is expected to obey. In such a system, the parent wins and the child loses. At the other extreme is the permissive home, in which the child wins and the parent loses. The alternative, Gordon says, is for the parent and the child to seek a solution that is acceptable to both and to keep trying until they find one. In this way, neither parent nor child loses and both win.

Criticisms of the Parent Effectiveness Training Approach

Although much is commendable about PET, parents may have problems with two of Gordon's suggestions. First, he recommends that because older children have a right to their own values, parents should not interfere with their dress, career plans, and sexual behavior. Some parents may feel they do have a right (and an obligation) to "interfere."

Second, the no-lose method of resolving conflict is sometimes unrealistic. Suppose a 16–year-old wants to spend the weekend at the beach with her boyfriend and her parents do not want her to do so. Gordon says to negotiate until a decision is reached that is acceptable to both. But what if neither the parents nor the daughter can suggest a compromise or shift their position? To encourage parents to find a mutually agreeable solution is commendable, but the specifics of how to do so in a particular situation are not always clear.

Socioteleological Approach

Alfred Adler, a physician and former student of Sigmund Freud, saw a parallel between psychological and physiological development. When a person loses her or his sight, the other senses (hearing, touch, taste) become more sensitive—they compensate for the loss. According to Adler, the same phenomenon occurs in the psychological realm. When an individual feels inferior in one area, she or he will strive to compensate and become superior in another. Rudolph Dreikurs, a student of Adler, has developed an approach to childrearing that alerts parents as to how their children might be trying to compensate for feelings of inferiority. Dreikurs's suggestions are based on Adler's theory.

Basic Perspective

According to Adler, it is understandable that most children feel they are inferior and weak. From the child's point of view, the world is filled with strong giants who tower above him or her. Because children feel powerless in the face of adult superiority, they try to compensate by gaining attention (making noise, becoming disruptive), exerting power (becoming aggressive, hostile), seeking revenge (becoming violent, hurting others), and acting inadequate (giving up, not trying). Adler suggested that such misbehavior is evidence that the child is discouraged or feels insecure about her or his place in the family. The term *socioteleological* refers to social striving or seeking a social goal—in the child's case, the goal of a secure place within the family.

Considerations for Childrearing

When parents observe misbehavior in their children, they should recognize it as an attempt to find security. According to Dreikurs, parents should not fall

Children must be taught to eat nutritious snacks instead of sweets.

Exhibit 17.2

FAMILY MEETINGS

The family meeting is a regularly scheduled meeting of all family members who want to attend. The purpose is to make plans for family chores and family fun, to express complaints and positive feelings, to resolve conflicts, and to make other decisions.

Guidelines for Family Meetings

1. Meet at a regularly scheduled time.
2. Treat all members as equals. Let everyone be heard.
3. Use reflective listening and I-messages to encourage members to express their feelings and beliefs clearly.
4. Pinpoint real issues. Avoid being sidetracked by other issues.
5. Encourage members by recognizing the good things that are happening in the family.
6. Remember to plan family fun and recreation.
7. Agree on the length of the meeting and keep it within the established limits.
8. Record plans and decisions that are made at the meeting. Post the record as a reminder.

Pitfalls to Avoid

1. Meeting only to handle crises; skipping meetings; changing meeting times.
2. Dominating by members who believe they have more rights.
3. Failing to listen to and encourage each other.
4. Dealing with symptoms (such as bickering and quarreling) instead of the purposes of the behavior.
5. Focusing on complaints and criticisms.
6. Limiting the meetings to job distribution and discipline.
7. Ignoring established time limits.
8. Failing to put agreements into action.

Source: *Systematic Training for Effective Parenting* (STEP) © 1982 by Don Dinkmeyer and Gary D. McKay. Reproduced by permission of American Guidance Service, Inc., Publishers' Bldg., Circle Pines, MN 55014.

The best way to make children is to make them happy.
—Oscar Wilde

into playing the child's game by, say, responding to a child's disruptiveness with anger, but should encourage the child, hold regular family councils, and let natural consequences occur. To encourage the child, the parents should be willing to let the child make mistakes. If John wants to help Dad carry logs to the fireplace, rather than Dad saying "You're too small to carry the logs," John should be allowed to try and encouraged to carry the size limb or stick that he can manage. Furthermore, Dad should praise John for his helpfulness.

Along with constant encouragement, the child should be included in a weekly family council (see Exhibit 17.2). During this meeting, such family issues as bedtimes, the appropriateness of between-meal snacks, assignment of chores, and family fun are discussed. The meeting is democratic; each family member has a vote. Such participation in family decision making is designed to enhance the self-concept of each child.

Finally, Dreikurs suggests that the parents let natural consequences occur for their child's behavior. If a daughter misses the school bus, she walks or is charged "taxi fare" out of her allowance. If she won't wear a coat and boots, she gets cold and wet. Of course, parents are to arrange suitable consequences when natural consequences will not occur or would be dangerous if they did. For example, if a child leaves the video games on the living room floor, they could be taken away for a month. "If we are not exposed to the natural consequences of our behavior, we will never learn the hardworking, cooperative behaviors that lead to social, economic, or personal success. . . . This is the kind of abuse that will cripple us throughout our lives" (Love & McVoy, 1981, p. 13).

Criticisms of the Socioteleological Approach

The socioteleological approach to childrearing has been criticized because it lacks supportive empirical research and is occasionally impractical. Regarding research, "The approach has been used and 'tested' clinically, but such research does not impress the empirical-minded. Science tends to pass over theories which fail to demonstrate their usefulness in predicting specific outcomes which can be demonstrated in nature" (Mead, 1976, p. 63). It is fair to say that some of the other childrearing approaches already discussed also lack solid empirical support.

The impracticality of the socioteleological approach is sometimes illustrated by letting the child take the natural consequences of his or her action. This may be an effective childrearing procedure for most behaviors, but it can backfire. Letting the child develop a sore throat in the hope that it will teach her or him the importance of wearing a raincoat in the rain is questionable.

Reality Therapy Approach

Based on the work of William Glasser and his parent involvement program (PIP), the *reality therapy* approach to childrearing focuses on the developing child and teenager.

Basic Perspective

Glasser suggests that the young child is irrationally narcissistic, emotionally precocious, and incapable of coping with frustration and stress. These qualities cause the behavioral problems children exhibit—from not cleaning their rooms to taking drugs. By irrational narcissism, Glasser means the child is completely self-centered and views everything in terms of "what's in it for me." Emotional precociousness means she or he is insensitive to the needs of others and seeks to manipulate others' emotions to his or her own ends. But Glasser sees the child's greatest character flaw as not being able to cope with stress and quitting rather than working through a problem. Children do not have the confidence in themselves to figure out what to do when something goes wrong or the perseverance to make a bad situation better.

In bringing up children, spend on them half as much money and twice as much time.
—Laurence Peter

Television is the villain behind these flaws. The hours children spend in front of this "mindless tube," according to Glasser, are destructive—not because the content of television is so awful, but because children are not using this time to interact with others, to develop social skills, to learn about life by experiencing it. They are living vicariously.

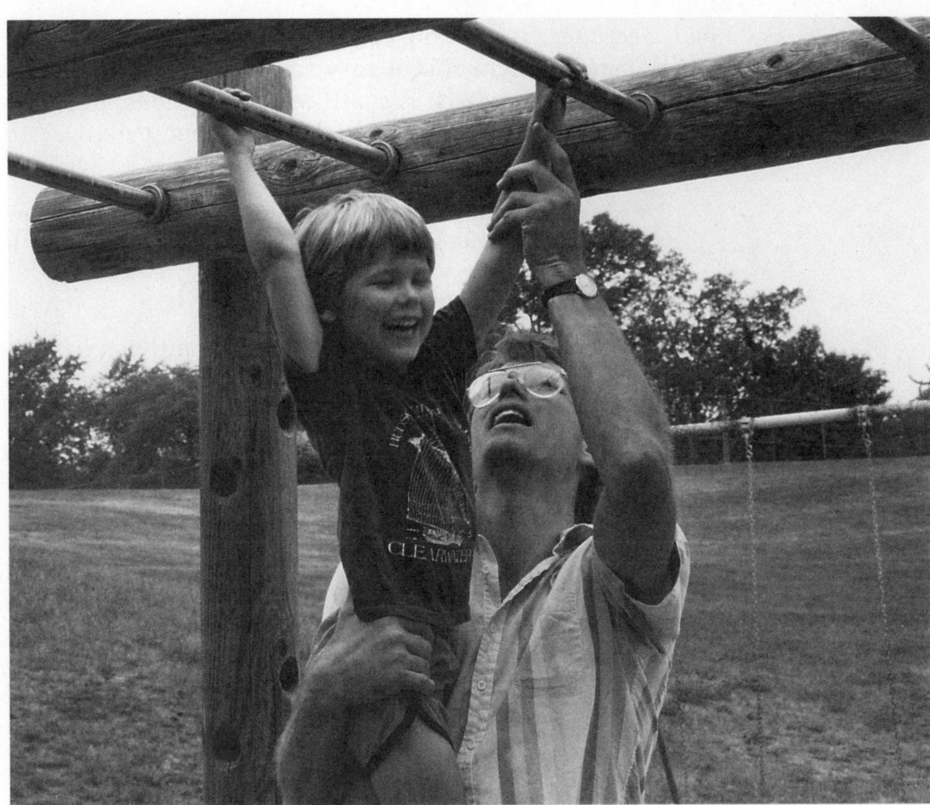

According to Dr. Glasser, spending time with your child is the most important thing you can do.

Considerations for Childrearing

Glasser recommends that parents understand that nothing they can do for their children is more valuable than spending time with them. This communicates to children that they are loved and valued, which is a prerequisite for developing their confidence to persevere in spite of setbacks. Spending time with children also helps them to learn social skills, to learn another person's point of view, and to learn to share with others. Participation in family rituals, such as Christmas, birthdays, vacations, Easter, and Sunday dinner, also have the effect of bonding family members to each other (Schvaneveldt & Lee, 1983).

The reality therapy approach to childrearing also emphasizes the right of children to make their own choices. Parents are urged to give children responsibility for their choices and to let them take the consequences. This principle is similar to the Adlerian principle of natural consequences. "My child has a right to fail in school," said one parent. This viewpoint acknowledges that only the child can decide what course of action to take (for example, whether to study or not) in life and that accepting the consequences for your own decisions is an effective way of learning how to make decisions.

Criticisms of the Reality Therapy Approach

Like most childrearing approaches, the reality therapy approach looks good on paper. Spending time with children, giving children the right to make their own decisions, and letting natural consequences follow are suggestions with which parents might find it easy to agree. However, the basic premise of the reality therapy approach is that the love relationship between the parent and the child is the critical variable that determines the way the child turns out. This premise is suspect. One parent said:

> I've spent half my life with my son, including regular fishing trips when he was a small boy and working with him in Scouts when he was older. His teacher told me the reason he is doing poorly in school is because I haven't spent enough time with him to show my love for him. Baloney!

Children are subject to a wide variety of influences, and parent behavior—regardless of how loving or stable it is—is only one aspect of the child's socialization.

In addition, as with the socioteleological approach, some parents may have a difficult time standing by waiting for their child to learn from her or his own decisions. For example, does a parent allow a 15–year–old to buy a motorcycle and learn through experience that turning curves too fast can cost a leg? Does a parent permit his or her child to be unconcerned about grades to the point of not being able to graduate? Does the parent let the child decide who his or her friends will be, even if these friends are known drug abusers?

Although you may not adhere to any one particular approach to childrearing, you do have a perspective on the permissiveness or strictness of child discipline. The Child Discipline Scale is designed to help you identify this perspective.

Responding to Teenage Drug Abuse

One of the greatest fears of today's parents is that their child will abuse drugs.

Data – Fifty-two percent of all adults polled say drug abuse is the number-one problem for children. (Harris, 1986)

For the drug abuser, the use of drugs or alcohol ultimately causes a problem in all areas of life—health, school, work, home, and social relationships. Parents *can* help to prevent their son or daughter from abusing drugs. If their prevention efforts fail, however, they should be ready to respond.

Drug Prevention—The Best Medicine

It is easier to do everything possible to ensure that your child does not begin to use drugs than it is to try to stop the drug use once it has begun. Some specific things that parents can do to ward off drug abuse in their children have been recommended by Louis Meador (1987), a drug-abuse specialist who works with teenagers and their families.

Be a Good Example

Parents who come home from a day at the office and drink liquor until bedtime are teaching their children that alcohol is used to relieve stress—the

Self-Assessment

Child Discipline Scale

This inventory is designed to measure the degree to which you have a permissive or strict view of childrearing. There are no right or wrong answers. After reading each sentence carefully, circle the number that best represents your view.

1 Strongly disagree
2 Mildly disagree
3 Undecided
4 Mildly agree
5 Strongly agree

	SD	MD	U	MA	SA
1. When you spare the rod, you spoil the child.	1	2	3	4	5
2. It is better for your children to view you as an authority than as a friend.	1	2	3	4	5
3. Parents let their children get away with too much.	1	2	3	4	5
4. One of the most important qualities a child can have is to be obedient.	1	2	3	4	5
5. Children should do as they are told without asking why.	1	2	3	4	5
6. If you aren't strict with a child, she or he won't respect you.	1	2	3	4	5
7. The only thing children really understand is a good spanking.	1	2	3	4	5
8. Parents who try to be buddy-buddy with their children lose their respect.	1	2	3	4	5
9. When children have done something bad, punishing them is more effective than talking with them about doing better the next time.	1	2	3	4	5
10. The Bible is a good guidebook for child discipline.	1	2	3	4	5

Scoring: Add the numbers you circled. 1 (strongly disagree) is the most permissive response you can make, and 5 (strongly agree) is the most strict response you can make. The lower your total score (10 is the lowest possible score), the more permissive your childrearing view; the higher your total score (50 is the highest possible score), the more strict you are about child discipline. A score of 30 total places you at the midpoint between being permissive and being strict.

more alcohol, the better. Regardless of what you say, your children will attend to what you do. And your telling them about the evils of alcohol won't fly.

Just as getting drunk models abuse of alcohol, moderate use of alcohol models drinking control. Children who are reared in homes in which their parents drink alcohol in moderation are most likely to avoid becoming alcoholics. On the other hand, children who are reared in homes in which one or both parents abuse alcohol or in homes in which alcohol is forbidden are most likely to become alcoholics. An alcoholic from a nondrinking home said, "My folks made a big thing out of never drinking alcohol and told me I was never to do it. I rebelled against them, started drinking at 17, and haven't quit."

Parents who use marijuana, cocaine, or other illegal drugs serve as role models for teenagers to use these same drugs. If your goal is for your child not to use any of these drugs, you should not use them yourself. To do so is to teach your child that drug use is acceptable behavior. And your saying "I'm older and know what I'm doing" won't mean much to your teenager.

Misuse of prescription drugs carries the same caveat. Although your physician may have prescribed tranquilizers to relieve stress, your taking more than the recommended dosage is similar to drinking more than a couple of cocktails or beers. If your children see you taking aspirin for a headache, valium for your nerves, and Dalmane to sleep, the message is clear—drugs are the answer to pain, stress, and insomnia.

There may also be a genetic link to the potential to abuse drugs. Individuals whose parents, grandparents, or siblings have a history of substance abuse or major depression are much more likely to abuse drugs themselves. Being reared by biological or nonbiological parents has less to do with a person becoming a substance abuser than having biological parents who abuse drugs.

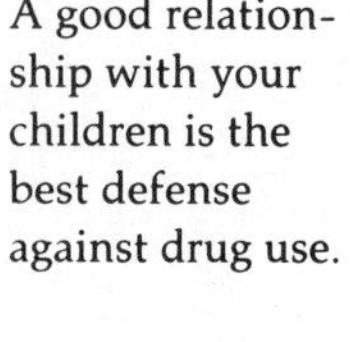
A good relationship with your children is the best defense against drug use.

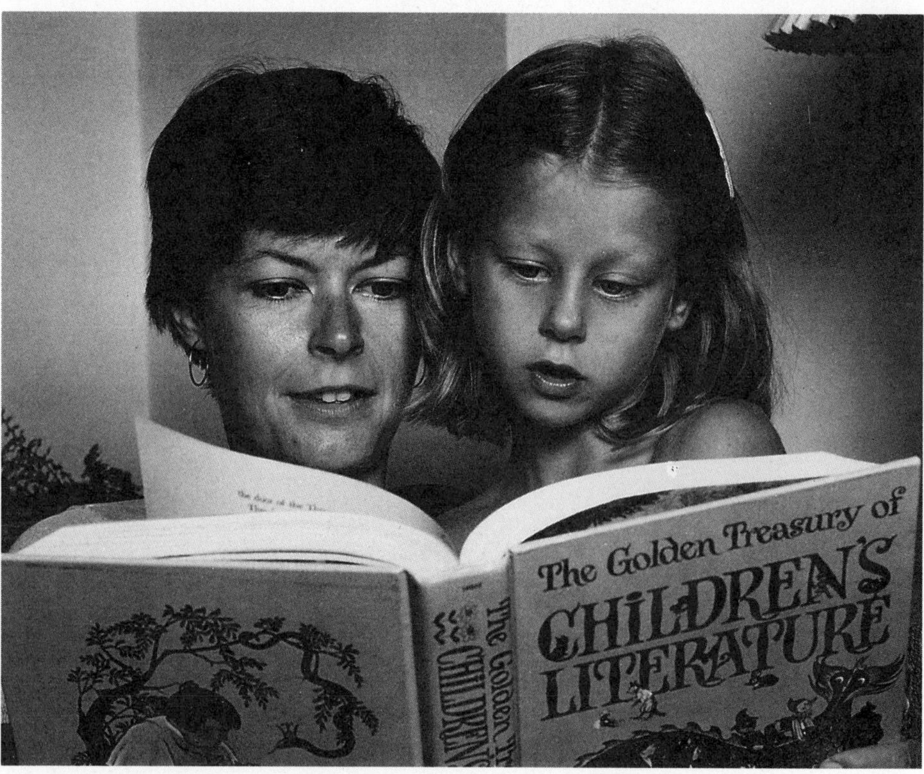

Data – Although it is a problem for all families, drug abuse is the number-one problem threatening the survival of the black family. (*Ebony*, 1986)

Some parents who once abused drugs but no longer do so wonder if they should tell their teenager of their earlier drug use. Two issues are at stake in such a situation. One, is it appropriate to lie to your teenager under any conditions? And two, what impact will the knowledge of your drug use have on your teenager's drug use? In regard to the first issue, one parent said that she "would never lie to her child because she would lose faith in me." But another parent said, "Everybody lies about something, and there may be some good reasons to lie to your kids about drugs." One of these "good" reasons follows:

> If you tell your child that you use or have used drugs, he or she may use the fact that you did to justify their doing so. And while you may be able to handle marijuana or cocaine or whatever, your teenager may not be able to do so. People have different biochemical makeups, and the drug a parent may not get addicted to the child might. So think carefully before you tell your child that you use or have used drugs. The drug may have an entirely different (and possibly addictive) effect on him or her.

An alternate perspective is to tell the truth. If you have used drugs, say so but explain the context of your doing so, the hazards, and the reasons you feel it is unwise to take drugs.

Keep Communication Channels Open

Teenagers who are troubled about school, work, and social relationships are more vulnerable to drug use than teenagers who make good grades, enjoy their after-school jobs, and have meaningful social relationships. The best way for parents to recognize that their teenager is becoming despondent is to keep the channels of communication with him or her open.

Open communication translates into less drug use. Children who enjoy their parents' approval are less likely to do something (drink, take drugs) if they know their parents will disapprove of the action. Good communication does not eliminate the possibility that children will drink or take drugs, but it does reduce the chance that they will.

When Drug Abuse Is Already Happening

A parent who becomes aware that a son or daughter is already involved in drugs should assess the situation. Drinking a beer at a party is not the same as getting drunk before school; taking a draw on a marijuana cigarette is not the same as having a bag of dope in a sock drawer. The parent should be careful not to overrespond to the smell of alcohol or something different from cigarette smoke in a child's room, for example. It is appropriate to ask, "What do I smell?," rather than accuse a son or daughter of drinking alcohol or smoking marijuana.

Assuming that the teenager says he or she had a beer or smoked some "dope," the parents' response will differ depending on their values. Some parents absolutely abhor the use of any alcohol or drugs; in these cases, they will tell the teenager this is completely unacceptable behavior, withdraw privileges ("you can't have the car for a month)," and encourage the teenager to recognize that alcohol and marijuana are drugs that are better left alone.

Other parents are more liberal and feel that moderate drug use is acceptable. "I've been using drugs since I was 18," said one 50–year-old parent. "And I've never missed a day at work. Nor has my efficiency dropped one iota. I am just very careful in terms of what drugs I take, how much, how often, and in what context. I think these are the more important issues."

If, however, a teenager has gone overboard and become a drug abuser (drugs are affecting his or her health, grades, and social relationships), the following steps, directed toward the parent, are indicated.

Confront Your Teenager

Armed with evidence (he or she is drunk or in possession of a bag of dope, a container of cocaine, pills, or some other drug), make your teenager aware that you know of the drug use. Cutting through your teenager's denial that he or she uses drugs is difficult for both teenager and parent.

Ask for Your Teenagers' Point of View

Be careful not to criticize or belittle your teenager, but ask him or her to explain why he or she drinks, smokes, snorts, or whatever. It is not unusual for teenagers to feel very guilty about what they are doing; once confronted by their parents, some teenagers are anxious to stop. "I drifted in over my head," said one teenager to her parents, "and I really am sick of it and want to stop."

Consult a Professional Drug-abuse Counselor

Drug abuse can be a difficult family problem, and there are no quick and easy solutions. Before choosing a course of action, consult with a drug-abuse specialist at your local mental-health center.

Make Your Position Clear

If your teenager is contrite and willing to stop drinking or using drugs, offer your love and support. Ask what you can do to make it easier for him or her to stop abusing alcohol or drugs.

But if your teenager is defiant and says that he or she is going to do whatever he or she wants, fight back. Drug abuse can ruin a life in terms of debilitating health, making it difficult to keep a job, and souring social relationships. As long as you have some control over your teenager's life, use it.

Make an Agreement

One alternative is to make it clear to your child that you will not tolerate drug use. One parent told her 16–year-old:

> Your father and I know that you get tired of us butting into your life. But we feel that drugs can harm you, and we ask that you stop as long as you are living with us. To ensure that you are not using drugs, we want you to have your urine analyzed weekly. If drug use has occurred, we are going to send you to an in-patient drug rehabilitation center.

If the teenager can stay drug-free without being admitted to an institutional environment, he or she should be encouraged to attend Narcotics Anonymous at least once weekly.

Narcotics Anonymous

Former drug abusers meet weekly in local chapters of Narcotics Anonymous (NA), patterned after Alcoholics Anonymous, to help each other continue to be drug-free. The premise of NA is that the best person to help someone who is abusing drugs is someone who once abused drugs. NA members of all ages, social classes, and educational levels provide a sense of support for each other to remain drug-free.

If the substance-abuse problem is alcohol, Alcoholics Anonymous (AA), is an appropriate support group (national headquarters mailing address: AA General Service Office; P.O. Box 459, Grand Central Station; New York, NY 10017). There are over 15,000 AA chapters nationwide; the one in your community can be contacted by looking in the Yellow Pages of your local telephone directory. Al-Anon is an organization that provides support for family members of drug abusers. Such support is often helpful to parents coping with a teenage drug abuser.

Other Issues Concerning Parents

Beyond the problem of drug abuse, parents are also concerned about the effects of society at large, day care, and public education on childrearing—and the pressure to produce a "superbaby."

Society at Large

Although the issue is complex, 74 percent of more than 30,000 respondents reported that family life is more difficult today than in previous years (Greer, 1986).

> *Data* – In a national survey, 75 percent of all adults (and almost 85 percent of all blacks) feel the problems children face today are greater than when they were growing up. (Harris, 1986)

Career-involved parents, divorce, economic hardship, drugs, and the absence of a religious or spiritual foundation, are regarded as the primary threats to family life today. One conservative parent said:

> When you look at the mess our society is in, it isn't a fit place to bring up a child any more. The television is filled with permissiveness; everybody is cheating on his wife or her husband or getting a divorce. And we've moved off the land into the big city, where there is plenty to get kids into trouble.

Day Care

Day care is defined as any of the many different types of arrangements that are used to provide supervision and care to children when the parent (usually the mother) is unable to do so. For the employed mother, the care of her child in her absence is of critical and primary concern. A relative is usually her first choice to care for her baby.

Data – In a study of 410 mothers who could not take care of their babies during the day, 63 percent said they left their babies in the care of relatives (mother, mother-in-law, father). (Floge, 1985)

As the child gets older the use of day-care options widen. Unlike Sweden where day-care centers are state-operated, parents in the United States must take care of the day-care needs of their children themselves. The greatest pattern of day care for children in America is the wide range of options used by mothers.

Data – In another study of employed mothers and day care, relatives, baby sitters, neighbors, older adults, older children, and spouses, were among the child-care options used. (ADIA, 1985/1986)

When parents use day-care centers, how confident can they be that their children will be well taken care of? The answer is mixed. In one study, 540 parents who had used day care for their children were asked to list any problems they encountered. The problems and the percentages of parents who reported each problem follow: inadequate child care, 44 percent; improper supervision, 35 percent; unsafe environment, 6 percent; physical abuse, 6 percent; and verbal abuse, 2 percent (Fuqua & Labensohn, 1986). However, in spite of these problems, most of the parents were "very satisfied" with the day-care arrangements they had made for their children. "Isolating the variables that constitute quality day care is a difficult task" (Bjorkman et al., 1986).

Consideration

Parents should ask for detailed information about the policies, activities, and caregivers of a particular day-care facility before enrolling their child. Parents should also visit the day-care center at unannounced times and ask for a list of names of parents who have children at the center. Day care can offer good care for children, but the parents should be careful in their selection. Cost is also a factor.

Data – More than 500 parents whose children were in commercial day-care centers spent as much as $20 per day, or $400 per month, for day-care. (Fuqua & Labensohn, 1986)

Regarding infants in day care, one researcher notes, "What is crucial is that infants have a consistent and warm relationship with their caregivers. . . . If there is a consensus regarding infant day care, it's that care of one baby by one sitter (the alternative preferred by parents) is probably the most desirable" (Meredith, 1986, p. 42). Day care does not adversely affect the infant–mother bond (Burchinal & Bryant, 1986).

Some parents tire of traditional day care and hire an *au pair.* These are European women (age 18 to 25) who help with child-care duties 5½ days a week for one year in exchange for room and board and the right to attend classes in their spare time. About 1,000 *au pairs* enter the United States annually. *Au pair* means "on par," or "equal"—the hosts must be willing to treat them as part of the family. The popularity of *au pairs* has also resulted in the training and hiring of American-born nannies. Families with children under the age of 3 are particularly interested in hiring an *au pair* or a nanny. (See Child Care in Resources and Organizations on page 623 for more information.)

Public Education

Parental concern continues when the children move beyond day care and into public education.

Data – It is estimated that by 1990, 86 percent of all students will be enrolled in public schools and 14 percent of all students will be enrolled in private schools. These are the same percentages as in 1985. (*Statistical Abstract of the United States,* 1987)

Considerable media attention has been given to the problems of public-school education. Some graduates of public high schools can't read, work simple math problems, or write an intelligible sentence. Parents feel frustrated when their children don't learn such basic skills. One parent said, "For all the money that is pumped into education, you would think more learning would take place."

The Superbaby Myth

In the hope of giving their infants a head start in the educational system, some parents who want their children to be "superbabies" are attracted to programs advertising that children can be taught to read by the age of 3. One such program, the Better Baby Reading Program, is marketed through the Encyclopedia Britannica. But researchers, found "no evidence documenting its long-term usefulness" (Zigler & Lang, 1985, p. 341).

Consideration

Children need time for their brains and bodies to develop before they are capable of performing complex cognitive tasks. Parents would be better advised to spend time playing with and enjoying their infants than trying to get them to read by the age of 3. If parents want to maximize the infant's learning potential, giving him or her objects to hold and manipulate teaches the infant about the properties of objects (hard, soft, pliable) and provides a good beginning.

Trends

New parents will continue to enter their childrearing role more or less naively, suggesting that most couples wait until they have a child to begin talking

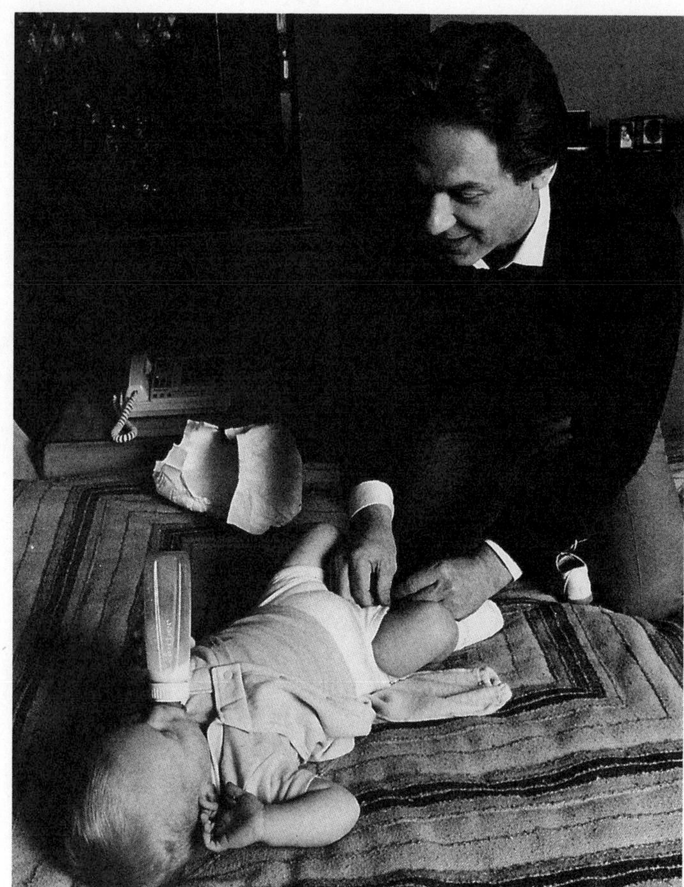

In the future, parenthood will more often be a shared experience.

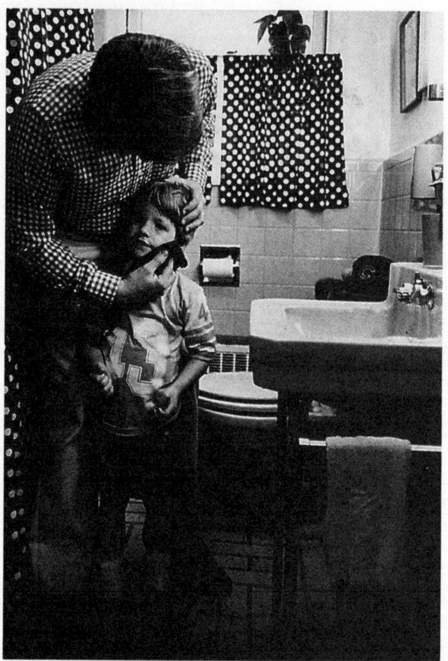

about their concerns about the childrearing role. Of course, no book, lecture, or course can adequately prepare a person for what it means to rear a child. Those who have had a great deal of responsibility for the care of younger siblings probably have a better idea than most.

For parents who find that the childrearing role is more than they had anticipated, a number of resources are available, including a "newsletter of video-based parenting education," *Active Parenting.* Parents can order videotapes on a variety of parenting concerns from this organization by telephone (1–800–235–7755; in Georgia, collect, 1–404–843–2723). These videos are also used in parenting workshops; a list of these workshops is also available from *Active Parenting.*

Working parents today are tending to use a wider range of options for child care than their parents, who left their children with their own parents. These options include day care, flex-time, job-sharing, and nannies.

Summary

Rearing children is one of the most demanding tasks an individual ever undertakes, and it requires that parents keep their role in perspective. Parenthood is only one stage in the person's marriage and life. In addition, parents are only one influence in the lives of their children; the joys and problems of childrearing change as the children mature; each child is different; and the goals of childrearing may differ. Some parents want obedient children; others want children who are independent and self-reliant. The latter goal is in the best interests of the child.

Extensive folklore has arisen to make the role of parent more palatable to adults to encourage a commitment to childrearing. Would-be parents are led to believe that childrearing is fun, that good parents will produce good children, that love is enough for successful parenting, and that their children will appreciate the sacrifices they make for them. These beliefs are not supported by facts.

There are a number of childrearing approaches to help parents with the problems of parenting. The developmental–maturational approach focuses on what the child will be able to do when and suggests that parents should not demand of children what they are developmentally unable to deliver. The behavioral approach assumes that behavior is learned and that parents can get their children to engage in the behavior they want by rewarding desirable behavior and punishing undesirable behavior. Parent effectiveness training focuses on the communication between parent and child and encourages the parents to negotiate with their children when conflicts occur. The socioteleological approach views the negative behavior of children as a result of feelings of inferiority and suggests regular family council meetings to give children a voice in what happens in the family. The reality therapy approach focuses on the necessity of letting children make their own choices and learning from them.

Beyond drug abuse, parents are also concerned about the ways in which the society at large, day care, public education, and the pressure to produce a "superbaby" affect childrearing.

New parents will continue to enter the parenting role naively, but they may make use of a large number of resources in the form of workshops, organizations, and books for parents who seek such help.

Questions for Reflection

1. Which childrearing approach appeals to you? Why?
2. How do you feel about putting your child in day care?
3. How do you feel about "spare the rod, and spoil the child" as a method of disciplining children? (This question will become more relevant after you read the Choices section which follows.)
4. As a parent, how would you respond to your teenager abusing drugs?

CHOICES

PARENTS ARE FACED with innumerable choices in rearing their children. These include which type of punishment to use, whether to reward positive behavior, how much freedom to give how soon, and how long to allow children to continue to live at home.

WHICH TYPE OF PUNISHMENT IS BEST?

Infants are unsocialized persons. They know only one way—their own. Parents who adopt the behavioral approach to childrearing believe that to learn appropriate behavior, developing infants and children must be rewarded for certain behaviors and punished for others. Although parents may agree that praise and privileges are ways of rewarding children for positive behavior, they may choose different forms of punishment.

Some parents (about 4 percent) have the "spare the rod, and spoil the child" philosophy and inflict physical pain on their children as punishment (Greer, 1986). Examples of such punishment include being beaten on the buttocks with a belt or leather strap, being whipped on the legs, buttocks, and back with a switch, and being slapped or knocked down. One parent said "If you don't give them a good beating now and then, they forget who's boss and they don't mind you. A good lickin' will snap a kid in line every time."

Other parents feel that corporal punishment is unnecessary or wrong and elect to put their children in "time out" (removing the child to a place of isolation) or to withhold privileges for inappropriate behavior:

> When my 6–year-old says 'Nah' rather than a polite 'No' or 'No ma'am,' I tell her to go to the bathroom. She knows that means she is being punished for being disrespectful. For her brother who didn't get home until 1:30 a.m. when he was supposed to be in at midnight, I took the car away from him for two weeks.

The decision to choose a corporal or noncorporal method of punishment should be based on the consequences of use. In general, the use of "time out" and withholding of privileges seem to be as effective in stopping undesirable behavior as corporal punishment. Young children who are consistently put in "time out" for inappropriate verbal behavior (saying "nah," talking back, having temper tantrums) decrease the frequency of those behaviors. Likewise, when meaningful privileges are withdrawn for inappropriate behavior (being late, not completing chores, drinking alcohol), the behaviors decrease.

Beatings and whippings will also decrease the negative verbal and nonverbal behaviors. But there is a major side effect. The person who is physically beaten learns to fear and avoid the punisher. One student recalled:

> My dad once beat me with his belt until I bled. I hated him for it and never wanted anything to do with him. And all I did was forget to bring his beer home.

Parents who don't want their children to become fearful and avoid them should consider noncorporal forms of punishment.

TO REWARD OR NOT REWARD POSITIVE BEHAVIOR?

Most parents agree that some form of punishment is necessary to curb a child's inappropriate behavior, but there is disagreement over whether positive behavior (taking out the trash, cleaning up one's room, making

(Continued)

good grades) should be rewarded by praise, extra privileges, or money. Some parents feel that a child should do the right things anyway and that to reward them is to bribe them. One parent said, "My kid is going to do what I say because I say so, not because I am going to give him something for doing it."

Other parents feel that both the child and the parent benefit when the parents reward the child for good behavior. Rewarding a child for a behavior will result in the child engaging in that behavior more often, so that the child develops a set of positive behaviors and feels good about herself or himself. The parents, in turn, feel good about the child.

Rather than ask whether it is good or bad to reward children for positive behavior, parents might ask, "What behavior do I want my child to engage in?" Once that behavior is identified, it is necessary to ensure that positive things happen when the behavior occurs and negative things happen when it doesn't. Children who are rewarded by praise or privileges for being polite, completing their chores, and making good grades and who are punished by having privileges withdrawn for the opposite behaviors will soon learn to engage in the behavior their parents want them to engage in.

How Much Freedom How Soon?

Becoming independent is one of the major tasks of adolescence. Successful parents may be defined as those who teach their children how to function as an independent adult in society. Parents accomplish this by learning to give less assistance to their offspring during adolescence. The parent who gives too little or too much help and the adolescent who takes too much or too little help will go through many adjustments before the adolescent becomes independent. One parent compared achieving a balance of freedom to flying a kite:

> If a parent lets out too much string too quickly, the kite will fall to the ground. But letting out the string slowly as the kite finds the wind and braces against it seems to make the kite soar. And once the kite achieves flight, the parent must let out even more string. If the kite line is kept too tight, it will snap and the kite will fall to the ground. So it is with the developing adolescent, letting out the line and waiting for the adolescent to adjust to that level of independence before letting out more line seems to work best for both parent and offspring.

How Long Should Children Live With Their Parents?

About 20 million young adults (age 18 to 29)—more men than women—continue to live with their parents; 3 million of them are between the ages of 25 and 29 (Glick & Lin, 1986). Their motivations are to save money, continue living in a stable environment, and avoid the psychological risk of going out on their own.

As long as offspring and parents agree with the arrangement, living with parents as an adult can be beneficial and enjoyable to both parties. But unless the rules of living together have been discussed and agreed on (most parents are concerned that their children not use drugs, not bring home late-night companions, and help with chores), parents often feel used and offspring often feel belittled. The choice to stay should be made in reference to maximizing and maintaining positive relationships with one's parents. If the young adult stays and saves money but damages the relationship with his or her parents in doing so, the price may be too high.

How Long Should Parents Let Adult Children Live With Them?

Parents view the dilemma of when the child should leave home from a different perspective. Most parents want to provide a home for their children but feel that it is in the best interest of the offspring to leave home and become independent—to learn to rely on his or her own resources—at some time.

Deciding when to nudge the reluctant offspring out of the nest isn't easy. Most parents gently encourage their offspring to get a job and an apartment. Others require their offspring to do work around the house (yard, laundry, food preparation and/or cleanup) or to pay rent. Still others resort to insisting that their adult children leave. "We have our own right to live," said one parent.

Perhaps the best choice for both parents and offspring is to make their feelings known to each other. Doing so avoids the buildup of resentments that may result in a heated argument and a permanent distancing of the relationship between the respective parties. Most parents (64 percent) feel good about their grown children returning home to live with them for a limited time (Greer, 1986).

Impact of Social Influences on Choices

How we behave as parents has more to do with the society in which we live than with our individual predispositions. "Spare the rod, and spoil the child," uninvolved fathers, and full-time mothers have been altered somewhat by the infusion of "time out for misbehavior," birthing fathers, and career women. Compared to past generations, today's parents are less likely to beat their children, fathers are more likely to be involved with their children, and women are more likely to be spending time outside the home earning money. The latter two changes have an economic base. Not only has motherhood been altered by the supposed necessity for the mother to work outside the home, but her doing so has put more pressure on the father to share in the parenting work load. Hence, forces beyond ourselves impact on our lives.

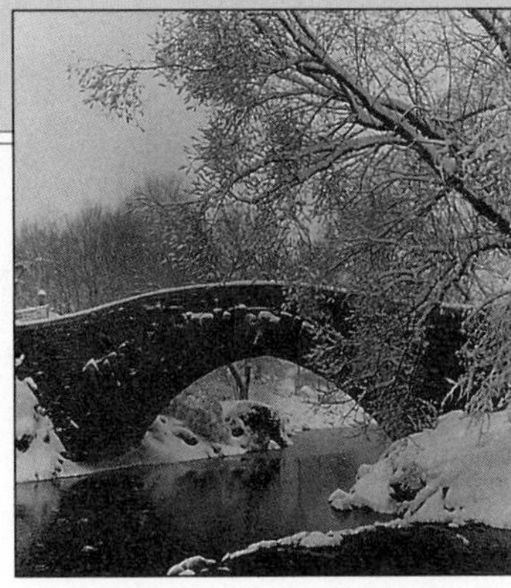

PART FIVE

TRANSITIONS

TRADITIONALLY, THE UNITED STATES has had an adversary system of divorce in which one party was found innocent and the other guilty. Under the "fault doctrine," it was necessary to prove that one spouse had performed some specific act that had been detrimental to the other spouse. For example, the wife might say (and prove), "He beat me" (physical cruelty), or "He won't give me money for the children" (nonsupport). Likewise, the husband might accuse his wife of having an affair (adultery). Under any of these circumstances, the "innocent party" would be granted a divorce.

In 1970, as an alternative to the adversary system of divorce, California initiated the "no-fault divorce," which allows spouses to terminate their marriage if either spouse feels that there are "irreconcilable differences." Under the no-fault system, spouses who don't want to live with each other because they are not happy, have grown apart, or don't love each other any more can get a divorce with relative ease.

By 1988 almost all states had adopted similar no-fault provisions. Other labels for "irreconcilable differences" include "irretrievable breakdown," "irremediable breakdown," and "no reasonable likelihood of preserving the marriage." Some states have adopted separation as a ground for divorce. Under this provision, the spouses only need to live apart for six months to one year (depending on the state) to provide evidence of "irreconcilable differences."

CHAPTER 18

Divorce, Widowhood, and Remarriage

Contents

Is It True?*

1. Employed wives are more likely to divorce than wives who do not work outside the home.
2. Researchers agree that the long-term effects of divorce on children are negative.
3. Lack of money is the most frequently reported problem encountered by widows.
4. Second marriages are more likely to end in divorce than first marriages.
5. Most divorcing fathers actively seek custody of their children.

*1=T; 2=F; 3=F; 4=T; 5=F.

Divorce

Divorce and death are the principal means by which marriages end. (Others are annulment and desertion.) Such endings are accompanied by many emotions—frustration, disappointment, grief, relief, hope—and sometimes by growth. In this chapter, we will explore the process of and adjustment to marital dissolution by divorce and death. We will also look at spouses who begin again through remarriage.

Data – Every year, there are more than 1 million divorces in the United States. The range is usually between 1,150,000 and 1,210,000. (*Statistical Abstract of the United States*, 1987)

Divorcees are people who have not achieved a good marriage; they are also people who would not settle for a bad one.
—Paul Bohannan

Preceding these divorces, spouses typically express feelings like:

I'm tired of waiting for things to get better. I'm afraid that 20 years from now we'll be in the same stale relationship. Let's separate.

I feel trapped and want out.

It's not that I think bad things about you; it's just that I don't think about you at all anymore.

I am involved in a new relationship and want a divorce.

What began at a wedding ceremony, usually with a minister, parents, and friends, ends in a courtroom with a judge, lawyers, and strangers. The reality of day-to-day living has failed to meet the hopeful expectations the partners shared during courtship.

In this section, we will look at the social and individual reasons for why spouses divorce. The social context of divorce has as much to do with divorce as the individuals who actually implement a divorce.

Causes of Divorce

Determining the causes of divorce is not easy. The reasons are embedded in the individuals, their interaction, and the society in which they live. First, let's look at the larger social context.

Societal Factors

A number of factors have combined to make divorce increasingly common in America. They include the following.

Changing Family Functions. Many of the protective, religious, educational, and recreational functions of the family have largely been taken over by outside agencies. Family members may now look to the police, the church or synagogue, the school, and commercial recreational facilities rather than to each other for fulfilling these needs. The result is that although meeting emotional needs remains a primary function of the family, there is less reason to keep the family together.

Decreased Economic Dependence of Wife. In the past, the unemployed wife was dependent on her husband for food and shelter. No matter how unhappy her marriage was, she could only think about divorce. Her husband literally represented her lifeline.

Finding gainful employment outside the home made it possible for the wife to afford to leave her husband if she wanted to. Now that almost 70 percent of all wives are employed (and this number is increasing), fewer and fewer wives are economically trapped in an unhappy marriage relationship. This economic independence sometimes translates into divorce. In one study comparing marriages in which the wives were employed with marriages in which the wives were not employed, the former were more likely to divorce (Menaghan, 1985).

There was a time when I felt a bit cocky when hearing about another's divorce. Their tragedy would never touch me. Now my marriage ends in what feels like disgrace.
—Ralph Detrick

An alternative explanation of the impact of the wife's employment on divorce suggests that her employment results in her spending less time on domestic chores, creating a sense of loss and aggravation for the husband. He complains, conflict ensues, and another stress has been added to the relationship. In one study, the researchers found that the amount of time the employed wife was away from the home had a greater impact on the chance for divorce than the amount of money she earned—the money that presumably provided her with economic independence (Spitze & South, 1985).

Fewer Moral and Religious Sanctions. The Catholic church no longer excommunicates divorced Catholics who remarry. Many priests and clergy recognize that divorce may be the only alternative in a particular marital relationship and attempt to minimize the guilt a member of their congregation may feel at the failure of his or her marriage. Increasingly, marriage is more often viewed in secular rather than in religious terms.

Divorce Models. As the number of divorced individuals in our society increases, the probability increases that a person's friends, parents, siblings, or children will be divorced. The more divorced people a person knows, the more normal divorce will seem to that person. The less deviant the person perceives divorce to be, the greater the probability that that person will divorce if his or her own marriage becomes strained.

Less Parental Control Over Mate Selection. In the past, American parents have had more control over whom their son or daughter married; such factors as family background, social class, and property were given priority. The result of such parentally controlled mate selection was that the partners had more in common than love feelings. Today, however, love may be the primary consideration in the decision to marry, and feelings of love are sometimes not enough to weather 50 years together.

Societal Goal of Happiness. The goal to be happy as a major reason to marry is encouraged in our society. When spouses stop having fun, they often feel there is no reason to stay married.

Data – Fifty-five percent of all women and men say a divorce is acceptable if the marriage isn't working out. (Roper Poll, 1985).

For over a third of all new spouses, the fun stops within the first five years (see Figure 18.1).

Consideration

The reason you stay married is not the same reason you get married. Most people marry for love, fun, and happiness. However, marriage blunts these emotions and focuses the spouses attentions on work and childrearing. Asian Americans and Mexican Americans have lower divorce rates than whites or blacks because they consider the family unit to be of greater value than their individual interests. To be unhappy is less likely to result in movement toward divorce for these groups.

Liberal Divorce Laws. California has one of the most liberal divorce laws in America. Marital partners who have no children and no more than $4,000 in debts, who have been married less than five years, whose community property does not exceed $12,000 in value, and who have waived alimony rights may fill out their own forms for dividing up the property. After a waiting period of six months, either the husband or wife returns to the court and asks that the judge declare the divorce legal.

All states now recognize some form of no-fault divorce (Freed & Walker, 1986). Although the legal terms are "irreconcilable differences" and "incompatibility," the reality is that spouses can get a divorce if they want to without having to prove that one of the partners is at fault (for example, adultery or drug addiction).

Individual Factors

Although various societal factors may make divorce a viable alternative to marital unhappiness, they are not sufficient to "cause" a divorce. One spouse

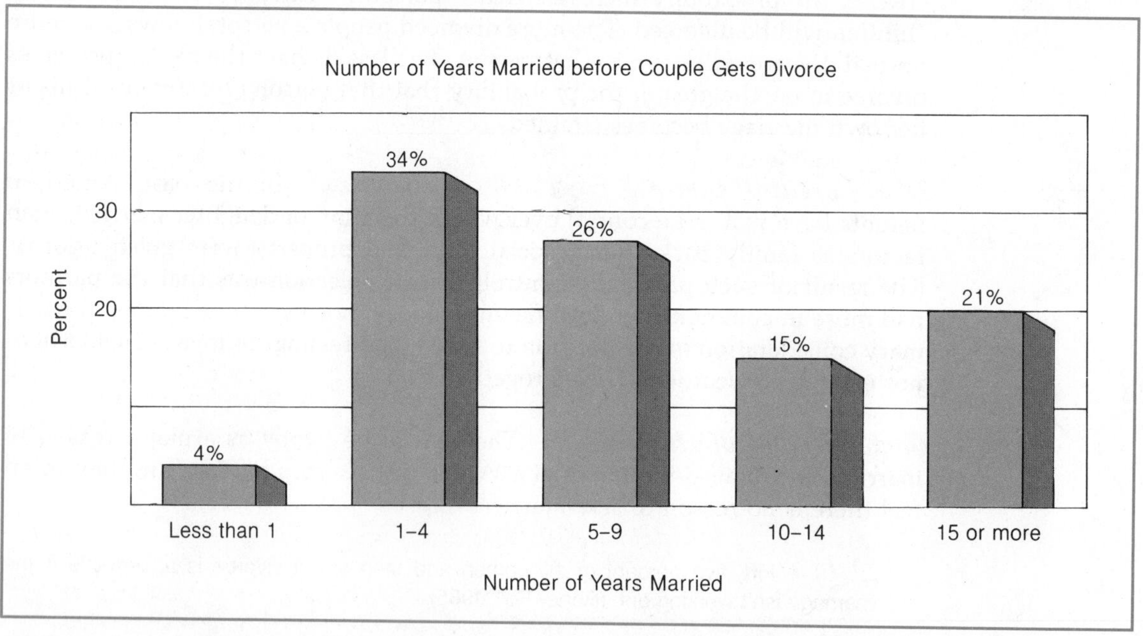

FIGURE 18.1 PERCENT OF MARRIED COUPLES DIVORCING BY DURATION OF MARRIAGE.

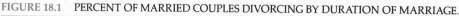

must actually initiate divorce proceedings. Reasons why a spouse might seek a divorce include the following.

If I had given as much to marriage as I gave to "The Tonight Show," I'd probably have a hell of a marriage. But the fact is, I haven't given that, and there you have the simple reason for the failure of my marriages: I put the energy into the show.
—Johnny Carson

Negative Behavior. People marry because they anticipate greater rewards from being married than from being single. During courtship, each partner engages in a high frequency of positive verbal and nonverbal behavior (compliments, eye contact, physical affection) toward each other. The good feelings the partners share as a result of these high-frequency positive behaviors encourage them to get married to ensure that each will be able to share the same experiences tomorrow.

Just as love feelings are based on positive behavior from the partner, hostile feelings are created when the partner engages in a high frequency of negative behavior. In one study of spouses who got divorced, wives were irritated by their husband's being too domineering, drinking too much, and being unfaithful. Husbands complained that their wives were overcommitted to their work, too involved with their relatives, and unfaithful (Kitson & Sussman, 1982). In another study, females complained of being basically unhappy and of having sexual and communication problems. In contrast, males said that drug abuse by themselves and their partner was a significant factor leading them to divorce (Cleek & Pearson, 1985).

When a spouse's negative behavior continues to the point of creating more costs than rewards in the relationship, either partner may begin to seek a more reinforcing situation. Divorce (being single again) or remarriage may appear to be a more attractive alternative than being married to the present spouse. The phrase "the seven year itch" refers to the fact that marriages often end during the seventh year—sometimes due to the interest of one or both partners in someone else.

Data – Of divorced couples, the median number of years most remained married was seven. (*Statistical Abstract of the United States,* 1987)

If you can't go around it, over it, or through it, you had better negotiate with it.
—Ashleigh Brilliant

Lack of Conflict Negotiation Skills. Although getting a divorce is one way to handle negative behavior, negotiating the reduction of the negative behavior and replacing it with more positive behavior is sometimes a more rewarding option. One wife said her husband never spent any time with her because he was always busy with his work. So she asked him what she could do to make him want to spend more time with her. He said she could stop criticizing him and approach him for lovemaking (he was always the initiator) twice a week. The exchange worked. He began to come home earlier and not go back to the office at night, and she stopped the criticizing and initiated lovemaking. The result was a change in behavior by both partners, with a subsequent change in their feelings toward each other. "I've got a husband who likes to spend time with me," said the wife. Her husband replied, "Yes, and I've got a wife who's fun to be with."

Consideration

On our wedding day, we get three things: a wedding license, a wedding ring, and a little red wagon. As we pull our little red wagon down the marital road, inevitably stones (conflicts) flip into the wagon. If we don't get the stones out of the wagon as they collect (if we don't have the negotiating skills to get the conflicts out of our marriage), the stones pile up and the wagon gets too heavy to pull. We give up and stop pulling the wagon—we get a divorce. Within a few years, we have remarried and have gotten another little red wagon into which new stones flip. Unless we develop negotiation skills to reduce the conflicts in our relationships, we are likely to repeat the cycle.

Radical Changes. "He's not the same man I married" is not an uncommon cry. People may undergo radical changes (philosophical or physical) after marriage. One minister married and decided seven years later that he did not like being a minister. He left the ministry, got a Ph.D. in psychology, and began to drink and have affairs. His wife, who had married him in the role of minister, now found herself married to a psychologist who spent his evenings at bars with other women. They divorced.

Spouses may also experience severe physical changes. One wife was in an automobile accident that broke her neck and put her in a wheelchair. "The car and my neck were not the only things that were wrecked," she said of the accident. "It changed our marriage. I was no longer the worker, companion, and lover I had been. We divorced."

Boredom. A 26-year-old woman who had been married for four years said, "It's not that my husband is terrible. I'm just tired of the same thing all the time. I dated a lot before I was married, and I miss the excitement of new people." "Satiated" best describes her feelings. She is bored, as though she had been watching the third rerun of a TV movie. She views divorce as a means of freeing herself from a stale relationship.

Extramarital Relationship. About 50 percent of all husbands and wives have intercourse with someone other than their spouse during their marriages. Spouses who feel mistreated by their partners or bored and trapped sometimes consider the alternative of a relationship with someone who is good to them, exciting, new, and who offers an escape from the role of spouse to the role of lover.

The vow of fidelity is an absurd commitment, but it is the heart of marriage.
—Father Robert Capon

Extramarital involvements sometimes hurry a decaying marriage toward divorce because the partner begins to contrast the new lover with the spouse. The spouse is often associated with negatives (bills, screaming children, nagging); the lover, almost exclusively with positives (clandestine candlelight dinners, new sex, emotional closeness). The choice is stacked in favor of the lover. Although most spouses do not leave their mate for a lover, the existence of an extramarital relationship may weaken the emotional tie between the spouses so that they are less inclined to stay married.

Negative behavior, lack of negotiation skills, radical changes, boredom, and extramarital relationships are only five of the reasons people say that they want to get divorced. Others include "can't hold a job," "too much drinking," "too authoritarian," "doesn't understand me," "lousy lover," "physical abuse," and "no longer in love." Regardless of the reason, the motivation is to get away from the spouse in order to live alone or with someone new.

Movement toward Divorce

Relationships go through certain stages when they are winding down. Figure 18.2 illustrates the progressive movement toward divorce. First, the partners in

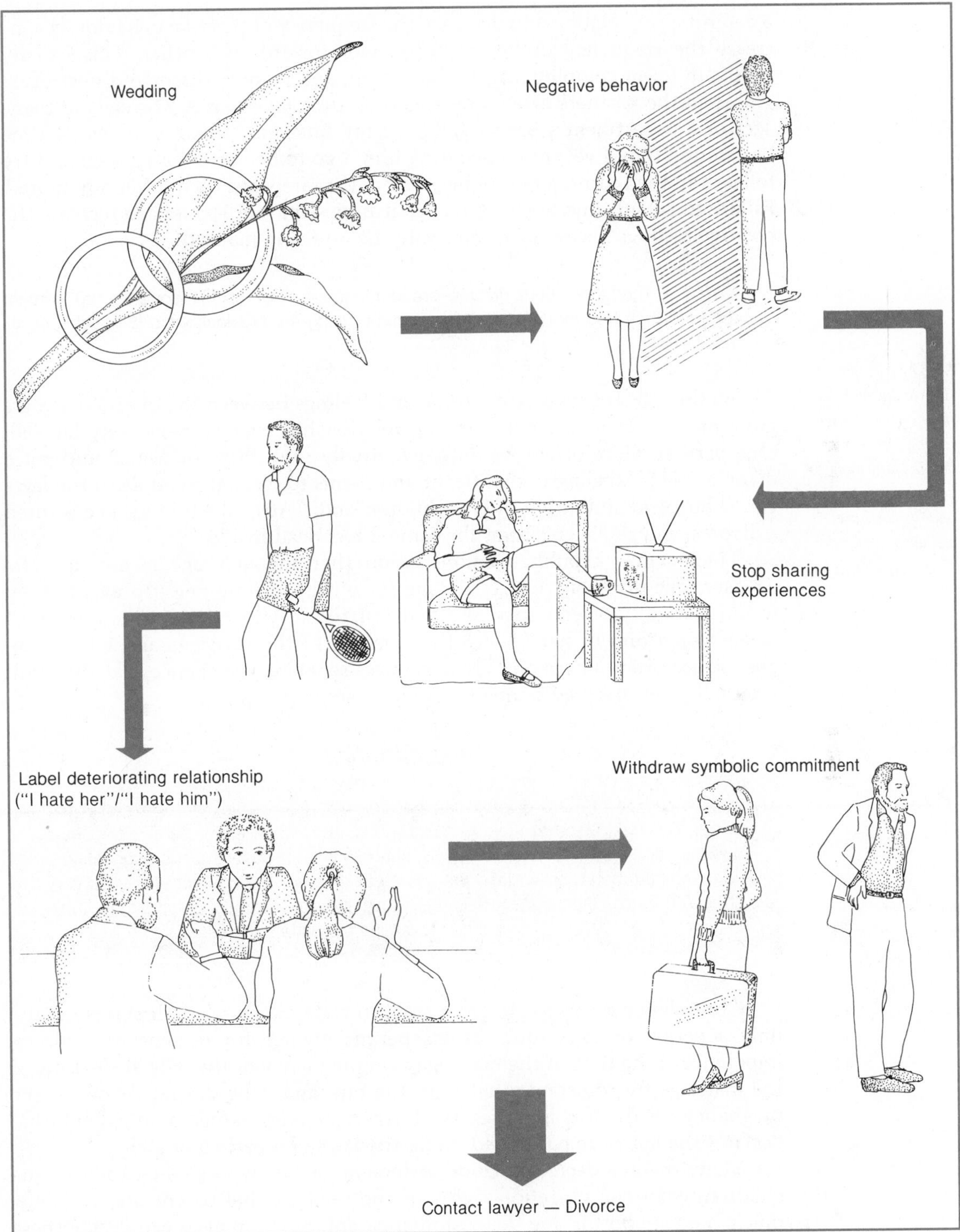

FIGURE 18.2 STAGES IN A DETERIORATING RELATIONSHIP.

a deteriorating relationship decrease the frequency of positive behavior and increase the frequency of negative behavior toward each other. This usually results in fewer compliments, less affection, and more criticism and hostility.

Then the partners often stop spending time together. A 32-year-old manager of a department store said, "Since my husband criticizes me every time I'm around him, I've started avoiding him. I go to bed after he's asleep and try to leave in the morning before he gets up. We rarely see each other any more." Failure to spend time together makes it impossible for spouses to recreate the positive feelings necessary to motivate them to stay married.

Data – Thoughts about divorce are not unusual. Out of 181 spouses, 20 percent reported they had thought about separation during the previous year. (Bugaighis et al., 1985–1986)

Moving from marriage to divorce is like traveling to a foreign country; few can afford the fare, and few know how to cope en route or what to expect when we arrive.
—Eleanor Dienstag

As thoughts of divorce continue and feelings between the marital partners grow more distant, the deteriorating relationship may be negatively labeled. One partner, more often the wife, eventually says, "I think we should get a divorce." This labeling is significant and seems to carry the couple to the lawyer. A husband and father of two children said, "After she told me she wanted a divorce, things haven't been the same. I feel dead inside."

Then comes a public demonstration that the marriage is ending. The spouses take off their rings, go alone (or with someone new) to events they would normally attend together, and tell those who call for the spouse, "I haven't seen him or her." Once the symbols of the marriage are withdrawn, one spouse often moves out. Once spouses separate, the chance that they will eventually get divorced dramatically increases.

Consideration

The progression toward divorce can be stopped at any point, but the earlier the better. The best place to stop it is in the beginning when either partner becomes upset at the behavior of the other. Talking about what is upsetting and negotiating a change in the behavior will take the source of negative feelings out of the relationship. Otherwise, the negative feelings move the spouses along toward the next stage of divorce, and the difficulty of reversing the pattern increases.

Grounds for divorce vary from state to state. Some no-fault states require only a period of separation; others permit divorce for reasons of adultery, impotence at the time of the marriage, and pregnancy of the wife at the time of the marriage by someone other than the husband if he did not know of the pregnancy. A divorce becomes final when a judge issues a judgment that declares the marriage has ended under the laws of a particular state.

Many divorce decrees include statements about who gets custody of the children, what the visitation rights of the noncustodial parent are, and how much child support is due the custodial parent. Some spouses can decide these issues themselves and have their decisions written into the divorce agreement. Other spouses are so hostile and noncommunicative that the judge must rule on issues of custody, visitation, and child support. Still other couples seek a middle ground—mediation. They are unable to reach a decision themselves but don't want a judge to decide, so they voluntarily go before a third party—a mediator—who helps the spouses reach decisions that are acceptable to both of them. Three states require mediation before the divorce is granted.

Characteristics of Divorced People

Spouses who get divorced tend to have different characteristics from those who stay married (Norton and Moorman, 1987; South and Spitze, 1986; Kitson et al., 1985). Some of these include:

1. Marrying in teens
2. Premarital pregnancy
3. Limited income
4. Having divorced parents
5. No high-school education
6. Having nothing in common
7. Not spending time together
8. Urban residence
9. Having no children
10. Having only female children
11. Having another partner available
12. Living in the western, southcentral, mountain, or Pacific region
13. Interreligious marriage
14. Interracial marriage
15. Low-status occupation
16. Courtship of less than one year
17. Being in a second marriage
18. Married less than five years
19. Having a seriously ill child
20. Having an alcoholic spouse
21. Not religiously devout
22. Having a child under age 2
23. Thinking seriously about divorce
24. Talking about divorce with the spouse
25. Being black

Being black is on the list because blacks have a disproportionate tendency to exhibit the characteristics associated with divorce (1–5, 15, 17, and 20.). Being Hispanic is not on the above list because the divorce rate among Mexican Americans, Cubans, and Puerto Ricans varies, depending on educational level (Frisbie, 1986).

Consideration

The above list of divorce characteristics should be viewed cautiously. Someone with all 25 characteristics could be happily married, just as someone with none of these characteristics could get divorced. Each of us is a potential candidate for divorce. Completing the Divorce Proneness Scale may help you to assess the probability of your getting a divorce.

Consequences of Divorce

For most people, divorce is one of the most devastating emotional experiences they encounter. Some reasons follow.

Self-Assessment

The Divorce Proneness Scale

This scale is designed to indicate the degree to which you are prone to get a divorce. There are no right or wrong answers. After reading each sentence carefully, circle the number that best represents your feelings.

1 Strongly agree
2 Mildly agree
3 Undecided
4 Mildly disagree
5 Strongly disagree

	SA	MA	U	MD	SD
1. My parents have a happy marriage.	1	2	3	4	5
2. My closest married friends have happy marriages.	1	2	3	4	5
3. My partner and I can negotiate our differences.	1	2	3	4	5
4. I plan to marry only once.	1	2	3	4	5
5. I am a religious person.	1	2	3	4	5
6. I will wait until my mid-twenties to marry.	1	2	3	4	5
7. I do not require a number of sexual relationships to be happy.	1	2	3	4	5
8. I think it best to marry only after I have known my partner for at least a year.	1	2	3	4	5
9. My parents approved of the person I married.	1	2	3	4	5
10. My partner and I have an adequate source of income to meet all of our expenses and some money left to play with.	1	2	3	4	5

Scoring: Add the numbers you circled. 1 (strongly agree) is the least divorce-prone response, and 5 (strongly disagree) is the most divorce-prone response. The lower your total score (10 is the lowest possible score), the less your chance of getting a divorce; the higher your score (50 is the highest possible score), the greater your chance of getting a divorce. A score of 30 places you at the midpoint between not getting and getting a divorce.

Loss, Disruptions, and Negative Labeling

A marriage and family counselor who divorced after 25 years of marriage said, "I knew all about divorce, except what it felt like." In spite of the prevalence of divorce and the suggestion that it is the path to greater self-actualization or fulfillment, most divorced people report some amount of personal disorganization, anxiety, unhappiness, and loneliness. "If I were miserable in a second marriage," said one spouse who was going through a divorce, "I'd stay married. I couldn't go through this again."

Feelings of depression and despair occur in response to three basic changes in the divorced person's life: termination of a major source of intimacy, disruption of the daily routine, and awareness of a new status—divorced person.

If you are married, you probably did so because you were in love and wanted to share your life with another. Like most people, you needed to experience feelings of intimacy in a world of secondary relationships. Others don't care about the intimate details of your life, nor do they have the background of a shared history to understand you. One reason divorce hurts is that you lose one of the few people who knew you and who, at least at one time, did care about you. Becoming aware that the marriage is not going to work out and thinking about divorce are the most difficult times in the divorce process.

Without forgiveness life is governed by . . . an endless cycle of resentment and retaliation.
—Roberto Assagioli

Divorce also shatters your daily routine and emphasizes your aloneness. Eating alone, sleeping alone, and driving alone to a friend's house for companionship are role adaptations made necessary by the destruction of your marital patterns. Depression and suicide are much more frequent among divorced persons than among married persons (Menaghan & Lieberman, 1986; Trovato, 1986).

Adjusting to and recovering from divorce usually takes two to four years following the separation:

The newly divorced are often lonely.

> It begins when you know you will live, but is marked by setbacks when new stressors such as holidays, problems with children, ex-spouses remarrying, dating experiences, and other changes occur . . .. You begin to act on your choices, and eventually become aware of growth, strength, and a new identity. (Johnson, 1986, p. 192)

Regarding gender differences in adjusting to a separation, two researchers have observed:

> Women begin their separations far more in favor of ending the marriage than men, and men appear to be more dependent and to make stronger efforts at reconciliation than women, again relatively early in the separation. After the early phase of the separation has passed, however, gender differences appear to diminish and neither frequency of contact nor any other aspect of the relationship appears to be gender-specific. (Bloom & Kindle, 1985, p. 380)

Telling others about the divorce isn't easy. In a study of 50 divorced members of Parents Without Partners, the respondents said that mothers, fathers, and coworkers were the most difficult to tell (Ratcliff, 1982). Although most reacted supportively, some were unwilling to accept that the person was getting a divorce. One woman who had been married for 23 years described what it was like to tell of her divorce:

> I think the hardest thing for me was breaking up the home and breaking down the image of the community that you had gone to church in, and had been on committees, etc. On the surface, everything looked fine. Everyone thought we were happy people. Most people would say, "You know you spent all those years together—you know you were happy—you're still happy." And I'd say, "Oh, yeah? Well look, how would you like to go live with him then?" (p. 42)

Two researchers observed some of the feelings and interactions that occurred when one set of parents was told that their daughter was getting a divorce:

> In the D family, after their tearful daughter told them she had separated, at one level, there was a form of parental rationalization that "It's tough for anyone to make a marriage work these days." On a different level, self-deprecation took hold: "If we had been better models, our child would not be so messed up." A vast amount of finger pointing took place, with Mr. D. yelling "If you were not such an incompetent, useless bore, *your* kid wouldn't be so screwed up." Mrs. D. countered with, "If you had been home more instead of hiding out in your plant, Judy would have known more about men and made a better choice." (Hyatt & Kaslow, 1985, p. 88)

Of course, divorce is not necessarily a negative experience. A wife and mother said, "It was, without a doubt, the happiest day of my life. I was finally free of him—I should have done it 20 years ago."

Consideration

Divorce seems to be an easier event to adjust to when certain conditions are present. These include ending the marriage, rather than having it ended by your partner; sharing the blame for the divorce, rather than blaming it on the spouse; not being emotionally involved with the ex-spouse and maintaining minimal contact with him or her after the divorce; having a positive self-concept and high self-esteem; maintaining social relationships with friends, relatives, and lovers; and not having a traditional family orientation.

Different factors also seem to account for the adjustment of custodial mothers and noncustodial fathers. Economic well-being is the primary factor for custodial mothers. Mothers who have ample money after divorce tend to be employed full-time, have higher educations, and fewer children. Noncustodial fathers evidence a better adjustment to divorce if they do not feel too restricted in terms of access to their children. Fathers whose ex-wives are uncooperative in granting them access to the children suffer the most (Buehler et al., 1985–1986).

Relationship with Ex-spouse

It is assumed that ex-spouses hate each other and have only hostile interactions with each other following a divorce. Researcher Constance Ahrons, who studied the actual relationships between 98 pairs of ex-spouses, has observed four patterns (Stark, 1986).

Perfect Pals. These ex-spouses (12 percent of the sample) continued to be involved in each other's lives. Neither spouse had remarried or was living with someone else. One such couple shared a duplex apartment, so that their children could come and go freely between the homes.

Cooperative Colleagues. Comprising 38 percent of the sample, these ex-spouses were able to minimize potential conflicts and to have a moderate amount of interaction. Basically, they made an effort to get along because it was in the best interest of the children.

Angry Associates. Unable to contain their anger and hostility, 25 percent of the sample had a moderate amount of interaction but most of it was unpleasant. They were unable to separate their roles of spouse and parent.

Fiery Foes. Another 25 percent of the sample consisted of ex-spouses who had little interaction but always fought when they did. Any interaction between them was hostile and bitter; neither was civil toward the other.

The pattern of relationship between ex-spouses is usually related to a new spouse. Some new spouses encourage positive relationships between their mates and ex-spouses (often because such relationships translate into more regular child support); other new spouses are threatened by such relationships.

Parenthood After Divorce

Data – More than 50 percent of all divorces involve children. More than 1 million children are affected by divorce annually. (National Center for Health Statistics, 1986)

For the mother who becomes a single parent (mothers are given custody in 90 percent of all divorce cases involving children), the transition may also be difficult. Due to the stress of earning an income and being solely responsible for the children, single mothers report more depression and decreased life satisfaction than married parents or single fathers (Burden, 1986). And when employed single mothers are compared to employed mothers in two-parent homes, single mothers report having much less time for themselves and very limited recreational time (Sanik & Mauldin, 1986). Of these stresses and lack of play time, one single mother said, "All of a sudden you recognize that you are on your own. You can't count on your ex-husband to pay child support, so you are stuck with paying the light bill out of your earnings."

Data – The income of a woman with children in a single-parent home is less than one-third of the income of a woman with children in a two-parent home. When single mothers with custody are compared to single fathers with custody, single mothers earn one-half of the income of single fathers. (Norton & Glick, 1986)

Most men earn higher incomes after divorce because their incomes were higher than the women's incomes during marriage. No-fault divorce means that all income and property acquired during the marriage is divided equally. However, because the woman usually gets custody, much of her income is spent in reference to the children. In effect, in most cases, divorce means that a mother must still take care of her children—but on half the amount of money she had when she was married (Weitzman, 1985). In response to this inequity, in 1986 a New York State Court of Appeals awarded Loretta O'Brien $188,000, or 40 percent of what the court determined her husband's medical license was worth. (O'Brien and her husband had been married nine years, during which time he earned his M.D. degree.) In effect, the court viewed the ability of O'Brien's husband to earn money as property that could be divided.

Wives who are not so lucky must depend on their ex-husbands for child-support payments. Many of these mothers end up with nothing at all. Although some men do pay child support, a surprising number do not.

Data – About one-fourth of all fathers who are required to pay child support pay nothing. (Nuta, 1986)

Those who do pay, pay only about one-third ($1,222) of the amount needed annually ($4,200) for a single child. (Wishik, 1986)

Parents who fail to make their child-support payments, may be required to make payments directly to the court. Alternatively, these payments may be withheld from the parent's paycheck, and back child support may be withheld from tax refunds that are due the parent. The federal child-support amendment, to be approved in 1988, requires that the state attach the wages of parents who fall one month behind in their child-support payments.

In addition to economic problems, a single parent must confront several other issues (see "Having a Child without a Spouse" on page 436). These issues include satisfying the emotional needs of children alone, satisfying adult emotional and sexual needs, and finding adequate child care. Reaching out to the extended family, which blacks are most likely to do, is helpful in coping with child-care concerns.

Single parents also worry about how divorce will affect their children. The research on this issue has produced mixed results. In one study comparing single-parent and two-parent homes, the researchers found that the quality of the environment for children one year after the separation or divorce was very similar in both homes (Rosenthal et al., 1985–1986). In another study of 60 families five years after divorce, about one-third of the children were happy and thriving; about one-third were doing reasonably well, and about one-third were depressed (Wallerstein & Kelly, 1980). Children's grades also drop following the divorce of their parents.

What makes the difference in the adjustment of the children of divorced parents is often in reference to how the parents treat each other and their children following the divorce. Children evidenced the best adjustment when parents continued a cordial relationship with each other and the custodial parent encouraged regular, dependable visits between the children and the noncustodial parent. In contrast, children whose parents continued their hostility after the divorce, resulting in infrequent visits or no contact with the noncustodial parent, were still carrying feelings of abandonment and rejection. Other researchers (Guidubaldi et al., 1986) have emphasized the importance of parents maintaining as positive a relationship as possible following a divorce.

The gender of the child may also be important in adjusting to a divorce. In general, female children seem to make a more successful adjustment than male children do. One explanation for this finding is that because wives get custody in most cases, their male children suffer from the lack of regular access to their fathers (Lowery & Settle, 1985).

Consideration

If you ever experience a divorce, you should be aware of the conditions under which divorce has the least negative effect on children:

1. The children understand that they are not personally responsible for the divorce. Many children blame themselves for their parents' breakup. ("My daddy left because he doesn't like me".)
2. Each parent continues to nurture a strong emotional tie with each child.
3. The divorce occurs when the children are very young (under 3 years) or grown up (18 or over). At these ages, the children are either too young to feel the emotional impact of divorce or old enough to perceive divorce as not unusual.
4. Each parent talks positively about the other parent to the children. The most destructive effect divorce can have on children occurs when one parent downgrades the other. A custodial parent who tries to turn the children against the noncustodial parent is only robbing the children of one of the few potentially meaningful emotional relationships in life. It is imperative that parents keep any hostile feelings they may have to themselves and give their children the opportunity to continue positive relationships with their noncustodial parent.
5. Access to the noncustodial parent is not forbidden. The ex-spouses continue to encourage regular contact of their child or children with the noncustodial parent. They do not encourage their children to regard the other parent as an uncle or aunt.
6. Access to the grandparents of the noncustodial parent is not forbidden. The custodial parent sometimes tries to punish the ex-spouse by withholding the children from the ex-spouse's parents. Such withholding is done at the expense of the grandchildren, who should not be deprived of the nurturance, support, and emotional security of the relationship with all of their grandparents.

Beyond the immediate impact of divorce, what are the long-term effects of divorce on children after they become adults? Research has shown conflicting results. In one study, when adults (ages 19 to 34) who were reared in single-parent homes were compared with similar-aged adults who were reared in two-parent homes, those from single-parent homes tended to be divorced, have less education, earn lower incomes, be unemployed, and have less prestigious jobs (Mueller & Cooper, 1986). Another nationwide study found lower psychological well-being (happiness, satisfaction with friends, satisfaction with family) associated with adult children of divorced parents compared to adult children whose parents stayed together (Glenn & Kramer, 1985).

However, another study of more than 8,000 adults compared those who were living with both parents and those who were living with only one parent at age 16. No significant differences were found between the two groups. Few long-term effects were noted as being associated with family disruption of any sort. The effects that were considered important were almost all positive, indicating that the individual may have been strengthened by the experience (Nock, 1982, p. 38).

Consideration

The differences in the findings of these studies may be related to the perception that an individual has of an event (divorce) and not to the event itself. Divorce, by itself, doesn't do anything to children. It is how the parents teach their children to regard the event and the children's relationship with the respective parents after the divorce that influences the eventual outcome.

Alternatives to Divorce

Divorce is not the only means of terminating a marriage. Others include annulment, separation (legal or informal), and desertion.

Annulment

The concept of annulment has its origin in the Roman Catholic church, which takes the position that marriage is indissoluble, except by death. An annulment states that no valid marriage ever existed and returns both parties to their premarital status. Any property that has been exchanged as part of the marriage arrangement is returned to the original owner. Neither party is obligated to support the other economically.

Common reasons for annulments are fraud, bigamy, under legal age, impotence, insanity, and lack of understanding. A university professor became involved in a relationship with one of his colleagues. During courtship he promised her that they would rear a "house full of babies." But after the marriage, she discovered that he had had a vasectomy several years earlier and had no intention of having more children. The marriage was annulled on the basis of fraud—his misrepresentation of himself to her. Most annulments are for fraud.

Bigamy is another basis for annulment. In our society, a person is allowed to be married to only one spouse at a time. If another marriage is contracted at the time a person is already married, the new spouse can have the marriage annulled. All 104 wives of confessed and convicted bigamist Giovanni Vigliotto were entitled to have their marriages to him annulled.

Most states have age requirements for marriage. When individuals are younger than the minimum age and marry without parental consent, the marriage may be annulled if either set of parents does not approve of the union. However, if neither set of parents or guardians disapproves of the marriage, it may be regarded as legal; the marriage is not automatically annulled.

Intercourse is a legal right of marriage. In some states, if a spouse is impotent, refuses to have intercourse, or is unable to do so for physical or psychological reasons, the other spouse can seek and may be granted an annulment.

Insanity and a lack of understanding of the marriage agreement are also reasons for annulment. Someone who is mentally deficient and incapable of understanding the meaning of a marriage ceremony can have a marriage annulled. However, being drunk at the time of the wedding is insufficient grounds for annulment.

Although annulments are granted by civil courts, a Catholic who divorces and wants to remarry in the Church must have the first marriage annulled by the Church. Grounds for Church annulment vary widely; the result is that a Catholic seeking to annul his or her first marriage must find a reason the Church will accept. In some cases, marriages have been annulled even though the couple has been married several years and has children. Julio Iglesias had his marriage of eight years (which included three children) annulled.

Legal Separation

An equally small proportion of unhappy relationships end in separation. Separations, or limited divorces, are sought by couples who, for religious or personal reasons, do not want a divorce or do not want one yet and who do not have grounds for an annulment. These couples contact a lawyer and ask that he or she draw up separation papers.

Typical items in a separation agreement include: (1) the husband and wife live separately; (2) their right to sexual intercourse with each other is ended; (3) the economic responsibilities of the spouses to each other is limited to the separation agreement; and (4) custody of the children is specified in the agreement, with visitation privileges granted the noncustodial parent. The spouses may have relationships with others, but neither party has the right to remarry. Although some couples live under this agreement until the death of one spouse, others draw up a separation agreement as a prelude to divorce. In some states, the fact that spouses have legally separated for one year is a ground for divorce.

Informal Separation

An informal separation is similar to a legal separation except that no lawyer is involved in the agreement. The husband and wife settle the issues of custody, visitation, alimony, and child support between themselves. Because no legal papers are drawn up, the couple is still married from the state's point of view.

Attorneys advise against an informal separation (unless it is temporary) to avoid subsequent legal problems. For example, after three years of an informal separation, a mother decided that she wanted custody of her son. Although the father would have been willing earlier to sign a separation agreement that would have given her legal custody of her son, he was now unwilling to do so. Each spouse hired a lawyer and had a bitter and expensive court fight.

Consideration

If marital partners decide that their marriage is not working out but feel that divorce is premature, they can get a legal separation. This specifies the important elements (custody, alimony, child support, visitation, and so on) of the relationship and cannot be changed arbitrarily by either partner. It is also important that each partner have a different lawyer when entering into a separation agreement. Rarely can one lawyer serve the needs of two divorcing spouses.

DESERTION

Desertion differs from informal separation in that the deserter walks out and breaks off all contact. Although either spouse may desert, it is usually the husband who does so. A major reason for deserting is to escape the increasing financial demands of a family. Desertion usually results in nonsupport, which is a crime.

The sudden desertion by a husband sometimes has more severe negative consequences for the wife than divorce would. Unlike the divorced woman, the deserted woman is not free to remarry for several years. In addition, she receives no child support or alimony payments, and the children are deprived of a father.

Desertion is not unique to husbands. Although infrequent, wives and mothers also leave their husbands and children. Their primary reason for doing so is to escape from an intolerable marriage and feeling trapped by the role of mother. "I'm tired of having to think about my children and my husband all the time—I want a life for myself," said one woman who deserted her family. "I want to live too." But such desertion is not without its consequences. Most mothers who desert their children feel extremely guilty.

Widowhood

A marriage relationship may also be ended by the death of one spouse. Women are more likely than men to be widowed and to become so in their mid-sixties.

Data – There are more than 11 million widowed females in contrast to more than 2 million widowed males in the United States. As a group, the widowed represent about 8 percent of the U.S. population. (*Statistical Abstract of the United States*, 1987)

The death of a spouse requires as much or more social and personal readjustment than any other crisis. One widow described her husband's death as "the most difficult tragedy of my life, which has caused a change in my life style, friends, and finances. . . . you never get over it completely. My husband has been dead 27 years, and I still think about him and the life we shared every day."

The Bereavement Process

Although every individual reacts somewhat differently, widows and widowers often go through several stages as they adjust to the death of their partner. Shock and disbelief represent the first stages. We all felt a sense of shock as we watched the Challenger spaceship explode before our eyes. Christa McAuliffe and her colleagues were dead. Even though we watched it over and over, we couldn't believe our eyes. Most widows also react with disbelief on the death of a spouse.

Death tugs at my ear and says, "Live, I am coming."
—Oliver Wendell Holmes, Sr.

After finally accepting the reality of death, they go on to the next stage of bereavement—deep sorrow and grief. "I can't tell you how lonely I am," said one widow. "I feel like there is a heavy weight inside me. It takes a huge effort just to get up and go through the daily routines. You won't understand what it's like until it happens to you." Coupled with these feelings is a profound disorientation. "Everything is up in the air now. I don't know who I am anymore," said one widower.

During this period of sorrow, grief, and disorientation, widows and widowers often fear mental and physical breakdowns and become inordinately dependent on others. "I guess I wanted someone with me all the time during those first weeks after Philip died," recalled one widow. "I was afraid of what I might do because I had no reason to go on living without him."

Although relatives, friends, and business associates are initially quite willing to assist the bereaved in every way possible, their support dwindles after a few weeks as they redirect their energies to their own families and job responsibilities. When such support is withdrawn, the bereaved often enter a new stage of grief as they are confronted with the reality of living without their mate and without continued help from others.

Widowhood is the most difficult life adjustment.

Consideration

The initial impact of a spouse's death is devastating, but most people can adjust to the loss. Time and other relationships seem to help. "It took about two years for me to get over the pain, loneliness, and self-pity I felt after she died," said one widower. "And I still get a wave of sadness at Christmas, the anniversary of her death, her birthday, and our wedding date. I'm remarried now, and that helps a lot to get over thinking about it every day." The widowed spouse might consider that the immediate and intense pain he or she feels at the time of the spouse's death is usually short-term.

Adjustment for Widows

Although both women and men go through the same stages of bereavement, each person responds differently to particular aspects of the adjustment. Many wives are married to husbands who make more money than they do, and a husband's death often means an end to the much-needed regular monthly check. "Aside from missing my husband terribly," recalls one widow, "it means I'll have to move out of this house because we didn't have insurance to pay off the house and my salary won't cover the house payment each month."

Other widows experience difficulties in making decisions. "Paul and I always talked everything over, and I depended on him to make the final decision. Now that he's gone, I can hardly decide which salad dressing to buy." Decisions about selling property, moving into smaller living quarters, and buying health insurance may be particularly difficult for the woman who has always depended on her husband to make such decisions.

But there are compensating factors for widows. The widow is more likely than the widower to derive emotional satisfaction from her children and grandchildren. She is also more likely to be welcome in the home of the son or daughter, where she can help with the household responsibilities.

In addition, widows have more people with whom they share a similar role than widowers do. Large churches may have Sunday school classes for widows; community centers offer special programs for them. Between interactions with other widows and with children and grandchildren, the widow is likely to continue her traditional domestic activities, which often give order and stability to her life. Although her husband is gone, what she does each day does not change that much. Nevertheless, loneliness can still be a problem.

Data – In a study of 36 widows, loneliness was the most frequently (55 percent) reported problem. (Haas-Hawkings et al., 1985)

Widowhood may also be an economic disaster.

Data – One out of every six widows can be officially classified as poor one year after widowhood. Widows who are least likely to experience poverty have a history of employment prior to the death of their spouses. (Smith & Zick, 1986)

Adjustment for Widowers

Whereas most wives expect to be a widow some day (and can have a psychological dress rehearsal), few husbands expect to be widowers. However, males who lose their spouses do not seem to face the economic hardship widows do. In a study of 27 widowers, money was not mentioned as one of the more serious concerns (Clark et al., 1986). The two most frequently cited problems were loneliness and accepting the fact that the mate had died.

Data – Out of 27 widowers, 63 percent reported that loneliness was the most difficult aspect of coping with the death of a spouse. (Clark et al., 1986)

Most of the men had found ways to help them cope with their loneliness. Over one-half of them saw their children at least once a week, and 85 percent reported having a "close" relationship with at least one child (see Exhibit 18.1). Over 70 percent had close friends they saw each week, and many were members of a social or religious organization.

When asked what they did to help them cope with the death of their spouses, most of these men cited being with their family, reading, and believing in God. Dating someone new also helped; almost one-half of these men had done so.

Preparation for Widowhood

Planning ahead for eventual widowhood may be difficult because it forces us to confront our own and our spouse's mortality. But as one widow said, "It's not as hard as making the arrangements later." There are several key areas to consider in preparing for the death of either spouse. Such preparation includes giving careful, early attention to wills, insurance, titles, and funeral expenses.

Wills

A will ensures that your money and property will be left to the people you want to have them. If you die intestate (without leaving a will), the state in which you lived will decide who gets what and how much. For example, suppose a married man with no children dies intestate. Although he may want his wife to have everything, she may get only half if the state law provides that his parents are entitled to half of his estate.

Consideration

Before drawing up a will, consult a lawyer. He or she will be familiar with laws relating to the distribution of property and the guardianship of children in your state. If you move to another state, you might have a lawyer there check your will to make sure that it conforms to the laws in that state.

Money is thicker than blood.

—Jack Wright, estate attorney

Under federal law, an estate tax (also known as an inheritance or transfer tax) return must be filed for every estate with gross assets of more than $600,000. And any tax due must be paid at the time the return is filed. Estates valued at less than $600,000 are not taxed.

Although a will is necessary in preparing for the death of a spouse, two additional documents are important when either spouse becomes incapaci-

Exhibit 18.1

CARING FOR WIDOWED OR ELDERLY PARENTS

Not all widows are elderly, and all elderly parents are not widowed. Nevertheless, adult children are often challenged with the responsibility of taking care of elderly parents (Dilworth-Anderson, 1987).

"With a great deal of difficulty," answered Jeff McAllister, Executive Director of the Pitt County Council on Aging in Greenville, North Carolina. I had asked him how children of aging parents can take care of them without disrupting their own marital lives. "We have to face it," he said, "there is just no easy or simple answer. It's a very complex problem." McAllister gave two examples:

> A wife whose widowed mother was 86 and could not walk because she had a broken hip. The wife had two children of her own. And with no siblings she had no brothers or sisters to help her care for her mother. She couldn't quit work to care for her mother because she needed the money. But the money she earned went to pay for the cost of having someone stay with her mother during the day when she was at work. Although there was no economic advantage to her working, she had to continue doing so to keep her own health insurance and retirement fund. Her husband was frustrated because she was always "exhausted."

> A husband whose mother had Alzheimer's disease was busy building his law practice and could not devote time to care for her. He was also an only child. So his mother came to live with him, his wife, and their young daughter. But the mother became irritable and irrational, and the wife (who did not work outside the home and was there to care for her all day) said that "she could not stand it any more."

As these examples indicate, caring for a dependent aging parent requires a great deal of effort, sacrifice, and decision making on the part of the 5 million adults in the United States who cope with this situation daily. And it is often the woman who ends up with the responsibility for her aging parent(s) while she is still taking care of her own children. Almost 60 percent of these women also have full-time jobs.

But males are not immune to the responsibility for aging parents. One son said he drives 2½ hours (one way) three days a week to get his father groceries, take him for a walk, and do his laundry. "I'm all he's got," said the son.

The emotional toll is heavy. Guilt, resentment, and anger are the most commonly reported feelings. The guilt comes from having promised the parents that they would be cared for when they became old and frail. Paying off the promise often entails more than the children ever expected. Or the offspring may feel guilty that they resent having to disrupt their own lives to care for their parents. Or they may feel guilty that they are angry about the frustration their parents are causing them. "I must be an awful person to begrudge taking my mother supper," said one daughter. "But I feel that my life is consumed by the demands she makes on me, and I have no time for myself."

Caring for a Widowed or Aging Parent—Some Suggestions

Be Realistic. Responding to the needs of an aging parent is not easy, and there is no magic solution. Don't be unhappy if there isn't a quick answer to every problem. Accept the fact that caring for an aging parent is one of the more difficult challenges you will ever face.

Involve Siblings. More than 85 percent of all adult children have brothers or sisters. Because some offspring live closer to or have

Exhibit 18.1

closer relationships with one or both parents, they may inadvertently wind up as almost total caretakers of their aging parents. It is a mistake not to involve your brothers and sisters in the care of parents. Tell them that your parents can no longer fend for themselves, and ask them to help you help them. If the siblings cannot offer practical support, they may be responsible enough to send money. Try to arrange it so that they send you a specified amount every month to help pay for the costs of caring for your parents. Whatever the nature of the support, ask for it.

Communicate Openly. It is important to keep communication channels open with your parents. Tell them how you feel, try to engage them in conversation, and don't "spring" anything on them. Some children decide on their own that it is time to put their parent in a nursing home, drive them to the door, and dump them. They avoid bringing up the subject of "nursing home" for fear that their parents will react with hurt and anger.

Express Love. Such open discussions with your parents may be difficult and should be tempered with expressions of love. Tell your parents that you love them. Touch them. Hug them. Show them that you care about them and intend to see that their needs are taken care of. Elderly people often spend a lot of time alone and sometimes wonder if anyone cares for them.

Investigate the Meals-on-Wheels Program. In the case of the woman with a full-time job and children of her own, the need for support in caring for an elderly parent is particularly great. Many communities offer a Meals-on-Wheels program in which the local council on aging will send a well-balanced meal twice a day to persons who are homebound, who can't prepare food for themselves, and who have no one to do it for them.

The Meals-on-Wheels program is particularly helpful to adults whose aging parents live in another town or state. "I called up the local council on aging in the county in which my mother lives," said one daughter, "told them I had a mother who lived there and who needed food and could they help. They took food to her door twice a day, every day. It was a lifesaver for both of us."

Investigate Elderly Day Care. Another way you can get a break from constant attention to the needs of your aging parent is through a program that provides a place for you to take your parent during the day. Elderly day care, available in some communities, allows the working adult to take his or her parent to the day-care center at 7:30 A.M. and return after work. The parent has shelter, food, and others to interact with throughout the day and can stay with the son or daughter at night. "This is a wonderful program for us," said one daughter. "This way we didn't have to put my mother in a nursing home but had full-time coverage for her."

Investigate Chore-service Program. Similar to the Meals-on-Wheels and elderly day-care programs, the chore-service program sends someone to your parent's home to do the chores that an aging parent cannot do by himself or herself. If you live in another town or state, you may be able to provide chore services for your aging parent long distance (for example, someone to mop the kitchen floor, clean the gutters, and grocery shop).

Meals-on-Wheels, elderly day care, and chore-service programs are not available in every city. You should contact your county Council on Aging or your local Social Services Department to determine the nearest location to you of self-help facilities for the elderly. Your parents' physician should also be aware of what resources for the elderly are available in your community.

(Continued)

Exhibit 18.1

Explore Organizations to Join. A number of organizations have evolved for persons who are caring for an aging parent. Children of Aging Parents (CAPS; 2761 Trenton Road; Levittown, PA 19056) has more than 12,000 members who are experiencing similar concerns. Joining such an organization helps to reduce the feeling that you are facing the problems of caring for an aging parent alone. An additional resource is the National Support Center for Families of the Aging (P.O. Box 245; Swarthmore, PA 19081). A newsletter, "Advice for Adults with Aging Parents," is available from Helpful Publications, Inc. (310 West Durham Street; Philadelphia, PA 19119).

tated. A Living Will is a document stating that should you become terminally ill, with no hope for recovery, you do not want your life prolonged by artificial means. A Living Will can be obtained from the Society for the Right to Die (250 West 57th Street, New York, NY 10107), a nonprofit organization. California, Idaho, and Wisconsin require that the document be resigned every five years; Georgia has a seven-year resigning requirement.

The second document, Power of Attorney, allows your spouse to sign papers on your behalf in the event that you become incapacitated and are unable to do so. For example, if you were brain dead and your spouse needed income, he or she could sell land that you owned if you had signed a Power of Attorney.

Insurance

Having made a will, check your life-insurance policy for amount, type of payment, and ownership of policy. Assuming that the insured feels that the face value of the policy is adequate, check to see if the payments are to be made monthly or in a lump sum. One widow was only allowed to receive monthly payments of $125 instead of the lump sum she needed to pay off her house.

Check your life-insurance policy for ownership. If the husband owns the policy and names the beneficiary as his wife (which is the usual case), the face value of the policy will be included in his estate and she may need to share the proceeds with the tax collector. If you are a man, you can keep money out of the tax collector's net by having your wife take out an insurance policy on your life. Because she is the owner of the policy, it is not included in your estate and hence is not taxable.

Titles

Just as life-insurance benefits can be saved from estate taxes, so can your house, car, and checking accounts. If these are listed in the wife's name, they are considered her property and consequently not part of the husband's estate. Of course, if the wife dies first, the husband will face the inheritance-tax problems she was to have avoided. So some balance of ownership is desirable. Retitling property to achieve a balance is only advisable, however, in a stable relationship. The transfer of ownership of large items followed by a divorce may create havoc.

Funeral Expenses

Currently, the cost of a funeral may range from $1,000 to $10,000, the average cost being around $5,000. This price includes embalming, casket, funeral service, use of the building for visitation, and cars for transportation to the cemetery.

The federal government now requires funeral homes to itemize the cost of their services and materials before an individual agrees to any arrangements. In addition, funeral homes are required to give price information over the telephone to permit customers to shop around. Embalming is often not necessary; it is usually required only if the death was caused by a specific contagious disease such as polio, diptheria, or tuberculosis.

Alternative ways to avoid traditional funeral expenses are donating the body to medical research, cremation, and joining a memorial society. If you want to consider body donation, contact a medical school near you and ask them the procedure for donating your body for medical research and teaching. This usually involves completing an application specifying your wish that your body be donated to a certain medical school. At the time of your death, your spouse would then contact a local mortician and ask him or her to make the necessary arrangements with the medical school. Although you have donated your body to medicine, the traditional funeral service may still be held, with your body being transferred to the medical school rather than to a cemetery afterward; or your body may be removed to the medical school immediately after death, and a memorial service may be held later. In either case, the medical school usually pays the embalming fee and the cost of transporting your body up to 200 miles.

Cremation is another alternative. The cost is usually about $200. As with body donation, a memorial service may be held at a cost of around $1,000.

Consideration

Some people feel uncomfortable with both body donation and cremation but don't want to pay the high price of a traditional funeral service. By joining a memorial society or a similar organization, they buy a predetermined package of funeral services at a fixed cost before their death. Details on the nearest society can be obtained by writing to the Continental Association of Funeral and Memorial Societies (1828 L Street, N.W., Suite 1100, Washington, DC 20036).

Remarriage

Marriage is like the army—everyone complains, but a surprising number reenlist.
—Laurence Peter

Although ending a marriage through divorce or death is traumatic for most people, life goes on. For the divorced and widowed, remarrying is an alternative that may ease recovery from the termination of a previous marriage.

Data –About 80 percent of all divorced persons eventually remarry, but they do not do so immediately. Most people feel more motivated to become involved in a new relationship about three years after their previous relationship has terminated. (Petronio & Endres, 1985–1986)

Data – Older women and women with children remarry at the slowest pace. (Teachman & Heckert, 1985)

Divorced men between the ages of 45 and 64 are four times more likely to remarry as women in the same age range. (Richardson, 1985)

Consideration

Although remarriage is often viewed as the best method of adjusting to a divorce, a comparison of divorced persons who remarried and who remained single showed no significant differences in the groups in terms of personal adjustment (Saul & Scherman, 1984).

The fact that a high percentage of divorced persons remarry emphasizes that spouses tire not of marriage but of the person they are married to. There is also an enormous amount of individual and couple pressure to make the next marriage work. Two researchers specify that there is a "remarriage myth" that:

> . . . marriage makes people significantly happy. This myth is dramatically reinstated at the time of remarriage. It is not only imperative that people be happy in their remarriages, but even happier than they were in their first marriages. A related remarriage myth is that if two people are happy and love each other enough, then everyone will be happy, including children, grandparents, and ex-spouses. (Coleman & Ganong, 1985, p. 118)

STAGES OF REMARRIAGE

Going from one spouse to another does not occur haphazardly. Rather, a person passes through identifiable stages on his or her way to a new partner (Roberts & Price, 1985–1986; Goetting, 1982).

Data – About forty percent of all marriages each year are remarriages (Weingarten, 1985).

Boundary Maintenance

Movement from divorce to remarriage is not a static event that happens in a brief ceremony and is over. Rather, ghosts of the first marriage in terms of the ex-spouse and, possibly, children must be dealt with. The parents must decide how to relate to the ex-spouse in order to maintain a good parenting relationship for the biological children and, at the same time, to keep an emotional distance to prevent problems from developing with the new partner. Some spouses continue to be emotionally attached to the ex-spouse and have difficulty breaking away.

Emotional Remarriage

The person begins to trust and love another person in a new relationship. Such feelings may come slowly as a result of negative experiences in the first marriage.

Psychic Remarriage

The person gives up the freedom and autonomy of being single again and develops a mental set conducive to pairing. This transition may be particularly difficult for the person who sought a divorce as a means to personal growth and autonomy. The individual may fear that getting remarried will put unwanted constraints on her or him.

Community Remarriage

This stage involves a change in focus from single friends to a new mate and other couples with whom the new pair will interact. The bonds of friendship established during the divorce period may be particularly valuable because they have lent support at a time of personal crisis. Care should be taken not to drop these friendships.

Parental Remarriage

Because most remarriages involve children, the nuances of living with someone else's children must usually be worked out. As we will note in Chapter 19, the role of the stepparent is ambiguous. Society offers few guidelines for the sharing of rights and responsibilities with the natural parent. The result is sometimes confusion, frustration, and resentment.

Partners bring their parental, economic, and legal responsibilities with them to a second marriage.

Economic Remarriage

The first time you buy a house, you see how pretty the paint is and buy it. The second time, you look to see if the basement has termites. It's the same with men.
—Lupe Velez

The second marriage may begin with economic responsibilities to the first marriage. Alimony and child support often threaten the harmony and sometimes even the economic survival of second marriages. One wife said that her paycheck was endorsed and mailed to her husband's first wife to cover his alimony and child-support payments. "It irritates me beyond description to be working for a woman who lived with my husband for seven years," she added. In another case, a remarried woman who was receiving inadequate child support from her ex-spouse felt too embarrassed to ask her new husband to pay for her son's braces.

Legal Remarriage

Partners in a second marriage may have legal responsibilities in the form of alimony and child-support payments to the first marriage. These responsibilities cannot be abandoned with the beginning of a new marriage. The individual must take on a new set of responsibilities while maintaining former responsibilities.

Legal documents that may be appropriate include an asset inventory (to establish what each new spouse owns and brings into the marriage), a premarital agreement (to specify what assets owned by whom will go to whom if the marriage ends in divorce or when it ends with the death of one spouse), and a living trust, in which assets from one spouse are transferred to a third party so that the new spouse will not be tempted to ask, "Can we use that money?"

Consideration

Some spouses feel it is not romantic to draw up legal documents specifying what will happen to the assets and money in a relationship. These spouses take the position that such an action smacks of distrust. But a lawyer and social worker who have dealt with the problems in remarriages said, "facing possible outcomes does not make them happen" (Bernstein & Collins, 1985, p. 389).

What is the likelihood for divorce among second marriages?

Data – Second marriages are particularly vulnerable to divorce. If both spouses are beginning a second marriage, with children from their previous marriages, the risk for divorce is much higher than it is if the spouses are marrying for the first time without children. (White et al., 1985)

Spouses who stay in their second marriages seem to be very similar to spouses in first marriages. In a study comparing second and first marriages, the researchers, observed that companionship, parental satisfaction, and general affect were the variables associated with marital satisfaction for both groups and that there was greater similarity than discrepancy when the two groups were compared (Leigh et al., 1985).

Consideration

An important factor that seems to contribute to the success of second marriages is a sufficient period of time (usually three to five years) between marriages. If remarriage occurs too soon or the new relationship begins while the emerging partner-to-be is still with the first spouse, the old relationship is more likely to impede heavily on the new.

REMARRIAGE FOR THE WIDOWED

Remarriage for the widowed is usually very different from remarriage for the divorced. The widowed are usually much older; their children are grown, and they are less likely to remarry.

A widow or widower may marry someone of similar age or someone who is radically older or younger. Marriages in which only one spouse is considerably older than the other are referred to as "May-December marriages"; these marriages were discussed in Chapter 9. Here, we will discuss only "December marriages," in which both spouses are elderly.

In a study of 24 elderly couples, the need to escape loneliness or the need for companionship was the primary motivation for remarriage (Vinick, 1978). The men reported a greater need to remarry than the women. Most of the spouses met through a mutual friend or relative (75 percent) and married less than a year after their partner's death (63 percent).

The children of the couples had mixed reactions to their remarriages. Most of the children were happy that their parents were happy and felt relieved that the companithe companionship needs of their elderly parent would now be met by someone on a more regular basis. But some children also disapproved of the marriage out of concern for their inheritance rights. "If that woman

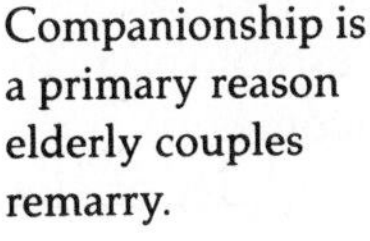

Companionship is a primary reason elderly couples remarry.

marries dad," said a woman with two children, "she'll get everything when he dies. I love him and hope he lives forever, but when he's gone, I want the farm."

More than 80 percent of the elderly spouses described themselves as being "very satisfied" or "satisfied" with their marriages. A typical response about how things were going was given by a woman who had been married two years: "We're like a couple of kids. We fool around—have fun. We go to dances and socialize a lot with our families. We enjoy life together. When you're with someone, you're happy" (Vinick, 1978, p. 362).

Most of the spouses had a live-and-let-live attitude toward each other. "It doesn't pay to get angry," "It takes two to make an argument," and "A person should contain his feelings" were common statements of these elderly spouses.

Trends

The number of divorces in the United States will peak around 1990. By then, the children of the baby-boom children will be ages 25 to 29—the age range when most divorces take place.

Divorce mediation will increase. In this process, the spouses meet with a counselor and lawyer team for the purpose of reducing their hostilities and reaching an out-of-court agreement on child support, custody, visitation rights, and property division issues. Such mediation avoids extended court fights and the buildup of extremely negative feelings between ex-spouses.

Legal changes will include more granting of joint custody, custody to the husband, and the assignment of child-support responsibilities to *both* parents. The legal precedent for joint child support has already been established. In *Silvia v. Silvia,* (1980) the Massachusetts court ruled that the incomes of both parents should be considered in assigning the economic responsibilities of the respective parents for the support of their children.

Finally, couples will find it even easier to get divorced through the use of do-it-yourself divorce kits. To avoid the $250–300 charged by an attorney for an uncontested divorce, a couple with no assets and no children will be able to complete their own divorce documents. (For those divorces involving property, children, and/or alimony, a lawyer should still be consulted.)

Summary

The divorce rate has increased in recent years. Societal factors contributing to such incrsuch increases include the loss of family functions, more employed wives, and liberal divorce laws. Individual factors include negative behavior, lack of conflict-negotiation skills, and extramarital relationships.

Certain categories of people have a higher probability than others of getting divorced. These include the premaritally pregnant, early married, black, and previously divorced.

For most, divorce represents a difficult transition. Loss of self-esteem, lack of money, and concern over children are among the potential consequences of divorce. But divorce may also represent a bridge from an unhappy relationship and personal confinement to new relationships and personal growth. For many, divorce is also the beginning of a new life.

Death terminates marriages that do not end by divorce, annulment, or desertion. Adjusting to the death of one's spouse is one of the most difficult life crises a person experiences. Although the trauma of widowhood cannot be avoided, it can be eased by attending to various concerns, such as wills, insurance, titles, and funeral arrangements. A great deal of money can often be saved by drawing up a will, making the wife the owner of the life insurance on her husband, putting property in the wife's name, and donating one's body to a medical school.

Many divorced and widowed people are in a stage of transition to another marriage. About 40 percent of all marriages are remarriages. Those who remarry and stay married report comparable marital happiness to those in their first marriages.

Trends regarding divorce include a peaking of the divorce number by 1990, an increase in the frequency of divorce mediation, and more couples opting for do-it-yourself divorces.

Questions for Reflection

1. To what degree do you share the characteristics of divorce-prone people? How do you feel these factors affect the probability that you will stay married or will eventually divorce?
2. Do you feel the people you know who have gotten divorced are glad they did so? Why do they feel this way? Do you think they are better off? Why or why not?
3. How comfortable would you be discussing funeral arrangements with your partner? Do you feel the potential money saved is worth the discomfort you might feel?

CHOICES

SINCE MORE THAN one-half of all divorces involve children, a basic decision to be made in a divorce is who gets custody of the children? The options include the mother, the father, or joint custody. The last decision involves additional choices.

WHO GETS THE CHILDREN? CUSTODY CRITERIA OF PARENTS

Nine out of 10 custody decisions after divorce result in one parent (usually the mother) receiving custody of the children with the other parent (usually the father) receiving visitation rights. This arrangement is usually decided on by the divorcing couple. "That's good," said one attorney, "because if spouses don't make their own decisions, the courts will make their choices for them."

The criteria that parents and judges use to determine who will get custody of the children include age of the children, gender of the children, emotional relationship of the parents with the children, time available to spend with the children, living conditions, income, and previous care (physical and emotional) of the children by the respective parents.

Who gets custody has implications not only for the child but also for the parents. Research demonstrates that the parent who gets custody of the child will continue to benefit from the child being emotionally attached to him or to her. Likewise, the emotional attachment of the child to the noncustodial parent decreases (White et al., 1985).

CUSTODY TO ONE PARENT?

When the parents disagree about who should have custody of the children, a judge must decide. In the past, preference has been given to the mother. Awarding custody to the mother, particularly of younger children, is based on the "tender-years doctrine," which holds that young children need their mother and it is in their best interests to live with her.

This doctrine was challenged by Ken Lewis, a divorced father of two daughters, who contended that the "tender-years doctrine" was an insidious example of sex discrimination. He won custody of his children on the grounds that the word *"mother"* is a verb and that he had demonstrated better mothering skills than the biological mother. Fathers for Equal Rights of Michigan and Canada, P.O. Box 2272, Southfield, MI 48037 is an organization for fathers seeking divorce and custody reform. Dr. Lewis (Child Custody Evaluation, Inc., P.O. Box 202, Glenride, PA 19038) now specializes in interviewing all parties involved in a custody case and making recommendations to the judge. He has evaluated over 600 cases, and the judges have followed his recommendations in over 90 percent of them.

Although in most cases, fathers agree that their wives should have custody of the children, some fathers want custody and contest the right of their wives to be the custodial caregivers. In one study (Greif, 1985) of over 1,000 custodial fathers, 20 percent actively sought custody. The other contexts in which the father ended up with the children were due to the ex-wife not wanting them (60 percent), the children choosing to live with their father (35 percent), or the father believing his ex-wife was not a competent parent (30 percent). One father who sought and was awarded custody of his son said of the single-fatherhood experience:

One of the most difficult things men have to learn when they become single custodial parents is to express these "softer" emotions. This problem is compounded by feelings of anger, resentment, sorrow, and fear, which many men cannot express when trying to cope with a child (or children) and trying to run a household. (Weinberg, 1985, p. 173)

Joint Custody

An alternative to sole custody that is increasingly being considered by parents and the courts is joint custody. At least 30 states have enacted legislation authorizing joint custody (Melli, 1986). Although one type of joint custody may involve the children spending half of their time in each parent's home, another type of joint custody results in giving the decision-making power to both parents but awarding the physical care of the children to one parent. For example, the court may dictate that the children live in the home of the mother but that the father and the mother have equal authority in terms of deciding where the children will go to school, in which religion they will be reared, which family doctor they will see, and so on. The intent is to permit each parent equal input into their children's lives.

Although the phrase "joint custody" sounds egalitarian, there are disadvantages to this arrangement. In some cases, the father uses the arrangement to avoid or reduce the amount of money he will be ordered by the court to pay in child support. Under a joint custody agreement, the father will be allowed to pay less because it is assumed that he will be keeping the children with him some of the time. Other fathers may use the threat of joint custody to get their wives to ask for limited amounts of alimony and child support. The implicit threat is, "If you ask for a lot of money, I will take the kids away from you as much as I can." Another disadvantage is that joint custody tends to put hostile ex-spouses in more frequent contact with each other, so that the marital war continues. What the children might have escaped being exposed to in a sole-parent custody decision, they are continually confronted with in a joint-custody decision.

But joint custody has a positive side. Ex-spouses may fight less if they have joint custody because there is no problem about who gets the children and other inequities of the sole-parent custody decision. Children will benefit from the resultant decrease in hostility between parents who have both "won" them.

Joint custody also allows both parents to continue to be involved in their children's lives. Unlike the sole-parent custody outcome, in which one parent (usually the mother) wins and the father is banished, children under joint custody may continue to benefit from the love and attention of both parents. Children in homes where joint custody has been awarded also have greater financial resources available to them than children in split-custody homes (Lowery & Settle, 1985).

Depending on the level of hostility between the ex-partners, their motivations for seeking sole or joint custody, and their relationship with their children, any arrangement could have positive or negative consequences for the spouses and the children. In those cases in which the spouses exhibit minimal hostility toward each other and have strong emotional attachments to their children, as well as the desire to remain an active influence in their children's lives, joint custody may be the best of all possible choices.

Relationship With Noncustodial Parent

The custodial parent has a choice to make in terms of what kind of relationship he or she will have with the noncustodial parent. Tra-

(Continued)

ditionally, custody "battles" have been hostile and bitter relationships between spouses, with one parent often trying to turn the children against the other parent. But everyone loses when this type relationship is allowed to develop (Greif, 1986). The parents continue to harbor negative feelings for each other, and the children are caught in the crossfire. They aren't free to develop or express love for either parent out of fear of disapproval from the other parent. Ex-spouses might consider the costs to their children of continuing to wage war and call a truce on their behalf. Everyone will profit from the choice.

Impact of Social Influences on Choices

Although we tend to think of divorce as an individual decision, the society in which the spouses live dictates whether or not divorce will occur. During the colonial period, the Puritans did not approve of spouses getting a divorce just because they were unhappy. In Massachusetts, there was an average of *one* divorce per year from 1639 to 1760 (Morgan, 1944). This is the ultimate example of social control on the private experience of marriage. Today, in contrast, you can get a divorce just because you don't like your partner (technically called "irreconcilable differences").

CHAPTER 19

Stepfamilies

Contents

Is It True?*

1. Stepfamilies have few unique characteristics; they are just like biological families.
2. People who stereotype stepfamilies as negative tend to live in a stepfamily.
3. It takes about six months for members of a stepfamily to feel a sense of family.
4. Most single mothers reported that the men they dated reacted negatively to their children.
5. Children in stepfamilies are more likely to get bad grades and use drugs than children in biological families.

*1=F; 2=F; 3=F; 4=F; 5=F.

With 50 percent of all spouses getting divorced, 80 percent of the divorced remarrying, and 55 percent of those who remarry coming to the new marriage with children from a previous marriage, stepfamilies are not unusual. In this chapter, we will examine how stepfamilies differ from biological families, how they are experienced from the viewpoint of women, men, and children, and the developmental tasks that must be accomplished to make a successful stepfamily. We will close the chapter with a look at the choices faced by those about to enter a stepfamily and suggest ways to make such decisions.

Definition and Types of Stepfamilies

Also referred to as a reconstituted, remarried, or binuclear family, a stepfamily is a married couple in which at least one of the spouses has had a child in a previous relationship. Stepfamilies are also known as blended families. The term "*blended*" is used because the new marriage relationship is blended with the children of at least one previous marriage.

How many stepfamilies are there?

Data – Although estimates vary, approximately 30 million American adults and 10 million children live in stepfamilies. (Cherlin & McCarthy, 1985)

Types of stepfamilies include the following:

The words "blended" and "reconstituted" remind you too much of the kitchen. It's as if you had to add water to make a new artificial family, something not quite as good as the real thing. We prefer the term stepfamily.
—John Visher

1. Families in which the children live with their remarried parent and stepparent. Such is the case of Roxie and Sherry who live with their recently remarried mother. Their stepfather is Mark.
2. Families in which the children from a previous marriage visit with their remarried parent and stepparent. Jack is the father of Roxie and Sherry. He has remarried and his children visit him and his new wife, Margaret, on weekends. When they visit, the four of them are a stepfamily.
3. An unmarried couple living together in which at least one of the partners has children from a previous relationship who live with or visit them. Susan and Bob are living together. Susan's daughter Michelle lives with them, and Bob's son visits them on weekends.

Unique Aspects of Stepfamilies

Stepfamilies are unique compared to couples who live with their own biological children. Some of these unique characteristics follow.

All Members Are Not Biologically Related

Unlike the biological family, in which the children are genetically related to both parents, children in the stepfamily are related to only one parent.

Data – About 16 percent of all children live with either a stepfather or a stepmother. (Cherlin & McCarthy, 1985)

Consideration

The significance to the stepfamily of the biological tie between parent and child is the strong emotional bond that accompanies it. Although stepparents can develop love feelings for their stepchildren, they sometimes do not. The different levels of emotional bonding parents and stepparents have with their children and stepchildren create a context for negative feelings and conflict. "If you don't love my daughter, you don't love me," said a biological mother to the child's stepfather.

STEPFAMILIES HAVE EXPERIENCED A CRISIS

Stepfamilies are born out of a crisis event. The children have been removed from one biological parent (whom they often desperately hope will reappear and reunite with the parent), and the spouse has experienced emotional disengagement and physical separation from a once-loved partner due to divorce or death. Jane, who is divorced with two children, said:

> It's been two years since I divorced Bill, and it's been hard for all of us. The children miss their father a great deal, and they still ask sometimes, "When are you and daddy getting back together?" It hurts me to know that they are separated from their father. But it would hurt even more for me to have to live with their father. Yet I miss being a family and look forward to getting remarried.

But when the remarriage comes, the problems aren't over. When stepfamilies are compared to first families, the spouses in stepfamilies tend to be less happy, the family members tend to feel less cohesive, and the family unit seems less able to resolve conflict (Pink & Wampler, 1985).

MEMBERS HAVE DIFFERENT BELIEFS AND VALUES

Children in a biological family have been exposed to a relatively consistent set of beliefs, values, and behavior patterns. When children enter a stepfamily, they "inherit" a new parent who brings a new way of living into the family unit. One stepchild confided:

> As long as my mother was alive, she cooked me plain ole meatloaf and potatoes for dinner. And her potatoes always were the real kind with lumps in them. My stepmother cooks all her meats in some fancy French wine sauce, and her potatoes are the instant variety. I don't like her cooking but didn't know how to tell her. And if I started to like her French cooking I might feel guilty because I would be betraying the memory of my mother.

Likewise, the new parent now lives with children who may have been reared differently from the way in which the stepparent would have reared them if he or she had been their parent all along. One stepfather explained:

> It's been a difficult adjustment for me living with Molly's kids. I was reared to say "Yes sir" and "Yes ma'am" to adults and taught my own kids to do that. But Molly's kids just say "yes" and "no." It rankles me to hear them say that, but I know they mean no disrespect by it. I've talked to Molly about it and she says she doesn't see anything

wrong with "yes" and "no" as long as it is said politely and that it is just something that I am going to have to live with.

Parent–Child Relationship Has a Longer History than the New Marriage

In the stepfamily, the relationships between the biological parent and children have existed longer than the relationships between the adults in the remarriage. Jane and her twin children have a nine-year relationship and are emotionally bonded to each other. But Jane has known her new partner only a year, and although her children like their new stepfather, they hardly know him.

Consideration

A parent's emotional bond with children (particularly if they are young and dependent) from a previous marriage may weaken a remarriage from the start. As one parent says, "Nothing and nobody is going to come between me and my kids." However, new spouses may view such bonding differently. One spouse said that such concern for one's own children was a sign of a caring and nurturing person. "I wouldn't want to live with anyone who didn't care about his kids." But another said, "I feel left out and that she cares more about her kids than me. I don't like the feeling of being an outsider."

In stepfamilies, the parent–child relationship has a longer history than the new husband–wife relationship.

Children Have Two Homes

Unlike children in the biological family who have one home they regard as theirs, children in stepfamilies have two homes they regard as theirs. In some cases of joint custody, children spend part of each week with one parent and part of each week with the other parent; they live with two sets of adult parents in two separate homes.

The respective adult couples may consider the time the children spend with the other couple to be a negative influence on the children. One remarried mother whose children spend a week with their father in the summer said:

> It takes them a week after they come home to settle down. He buys them everything, takes them to movies and pony shows, and shows them a terrific time. They come back here, and it's rather drab. I dread their seeing their father because he interferes with the type of stable family life my new husband and I am trying to provide for them. (I won't go into the fact that my ex has a girlfriend who lives with him.)

Children in these relationships often feel torn. One child said:

> I love both my mom and my dad but feel like I'm not supposed to enjoy either of them when I'm with them. My mom makes me feel guilty if I act like I enjoy being with my father on Saturdays, and my dad can't understand why I would rather live with my mom. It's a real bind.

Money from Ex-Spouse May Be a Source of Conflict

In some stepfamilies the ex-spouse is expected to send child-support payments to the parent who has custody of the children. Less than one-half of these fathers send any money; those who do may be irregular in their payments. Even the amount of money awarded may be inadequate.

> *Data* – The average amount of money awarded for child support each year is $1,928. (Wishik, 1986)

Consideration

> The ex-husband sending money to the biological mother creates the illusion for the stepfather that the ex-husband will take care of the expenses for the children. In reality, child-support payments cover only a fraction of what is actually spent on a child, so that the new stepfather may feel burdened with more financial responsibility for his stepchildren than he bargained for. This may engender negative feelings toward the wife in the new marriage relationship.

Money to Ex-Spouse May Be a Source of Conflict

The other side of child support is the remarried father who pays money to his ex-wife, who has custody of their children. One researcher studied 101 divorced men and observed that their remarriage was associated with an increase in voluntary support payments (Tropf, 1984).

One remarried father sent his ex-wife $500 each month in child support for their two children. But his new wife became upset that this money left their marriage every month and could not be used to buy the things they wanted. She eventually told her husband that if he were going to send his money to a wife he hated for children he never saw, she was going to leave him. The husband stopped sending the money. His ex-wife did not take legal action because she wanted him out of her life and didn't value the money.

New Relationships Are in Flux

Each member of a new stepfamily has many adjustments to make. Issues that must be dealt with include how the mate feels about the partner's children from a former marriage, how the children feel about the new stepparent, and how the newly married spouse feels about the spouse sending alimony and child-support payments to an ex-wife. One researcher reports that it takes at least two years for newly remarried spouses to feel comfortable together—to feel that they are a team as strong as the parent–child team. It takes four to five years for the whole family to feel comfortable, to have a shared history, and to feel inside rather than outside the family (Osborne, 1983).

Stepfamilies Are Stigmatized

We are all familiar with the wicked stepmother in *Cinderella.* The fairy tale certainly gives us the impression that to be in a stepfamily with stepparents is a bad thing. Such bad press has affected stepfamilies to the degree that remar-

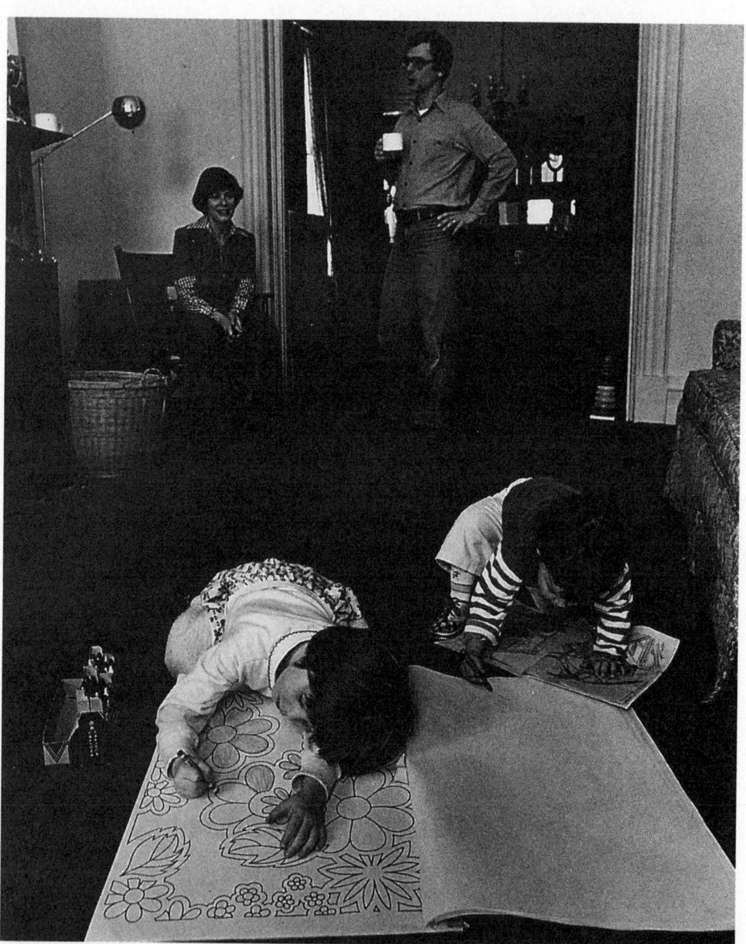

Stepparents have no child-free period.

ried couples often hide the fact that their children are not biologically theirs. One remarried mother said:

> We moved to another state so no one would know that the children were from my former marriage. There is something better about my new husband saying "This is my son and daughter" rather than "This is my stepson and stepdaughter." The latter kind of assumes that there is something wrong with us (because we're divorced) and that something is wrong with the kids (they don't live in a "real family").

Those most likely to negatively stereotype stepfamilies don't live in a stepfamily (Fine, 1986).

Stepchildren are also stigmatized. One researcher observes that:

> . . . stepchildren may be among the most negatively stereotyped children in our society . . .. It may be that the frequent use of "stepchild" to mean poor, neglected, and ignored has had an insidious impact . . .. (Bryan et al., 1986, p. 173)

Consideration

Although stepfamilies are stigmatized, a study of 80 stepfamilies reported that the husbands and wives were aware of their problems, were able to suggest changes, and perceived themselves as strong and successful. The researchers concluded that any suggestion that a stepfamily is inferior is inappropriate and is dysfunctional to that stepfamily's adjustment. (Knaub et al., 1984)

Stepparents Have No Child-Free Period

Unlike the biological family in which the newly married couple have their first child about 2½ years after their wedding, the remarried couple begin their marriage with children in the house. "We've never been alone," said one wife. "We wouldn't know what it is like."

The differences between biological families and stepfamilies are summarized in Table 19.1.

TABLE 19.1 DIFFERENCES BETWEEN BIOLOGICAL FAMILIES AND STEPFAMILIES

Biological Families	*Stepfamilies*
1. Children are biologically related to both parents.	1. Children are biologically related to only one parent.
2. Both biological parents live with children.	2. One biological parent does not live with children as a result of divorce or death.
3. Beliefs and values of members tend to be similar.	3. Beliefs and values of members are more likely to be different due to different backgrounds.
4. Relationship between adults has existed longer than relationship between children.	4. Relationship between children and parents has existed longer than relationship between adults.
5. Children have one home they regard as theirs.	5. Children have two homes they regard as theirs.
6. The family's economic resources come from within the family unit.	6. Some economic resources come from ex-spouse.
7. All money generated stays in the family.	7. Some money generated may leave the family in the form of alimony or child support.
8. Relationships are relatively stable.	8. Relationships are in flux: new adults adjusting to each other; children adjusting to stepparent; stepparent adjusting to stepchildren.
9. No stigma attached to biological family.	9. Stepfamilies are stigmatized.
10. Spouses had child-free period.	10. Spouses had no child-free period.

Strengths of Stepfamilies

Stepfamilies have both strengths and weaknesses. Strengths include early reality coping by children, their exposure to a variety of behavior patterns, their observation of a happy remarriage, adaptation to stepsibling relationships inside the family unit, and greater objectivity on the part of the stepparent. (Coleman et al., 1985; Coleman & Ganong, 1987).

Early Reality Coping

Children in stepfamilies learn about life's realities early. Whereas many biological children never have to cope with separation, divorce, and death, stepchildren have been around the track. They have had the first-hand experience of losing someone close to them. More important, they have learned that life goes on no matter what happens and that transitions to new relationships can be for the better. One daughter said:

> Looking back on my parents' divorce, I wish they had done it long ago. While I miss my dad and am sorry that I don't see him more often, I was always upset listening to my parents argue. They would yell and scream, and it would end with my mom crying. It was a lot more peaceful (and I know my mom was a lot more happy) after they got divorced. Besides, I like my stepdaddy. Although he isn't my real dad, I know he cares about me.

We all have a picture of a family. It is usually not a stepfamily.
—Judy Osborne

Exposure to a Variety of Behavior Patterns

Children in stepfamilies also experience a variety of behaviors, values, and life styles. They have had the advantage of living on the inside of two families. One 12-year-old said:

> My real dad didn't like sports and rarely took me anywhere. My stepdad is different. He likes to take me fishing and roller skating. He recently bought me a knife and is showing me how to whittle a stake for our tent when we go camping this summer.

Parent Happier

Single parenting can be a demanding and exhausting experience. Remarriage can ease the stress of parenting and provide a happier context for the parent. Stepchildren often witness their parent's transition from a state of unhappiness to a state of happiness.

Adaptation to Stepsiblings

Children learning how to get along with other children in an intimate environment is another beneficial experience provided by the stepfamily. The child's world may also be expanded by new playmates and companions. This is a particular benefit for an only child whose parent marries a person with one or more children.

Stepparent More Objective

Due to the biological tie between a parent and a child, some parents seem to be incapable of discussing certain issues or topics. A stepparent often has the advantage of not being emotionally involved and can relate to the child at a different level. One 13-year-old said of the relationship with her father's new wife:

> She went through her own parents' divorce and knows what it's like for me to be going through my dad's divorce. She is the only one I can really talk to about this issue. Both my dad and mom are too emotional about the subject to be able to talk about it.

Weaknesses of Stepfamilies

Weaknesses of stepfamilies include unrealistic expectations, the necessity of continually dealing with an ex-spouse, and the complexity of issues.

Unrealistic Expectations

Both spouses in the remarriage may expect their present marriage to right all previous relationship disappointments—both parental and past marital failures. One spouse said:

> I was looking for a fresh start. I felt like a failure because I was divorced and separated from my kids. I wanted so desperately to be remarried and to be happy with my new wife and family. But it didn't work out that way. She had a problem with being faithful and her kids never looked on me as their dad.

Consideration

In a stepfamily expectations run high about everybody accepting everybody else. He is supposed to like her children, she is supposed to like his, and the children are supposed to like their new stepparent and stepsiblings. But "supposed to" expectations are no more likely to be fulfilled in a remarriage than they are in a first marriage.

Sometimes the expectations become requirements. "If you can't accept my son, there is no sense in us staying married," said one parent. To expect that another adult will automatically love your child just because the child is yours is unrealistic. As noted earlier, it takes between four and five years for members of a stepfamily to develop a sense of family.

Dealing with the Ex-Spouse

Data – In a study of 200 second wives, 26 percent reported that their husband's ex-wife was the primary problem in their relationship. (Walker, 1984)

I don't have all the fond memories of you when you were a young child, so don't expect me to enjoy these teen years without some good years to balance them.

—Stepmother to Stepdaughter

Another weakness of stepfamilies is dealing with the ex-spouse—the visible reminder of the first marriage who calls and comes by to pick up the children. Although new spouses may intellectually understand the necessity of such interaction between their spouse and the spouse's former husband or wife, emotionally they may feel jealous of the tie to the previous marriage:

> I can't stand it when his ex-wife calls and comes to visit the kids. I've asked my husband to go into another room to talk when she calls, and I go to another room when she comes to pick up the kids. This thing gets me upset every time.

Complexity of Issues

Remarriages with stepchildren involve twice as many former in-laws, ex-spouses, and children as first marriages do. Managing these relationships and the issues they can create becomes difficult for the most skilled partner. For many, the strain becomes overwhelming.

Married couples who have stepchildren living with them more often wish that they could live away from their children, say their children give them problems, are less satisfied with their spouse's relationship to their children, and think their marriage has a negative effect on their children.

Data – Remarried spouses with stepchildren are twice as likely to say they would not marry again as remarried spouses without stepchildren. Marriages in which both spouses have been married before and have had children in their first marriages are characterized by the greatest strain and dissatisfaction. (White & Booth, 1985)

The researchers noted that one answer to the strain created by stepchildren is to send them away to the other parent or to encourage them to become as independent as possible and move out. When stepchildren are gone, the marital quality of the spouses tends to return.

Women in Stepfamilies

Some of the concerns women in stepfamilies have include accepting the new partner's children, adjusting to alimony and child-support payments to an ex-wife, having the new partner accept her children and having her children accept him, and having another child in the new marriage.

Accepting Partner's Children

"She'd better think a long time before she marries a guy with kids," said one 29–year-old woman who had done so.

Data – In a study of 200 second wives, 35 percent reported children from the husband's first marriage to be the top problem in their relationship. (Walker, 1984)

This stepmother went on to explain:

> It's really difficult to love someone else's children. Particularly if the kid isn't very likable. A year after we were married, my husband's 9-year-old daughter visited us for a summer. It was a nightmare. She didn't like anything I cooked, was always dragging around making us late when we had to go somewhere, kept her room a mess, and acted like a gum-chewing smart aleck. I hated her, but felt guilty because I wanted to have feelings of love and tenderness. Instead, I was jealous of the relationship she had with her father, and I wanted to get rid of her. I began counting how many days until she would be gone.
>
> You can hide your dislike for awhile, but eventually you must tell your partner how you feel. I was lucky. My husband also thought his daughter was horrible to live with and wasn't turned off by my feelings. He told her if she couldn't act more civil, she couldn't come back. The message to every woman about to marry a guy with kids is to be aware that your man is a package deal and that the kid is in the package.

Adjusting to Alimony and Child Support

Data – In a study of 200 second wives, 21 percent reported financial problems to be the top problem in their relationship. (Walker, 1984)

In addition to the potential problems of not liking the partner's children, there may be problems of alimony and child support. As noted earlier, it is not unusual for a wife to become upset when her husband mails one-quarter or one-third of his income to a woman with whom he used to live. This amount of money is often equal to the current wife's earnings. Some wives in this position see themselves as working for their husband's ex-wife—a perception that is very likely to create conflict.

New Partner Accepting Her Children and Their Accepting Him

In this situation, a divorced or widowed woman has custody of her children and remarries a man without children. Her main concerns are how her new husband will accept her children and how the children will accept him. The ages of the children are important in these adjustments. If the children are young (age 3 or younger), they will usually accept any new adult into the natural parent's life. On the other hand, if the children are in adolescence, they are struggling for independence from their natural parents and do not want any new authority figures in their lives.

Whether the new spouse will accept the children is unpredictable. Some men enjoy children and relate to them easily, as did the man who built a new house "for my new family." Other men find it difficult to enjoy children, particularly those with whom they have no biological link. One man told his fiancée, "If those kids are going to live with us, I don't want to be married to you."

Data – When women with children (in a Cosmopolitan survey of 65,000) were asked how the men they dated reacted to their children, 58 percent said "with pleasure," 38 percent said "politely but not warmly," and 4 percent said "indifferent or resentful." (Bowe, 1986)

Having Another Child

Another important issue may be whether the new husband wants to have a child with the new wife. Some men delight in the prospect of a child with their new wife. Others feel that they have had enough children and do not want any more. One husband in a second marriage said, "I've got two kids of my own, and I certainly don't want any more. But my new wife wants one, so I guess we'll have one."

Men in Stepfamilies

Three combinations (among others) of men in stepfamilies are those with or without custody of their children who marry a woman with or without children.

Man without Custody Married to a Woman without Children

A frequent stepfamily situation is the divorced man who is separated from his children and who is remarried to a woman without children. The husband is often concerned about the possibility that his new wife will resent his children visiting him or his visiting them.

Data – In a study of 101 divorced fathers, of those who were remarried, 47 percent saw their children at least once a month. (Tropf, 1984)

Another concern is whether the new wife will accept the fact that her husband will be sending between one-quarter and one-third of his income to his ex-wife in the form of child-support payments. In addition, the new wife is typically younger and childless, and she may want children of her own. One divorced man said:

> I feel awful not being able to see my kids, and I mope around the house a lot on weekends. When the time comes for them to visit, I get excited and really look forward to it. But my wife doesn't. She's tried to enjoy them, but I know that she resents the relationship I have with them and their intrusion into our marriage. And the money has become a real problem. I send in child support the amount she makes each month. She told me that we could be living in a nice house for the money we are spending on "those kids." She's talking about "my kids."

Man with Custody Married to a Woman with Children

As more men are awarded custody of their children, an increasing number of stepfamilies will include two sets of children. Because the number of relation-

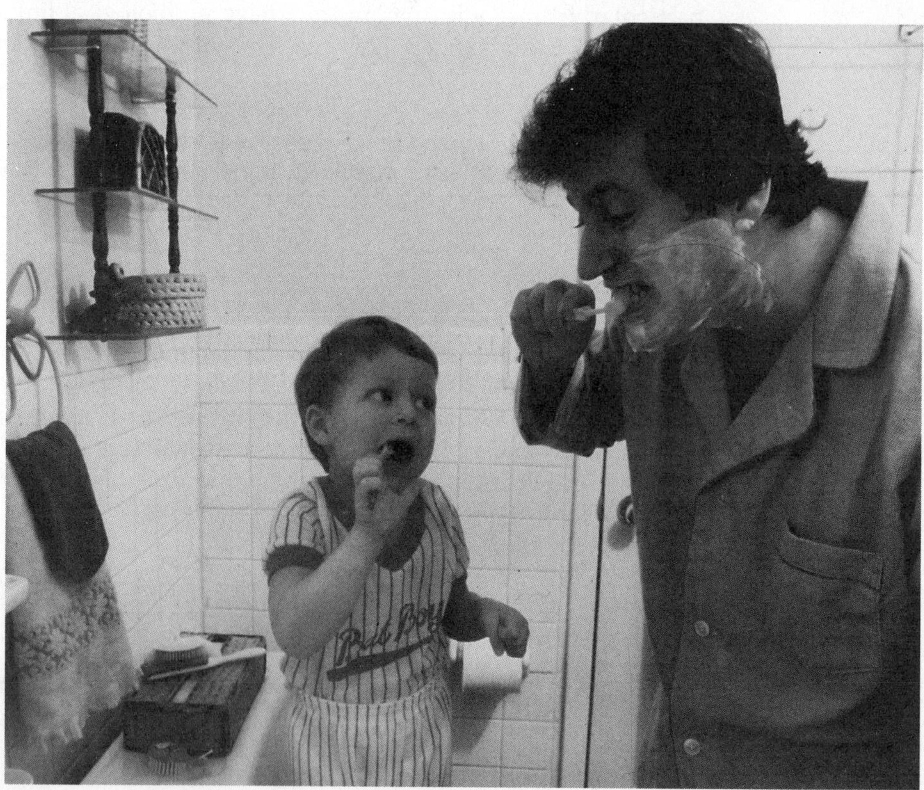

A woman marrying a divorced man who is a father must be aware of the strong bond he has with his children.

ships to manage increases with each new person who is added to the family, such stepfamilies have most of the potential problems of stepfamilies: the adjustments of the spouses to their respective sets of stepchildren, coupled with the stepchildrens' adjustments to their new stepparent and stepsiblings. The problems that these stepfamilies avoid are child-support payments and a lack of knowledge on the part of the adults as to what the parent–child bond is all about.

MAN WITHOUT CHILDREN MARRIED TO A WOMAN WITH CHILDREN

The adjustments of the never-married, divorced, or widowed man without children who marries a woman with children are primarily related to her children, their acceptance of him, and his awareness that his wife is emotionally bonded to her children. Unlike child-free marital partners, who are bonded only to each other, the husband entering a relationship with a woman who has children must accept her attachment with her children from the outset. One husband said:

> By the time we decided to get married, I was already acquainted with her three children: George, who was 8, Billy, who was 6, and Susie, who was 3. I was sure they would accept me as their father, because they seemed to view me as a friend. I also assumed that every child needs and wants a father. I liked kids, especially these kids, and I expected no trouble. I was, in a word, naive. (Gorman, 1983, p. 2.)

Their daddy is still very much present in their lives, their personalities, their memories and their momentos. There is no attempt to block him out and his name is daddy. But I am concerned about what I am to be called. I want to be daddy.
—Tony Gorman, a stepfather

Two researchers compared the quality of the relationship between the stepfather and his new wife's children with the relationship between the biological father and his own children. The stepfathers reported much less positive communication and more negative communication (Pink & Wampler, 1985).

Stepfathers who report satisfaction in their parenting roles have good communication with the stepchildren, spend time with the stepchildren, and are involved in the discipline of the stepchild, with the spouse's support (Pasley, 1985).

Another stepfather said:

> You better like children a lot if you marry a woman who already has children. I do love kids, and it has worked out for us. But it hasn't been easy. I love for her to nurture her children and am not jealous of the time it takes to do so. Money is our problem. I'm always asked to pay for things the kids want, even though they are her kids. Just this last week, we found out that Marcy will need braces. That's $2,700, and since my wife's ex-husband doesn't pay a cent in child support, I end up with the bill.
>
> The good news is you have an instant family. You have kids you can do things with. And you're more like a friend to them than a parent.

Consideration

Here are some questions a man without children might ask a woman who has children:

1. How do you expect me to relate to your children? Am I supposed to be their friend, daddy, or what?
2. How do you feel about having another child? How many more are you willing to have?
3. How much money do you get in alimony and child support from your ex-husband? How long will this last?

4. What expenses of the children do you expect me to pay for? Who is going to pay for their college expenses?
5. How often will you be in contact with your ex-husband? How will you help me handle my jealousy if it becomes a problem?

Children in Stepfamilies

Data – About 35 percent of all children in the United States will live with a stepparent during a part of their childhood. (Glick, 1984)

Stepchildren have viewpoints and must make adjustments of their own when their parents remarry. They have experienced the transition from a family in which their biological parents lived together to living alone with one parent (usually the mother) to a stepfamily with a new stepparent.

Some adjustments revolve around feeling abandoned, divided loyalties, discipline, and stepsiblings.

Feeling Abandoned

Some stepchildren feel that they have been abandoned twice—once when their parents got divorced and again when the remaining parent turned his or her attention to a new adult partner in a remarriage. One adolescent explained:

> It hurt me when my parents got divorced and my dad moved out. I really missed him and felt he really didn't care about my feelings. But we adjusted with just my mom, and when everything was going right again, she gets involved with this new guy and we've got baby sitters all the time. I feel like I've lost both parents in two years.

Consideration

Coping with feelings of abandonment is not easy. It is best if the remaining parent assures the children that the divorce was not their fault and that they are loved a great deal by both parents. In addition, the remaining parent should be careful not to abandon the children to baby sitters but to find a balance between spending time with the new partner and spending time with the children.

Divided Loyalties

Data – More than 50 percent of 103 adolescents living in stepfamilies reported they had experienced feelings of divided loyalty. (Lutz, 1983)

Sometimes the children develop an attachment for a stepparent that is more positive than the relationship with the natural parent of the same gender. When these feelings develop, the children may feel they are in a bind. One adolescent boy explained:

> My real dad left my mother when I was 6, and my mom remarried. My stepdad has always been good to me, and I really prefer to be with him. But when my dad comes to

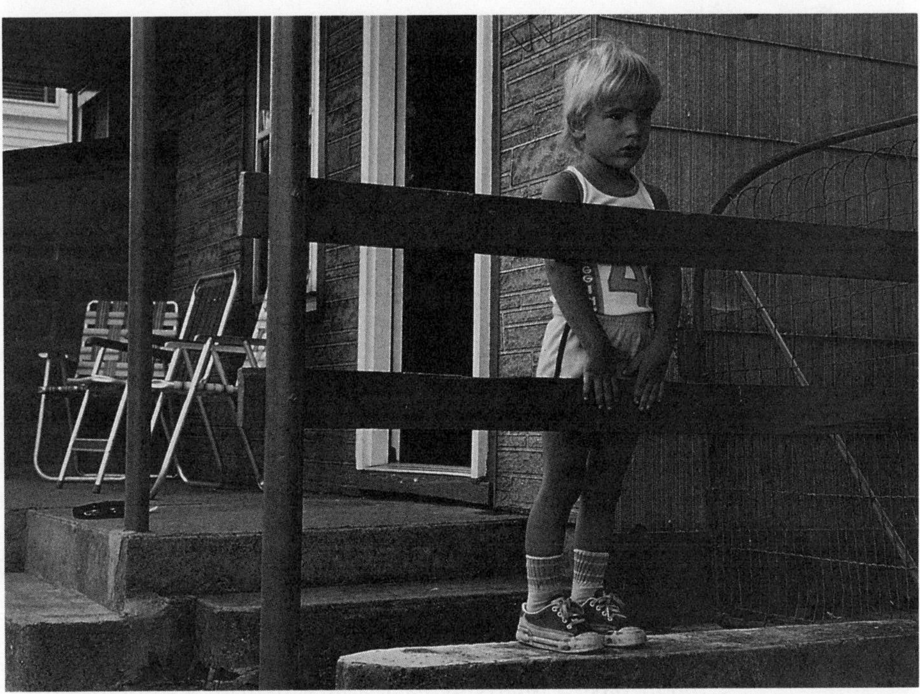

Children in stepfamilies sometimes feel abandoned.

> pick me up on weekends, I have to go. It's very uncomfortable for me, but I don't know how to tell him I would just as soon he not come around.

For some adolescents, the more they care for the stepparent, the guiltier they feel, so they may try to hide their attachment. The stepparent may be aware of both positive and negative feelings coming from the child.

Stepchildren may also resent the new stepparent and feel that he or she is trying to rob them of their biological parent's love. One 14–year-old said:

> My new stepdad made me feel guilty when I told him that I wanted to spend the summer with my dad. It was almost as though I was not supposed to have feelings for my real dad. I was in a bind. If I showed that I cared about my real dad, my stepdad would stop talking to me. If I didn't show the emotion I felt when my dad called to talk, I felt I was betraying myself and him.

Discipline

"Adjusting to living with a new set of rules from your stepparent," "accepting discipline from a stepparent," and "dealing with the expectations of your stepparent" are situations 80 percent of more than 100 adolescents in stepfamilies said they had experienced (Lutz, 1983). Their main problem was accepting rules from an "outsider":

> I resented my stepdad telling me what to do. He wasn't my real dad, and I didn't want my mom to marry him anyway. It's been a problem ever since he moved in. I liked it better when my mom was a single parent. It seems as though we were all happier then.

Stepsiblings

Stepchildren experience higher levels of stress in stepfamilies if they have stepsiblings than if they do not (Lutz, 1983). The stress seems to be a result of more arguments among the adults when both sets of children are present and the perception that parents are more fair with their own children:

> I could bounce the ball in the den and my stepdad would jump all over me. But let my stepsister bounce it and he wouldn't say a word. All I want is to be treated fairly, and that's not what's happening in this family.

Given that children who live in stepfamilies are exposed to a different set of learning experiences than children who live with their biological parents, what are the differences in developmental outcome for the two groups? Studies disagree. Some studies indicate that children in stepfamilies have more difficulties; other studies conclude that there are no differences in outcome between the two groups (Skeen et al., 1985).

In a review of 33 studies on this issue, the researchers concluded:

> Overall, few differences were found between children reared in stepfather families and those reared in biological families on measures of stability, self-sufficiency, dominance, delinquency, personality characteristics, school behavior, grades, friends, psychosocial functioning, drug use, psychosomatic complaints, self-concept, attitudes toward marital roles and family size, and interpersonal behavior. (Pasley, 1985, p. 296)

In general, stepfamilies for men, women, and children are difficult. The Stepfamily Success Scale provides a way to predict the degree to which you might have a relatively easy adjustment in a stepfamily.

Developmental Tasks for Stepfamilies

A developmental task is a skill that, if mastered, allows the family to grow as a cohesive unit. Developmental tasks that are not mastered will bring the family closer to the point of disintegration. Some of the more important developmental tasks for stepfamilies are discussed in this section.

Nurture New Marriage Relationship

If two people who love each other let a single instant wedge itself between them, it grows—it becomes a month, a year, a century; it becomes too late.

—Jean Giraudoux

Because the demands of family interaction can become intense—even excessive—it is important that the new wife and husband allocate time to be alone to nurture their relationship. They must take time to communicate, to share their lives, and to have fun. One remarried couple goes out on a date each Saturday night for dinner and a movie—without the children. "If you don't spend time alone with your partner, you won't have one," said one stepparent.

Decide about Money

Money is an issue of potential conflict in stepfamilies because it is a scarce resource and several people want to use it for their respective needs. The father wants a new computer; the mother wants a new car; the mother's children want bunk beds, a new stereo, and a satellite dish; the father's children want a larger room, clothes, and a phone. How do the newly married couple and their children decide how money should be spent? There are two patterns of spending in stepfamilies (Fishman, 1983).

Self-Assessment

Stepfamily Success Scale

This scale is designed to measure the degree to which you and your partner might expect to have a successful stepfamily. There are no right or wrong answers. After reading each sentence carefully, circle the number that best represents your feelings.

1 Strongly disagree
2 Mildly disagree
3 Undecided
4 Mildly agree
5 Strongly agree

	SD	MD	U	MA	SA
1. I am a flexible person.	1	2	3	4	5
2. I am not a jealous person.	1	2	3	4	5
3. I am a patient person.	1	2	3	4	5
4. My partner is a flexible person.	1	2	3	4	5
5. My partner is not a jealous person.	1	2	3	4	5
6. My partner is a patient person.	1	2	3	4	5
7. My partner values our relationship more than the relationship with his or her children.	1	2	3	4	5
8. My partner understands that it is not easy for me to love someone else's children.	1	2	3	4	5
9. I value the relationship with my partner more than the relationship with my children.	1	2	3	4	5
10. I understand that it will be difficult for my partner to love my children as much as I do.	1	2	3	4	5
11. My partner and I will put our money in a common fund and use it for both of our children as necessary.	1	2	3	4	5
12. My children and those of my partner will live with the ex-spouse.	1	2	3	4	5
13. We will have plenty of money in our stepfamily.	1	2	3	4	5
14. I feel positively about my partner's children.	1	2	3	4	5
15. My partner feels positively about my children.	1	2	3	4	5
16. My children and those of my partner feel positively about each other.	1	2	3	4	5

(Continued)

Self-Assessment

17. My partner and I will begin our stepfamily in a place that neither of us has lived before.	1	2	3	4	5
18. My partner and I agree on how to discipline our children.	1	2	3	4	5
19. My children feel positively about my new partner.	1	2	3	4	5
20. My partner's children feel positively about me.	1	2	3	4	5

Scoring: Add the numbers you circled. 1 (strongly disagree) is the most negative response you can make, and 5 (strongly agree) is the most positive response you can make. The lower your total score (20 is the lowest possible score), the greater the number of potential problems and the lower the chance of success in a stepfamily with this partner. The higher your total score (100 is the highest possible score), the greater the chance of success in a stepfamily with this partner. A score of 60 places you at the midpoint between the extremes of having a difficult or an easy stepfamily experience.

Common Money Pot Pattern

Under this arrangement, the marital partners put both their incomes from all sources (including alimony and child support) into a common pot and distribute money from it to themselves and the children, without concern for who earned the money or whose child it will be spent on. Figure 19.1 shows how this family conceptualizes the distribution of their money.

One spouse commented:

> We see ourselves as one family, not as two families living under one roof. If any one of the children needs something, we decide on a case-by-case basis whether or not we will purchase that item. We don't consider that it is "his" child or "my" child but what is the need of the child in reference to the whole family. And just because I make more money than my husband, I don't feel that I have a greater right to spend more of the money on "my children."

The safest way to double your money is to fold it over once and put it in your pocket.
—Frank McKinney Hubbard

The common money pot pattern provides for a feeling of solidarity and family unity. The problems that arise when two families "line up" against each other are minimized. On the other hand, sacrifices and compromises must be made, and this can produce a lot of tension. In one case, the mother wanted to spend $800 to attend a professional conference, but this meant her husband's son wouldn't have the money to attend computer camp that summer. She decided not to attend the conference, but felt as though her career was suffering because of her stepson.

Two Money Pot Pattern

Under this arrangement, money is distributed primarily according to the biological identity of the children and only secondarily according to need. Figure 19.2 describes this pattern.

FIGURE 19.1
THE COMMON MONEY POT PATTERN

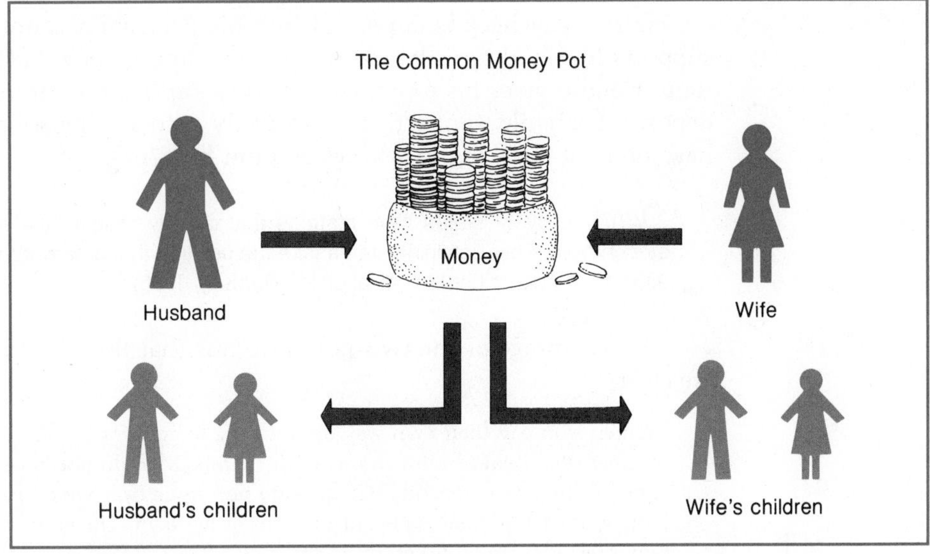

Source: Fishman, 1983.

Fishman (1983) describes the money arrangement of Sheila and Harry, a remarried couple. She has three sons by a previous marriage; he has a daughter who does not live with them. Of their economic arrangement, Sheila said:

> When it comes to money, we take care of our own. Harry gives me $25 every week for his share of food and small expenses—dry-cleaning his clothes, things like that. I add the $200 a week I get from child support. Out of this total, I run the house and pay for clothes for the boys and myself. Harry pays the fixed expenses—mortgage, gas and electric, and he supports his own child. (p. 364)

FIGURE 19.2
THE TWO MONEY POT PATTERN

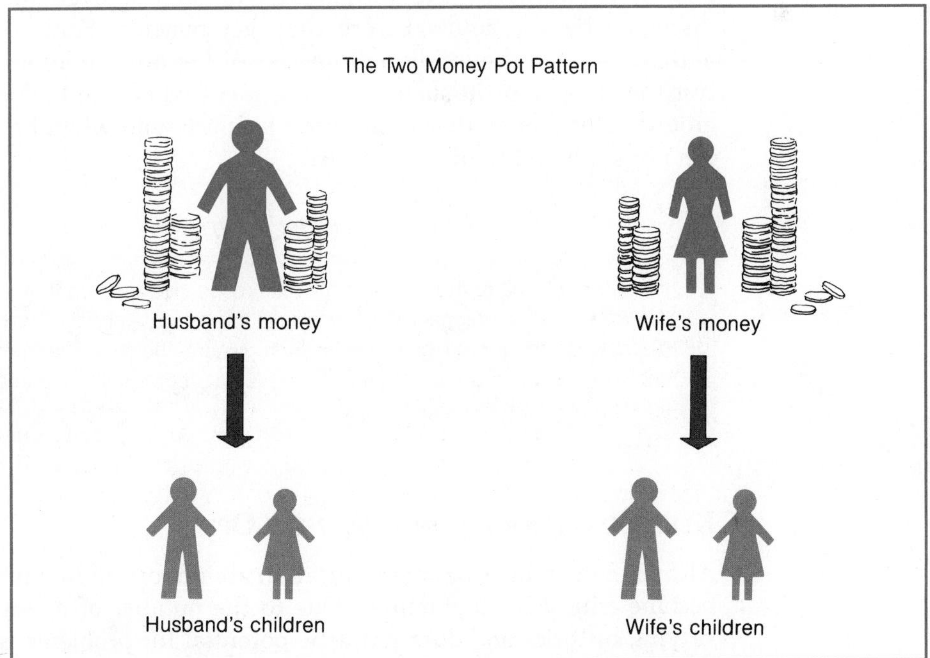

Source: Fishman, 1983.

Harry's paycheck is deposited into his personal account, out of which he supports his child directly, giving her spending money and paying school tuition. He also gives his ex-wife a monthly stipend for Ginny's support. Sheila deposits her child-support check directly into her personal account. "They have no joint checking or savings account" (p. 364).

Data – Only 14 states have statutes that directly obligate the stepparent to support stepchildren. The remaining states take the position that a parent's money should first be allocated to his or her biological child. (Ramsey, 1986)

The advantage of the two-pot pattern is that the economic responsibilities are clear:

> Women who pay their own way do not have to account to a husband for the purchase of a personal item or a lunch out with friends. Men do not have to produce extra income to finance a stepchild. Couples do not argue over which partner is in control of money, as each partner is in control of his or her own. The very structure of their economy precludes this conflict. (p. 365.)

Consideration

> Neither the one- nor the two-pot economic model is superior. They both have their advantages and limitations. What is important is that each family assess its situation and use the model that best fits its needs.

Decide Who May Discipline Whom

How much authority the stepparent will exercise over the children must be discussed by the adults before they get married. Some couples divide the authority—each spouse disciplining his or her own children. But children may test the stepparent in such an arrangement when the biological parent is not around. One stepmother said, "Jim's kids are wild when he isn't here because I'm not supposed to discipline them."

Consideration

> It is often helpful for the adults to tell their respective children that they must respect the wishes of the stepparent. Stepparents can't grab authority. They must become a partner with the natural parent, who then gives authority to the new spouse. Unless children view each parent as an authority figure, they are likely to undermine the relationship between the adults.

Keep Communication Channels Open

Although open lines of communication are important in any relationship, they become critical in stepfamilies. Due to the number of new relationships with varying histories and durations, the potential for problems is high. To prevent misunderstandings from festering, family members should understand that it is all right not to like something and agree on a means of telling others how they are feeling. Some families do this through a family council meeting.

SUPPORT CHILD'S RELATIONSHIP WITH ABSENT PARENT

Because a continued relationship with the absent biological parent is critical to the emotional well-being of the child, ex-spouses and stepparents should encourage that relationship. Regardless of the feelings the spouse and new partner may have about the ex-spouse, the children should be encouraged to talk with and see the biological parent.

Consideration

In addition, the stepparent needs to communicate to the child that he or she is not trying to take the place of the biological parent but wants to be an additional person in the child's life who can, in time, become a friend. Suggesting that the child call the stepparent by a name the child feels comfortable with may help to encourage a friendly rather than an authoritarian relationship. Many stepparents recognize that it would be a mistake to force their stepchildren to call them "mom" or "dad" and ask the children to call them by their first name.

SUPPORT CHILD'S RELATIONSHIP WITH NATURAL GRANDPARENTS

A child's continued relationship with her or his natural grandparents is also in the best interest of that child. This is one of the more stable relationships in the stepchild's changing world of adult relationships. Regardless of how ex-spouses feel about their former in-laws, they should encourage such relationships. One mother said, "Although I am uncomfortable around my ex-in-laws, I know my children enjoy visiting them, so I encourage their relationship."

Trends

Stepfamilies will become an increasingly visible phenomenon in American society. Schoolchildren play with other children in stepfamilies, and adults have friends, relatives, and coworkers who are remarrying and beginning stepfamilies. As a result, stepfamilies will become more normative and lose the stigma they now carry.

Stepfamilies will continue to reach out for help. Members of stepfamilies have already established national organizations for support. These include the Stepfamily Association of America (28 Allegheny Avenue, Suite 1307; Baltimore, MD 21204) and Stepfamily Foundation (333 West End Avenue; New York, NY 10023). Stepfamily Associates (353 Walnut Street; Brookline, MA 02146) is a private organization that offers workshops and group meetings in which stepfamily members can discuss their various concerns. Finally, for wives who do not have custody of their children or who are remarried to husbands who do not have custody of their children, Second Wife, First Class (2527 South Randolph; Indianapolis, IN 46203) has been established.

Summary

A stepfamily is a married couple in which at least one of the spouses has had a child in a previous relationship. These families include those in which the children live with their remarried parent and stepparent, those in which the children only visit their remarried parent and stepparent, and those in which the children of divorced parents either live with the remarried partners or visit.

There are a number of differences between biological families and stepfamilies. In stepfamilies, the members are not all biologically related; they may have different values; they have experienced a crisis (divorce or death); and they are stigmatized as a stepfamily. In addition, the adults have never had a child-free period and have known each other a shorter period of time than the parents have known their children.

Stepfamilies have both strengths and weaknesses. The strengths include early reality testing, exposure to a variety of behavior patterns, the observation of a happy remarriage, learning to mesh with stepsiblings in an intimate family environment, and greater objectivity on the part of the stepparent. The weaknesses include the adults having unrealistic expectations, the occasional presence of the ex-spouse, and the complexity of issues.

Women, men, and children sometimes experience stepfamily living differently. For women, learning to get along with the husband's children, not being resentful of his relationship with his children, and adapting to the fact that one-quarter to one-third of his income will be sent to his ex-wife as alimony or child support are skills the new wife must develop. She may also want children with her new partner or may bring her own children into the remarriage. In the latter case, she is anxious that her new husband will accept her children.

Men in stepfamilies have similar concerns. Getting along with their wife's children, paying for many of the expenses of their stepchildren, having their new partner accept their own children, and dealing with the issue of having more children are among them.

Children must cope with feeling abandoned and problems of divided loyalties, discipline, and stepsiblings.

Developmental tasks for stepfamilies include nurturing the new marriage relationship, deciding whose money will be spent on whose children, deciding who will discipline the children and how, keeping communication channels open, and supporting the child's relationship with the absent parent and natural grandparents.

Trends include the increased visibility of stepfamilies. By 1990, there will be more single-parent homes and stepfamilies than two-parent and biological homes. Such visibility will result in greater acceptance and less stigmatization. In addition, stepfamilies will continue to support each other through various organizations.

Questions for Reflection

1. How capable do you think you are of loving someone else's children?
2. How accepting would you be of a new spouse who could not accept your children?
3. How would you feel if your stepchildren never accepted you as a member of the family? What could you do to try to change their attitude?

CHOICES

NEVER-MARRIED AND divorced individuals with children have choices to make about entering a stepfamily. The various issues for each of these individuals to consider follow.

Should a Never-Married Man Marry a Divorced Woman With Children?

The following diagrams, which were first presented in Chapter 4, emphasize the positive and negative consequences of a "yes" or "no" decision. They are helpful in making many kinds of decisions. First, we suggest how they may help the single man in deciding whether to marry a divorced woman with children.

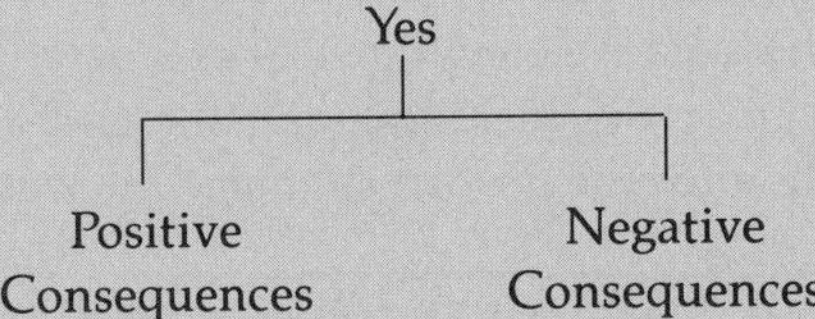

Yes

The positive consequences of marrying a divorced woman with children include continuing the love relationship with the woman, having a ready-made family, and avoiding the pain of living without the beloved. Because the man making such a decision will be emotionally involved with the woman, a major factor in his decision will be his emotional outlook. One man said:

> I love her and want to be with her, whether she has kids or not. If you try to add and subtract everything about human relationships as though you are keeping a ledger, you are missing the point. My happiness depends on my being with her, and marriage means that we will continue our lives together, since we don't believe in living together.

In addition to being able to live with the loved person in a marriage relationship, another positive consequence of marrying a divorced person with children is having a ready-made family. "I've always wanted children, and I think her kids are great," said a prospective groom. "We've been camping together as a family, and it was nothing but fun. I don't see any problem down the road with these kids."

Another positive outcome is avoiding a negative one:

> If I don't marry her, I'm forced to go back to bars and talk to people I'm not interested in. I love her, and deciding not to marry her would mean loneliness and pain.

Every decision has positive and negative consequences. What are the negative consequences of deciding to marry a divorced woman with children? The emotional bond between the woman and her children, the presence of an ex-husband who may be calling and coming by to get the kids, and the costs associated with rearing the children are potential problems. One man who married (and subsequently divorced) a woman with two children said:

> It didn't work out for us. I was jealous of the time she gave to her own kids and knew that I was always second. I also didn't like her ex around, even though it was for a brief time each week. Just to see the guy who had sex with my wife for 15 years unnerved me. And the money was a real problem. Her ex never paid enough child support to cover what the kids cost, and I got tired of paying for kids who weren't really mine. Besides, they both

(Continued)

needed braces, and that got us deeply in debt. I'd say marrying a woman with kids isn't worth it, no matter how much you love her.

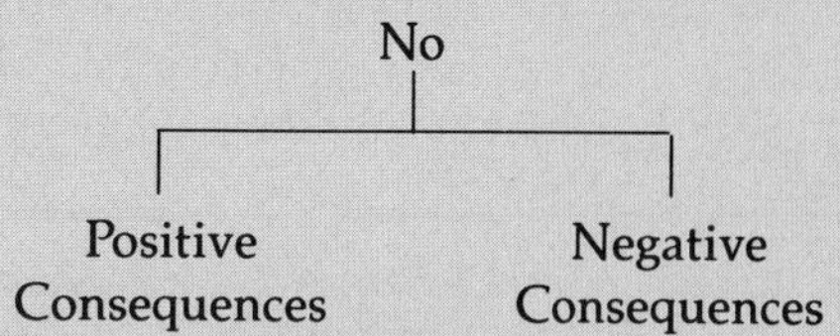

No

Suppose the man decides not to marry the divorced woman with children. What are the positive and negative consequences of his decision? On the positive side, he has avoided the potential problems of feeling jealous of the bond between the woman and her children, of having to deal with an ex-spouse, and of feeling financially responsible for children that are not biologically his. By making a single decision, he has avoided a lot of potential headaches (and maybe a divorce, since 60 percent of these marriages do not last).

On the other hand, there are some losses associated with deciding not to marry her. The primary one is the emotional pain he would feel as a result of terminating the relationship with her. "In these situations," said one man, "I'm a real sucker for romance. I do what I feel every time. And living without this woman is something I can't do."

After listing the positive and negative consequences of a "yes" and "no" decision, a final decision can be made by examining how the consequences look on paper. Assign weights to the different consequences if necessary. For example, on a 10-point scale (10 = tops), how important is it to have a ready-made family, to continue the love relationship, or to avoid going in debt over children who are not biologically yours? Getting the issues on paper and looking at them sometimes makes it easy to make a decision.

How the decision feels is also important. Regardless of how it looks on paper, your feelings will play an important role in determining the final decision. "If the decision doesn't feel right in your heart, it isn't right," said one person.

Should a Never-Married Woman Marry a Divorced Man With Children?

It is not unusual for a single woman to become emotionally involved with a divorced man who has children. Although the ex-wife frequently has custody of their children, they may visit and he will probably pay child support. The process just described is helpful in examining the issues involved (see earlier diagrams).

Yes

The positive consequences for the single woman marrying a divorced man with children would be similar to those of the single man marrying a divorced woman with children: continuing the love relationship, benefiting from a ready-made family, and avoiding the pain of losing the partner.

The negative consequences of a "yes" decision may also include competing with the children for the husband's time. One woman said:

> Since we both worked all week, I wanted the weekend to enjoy by ourselves. But he wanted his kids to visit us on weekends. I went along with it for awhile, but finally told him I didn't like it. He said, "My kids are coming to this house every Saturday as long as they want to. If you don't like it, leave." I tried to get along with them, but I just ended up cooking and doing the laundry for them. I felt like a maid for his kids, who were interfering in our marriage.

No

The positive outcome of a decision not to marry a divorced man with children is avoiding the problems of stepchildren visiting frequently and taking money out of the marriage and giving it to the husband's ex-wife.

The negative consequence of deciding not to marry is the flood of bad feelings—loneliness, depression, and pain—that often follow a decision to walk away from an emotionally important relationship.

It is critical to keep in mind that no decision will have all positive or negative consequences. Every decision will involve trade-offs.

Should a Divorced Woman With Children and a Divorced Man With Children Marry?

Divorced people sometimes prefer each other because they know the person has an experiential understanding of the divorced state. "I won't date single people," said one divorced woman. "They have no appreciation for what it is like to be divorced and they certainly don't know anything about the parent–child bond." Marrying someone with children has its own problems. (Refer again to the earlier diagrams.)

Yes
Marrying someone who understands divorce and children is perhaps the greatest benefit of deciding to marry a divorced person with children. Because they know how intense the parent–child bond is, they are not as likely to feel jealous of this relationship. In addition, they have ex-spouses too and can empathize with the need and discomfort of interacting with an ex.

Mother and father role models for each other's children are also a benefit for adults and children. "I need a mother for my kids, and she needs a daddy for hers, so it's a good trade-off," said one father. "I wouldn't say I'm getting married for that reason, but it sure is a plus."

The negative consequences of a decision to blend two families together are problems of the wife's children accepting their stepfather, the husband's children accepting their stepmother, and the children accepting each other. These factors will influence the degree to which the new family "jells" and becomes a cohesive unit. To expect that such a fusion will occur quickly and smoothly is unrealistic.

No
The decision against blending two families will result in avoiding the potentially negative consequences just described. On the other hand, such a decision will terminate an emotional relationship with someone who knows what divorce, children, and single parenting are all about.

Impact of Social Influences on Choices

Our society has not decided how it feels about stepfamilies. On the one hand, they are stigmatized as being less than a "real" family in which the adults have been married one time to each other and have their own children living with them. But with 60 percent of the divorces occurring in such "real" families with children, stepfamilies are no longer an anomaly.

The degree to which an individual who lives in a stepfamily does not stigmatize himself or herself will be influenced by whether he or she has friends who are also in stepfamilies. Grade-school kids often have playmates whose parents are divorced or remarried. As these children grow up, the stigmas of divorce and living in a stepfamily will be muted.

PART SIX

SPECIAL TOPICS

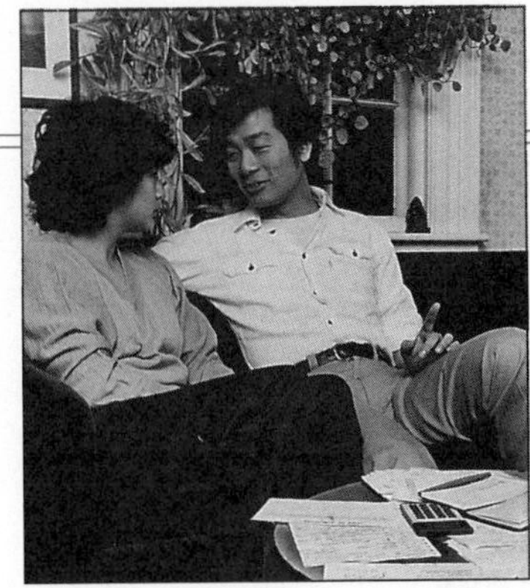

SPECIAL TOPIC 1

Budgeting, Investing, Life Insurance, and Credit

Contents

ONE ASPECT OF marriage is that it is an economic partnership in which the spouses conduct the business of getting and spending money. Problems may arise when this scarce resource is not managed properly. Here, we will consider possible ways to prevent spending more than you and your partner are making and how to invest money for future needs.

Developing a Budget

Developing a budget is a way of planning your spending. Since money spent on X cannot be spent on Y, budgeting requires conscious value choices about which bills should be paid, what items should be bought, and what expenditures should be delayed. Couples need to develop a budget if they are always out of money long before their next paycheck, if they cannot make partial payments or pay off existing bills but keep incurring new debts, or if they cannot save money.

Consideration

The advantages of developing and following a budget include having money available when you need it, avoiding unnecessary debt, and saving money.

To develop a budget (see Table ST1.1), list and add up all your monthly take-home (after-tax) income from all sources. This figure should represent the amount of money your family will actually have to spend each month. Next, list and add up all of your fixed monthly expenses, such as rent, utilities, telephone, and car payment. Other fixed expenses include such items as life, health, and car insurance. You may not receive a bill for some of these expenses every month, so divide the yearly cost of each item by 12 so that you can budget it on a monthly basis. For example, if your annual life insurance premium is $240, you should budget $20 per month for that expense.

Set aside a minimum of 5 percent of your monthly income—and more, if possible—for savings, and include this sum in your fixed expenses. By putting a fixed amount in a savings account each month, you will not only have money available for large purchases, such as a car or a major home appliance, but you will also have an emergency fund to cover unforeseen expenses like those caused by an extended illness or a long-distance move. The size of an emergency fund should be about twice your monthly income. Although you can personally set aside some of your monthly income for savings, an alternative is to instruct the bank to transfer a certain sum each month from your checking account to your savings account, or you can join a payroll savings plan. Under the latter arrangement, a portion of your monthly salary is automatically deposited in your savings account without ever passing through your hands. "I always have the bank put money in a separate account," said one spouse. "If I don't, there won't be any savings. As soon as I get money, I spend it. I just can't keep money."

TABLE ST1.1 MONTHLY BUDGET FOR TWO–INCOME COUPLE:

Both Spouses Employed Full Time		
Sources of Income		
Husband's take-home pay		$1,480
Wife's take-home pay		920
Interest earned on savings		17
	TOTAL	$2,417
Fixed Expenses		
Rent		$ 350
Utilities		90
Telephone		50
Insurance		85
Car payments and expenses		290
Furniture payments		80
Savings		200
	TOTAL	$1,145
	DIFFERENCE	$1,272
	(Amount available for day-to-day expenses)	
Day-to-Day and Discretionary Expenses		
Food		$ 250
Clothes		170
Personal care		90
Recreation		120
Miscellaneous		110
	TOTAL	$ 740

This dual-income couple should have $532 extra at the end of each month. The reality is that many couples can't or don't live within their income and go into debt each month.

After adding together all your fixed monthly expenses, including savings, subtract this amount from your monthly take-home income. What remains can be used for such day-to-day expenses as food (groceries and restaurant meals), clothes (including laundry, dry cleaning, alterations, and new clothes), personal care (barber and hairdresser, toilet articles, cosmetics), and recreation (theater, movies, concerts, books, magazines).

Consideration

If you come out even at the end of the month, you are living within your means. If you have money left over, you are living below your means. If you had to tap your savings or borrow money to pay your bills last month, you are living beyond your means. Knowing whether you are living within, below, or above your means depends on keeping accurate records.

And remember, you must pay taxes on what you earn. The following shows how much:

TAXABLE INCOME 1988 AND BEYOND

Rate	*Joint Return*	*Single Return*
15%	$0–$29,750	$0–$17,850
28%	$29,751 and up	$17,851 and up

There is a 5 percent surcharge imposed on incomes of $71,900–149,250 for joint returns and $43,150–89,560 for single returns.

Investing

Saving should be a part of every budget. By allocating a specific amount of your monthly income to savings, having your employer do so through the payroll savings plan, or putting your change in a container on your dresser every evening, you can accumulate money for both short-term (vacation, down payment on a house) and long-term (college education for children, retirement income) goals.

Consideration

Loose change in a container on your dresser is not earning you the money it could. By investing, you use money to make more money. All investments must be considered in terms of their risk and potential yield. In general, the higher the rate of return on an investment, the greater the risk. Putting your money in a bank or savings and loan institution is risk-free because your deposit is insured by the federal government.

Another way to invest money and receive a fairly stable return is to buy a blue-chip stock, such as American Telephone & Telegraph or Eastman Kodak. The value of these stocks is likely to increase. Also, some stocks have the potential to appreciate and pay dividends as well. Although there is greater potential return on these investment stocks than on money placed in a savings

Investing money is a way of making money.

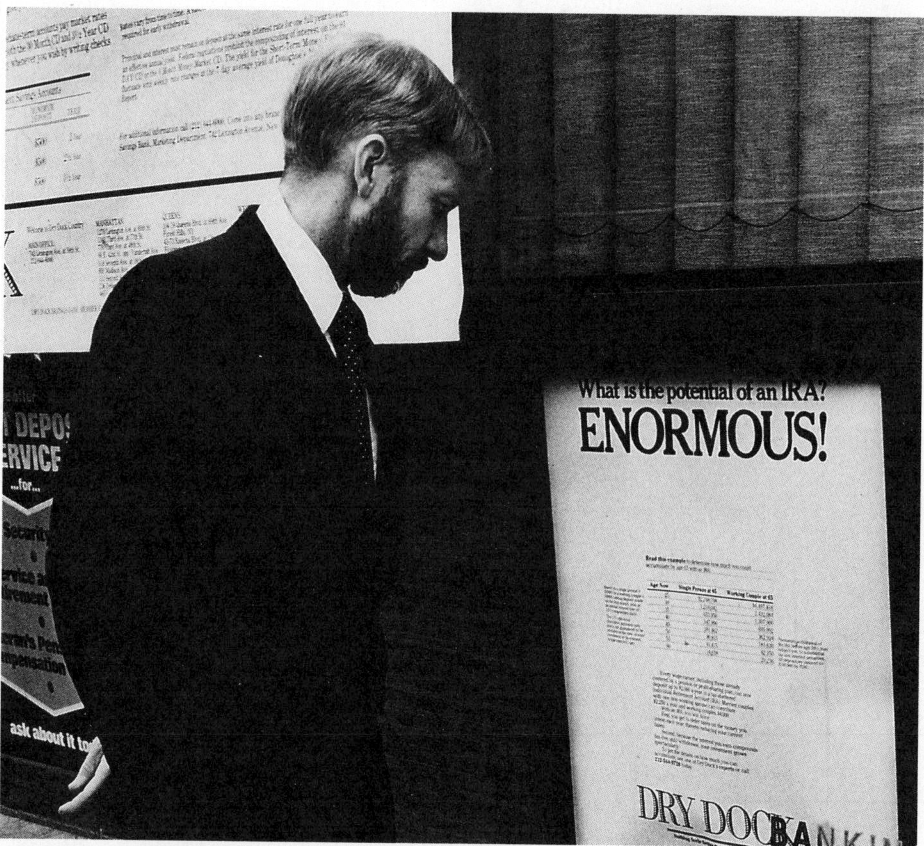

account at the bank, there is also a risk to the investor. For example, if Nikon Camera invented a new film that offered superior quality at a lower cost, Kodak stock might plummet and take your money with it.

There is an even greater risk with speculative stocks—stocks that can radically increase or decrease in value within a short time. Suppose you could afford to lose $500 and were willing to gamble on a high return. You could buy 100 shares of stock at slightly below $5 per share. If the stock is selling for $10 one year later, your original investment would double in value: you would now have $1,000 from your initial investment of $500. But if the stock is selling for $1 per share one year later, you would only realize $100 on your $500 investment. You can lose money as fast as you can gain it. One spouse invested in a company specializing in bananas and looked forward to tripling her investment. But less than a week after she purchased the stock, a hurricane in Puerto Rico wiped out the banana crop, and the value of her stock dropped sharply.

Consideration

Don't invest in speculative stocks unless you can afford to lose the money.

Fortunately, investment opportunities are not limited to banks and stocks. Table ST1.2 illustrates several investment alternatives and furnishes information on other factors that you should consider in deciding on an investment. In addition to risk and return on investment, the *liquidity*, or the ease with which your investment can be converted into cash, is an important consideration. Stocks and bonds can be sold quickly to provide cash in hand. In contrast, if you have invested in a building or land, you must find a buyer who is willing to pay the price that you are asking for your asset before you can convert it to cash.

The amount of your time that is required to make your investment grow is also important. A real estate investment can give you a considerable return on your money, but it may also demand a lot of your time—perusing the newspaper, arranging for loans, placing ads, and showing the house, not to mention fixing leaky faucets, mowing grass, and painting rooms.

TABLE ST1.2 SOME INVESTMENT ALTERNATIVES

Type	*Risk/Yield*	*Liquidity*	*Management*	*Tax Aspects*
Savings account	Low/6%	Immediate	Self	Interest is taxed.
Treasury bill	Low/6%	3 months to a year	Self	Interest is taxed.
Money market	Low/7%	One week	Broker	Interest is taxed.
Annuity	Low/9%	Retirement	Company	Tax is deferred.
Real estate	Depends/0–25%	Months/years	Self or other	Good tax advantage.
Mutual fund	Moderate/3–30%	One week	Agent	Lower tax if held.
Stocks	Depends/0–100%	One week	Broker	Depends on investment.
Life insurance	Low/6%	Years	Agent	Depends on investment.
Bonds	Depends/8–10%	One week	Broker	Depends on investment.
IRA	Low/6–8%	Retirement	Broker	Deferred.
Certificate of Deposit (CD)	Low/6–8%	Variable	Self	Interest is taxed.

Also, consider the maturity date of your investment. For example, suppose you invest in a six-year certificate at a savings bank. Although the bank will pay you, say, 12-percent interest and guarantee your investment, you can't get your principle (the money you deposited) or the interest until the six years is up unless you are willing to pay a substantial penalty. Regular savings accounts have no maturity date. You can withdraw any amount of your money from your savings account at the bank whenever you want it, but you may earn only, say, 6-percent interest on the money while it remains in the account.

A final investment consideration is taxation. Investment decisions should be made on the basis not of how much money you can make but of how much money you can keep. Tax angles should be considered as carefully as risk and yield issues.

Consideration

Unless you are majoring in business or banking and have some expertise in money management, it may be wise to ask a broker in an investment firm like Merrill Lynch, Smith Barney, or E.F. Hutton to advise you. A financial advisor can tailor your investment program to accommodate your specific needs (high yield but low risk, go for broke, or whatever). Although there will be a commission if you decide to buy through the broker, there is usually no charge for the consultation. Discount brokers are available if you need no investment advice. Most banks have such brokers.

Although savings, life insurance, real estate, and stock investments are probably familiar forms of investment to you, the other types of investments listed in Table ST1.2 may need further clarification.

Annuities provide a monthly income after age 65 (or earlier if desired) in exchange for your investment of monthly premiums during your working years. For example, a 65-year-old man may receive $100 per month as long as he lives (or a lump sum) if he has paid the insurance company $238 annually since age 30.

Bonds are issued by corporations and federal, state, and local governments that need money. In exchange for your money, you get a piece of paper that entitles you to the return of the sum you lend at a specified date (up to 30 years) plus interest on that money. Although bonds are safer than stocks, you could lose all your money if the corporation you lend the money to goes bankrupt. United States Savings Bonds are safe but pay a comparatively low rate of interest.

Mutual funds offer a way of investing in a number of common stocks, corporate bonds, or government bonds at the same time. You invest your money in shares of the mutual fund, whose directors invest the fund's capital in various securities. If the securities they select increase in price, so does the value of your shares in the mutual fund, and vice versa.

Anyone who thinks there's safety in numbers hasn't looked at the stock-market pages.
—Irene Porter

Treasury bills (T-bills) are issued by the Federal Reserve Bank. You pay a lower price for the bill than its cash value. For example, you may pay $900 for a T-bill that will be worth $1,000 on maturity. Maturity of the bill occurs at three, six, nine, or 12 months. The longer the wait, the more money paid on the investment.

Money market investments require a payment of $5,000 or more to a stockbroker who uses your money, together with the money others wish to invest, to purchase high-interest securities. Your money can be withdrawn in any amount at any time. As with all investments, you pay a fee to the broker or agent for investing your money. In the past several years, increasing numbers of people have put their money in money market funds.

Individual retirement accounts (IRAs) permit you to set aside up to $2,000 each year for your personal retirement fund. The money you put in your IRA is not automatically tax-free. (You must meet certain criteria restrictions.) Each spouse can open his or her own IRA.

Certificates of deposit (CDs) are insured deposits given to the bank that earn interest at a rate from one day to several years. These high-yield, low-risk investments have become extremely popular. A minimum investment of $500 or more is usually required.

Life Insurance

In addition to saving and investing, it is important to be knowledgeable about life insurance. The major purpose of life insurance is to provide income for dependents when the primary wage earner dies. With dual-income couples, life insurance is often necessary to prevent having to give up their home when one wage earner dies. Otherwise, the remaining wage earner may not be able to make the necessary mortgage payments.

Consideration

Unmarried, child-free, college students probably do not need life insurance. No one is dependent on them for economic support. However, the argument used by some insurance agents who sell campus policies is that college students should buy life insurance while they are young when the premiums are low and when insurability is guaranteed. Still, consumer advocates suggest that life insurance for unmarried, child-free college students is not necessary.

When it is a question of money, everybody is of the same religion.

—Voltaire

When considering income protection for dependents, there are two basic types of life insurance policies: (1) term insurance and (2) insurance-plus-investment. As the name implies, term insurance offers protection for a specific time period (usually one, five, 10, or 20 years). At the end of the time period, the protection stops. Although a term-insurance policy offers the greatest amount of protection for the least cost, it does not build up cash value (money the insured would get if he or she surrendered the policy for cash).

Insurance-plus-investment policies are sold under various names. The first is straight life, ordinary life, or whole life, in which the individual pays a stated premium (based on age and health) as long as he or she lives. When the insured dies, the beneficiary is paid the face value of the policy (the amount of insurance originally purchased). During the life of the insured, the policy also builds up a cash value (which is tax-free), which permits the insured to borrow money from the insurance company at a low rate of interest. A second type of life insurance is a limited-payment policy, in which the premiums are paid up after a certain number of years (usually 20) or when the insured reaches a certain age (usually 60 or 65). As with straight, ordinary-life, or whole-life policies, limited-payment policies build up a cash value, and the face value of the policy is not paid until the insured dies. The third type of life insurance is endowment insurance, in which the premiums are paid up after a stated number of years and can be cashed in at a stated age.

Regardless of how they are sold, insurance-plus-investment policies divide the premium paid by the insured. Part pays for the actual life insurance, and part is invested for the insured, giving the policy a cash value. Unlike term insurance, insurance-plus-investment policies are not canceled at age 65.

Which type of policy, term or insurance-plus-investment, should you buy? An insurance agent is likely to suggest the latter and point out the advantages of cash value, continued protection beyond age 65, and level premiums. But the agent has a personal incentive for your buying an insurance-plus-investment policy. The commission he or she gets on this type of policy is much higher than it is on a term-insurance policy.

Consideration

A strong argument can be made for buying term insurance and investing the additional money that would be needed to pay for the more expensive insurance-plus-investment policy.

The annual premium for $50,000 worth of renewable term insurance at age 25 is about $175. The same coverage offered in an ordinary life policy—the most common insurance-plus-investment policy—costs $668 annually, so the difference is $493 per year. If you put this money in the bank at a minimum interest rate of 5 percent, at the end of five years you will have $2,860.32. In contrast, the cash value of an ordinary-life policy after five years is $2,350. But to get this money, you have to pay the insurance company interest to borrow it. If you don't want to pay the interest, the company will give you this amount but cancel your policy. In effect, you lose your insurance protection if you receive the cash value of your policy. With term insurance, you have the $2,860.32 in the bank earning interest, and you can withdraw it any time without affecting your insurance program.

It should be clear that for term insurance to be cheaper, you must invest the money you would otherwise be paying for an ordinary life insurance policy. If you can't discipline yourself to save, buy an insurance-plus-investment policy, which will ensure savings.

Finally, what about the fact that term insurance stops when you are 65, just as you are moving closer to death and needing the protection more? Again, by investing the money that you would otherwise have spent on an insurance-plus-investment policy, you will have as much or more money for your beneficiary than your insurance-plus-investment policy would earn.

Whether you buy a term policy, an insurance-plus-investment policy, or both, there are three options to consider: guaranteed insurability, waiver of premiums, and double or triple indemnity. All are inexpensive and generally should be included in a life insurance policy.

Guaranteed insurability means that the company will sell you more insurance in the future, regardless of your medical condition. For example, suppose you develop cancer after you buy a policy for $10,000. If the guaranteed insurability provision is in your contract, you can buy additional insurance. If not, the company can refuse you more insurance.

Waiver of premiums provides that your premiums will be paid by the company if you become disabled for six months or longer and are unable to earn an income. Such an option ensures that your policy will stay in force because the premiums will be paid. Otherwise, the company will cancel your policy.

Double or triple indemnity means that if you die as the result of an accident, the company will pay your beneficiary twice or three times the face value of your policy.

An additional item you might consider adding to your life insurance policy is a *disability income rider.* If the wage earner becomes disabled and cannot work, the financial consequences for the family are the same as though he or she were dead. With disability insurance, the wage earner can continue to provide for the family up to a maximum of $3,500 per month or two-thirds of his or her salary, whichever is smaller. If the wage earner is disabled by accidental injury, payments are made for life. If illness is the cause, payments may be made only to age 65. A 27-year-old spouse and parent who was paralyzed in an automobile accident said, "It was the biggest mistake of my life to think I needed only life insurance to protect my family. Disability insurance turned out to be more important."

Consideration

In deciding to buy life insurance, it may be helpful to keep four issues in mind:

1. Compare prices. All policies and prices are not the same. In some cases, the higher premiums are for lower coverage.
2. Select your agent carefully. Only one in 10 life insurance agents stay in the business. The person you buy life insurance from today may be in the real estate business tomorrow. Choose an agent who has been selling life insurance for at least 10 years.
3. Seek group rates. Group life insurance is the least expensive coverage. See if your employer offers a group plan.
4. Proceed slowly. Don't rush into buying an insurance policy. Consult several agents, read *Consumer Reports,* and talk with friends to find out what they are doing about their insurance needs.

Credit

You use credit when you take an item home today and pay for it later. The amount you pay later will depend on the arrangement you make with the seller. Suppose you want to buy a color television set that costs $600. Unless you pay cash, the seller will set up one of three types of credit accounts with you: installment, revolving charge, or open charge.

Under the installment plan, you make a down payment and sign a contract to pay the rest of the money in monthly installments. You and the seller negotiate the period of time over which the payments will be spread and the amount you will pay each month. The seller adds a finance charge to the cash price of the television set and remains the legal owner of the set until you have made your last payment. Most department stores, appliance and furniture stores, and automobile dealers offer installment credit. The cost of buying the $600 color television set can be calculated as illustrated in Table ST1.3.

Instead of buying your $600 television on the installment plan, you might want to buy it on the revolving charge plan. Most credit cards, such as MasterCard, and Visa, represent revolving charge accounts that permit you to buy on credit up to a stated amount during each month. At the end of the month, you may pay the total amount you owe, any amount over the stated "minimum payment due," or the minimum payment. If you choose to pay less than the full amount, the cost of the credit on the unpaid amount is 1.5 percent per month, or 18 percent per year. For instance, if you pay $100 per month for your television for six months, you will still owe $31.62 to be paid the next month, for a total cost (television plus finance charges) of $631.62.

You can also purchase items on an open charge (30–day) account. Under this system you agree to pay in full within 30 days. Since there is no direct service charge or interest for this type of account, the television set would cost only the purchase price. As examples, Sears and J.C. Penney offer open charge (30–day) accounts. If you do not pay the full amount in 30 days, a finance charge is placed on the remaining balance. Both the use of revolving-charge and open-charge accounts are wise if you pay off the bill before finance charges begin. In deciding which type of credit account to use, remember that credit usually costs money; the longer you take to pay for an item, the more the item will cost you. Exhibit ST1.1 describes the high cost of credit and one way parents of young married couples can help to reduce this burden. In 1988, only 40 percent of all interest payments on consumer debt will be tax-deductible; in 1989, 20 percent; in 1990, 10 percent; and by 1991, zero.

In the long run, using credit often costs more.

TABLE ST1.3 CALCULATING THE COST OF INSTALLMENT CREDIT

1. The amount to be financed:		
	Cash price	$600.00
	− down payment (if any)	−50.00
	Amount to be financed	$550.00
2. The amount to be paid:		
	Monthly payments	$ 35.00
	× number of payments	× 18
	Total amount repaid	$630.00
3. The cost of the credit:		
	Total amount repaid	$630.00
	− amount financed	−550.00
	Cost of credit	$ 80.00
4. The total cost of the color TV:		
	Total amount repaid	$630.00
	+ down payment (if any)	+ 50.00
	Total cost of TV	$680.00

THREE Cs OF CREDIT

Whether you can get credit will depend on the rating you receive on the "three Cs": character, capacity, and capital. *Character* refers to your honesty, sense of responsibility, soundness of judgment, and trustworthiness. *Capacity* refers to your ability to pay the bill when it is due. Such issues as the amount of money you earn and the length of time you have held a job will be considered in evaluating your capacity to pay. *Capital* refers to such assets as bank accounts, stocks, bonds, money market funds, real estate, and so on.

Consideration

It is particularly important that a married woman establish a credit rating in her own name in case she becomes widowed or divorced. Otherwise, her credit will depend on her husband; if he dies or divorces her, she will have no credit of her own. Although the law now furnishes some protection against financial discrimination by lenders, it remains the responsibility of the individual to establish his or her own credit rating.

Exhibit ST1.1

THE HIGH COST OF INTEREST OVER TIME

"What hurts young families so often is the high rate of interest they get saddled with over a 30–year–period when they buy a house," said one father of two children. "House payments in the early years are mostly interest, so it takes forever for the kids to pay off the principal."

The first payment on a $65,000 loan at 10–percent interest for 30 years is $570.42. Only $28.75 of this amount is applied to the principal. The remainder ($541.67) is interest. Taxes and fire insurance are an additional $50 and $20, respectively, per month. To shorten the total number of years during which a family must pay the bank $570.42 every month, spouses or parents can make separate monthly payments that are applied specifically to the principal. The sooner the principal is paid off, the sooner all payments will stop.

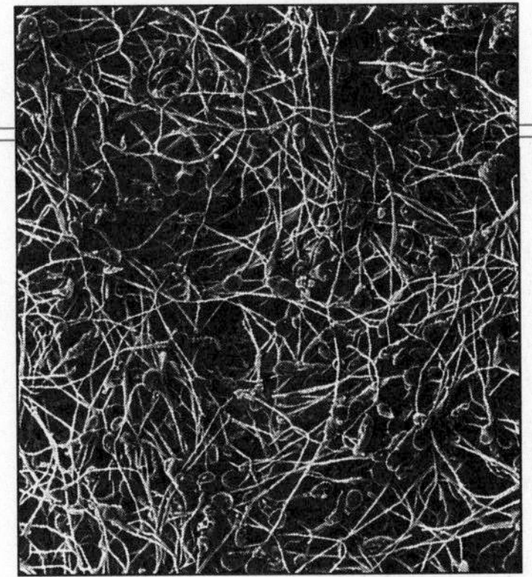

Sexual Anatomy and Physiology

Contents

In the culture in which we live, it is the custom to be least informed upon that subject concerning which every individual should know most—namely, the structure and functions of his/her own body.
—Ashley Montague

IF WE THINK of the human body as a special type of machine, *anatomy* refers to that machine's parts and *physiology* refers to how the parts work. In this topic, we will review the sexual anatomy and physiology of women and men and the reproductive process.

Female External Anatomy and Physiology

The external female genitalia are collectively known as the *vulva* (VUHL-vuh), a Latin term meaning "covering." The vulva consists of the mons veneris, the labia, the clitoris, and the vaginal and urethral openings (see Figure ST2.1). Like faces, the female genitalia differ in size, shape, and color, resulting in considerable variability in appearance.

Mons Veneris

The soft cushion of fatty tissue overlaying the pubic bone is called the *mons veneris* (mahns-vuh-NAIR-ihs), also known as the *mons pubis.* This area becomes covered with hair at puberty and has numerous nerve endings. The purpose of the mons is to protect the pubic region during sexual intercourse.

Labia

In the sexually unstimulated state, the urethral and vaginal openings are protected by the *labia majora* (LAY-bee-uh muh-JOR-uh), or "major lips"—two elongated folds of fatty tissue that extend from the mons to the *perineum,* the area of skin between the opening of the vagina and the anus. Located between the labia majora are two additional hairless folds of skin, called the *labia minora* (muh-NOR-uh), or "minor lips," that cover the urethral and vaginal openings and join at the top to form the hood of the clitoris. Both sets of labia—particularly the inner labia minora—have a rich supply of nerve endings that are sensitive to sexual stimulation.

FIGURE ST2.1 EXTERNAL FEMALE GENITALIA

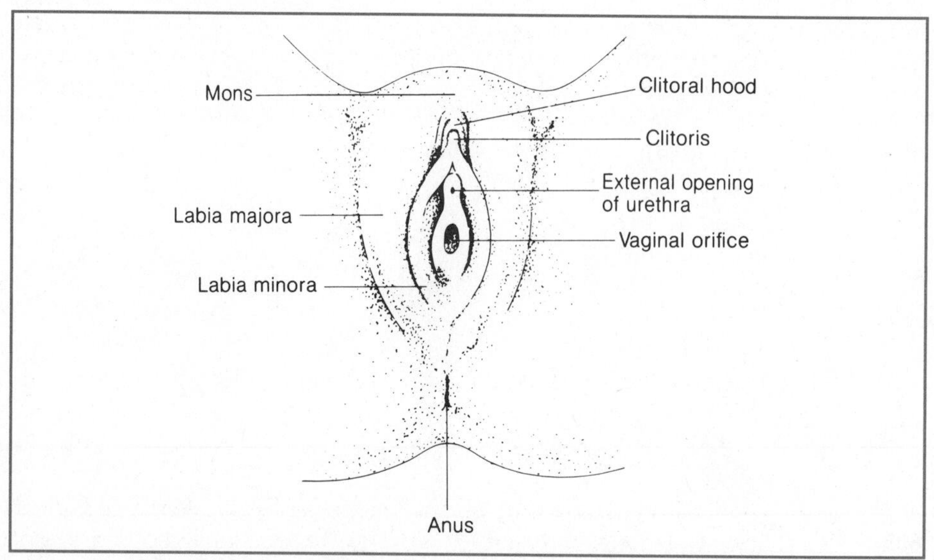

Clitoris

At the top of the labia minora is the *clitoris* (KLIHT-uh-ruhs), which also has a rich supply of nerve endings. The clitoris is the site of sexual excitement in the female and, like the penis, becomes erect during sexual excitation.

Vaginal Opening

The area between the labia minora is called the *vestibule.* This includes the urethral opening and the vaginal opening, or *introitus* (ihn-TROH-ih-tuhs), neither of which is visible unless the labia minora are parted. Like the anus, the vaginal opening is surrounded by a ring of sphincter muscles. Although the vaginal opening can expand to accommodate the passage of a baby at childbirth, under conditions of tension these muscles involuntarily contract, making it difficult to insert an object, including a tampon, into the vagina. The vaginal opening may be covered by a *hymen,* a thin membrane.

Consideration

Probably no other body part has caused as much grief to so many women as the hymen, which has been regarded throughout history as proof of virginity. A newly wed woman who was thought to be without a hymen was often returned to her parents, disgraced by exile, or even tortured and killed. It has been a common practice in many societies to parade a bloody bedsheet after the wedding night as proof of the bride's virginity. The anxieties caused by the absence of a hymen persist even today; in Japan and other countries, sexually experienced women may have a plastic surgeon reconstruct a hymen before marriage. Yet the hymen is really a poor indicator of virtue. Some women are born without a hymen or with incomplete hymens. In others, the hymen is accidentally ruptured by vigorous physical activity or insertion of a tampon. In some women, the hymen may not tear but only stretch during sexual intercourse. Even most doctors cannot easily determine whether a female is a virgin.

Urethral Opening

Just above the vaginal opening is the urethral opening where urine passes from the body. A short tube, the *urethra,* connects the bladder (where urine collects) with the urethral opening. Because of the shorter length of the female urethra and its close proximity to the anus, women are more susceptible than men to cystitis, a bladder inflammation.

Female Internal Anatomy and Physiology

The internal sex organs of the female include the vagina, uterus, and paired Fallopian tubes and ovaries (see Figure ST2.2).

Vagina

Leading from the vaginal opening into the woman's body is the *vagina,* a thin walled elastic canal. In addition to receiving the penis during intercourse, the vagina functions as a passageway for menstrual flow and as the birth canal. The walls of the vagina are normally collapsed. Thus the vagina is actually a potential space.

Consideration

The vagina is a self-cleansing organ. The bacteria that are found naturally in the vagina help to destroy other potentially harmful bacteria. In addition, secretions from the vaginal walls help to maintain its normally acidic environment. The use of feminine hygiene sprays, as well as excessive douching, may cause irritation, allergic reactions, and in some cases, vaginal infection by altering the normal chemical balance of the vagina.

Some researchers believe that there is an extremely sensitive area in the front wall of the vagina 1 to 2 inches into the vaginal opening. The spot swells during stimulation, and although a woman's initial response may be a need to urinate, continued stimulation generally leads to orgasm (Perry & Whipple, 1981). Other researchers disagree about the existence of the so-called "Grafenberg spot," or "G spot," named for gynecologist Ernest Grafenberg who discovered it:

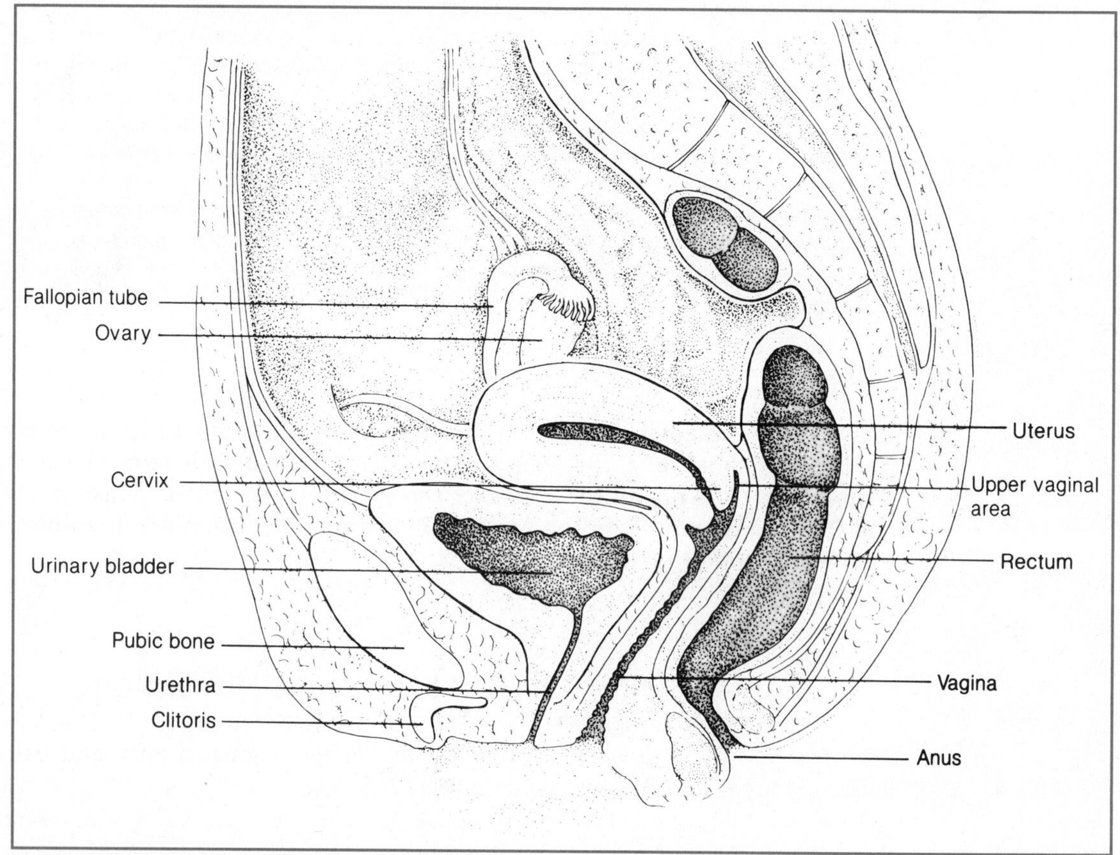

FIGURE ST2.2 INTERNAL FEMALE SEXUAL AND REPRODUCTIVE ORGANS

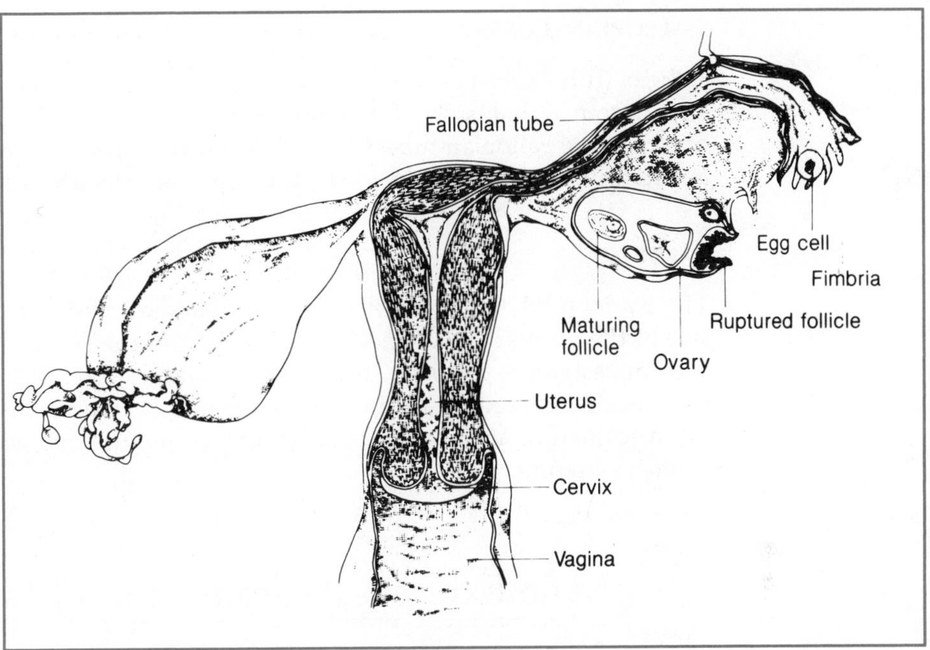

FIGURE ST2.3 THE ANATOMICAL RELATIONSHIPS OF THE VAGINA, CERVIX, UTERUS, FALLOPIAN TUBES, AND OVARIES

The ovaries are secured in the abdominal cavity by ligaments. The right ovary in the diagram has been opened to illustrate the progressive stages in the development of a follicle. A follicle has just ruptured, and the mature egg cell is swept into the funneled end of the Fallopian tube, the *fimbria*, by the action of cilia.

> The "G spot" does *not* exist as such, and the potential professional use of this term would be not only incorrect but also misleading. . . . The *entire* extent of the anterior wall of the vagina (rather than *one* specific spot), as well as the more deeply situated tissues, *including* the urinary bladder and urethral region, are extremely sensitive, being richly endowed with nerve endings. (Hock, 1983, p. 166)

In one study, 48 women volunteered to allow one of several physicians to stimulate them digitally to assess the degree to which they felt erotic sensitivity in their vaginas. Of the 48 women, 45 reported erotic sensitivity located, in most cases, on the anterior wall of the vagina; of those, 66.7 percent either reached orgasm or requested the physician to stop stimulation short of orgasm. The researchers concluded that the study supported the idea of erotic sensitivity in the vagina but that it did not support the idea of a particular location (Alzate & Dippsy, 1984).

Uterus

The *uterus* (YOOT-uh-ruhs), or *womb,* resembles a small, inverted pear, which measures about 3 inches long and 3 inches wide at the top in women who have not given birth. A fertilized egg becomes implanted in the wall of the uterus and continues to grow and develop there until delivery. At the lower end of the uterus is the *cervix,* an opening that leads into the vagina.

Fallopian Tubes

Fallopian (fuh-LOH-pee-uhn) *tubes* (see Figure ST2.3) extend about 4 inches laterally from either side of the uterus to the ovaries. Fertilization normally occurs in the Fallopian tubes. The tubes transport the *ovum,* or egg, by means of *cilia* (hairlike structures) down the tube and into the uterus.

Ovaries

The *ovaries* (OH-vuhr-eez) are two almond-shaped structures, one on either side of the uterus. The ovaries produce eggs and the female hormones estrogen and progesterone. At birth, the ovaries contain about 400,000 immature ova total, each enclosed in a thin capsule forming a follicle. Some of the follicles begin to mature at puberty; only about 400 mature ova will be released in a woman's lifetime.

Male External Anatomy and Physiology

Although they differ in appearance, many structures of the male (see Figure ST2.4) and female genitals develop from the same embryonic tissue (the penis and the clitoris, for example).

Penis

The *penis* (PEE-nihs) is the primary male sexual organ. In the unaroused state, the penis is soft and hangs between the legs. When sexually stimulated, the penis enlarges and becomes erect, enabling penetration of the vagina. The penis functions not only to deposit sperm in the female's vagina but also as a passageway from the bladder to eliminate urine. In cross section, the penis can be seen to consist of three parallel cylinders of tissue containing many cavities, two *corpora cavernosa* (cavernous bodies) and a *corpus spongiosum* (spongy body) through which the urethra passes. The penis has numerous blood vessels; when stimulated, the arteries dilate and blood enters faster than it can leave. The cavities of the cavernous and spongy bodies fill with blood, and pressure against the fibrous membranes causes the penis to become erect. The head of the penis is called the *glans.* At birth, the glans is covered by *foreskin.* The surgical procedure in which the foreskin is pulled forward and cut off is known as *circumcision.*

Consideration

Circumcision was performed by the Egyptians as early as 4000 B.C. and was an early religious rite for members of the Jewish and Moslem faiths. To Jewish people, circumcision symbolizes the covenant with God made by Abraham. Today, the primary reason for performing circumcision is to ensure proper hygiene. The smegma that can build up under the foreskin is a potential breeding ground for infection. But circumcision is a rather drastic procedure merely to ensure proper hygiene, which, as the Academy of Pediatrics suggests, can just as easily be accomplished by pulling back the foreskin and cleaning the glans during normal bathing. However, circumcision is indicated when the foreskin will not retract.

SCROTUM

The *scrotum* (SCROH-tuhm) is the sac located below the penis, which contains the *testes.* Beneath the skin covering the scrotum is a thin layer of muscle fibers that contract when it is cold, helping to draw the testes (testicles) closer to the body to keep the temperature of the sperm constant. Sperm can only be produced at a temperature several degrees lower than normal body temperature; any prolonged variation can result in sterility.

Consideration

It is particularly hazardous for a male to contract a case of the mumps, a viral infection that often causes swelling of the testicles. The sheath in which the testes are enclosed does not readily expand, and the resulting pressure can cause sterility.

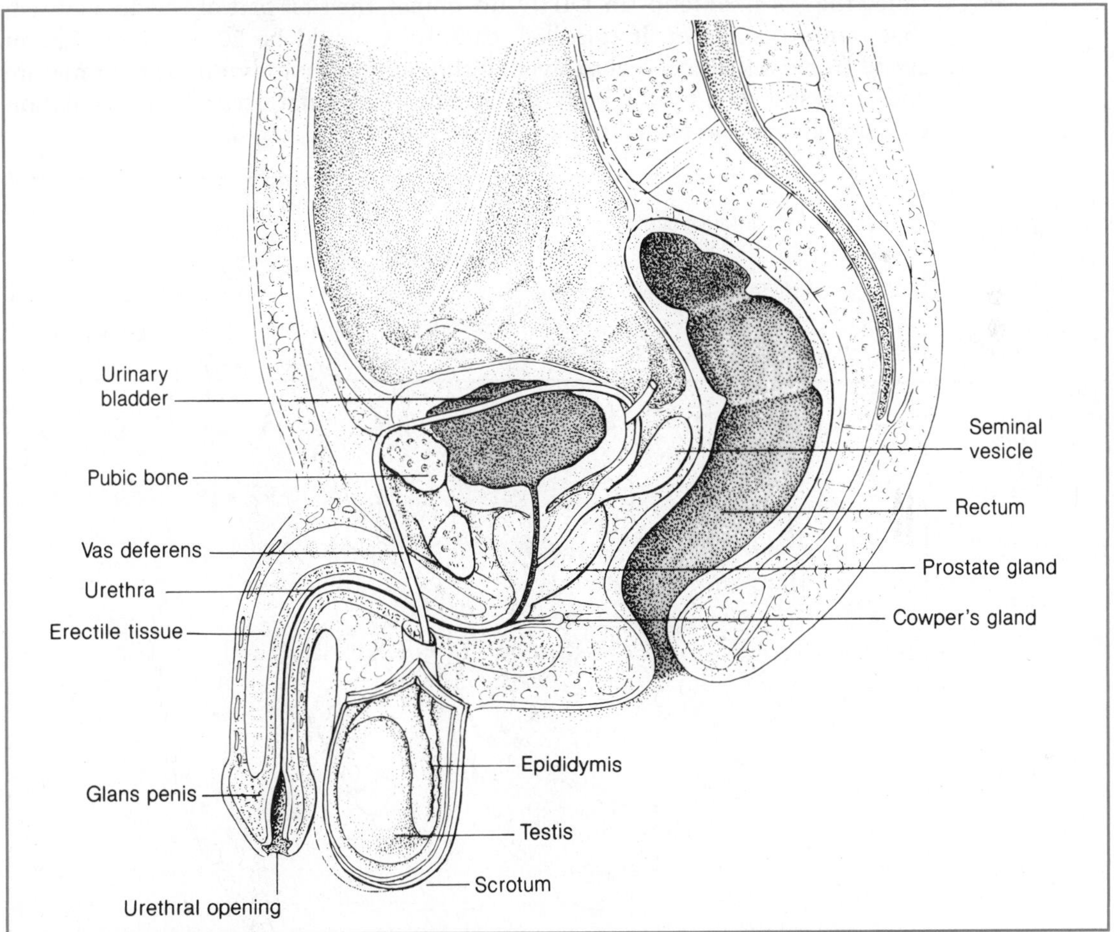

FIGURE ST2.4 INTERNAL AND EXTERNAL MALE SEXUAL ORGANS

Male Internal Anatomy and Physiology

The male internal organs, often referred to as the reproductive organs, include the testes, where the sperm is produced, a duct system to transport the sperm out of the body, and some additional structures that produce the seminal fluid in which the sperm is mixed before ejaculation.

TESTES

The male gonads—the paired testes, or testicles—develop from the same embryonic tissue as the female gonads (the ovaries). The two oval-shaped testicles are suspended in the scrotum by the *spermatic cord* and enclosed within a fibrous sheath. The function of the testes is to produce spermatozoa and male hormones, primarily testosterone (see Figure ST2.5).

DUCT SYSTEM

Several hundred *seminiferous tubules* come together to form a tube in each testicle called the *epididymis* (ehp-uh-DIHD-uh-muhs), the first part of the duct system that transports sperm. If uncoiled, each tube would be 20 feet long. Sperm spend from two to six weeks traveling through the epididymus as they mature and are reabsorbed by the body if ejaculation does not occur. One ejaculation contains an average of 360 million sperm cells.

FIGURE ST2.5 INTERNAL STRUCTURES OF THE HUMAN MALE TESTES, ILLUSTRATING THE COMPLEX OF DUCTS INVOLVED IN SPERM MANUFACTURE AND TRANSPORT

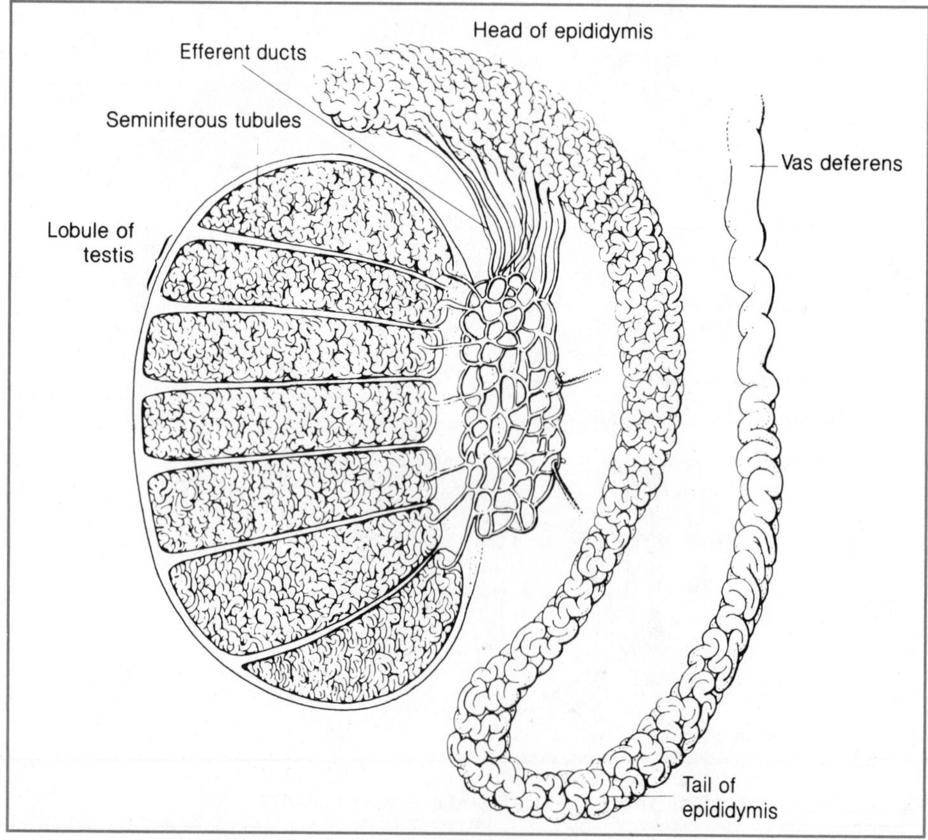

The sperm leave the scrotum through the second part of the duct system, the *vas deferens* (vas-DEF-uh-renz). These 14- to 16-inch paired ducts transport the sperm from the epididymis up and over the bladder to the prostate gland. Rhythmic contractions during ejaculation force the sperm into the paired ejaculatory ducts that run through the prostate gland. The entire length of this portion of the duct system is less than 1 inch. It is here that the sperm mix with seminal fluid to form *semen* before being propelled to the outside through the urethra.

Seminal Vesicles and Prostate Gland

The *seminal vesicles* resemble two small sacs, each about 2 inches in length, located behind the bladder. These vesicles secrete their own fluids, which empty into the ejaculatory duct to mix with sperm and fluids from the prostate gland.

Most of the seminal fluid comes from the *prostate gland,* a chestnut-sized structure located below the bladder and in front of the rectum. The fluid is alkaline and serves to protect the sperm in the more acidic environments of the male urethra and female vagina.

A small amount of clear, sticky fluid is also secreted into the urethra before ejaculation by two pea-sized *Cowper's,* or *bulbourethral, glands* located below the prostate gland. This protein rich fluid prolongs sperm life.

Consideration

The fluid secreted by the Cowper's glands can often be noticed on the tip of the penis during sexual arousal. It may contain stray sperm, so that withdrawal of the penis from the vagina before ejaculation is a risky method of birth control.

Sexually Transmitted Diseases (STDs)

Contents

SEXUALLY TRANSMITTED DISEASES (STDs) are also known as *venereal diseases.* Venus was the Roman goddess of love, and since some diseases are transmitted through various acts of love (kissing, cunnilingus, fellatio, intercourse), the term "venereal" (from Venus) has been used to describe such diseases. STDs are also referred to as *social diseases,* because they are contracted primarily through sociosexual contact. In effect, any person who has physical or sexual contact with someone who has a sexually transmitted disease may get that disease. The exposure may be through heterosexual or homosexual contacts. Table ST3.1 lists some of the myths and facts about STDs. We will review some of the more common STDs in the following sections.

Gonorrhea

Also known as "the clap," "the whites," and "morning drop," gonorrhea is the second most communicable disease in the United States (the first is the common cold). *Communicable* means that, like the common cold, the disease is easily "caught" from someone who has it.

Data – About 900,000 cases of gonorrhea are reported every year. Most new cases are contracted by people between the ages of 20–24. (U.S. Department of Health and Human Services, 1985)

Individuals most often contract gonorrhea through having genital contact with someone who is carrying the *gonococcus* (gahn-uh-KAH-us) *bacteria.* These bacteria live in the urethra and around the cervix of the female and in the urinary tract of the male. During intercourse, some of the bacteria are transferred from the mucous membranes inside the urethra of one gender to the other. The bacteria may also enter the throat during oral–genital contact or the rectum during anal intercourse.

TABLE ST3.1 MYTHS AND FACTS ABOUT SEXUALLY TRANSMITTED DISEASES (STDs)

Myth	*Fact*
STDs in the genitals cannot be transmitted to the mouth, and vice versa.	Transmission of STD infections from mouth to genitals and vice versa does occur.
If you have syphilis or gonorrhea, you will know it.	Some infected people show no signs of having syphilis or gonorrhea until many years later.
You can avoid having to see a physician by treating your suspected STD infection at home.	Only a physician can recommend a treatment plan for STDs.
You cannot have more than one STD at a time.	More than one-half of the women who visited one STD clinic had two or more STDs.
Birth-control pills protect you from STDs.	Birth-control pills may increase a woman's chance of contracting various STDs when exposed.
Once you have been cured of an STD, you cannot get it again.	You can get an STD infection any time you come into contact with it, whether you have already had it or not.
Syphilis and gonorrhea can be contracted by contact with a toilet seat.	The germs of these diseases cannot live in the open air.

Although some infected men show no signs, 80 percent do so between three and eight days after exposure. They begin to discharge a thick, white pus from the penis and to feel pain or discomfort during urination. They may also have swollen lymph glands in the groin. Women are more likely to show no signs of the infection, but when they do, they are sometimes in the form of a discharge from the vagina along with a burning sensation. More often, a woman becomes aware of gonorrhea only after she feels extreme discomfort, which is a result of the untreated infection traveling up into her uterus and Fallopian tubes. *Pelvic inflammatory disease* (PID) is the term used to describe the inflammation in these areas caused by the gonococci or other bacteria.

Consideration

Undetected and untreated gonorrhea is dangerous. Not only does the infected person pass on this disease to the next partner, but other undesirable consequences may also result. The bacteria may affect the brain, joints, and reproductive systems. Both men and women may develop meningitis (inflammation of the tissues surrounding the brain and spinal cord), arthritis, and sterility. In men, the urethra may become blocked, necessitating frequent visits to a physician to clear the passage for urination. Infected women may have spontaneous abortions and premature or stillborn infants.

Syphilis

Although syphilis is less prevalent than gonorrhea, the effects of syphilis are more devastating and include mental illness, blindness, heart disease—even death. The *spirochete* (SPY-roh-keet) *bacteria* —the villain germs—enter the body through mucous membranes that line various body openings. With your tongue, feel the inside of your cheek. This is a layer of mucous membrane—the substance in which spirochetes thrive. Similar membranes are in the vagina and urethra of the penis. If you kiss or have genital contact with someone harboring these bacteria, they can be absorbed into your mucous membranes and cause syphilitic infection. Your syphilis will then progress through at least three or four stages.

Data – About 70,000 cases of syphilis are reported every year. (U.S. Department of Health and Human Services, 1985).

In stage one (primary-stage syphilis), a small sore will appear at the site of the infection between 10 and 90 days after exposure. The *chancre* (SHANK–er), as it is called, shows on the tip of the man's penis, in the labia or cervix of the woman, or in either partner's mouth or rectum. The chancre neither hurts nor itches, and if left untreated, will disappear in three to five weeks. This disappearance encourages the person to believe that she or he is cured—one of the tricky aspects of syphilis. In reality, the disease is still present and doing great harm, even though there are no visible signs.

During the second stage (secondary-stage syphilis), beginning from two to 12 weeks after the chancre has disappeared, other signs of syphilis appear in the form of a rash all over the body or just on the hands or feet. Welts and sores may also occur, as well as fever, headaches, sore throat, and hair loss. Syphilis has been called "the great imitator" because it mimics so many other diseases (for example, infectious mononucleosis, cancer, and psoriasis). Whatever the symptoms, they too will disappear without treatment. The person may again be tricked into believing that nothing is wrong.

For about two-thirds of those with late, untreated syphilis (latent-stage syphilis), the disease seems to have gone away and left no subsequent effects. However, the spirochetes are still in the body and can attack any organ at any time. For the other one-third, serious harm results. Tertiary syphilis—the third stage—may disable or kill. Heart disease, blindness, brain damage, loss of bowel and bladder control, difficulty in walking, and impotence may result.

Aside from avoiding contact with a person infected with syphilis, early detection and treatment is essential. Blood tests and examination of material from the infected site can help to verify the existence of syphilis. But such tests are not always accurate. Blood tests reveal the presence of antibodies, not spirochetes, and it sometimes takes three months before the body produces detectable antibodies. Sometimes there is no chancre anywhere on the person's body.

Treatment for syphilis is similar to that for gonorrhea. Penicillin or other antibiotics (for those allergic to penicillin) are effective. Infected persons treated in the early stages can be completely cured with no ill effects. If the syphilis has progressed into the later stages, any damage that has been done cannot be repaired.

Consideration

Another problem with syphilis is the effect it has on the newborn of an infected woman. If the pregnant woman does not receive treatment, her baby is likely to be born with congenital syphilis. If she is treated by the eighteenth week of pregnancy, the fetus will not be affected.

Genital Herpes

Herpes refers to more than 50 viruses related by size, shape, internal composition, and structure. One such herpes is *genital herpes.* Whereas the disease has been known for at least 2,000 years, media attention to genital herpes is relatively new. Also known as *herpes simplex virus type 2* (HSV–2), genital herpes is a viral infection that is usually transmitted during sexual contact. Symptoms occur in the form of a cluster of small, painful blisters or sores on the penis or around the anus in men. In women, the blisters usually appear around the vagina but may also develop inside the vagina, on the cervix, and sometimes on the anus.

Another type of herpes, *labial* or *lip herpes,* originates in the mouth. Herpes simplex virus type 1 (HSV–1) is a biologically different virus with which people are more familiar as cold sores on the lips. These sores can be transferred to the genitals by the fingers or by oral-genital contact. In the past, genital and lip herpes had site specificity; HSV–1 was always found on the lips or in the mouth, and HSV–2 was always found in the genitals. But because of the increase in fellatio and cunnilingus, HSV–1 herpes may be found in the genitals and HSV–2 may be found in the lips.

Data – There are more than 450,000 physician-patient consultations about genital herpes annually. (Department of Health and Human Services, 1986a)

The first symptoms of genital herpes appear a couple of days to three weeks after exposure. At first, these symptoms may include an itching or burning sensation during urination, followed by headache, fever, aches, swollen glands, and—in women—vaginal discharge. The symptoms worsen over about 10 days, during which there is a skin eruption, followed by the appearance of painful sores, which soon break open and become extremely painful during genital contact or when touched. The acute illness may last from three to six weeks. "I've got herpes," said one sufferer, "and it's a very uneven discomfort. Somedays I'm okay, but other days I'm miserable."

As with syphilis, the symptoms of genital herpes subside (the sores dry up, scab over, and disappear) and the persons feels good again. But the virus settles in the nerve cells in the spinal column and may cause repeated outbreaks of the symptoms in about one-third of those infected.

Stress, menstruation, sunburn, fatigue, and the presence of other infections seem to be related to the reappearance of the virus. Although such recurrences are usually milder and of shorter duration than the initial outbreak, the resurfacing of the virus may occur throughout the person's life. "It's not knowing when the thing is going to come back that's the bad part about herpes," said one woman.

Consideration

The herpes virus is usually contagious during the time that a person has visible sores but not when the skin is healed. However, the infected person may have a mild recurrence yet be unaware that she or he is contagious. Aside from visible sores, itching, burning, or tingling sensations at the sore site also suggest that the person is contagious.

At the time of this writing, there is no cure for herpes. Because it is a virus, it does not respond to antibiotics as syphilis and gonorrhea do. A few procedures that help to relieve the symptoms and promote healing of the sores include seeing a physician to look for and treat any other genital infections near the herpes sores, keeping the sores clean and dry, taking hot sitz baths three times a day, and wearing loose-fitting cotton underwear to enhance air circulation. Proper nutrition, adequate sleep and exercise, and avoiding physical or mental stress help people to cope better with recurrences.

Acyclovir, marketed as Zovirax, is an ointment that can be applied directly on the sores, helps to relieve pain, speed healing, and reduce the amount of time that live viruses are present in the sores. A more effective tablet form of acyclovir which significantly reduces the rate of recurring episodes of genital herpes is also available. Once acyclovir is stopped, the herpetic recurrences resume. Acyclovir seems to make the symptoms of first-episode genital herpes more manageable, but it is less effective during subsequent outbreaks. Immu Vir—an alternative to acyclovir—is primarily for use by persons who have frequent outbreaks of genital herpes (once a month or more). This ointment is designed to reduce pain, healing time, and number of outbreaks. The drug has no known side effects.

Consideration

A person with genital herpes can prevent infecting someone else by avoiding genital contact until the sores have healed. It is also recommended that the male use a condom and the female use a diaphragm for two weeks after the sores have healed. But using the condom or diaphragm is not completely effective, because the herpes virus can pass through these synthetic membranes.

Coping with the psychological and emotional aspects of having genital herpes is often more difficult than coping with the physical aspects of the disease. Herpes victims typically go through a predictable pattern of shock, anger, bitterness, and depression. The latter may result in social withdrawal—not only from sexual encounters, but also from friends who are not sexual partners. Getting accurate information about the disease, dealing with a negative self-image, and learning how to tell someone who is sexually interested in them that they have herpes are among the problems facing herpes sufferers.

Chlamydia

Chlamydia (clah-MID-i-ah) has been described as the "the silent disease." It refers to one of two types of infection: (1) *Chlamydia trachomatis,* which may cause infections in the genitals, eyes, and lungs of humans, and (2) *Chlamydia psittici,* which primarily infects birds.

In this discussion, we will focus on *Chlamydia trachomatis,* or the CT variety. Public attention has been focused on CT as a result of gynecologists and urologists who, after seeing increasing numbers of sexually transmitted diseases that were not caused by gonorrhea, syphilis, or genital herpes, became aware of the devastating consequences of untreated chlamydial infections.

Several facts about chlamydia include:

1. *Chlamydia is a bacteria.* CT was once thought to be a virus, but improved laboratory techniques have permitted medical researchers to identify CT as a bacteria. The good news about this discovery is that bacteria can be successfully treated with antibiotics; a virus cannot be.
2. *Chlamydia is transmittable.* CT is easily transmitted from person to person via sexual contact. The microorganisms are most often found in the urethra of the male, the cervix, uterus, and Fallopian tubes of the female, or the rectums of either men or women. In addition to direct contact, CT

infections can occur indirectly by contact with, as examples, a towel, a handkerchief, or the side of a hot tub in which the bacteria are present.

Genital to eye transmission of the bacteria can also occur. If a person with a genital CT infection rubs his or her own eye or the eye of a partner after touching infected genitals, the bacteria can be transferred to the eye, and vice versa. Finally, infants can get CT as they pass through the cervix of their infected mothers during delivery.

3. *Numbers infected by chlamydia.* Because chlamydial infections are not reportable diseases in the United States, no national statistics on the disease are available and its prevalence must be estimated. The best estimates suggest that more people are infected with CT each year than all other sexually transmitted diseases combined.

   Worldwide, it is estimated that 300 million people contract sexually transmitted chlamydial infections each year. When the eye infection, *chlamydial trachoma,* is considered, over 500 million cases are contracted yearly. At least 2 million of the 200 million people who contract *chlamydial trachoma* each year are permanently blinded by the infection; most of these people live in Asia and Africa. The rate of blindness due to chlamydial infections in the United States is much lower, due to climate and the medication readily available to control the infection.
4. *Chlamydia occurs as a multiple infection.* Chlamydial infections rarely occur by themselves. One-half of all persons infected with gonorrhea also have CT. In most cases, only the gonorrhea is treated, leaving the CT to flourish and be transferred to subsequent sexual partners.
5. *Chlamydia is asymptomatic.* Women and men who are infected with CT usually do not know that they have the disease. The result is that they infect new partners unknowingly, who infect others unknowingly—and unendingly. CT rarely shows obvious symptoms, which accounts for its being known as "the silent disease."
6. *Chlamydia is curable if treated early.* Although delayed treatment can be devastating, CT is curable if it is diagnosed and treated before the bacteria has had a chance to flourish. CT has often been overlooked as a cause of genital infection, because laboratory tests were not sensitive and accurate enough to reveal the presence of this bacteria until recently.
7. *Persons likely to get chlamydia.* Heterosexuals, homosexuals, and bisexuals who have intercourse or oral or anal sex with several partners are more likely to contract chlamydia than people in these groups who restrict their sexual activity to one person. Individuals who have several sexual partners are also more likely to be having sex with people who also have several sexual partners—thus compounding the risk. In general, the greater the number of sexual partners, the greater the risk of contracting CT.
8. *Diagnosing chlamydia.* Although CT often exhibits no symptoms, symptoms do occur in some cases of CT. In men, the symptoms include pus from the penis, a sore on the penis, sore testis, or a bloody stool. In women, symptoms include low back pain, pelvic pain, a boil on the vaginal lip, or a bloody discharge. Symptoms in either gender include a sore on the tongue, a sore on the finger, pain during urination, or the sensation of needing to urinate frequently. Even in the absence of such

symptoms, a person who has had sex with an individual who has multiple sex partners should consult a physician. The presence of chlamydia can be determined by a laboratory test, using Chlamydiazyme, within 24 hours. The physician can then prescribe antibiotics as appropriate. (Chlamydia can be cured with tetracycline.)

Acquired Immune Deficiency Syndrome (AIDS)

Acquired immune deficiency syndrome (AIDS) represents the appearance in previously healthy individuals of various aggressive infections and malignancies. AIDS was first seen among homosexual and bisexual males with multiple sex partners (still the predominant victims), hemophiliacs, Haitian immigrants to the United States, and intravenous drug users.

Heterosexual women and men may now transmit the virus. Only a small percentage of AIDS victims have been infected during a blood transfusion. Fresh blood, semen, preseminal fluid, tears, and saliva infected with HTLV–III (human T–cell lymphotrophic virus III), also referred to as AIDS virus, must enter the bloodstream for the virus to be transmitted from one person to another. The AIDS virus is not superficially transmitted. Transmission can only occur if a "critical amount of an infected body fluid gains access to an individual's bloodstream through tissue capable of absorbing it. Rectal and vaginal linings are in this group" (Campbell, 1986).

Data – Less than 2 percent of all AIDS cases are thought to be transfusion-related. (Fincher, 1986)

The average incubation period from inoculation to development of AIDS in blood-transfusion patients is estimated to be five years. (Campbell, 1986)

AIDS attacks the immune system of the body and makes it vulnerable to infection. The incubation period for AIDS ranges from a few months to about two years. Symptoms of AIDS include swollen glands, persistent fever, persistent dry cough, bruiselike markings on the skin, weight loss, night sweats, and persistent diarrhea. *Kaposi's sarcoma* (KS), a type of cancer, and *Pneumocystis carinii pneumonia* (PCP) have been associated with AIDS.

AIDS patients often die because their bodies become incapable of combating other diseases and infections. Of those who contract AIDS, 80 percent are dead within three years.

A vaccine to prevent AIDS is currently being developed by medical researchers. A test, ELISA (enxyme-linked immunosorbent assay), can now assess the presence of antibodies in the bloodstream of a person who has been exposed to AIDS. This test does not confirm that the person has or will develop AIDS. However, the test should be taken by pregnant women who have been exposed to high-risk groups, because the AIDS virus can be passed on to their babies (Department of Health and Human Services, 1986b).

Consideration

To avoid getting AIDS, sexual intercourse, anal intercourse, and oral sex with persons in high-risk categories (homosexual and bisexual males; prostitutes; hemophiliacs; heterosexual partners in high-risk groups; heterosexuals exposed to high-risk partners) should be avoided. The current thinking is if you have sex with someone, you are having sex with everyone that person has had sex with in the last 10 years.

Once AIDS is contracted, the outlook is bleak.

Data – More than 35,000 people have been diagnosed as having AIDS, and more than 20,000 of those known to be infected with the AIDS virus have died by 1988. By 1991, more than 270,000 people will have been stricken, and more than 179,000 will have died. Regarding treatment, there is some evidence that the drug Azidothymidine (AZT) is useful in treating those infected with AIDS. However, AZT is not a cure and some AIDS victims are not helped by AZT.

The fear of contracting AIDS has begun to influence sexual choices.

Data – In a CBS poll of more than 800 respondents, one in four have altered their sexual behavior due to the fear of AIDS. (CBS Poll, 1986)

Getting Help

If you suspect that you have had contact with someone who has a sexually transmitted disease or if you have any symptoms of the STDs discussed in this Special Topic section, call the toll-free national VD hotline at 800–227–8922. You will not be asked to identify yourself; you will be given information about your symptoms and told to contact STD clinics in your area that offer confidential, free treatment.

A newsletter, *The Helper,* is published quarterly to provide the latest information for herpes sufferers. The newsletter can be obtained by writing to HELP (Herpetics Engaged in Living Productively); 260 Sheridan Avenue; Palo Alto, CA 94306. Herpes information is also available at 415–328–7710.

Duke University in Durham, North Carolina, has opened an AIDS clinic to treat AIDS victims (919–684–2660). For special information about AIDS, call 800–342–2437; in Washington, D.C. call 646–8182.

Consideration

In addition to getting medical attention or advice for yourself and your sexual partner, sexual contact with others should be avoided until your infection is cured or is no longer contagious. You should also exercise care if you masturbate. For example, if you accidentally touch a herpes sore during masturbation, be careful not to put your finger near your mouth or eye before washing your hands.

Prevention

The best way to avoid getting a sexually transmitted disease is to avoid sexual contact or to have contact only with partners who are not infected. This means restricting your sexual contacts to those who limit their relationships to one person. The person most likely to get a sexually transmitted disease has sexual relations with a number of partners or with a partner who has a variety of partners.

In addition to restricting sexual contacts, putting on a condom before the penis touches the partner's body will make it difficult for sexually transmitted diseases, including genital herpes, to pass from one person to another. After genital contact, it is also a good idea for the partners to urinate and to wash their genitals with soap and hot water.

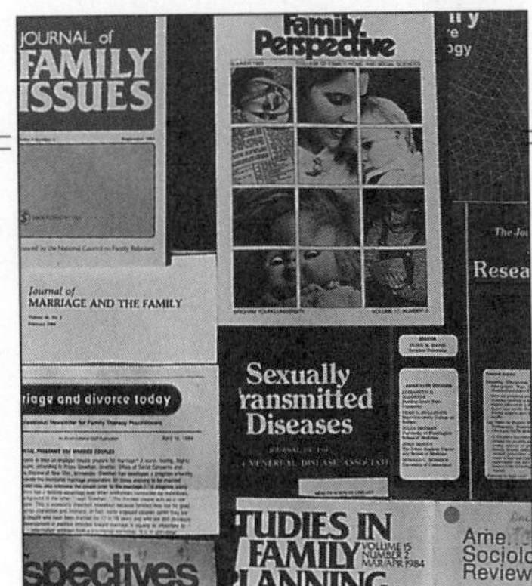

SPECIAL TOPIC 4

Resources and Organizations

Abortion*

Pro Choice

National Abortion Rights Action League
1424 K St., N.W.
Washington, DC 20005
Phone: 202–347–7774

Pro Life

National Right to Life Committee
419 Seventh St., N.W.
Washington, DC 20045
Phone: 202–626–8800

Birth Alternatives

Nurse–Midwives
American College of Nurse–Midwives
1522 K St., N.W., Suite 1120
Washington, DC 20005
Phone: 202–347–5445

Breastfeeding

LaLeche International, Inc.
9616 Minneapolis Ave.
Franklin Park, IL 60123
Phone: 312–455–7730

Child Abuse

National Committee for Prevention of Child Abuse
332 South Michigan Ave., Suite 1250
Chicago, IL 60604–4357
Phone: 312–663–3520

National Child Abuse Hotline
Phone: 800–422–4453

Child Care

Au Pair in America
100 Greenwich Ave.
Greenwich, CT 06830

Child Custody

Joint Custody Association
10606 Wilkins Ave.
Los Angeles, CA 90024
Phone: 213–475–5352

Divorced Mothers

Mothers without Custody
P.O. Box 56762
Houston, TX 77256–6762
Phone: 301–552–2319

Drugs

Cocaine National Treatment and Referral Information Service
Phone: 800–262–2463

Drug Abuse Hotline
Phone: 800–241–9746

Family Planning

Planned Parenthood Federation of America
2010 Massachusetts Ave., N.W.
Washington, DC 20036
Phone: 202–785–3351

Fertility

American Fertility Foundation
2131 Magnolia Ave., Suite 201
Birmingham, AL 35256
Phone: 205–251–9764

Resolve Inc.
5 Water St.
Arlington, MA
Phone: 617–643–2424

*These addresses and phone numbers were accurate at the time this section was printed.

Gender Equality

National Organization for Changing Men
P.O. Box 451
Watseka, IL 60970
Phone: 815–347–2279

National Organization for Women
1401 New York Ave., N.W.
Washington, DC 20004
Phone: 202–347–2279

Genetic Counseling

National Foundation for Jewish
Genetic Disease
45 Sutton Place South
New York, NY 10003
Phone: 212–371–1030

Healthy Baby

Healthy Mothers–Healthy Babies Coalition
Department of Public Affairs
600 Maryland Ave., S.W.
Washington, DC 20024
Phone: 202–638–5577

Homosexual Life Style

Parents and Friends of Lesbians and Gays
P.O. Box 24565
Los Angeles, CA 90024
Phone: 213–472–8952

Incest Prevention

Committee for Children
P.O. Box 15190
Seattle, WA 98115
Phone: 206–322–5050

Interracial Parenting

Council on Interracial Books for Children
1841 Broadway
New York, NY 10023
Phone: 212–757–5339

Marriage Enrichment

Training in Marriage Enrichment
American Guidance Service
Publisher's Building
P.O. Box 99
Circle Pines, MN 55014–1796
Phone: 612–786–4343

Marriage Therapy

American Association for Marriage
and Family Therapy
1717 K St., N.W., Suite 407
Washington, DC 20006
Phone: 202–429–1825

Mediation

Divorce Mediation Services
Association of Family and Conciliation Court
1227 Spruce St.
Boulder, CO
Phone: 303–447–8116

Ovum Transfer

Harbor–UCLA Medical Center
1000 West Carson St.
Torrance, CA 90509
Phone: 213–533–2345

Sex Education

Sex Information and Education Council
of the United States (SIECUS)
80 Fifth Ave.
New York, NY 10011
Phone: 212–929–2300

Sexual Therapy

American Association of Sex Educators,
Counselors, and Therapists (AASECT)
2000 N St., N.W., Suite 110
Washington, DC 20036

Masters and Johnson Institute
24 South Kings Highway
St. Louis, MO 63108
Phone: 314–361–2277

Loyola Sexual Dysfunction Clinic
Loyola University Hospital
2160 South First Ave.
Maywood, IL 60153
Phone: 312–531–3000

Sexual Dependency Unit
4101 Golden Valley
Minneapolis, MN 55422
Phone: 612–588–2771

Sexually Transmitted Diseases

AIDS Hotline
Phone: 800–342–AIDS

AZT Hotline
Phone: 800–843–9388

Centers for Disease Control
Technical Information Services
Bureau of State Services
Atlanta, GA 30333
Phone: 404–329–3311

Herpes Resource Information
260 Sheridan Ave.
Palo Alto, CA 94302
Phone: 415–328–7710

National VD Hotline
Phone: 800–227–8922
(in California: 800–982–5883)

Single Parenthood

Parents without Partners International
8807 Colesville Rd.
Silver Springs, MD 20910
Phone: 301–588–9354

Single Mothers by Choice
P.O. Box 7788, FDR Station
New York, NY 10150
Phone: 212–988–0993

Stepfamilies

Stepfamily Association of America, Inc.
28 Allegheny Ave., Suite 1307
Baltimore, MD 21204
Phone: 301–823–7570

Sterilization

Association for Voluntary
Sterilization, Inc.
122 East 42nd St.
New York, NY 10017
Phone: 212–573–8322

Test-tube Fertilization

Eastern Virginia Medical School
Norfolk General Hospital
Howard and Georgeanna Jones
Institute for Reproductive Medicine
825 Fairfax Ave.
Norfolk, VA 23507
Phone: 804–446–8948

Widowhood

Widowed Person's Service
American Association of Retired Persons
1909 K St., N.W.
Washington, DC 20049
Phone: 202–872–4700

References

PREFACE AND CHAPTER 1

Anderson, S. Cohesion, adaptability and communication: A test of an Olson circumplex model hypothesis. *Family Relations,* 1986, *35,* 289–293.

Axelson, L. Department of Family and Child Development, Virginia Polytechnic and State University, Blacksburg, Virginia. Personal communication, 1987.

Bean, F.D., Stephen, E.H., & Opitz, W. The Mexican origin population in the United States: A demographic overview. In De La Garza, R.O., F.D. Bean, C.M. Bonjean, R. Romo, and R. Alvarez (Eds.), *The Mexican American experience: An interdisciplinary anthology.* Austin, Texas: University of Texas Press, 1985. Pp. 33–56.

Brecher, E.M., & Brecher, J. Extracting valid sexological findings from severely flawed and biased population samples. *The Journal of Sex Research,* 1986, *22,* 6–20.

Hewlett, S.A. *A lesser life: The myth of women's liberation in America.* New York: William Morrow, 1986.

Hirschman, C., & Wong, M.G. The extraordinary educational attainment of Asian Americans: A search for historical evidence and explanations. *Social Forces,* 1986, *65,* 1–27.

Kohn, A. *False prophets.* New York: Basil Blackwell, 1987.

McLemore, S.D., & Romo, R. The origins and development of the Mexican American people. In De La Garza, R.O., F.D. Bean, C.M. Bonjean, R. Romo, and R. Alvarez (Eds.), *The Mexican American experience: An interdisciplinary anthology.* Austin, Texas: University of Texas Press, 1985. Pp. 3–33.

Mindel, C.H., & Habenstein, R.W. (Eds.), *Ethnic families in America: Patterns and variations,* 2d ed. New York: Elsevier, 1981.

National Center for Health Statistics: Births, marriages, divorces, and deaths for October 1986. *Monthly Vital Statistics Report, 35,* 10. DHHS Pub. No. (PHS), 87–1120. Hyattsville, Md.: U.S. Public Health Service, January 1987.

Norton, A.J., & Moorman, J.E. Current trends in marriage and divorce among American women. *Journal of Marriage and the Family,* 1987, *49,* 3–14.

Poussaint, A.F. Save the fathers. *Ebony,* August 1986, p. 43 et passim.

Staples, R. (Ed.). *The black family* (third edition). Belmont, Calif.: Wadsworth Publishing, 1987.

Staples, R., & Mirande, A. Racial and cultural variations among American families: A decennial review of the literature on minority families. *Journal of Marriage and the Family,* 1980, *42,* 157–173.

Statistical Abstract of the United States, 1987, 107th ed. Washington, D.C.: U.S. Bureau of the Census, 1986.

Tienda, M., & Ortiz, V. Hispancity and the 1980 census. *Social Science Quarterly,* 1986, *67,* 3–30.

Trotter, R.J. Stop blaming yourself. *Psychology Today,* February 1987, pp. 31–39.

Ts'ai, Y. *Family and property in Sung China.* Patricia B. Ebrey, Trans. Princeton, New Jersey: Princeton University Press, 1984.

Williams, D.A. Black problems become white. *Newsweek,* August 18, 1986, p. 7.

Zinn, M.B. Chicano men and masculinity. *The Journal of Ethnic Studies,* 1986, *10,* 29–44.

CHAPTER 2

Buehler, C.J., & Wells, B. Counseling the romantic. *Family Relations,* 1981, *30,* 452–458.

Davidson, B., Balswick, J., & Halverson, C. Affective self-disclosure and marital adjustment: A test of equity theory. *Journal of Marriage and the Family,* 1983, *45,* 93–102.

De Moja, C.A. Anxiety, self-confidence, jealousy, and romantic attitudes toward love in Italian undergraduates. *Psychological Reports,* 1986, *58,* 138.

Duffy, S.M., & Rusbult, C.E. Satisfaction and commitment in homosexual and heterosexual relationships. *Journal of Homosexuality,* 1985/1986, *12,* 1–24.

Family Protection Act. H.R. 614, a Bill introduced into the 98th Congress, 1983, in the House of Representatives by Mr. Hansen of Idaho.

Freedman, J.L. *Happy people.* New York: Harcourt Brace Jovanovich, 1978.

Green, R. Sexual identity of 37 children raised by homosexual or transsexual parents. *American Journal of Psychiatry,* 1978, *135,* 692–697.

Hansen, G.L. Marital satisfaction and jealousy among men. *Psychological Reports,* 1983, *52,* 363–366.

Hansen, G.L. Perceived threats and marital jealousy. *Social Psychology Quarterly,* 1985, *48,* 262–268.

Harry, J., & Lovely, R. Gay marriages and communities of sexual orientation. *Alternative Lifestyles,* 1979, *2,* 177–200.

Jay, K., & Young, A. *The gay report.* New York: Summit Books, 1979.

Jorgensen, S.R., & Gaudy, J.C. Self-disclosure and satisfaction in marriage: The relation examined. *Family Relations,* 1980, *29,* 281–288.

Kemper, T.D., & Bologh, R.W. What do you get when you fall in love? Some health status effects. *Sociology of Health and Illness,* 1981, *3,* 72–88.

Kinsey, A.C., Pomeroy, W.B., Martin, C.E., & Gebhard, P.H. *Sexual behavior in the human female.* Philadelphia: W.B. Saunders, 1953. Reprinted by permission of the Kinsey Institute for Research in Sex, Gender, and Reproduction, Inc. (Book reprinted in 1970 by Pocket Books).

Knox, D. Conceptions of love at three developmental levels. *Family Life Coordinator,* 1970, *19,* 151–157.

————. *What kind of love is yours?* Unpublished study, Department of Sociology, Anthropology, and Economics, East Carolina University, 1982.

————, & Sporakowski, M.J. Attitudes of college students toward love. *Journal of Marriage and the Family,* 1968, *30,* 638–642.

Lewis, R.A., Kosac, E.B., Milardo, R.M., & Grosnick, W.A. Commitment in same-sex love relationships. *Alternative Lifestyles,* 1981, *4,* 22–42.

Liebowitz, M. *The chemistry of love.* Boston, Mass.: Little, Brown, 1983.

Lockhart, B.D. The "other" intimacy. *Family Perspective,* 1983, *17,* 35–39.

Loewenstein, S.F. On the diversity of love-object orientations among women. *Journal of Social Work & Human Sexuality,* 1985, *3,* 7–24.

Lynch, J.J. *The broken heart: The medical consequences of loneliness in America.* New York: Basic Books, 1977.

Masters, W.H. & Johnson, V.E. *Human sexual response.* Boston, Mass.: Little, Brown, 1966.

Meredith, N. The gay dilemma. *Psychology Today,* January 1984, pp. 56–62.

Mirchandani, V.K. Attitudes toward love among blacks. Unpublished Master's thesis, East Carolina University, Greenville, N.C., 1973.

Money, J. *Love and sickness.* Baltimore: Johns Hopkins University Press, 1980.

Peele, S., & Brodsky, A. *Love and addiction.* New York: New American Library, 1976.

Peplau, L.A. What homosexuals want in relationships. *Psychology Today,* March 1981, pp. 28–38.

Petersen, J.R., Kretchmer, A., Hellis, B., Lever, J., & Hertz, B. The *Playboy* reader's sex survey, Part 1. *Playboy,* January 1983a, p. 108 et passim.

Pines, A., & Aronson, E. Antecedents, correlates, and consequences of sexual jealousy. *Journal of Personality,* 1983, *51,* 108–109.

Rettig, K.D., & Bubolz, M.M. Interpersonal resource exchanges as indicators of quality of marriage. *Journal of Marriage and the Family,* 1983, *45,* 497–509.

Rose, S. Is romance dysfunctional? *International Journal of Women's Studies,* 1985, *8,* 250–265.

Rubenstein, C. The modern art of courtly love. *Psychology Today,* July 1983, pp. 40–49.

Rubin, Z., Hill, C.T., Peplau, L.A., & Dunkel-Schetter, C. Self-disclosure in dating couples: Sex roles and the ethic of openness. *Journal of Marriage and the Family,* 1980, *42,* 305–318.

Schacter, S. The interaction of cognitive and physiological determinants of emotional state. In Berkowitz, L. (Ed.), *Advances in experimental social psychology.* New York: Academic Press, 1964. Pp. 49–80.

Simmons, C.H., Kolke, A.V., and Shimizu, H. Attitudes toward romantic love among American, German, and Japanese students. *The Journal of Social Psychology,* 1986, *126,* 327–336.

Statistical Abstract of the United States, 1987, 107th ed. Washington, D.C.: U.S. Bureau of the Census, 1986.

Sternberg, R.J. A triangular theory of love. *Psychological Review,* 1986, *93,* 119–135.

Stewart, S.A. Sex is casual, despite new concerns. *USA Today,* 1986c, p. 5d.

Story, M.D. A comparison of university student experience with various sexual outlets in 1974 and 1984. *Journal of Sex Education and Therapy,* 1985, *11,* 35–41.

Trotter, R.J. The three faces of love. *Psychology Today,* September 1986, pp. 46–54.

Vannoy, R. *Sex without love: A philosophical exploration.* Buffalo, N.Y.: Prometheus Books, 1980.

Walsh, A. Love and human authenticity in the works of Freud, Marx, and Maslow. *Free Inquiry in Creative Sociology,* 1986, *14,* 21–26.

Walster, E., & Walster, G.W. *A new look at love.* Reading, Mass.: Addison-Wesley, 1978.

Zinik, G. Identity conflict or adaptive flexibility? Bisexuality reconsidered. *Journal of Homosexuality,* 1985, *11,* 7–20.

CHAPTER 3

Albert, A.A., & Porter, J.R. Children's gender role stereotypes. *Journal of Cross-Cultural Psychology,* 1986, *17,* 45–66.

Alperson, B.L., & Friedman, W.J. Some aspects of the interpersonal phenomenology of heterosexual dyads with respect to sex-role stereotypes. *Sex Roles,* 1983, *9,* 453–474.

Alvarez, R. The psycho-historical and socioeconomic development of the Chicano community in the United States. In R.O. De La Garga, F.D. Bean, C.M. Bonjean, R. Romo, & R. Alvarez (Eds.). *The Mexican American experience.* Austin: University of Texas Press, 1985. Pp. 32–56.

Astrachan, A. *How men feel.* New York: Anchor Press, 1986.

Bales, F. Television use and confidence in television by blacks and whites in four selected years. *Journal of Black Studies,* 1986, *16,* 283–291.

Baca Zinn, M. Gender and ethnic identity among Chicanos. *Frontiers,* 1980, *2,* 18–24.

Billingham, R.E., & Sack, A.R. Gender differences in college students' willingness to participate in alternative marriage and family relationships. *Family Perspective,* 1986, *20,* 37–44.

Bonkowski, S.E., Boomhower, S.J., & Bequette, S.Q. What you don't know *can* hurt you: Unexpressed fears and feelings of children from divorcing families. *Journal of Divorce,* 1985, *9,* 33–46.

Bouchard, T.J. Do environmental similarities explain the similarity in intelligence of identical twins reared apart? *Intelligence,* 1983, *7,* 175–184.

Bouchard, T.J., Eckert, E., Resnick, S., & Keys, M. The Minnesota study of twins reared apart: Project description and sample results. *Intelligence,* 1980. Reprinted by permission.

Caplan, P.J. Single life and married life. *International Journal of Women's Studies,* 1985, *8,* 6–11.

Cash, T.F., Winstead, C.A., & Janda, L.H. The great American shape-up. *Psychology Today,* April 1986, 30–37.

Caulfield, M.D. Sexuality in human evolution: What is "natural" in sex? *Feminist Studies,* 1985, *11,* 343–364.

Chafetz, J.S., & Dworkin, A.G. Work pressure similarity for homemakers, managers, and professionals. *Free Inquiry in Creative Sociology,* 1984, *12,* 47–50.

Cleaver, G. Marriage enrichment by means of a structured communication program. *Family Relations,* 1987, *36,* 49–54.

Cloninger, C.R. Is there a genetic predisposition to behavior?: Adoption study. *Marriage and Divorce Today,* 1986, 11(31), 3–4.

Crossman, S.M., & Edmondson, J.E. Personal and family resources supportive of displaced homemakers' financial adjustment. *Family Relations,* 1985, *34,* 365–474.

Fabes, R.A., & Laner, M.R. How the sexes perceive each other. *Sex Roles,* 1986, 15(3/4), 129–143.

Farrell, W. *Why men are the way they are.* New York: McGraw-Hill, 1986.

Frankel, F., & Rathvon, S. *Whatever happened to Cinderella?* New York: St. Martin's Press, 1980.

Freud, S. *New introductory lectures in psychoanalysis.* (J. Strachey, Ed. and trans.). New York: W.W. Norton, 1965. Originally published, 1933.

__________. Some psychological consequences of an anatomical distinction between the sexes (1925). In J. Strouse (Ed.). *Women and analysis.* New York: Grossman, 1974.

Gerdes, E.P., & Garber, D.M. Sex bias in hiring: Effects of job demands and applicant competence. *Sex Roles,* 1983, *9,* 307–319.

Gilson, E., and Kane, S. *Unnecessary choices.* New York: William Morrow, 1987.

Green, R. Sexual identity of 37 children raised by homosexual or transsexual parents. *American Journal of Psychiatry,* 1978, *135,* 692–697.

Greenglass, E.R. A social-psychological view of marriage for women. *International Journal of Women's Studies,* 1985, *8,* 24–31.

Greif, G.L. Children and housework in the single father family. *Family Relations,* 1985, *34,* 353–357.

Haggstrom, G.W., Kanouse, D.E., & Morrison, P.A. Accounting for the educational shortfall of mothers. *Journal of Marriage and the Family,* 1986, *48,* 175–186.

Hall, E. June Reinisch: New directions for the Kinsey Institute. *Psychology Today,* June 1986, 33–39.

Harvey, P.A. Evolution or creation of sex roles: Do they pay the same? *Free Inquiry in Creative Sociology,* 1986, *14,* 93–99.

Harvey, P.H. Macho and his mate. *Free Inquiry in Creative Sociology,* 1983, *11,* 167–170.

Herzog, A.R., Bachman, J.G., & Johnston, L.D. Paid work, child care, and housework: A national survey of high-school seniors' preferences for sharing responsibilities between husband and wife. *Sex Roles,* 1983, *9,* 109–135.

Kalin, R., & Lloyd, C.A. Sex role identity, sex-role ideology, and marital adjustment. *International Journal of Women's Studies,* 1985, *8,* 32–39.

Kenkel, W.F., & Gage, B.A. The restricted and gender-typed occupational aspirations of young women: Can they be modified? *Family Relations,* 1983, *32,* 129–138.

Keown, A.L., & Keown, C.F. Factors of success for women in business. *International Journal of Women's Studies,* 1985, *8,* 278–285.

Kessler, R.C., & Neighbors, H.W. A new perspective on the relationships among race, social class, and psychological distress. *Journal of Health and Social Behavior,* 1986, *27,* 107–115.

Kniesner, T. The feminization of poverty. *Social Science,* 1986, *71,* 6–10.

Koberg, C.S. Sex and situational influences on the use of power: A follow-up study. *Sex Roles,* 1985, *13,* 625–640.

Kohlberg, L. A cognitive-developmental analysis of children's sex-role concepts and attitudes. In E.E. Macoby (Ed.). *The development of sex differences.* Stanford, Calif.: Stanford University Press, 1966.

____________. State and sequence: The cognitive-developmental approach to socialization. In D.A. Goslin (Ed.). *Handbook of socialization theory and research.* Chicago: Rand McNally, 1969. Pp. 347–480.

Kohn, A. How to succeed without even trying. *Psychology Today,* September 1986, 22–28.

Marshall, M.M.S. Marital power, role expectations, and marital adjustment. *International Journal of Women's Studies,* 1985, *8,* 40–46.

McBroom, W.H. Changes in role orientation of women. *Journal of Family Issues,* 1986, *7,* 149–159.

McVicar, P., & Herman, A. Assertiveness, self-actualization, and locus of control in women. *Sex Roles,* 1983, *9,* 555–562.

Mednick, S. Crime in the family tree. *Psychology Today,* March 1985, 58–61.

Mintz, L.B., & Betz, N.E. Sex differences in the nature, realism, and correlates of body image. *Sex Roles,* 1986, 15(3/4), 185–195.

Mirowsky, J. Depression and marital power: An equity model. *American Journal of Sociology,* 1985, *91,* 557–592.

Moore, H. Job satisfaction and women's spheres of work. *Sex Roles,* 1985, *13,* 663–678.

Paludi, M.A., & Bauer, W.D. Goldberg revisited: What's in an author's name? *Sex Roles,* 1983, *9,* 387–396.

Petersen, D.M., & Dressel, P.L. Equal time for women: Social notes on the male strip show. *Urban Life,* 1982, *11,* 185–208.

Rabine, L.W. Romance in the age of electronics: Harlequin Enterprises. *Feminist Studies,* 1985, *11,* 39–60.

Rhodes, A.L. Effects of religious denomination on sex differences in occupational expectations. *Sex Roles,* 1983, *9,* 93–108.

Ridley, C.A., Lamke, L.K., Avery, A.W., & Harrell, J.E. The effects of interpersonal skills training on sex-role identity of premarital dating partners. *Journal of Research and Personality,* 1982, *16,* 335–342.

Riemer, J.W., & Bridwell, L.M. How women survive in nontraditional occupations. *Free Inquiry in Creative Sociology,* 1982, *10,* 153–158.

Robinson, C.C., & Morris, J.T. The gender-stereotyped nature of Christmas toys received by 36–, 48–, and 60–month old children: A comparison between nonrequested vs. requested toys. *Sex Roles,* 1986, 15(1/2), 21–32.

Rombough, S., & Ventimiglia, J.C. Sexism: A tri-dimensional phenomenon. *Sex Roles,* 1981, *7,* 747–755.

Rubenstein, C. What's become of the American family? *Family Circle,* October 1985, 24 et passim.

Sadker, M., & Sadker, D. Sexism in the schoolroom of the '80s. *Psychology Today,* March 1985, 54–57.

Salholz, E., Ambramson, P., Doherty, S., Michael, R., & Weathers, D. Feminism's Identity Crisis. *Newsweek,* March 31, 1986, 58–59.

Sanchez, A.R., & King, M. Mexican Americans' use of counseling services: Cultural and institutional factors. *Journal of College Student Personnel,* 1986, *27,* 344–349.

Sheppard, M.A., Wright, D., & Goodstadt, M.S. *Adolescence,* 1985, *22,* 949–958.

Stainton, M.C. The fetus: A growing member of the family. *Family Relations,* 1985, *34,* 321–326.

Statistical Abstract of the United States, 1987, 107th ed. Washington, D.C.: U.S. Bureau of the Census, 1986.

Stump, J.B. *What's the difference?* New York: William Morrow, 1985.

Sun-Hee, L. Women and education in Korea. *Korea Journal,* 1985, *25,* 16–24.

Thompson, C. A new vision of masculinity. *Family Life Educator,* 1986, *4,* 4–7.

Thompson, J.K. Larger than life. *Psychology Today,* April 1986, 39–44.

Usher, S., & Fels, M. The challenge of feminism and career for the middle-aged woman. *International Journal of Women's Studies,* 1985, *8,* 47–57.

Verbrugge, L.M. Gender and health: An update on hypotheses and evidence. *Journal of Health and Social Behavior,* 1985, *26,* 156–182.

Wagner, D.G., Ford, R.S., & Ford, T.W. Can gender differences in equality be reduced? *American Sociological Review,* 1986, *51,* 47–61.

Wilson, K., & Knox, D. Sex role identity and dating appeal. Paper presented at the annual meeting of the National Council on Family Relations, Milwaukee, Wis., 1981. Used by permission.

CHAPTER 4

Atwater, L. *The extramarital connection: Sex, intimacy, identity.* New York: Irvington Publishers, 1982.

Bachrach, C.A., & Horn, M.C. Marriage and first intercourse, marital dissolution and remarriage: United States, 1982. *Advance Data from Vital and Health Statistics,* 1985, No. 107.

Beach, S.R.H., Jouriles, E.N., & O'Leary, K.D. Extramarital sex: Impact on depression and commitment in couples seeking marital therapy. *Journal of Sex and Marital Therapy,* 1985, *11,* 99–108.

Belcastro, P.A. Sexual behavior differences between black and white students. *The Journal of Sex Research,* 1985, *21,* 56–67.

Bell, R.R., & Coughey, K. Premarital sexual experience among college females, 1958, 1968, and 1978. *Family Relations,* 1980, *29,* 353–357.

Bermant, G. Sexual behavior: Hard times with the Coolidge Effect. In M.H. Siegel & H.P. Zeigler (Eds.), *Psychological research. The inside story.* New York: Harper & Row, 1976.

Blumstein, P., & Schwartz, P. *American couples.* New York: William Morrow, 1983.

Booth, A., Brinkerhoff, D.B., & White, L.K. The impact of parental divorce on courtship. *Journal of Marriage and the Family,* 1984, *46,* 85–94.

Bowe, C. What are men like today? *Cosmopolitan,* May 1986, pp. 263 et passim.

Britton, T. Lenoir Community College, Kinston, N.C. Personal communication, 1984.

Brown, S.V. Premarital sexual permissiveness among black adolescent females. *Social Psychology Quarterly,* 1985, *48,* 381–387.

Cook, K., Kretchmer, A., Nellis, B., Petersen, J.R., Lever, J., & Hertz, R. The *Playboy* reader's sex survey, Part 5. *Playboy,* October 1983, p. 92.

Crenshaw, T. AIDS today. *Fast Copy.* NBC (National Broadcasting Company) Television, May 18, 1986.

Darling, C.A., & Davidson, J., Sr. Female sexual satisfaction: The effect of sexual experience. Paper presented at the Southern Sociological Society, Knoxville, Tennessee, 1984. Used by permission.

Diederen, I., & Rorer, L. Do attitudes and background influence college students' sexual behavior? Paper presented at the annual meeting of the American Psychological Association, Washington, D.C., 1982. Used by permission.

Earle, J.R., & Perricone, P.J. Correlates of premarital intercourse at a small southern university: Survey data for 1970, 1975, and 1981. Unpublished manuscript, 1982. Used by permission.

__________. Premarital sexuality: A ten-year study of attitudes and behavior on a small university campus. *The Journal of Sex Research,* 1986, *22,* 304–310.

Encyclopedia of Associations, 20th ed. Detroit, Mich.: Gale Research Co., 1986.

Falwell, J. Falwell addresses nation live on moral and spiritual state of the union. *Moral Majority Report,* 1984, 5(3), s–1.

Gallup Report—Premarital sex. Report No. 237. Princeton, N.J.: June 1985, p. 28.

Graham, S. Lecture to young men, on chasity, intended also for the serious consideration of parents and guardians, 10th ed. Boston: C.H. Pierce, 1848.

Green, V. Experiential factors in childhood and adolescent sexual behavior: Family interaction and previous sexual experiences. *The Journal of Sex Research,* 1985, *27,* 157–182.

Greenblat, C.S. The salience of sexuality in the early years of marriage. *Journal of Marriage and the Family,* 1983, *45,* 289–299.

Herold, E.S., & Way, L. Oral-genital sexual behavior in a sample of university females. *Journal of Sex Research,* 1983, *19,* 327–338.

Hill, C.T., Rubin, Z., & Peplau, L.A. Breakups before marriage: The end of 103 affairs. *Journal of Social Issues,* 1976, *32,* 147–168.

Hite, S. *The Hite report: A nationwide study of female sexuality.* New York: Dell, 1977.

Hudson, W.W., Murphy, G.J., & Nurius, P.S. A short-form scale to measure liberal vs. conservative orientations toward human sexual expression. *Journal of Sex Research,* 1983, *19,* 258–272.

Jasso, G. Marital coital frequency and the passage of time: Estimating the separate effects of spouses' ages and marital duration, birth and marriage cohorts, and period influences. *American Sociological Review,* 1985, *50,* 224–241.

Kent, M. *How to marry the man of your choice.* New York: Warner Books, 1986.

Kinnaird, K.L., & Gerrard, M. Premarital sexual behavior and attitudes toward marriage and divorce among young women as a function of their mothers' marital status. *Journal of Marriage and the Family,* 1986, *48,* 757–764.

Knox, D., & Wilson, K. Dating behaviors of university students. *Family Relations,* 1981, *30,* 83–86.

__________. Dating problems of university students. *College Student Journal,* 1983, *17,* 225–228.

Koblinsky, S.A., & Palmeter, J.G. Sex-role orientation, mother's expression of affection toward spouse, and college women's attitudes toward sexual behaviors. *Journal of Sex Research,* 1984, *20,* 32–43.

Marsman, J.C., & Herold, E.S. Attitudes toward sex education and values in sex education. *Family Relations,* 1986, *35,* 357–362.

Miller, B.C., McCoy, J.K., Olson, T.D., & Wallace, C.M. Parental discipline and control attempts in relation to adolescent sexual attitudes and behavior. *Journal of Marriage and the Family,* 1986, *48,* 503–512.

Moore, Kristin A., Peterson, J.L., & Fuistenberg, F.F. Parental attitudes and the occurence of early sexual activity. *Journal of Marriage and the Family,* 1986, *48,* 777–782.

Moral Majority Report: What does Moral Majority believe about equal rights?, Censorship? Gays? March 1984, 5(3), 21.

National Center for Health Statistics: Advance report of final natality statistics, 1984. *Monthly Vital Statistics Report,* 35(4). Supp. DHHS Pub. No. (PHS) 86–1120. Hyattsville, Md.: U.S. Public Health Service, July 18, 1986.

Notzer, N., Levran, D., Mashiach, S., & Soffer, S. Effect of religiosity on sex attitudes, experience, and contraception among university students. *Journal of Sex and Marital Therapy,* 1984, *10,* 57–62.

Nurius, P.S., & Hudson, W.W. A sexual profile of social groups. *Journal of Sex Education and Therapy,* 1982, 8(2), 15–30.

Petersen, J.R., Kretchmer, A., Nellis, B., Lever, J., & Hertz, R. The *Playboy* reader's sex survey, Part 2. *Playboy,* March 1983b, p. 90.

Petersen, K.S. Single men say easy sex is unsafe. *USA Today,* July 7, 1986, p. 1.

Phillis, D.E., & Gromko, M.K. Sex differences in sexual activity: Reality or illusion? *The Journal of Sex Research,* 1985, *27,* 437–443.

Ratcliff, B., & Knox, D. University students motivations for intercourse. Paper, Southern Sociological Society, Memphis, Tenn., 1982. Used by permission.

Richardson, L. *The new other woman.* New York: The Free Press, 1985.

Roper Organization. *The 1985 Virginia Slims American women's opinion poll.* New York, 1985.

Sack, A.R., Keller, J.F., & Hinkle, D.E. Premarital sexual intercourse: A test of the effects of peer group, religiosity, and sexual guilt. *Journal of Sex Research,* 1984, *20,* 168–185.

Schaefer, L. Women and extramarital affairs. *Sexuality Today,* 1981, 4(13), 3.

Sheehan, M.K., Ostwald, S.K., & Rothenberger, J. Perceptions of sexual responsibility: Do young men and women agree? *Pediatric Nursing,* 1986, *12,* 17–21.

Sherwin, R., & Corbett, S. Campus sexual norms and dating relationships: A trend analysis. *Journal of Sex Research,* 1985, *21,* 258–274.

Spanier, G.B., & Margolis, R.L. Marital separation and extramarital sexual behavior. *Journal of Sex Research,* 1983, *19,* 23–48.

Staples, R. Black masculinity, hypersexuality, and sexual aggression. In Robert Staples (Ed.), *The Black Family.* Belmont, Calif.: Wadsworth Publishing, 1986. Pp. 57–63.

Starr, B.D., & Weiner, M.B. *The Starr-Weiner report on sex and sexuality in the mature years.* New York: McGraw-Hill, 1982.

Stewart, S.A. Sex is casual, despite new concerns. *USA Today,* May 15, 1986, p. 5D.

Story, Marilyn D. A comparison of university-student experience with various sexual outlets in 1974 and 1984. *Journal of Sex Education and Therapy,* 1985, *11,* 35–41.

Symons, D. *The evolution of human sexuality.* New York: Oxford University Press, 1979.

Thompson, A.P. Emotional and sexual components of extramarital relations. *Journal of Marriage and the Family,* 1984, *46,* 35–42.

____________. Extramarital sex: A review of the research literature. *Journal of Sex Research,* 1983, *19,* 1–22.

Tissot, S.A. (1766). *Onania, or a treatise upon the disorders produced by masturbation.* (A. Hume, Trans.). London: J. Pridden. (Original work published in 1758).

Weiss, D.L. Affective reactions of women to their initial experience of coitus. *Journal of Sex Research,* 1983, *19,* 209–237.

Weiss, D.L., & Jurich, J. Size of community of residence as a predictor of attitudes toward extramarital sexual relations. *Journal of Marriage and the Family,* 1985, *47,* 173–178.

Wheeler, J., & Kilmann, P.R. Comarital sexual behavior: Individual and relationship variables. *Archives of Sexual Behavior,* 1983, *12,* 295–306.

Women's Views Study. 1 Sex, money, politics, family—Where are women now? *Glamour,* January 1984, p. 144.

Yablonsky, L. *The extra-sex factor: Why over half of America's married men play around.* New York: Times Books, 1979.

Young, M. Religiosity and satisfaction with virginity among college men and women. *Journal of College Student Personnel,* 1986, *27,* 339–344.

Zelnik, M., & Kantner, J.F. Sexual activity, contraceptive use, and pregnancy among metropolitan-area teenagers: 1971–1979. *Family Planning Perspectives,* 1980, *12,* 230–237.

Zelnik, M., Koenig, M.A., & Kim, Y.J. Sources of prescription contraceptives and subsequent pregnancy among young women. *Family Planning Perspectives,* 1984, *16,* 6–13.

Zelnik, M., & Shah, F.K. First intercourse among young Americans. *Family Planning Perspectives,* 1983, *15,* 64–70.

CHAPTER 5

Austrom, D., & Hanel, K. Psychological issues of single life in Canada: An exploratory study. *International Journal of Women's Studies,* 1985, *8,* 12–23.

Block, S. *Advertising for love: How to play the personals.* New York: William Morrow, 1985.

Bowe, C. What are men like today? *Cosmopolitan,* May 1986, pp. 263 et passim.

Bulcroft, K., & O'Conner-Roden, M. Never too late. *Psychology Today,* June 1986, 66–69.

Buss, D.M. Human mate selection. *American Scientist,* 1985, *73,* 47–51.

Cassell, C. Sex-ratio imbalance creates fearful women. *Sexuality Today,* 1986, 9(24), 1.

Daniel, H.J., III, O'Brien, K.F., McCabe, R.B., and Quinter, V.E. Values in mate selection: A 1984 campus survey. *College Student Journal,* 1985, *19,* 44–50.

Farley, F. The big T in personality. *Psychology Today,* May 1986, 43–52.

Gilmartin, B.G. Some family antecedents of severe shyness. *Family Relations,* 1985, *34,* 429–438.

Greenglass, E.R. A social–psychological view of marriage for women. *International Journal of Women's Studies,* 1985, *8,* 24–31.

Harriman, L.C. Application of mate-selection theories in the classroom. *Family Perspective,* 1982, *16,* 91–92.

Janda, L.H., O'Gray, K.E., & Barnhart, S.A. Effects of sexual attitudes and physical attractiveness on person perception of men and women. *Sex Roles,* 1981, *7,* 189–199.

Jedlicka, D. Indirect parental influence on mate choice: A test of the psychoanalytic theory. *Journal of Marriage and the Family,* 1984, *46,* 65–70.

Kent, M. *How to marry the man of your choice.* New York: Warner Books, 1986.

Knox, D., & Daniel, H.J., III. Gender differences in expressions of sexuality. *International Journal of Modern Sociology,* 1986, *16,* 95–102.

Knox, D., & Wilson, K. Dating problems of university students. *College Student Journal,* 1983, *17,* 225–228.

Laner, M.R. Competition in courtship. *Family Relations,* 1986, *35,* 275–279.

Lawlor, Julia. Is brokering love or exploitation? *USA Today,* November 18, 1986, p. 1.

Leslie, L.A., Huston, T.L., & Johnson, M.P. Parental reactions to dating relationships: Do they make a difference? *Journal of Marriage and the Family,* 1986, *48,* 57–66.

Lloyd, S.A., Cate, R.M., & Henton, J.M. Predicting premarital relationship stability: A methodological refinement. *Journal of Marriage and the Family,* 1984, *46,* 71–76.

Meyer, J.P., & Pepper, S. Need compatibility and marital adjustment in young married couples. *Journal of Personality and Social Psychology,* 1977, *35,* 331–342.

Moore, M.M. Nonverbal courtship patterns in women: Context and consequences. *Ethology and Sociobiology,* 1985, *6,* 237–247.

Murray, T.E. The language of singles bars. *American Speech,* 1985, *60,* 17–30.

Nye, F.I. Family minitheories as special instances of choice and exchange theory. *Journal of Marriage and the Family,* 1980, *42,* 479–489.

Rodgers, R.H., & Conrad, L.M. Courtship for remarriage: Influences on family reorganization after divorce. *Journal of Marriage and the Family,* 1986, *48,* 767–775.

Statistical Abstract of the United States, 1987, 107th ed. Washington, D.C.: U.S. Bureau of the Census, 1986.

Stewart, S.A. A world of good times, new experiences. *USA Today,* May 14, 1986b, p. 5–D.

U.S. Bureau of the Census. Marital status and living arrangements: March 1985. *Current Population Reports,* Series P–20, No. 410. Washington, D.C.: U.S. Government Printing Office, 1986.

Waller, W., & Hill, R. *The family: A dynamic interpretation.* New York: Holt, Rinehart & Winston, 1951.

Winch, R.F. The theory of complementary needs in mate selection. Final results on the test of the general hypothesis. *American Sociological Review,* 1955, *20,* 552–555.

Woodfin, M.H., & Tinling, J. (Eds.). *Another secret diary of William Bryd of Westover, 1739–1741.* Richmond, Va.: 1942.

CHAPTER 6

Austrom, D., & Hanel, K. Psychological issues of single life in Canada: An exploratory study. *International Journal of Women's Studies,* 1985, *8,* 12–23.

Bean, F.D., Stephen, E.H., & Opitz, W. The Mexican origin population in the United States: A demographic overview. In R.O. De La Garza, F.D. Bean, C.M. Bonjean, R. Romo, and R. Alvarez (Eds.), *The Mexican American experience.* Austin: University of Texas Press, 1985. Pp. 57–75.

Billingham, R.E., & Sack, A.R. Gender differences in college students' willingness to participate in alternative marriage and family relationships. *Family Perspective.* 1986, *20,* 37–44.

Bulcroft, K., & O'Connor, M.R. The importance of dating relationships on quality of life for older persons. *Family Relations,* 1986, *35,* 397–402.

Cockrum, J., & White, P. Influences on the life satisfaction of never-married men and women. *Family Relations,* 1985, *34,* 551–556.

Directory of intentional communities. *Communities.* Stelle, Il.: Community Publications Co-operative, 1985.

Feinson, M.C. Aging and mental health. *Research on Aging,* 1985, *7,* 155–174.

Greenglass, E.R. A social-psychological view of marriage for women. *International Journal of Women's Studies,* 1985, *8,* 24–31.

Harayda, J. *The joy of being single.* New York: Doubleday, 1986.

Jankowski, L. Marriage satisfying, 65% say. *USA Today,* 1985, p. A–1.

Johnson, C.L. The impact of illness on late-life marriages. *Journal of Marriage and the Family,* 1985, *47,* 165–172.

Keith, P.M. Isolation of the unmarried in later life. *Family Relations,* 1986, *35,* 389–396.

Levine, S.V. Radical departures. *Psychology Today,* August 1984, pp. 20–27.

Richardson, L. *The new other woman.* New York: The Free Press, 1985.

Rollins, J. Single men and women: Differences and similarities. *Family Perspective,* 1986, *20,* 117–124.

Roper Organization, *The 1985 Virginia Slims American women's opinion poll,* New York: 1985.

Statistical Abstract of the United States, 1987, 107th ed. Washington, D.C.: U.S. Bureau of the Census, 1986.

Stewart, S.A. They want an upscale, happy future. *USA Today,* May 13, 1986, p. A–2.

U.S. Bureau of the Census. Marital status and living arrangements: March 1985. *Current Population Reports,* Series P–20, No. 410. Washington, D.C.: U.S. Government Printing Office, 1986.

Van Deusen, E.L. *Contract cohabitation.* New York: Grove Press, 1974.

CHAPTER 7

Billingham, R.E., & Sack, A.R. Gender differences in college student's willingness to participate in alternative marriage and family relationships. *Family Perspective,* 1986, *20,* 37–44.

Bowe, C. What are men like today? *Cosmopolitan,* May 1986, pp. 263 et passim.

Bulcroft, K., & O'Conner-Roden, M. Never too late. *Psychology Today,* June 1986, 66–69.

DeMaris, A., & Leslie, G.R. Cohabitation with the future spouse: Its influence upon marital satisfaction and communication. *Journal of Marriage and the Family,* 1984, *46,* 77–84.

Freed, D.J., & Walker, T.B. Family law in the fifty states: An overview. *Family Law Quarterly,* 1986, *19,* 331–442.

Glick, P.C. How American families are changing. *American Demographics,* 1984, 6(1), 20–25.

Gwartney-Gibbs, P.A. The institutionalization of premarital cohabitation: Estimates from marriage license applications, 1970 and 1980. *Journal of Marriage and the Family,* 1986, *48,* 423–433.

Hill, C.T., Rubin, Z., & Peplau, L.A. Breakups before marriage: The end of 103 affairs. *Journal of Social Issues,* 1976, *32,* 147–168.

Jacques, J.M., & Chason, K.J. Cohabitation: Its impact on marital success. *Family Relations,* 1979, 28(1), 35–39.

Khoo, S. Living together as married: A profile of de facto couples in Australia. *Journal of Marriage and the Family,* 1987, *36,* 185–191.

Kotkin, M. To marry or live together. *Life styles: A journal of changing patterns,* 1985, *7,* 156–170.

Macklin, E.D. Nontraditional family forms: A decade of research. *Journal of Marriage and the Family,* 1980, 42(4), 905–922.

Markowski, E.M., & Johnston, M.J. Behavior, temperament, perceived temperament, and idealization of cohabitating couples who married. *International Journal of Sociology,* 1980, *10,* 115–125.

Myricks, N. Palimony: The impact of *Marvin* v. *Marvin. Family Relations,* 1980, 29(2), 210–215.

Ridley, C.A., Peterman, D.J., & Avery, A.W. Cohabitation: Does it make for a better marriage? *Family Coordinator,* 1978, *27,* 129–136.

Risman, B.J., Hill, C.T., Rubin, Z., & Peplau, L.A. Living together in college: Implications for courtship. *Journal of Marriage and the Family,* 1981, 43(1), 77–83.

Statistical Abstract of the United States, 1987, 107th ed. Washington, D.C.: U.S. Bureau of the Census, 1986.

U.S. Bureau of the Census. Marital Status and Living Arrangements: March 1985. *Current Population Reports,* Series P–20, No. 410. Washington, D.C.: U.S. Government Printing Office, 1986.

Watson, R.E.L. Premarital cohabitation vs. traditional courtship: Their effects on subsequent marital adjustment. *Family Relations,* 1983, *32,* 139–147.

Watson, R.E.L., and DeMeo, P.W. Premarital cohabitation vs. traditional courtship and subsequent marital adjustment: A replication and followup. *Family Relations*, 1987, *36*, 193–197.

Yamaguchi, K., & Kandel, D.B. Dynamic relationships between premarital cohabitation and illicit drug use: An event–history analysis of role selection and role socialization. *American Sociological Review,* 1985, *50,* 530–546.

CHAPTER 8

Adams, B.N., and Cromwell, R.E. Morning and night people in the family: A preliminary statement. *The Family Coordinator* 27 (1978): 5–13.

Bitter, R.G. Late marriage and marital instability: The effects of heterogeneity and inflexibility. *Journal of Marriage and the Family,* 48 (1986): 631–40.

Booth, A., and Edwards, J.N. Age at marriage and marital instability. *Journal of Marriage and the Family,* 47 (1985): 67–75.

Buckner, L.P., and Salts, C.J. A premarital assessment program. *Family Relations,* 34 (1985): 513–20.

Carpenter, D., and Knox, D. Relationship maintenance of college students separated during courtship. *The College Student Journal,* 20 (1986): 86–88.

Darnley, F. Periodicity in the family. *Family Relations,* 30 (1981): 31–37.

Freed, D.J., and Walker, T.B. *Family Law Quarterly,* 19 (1986): 331–442.

Freedman, M. Ritual aspects of Chinese kinship and marriage. *In Family and Kinship in Chinese Society.* Edited by M. Freedman. Stanford, Calif.: Stanford University Press, 1970, pp. 163–87.

Glick, P.C. How American families are changing. *American Demographics* 6 (1984): 20–27.

Grover, K.J., Russell, C.S., Schumm, W.R., and Paff-Bergen, L.A. Mate selection processes and marital satisfaction. *Family Relations,* 34 (1985): 383–86.

Hatch, R.C., James, D.E., and Schumm, W.R. Spiritual intimacy and marital satisfaction. *Family Relations,* 35 (1986): 539–45.

Knox, D. Breaking up: The cover story versus the real story. *Free Inquiry in Creative Sociology,* 13 (1985): 131–32.

Lear, M.W. How many choices do women really have? *Woman's Day,* November 11, 1986, pp. 109 et passim.

Leigh, G.K., Holman, T.B., and Burr, W.R. An empirical test of sequence in Murstein's SVR theory of mate selection. *Family Relations,* 33 (1984): 225–31.

Maneker, J.S., and Rankin, R.P. Education, age at marriage, and marital duration: Is there a relationship? *Journal of Marriage and the Family,* 47 (1985): 675–83.

Mitchell, M. *Gone With the Wind.* New York: Macmillan, 1977.

Murstein, B.I., and Brust, R.G. Humor and interpersonal attraction. *Journal of Personality Assessment,* 49 (1985): 637–40.

Norment, L. Resolve tensions between black men and women. *Ebony* (August 1986): 153–56.

Pelzel, J.C. Japanese kinship: A comparison. In *Family and Kinship in Chinese Society.* Edited by M. Freedman. Stanford, Calif.: Stanford University Press, 1970, pp. 227–48.

Rosenblatt, P.C., & Keller, L.O. Economic vulnerability and economic stress in farm couples. *Family Relations,* 1983, *32,* 567–573.

Rubin, Z., Peplau, L.A., and Hill, C.T. Loving and leaving: sex differences in romantic attachments. *Sex Roles,* 7 (1981): 821–35.

Sammons, R.A., Jr. Cognitive marriage therapy. Chicago: American Psychiatric Association (annual meeting), 1987.

Stewart, S.A. They see an upscale, happy future. *USA Today* (May 13, 1986): A–2.

Statistical Abstract of the United States, 1987, 107th ed. Washington, DC: U.S. Bureau of the Census, 1986.

Wasow, M. Support groups for family caregivers of patients with Alzheimer's disease. *Social Work,* 31 (1986): 93–97.

CHAPTER 9

Ade-Ridder, L. Quality of marriage: A comparison between golden-wedding couples and couples married less than fifty years. *Lifestyles: Journal of Changing Patterns,* 1985, *7,* 224–237.

Alder, C. The timing of marriage and educational attainment. Paper presented to the American Sociological Association, San Francisco, 1982.

Alvirez, D., Bean, F.D., & Williams, D. The Mexican American family. In Charles H. Mindel and Robert W. Habenstein (Eds.), *Ethnic Families in America,* 3rd ed. New York: Elsevier, 1981, pp. 269–292.

Ammons, P., & Stinnett, N. The vital marriage: A closer look. *Family Relations,* 1980, 29(1), 37–42.

Aschenbrenner, J., & Carr, C. H. Conjugal relationships in the context of the black extended family. *Alternative Lifestyles,* 1980, 3(4), 463–484.

Ball, R.E., & Robbins, L. Black husbands' satisfaction with their family life. *Journal of Marriage and the Family,* 1986a, *48,* 849–855.

Ball, R.E., & Robbins, L. Marital status and life satisfaction among black Americans. *Journal of Marriage and the Family,* 1986b, *48,* 389–394.

Berkove, G.F. Perceptions of husband support by returning women students. *Family Relations,* 1979, 28(4), 451–457.

Brigman, K.M.L., Schons, J., & Stinnett, N. Strengths of families in a society under stress: A study of strong families in Iraq. *Family Perspective,* 1986, *20,* 61–73.

Brubaker, T.H., & Kinsel, B.I. Who is responsible for household tasks in long-term marriages of the "young–old" elderly? *Lifestyles: Journal of Changing Patterns,* 1985, *7,* 238–247.

CBS News. The vanishing family: Crisis in black families. "CBS Reports," March 26, 1986.

Cole, C.L. Relationship quality in long-term marriages: A comparison of high-quality and low-quality marriages. *Lifestyles: Journal of Changing Patterns,* 1985, *7,* 248–257.

Cuber, J.F. & Harroff, P.B. *Sex and the significant Americans.* Baltimore, Md.: Penguin Books, 1965.

Egelman, W., & Berlage, G. Catholic college students' attitudes toward interfaith marriage: An exploratory study. Paper presented to the Southern Sociological Society, Memphis, 1982.

Feinson, M.C. Aging and mental health. *Research on Aging,* 1985, *7,* 155–174.

Glenn, N.D. Interreligious marriage in the United States: Patterns and recent trends. *Journal of Marriage and the Family,* 1982, 44(3), 555–566.

Gray-Little, B.G. Marital quality and power processes among black couples. *Journal of Marriage and the Family,* 1982, 44(3), 633–646.

Harrington, W. What color are our children? *Washington Post Magazine,* October 17, 1982, p. 10 et passim.

Huston-Hoburg, L., & Strange, C. Spouse support among male and female returning adult students. *Journal of College Student Personnel,* 1986, *27,* 388–394.

Johnson, M.P., & Leslie, L. Couple involvement and network structure: A test of the dyadic withdrawal hypothesis. *Social Psychology Quarterly,* 1982, 45(1), 34–43.

Johnson, R.C., & Nagoshi, C.T. The adjustment of offspring of within-group and interracial/intercultural marriages: A comparison of personality factors. *Journal of Marriage and the Family,* 1986, *48,* 279–284.

Kantrowitz, B. The ultimate assimilation. *Newsweek,* November 24, 1986, p. 80.

Kelly, S. Returning to college. *Family Relations,* 1982, 31(2), 287–294.

Koopman-Boyden, P.G., & Abbott, M. Expectations for household task allocation and actual task allocation: A New Zealand study. *Journal of Marriage and the Family,* 1985, *47,* 211–219.

Landry, B., & Jendrek, M.P. The employment of wives in middle-class black families. *Journal of Marriage and the Family,* 1978, 40(4), 787–797.

Ma, Li. Family ties as related to academic performance of college students. *College Student Journal,* 1983, *17,* 308–316.

McAdoo, H.P. Stress-absorbing systems in black families. *Family Relations,* 1982, 31(4), 478–488.

McRoy, S., & Fisher, V. Marital adjustment of graduate-student couples. *Family Relations,* 1982, 31(1), 37–41.

Price-Bonham, S., & Balswick, J.O. The noninstitutions: Divorce, desertion, and remarriage. *Journal of Marriage and the Family,* 1980, 42(4), 959–972.

Sanders, G.F., & Walters, J. Life satisfaction and family strengths of older couples. *Lifestyles: Journal of Changing Patterns,* 1985, *7,* 194–206.

Schwartz, S. Earnings capacity and the trend in inequality among black men. *Human Resources,* 1986, *22,* 44–63.

Staples, R., & Mirande, A. Racial and cultural variations among American families: A decennial review of the literature on minority families. *Journal of Marriage and the Family,* November 1980, 887–903.

Statistical Abstract of the United States, 1987, 107th ed. Washington, D.C.: U.S. Bureau of the Census, 1986.

Stinnett, N., Sanders, G., DeFrain, J., & Parkhurst, A. A nationwide study of families who perceive themselves as strong. *Family Perspective,* 1982, 16(1), 15–22.

Taylor, R.J. Receipt of support from family among black Americans: Demographic and familial differences. *Journal of Marriage and the Family,* 1986, *48,* 67–77.

Tryban, G.M. Effects of work and retirement within long-term marital relationships. *Lifestyles: Journal of Changing Patterns,* 1985, *7,* 207–223.

U.S. Bureau of the Census. Marital Status and living arrangements: March 1985. Current Population Reports, Series P–20, No. 410. Washington, D.C.: U.S. Government Printing Office, 1986.

Van Meter, M.J.S., & Agronow, S.J. The stress of multiple roles: The case for role strain among married college women. *Family Relations,* 1982, 31(1), 131–138.

Vega, W.A., Patterson, T., Sallis, J., Nader, P., Atkins, C., & Abramson, I. Cohesion and adaptability in Mexican American and Anglo families. *Journal of Marriage and the Family,* 1986, *48,* 857–867.

Vera, H., Berardo, D.H., and Berardo, F.M. Age heterogamy in marriage. *Journal of Marriage and the Family,* 1985, *47,* 553–566.

CHAPTER 10

Atkinson, M.P., & Boles, J. WASP (Wives as Senior Partners). *Journal of Marriage and the Family,* 1984, *46,* 861–870.

Beer, W.R. *Househusbands.* South Hadley, Mass.: Bergin & Garvey, 1984.

Berardo, D.H. Dual-career families: A comparison with dual-occupation and traditional families. Paper presented at the National Council on Family Relations, Washington, D.C., 1982.

Berg, B. *The crisis of the working mother.* New York: Summit Books, 1986.

Billingham, R.E., & Sack, A.R. Gender differences in college students' willingness to participate in alternative marriage and family relationships. *Family Perspective,* 1986, *20,* 37–44.

Bird, G.A., & Bird, G.W. Determinants of mobility in two-earner families: Does the wife's income count? *Journal of Marriage and the Family,* 1985, *47,* 753–758.

Bird, G.W., & Ford, R. Sources of role strain among dual-career couples. *Home Economics Research Journal,* 1985, *14,* 187–194.

Bird, G.W., Bird, G.A., & Scruggs, M. Determinants of family task sharing: A study of husbands and wives. *Journal of Marriage and the Family,* 1984, *46,* 345–355.

Blumstein, P., & Schwartz, P. *American couples.* New York: William Morrow, 1983.

Bowe, C. What are men like today? *Cosmopolitan,* May 1986, pp. 263 et passim.

Chafe, W.H. Looking backward in order to look forward: Women, work, and social values in America. In J.M. Dreps (Ed.), *Women and the American economy: A look to the 1980s.* Englewood Cliffs, N.J.: Prentice-Hall, 1976. Pp. 6–30.

Edmondson, B. Superwomen say enough is enough. *American Demographics,* 1986, *8,* 18.

Garbarino, J. Can American families afford the luxury of childhood? *Child Welfare,* 1986, *65,* 119–128.

Gaylin, J. Do kids need a stay-at-home mom? *Redbook,* August 1986, pp. 78–79.

Gerber, L.A. *Married to their careers.* New York: Tavistock Publications, 1983.

Gerstel, N., & Gross, H. *Commuter marriage.* New York: The Gilford Press, 1984.

Gilson, E., and Kane, S. *Unnecessary Choices.* New York: William Morrow, 1987.

Glenn, E.N. Split household, small producer, and dual wage earner: An analysis of Chinese American family strategies. *Journal of Marriage and the Family,* 1983, *45,* 35–46.

Greenstein, T.N. Social–psychological factors in perinatal labor-force participation. *Journal of Marriage and the Family,* 1986, *48,* 565–571.

Hewlett, S.A. *A lesser life: The myth of women's liberation in America.* New York: William Morrow, 1986.

Hibbard, J.H., & Pope, C.R. Employment status, employment characteristics, and women's health. *Women and Health,* 1985, *10,* 59–78.

Imig, D.R., & Imig, G.L. Influences of family management and spousal perceptions on stressor pile-up. *Family Relations,* 1985, *35,* 227–232.

Keown, A.L., & Keown, C.F. Factors of success for women in business. *International Journal of Women's Studies,* 1985, *8,* 278–285.

Knaub, P.K. Growing up in a dual-career family: The children's perceptions. *Family Relations,* 1986, *35,* 431–437.

Maiolo, J. Department of Sociology and Anthropology, East Carolina University. Personal communication, 1982.

Mathis, J.L. Physician-physician marriages. *Medical Aspects of Human Sexuality,* January 1984, 185–196.

McLanahan, S.S., & Glass, J.L. A note on the trend in sex differences in psychological distress. *Journal of Health and Social Behavior,* 1985, *26,* 328–336.

Meredith, D. The nine-to-five dilemma. *Psychology Today,* February 1986, 36–44.

Mikitka, K.F., & Koblinsky, S.A. Job-sharing couples in academia: Career and family life styles. *Home Economics Research Journal,* 1985, *14,* 195–207.

Newsweek Poll. How women view work, motherhood, and feminism. *Newsweek,* March 31, 1986, p. 51.

Orthner, D.K., & Pittman, J.F. Family contributions to work commitment. *Journal of Marriage and the Family,* 1986, *48,* 573–581.

Ortiz, V., & Cooney, R.S. Sex-role attitudes and labor-force anticipation among young Hispanic females and non-Hispanic white friends. In R.O. De La Garga, F.D. Bean, E.M. Bonjean, R. Romo, & R. Alvarez, *The Mexican American experience.* Austin, Texas: University of Texas Press, 1985. Pp. 174–182.

Pleck, J.H., & Staines, G.L. Work schedules and family life in two-earner couples. *Journal of Family Studies,* 1985, *6,* 61–82.

Reading, J., & Amatea, E.S. Role deviance or role diversification: Reassessing the psychosocial factors affecting the parenthood choice of career-oriented women. *Journal of Marriage and the Family,* 1986, *48,* 255–260.

Rextoat, C. Women's work expectations and labor-market experience in early and middle family life-cycle stages. *Journal of Marriage and the Family,* 1985, *47,* 131–142.

Robinson, B.E., Rowland, B.H., & Coleman, M. Taking action for latch-key children and their families. *Family Relations,* 1986, *35,* 473–478.

Rodman, H., & Cole, C. Latch-key children: A review of policy and resources. *Family Relations,* 1987, *36,* 101–105.

Roper Organization. *The 1985 Virginia Slims American women's opinion poll.* New York: Roper Organization 1985.

Rubenstein, C. Real men don't earn less than their wives. *Psychology Today,* November 1982, pp. 36–41.

Rubin, Z. Are working wives hazardous to their husbands' mental health? *Psychology Today,* May 1983, pp. 70–72.

Sack, A.R., & Liddell, M.B. Marital adjustment and division of labor of professional women. *Family Perspective,* 1985, *19,* 151–160.

Sawon, H. Korean women at work. *Korean Journal,* 1984, *24,* 4–37.

Schaninger, C.M., & Buss, W.C. A longitudinal comparison of consumption and finance handling between happily married and divorced couples. *Journal of Marriage and the Family,* 1986, *48,* 129–136.

Schumm, W.R., & Bugaighis, M.A. Marital quality over the marital career: Alternative explanations. *Journal of Marriage and the Family,* 1986, *48,* 165–168.

Selkow, P. Mom's jobs, kids' careers. Reported in *Psychology Today* by Diana Zuckerman, February 1985, p. 6.

Sharda, B.D., & Nangle, B. Marital effects on occupational attainment. *Journal of Family Issues,* 1981, 2(1), 148–163.

Smith, A.D., & Reid, W.J. Role-sharing marriage. New York: Columbia University Press, 1986.

Smith, D.S. Wife employment and marital adjustment: A cumulation of results. *Family Relations,* 1985, *34,* 483–490.

Sorensen, G., Pirie, P., Folsom, A., Luepker, R., & Jacobs, D. Sex differences in the relationship between work and health: The Minnesota heart survey. *Journal of Health and Social Behavior,* 1985, *26,* 379–394.

Staines, G.L., Pottick, K., & Fudge, D.A. Wives' employment and husbands' attitudes toward work and life. *Journal of Applied Psychology,* 1986, *71,* 118–128.

Statham, A., & Larrick, D. Changing family roles: Implication for married women's earnings. *Family Perspective,* 1986, *20,* 13–25.

Statistical Abstract of the United States, 1987, 107th ed. Washington, D.C.: U.S. Bureau of the Census, 1986.

Stewart, S.A. They see an upscale, happy future. *USA Today,* May 13, 1986, p. A–2.

Stokes, J.P., & Peyton, J.S. Attitudinal differences between full-time homemakers and women who work outside the home. *Sex Roles,* 1986, 15 (5/6), 299–310.

Straits, B.C. Factors influencing college women's responses to fertility decision-making vignettes. *Journal of Marriage and the Family,* 1985, *47,* 585–596.

Thornton, A., & Freedman, D. The changing American family. *Population Bulletin,* 1983, *38,* 4.

Ulrichson, A.M., & Hira, T. The impact of financial problems on family relationships. *Family Perspective,* 1985, *19,* 177–187.

U.S. Bureau of the Census. Wives who earn more than their husbands. *Special Demographic Analyses,* CDS–80–9. Washington, D.C.: U.S. Government Printing Office, 1983.

White, P., Mascalo, A., Thomas, S., & Shoun, S. Husbands' and wives' perceptions of marital intimacy and wives' stresses in dual-career marriages. *Family Perspective,* 1986, *20,* 27–35.

CHAPTER 11

Ade-Ridder, L. Quality of marriage: A comparison between golden-wedding couples and couples married less than fifty years. *Lifestyles,* 1985, *7,* 224–237.

Appell, R.A. Importance of the neurological examination in erectile dysfunction. *Medical Aspects of Human Sexuality,* 1986, *20,* 32–36.

Ash, P. Healthy sexuality and good health. *Sexuality Today,* 1986, 9(24), 1.

Barbach, L., & Flaherty, M. Group treatment of situationally orgasmic women. *Journal of Sex and Marital Therapy,* 1980, *6,* 19–29.

Brewer, J.S. Duration of intromission and female orgasm rates. *Medical Aspects of Human Sexuality,* 1981, 15(4), 70–71.

Butler, R.N., & Lewis, M.I. *Sex after sixty.* New York: Harper & Row, 1976.

Clement, U., & Schmidt, G. The outcome of couple therapy for sexual dysfunctions using three different formats. *Journal of Sex and Marital Therapy,* 1983, *9,* 67–78.

Coleman, E., Listiak, A., Braatz, G., and Lange, P. Effects of penile implant surgery on ejaculation and orgasm. *Journal of Sex and Marital Therapy,* 1985, *11,* 199–205.

Duddle, C.M., & Ingram, A. Treating sexual dysfunction in couple's groups. In R. Forleo & W. Pasini (Eds.), *Medical sexology.* Littleton, Mass.: PSG Publishing, 1980. Pp. 598–605.

Gebhard, P.H. Human sexual behavior: A summary statement. In D.S. Marshall & R.C. Suggs (Eds.), *Human sexual behavior.* Englewood Cliffs, N.J.: Prentice-Hall, 1972. Pp. 206–217.

Golden, J.S., Price, S., Heinrich, A.G., & Lobitz, W.C. Group vs. couple treatment of sexual dysfunctions. *Archive of Sexual Behavior,* 1978, *7,* 593–602.

Greenblatt, C.S. The salience of sexuality in the early years of marriage. *Journal of Marriage and the Family,* 1983, *4,* 289–299.

Grosskopf, D. *Sex and the married woman.* New York: Wallaby Books, 1983.

Hatfield, E., Greenberger, D., Traupmann, J., & Lambert, P. Equity and sexual satisfaction in recently married couples. *Journal of Sex Research,* 1982, *18,* 18–32.

Hegeler, S., & Mortensen, M. Sexual behavior in elderly Danish males. In R. Gemme and C. Wheeler (Eds.), *Progress in sexology.* New York: Plenum Press, 1977. Pp. 285–292.

Heiman, J.R., Gladue, B.A., Roberts, C.W., & LoPiccolo, J. Historical and current factors discriminating sexually functional from sexually dysfunctional married couples. *Journal of Marital and Family Therapy,* 1986, *12,* 163–174.

Hite, S. *The Hite report on male sexuality.* New York: Alfred A. Knopf, 1981.

Hong, L.K. Survival of the fastest: On the origin of premature ejaculation. *Journal of Sex Research.* 1984, *20,* 109–122.

Johnson, F.A., Kaplan, E.A., & Tusel, D.J. Sexual dysfunction in the "two-career" family. *Medical Aspects of Human Sexuality,* 1979, 13(1), 7–17.

Kaplan, H. The classification of the female sexual dysfunctions. *Journal of Sex and Marital Therapy,* 1974, 1(2), 124–138.

Kilmann, P.R., Boland, J.P., Norton, S.P., Davidson, E., & Caid, C. Perspectives of sex therapy outcome: A survey of AASECT providers. *Journal of Sex and Marital Therapy,* 1986, *12,* 116–138.

Kilmann, P.R., Mills, K.H., Caid, C., Bella, B., Davidson, E., & Wanlass, R. The sexual interaction of women with secondary orgasmic dysfunction and their partners. *Archives of Sexual Behavior,* 1984, *13,* 41–49.

Kivett, V.R. Grandfathers and grandchildren: Patterns of association, helping, and psychological closeness. *Family Relations,* 1985, *34,* 565–571.

Kolodny, R.C., Masters, W.H., & Johnson, V.E. *Sex and Human Loving.* Boston: Little, Brown, 1986.

Masters, W.H., & Johnson, V.E. *Human sexual inadequacy.* Boston: Little, Brown, 1970.

McCarthy, B.W. Sexual dysfunctions and dissatisfactions among middle-years couples. *Journal of Sex Education and Therapy,* 1982, 8(2), 9–12.

Meeks, G.R. Easing the climacteric. *Medical Aspects of Human Sexuality,* 1986, *20,* 88–107.

Mehlman, S.K., Baucom, D.H., & Anderson, D. Effectiveness of cotherapists versus single therapists and immediate versus delayed treatment in behavioral marital therapy. *Journal of Consulting and Clinical Psychology,* 1983, *51,* 258–266.

Mehrabian, A. & Stanton-Mohr, L. Effects of emotional state on sexual desire and sexual dysfunction. *Motivation and Emotion,* 1985, *9,* 315–330.

Merriam, A.P. Aspects of sexual behavior among the Bala (Basongye). In D.S. Marshall & R.C. Suggs (Eds.) *Human sexual behavior.* Englewood Cliffs, N.J.: Prentice-Hall, 1972. Pp. 71–102.

Nathan, E.P., & Joanning, H.H. Enhancing marital sexuality: An evaluation of a program for the sexual enrichment of normal couples. *Journal of Sex and Marital Therapy,* 1985, *11,* 157–164.

Olds, S.W. *The eternal garden: Seasons of our sexuality.* New York: Random House, 1985.

Patton, D., & Waring, E.M. Sex and marital intimacy. *Journal of Sex and Marital Therapy,* 1985, *11,* 176–184.

Peter, L. *Peter's almanac.* New York: William Morrow, 1982.

Petersen, J.R., Kretchmer, A., Nellis, B., Lever, J., & Hertz, R. The *Playboy* reader's sex survey, Part 1. *Playboy,* January 1983a, p. 108 et passim.

Petersen, J.R., Kretchmer, A., Nellis, B., Lever J., & Hertz, R. The *Playboy* reader's sex survey, Part 2. *Playboy*, March 1983b, p. 90 et passim.

Rossman, I. Sexuality and aging: An internist's perspective. In R.L. Solnick (Ed.), *Sexuality and aging.* Los Angeles: Ethel Percy Andus Gerontology Center, University of Southern California, 1978. Pp. 66–77.

Scales, P. The changing context of sexuality education: Paradigms and challenges for alternative futures. *Family Relations,* 1986, *35,* 265–274.

Scharlach, A.S. From supermoms to superdaughters. *Marriage and Divorce Today,* 1986, 11(32), 1–2.

Sholty, M.J., Ephross, P.H., Plant, S.M., Fischman, S.H., Charnas, J.F., & Cody, C.A. Female orgasmic experience: A subjective study. *Archives of Sexual Behavior,* 1984, *13,* 155–164.

Shortle, B., & Jewelewicz, R. Psychogenic vaginismus. *Medical Aspects of Human Sexuality,* 1986, *20,* 82–87.

Sidi, A.A., Cameron, J.S., Duffy, L.M., & Lauge, P.H. Intracavernous drug-induced erections in the management of male dysfunction: Experience with 100 patients. *Journal of Urology,* 1986, *135,* 704–706.

Starr, B.D., & Weiner, M.B. *The Starr-Weiner report on sex and sexuality in the mature years.* New York: McGraw-Hill, 1982.

Statistical Abstract of the United States, 1987, 107th ed. Washington, D.C.: U.S. Bureau of the Census, 1986.

Stephens, W.N. *The family in cross-cultural perspective.* Washington, D.C.: University Press of America, 1982.

Stuart, F.M., Hammond, C., & Pett, M.A. Psychological characteristics of women with inhibited sexual desire. *Journal of Sex & Marital Therapy,* 1986, *12,* 108–115.

Talmadge, L.D., & Talmadge, W.C. Relational sexuality: An understanding of low sexual desire. *Journal of Sex and Marital Therapy,* 1986, *12,* 3–21.

Winn, R.L., & Newton, N. Sexuality in aging: A study of 106 cultures. *Archives of Sexual Behavior,* 1982, *11,* 283–298.

CHAPTER 12

Alberts, J.K. The role of couples' conversations in relational development: A content analysis of courtship talk in Harlequin romance novels. *Communication Quarterly,* 1986, *34,* 127–142.

Alford, R.D. Intimacy and disputing styles within kin and nonkin relationships. *Journal of Family Issues,* 1982, *3,* 361–374.

Altschuler, M., & Krueger, D.W. Game playing that destroys marriages. *Medical Aspects of Human Sexuality,* 1986, *20,* 63–76.

Anderson, S.A., Atilano, R.B., Bergen, L.P., Russell, C.S., & Jurich, A.P. Dropping out of marriage and family therapy: Intervention strategies and spouses' perceptions. *The American Journal of Family Therapy,* 1985, *13,* 39–53.

Balswick, J. Explaining inexpressive males: A reply to L'Abate. *Family Relations,* 1980, *29,* 231–233.

Beach, S.R.H., & O'Leary, D. The treatment of depression occurring in the context of marital discord. *Behavior Therapy,* 1986, *17,* 43–49.

Bell, D.C., Chafetz, J.S., & Horn, L.H. Marital conflict resolution: A study of strategies and outcomes. *Journal of Family Issues,* 1982, *3,* 111–132.

Belsky, J., Perry-Jenkins, M., & Crouter, A.C. The work–family interface and marital change across the transition to parenthood. *Journal of Family Issues,* 1985, *6,* 205–220.

Brandt, A. Avoiding couple karate: Lessons in the marital arts. *Psychology Today,* October 1982, pp. 38–43.

Brodbar-Nemzer, J.Y. Divorce and group commitment: The case of the Jews. *Journal of Marriage and the Family,* 1986, *48,* 329–340.

Crane, D.R., Griffin, W., & Hill, R.D. Influence of therapist skills on client perceptions of marriage and family therapy outcome: Implications for supervision. *Journal of Marital and Family Therapy,* 1986, *12,* 91–96.

Doherty, W.J., Lester, M.E., & Leigh, G. Marriage encounter weekends: Couples who win and couples who lose. *Journal of Marriage and Family Therapy,* 1986, *12,* 49–61.

Galvin, K.M., & Brommel, B.J. *Family communication: Cohesion and change.* Glenview, Ill.: Scott, Foresman, 1982.

Ganahl, G.F., Ferguson, L.R., & L. L'Abate, Training in family therapy. In L. L'Abate (Ed.), *Handbook of family psychology and therapy.* Homewood, Ill.: Dorsey Press, 1985. Pp. 961–988.

Glenn, N.D., & McLanahan, S. Children and marital happiness: A further specification of the relationship. *Journal of Marriage and the Family,* 1982, *44,* 63–72.

Greer, K. Today's parents. How well are they doing? *Better Homes and Gardens,* October 1986, pp. 36–46.

Grover, K.J., Paff-Bergen, L.A., Russell, C.S., and Schumm, W.R. The Kansas Marital Satisfaction Scale: A further brief report. *Psychological Reports,* 1984, *54,* 629–630.

Gurman, A.S., & Kniskern, D.P. Commentary on Wells and Giannetti article on individual marital therapy. *Family Process,* 1986, *25,* 51–62.

Hayes, M.P., Stinnett, N., & DeFrain, J. Learning about marriage from the divorced. *Journal of Divorce,* 1981, *4,* 23–29.

Hennon, C.B. Conflict management within cohabitation relationships. *Alternative Lifestyles,* 1981, *4,* 467–486.

Honeycutt, J.M., Wilson, C., & Parker, C. Effects of sex and degrees of happiness on perceived styles of communication in and out of the marital relationship. *Journal of Marriage and the Family,* 1982, *44,* 395–406.

Julius, M. Marital stress and suppressed anger linked to death of spouses. *Marriage and Divorce Today,* 1986, 11(35), 1–2.

Klagsbrun, F. *Married people: Staying together in the age of divorce.* New York: Bantam Books, 1985.

Knox, D., & Wilson, K. Dating problems of university students. *College Student Journal,* 1983, *17,* 225–228.

Kramarae, C. *Women and men speaking.* New York: Newbury House, 1981.

Lederer, W.J., & Jackson, D.D. *The mirages of marriage.* New York: W.W. Norton, 1968.

Lester, M.E., & Doherty, W.J. Couple's long-term evaluations of their marriage-encounter experience. *Journal of Marriage and the Family,* 1983, *9,* 183–188.

Marotz-Baden, R., & Colvin, P.L. Coping strategies: A rural–urban comparison. *Family Relations,* 1986, *35,* 281–288.

Martin, D., & Martin, M. Selected attitudes toward marriage and family life among college students. *Family Relations,* 1984, *33,* 293–300.

Massey, R.F. What/who is the family system? *The American Journal of Family Therapy,* 1986, *14,* 23–39.

Meeks, S., Arnkoff, D.B., Glass, C.R., & Notarius, C.I. Wives' employment status, hassles, communication, and relational efficacy: Intra- versus extra-relationship factors and marital adjustment. *Family Relations,* 1986, *35,* 249–255.

Menaghan, E.G. Coping with marital problems: Assessing effectiveness. Paper presented at the annual meeting of the American Sociological Association, 1982. Used by permission.

Moffitt, P.F., Spence, N.D., & Boldney, R.D. Mental health in marriage: The roles of need for affiliation, sensitivity to rejection, and other factors. *Journal of Clinical Psychology,* 1986, *42,* 68–76.

Notarius, C.I., & Johnson, J.S. Emotional expression in husbands and wives. *Journal of Marriage and the Family,* 1982, *44,* 483–489.

Rao, V.V.P., & Rao, N. Correlates of marital happiness: A longitudinal analysis. *Free Inquiry in Creative Sociology,* 1986, *14,* 3–8.

Rothman, J., Gant, L.M., & Hnat, S.A. Mexican American family culture. *Social Service Review,* June 1985, pp. 197–215.

Rubin, L. *Intimate strangers: Men and women together.* New York: Harper & Row, 1983.

Schumm, W.R., Barnes, H.L., Bollman, S.R., Jurich, A.P., & Bugaighis, M.A. Self-disclosure and marital satisfaction revisited. *Family Relations,* 1986, *35,* 241–247.

Schumm, W.R., Jurich, A.P., Bollman, S.R., & Bugaighis, M.A. His and her marriage revisited. *Journal of Family Issues,* 1985, *6,* 221–227.

Schumm, W.R., Nichols, C.W., Schectman, K.L., & Grigsby, C.C. Characteristics of responses to the Kansas Marital Satisfaction Scale by a sample of 84 married mothers. *Psychological Reports,* 1983, *53,* 567–572.

Schumm, W.R., Paff-Bergen, L.A., Hatch, R.C., Obiorah, F.C., Copeland, J.M., Meens, L.D., & Bugaighis, M.A. Concurrent and discriminant validity of the Kansas Marital Satisfaction Scale. *Journal of Marriage and the Family,* 1986, *48,* 381–387.

Schumm, W.R., Scanlon, E.D., Crow, C.L., Green, D.M., & Buckler, D.L. Characteristics of the Kansas Marital Satisfaction Scale in a sample of 79 married couples. *Psychological Reports,* 1983, *53,* 583–588.

Scoresby, A.L. *The marriage dialogue.* Reading, Mass.: Addison-Wesley, 1977.

Secord, P.F., & Ghee, K. Implications of the black marriage market for marital conflict. *Journal of Family Issues,* 1986, *7,* 21–30.

Sherman, M.A., & Haas, A. Man to man, woman to woman. *Psychology Today,* June 1984, pp. 72–73.

Stuart, R.B. *Helping couples change.* New York: Guilford Press, 1980.

Tiggle, R.B., Peters, M.D., Kelley, H.H., and Vincent, J. Correlational and discrepancy indices of understanding and their relation to marital satisfaction. *Journal of Marriage and the Family,* 1982, *44,* 209–216.

U.S. Bureau of the Census, 1984. Marital status and living arrangements: March 1983. *Current Population Reports,* Series P–20, No. 389. Washington, D.C.: U.S. Government Printing Office, 1983.

Warner, R. Hard Times and schizophrenia. *Psychology Today,* June 1986, pp. 51–52.

Wells, R.A., & Giannetti, V.J. Individual marital therapy: A critical reappraisal. *Family Process,* 1986, *25,* 43–51.

White, L.K., Booth, A., & Edwards, J.N. Children & marital happiness: Why the negative correlation? *Journal of Family Issues,* 1986, *7,* 131–147.

Wilson, M.R., & Filsinger, E.E. Religiosity and marital adjustment: Multidimensional interrelationships. *Journal of Marriage and the Family,* 1986, *48,* 147–151.

Zilbergeld, B. *The shrinking of America, Myths of psychological change.* Boston, Mass.: Little, Brown, 1983.

CHAPTER 13

Barth, R.P., Blythe, B.J., Schinke, S.P., & Schilling, R.F., II. Self-control training with maltreating parents. *Child Welfare,* 1983, *72,* 313–324.

Berk, R.A., Newton, P.J., & Berk, S.F. What a difference a day makes: An empirical study of the impact of shelters for battered women. *Journal of Marriage and the Family,* 1986, *48,* 481–490.

Browne, A., & Finkelhor, D. Impact of child sexual abuse: A review of the research. *Psychological Bulletin,* 1986, *99,* 66–77.

Browning, J., & Dutton, D. Assessment of wife assault with the Conflict Tactics Scale: Using couple data to quantify the differential reporting effect. *Journal of Marriage and the Family,* 1986, *48,* 375–379.

Burgess, R.L., & Garbarino, J. Doing what comes naturally? An evolutionary perspective on child abuse? In D. Finkelhor, R.J. Gelles, G.T. Hotaling, & M.A. Straus (Eds.), *The dark side of families: Current family violence research.* Beverly Hills, Calif.: Sage Publications, 1983. Pp. 88–101.

Cameron, P., Coburn, W., Larson, H., Proctor, K., Forde, N. & Cameron, K. Child molestation and homosexuality. *Psychological Reports,* 1986, *58,* 327–337.

Daly, M., & Wilson, M. Child abuse and other risks of not living with both parents. *Ethology and Sociobiology,* 1985, *6,* 197–210.

Downing, L.C. Substantiated reports of child abuse and neglect. *Free Inquiry in Creative Sociology,* 1982, *10,* 197–201.

Eastman, P. Elders under siege. *Psychology Today,* January 1984, p. 30.

Edleson, J.L., & Brygger, M.P. Gender differences in reporting of battering incidences. *Family Relations,* 1986, *35,* 383–388.

Edleson, J.L., Eisikovits, Z., & Guttmann, E. Men who batter women. *Journal of Family Issues,* 1985, *6,* 229–247.

Elder Abuse Report. Worchester, Mass.: University of Massachusetts Medical Center, University Center on Aging, 1986.

Engfer, A., & Schneewind, K.A. Causes and consequences of harsh parental punishment. *Child Abuse & Neglect: The International Journal,* 1982, *6,* 129–140.

Estroff, S. Kinship and conflict: Child sexual abuse as a family problem. *Social Science,* 1986, *71,* 11–15.

Finkelhor, D. Sex among siblings: A survey on prevalence, variety, and effects. *Archives of Sexual Behavior,* 1980, *9,* 171–194.

Finkelhor, D., & Yllo, K. Forced sex in marriage: A preliminary research report. *Crime and Delinquency.* July 1982, 459–478.

Finkelhor, D., & Yllo, K. Rape in marriage: A sociological view. In D. Finkelhor, R.J. Gelles, G.T. Hotaling, & M.A. Straus (Eds.), *The dark side of families: Current family violence research.* Beverly Hills, Calif.: Sage, 1983. Pp. 119–130.

Garbarino, J. Can we measure success in preventing child abuse? Issues in policy, programming, and research. *Child Abuse & Neglect,* 1986, *10,* 143–156.

Garbarino, J., & Ebata, A. The significance of ethnic and cultural differences in maltreatment. *Journal of Marriage and the Family,* 1983, *45,* 773–783.

Giarretto, H. A comprehensive child sexual-abuse treatment program. *Child Abuse and Neglect,* 1982, *6,* 263–278.

Goldstein, D., & Rosenbaum, A. An evaluation of the self-esteem of maritally violent men. *Family Relations,* 1985, *34,* 425–428.

Helfer, R.E. A review of the literature on the prevention of child abuse and neglect. *Child Abuse and Neglect,* 1982, *6,* 251–262.

Herrenkohl, E.C., Herrenkohl, R.C., & Toedter, L.J. Perspectives on the intergenerational transmission of abuse. In D. Finkelhor, R.J. Gelles, G.T. Hotaling, & M.A. Straus (Eds.), *The dark side of families: Current family violence research.* Beverly Hills, Calif.: Sage, 1983, Pp. 305–316.

Jehu, D., Gazan, M., and Klassen, C. Common therapeutic targets among women who were sexually abused in childhood. *Journal of Social Work and Human Sexuality,* spring 1985, *3,* 25–45.

Kalmuss, D. The intergenerational transmission of marital aggression. *Journal of Marriage and the Family,* 1984, *46,* 11–19.

Kalmuss, D., & Seltzer, J.A. Continuity of marital behavior in remarriage: The case of spouse abuse. *Journal of Marriage and the Family,* 1986, *48,* 113–120.

Knox, D., & Wilson, K. Dating problems of university students. *College Student Journal,* 1983, *17,* 225–228.

Kohn, A. Shattered innocence. *Psychology Today,* February 1987, pp. 54–58.

Krugman, R.D., Lenherr, M., Betz, B.A., & Fryer, G.E. The relationship between unemployment and physical abuse of children. *Child Abuse and Neglect,* 1986, *10,* 415–418.

Lane, K.E., & Gwartney-Gibbs, P.A. Violence in the context of dating and sex. *Journal of Family Issues,* 1985, *6,* 45–59.

Lewin, M. Unwanted intercourse: The difficulty of saying no. *Psychology of Women Quarterly,* 1985, *9,* 184–192.

Makepeace, J.M. Gender differences in courtship violence victimization. *Family Relations,* 1986, *35,* 383–388.

Makepeace, J.M. Social factor and victim-offender differences in courtship violence. *Family Relations,* 1987, *36,* 87–91.

Matthews, W., and Ellis, G. Parental television viewing and abusive childrearing attitudes and behaviors: Modeling vs. symbolic interaction as theoretical explanations. *Family Perspective,* 1985, *19,* 189–202.

McKinney, K. Measures of verbal, physical, and sexual dating violence by gender. *Free Inquiry in Creative Sociology,* 1986, *14,* 55–60.

Merrick, J. Physical punishment of children in Denmark: An historical perspective. *Child Abuse and Neglect,* 1986, *10,* 263–264.

Myer, M.H. A new look at mothers of incest victims. *Journal of Social Work and Human Sexuality,* spring 1985, *3,* 47–58.

Oates, R.K., Davis, A.A., & Ryan, M.G. Predictive factors for child abuse. In R.J. Gelles & C.P. Cornell (Eds.), *International perspectives on family violence,* 1983. Pp. 97–106.

O'Toole, R., Turbett, J.P., Linz, M., & Mehta, S.S. Defining parent abuse and neglect. *Free Inquiry in Creative Sociology,* 1983, *11,* 156–158.

Roscoe, B., & Benaske, N. Courtship violence experienced by abused wives: Similarities in patterns of abuse. *Family Relations,* 1985, *34,* 419–424.

Russell, D. *Rape in marriage.* New York: Macmillan, 1982.

Sarrel, P., & Masters, W. Sexual molestation of men by women. *Archives of Sexual Behavior,* 1982, *11,* 117–131.

Schumm, W.R., Martin, M.J., Bollman, S.R., & Jurich, A.P. Classifying family violence. *Journal of Family Issues,* 1982, *3,* 319–340.

Sherman, L.W., & Berk, R.A. *Police Foundation report 1: The Minneapolis domestic violence experiment,* 1984. Used by permission of L.W. Sherman.

Smith, S.M., & Hansen, R. 134 battered children: A medical and psychological study. In R.J. Gelles & C.P. Cornell (Eds.), *International perspectives on family violence,* 1983. Pp. 83–96.

Straus, M.F., & Gelles, R.J. Societal change and change in family violence from 1975 to 1985 as revealed by two national surveys. *Journal of Marriage and the Family,* 1986, *48,* 465–480.

Strube, M.J., & Barbour, L.S. The decision to leave an abusive relationship: Economic dependence and psychological commitment. *Journal of Marriage and the Family,* 1983, *45,* 785–793.

Timnick, L. Fatal means for children to end child abuse. *Los Angeles Times,* August 31, 1986. Part II, p. 2.

Washburne, C.K. A feminist analysis of child abuse and neglect. In D. Finkelhor, R.J. Gelles, G.T. Hotaling, & M.A. Straus (Eds.), *The dark side of families: Current family violence research.* Beverly Hills, Calif.: Sage Publications, 1983. Pp. 289–292.

Wilson, K., & Faison, R. Victims of sexual assault during courtship. Unpublished paper, Department of Sociology, Anthropology, and Economics, East Carolina University, 1983.

Wyatt, G.E., & Peters, S.D. Issues in the definition of child sexual abuse in prevalence research. *Child Abuse and Neglect,* 1986, *10,* 231–240.

Yates, A., Hull, J.W., & Huebner, R.B. Predicting the abusive parents response to intervention. *Child Abuse and Neglect,* 1983, *7,* 37–44.

Ziegert, K.A. The Swedish prohibition of corporal punishment: A preliminary report. *Journal of Marriage and the Family,* 1983, *45,* 917–926.

CHAPTER 14

Abbott, D.A., & Brody, G.H. The relation of child age, gender, and number of children to the marital adjustment of wives. *Journal of Marriage and the Family,* 1985, *47,* 77–84.

Bell, J.E., & Eisenberg, N. Life satisfaction in midlife childless and empty-nest men and women. *Lifestyles: A Journal of Changing Patterns,* 1985, *7,* 146–155.

Billingham, R.E., & Sack, A.R. Gender differences in college students' willingness to participate in alternative marriage and family relationships. *Family Perspective,* 1986, *20,* 37–44.

Bloom, D.E., & Bennett, N.G. Childless couples. *American Demographics,* 1986, *8,* 23 et passim.

Bongaarts, J. Building a family: Unplanned events. *Studies in Family Planning,* 1984, *15,* 14–19.

Callan, V.J. Comparisons of mothers of one child by choice with mothers wanting a second birth. *Journal of Marriage and the Family,* 1985, *47,* 155–164.

Callan, V.J. The impact of the first birth: Married and single women preferring childlessness, one child, or two children. *Journal of Marriage and the Family,* 1986, *48,* 261–269.
Campbell, E. *The Childless Marriage.* New York: Methuen, 1985.
Chen, X. The one-child population policy, modernization, and the extended Chinese family. *Journal of Marriage and the Family,* 1985, *47,* 193–202.
Falbo, T., & Polit-O'Harra, D.F. Only children: What do we know about them? *Pediatric Nursing,* 1985, *11,* 356–360.
Hanson, S.H., & Sporakowski, M.J. Single-parent families. *Family Relations,* 1986, *35,* 3–8.
Hawke, S., & Knox, D. *One child by choice.* Englewood Cliffs, N.J.: Prentice-Hall, 1977.
Hogge, W.A., Schonberg, S.A., & Golbus, M.S. Chorion villus sampling: The experiences of 1,000 cases. *American Journal of Obstetrics and Gynecology,* 1986, *154,* 1249–1252.
Kantrowitz, B., & Greenberg, N.F. Only but not lonely. *Newsweek,* June 16, 1986, pp. 66–67.
Knox, D., & Wilson, K. The differences between having one and two children. *Family Coordinator,* 1978, *27,* 23–25.
LeMasters, E.E., & DeFrain, J. *Parents in contemporary America.* Homewood, Ill.: Dorsey Press, 1983.
Marini, M.M. Effects of the number and spacing of children on marital and parental satisfaction. *Demography,* 1980, *17,* 225–242.
Matthews, R., & Matthews, A.M. Infertility and involuntary childlessness: The transition to nonparenthood. *Journal of Marriage and the Family,* 1986, *48,* 641–650.
McGhee, J.L. The effects of siblings on the life satisfaction of the rural elderly. *Journal of Marriage and the Family,* 1985, *47,* 85–91.
McLaughlin, S.D., & Micklin, M. The timing of the first birth and changes in personal efficacy. *Journal of Marriage and the Family,* 1983, *45,* 47–55.
National Center for Health Statistics. Births, marriages, divorces, and deaths for March 1987. *Monthly Vital Statistics Report,* 36(3), DHHS Pub. No. (PHS) 87–1120. Hyattsville, Md.: Public Health Service, June 22, 1987.
National Center for Health Statistics. Births, marriages, divorces, and deaths for April 1986. *Monthly Vital Statistics Report* 35(4), DHHS Pub. No. (PHS) 86–1120. Hyattsville, Md.: Public Health Service, July 17, 1986a.
National Center for Health Statistics. Advance report of final natality statistics, 1984. *Monthly Vital Statistics Report* 35(4) Supp. DHHS Pub. No. (PHS) 86–1120. Hyattsville, Md.: Public Health Service, July 18, 1986b.
Population update. *Population Today,* 1986, *14,* 13.
Powledge, T.M. Windows of the womb. *Psychology Today,* March 1983, pp. 37–42.
Pratt, W.C., & Horn, M.C. Wanted and unwanted childbearing: United States, 1973–1982. *Advance Data from Vital Statistics,* 1985, No. 108.
Ramu, G.N. Voluntarily childless and parental couples: A comparison of their life-style characteristics. *Lifestyles: A Journal of Changing Patterns,* 1985, *7,* 130–145.
Rempel, J. Childless elderly. *Journal of Marriage and the Family,* 1985, *47,* 343–348.
Renvoize, J. *Going solo: Single mothers by choice.* London: Routledge & Kegan Paul, 1985.
Risman, B.J. Can men "mother"? Life as a single father. *Family Relations,* 1986, *35,* 95–102.
Rogers, C.C., & O'Connell, M. Child-spacing among birth cohorts of American women (1905–1959). U.S. Bureau of the Census, Series P–20, No. 385. Washington, D.C.: U.S. Government Printing Office, 1984.
Roper Organization. *The 1985 Virginia Slims American women's opinion poll,* New York, 1985.
Rothman, J., Gant, L.M., and Hnat, S.A. Mexican American family culture. *Social Service Review,* June 1985, pp. 197–215.
Seashore, M.R. Counseling prospective parents about possible genetic disorders in offspring. *Medical Aspects of Human Sexuality,* 1980, 14(11), 97–98.
Statistical Abstract of the United States, 1987, 107th ed. Washington, D.C.: U.S. Bureau of the Census, 1986.
Stewart, S.A. They see an upscale, happy future. *USA Today,* May 13, 1986, p. A–2.
Uzzell, O. Family planning: The artificial control of gender. *Family Perspective,* 1985, *19,* 279–282.

CHAPTER 15

Atkinson, L.E., Lincoln, R., & Forrest, J.D. The next contraceptive revolution. *Family Planning Perspectives,* 1986, *18,* 19–26.

Baetsen, K.L. A comparative MMPI study of abortion-seeking women and those who intend to carry their pregnancies to term. *Family Practice Research Journal,* 1985, *4,* 199–207.

Berger, C., Jacques, J., Brender, W., Gold, D., & Andres, D. Contraceptive knowledge and use of birth control as a function of sex guilt. *International Journal of Women's Studies,* 1985, *8,* 32–39.

Blackmun, H. Governments have no right to block freedom of choice. *USA Today,* June 12, 1986, p. 9–A.

Collins, M. Today: New choice for women. *USA Today,* July 7, 1986.

Dawson, D.A. The effects of sex education on adolescent behavior. *Family Planning Perspectives,* 1986, 18(4), 162–170.

Donovan, P. Letting the people decide: How the antiabortion referenda fared. *Family Planning Perspectives,* 1986, 18(3), 127–128.

Dunn, P.C., & Ryan, I.J., and O'Brien, K. College students level of acceptability of the new medical science of conception and problems of infertility. Accepted by *Journal of Sex Research.* In press.

Edmondson, B. Golden Cradle advertises adoption. *American Demographics,* 1986, *8,* 18.

Forrest, J.D. The end of IUD marketing in the United States: What does it mean for American women? *Family Planning Perspectives,* 1986, *18,* 52–57.

Gordon, S. What kids need to know. *Psychology Today,* October 1986, 20(10), 22–27.

Greenberg, J.S., Bruess, C.E., & Sands, D.W. *Sexuality: Insights and Issues.* Dubuque, Iowa: William C. Brown, 1986.

Harper, T. Surrogate motherhood: Should we follow this U.S. example? *Institute of Family Studies,* April 1985, 11–12.

Height, D. Black families. *USA Today,* September 25, 1986, p. 7–A.

Henshaw, S.K. Trends in abortions, 1982–1984. *Family Planning Perspectives,* 1986, *18,* 34.

Hornick, J.P., Devlin, M.C., Downey, M.K., & Baynham, T. Successful and unsuccessful contraceptors: A multivariate typology. *Journal of Social Work and Human Sexuality,* winter 1985–1986, *4,* 17–34.

Lodl, K.M., McGettigan, A., & Bucy, J. Women's responses to abortion: Implications for post-abortion support groups. *Journal of Social Work and Human Sexuality,* spring 1985, *3,* 119–132.

Marsiglio, W., & Mott, F.L. The impact of sex education on sexual activity, contraceptive use, and premarital pregnancy among American teenagers. *Family Planning Perspectives,* 1986, 18(4), 151–162.

National Center for Health Statistics, E. Powell-Griner. Induced terminations of pregnancy: Reporting states, 1982 and 1983. *Monthly Vital Statistics Report.* Vol. 35, No. 3, Supp. DHHS Pub. No. 86–1120. Hyattsville, Md.: Public Health Service, July 14, 1986.

Ory, H.W. Mortality associated with fertility and fertility control. *Family Planning Perspectives,* 1983, *15,* 57–63.

Abortion in the United States. *Population Today,* 1985, *13,* 2 et passim.

Riche, M.F. The adoption story. *American Demographics,* 1986, *8,* 42–45.

Rivara, E.P., Sweeney, P.J., & Henderson, B.F. A study of low socioeconomic status, black teenage fathers, and their nonfather peers. *Pediatrics,* 1985, 75(4), 648–656.

Sheehan, M.K., Ostwald, S.K., & Rothenberger, J. Perceptions of sexual responsibility: Do young men and women agree? *Pediatric Nursing,* 1986, *12,* 17–21.

Smith, T.W. National Opinion Research Center. General Social Surveys, August 1985.

Stark, E. Young, innocent, and pregnant. *Psychology Today,* October 1986, 20(10), 28–35.

Statistical Abstract of the United States, 1987, 107th ed. Washington, D.C.: U.S. Bureau of the Census, 1986.

Stewart, S.A. Sex is casual, despite new concerns. *USA Today Poll,* May 15, 1986.

Tanfer, K., and Rosenbaum, E. Contraceptive perceptions and method choice among young single women in the United States. *Studies in Family Planning,* November/December 1986, 17(6), 269–277.

Torres, A., Donovan, P., Dittes, N., & Forrest, J.D. Public benefits and costs of government funding for abortion. *Family Planning Perspectives,* 1986, 18(3), 111–118.

Zabin, L.S., Hirsch, M.B., Smith, E.A., Street, R., & Hardy, J.B. Evaluation of a pregnancy-prevention program for urban teenagers. *Family Planning Perspectives,* 1986, 18(3), 119–126.

CHAPTER 16

Assor, A., & Assor, T. Emotional involvement in marriage during the last trimester of the first pregnancy: A comparison of husbands and wives. *The Journal of Psychology,* 1985, *119,* 243–252.

Brazelton, T.B. *Working and caring.* New York: Addison-Wesley, 1985.

Bryant, N.B., & Collins, C.J. Human sexuality and feminism: A new approach to perinatal social work. *Journal of Social Work and Human Sexuality,* spring 1985, *3,* 103–117.

Cohen, N.W., and Estner, L.J. *Silent knife.* South Hadley, Mass.: Bergin & Garvey, 1983.

Cosby, B. *Fatherhood.* New York: Doubleday, 1986.

Cowan, C.P., Cowan, P.A., Heming, G., Garrett, E., Coysh, W.S., Curtis-Boles, H., & Boles, A.J., III. Transitions to parenthood: His, hers, and theirs. *Journal of Family Issues,* 1985, *6,* 451–482.

Crooks, R., and Bauer, K. *Our sexuality.* Menlo Park, Calif.: Benjamin-Cummings, 1984.

Dail, P.W., & Way, W.L. What do parents observe about parenting from prime-time television. *Family Relations,* 1985, *34,* 491–499.

Donovan, P. New reproductive technologies: Some legal dilemmas. *Family Planning Perspectives,* 1986, *18,* 57–60.

Dunn, P.C., Ryan, I.J., & O'Brien, K. College students level of acceptability of the new medical science of conception and problems of infertility. Accepted by Journal of Sex Research. In press.

Edmondson, B. Golden Cradle advertises adoption. *American Demographics,* 1986, *8,* 18.

Goldberg, W.A., Michaels, G.Y., & Lamb, M.E. Husbands' and wives' adjustment to pregnancy and first parenthood. *Journal of Family Issues,* 1985, *6,* 483–504.

Greenberg, J.S., Bruess, C.E., & Sands, D.W. *Sexuality: insights and issues.* Dubuque, Iowa: William C. Brown, 1986.

Greer, K. Today's parents: How well are they doing? *Better Homes and Gardens,* October 1986, pp. 36–46.

Grudzinskas, J.G., & Atkinson, L. Sexual function during the puerperium. *Archives of Sexual Behavior,* 1984, *13,* 85–91.

Hanson, S.M.H., & Bozett, F.W., eds. *Dimensions of fatherhood.* Beverly Hills, Calif.: Sage Publications, 1985.

Harper, T. Surrogate motherhood: Should we follow this U.S. example? *Institute of Family Studies,* April 1985, 11–12.

Harriman, L.C. Marital adjustment as related to personal and marital changes accompanying parenthood. *Family Relations,* 1986, *35,* 233–239.

Hinds, M.W., Bergeisen, G.H., & Allen, D.T. *Journal of the American Medical Association,* 1985, *253,* 1578–1582.

Jensen, M., & Bobak, I. *Maternity and Gynecologic Care.* St. Louis: C.V. Mosby, 1985.

Kraus, M.A., & Redman, E.S. Postpartum depression: An interactional view. *Journal of Marital and Family Therapy,* 1986, *12,* 63–74.

LaRossa, R. The transition to parenthood and the social reality of time. *Journal of Marriage and the Family,* 1983, *45,* 579–589.

Lumley, J. Preschool siblings at birth: Short-term effects. *Birth Issues in Perinatal Care and Education,* 1983, *10,* 11–16.

McAdoo, J.L. A black perspective on the father's role in child development. In Robert A. Lewis and Marvin B. Sussman, eds. *Marriage and Family Review,* 1985/1986, *9,* 117–133.

McHale, S.M., & Huston, T.L. The effect of the transition to parenthood on the marriage relationship. *Journal of Family Issues,* 1985, *6,* 409–434.

McKim, M.K. Transition to what? New parents' problems in the first year. *Family Relations,* 1987, *36,* 22–25.

National Center for Health Statistics: Advance report of final divorce statistics, 1984. *Monthly Vital Statistics Report,* 35(6), Supp. DHHS Pub. No. (PHS) 86–1120. Hyattsville, Md.: Public Health Service, September 25, 1986.

Riche, M.F. The adoption story. *American Demographics,* 1986, *8,* 42–45.

Ricks, S.S. Father–infant interactions: A review of empirical research. *Family Relations,* 1985, *34,* 505–511.

Sacks, S.R., & Donnerfeld, P.B. Parental choice of alternative birth environments and attitudes toward childrearing philosophy. *Journal of Marriage and the Family,* 1984, *46,* 469–475.

Shapiro, J.L. The expectant father. *Psychology Today,* January 1987, 36–42.

Sharpe, R. Baby M case good advertising. *USA Today,* February 17, 1987, p. 1.

Stainton, M.C. The fetus: A growing member of the family. *Family Relations,* 1985, *34,* 321–326.

Statistical Abstract of the United States, 1987, 107th ed. Washington, D.C.: U.S. Bureau of the Census, 1986.

Ventura, J.H. The stresses of parenthood reexamined. *Family Relations,* 1987, *36,* 26–33.

Waite, L.J., Haggstrom, G.W., & Kanouse, D.E. The consequences of parenthood for the marital stability of young adults. *American Sociological Review,* 1985, *50,* 850–857.

White, L.K., & Booth, A. The transition to parenthood and marital quality. *Journal of Family Issues,* 1985, *6,* 435–450.

Wilkie, C.F., & Ames, E.W. The relationship of infant crying to parental stress in the transition to parenthood. *Journal of Marriage and the Family,* 1986, *48,* 545–550.

CHAPTER 17

Abramovitch, R., Corter, C., Peoler, D.J., & Stanhope, L. Sibling and peer interaction: A final follow-up and a comparison. *Child Development,* 1986, *57,* 217–229.

ADIA Research Department. Child care and the clerical workforce 1985/1986 National Survey. ADIA Personnel Services; P.O. Box 2768; Menlo Park, Calif. 94026.

Bankart, C.P., & Bankart, B.M. Japanese children's perceptions of their parents. *Sex Roles,* 1985, *13,* 679–690.

Bjorkman, S., Poteat, M., & Snow, C.W. Environmental ratings and children's social behavior: Implications for the assessment of day-care quality. *American Journal of Orthopsychiatry,* 1986, *56,* 271–277.

Bronstein, P. Differences in mothers' and fathers' behaviors toward children: A cross-cultural comparison. *Developmental Psychology,* 1984, *20,* 995–1003.

Burchinal, M., & Bryant, D. Does early day care affect infant–mother attachment levels? Poster session, American Psychological Association, September 1986. Used by permission of M. Burchinal.

Ebony. Massive abuse of illegal drugs must be stopped. August 1986, pp. 149–150.

Floge, L. The dynamics of child-care use and some implications for women's employment. *Journal of Marriage and the Family,* 1985, *47,* 143–154.

Fuqua, R.W., & Labensohn, D. Parents as consumers of child care. *Family Relations,* 1986, *35,* 295–303.

Glick, P.C., & Lin, S. More young adults are living with their parents: Who are they? *Journal of Marriage and the Family,* 1986, *48,* 107–112.

Goldscheider, F.K., & LeBourdais, C. Recent social trends: The decline in age at leaving home, 1920–1979. *Sociology and Social Research,* 1986, 70(2), 143–145.

Greer, K. Today's parents: How well are they doing? *Better Homes and Gardens,* October 1986, pp. 36–46.

Grigsby, J., & McGowan, J.B. Still in the nest: Adult children living with their parents. *Sociology and Social Research,* 1986, 70(2), 146–148.

Haffey, N.A., & Levant, R.F. The differential effectiveness of two models of skills training for working class parents. *Family Relations,* 1984, *33,* 209–216.

Harris, L. National poll on parenthood. *USA Today,* September 24, 1986, p. 1.

Hewlett, S.A. *A lesser life: The myth of women's liberation in America.* New York: Morrow, 1986.

Hughes, R.J. The informal help-giving of home and center child-care providers. *Family Relations,* 1985, *34,* 359–366.

Kliman, D.S., & Vukelich, C. Mothers and fathers: Expectations for infants. *Family Relations,* 1985, *34,* 305–313.

LeMasters, E.E., and DeFrain, J. *Parents in contemporary America: A sympathetic view.* Homewood, Ill.: Dorsey Press, 1983.

Love, N.W., Jr., and McVoy, J.H. Child abuse by the unaware. *Marriage and Family Living,* 1981, 65(11), 12–29.

Mead, D.E. *Six approaches to child rearing.* Provo, Utah: Brigham Young University Press, 1976.

Meador, L. Drug abuse in the family. Presentation, East Carolina University, Greenville, North Carolina, January 21, 1987. Used by permission.

Meredith, D. The nine-to-five dilemma. *Psychology Today,* February 1986, pp. 37–44.

Meyerhoff, M.K., & White, B.L. Making the grade as parents. *Psychology Today,* September 1986, pp. 38–45.

Parks, P.L., & Smeriglio, V.L. Relationships among parenting knowledge, quality of stimulation in the home, and infant development. *Family Relations,* 1986, *35,* 411–416.

Ramirez Barranti, C.C. The grandparent/grandchild relationship: Family resource in an era of voluntary bonds. *Family Relations,* 1985, *34,* 343–352.

Rutter, M. Resilient children. *Psychology Today,* March 1984, pp. 57–65.

Scarr, S. What's a parent to do? *Psychology Today,* May 1984, pp. 58–63.

Schroeder, A.B., & Brocato, B.R. Television and the family interaction. *Free Inquiry in Creative Sociology,* 1983, *11,* 61–64.

Schvaneveldt, J.D., & Lee, T.R. The emergence and practices of ritual in the American family. *Family Perspective,* 1983, *17,* 137–143.

Shea, J. Department of Child Development and Family Relations, East Carolina University, Greenville, North Carolina. Personal communication, 1984. Used by permission.

Statistical Abstract of the United States, 1987, 107th ed. Washington, D.C.: U.S. Bureau of the Census, 1986.

Thompson, L., Acock, A.C., & Clark, K. Do parents know their children? The ability of mothers and fathers to gauge the attitudes of their young adult children. *Family Relations,* 1985, *34,* 315–320.

Weisner, T.S., & Eiduson, B.T. The children of the '60s as parents. *Psychology Today,* January 1986, pp. 60–66.

York, P., & York, D. Toughlove. *Family Therapy Networker.* September-October 1982, pp. 32–37.

Zigler, E., & Lang, M.E. The emergence of "superbaby": A good thing? *Pediatric Nursing,* 1985, *11,* 337–341.

CHAPTER 18

Bernstein, B.E., & Collins, S.K. Remarriage counseling: Lawyer and therapist's help with the second time around. *Family Relations,* 1985, *34,* 387–391.

Bloom, B.L., & Kindle, K.R. Demographic factors in the continuing relationship between former spouses. *Family Relations,* 1985, *34,* 375–381.

Booth, A., Johnson, D.R., White, L.K., & Edwards, J.N. Predicting divorce and permanent separation. *Journal of Family Issues,* 1985, *6,* 331–346.

Buehler, C.A., Hogan, M.J., Robinson, B.E., & Levy, R.J. The parental divorce transition: Divorce-related stressors and well-being. *Journal of Divorce,* 1985–1986, *9,* 61–81.

Bugaighis, M.A., Schumm, W.R., Jurich, A.P., & Bollman, S.R. Factors associated with thoughts of marital separation. *Journal of Divorce,* 1985–1986, *9,* 49–59.

Burden, D.S. Single parents and the work setting: The impact of multiple job and home-life responsibilities. *Family Relations,* 1986, *35,* 37–44.

Clark, P.G., Siviski, R.W., & Weiner, R. Coping strategies of widowers in the first year. *Family Relations,* 1986, *35,* 425–430.

Cleek, M.G., & Pearson, T.A. Perceived causes of divorce: An analysis of interrelationships. *Journal of Marriage and the Family,* 1985, *47,* 179–183.

Coleman, M., & Ganong, L.H. Remarriage myths: Implications for the helping professions. *Journal of Counseling and Development,* 1985, *64,* 116–120.

Dilworth-Anderson, P. Effectiveness of family support-group involvement in adult day care. *Family Relations,* 1987, *36,* 78–81.

Ferreiro, B.W., Warren, N.J., & Konanc, J.T. ADAP: A divorce-assessment proposal. *Family Relations,* 1986, *35,* 439–448.

Freed, D.J., & Walker, T.B. Family law in the fifty states. *Family Law Quarterly,* 1986, *19,* 331–441.

Frisbie, W.P. Variation in patterns of marital instability among Hispanics. *Journal of Marriage and the Family,* 1986, *48,* 99–106.

Glenn, N.D., & Kramer, K.B. The psychological well-being of adult children of divorce. *Journal of Marriage and the Family,* 1985, *47,* 905–912.

Goetting, A. The six stations of remarriage: Developmental tasks of remarriage after divorce. *Family Coordinator,* 1982, *31,* 213–222.

Greer, K. Today's parents: How well are they doing? *Better Homes and Gardens,* October 1986, pp. 36–46.

Greif, G.L. *Single fathers.* Lexington, Mass.: Lexington Books, 1985a.

Greif, G.L. Single fathers rearing children. *Journal of Marriage and the Family,* 1985b, *47,* 185–191.

Guidubaldi, J., Cleminshaw, H.K., Perry, J.D., Nastasi, B.K., & Lightel, J. The role of selected family-environment factors in children's post-divorce adjustment. *Family Relations,* 1986, *35,* 141–151.

Haas-Hawkings, G., Sangster, S., Ziegler, M., & Reid, D. A study of relatively immediate adjustment to widowhood in late life. *International Journal of Women's Studies,* 1985, *8,* 158–165.

Hyatt, R., & Kaslow, F. The impact of childrens' divorce on parents: And some contributing factors. *Journal of Divorce,* 1985, *9,* 79–92.

Johnson, B.H. Single mothers following separation and divorce: Making it on your own. *Family Relations,* 1986, *35,* 189–197.

Kitson, G.C. Marital discord and marital separation: A county survey. *Journal of Marriage and the Family,* 1985, *47,* 693–700.

Kitson, G.C., Babri, K.B., & Roach, M.J. Who divorces and why. *Journal of Family Issues,* 1985, *6,* 255–293.

Kitson, G.C., & Sussman, M.B. Marital complaints, demographic characteristics, and symptoms of mental distress in divorce. *Journal of Marriage and the Family,* 1982, *44,* 87–101.

Leigh, G.K., Ladehoff, G.S., Howie, A.T., & Christians, D.L. Correlates of marital satisfaction among men and women in intact first marriage and remarriage. *Family Perspective,* 1985, *19,* 139–149.

Lowery, C.R., & Settle, S.A. Effects of divorce on children: Differential impact of custody and visitation patterns. *Family Relations,* 1985, *34,* 455–463.

Melli, M.S. The changing legal status of the single parent. *Family Relations,* 1986, *35,* 31–35.

Menaghan, E.G. Depressive affect and subsequent divorce. *Journal of Family Issues,* 1985, *6,* 295–306.

Menaghan, E.G., & Lieberman, M.A. Changes in depression following divorce: A panel study. *Journal of Marriage and the Family,* 1986, *48,* 319–329.

Morgan, E.S. *The Puritan Family,* Boston: Public Library, 1944.

Mueller, D.P., & Cooper, P.W. Children of single-parent families: How they fare as young adults. *Family Relations,* 1986, *35,* 169–176.

National Center for Health Statistics. Advance report of final divorce statistics, 1984. *Monthly Vital Statistics Report,* 35(6), Supp. DHHS Pub. No. (PHS) 86–1120. Hyattsville, Md.: Public Health Service, September 25, 1986.

Nock, S.L. Enduring effect of marital disruption and subsequent living arrangements. *Journal of Family Issues,* 1982, *3,* 25–40.

Norton, A.J., & Glick, P.C. One-parent families: A social and economic profile. *Family Relations,* 1986, *35,* 9–17.

Norton, A.J., and Moorman, J.E. Current trends in marriage and divorce among American women. *Journal of Marriage and the Family,* 1987, *49,* 3–14.

Nuta, V.R. Emotional aspects of child-support enforcement. *Family Relations,* 1986, *35,* 177–182.

Petronio, S., & Endres, T. Dating and the single parent: Communication in the social network. *Journal of Divorce,* 1985–1986, *9,* 83–103.

Ratcliff, B.B. *Patterns of divorce disclosure.* Unpublished thesis, Department of Sociology and Anthropology, East Carolina University, Greenville, North Carolina, 1982.

Richardson, L. *The new other woman.* New York: The Free Press, 1985.

Roberts, T.W., & Price, S.J. A systems analysis of the remarriage process: Implications for the clinician. *Journal of Divorce,* 1985–1986, *9,* 1–25.

Roper Organization. *The 1985 Virginia Slims American women's opinion poll,* New York, 1985.

Rosenthal, D., Leigh, G.K., & Elardo, R. Home environment of three- to six-year-old children from father-absent and two-parent families. *Journal of Divorce,* 1985–1986, *9,* 41–48.

Sanik, M.M., & Mauldin, T. Single- versus two-parent families: A comparison of mothers' time. *Family Relations,* 1986, *35,* 53–56.

Saul, S.C., & Scherman, A. Divorce grief and personal adjustment in divorced persons who remarry or remain single. *Journal of Divorce,* 1984, 7(3), 75–85.

Smith, K.R., & Zick, C.D. The incidence of poverty among the recently widowed: Mediating factors in the life course. *Journal of Marriage and the Family,* 1986, *48,* 619–630.

South, S.J., & Spitze, G. Divorce determinants. *American Sociological Review,* 1986, *51,* 583–590.

Spitze, G., & South, S.J. Women's employment, time expenditure, and divorce. *Journal of Family Issues,* 1985, *6,* 307–329.

Stark, E. Friends through it all. *Psychology Today,* May 1986, pp. 54–60.

Statistical Abstract of the United States, 1987, 107th ed. Washington, D.C.: U.S. Bureau of the Census, 1986.

Teachman, J.D., & Heckert, A. The impact of age and children on remarriage. *Journal of Family Issues,* 1985, *6,* 185–203.

Trovato, F. The relationship between marital dissolution and suicide: The Canadian case. *Journal of Marriage and the Family,* 1986, *48,* 341–348.

Vinick, B. Remarriage in old age. *The Family Coordinator,* 1978, *27,* 359–363.

Wallerstein, J.S., & Kelly, J.B. *Surviving the break-up: How children actually cope with divorce.* New York: Basic Books, 1980.

Weinberg, T. Single fatherhood: How is it different? *Pediatric Nursing,* 1985, *11,* 173–176.

Weingarten, H.R. Marital status and well-being: A national study comparing first-married, currently divorced, and remarried adults. *Journal of Marriage and the Family,* 1985, *47,* 653–661.

Weitzman, L. *The divorce revolution.* Riverside, N.J.: The Free Press, 1985.

White, L.K., & Booth, A. Stepchildren in remarriages. *American Sociological Review,* 1985, *50,* 689–698.

White, L.K., Brinkerhoff, D.B., & Booth, A. The effect of marital disruption on child's attachment to parents. *Journal of Family Issues,* 1985, 6(1), 5–22.

Wishik, H.R. Economics of divorce. *Family Law Quarterly,* 1986, *20,* 79–107.

CHAPTER 19

Bowe, C. What are men like today? *Cosmopolitan,* May 1986, pp. 263 et passim.

Bryan, L.R., Coleman, M., Ganong, L.H., & Bryan, S.H. Person perception: Family structure as a cue for stereotyping. *Journal of Marriage and the Family,* 1986, *48,* 169–174.

Cherlin, A., & McCarthy, J. Remarried couple households: Data from the June 1980 Current Population Survey. *Journal of Marriage and the Family,* 1985, *47,* 23–30.

Coleman, M., and Ganong, L.H. An evaluation of the stepfamily self-help literature for children and adolescents. *Family Relations,* 1987, *36,* 61–65.

Coleman, M., Ganong, L.H., & Gingrich, R. Stepfamily strengths: A review of popular literature. *Family Relations,* 1985, *35,* 583–588.

Fine, M.A. Perceptions of stepparents: Variation in stereotypes as a function of current family structure. *Journal of Marriage and the Family,* 1986, *48,* 537–544.

Fishman, B. The economic behavior of stepfamilies. *Family Relations,* 1983, *32,* 359–366. ©National Council on Family Relations, Fairview Community School Center (1910 West County Road B, Suite 147; St. Paul, MN 55113.) Reprinted by permission.

Glick, P.C. How American families are changing. *American Demographics,* 1984, 6(1), 20–25.

Gorman, T. *Stepfather*. Boulder, Co.: Gentle Touch Press, 1983.

Knaub, P.K., Hanna, S.L., & Stinnett, N. Strengths of remarried families. *Journal of Divorce,* 1984, 7(3), 41–55.

Lutz, P. The stepfamily: An adolescent perspective. *Family Relations,* 1983, *32,* 367–375.

Morrison, K., & Thompson-Guppy, A. (with Patricia Bell). *Stepmothers: Exploring the myth.* Ottawa, Ontario: Canadian Council on Social Development, 1985.

Osborne, J. How to provide effective help for remarried couples. *Marriage and Divorce Today,* 1983, 8(52), 2–3.

Pasley, K. Stepfathers. In S.M.H. Hanson & F.W. Bozett, *Dimensions of fatherhood.* Beverly Hills, Calif.: Sage Publications, 1985, 288–306.

Pink, J.E.T., & Wampler, K.S. Problem areas in stepfamilies: Cohesion, adaptability, and the stepfather–adolescent relationship. *Family Relations,* 1985, *34,* 327–335.

Ramsey, S.H. Stepparent support of stepchildren: The changing legal context and the need for empirical policy research. *Family Relations,* 1986, *35,* 363–369.

Skeen, P., Covi, R.B., & Robinson, B.E. Stepfamilies: A review of the literature with suggestions for practitioners. *Journal of Counseling and Development,* 1985, *64,* 121–125.

Tropf, W.D. An exploratory examination of the effect of remarriage on child support and personal contacts. *Journal of Divorce,* 1984, 7(3), 57–73.

Walker, G. *Second wife, second best?* New York: Doubleday, 1984.

White, L.K., & Booth, A. The quality and stability of remarriages: The role of stepchildren. *American Sociological Review,* 1985, *50,* 689–698.

Wishik, H.R. Economics of divorce: An exploratory study. *Family Law Quarterly,* 1986, *20,* 79–107.

SPECIAL TOPICS

Alzate, H. Vaginal eroticism and female orgasm: A current appraisal. *Journal of Sex and Marital Therapy,* 1985, *4,* 271–284.

Alzate, H., & Dippsy, M.L. Vaginal erotic sensitivity. *Journal of Sex and Marital Therapy,* 1984, *10,* 49–56.

CBS Poll. AIDS. CBS Television, October 22, 1986.

Campbell, J.M. Sexual guidelines for persons with AIDS and at risk for AIDS. *Human Sexuality,* special issue on the physician's guide to sexual counseling. March 1986, 100–103.

Department of Health and Human Services. Sexually transmitted disease statistics, 1984. Atlanta: Public Health Service, Centers for Disease Control, 1984.

Department of Health and Human Services. Genital herpes infection—United States, 1966–1984. Morbidity and Mortality Weekly Report. Atlanta: Public Health Service, Centers for Disease Control, June 20, 1986a, *35,* 402–404.

Department of Health and Human Services. AIDS Guidelines. Morbidity and Mortality Weekly Report, November 1982 through December 1985. Atlanta: Public Health Service, Centers for Disease Control, February, 1986b.

Fincher, R.E. Interval between transfusion and appearance of ARC or AIDS, *Medical Aspects of Human Sexuality,* 1986, *20,* 61.

Hock, Z. The G Spot. *Journal of Sex and Marital Therapy,* 1983, *9,* 166–167.

Perry, J.D., & Whipple, B. Pelvic muscle strength of female ejaculation: Evidence in support of a new theory of orgasm. *Journal of Sex Research,* 1981, *17,* 22–39.

Polk, B.F. AIDS: Proof lacking of female to male transmission. *Medical Aspects of Human Sexuality,* 1986, *20,* 61.

Index

PHOTO CREDITS

1 © Roy Morsch, The Stock Market. **3** © Jeffry W. Myers, FPG. **7** © C.C. Garcia, FPG. **10** Sybil Shelton, Peter Arnold, Inc. **17** © Elizabeth Crews, Stock, Boston. **25** © Jeff Albertson, Stock, Boston. **31** © Richard Dunoff, The Stock Market. **34** © 1985 Thomas Coard, EKM-Nepenthe. **36** © Jean-Claude Lejeune, Stock, Boston. **39** Richard Laird, FPG. **44** Sybil Shelton, Peter Arnold, Inc. **48** (left) © Barbara Alper, Stock, Boston; (right) © Roy Morsch, The Stock Market. **63** © Jean-Claude Lejeune, Stock, Boston. **70** © 1984 Peter Menzel, Stock, Boston. **71** © Jane Scherr, Jeroboam, Inc. **74** © Hazel Hankin, Stock, Boston. **76** © Elizabeth Crews, Stock, Boston. **80** © Barbara Alper, Stock, Boston. **84** David Aronson, Stock, Boston. **86** Owen Franken, Stock, Boston. **95** © 1987 Joel Baldwin, The Stock Market. **100** © David Powers, Stock, Boston. **102** Lionel J-M Delvingne, Stock, Boston. **109** (top) © Tom Ballard, EKM-Nepenthe; (right) © Michael Siluk, EKM-Nepenthe; (left) © 1985 David Stoecklein, The Stock Market. **119** Barbara Pfeffer, Peter Arnold, Inc. **123** © 1984 Peter Menzel, Stock, Boston. **131** Spencer Grant, Stock, Boston. **133** © Ken Nahoun, The Stock Market. **139** © Budd Gray, Jeroboam, Inc. **144** © Frank Siteman, Stock, Boston. **149** © Frank Siteman, Jeroboam, Inc. **163** David S. Strickler, The Picture Cube. **166** © 1979 Michael Malyszko, Stock, Boston. **167** © 1978 Erika Stone, Peter Arnold, Inc. **171** © Eric Kroll, Taurus Photos, Inc. **174** Susie Fitzhugh, Stock, Boston. **179** © Jeff Albertson, Stock, Boston. **185** © 1979 Michael Malyszko, Stock, Boston. **187** Sybil Shelton, Peter Arnold, Inc. **189** Sybil Shelton, Peter Arnold, Inc. **191** © 1979 Carolyn A. McKeone, FPG. **205** © Werner H. Müller, Peter Arnold, Inc. **207** Emilio A. Mercado, Jeroboam, Inc. **215** © 1980 Frank Siteman, Jeroboam, Inc. **218** © 1983 Frank Siteman, Stock, Boston. **220** © J. Berndt, Stock, Boston. **227** Michael Hayman, Stock, Boston. **237** © Barbara Alper, Stock, Boston. **239** Ellis Herwig, The Picture Cube. **241** © Elizabeth Crews, Stock, Boston. **246** © Frank Siteman, Jeroboam, Inc. **253** Karen Rosenthal, Stock, Boston. **258** © 1981 David Hundley, The Stock Market. **263** © Ginger Chih, Peter Arnold, Inc. **273** © Cathy Cheney, EKM-Nepenthe. **277** Carolyn A. McKeone, FPG. **279** © Jeffry W. Myers, FPG. **284** © 1981 Judy S. Gelles, Stock, Boston. **290** Laurie Cameron, Jeroboam, Inc. **298** Peter Vandermark, Stock, Boston. **307** Jeff Albertson, Stock, Boston. **311** © Jeffry W. Myers, Stock, Boston. **319** © Jean-Claude Lejeune, Stock, Boston. **326** Willie L. Hill, Jr., FPG. **328** © Frank Siteman, Stock, Boston. **337** © Frank Siteman, Stock, Boston. **339** Christopher S. Johnson, Stock, Boston. **345** Ginger Chih, Peter Arnold, Inc. **346** Fredrik D. Bodin, Stock, Boston. **356** Carolyn A. McKeone, FPG. **367** © 1982 Frank D. Smith, Jeroboam, Inc. **383** © Gerard Fritz, Jeroboam, Inc. **386** Sybil Shelton, Peter Arnold, Inc. **394** Mike Valeri, FPG. **397** James Holland, Stock, Boston. **405** © Bohdan Hrynewych, Stock, Boston. **411** Michael Hayman, Stock, Boston. **413** © 1986 Bob Hahn, Taurus Photos, Inc. **415** © Ginger Chih, Peter Arnold, Inc. **426** © George W. Gardner, Stock, Boston. **430** © Jean-Claude Lejeune, Stock, Boston. **431** © Kit Hedman, Jeroboam, Inc. **432** David S. Strickler, The Picture Cube. **439** Courtesy of Andrew Y. Silverman, Lenox Hill Hospital, New York. **440** © Frank Siteman, Stock, Boston. **458** (left) © 1986 Mike Valeri, FPG; (right) © Gale Zucker, Stock, Boston. **459** © Paul Fortin, Stock, Boston. **465** © Barbara Alper, Stock, Boston. **472** Steve Hanson, Stock, Boston. **473** © 1976 Elizabeth Hamlin, Stock, Boston. **477** © 1980 Suzanne Arms, Jeroboam, Inc. **485** Michael Weisbrot, Stock, Boston. **488** Carolyn A. McKeone, FPG. **491** Michael Weisbrot, Stock, Boston. **495** © Elizabeth Crews, Stock, Boston. **497** © Ginger Chih, Peter Arnold, Inc. **500** George Bellerose, Stock, Boston. **508** Peter Vandermark, Stock, Boston. **511** © Linda Benedict Jones, The Picture Cube. **514** © Jean-Claude Lejeune, Stock, Boston. **520** (left) © Erika Stone, Peter Arnold, Inc.; (right) James H. Karales, Peter Arnold, Inc.; (bottom) © Erika Stone, Peter Arnold, Inc. **527** © Joseph Schuyler, Stock, Boston. **529** © Erika Stone, Peter Arnold, Inc. **539** Carolyn A. McKeone, FPG. **547** © Don Ivers, Jeroboam, Inc. **555** © Bonnie Griffith, The Picture Cube. **557** © Pamela Price, The Picture Cube. **563** © Ginger Chih, Peter Arnold, Inc. **566** Barbara Pfeffer, Peter Arnold, Inc. **568** Jean-Claude Lejeune, Stock, Boston. **574** © 1985 Barbara Kirk, The Stock Market. **577** © 1983 Deborah Kahn, Stock, Boston. **591** Frank Siteman, EKM-Nepenthe. **594** © Hazel Hankin, Stock, Boston. **600** © 1982 Robert V. Eckert, Jr., Stock, Boston. **603** © 1982 David Scharf, Peter Arnold, Inc. **613** Peter Keegan, FPG.